W9-BQI-616

THE TIDES OF HISTORY

JACQUES PIRENNE

THE TIDES OF HISTORY

VOLUME I

FROM THE BEGINNINGS TO ISLAM

TRANSLATED FROM THE FRENCH BY LOVETT EDWARDS

NEW YORK
E. P. DUTTON & CO., INC.
1962

FIRST EDITION

Translated from LES GRANDS COURANTS DE L'HISTOIRE UNIVERSELLE: (*Nouvelle édition revue et augmentée*)

Library of Congress Catalog Card Number: 62-7800

PREFACE

History is essentially a continuity and a unity; a continuity that goes on, without men being able to escape it, from generation to generation, and which links our own times to the most distant epochs; a unity, since in any society the life of each man is bound up with the lives of all others, even as, in the community of nations, the history of each nation develops, without even being aware of it, as a part of the history of all the nations of the universe.

The words of Christ, the words of Buddha, which were heard by only a few thousand Jews or Hindus, have changed the course of the entire world. The discovery of the steam-engine in England altered the destiny of all countries. What is so obvious in such well-known cases is no less true of all the other factors that have modified the thinking or the ways of life of a specific people; their influence makes itself felt in all parts of the world, even as sound-waves, once emitted, fill the whole atmosphere.

For this reason humanity unconsciously takes account of this interdependence which links, in time and space, all men now living with those who have lived; and it is for this reason that in great periods of crisis or of climax universal histories are written.

The first to be written in antiquity was that of Herodotus in the Vth century BC, for this enquiry into the customs and life of all the peoples, civilized or barbarian, then known to the Greeks, was in fact a universal history; it was one of the most grandiose and disinterested attempts to bring men together, at the very moment when Darius for the first time envisaged the union of all peoples in a universal Empire which would not be subject to any national or racial hegemony.

Later, at the time when the Hellenistic kingdoms were ending the great wars they had waged among themselves to conquer the mastery of the seas, without achieving any other result than their own ruin to the advantage of Rome, Polybius (207–125 BC) sketched out a wide review of the historical factors which led to the Roman victory. With magnificent objectivity, he sought for the causes that united events and tried to penetrate the meaning of the evolution of states and cities, and laid the foundations of real historical science by defining, to a certain degree, the laws which govern societies.

In the history of humanity the advent of the Roman Empire marks the culmination of this irresistible tendency of all societies to enlarge their horizons. Contemporaries understood all its grandeur and set themselves to study their origins, diverse or common, in order to comprehend fully this unique civilization that had forced itself upon them. That is why universal histories abounded in the first century BC and the first century AD. These were, in Greek, the histories of Diodorus (born about 90 BC), of Nicholas of Damascus (born about 64 BC), of Strabo, during the reign of Tiberius and, in Latin, of Trogus Pompeius which appeared under Augustus.

Later, the universal balance established seemed a natural thing to men; the Empire had eclipsed the past and historians no longer concerned themselves with anything save Roman history.

But the great crises which ended in the triumph of Christianity and ushered in the decadence of that Empire that had been thought eternal, led men once more to turn to the past and to ask of history an explanation of the fact of Christianity. But meanwhile mysticism had destroyed the scientific spirit, and the Aquitanian priest Sulpicius Severus (365–425) and even that great spirit the Spanish priest Paul Orosius (417), when writing their universal histories, were no longer seeking to understand their times by a study of their origins and of the development of which they were the culmination—as Polybius had done—but only to find in them the proof and justification of Christian faith. Like Christianity, Islam in the *History of the World* written by the Persian Kelbi (819) based itself on a vision of universal history; and when Islam, after having known a period of brilliant civilization, began its long and profound decadence, it produced, before its thinking congealed, a last great work, the *Universal History* of Ibn Khaldun, in the 15th century.

After Paul Orosius, history took, among the Christians, that apologetic character of which, in the 17th century, Bossuet was to be the most illustrious representative. But it is remarkable that, at the moment when the Greco-Roman world was setting out on the new path opened for it by the words of Christ, it should have wanted to revise all its convictions and link its faith, in the manner of St. Augustine in his *City of God*, to the mass of historical evidence, in order to give it its place in the story of mankind, henceforth envisaged as determined by the Divine Will.

From that time history ceased to be a science until in the 16th century Jean Bodin revived, by the comparative study of institutions, a sense of evolution and of the interdependence of peoples. In the 17th century, historical writing turned, with Bossuet, towards a universalist conception, related to the classical character of literature, and was to find its culmination in the admirable *Essai sur les moeurs et l'esprit des nations* (1756) wherein

Voltaire attempted a vast synthesis of the history of the entire universe from the 9th to the 17th century. Condorcet, in his *Esquisse d'un tableau historique des progrès de l'esprit humain*, tried in his turn to establish a law for the development of societies whose progress he related to that of knowledge. But the greatest historical work of the 18th century is certainly the *Scienza Nova* of the Neapolitan Vico who tried to extract the first elements of a philosophy of history from the evolution of peoples, and whose influence on the philosophy of Auguste Comte was to be so great.

It seemed that history was going to attempt to tie together once more the countless threads that united the great civilizations to one another and to reveal the deep sense of those great political, social and moral currents that have influenced the life of men, peoples and all humanity.

But in the 19th century history acquired a new outlook. From the 16th century onward the formation of national states drove historians more and more towards the study of national history. Erudition, by making history a technical study, helped to break it up into specialized branches. Furthermore, modern Europe exercised over the world so uncontested a leadership that—save for specialists—men ceased to be interested in anything that was not European. But the 19th century was the great century of history, which sought out new paths, understood the importance of the economic factor and examined religious and philosophical problems. That was the moment when Germany, a latecomer in the concert of European powers, elaborated, according to the ideas of Fichte, the theory of nationalism that won over her universities. Following the example of Sybel and Treitschke, German historians made themselves the apostles of Prussian hegemony. And then, as nationalism penetrated into the western countries under the influence of Hegel, history, consciously or not, placed itself more and more at the service of politics. That is why it has sometimes been possible to say that history has fanned the hatreds that set the peoples against one another. And it is true that in regarding history as essentially an apologia of their own country, the 'nationalist' historians no longer tried to understand other peoples and other races and disdained or were ignorant of other civilizations. Under the influence of the German school, turned naturally towards its own past, the mediaevalists—with the exception of Fustel de Coulanges, the greatest of his time—traced back to the German invasions all the characteristic traits of the history of Europe, and the notion of the historical continuity between our civilization and the ancient civilizations was broken.

In recent times nationalist or political conceptions have been more and more frequently imposed upon history, and science has put into operation an immense apparatus of erudition to reach, in many cases, a methodical and systematic deformation of historical realities. Learned works have been written to demonstrate preconceived political theories; learning has placed itself at the service of error.

Without doubt the greater number of real historians have escaped this contagion. But synthesis having more and more taken on the appearance of political apologia or propaganda, it has become a more and more widespread idea that learning must disengage itself from general ideas to devote itself essentially to questions of analysis.

Nevertheless, in opposition to nationalist theories, a movement for the study of universal history developed in the second half of the 19th century, which was to become greatly accentuated after the 1914–18 war. Above all in this last quarter of a century, a series of great collections have appeared devoted to the history of the world, amongst which that edited by Gustave Glotz takes pride of place. The crisis which began with the 1914 war rendered humanity conscious of the unity imposed on it and the necessity of revising our historical conceptions by comparing our civilization with those of other races and of other times. Wells and Jorga both wrote universal histories.

The idea of evolution has, on the other hand, taken on fresh importance. Vico and Auguste Comte have applied it to history, Bergson has shown its importance in the genesis of thought and Einstein, by introducing it into the physical sciences, has shaken them to their foundations.

Another important fact was the introduction into history of philosophical conceptions, such as historical materialism which derives from Marx and to which other conceptions have replied, spiritual such as that which Grousset has made use of in his *Bilan de l'histoire*, or sociological like the vast enquiry undertaken by Toynbee who tries, basing himself on history, to determine the factors that govern the growth and evolution of society.

History has turned, completely, towards the study of humanity as envisaged in its growth. But the study of growth cannot result in scientific conclusions, above all when moral factors are in question, save by comparison. History, in order to become a science of human growth, must be able to make comparisons. It can only do so by making itself more and more universal.

The special studies which have been made up to the present render possible an attempt at a general synthesis. If I have tried to do this, it is because I have thought that it was not without use, at a moment when all values have been called in question, to link the history of modern times with that of antiquity, in the course of which problems have been posed that still await a solution.

Without doubt the circumstances in which they were posed three thousand or two thousand years ago are no longer those of today; technical achievement has profoundly changed the world. But I believe, none the less, that the human aspect of problems has changed far less than appears at first glance.

Even if man by the aid of science has made himself master of the world and has transformed everything about him, he himself, in his deeper instincts, has not changed. But the true aim of historical research is a knowledge of the factors that control men living in societies. The study of the history of ancient times, even as that of modern times, is therefore to study man himself and human society through the cycles of evolution of which we can study the origins, the apogee and the decadence. Without doubt it is painful to have to say that, if science has progressed, the moral values of man, even after two thousand years of effort by Christianity, have not improved.

In the 19th century men believed that progress would go on for ever and imagined that the world would never again see the massacre of conquered peoples, the extermination of one race by another with no other reason than ethnic hate like that between dogs and cats; that mass deportations of vanquished peoples into slavery, the sack of cities by fire and sword, the use of torture and the indifference of those who were not affected, were all things which could never return. Yet, none the less, men have gone back to such methods of war. Does the fact that they practise them scientifically make them any the less barbarous?

We must conclude that progress is not continuous and that civilization is very frail. Confronted by the abyss into which humanity has fallen, should we not take stock and examine our consciences? There is no other way to do so, in my opinion, than to follow, through the universal history of the first six thousand years of man, the long adventure of humanity.

Only universal history, by comparing all civilizations, of all times and of all races, can cause some sort of philosophy of history to become apparent, and thus lead to sociological, scientific and moral conclusions. It alone is capable, by revealing to us that neither our country nor our race nor our age has achieved a civilization in all ways superior to all that has gone before, of eradicating those prejudices of religion, race and language, of political, social or mystical ideologies, that have not ceased to drive men into vain massacres and to degrade, by hatred, all ideals, even the noblest and those which have no other aim than the triumph of tolerance and love.

Universal history also is alone able, by developing before our eyes the great cycles of human evolution, to make us understand at what point in evolution we are today. That, I think, is the essential question. For it is on knowledge of the necessities and possibilities of our time that the value of future peace depends.

Is it possible to deduce from the past the outlines of the future? I think it is. Without doubt, history is complex. Humanity is not a homogeneous whole. Sometimes it is divided into groups unknown, foreign and hostile to one another, each evolving in its own manner; sometimes it is harmonized into a magnificent balance.

The progressive periods of civilization are those that enlarge the horizons of the human community, creating a material and moral solidarity between more and more numerous peoples, and breaking down the barriers that incomprehension, fanaticism or the mere impossibility of communication have set up between men. The culmination of history, to which all its active forces instinctively tend, is universal association in a stable and peaceful balance, such as was nearest to realization at the close of ancient times, in that period which I have called 'The Era of the Empires'.

Periods of decadence are those in which the great communities disintegrate and when society, like a dead body, decomposes and dissolves.

Can one therefore conclude that humanity is governed by laws against which it is impossible to react? I do not think so. Determination and historical materialism have certainly helped in the development of this horrible cynicism, known to us under the name of realism, which has made us lose all sense of moral values and no longer believe in anything save the necessity of material order. However, I am convinced that if determinism must be discarded, equally we cannot allow ourselves to believe that human societies can model themselves on a plan elaborated by theorists who claim to give the world a final and perfect order.

The study of universal history establishes, without any possible doubt, that the evolution of society, like that of individuals, obeys laws by which certain social forms follow from certain economic conditions, and which fix constant relations between the changes of public and private law. In other words, there is a balance between various aspects of a society that cannot be broken without submitting it to violent crises. Equally there are, in the evolution of peoples, stages that follow one another necessarily, since one is the result of the other. There are social reactions even as there are chemical reactions. The problem consists in knowing whether these reactions are immutable, or if the intervention of human genius can modify them. To me, the answer does not seem to be in doubt. A social reaction depends on psychological, economic, social and moral elements, and if one of these elements changes, then the reaction is definitely influenced. Over certain of these elements we have little or no power. We cannot, for example, prevent men from being compelled by certain physical necessities that rule their existence and in consequence their instincts, which explains why human nature does not change. But it is possible to transform the economic conditions of life by technical inventions, to make social deficiencies disappear by laws that organize more efficiently the distribution of wealth and to create higher sentiments in men's hearts by giving them a moral ideal.

The lesson that we can draw from history is precisely to allow us to understand which are the elements that appear immutable in human evolution because inherent in the very nature of man, and in what measure individual actions can influence society. Societies must therefore admit the necessity of certain laws of evolution, even as each one of us accepts that he must live according to his times. We must not imagine that in extending similar institutions to peoples whose evolution is at a different stage we can thereby give them an identical civilization. It would be vain, for example, to want to introduce parliamentary democracy to a people living under a full feudal régime. Institutions are, in fact, only the reflection of a certain degree of evolution. A social change cannot be carried out or maintained save insofar as it is accompanied by a parallel change in moral ideals.

But to admit that societies are determined by the stage of their evolution is not to deny that one can influence the level of their civilization. The social framework of a society is not the expression of its civilization. It is only its support. What makes a work of art is not the frame, whether it be of oak, of ebony or of gilt, but the picture within it. It is the same for societies; the essential is not their form, but the human conception that accompanies it. The same social form can create an ideal of justice or constitute an instrument of oppression, be favourable to the blossoming of a great intellectual and artistic upsurge or, on the contrary, tarnish all spiritual forces to the benefit of mere material considerations.

The social question is without doubt essential, but what must dominate it, under penalty of stopping all progress, is respect for human personality, by giving to every man the maximum of security, dignity and well-being; for if it be true that civilization is above all based on moral ideas, it must be admitted that its aim is to increase the individual value of man and not to make him an ant in an antheap.

These few considerations will serve to explain to the reader the manner in which I have conceived this work. I have tried to follow, through the centuries and among all peoples, the development of economic and social conditions that form the basis of societies, and to show how justice and public and private institutions are derived from it. I have tried at the same time to follow the action of religious, moral, philosophical and scientific ideas that were the work of great individuals whose influence on the development of peoples has created humanity out of the human masses.

Perhaps in following this drama of history, we shall be painfully struck by the weaknesses, the follies, the cruelties that have never ceased to accompany it and will be tempted to think, at first, on the vanity of human effort when faced with the successive ruins of the most advanced civilizations.

We must, it is true, resign ourselves to accept the world as it is, a place where death necessarily accompanies life. But if we resign ourselves to admitting that the plane upon which the activities of man are exercised is that of a savagery which exists everywhere around us in nature, and that the task of civilization consists precisely in breaking free of this, then it seems to me difficult not to be filled with admiration, confidence and enthusiasm at the admirable work of creation that human beings in the course of several thousand years have been able to achieve. Often listening only to their own interests, they have devoted themselves to the conquest of seas and continents, have come into contact with one another, have established a system of trade that has introduced into life a refinement and a variety whence have come art and thought. In the midst of a savage contest of instincts, individual consciences have been formed and with them have appeared charity and the idea of the oneness of humanity. It was on these bases that blossomed the great religions of Egypt, of Persia, of India, the moral ideas of the Stoics, and finally Christianity.

Is it not a wonderful spectacle to see men progressively liberating themselves from their primitive savagery and developing until they are able to conceive divinity and the infinite, to discover the laws that control the worlds and matter, and being able, without having been forced by any necessity, to express in immortal works of art that thirst for the ideal that instinctively fills the human heart and which is the true, if not the only, source of civilization?

Thus the view that emerges from history is, despite everything, optimistic, for it teaches us that empires built through centuries of evolution—and of which their statesmen and warriors have thought themselves the originators—have fallen, yet ideas, once conceived, are not lost. Through all the ups and downs of history an immense hoard of moral values has little by little been created, to the formation of which all races and all generations have contributed. It has happened that certain epochs have left this hoard unexploited, yet it has existed none the less and succeeding generations have found it again. For it is the greatness of spiritual values that, once discovered, they exist in themselves, always ready to shine forth to those men of goodwill who turn to them.

I would like to thank M. Ernest Stein, Professor at Louvain University, who was good enough to put at my disposal the still unpublished manuscript of Volume II of his *Histoire du Bas Empire romain*, and also my son Pierre who drew the maps for this volume.

I have thought it preferable not to give the reader any references, although I have often departed from generally accepted views, especially insofar as the history of Egypt and the Orient is concerned. The justification for my viewpoint may be found in my *Histoire des Institutions et du Droit privé de l'Ancienne Egypte* (3 vols. Brussels, 1932–1935)

JACQUES PIRENNE

CONTENTS

MAPS

Folders

at end of book

PART ONE

THE CONTINENTAL ERA

BOOK I

The Formation of the Great States
from the
Origins to the XXth Century BC
and
the First Aryan Invasion from the XXth
to the XVIth Century BC

CHAPTER I
THE ORIGINS

EARLIEST TRADITIONS

IT is in the three river basins of the Nile, the Euphrates and Tigris, and the Indus that civilization appears in the IVth millenary BC in an already highly developed form. Agriculture, urban life, trade, navigation and writing already existed. This means that civilization was already, at that time, extremely ancient and was the result of an evolution of several thousand years.

The oriental peoples of the most ancient civilizations preserve the tradition of a history lost in the night of time. But Babylon and China alone give a duration to these distant and mythical epochs. Berosius[1] relates that after a period of anarchy lasting 1,680,000 years the first social groups made their appearance, and slowly changed in the course of the 432,000 years before the Sumerian deluge[2] when real history begins.

The Chinese tradition is still more interesting, since it tries to follow the main stages of the world and of civilization; in the beginning was creation when the sky, the earth and living beings first appeared; life began during the reign of the 'august families of heaven', and then passed under the rule of the 'august families of the earth' before finally attaining that of the 'august families of men'. After this mythical period, reckoned at 594,000 years, humanity was already becoming civilized, and had spent hundreds of centuries learning to make huts, to discover fire and to invent the wheel. About the XLVth century BC men practised stock-breeding, learned to count, established a calendar and organized marriage; in the XXXIInd century came the culture of cereals, the art of medicine, the first markets; in the XXVIth century came writing, arithmetic, astronomy, the use of carts and boats, the building of houses and palaces, silk-weaving, in short what we call civilization.

[1] A Babylonian historian who wrote about 280 BC.

[2] Sumeria is the delta country of the Euphrates and Tigris. The Sumerian 'deluge' dates from about 3000 BC.

These traditions show a knowledge of human history and scientific ideas much more advanced than those of the Bible, which dates the creation of the world only about two thousand years before the Sumerian deluge. This may be explained by the late epoch in which the Hebrew people attained a sedentary civilization.

These historical myths are accompanied, among the Sumerians, by very ancient traditions: 'Human kind, when it was created, did not know bread to eat nor garments to cover itself. The people walked on all fours and ate grass with their mouths like sheep and drank the water of the ditches'.

The Odyssey evokes the cave age when 'from the summit of high mountains or from the depths of caves each man, without concern for his fellow, laid down the law to his children and his wife'—IX.115.

FROM NOMADISM TO SEDENTARY CIVILIZATION

As for the Egyptians, they remembered that before settling in the Nile Valley they had known a nomadic life. It must have been somewhat similar to the age of the Patriarchs as described in the Bible.

While they were still living as nomads on the high plateaux, today desert, the future inhabitants of Egypt, who came from Africa, Asia and Europe to form an extraordinary amalgam of races[1], held the religious ideas that are to be found among all the peoples of the ancient East; they venerated the forces of Nature that they subordinated to a great mother-goddess, the image of fecundity. In short, what men first adored was Life.[2]

Little by little, it is impossible to say when or where, they conceived, alongside the life that was evident around them, a life-principle. This conception was translated on the religious plane into a belief in a male god, a fecundating god who first appeared as subordinate to the mother-goddess but who gradually took the dominant place as a creator-god. This stage of evolution must have been reached about the time of the stabilization of the nomad peoples in the Nile Valley. The stabilization resulted in the founding of villages and the principle of patriarchal marriage, an institution that had its parallel in religious ideas; the cult of the mother-goddess was replaced by one venerating a pair of gods, the heaven-god

[1] It is impossible to give any precise details on the races of Egypt, whose population was made up of a mixture that recalls the language, composed of Semitic, Berber and Bantu elements. The negroid type, of which very definite traces have been found dating from the prehistoric epoch of Upper Egypt, has never ceased to lose ground before the non-negroids of the Delta and Middle Egypt.

[2] No trace has been found in Egypt of a totemic civilization; the clan and the totem were totally unknown there.

and the earth-goddess,[1] symbol of the primordial world; the son who was shortly afterwards attributed to them represented the created world.

The idea of a great creator-god, the god of Heaven, was also that of the Aryans—he is the Diaous of the Indo-Mitannians, the Zeus of the Greeks and the Jupiter of the Latins—as well as of the Mongols and the peoples of the Asiatic steppes.

The régime of the village and the patriarchal family was based on agriculture; and agriculture gave rise to a cult common to all the peoples of the ancient East whatever their race—nature-worship. Dedicated to the god of vegetation, born in the springtime to die in autumn and to be reborn in the following spring, it was to develop in Egypt around the cult of Osiris.

Osiris is not the great creator-god, he is only the manifestation of the principle of fecundity in the world of vegetation; he was therefore quite naturally regarded as the son of Heaven and Earth.

The period of stabilization is the great stage in the life of peoples. Nomads know a type of society which, once it has realized the cohesion of the tribe around the chiefs of the clan from whom, when necessity arises, a military 'king' is chosen, does not develop because conditions of life do not change. The nomads described twenty centuries before Christ in the Egyptian texts are exactly similar to those, Aryans, Mongols, Turks or Semites, who were so often to pour their devastating hordes across the sedentary lands. Stabilization, on the contrary, by introducing the idea of property, of private ownership of land, of the community of interest which creates neighbourliness and which little by little replaces that of blood and finally of the family, makes civilization advance rapidly.

Therefore the Egyptians attributed to Osiris, the god of vegetation, the invention not only of culture but also of marriage, morals and law.

If all peoples had known nature worship, not all had conceived it in the same manner. Those who, like the Egyptians, made of it from the first a cult with moral aims are rare. Osiris, who brought civilization to man, is the god of good. He is at the same time god of life and of death. Dead, he is confided to the earth—symbolized by the grain—and with the spring vegetation he is born again. But man too, once dead, is buried and confided to Mother Earth, whence Osiris is born. Becoming a part of the Great All that is the Earth, he too will follow its laws and, like the plants, like Osiris, he will rise again.

The idea of resurrection is perhaps at first conceived in the form of

[1] In later times the sky becomes a goddess, Nout, and the earth a god, Geb, the great creator-god being by then symbolized by the sun, Ra.

metempsychosis, the dead man being reborn, though not necessarily in his original form. But as Osiris becomes progressively more and more the god of the dead, the dead are assimilated to him; the dead henceforward must, like Osiris, be reborn with their own personality; on one condition, however, that of being able to be assimilated to Osiris. For Osiris is the god of good. Resurrection will therefore be reserved to men who, in the course of this life, have practised virtue.

Thus nature worship was transformed, among the Egyptians, into a religion that assigns an eternal sense to human life; the resurrection in the world over which the god Osiris presides.

THE FORMATION OF THE VILLAGE AND OF THE SEIGNIORIAL RÉGIME

Stabilization formed communities settled on limited areas. The political group is born, symbolized by an emblem—the Egyptian ensigns—and protected by the great mother-goddess or some other local god, since the cult of the forces of nature surrounds men with divine manifestations. In its origin, social life has no sanction other than the cult. Every group is therefore of religious origin. That is why stabilization splits up the cult into as many various forms as there are social, that is to say political, communities. The leader of the community, the king, is a priest who has no power other than that which he holds from the deity. This local divinity is usually the great mother-goddess. But, venerated in her local aspect, she gives birth to a number of goddesses who, little by little, take on distinct personalities.[1] The cult of the *nome*[2] in Egypt—similar to the cult of the city in Greece three thousand years later—is born. It is a phenomenon common to all the ancient East.

THE EGYPTIAN NOMES

The Egyptian *nomes* banded together, or fought with one another; and so were born, by agreement or by force, confederations which were the first real political states.

At first these confederations were based on landholding and founded on a social hierarchy that made the possessor of the soil the master of those who, in order to live, had to ask him for the use of it.

The nomad group already knew social differences; the chiefs of families

[1] It was the same in Syria, in Mesopotamia, in Greece.
[2] The Egyptian '*nome*' is, in origin, the equivalent of the Greek city.

formed a nobility, the vanquished were semi-servile dependents. Attachment to the soil and the idea of landed property which derived from it made the nobility a landowning class. Thenceforward, the group was divided not only into nobles or free men and dependents, but into rich and poor, the rich who possessed most land becoming quite naturally the lords. Among these lords, some were more, some less, powerful. They formed a hierarchy, fought among themselves to assert their leadership, formed groups under the authority of the strongest. A manorial system was thus little by little set up which, on the political plane, took the form of a type of feudalism. This development is universal. It is to be found in all the ancient East, in India, in China, and it will be in this form that the first social and political organizations will emerge among the Germans on the farther side of the Rhine between the 5th and 12th centuries AD.

CHAPTER II
THE FIRST URBAN CIVILIZATIONS

THE NILE DELTA

IN the fourth millenary BC the sea and the rivers were a beneficent influence on the agricultural populations in the deltas of the Nile, in Mesopotamia and in the Valley of the Indus. The waterways favoured trade, and markets were created. Fishing developed along the sea-coasts, then coastal shipping, piracy and trade. From the most ancient times Egypt was in touch, by sea, with the Syrian coast. Egypt lacked timber and the Syrians were only too willing to exploit their magnificent forests of pine and cedar; the Egyptians had a grain surplus, and international trade thenceforth appeared. Navigation created a new social class, of sailors and traders; the fishing centres turned into merchant cities. In the Nile delta Metelis, the first port to trade with Asia, became supreme in the ancient landholding confederation formed on the Libyan frontier. Cities were founded on the principal branches of the Nile, Mendes, Busiris, Athribis, Sais, Bubastis, Hermopolis, Letopolis, Butos and many others. Contact with the sea multiplied internal activity. Husbandry developed in order to furnish the navigators with return freights; and, after it, industry. A middle class was created which lived by trade and was animated by a spirit of adventure. Colonies were established along the Nile; expeditions setting off from the Delta went up the river as far as Nubia to search for gold.

At the place where the branches of the Nile joined, an important market, Letopolis, arose. And as transactions were only possible when sanctioned by religion, the merchants of all the cities set up shrines there. So was born, opposite Letopolis, the Holy City of Egypt, Heliopolis, where all the cults met and fused. A priesthood was formed there which, by combining the national cults, laid the foundations of a theology; and since the cult was the sanction of law, a legal tradition developed there parallel with the religious tradition.

In the cities where the ancient landowning nobility was dominant, a conflict with the new middle class became inevitable. The nobility rallied around the city cult; the middle class, made up of heterogeneous elements, practised nature worship, the universal cult which, by contact with Syrian nature worship, was already saturated with Asiatic forms. For trade, by developing exchanges between different peoples, hastened the formation of an international religion which, quite naturally, would be nature worship since all peoples knew it.

When the balance between the economic or numerical power of the ancient nobles and that of the middle class breaks down, social revolution becomes imminent. The oldest of these revolutions known to us was the one which triumphed at Busiris in the Delta. There the aristocracy had to give way to the new commercial class, the local cult was replaced by that of Osiris, and a new royalty appeared, as a reaction against the former aristocratic power, founded on the popular and universal Osiris cult. The social transformation which took place at Busiris spread through all the towns of Lower Egypt. Royalty of the Osirian type triumphed everywhere. Urban customs were codified. And at Heliopolis, theology recognized Osiris as the royal god, thus legitimatizing the newly established power.

Among the principal cities, each the centre of a federation, a struggle for leadership broke out. After Busiris, Letopolis, Sais, Hermopolis, Butos, exercised it successively. But each time the monarchy, created by force, asked for recognition at Heliopolis. Heliopolis thus became the guardian of legitimate power and the custom arose for kings to go there to be anointed.

At Busiris, royalty had first of all taken an elective form. But, as it became stronger, it became hereditary. In the cities where democratic evolution continued, the royal power was replaced by that of elected magistrates, the 'ten men'. When Butos took over the leadership, there was only one king in the Delta; thus monarchy was created.

THE BASIN OF THE INDUS

While urban civilization born of overseas trade was developing in Lower Egypt, the delta and the lower valley of the Indus were covered with cities which, from the IVth millenary BC, attained such a development, with their many-storeyed houses, their public baths, their drainage systems, that they already, at that time, represented the zenith of a very ancient economic and social evolution.

Urban civilization had taken possession of the basin of the Indus as far

Map No. 1

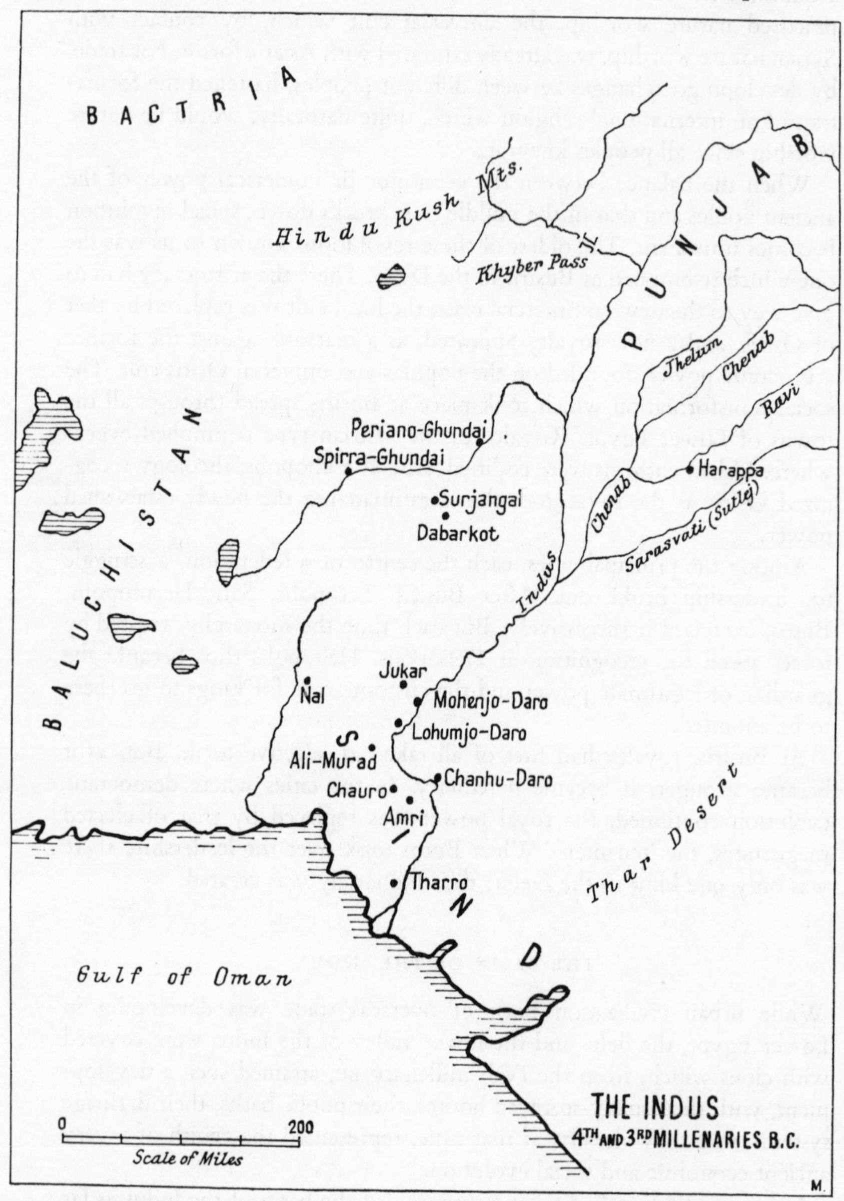
BACTRIA
BALUCHISTAN
Hindu Kush Mts.
Khyber Pass
PUNJAB
Jhelum
Chenab
Ravi
Periano-Ghundai
Spirra-Ghundai
Surjangal
Dabarkot
Harappa
Chenab
Indus
Sarasvati (Sutlej)
Jukar
Nal
Mohenjo-Daro
Lohumjo-Daro
SIND
Ali-Murad
Chanhu-Daro
Chauro
Amri
Thar Desert
Tharro
Gulf of Oman
0
200
Scale of Miles
THE INDUS
4TH AND 3RD MILLENARIES B.C.
M.

as the Punjab itself, where the great commercial city of Harappa was founded.

It seems that there had been among the great cities—as in Egypt—a struggle for leadership which, always going farther and farther up the valley, passed from Amri to Mohenjo-Daro and finally to Harappa. Then, perhaps, the great urban civilization of the Dravidians became decadent, at least in the Punjab, for its centre returned to the lower Indus Valley at Chamhou-Daro.

The basins of the Indus and the Saravasti represent an area of civilization far more extensive than that of the Nile Valley or Mesopotamia. Its peak was about 2,900 BC, when it extended widely towards Baluchistan; and it must be assumed that, at that distant epoch, it had reached the basin of the Narbada on the Malabar coast, on whose estuary the trade centres of Barygaza (Baroch) and Suppara (the Ophir of the Bible) north of Bombay were to know so great an expansion.

Perhaps, granted its extent and the level of its city life, the Indus civilization is the most ancient known to us. It was, furthermore, very similar to that of Ancient Egypt. The cult there was dominated by a mother-goddess and a god of fecundity, whose three-headed representation foreshadows the god Shiva, as well as by a nature deity with the phallus and the sacred tree as emblems, as they were in Egypt. Hieroglyphic writing was also largely in use and there were continual exchanges overseas.

The towns of the Indus seem more advanced, therefore more ancient, than those of the Mesopotamian delta. Perhaps the Mesopotamian cities were born out of contact with the Indus; tradition indeed relates that civilization was brought to the Land of Sumeria by a man-fish from the Persian Gulf.

Moreover, certain relations and perhaps also resemblances of race exist between them.

The Dravidian society of the Indus probably owed its rapid development to the fact that it looked both seaward and towards the continent; it imported iron from Rajputana, amazonite from Kashmir and jade from eastern Turkestan—which proves that caravan routes penetrated deeply into Central Asia even before the XXXth century BC—and exported them by sea, especially to the Mesopotamian cities.

THE DELTA OF THE EUPHRATES AND TIGRIS

The population of the Mesopotamian delta recalls in its formation that of the Nile. It seems to have come from the Iranian plateau, as the river silt progressively created habitable lands. Perhaps it was the same immigration that, coming from Iran, reached, by way of the region of Carchemish, the Mediterranean coast, where it is found at Ugarit in Syria.

Another immigration, this time Semitic, reached the Euphrates and Tigris valleys from the west; it was thus that Akkad was peopled by the same Semitic race as that which occupied almost the whole of Syria, very different in ethnic origin and language from the Sumerians.

The Sumerians of the Delta were the first to become settled, both because of the fertility of the soil and the proximity of the sea. The first achievements of civilization, agriculture, flint-working, clay moulding and metalwork, came to them from the land. But it is from the moment when trade led them to adventure on the sea—whence perhaps came immigrants also—that the cities appeared.

The civilization of the Sumerians recalls that of Egypt and the Indus as much from the religious as from the social viewpoint. Their religious ideas were centred on the cult of a mother-goddess, of whom Ishtar is the type, and of a great creator-god who, in the urban epoch, was to take a solar aspect under the name of Shamash. This cult broke into various local religions devoted to families of gods who, despite their common origin, ended by differing from one another.

Urban civilization developed in the IVth millenary in Sumeria in direct contact with the Indus. It is on the coast that the first city appears, Eridu, turned seaward, a phenomenon identical with that which had led to the founding of Metelis in Egypt. Then there was Ur, at the mouth of the Euphrates, and on the confluent branches of the two rivers, Uruk, Larsa, Suruppak, Lagash, Badtibirra-Ki, Umma. Struggles for leadership took place between these larger cities. After Eridu, the industrial city of Badtibirra-Ki, whose prosperity was derived from its copper work, took the lead. Doubtless because of its industrial activity and its artisan population, its middle class was the first to set in motion the social revolution, which led, as at Busiris in Egypt, to a new urban régime symbolized by the triumph of the nature god Dumuzi who, like his Egyptian counterpart, Osiris, was to become the royal god.

The development of the land of Sumeria was brusquely halted by a series of great floods that destroyed the principal cities of the Delta between the XXXVth and XXXth centuries BC. Evolution, however, was to begin again at once,[1] and to reach its highest point in the IIIrd millenary.

[1] See my *Civilisations antiques*, 2nd edition, Paris, 1958.

CHAPTER III

RISE AND FALL OF THE ANCIENT EMPIRE IN EGYPT

THE CENTRALIZED MONARCHY OF LOWER EGYPT

AT the end of the IVth millenary BC the Egyptian Delta formed a unified kingdom under the dynasty of Butos. The first centralized monarchical state was being built there in a form, both religious and political, based on a civil law by which the Egyptian monarchy lived for more than thirty centuries. It was the most grandiose in its continuity of all the achievements of human history.

No traces of feudal or seigniorial organization remained in the kingdom of Butos. The king was the sole source of all power, which he exercised by means of a central government presided over by a Chancellor. The old hereditary nobility was replaced by officers of state; social duties were taken from the aristocracy of birth and handed over to salaried officials; the social hierarchy disappeared, but a financial order, supported by taxes on income, was introduced. The disappearance of the nobility heralded the advent of an individualist régime; family responsibility became looser, intellectual culture developed, writing, born in the form of a primitive picture-script, became fixed, wealth became more and more transferable, civil status and the census of 'gold and fields' were organized by the State; the calendar was established, the decimal system became universal. In short, society advanced, and art, technical achievement and law developed.

SOLAR THEOLOGY

As power became centralized, so religion evolved towards a pantheist monotheism. The establishment of a theory of power went hand in hand with the establishment of a solar theology, which was to reach its most highly developed form under the Ancient Empire. It was one of the most exalted achievements not only of Egyptian, but of human, thought. It was to mark with its imprint the whole history of Egypt and exercise a profound and undeniable influence on Greek philosophy and Jewish ethics.

From the cult of the forces of Nature, of the mother-goddess and the creator-god, was to emerge a co-ordinated and wonderfully exalted idealism.

In the beginning was chaos (Noun) wherein the spirit of the world (Atum) was diffused and unconscious of itself. Matter and spirit therefore have not been created; they are of all time. Creation is only the consciousness that the spirit of the world takes upon itself, freeing itself from chaos, light separating itself from darkness.

Ra, the consciousness of the world, conceives it. And, in conceiving, he creates it. The created world is nothing save the materialization of the divine thought. The genealogy of the gods symbolizes the evolution of matter passing from chaos into form.

All that exists 'has come out of the eyes and mouth' of Ra; which means that beings emerge from initial chaos progressively as Ra sees them, that is to say conceives them; and names them, that is to say wills them. On this theological conception the priests of Memphis, from the Ancient Empire onward, elaborated a theory of will, of which the text has come down to us.

Thus appeared the elements, proceeding one from another; air and fire, the divinities Shu and Tefnet, the earth and the heavens, the god Geb and the goddess Nut, which the air, Shu, keeps apart.

But from the time that the elements existed, that is to say from the time that the divine concept was made concrete in material form, good and evil appeared, opposed to one another in a constant struggle. The good, the god Osiris, is life, fruitfulness, knowledge; the evil, the god Seth, is death, sterility, injustice.

Once the elements had been separated, the work of creation was completed by successive materializations whence proceeded all beings; at first the gods, that is to say the concepts—such as Maat, justice, daughter of Ra—then living beings, firstly and foremostly men; then things endowed with a personality, with a 'form' given them by the divine consciousness constantly creative, since, by the sole fact of its existence, the thought of Ra does not cease to conceive, that is to say to create.

Thus, for the Egyptian, realities are concepts; sentient things are only imperfect and transitory manifestations of the divine thought. The world, the material projection of the knowledge and the will of the great creative principle, identified with the solar god Ra, is in its essence as perfect as possible. Goodness, knowledge and life merge into one another. Egyptian idealism results in an optimistic view of the world.

Without doubt evil exists. This is due to the fact that matter is finite.

In Ra opposites are reconciled, 'the being and the non-being', the past and the future; he is the absolute. Sentient beings, on the contrary, are material and, in consequence, finite. In them life struggles against death, that is to say knowledge against injustice, good against evil, form against chaos, the future against the past. The divine consciousness creates matter, but matter tends towards the void. And the world continues to exist only because the consciousness which penetrates it does not cease to recreate it.

Every being, as a part of the All, includes at the same time matter (khet) and spirit (ka) and from the union of these two elements is born the form, the individuality of the being, its soul (ba). Man, microcosm of the universe, is formed of perishable matter and immortal spirit, but these two elements are only momentarily united; their union realized by the divine consciousness gives birth to the individual soul. The soul has its origin in the divine will; its aim is to return to the absolute spirit whence it proceeded, which is Ra, freeing itself from the original impurity of matter and from the impurity with which every man covers himself by sin.

Since the divine spirit is in every being in the form of *ka*, man, in order to possess knowledge and to practise good, must turn to the great god Ra. Knowledge and morality are from Ra, placed in us by him, that is to say revealed.

In order to win eternal life, therefore, every Egyptian must live according to the will of Ra. The king must ensure the triumph of the divine *ka* that is in him by assuring the reign of justice—which is the justification of his absolutism—even as every man must make the divine will manifest by practising charity. This is explained in the records of works of charity engraved on tombs from the IIIrd millenary BC. 'I have given him who was hungry to eat, I have given him who was thirsty to drink, I have clothed him who was naked, I have taken across the Nile him who had no boat, I have buried him who had no sons.'

After this life, the soul of the king, even as that of his humblest subject, will be judged before the tribunal of the gods, presided over by Justice, and in the presence of the whole universe, represented by the god Earth and the goddess Heaven. If the soul is judged pure, it will live eternally, that is to say that its personality, become spirit, will exist in the glory of the divine absolute; if it has allowed itself to be weighed down by impure matter, it will disappear.

The moral conceptions of the Egyptians are in fact centred on the other world which is attained by the practice of good. The individual consciousness alone can save human beings by revealing to them the universal values placed by the divine consciousness at the source of all life.

THE OSIRIAN RITE

This struggle of good against evil, which is to give man eternal life, is symbolized in the myth of Osiris who was to become, in the course of centuries, the great spiritual ferment for the Oriental and Greek peoples. Osiris, the former nature god, had at first presided over the constant renewal of nature. From this renewal men conceived the idea that life naturally succeeded death, as much for men as for the vegetable world. So was formed the idea of a resurrection of men after their death in another world, in which presided Osiris, the god of vegetation. Osiris thus becomes the God of the Dead, the God of life beyond the grave. As a benefactor of humanity, he was credited with the invention of the first laws given to men. Around Osiris, half-god, half-man, the myth of the struggle of the good against the evil inherent in life was created. In this myth Osiris, or good, is said to have been killed by his brother Seth, that is evil. But Isis, the wife of Osiris and the goddess of love, recalls him to life; then, in a great outburst, Osiris appeals to the god Ra, by whom he is embraced and their two souls become one. Good, thenceforth, is identified with the eternal principle of creation. The death of the god assures the final triumph of Good in the created world.

The drama of the struggle between good and evil is ceaselessly renewed; the good, practised by imperfect man, succumbs of necessity to evil; love alone can lead man towards the divine, comforting him after his weaknesses; by love man attains to the faith which, by uniting his soul to the divine, prepares for him eternal life.

Thus the nature cult, devoted at first to fruitfulness alone, has arisen to the most exalted mysticism, which was little by little to penetrate the 'mysteries' that prepared the world, three thousand years later, to receive Christianity.

It is clear that the Egyptian theology did not build only a religion, but also a general view of the world which united in a single whole the ideas of divinity, morality and the theory of power. Egypt was never to abandon this unitary conception. It is the secret of the wonderful continuity of her civilization.

THE FEUDAL MONARCHY IN UPPER EGYPT

While urban civilization was developing in the Delta, Upper Egypt, landholding and feudal, was grouped around the Princes of Ombos. They owed their position of leadership to their control of the Nubian gold market. The colonies founded by the cities of the North brought trade into the valley. They fought with the feudal lords; and at Koptos, where the caravan route from the Red Sea to the Nile had created the principal market of Upper Egypt, a monarchy was set up, supported by the merchant colonies in reaction against the feudal lords of the South. Soon translated to Nekhen and supported by the kings of Butos, it unified the whole of Upper Egypt in a single monarchy.

Like the kings of Butos, the feudal kings of Nekhen had their power confirmed at Heliopolis where they went to be anointed; Heliopolis thus became the uncontested arbiter of the whole country.

Under the monarchy the South began to be civilized. The king, in order to reduce the power of the feudal lords, surrounded himself with ten great vassals, with whose help he held the whole country in his hands, created a royal army and organized a rudimentary administration under a chancellor.

Meanwhile in the North the cities resisted the royal policy of centralization; and the kingdom of Butos collapsed in a struggle against the great cities, jealous of their autonomy. The fall of the monarchy left the Asiatic frontier open to the invasions of the nomads. The kings of the South intervened and conquered, one after the other, the rich cities of the Delta which, divided amongst themselves, were unable to form a league for their own defence.

Thus, about 3000 BC, Menes united the 'red crown' of the North and the 'white crown' of the South; Egypt was unified.

THE UNIFIED MONARCHY

Egypt once unified, the mission of the Holy City of Heliopolis was ended. It had prepared, by its role as arbiter, a legitimate power which gradually grew greater until it dominated all Egypt which thenceforward entered into a new era of her history, that of the absolute monarchy. This is the era usually known as the Ancient Empire.

For five centuries the first two dynasties went on unifying monarchical institutions by destroying feudalism in the south and the autonomy of the cities of the north. But, unified territorially by the feudal kings of the south, Egypt was also to become unified legally, politically and economically by the extension to the whole country of centralized institutions, by an individualist common law and by the economic organization of the Delta.

The monarchy established a theory of power which, while liberating itself from sacerdotal sanction, found its justification in the sacred character

Map No. 2

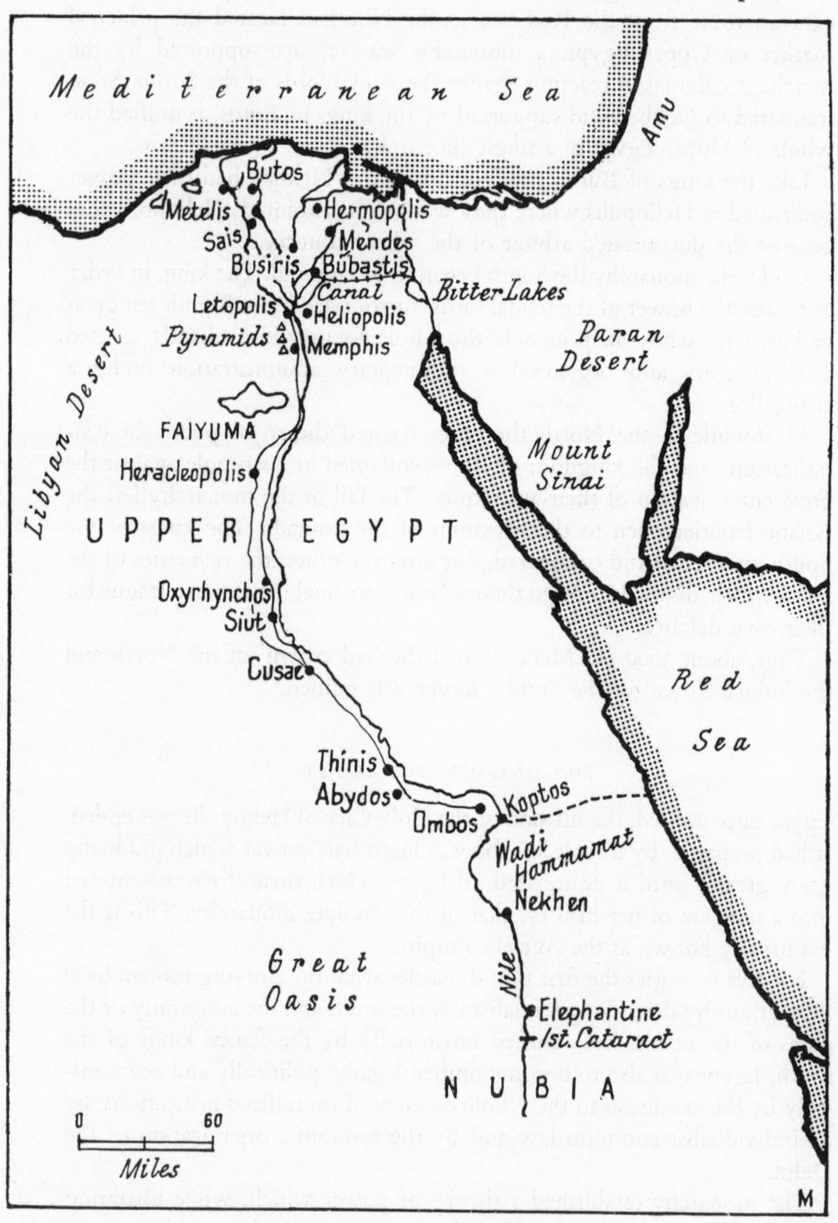

Egypt in the 4th and 3rd Millenaries BC.

transmitted hereditarily in the dynasty; the central government was developed on a basis of bureaucracy and the king achieved his absolutism by dispensing with every hereditary power other than his own, that is to say by suppressing every class distinction and thus giving all citizens equal rights.

THE LIBERAL PERIOD

The monarchy reached its zenith under the IIIrd dynasty (about 2778–2723 BC). The Chancellor was the highest dignitary in the State. The ancient feudal council of the ten great vassals of the South became a real Cabinet with Ministers presiding over the great departments of the central administration: the Chancellery, Finance, the Registry, Public Works, Administration of the Royal Domains, the Irrigation Service, Religion, Military Supply. All these departments had branches in the forty-two provinces of the country, placed under the authority of governors. The officials, appointed by royal decree, were paid and were subject to a rigorous grading; they had to work their way upward from the lowest rank. The tax system was calculated on a property basis established after declarations to which all taxpayers were subject: civil status and the public registers were organized by the State. Courts of Notables presided over by the provincial governors administered justice; under the Vth dynasty, appeals from their decisions could be made to 'the High Court of the Six Chambers' at Memphis, made up of the Ministers and professional judges. The procedure was entirely written and in every court a Clerk of the Court had charge of the archives, while the registers of civil status were confided to special magistrates. The penal code was not severe, a thing remarkable in itself and which showed a high degree of civilization. For the thousand years that the Ancient Empire lasted, we know no account of, or representation of, the death penalty.

The courts, like the administration, applied the law promulgated by the king and drawn up by him with the help of Privy Councillors who formed a real Legislative Council.

All Egyptians had equal rights before the law. There were no nobles amongst them and no slaves. Private slavery did not exist in Egypt at this time. Only the State made use of prisoners of war as public slaves in the quarries and on the Crown lands, but the workers, normally, were free.

An individualist common law corresponded to this public egalitarian civil law. The family, strictly monogamous—only the king had several legitimate wives—was based on the legal equality of the spouses. Marital authority or paternal authority did not exist; the law of the Ancient Empire did not recognize the privilege of age nor the privilege of the male. The right of wills was free and the laws of succession similar for sons and for daughters.

Private property, both fixed and movable, was alienable and the laws of succession continually parcelled it out. Smallholdings were the rule; large estates were rare and did not exceed about two hundred and fifty acres. Leases were concluded for a single year (the rising of the Nile did not allow a crop rotation) and were registered, as were also labour contracts stipulated by the workers.

Agriculture, highly developed, assured the existence of a population of several million souls. But the activity of the cities also played a considerable role in the country's economy. The large towns of the Delta numbered several tens of thousands of inhabitants employed in trade and industry; among the urban middle classes were wealthy ship-owners and modest craftsmen, all fellow-citizens, and wealth was won and lost quickly. Trade was mainly by sea; the export of corn and manufactured products provided return freights for the import of timber and raw materials from Syria. Trade with Byblos, the great industrial centre where Egyptian traders met Sumerian business men, and with the interior of the country, was also in private hands. The king, however, carried on State trading with some distant countries. The Administration of Public Works and that of the Finances organized in common the despatch of expeditions by way of the Red Sea to the Land of Punt, the Somali and Arabian coasts, where, it seems, the Egyptians went to obtain African and Indian products. In Nubia, the king carried on a colonial policy; caravans went there to search for ebony, ivory and gold. In Sinai, the copper and turquoise mines were a State monopoly.

To assure the safety of the country, the army was made up of recruits divided into tactical units under the command of career-officers—the generals were nearly always sons or relations of the king—and was stationed in citadels on the frontiers. Their supply and equipment was administered by the 'arsenals'. Frontier-zones placed under the control of generals covered the country on the desert side.

From the IIIrd dynasty onward, cultural and artistic development was as remarkable as that of trade and law; the sacred precinct of Sakkara, the most ancient architectural complex that the past has left to us, was one of the most beautiful creations of all antiquity; it opens the period of artistic greatness that Egypt was to know under the Ancient Empire.

ABSOLUTIST EVOLUTION

The monarchy, borne onward by the centralization of power, evolved towards absolutism. Save for the king, only one independent power existed; the priesthood, a power the more considerable in that the monarchy found its justification in a divine origin. The kings of the IVth dynasty (2723–2563 BC)—who built the Great Pyramids of Gizeh—mastered the priesthood after a radical religious and dynastic reform. Pushing forward audaciously the double evolution, monotheist and absolutist, Cheops concentrated all the cults around that of the one god Ra, of whom he proclaimed himself at the same time the son and the incarnation, and breaking the opposition of the priesthood subjected it to the royal authority. This concentration of power was accompanied by a transformation of the principles of civil law. Shut away within the administrative hierarchy that it had itself created, the monarchy had either to resign itself to becoming integrated with the administration, or break its power by placing over it a government responsible to the sole will of the king. That is what the Pharaohs of the IVth dynasty did. The chancellor, up till then an official, was replaced by a 'supreme judge-vizier' chosen outside the official bureaucracy and who was to be the instrument of the personal power of the king.

Identified with Ra, the Pharaoh set up a cult which became the official State religion. A royal priesthood was established, and the cult of the god-king, assimilated to the great solar god, was organized in all the temples. The palace became a sanctuary, the court officials took precedence over those of the administration and, quite naturally, the royal priesthood assumed a leading position in the State.

But the opposition of the priesthood of the ancient cults was not disarmed; the struggle that followed ended, we do not know for what reasons, in its victory and under the Vth dynasty (2563–2423 BC) there was a return to the earlier religious tradition. The solar theology was forced to reconcile itself with all the archaisms that encumbered it and the texts engraved in the pyramids of the Vth dynasty mark a return to the faith of olden times.

THE FORMATION OF AN OLIGARCHY

The Vth dynasty (2563–2423 BC), which seems to have owed its throne to the support of the priesthood, reveals a clearly religious orientation. The monarchy takes the form of a theocracy. The royal priesthood, which was now the foundation of absolutism, is transformed into a privileged oligarchy. The duties carried out by the priesthood, rewarded by grants and benefices in land, become hereditary; the same families fill several posts in the priesthood and, while multiplying their stipends, become little by little a class of large landowners. The temples that celebrated the royal cult were granted larger and larger donations taken from the crown lands.

On the other hand, absolutism, by creating royal appointments outside the framework of the bureaucracy, favoured the monopoly of high offices by the families of the new priestly nobility. The personal power of the king, backed up by privy councillors superimposed on the administration, passed in reality into their hands. The king soon became even more subject to the rule of this oligarchy than previously to that of the bureaucracy. The vizierate was monopolized by certain families. The government of the *nomes* was granted by the viziers to their sons who, by-passing the grades of the former official regime, distorted the whole administrative apparatus of the State.

Like the priestly functions, the high offices of state had a tendency to become hereditary.

Having taken possession of civil and religious power, the oligarchy obtained tax exemption also. The funeral foundations, set up to celebrate the cult of dead kings, and also the temples were granted privileges of tax exemption which, growing more extensive, ended by assuming all the rights over the royal domains. The temples, whose lands never ceased to grow larger to the detriment of the treasury, ended by becoming states within the state.

The delegation by the king of his sovereign powers constitutes, in the civil law of the time, a new idea. By the end of the Vth dynasty it had been transferred to the administrative plane and the 'benefice-function' first appeared; the King confided to certain high priests or to a general returning victorious from Palestine the hereditary government of certain provinces of Upper Egypt. Thenceforward the fate of the administrative apparatus created by the monarchy to escape from the hereditary power of the nobles was sealed. The evolution of civil law was turned inside out. Up to the IVth dynasty the monarchy had always continued to centralize all the power in its own hands until the formulation of the principle of absolutism; absolutism had only been able to assert itself through royal agents; these, now become an oligarchy by the very fact that they by-passed the administrative duties of the State, were transformed into a new nobility that was to dismember the sovereign power.

At the same time, this nobility, more and more richly endowed with benefices, became a class of large landowners exempt from taxes and who, by virtue of this immunity, exercised the royal jurisdiction over the tenants of their domains. From landowners they became lords. They no longer engaged tenants save on long term; leases, hitherto annual, were drawn up for life, then for two lives and finally became hereditary tenure. Thus between the landowner and his tenants a hereditary bond was created that destroyed the ancient legal equality and replaced it by a system of social classes; the population was henceforth composed of privileged nobles, of tenants who, dependent on their lord, gradually became serfs, and free men who, outside the seigniorial domains, continued to live independently.

But since the nobles enjoyed tax immunity, all the weight of the taxes fell upon the smallholders. Ruined and in debt, these could only sell their lands to the great landowners if they—since at the same time they held the high offices of state—did not force them to relinquish them. Thus smallholdings tended to disappear.

This social evolution affected private law. Land became the basis of personal status. The heredity of priestly offices, duties and livings led to a new system of inheritance, based on primogeniture. The noble families were closely concentrated about their inherited lands under the authority of the head of the family. Individualism recoiled before the new seigniorial theory of family responsibility.

THE OLIGARCHY DISMEMBERS THE MONARCHY

The oligarchy of nobles became so powerful that, when the Vth dynasty came to an end, it seems that the new reigning family was recruited from its ranks. The VIth dynasty (2423–2263 BC) led to the final triumph of the nobility over the monarchy.

The advent of King Teti led to a radical reform of the constitution; feudal rule replaced bureaucratic rule in the government of the Southern provinces. One after the other, the *nomes* were granted by decree to hereditary officials who took the title of prince, exercised sovereign power by virtue of the investiture given them by the king and were linked to the royal authority only by an oath of fidelity. In the provinces, now become autonomous principalities, the feudal principle was extended to the fiefs, at first territorial and later administrative. The prince conferred duties within his jurisdiction on relations or 'vassals' as hereditary fiefs. The feudal system thus replaced, little by little, the administrative system.

The army too became feudalized, each prince and each tax-free temple levying recruits within its own jurisdiction. To mobilize the army, the king could do no more than summon the princes and the high priests. However he retained more direct authority in Lower Egypt where the existence of the cities prevented the feudalization of the country. He also remained master of Nubia, where he levied mercenary troops and kept for himself the produce of the goldmines and the tribute paid by the Nubian chiefs. To assure himself of this he entrusted the defence of Elephantine, the Nubian frontier province, to generals of the mercenary troops. But these in their turn became feudal and turned themselves into Princes of Elephantine. From then onwards, the king lost all power in Upper Egypt.

At the same time he lost control of the government. In order to resist the dismemberment of their sovereignty, Kings Teti and Pepi I concentrated all the powers of the state in the hands of their viziers, whom they tried to choose from outside the ranks of the territorial nobility. This concentration was all the more necessary since the tax revenues had been monopolized by the princes, and the king could no longer meet the heavy expenses of the administration. He still kept, however, the taxes due to him from Lower Egypt, thanks to which the monarchy managed to hold out against the feudal lords.

But the viziers, now become real Mayors of the Palace, placed the king under their guardianship and profited by their power to make him grant them hereditary governorships also. Thus the vizierate became a part of the feudal oligarchy and there was nothing left for the king to do save to ally himself to the most powerful of the feudal lords by marrying their daughters. This King Pepi I did. But the princes thus allied to the royal family profited by their situation to obtain hereditary governorships in the *nomes* of Lower Egypt. Thus first the Princes of Thinis and then those of Koptos replaced the king *de facto*, leaving him only a nominal authority.

EGYPT SLIDES INTO FEUDALISM

Having become hereditary, the provinces broke away from the king. The princes no longer administered justice in his name, but in the name of the local god, of whom they were at the same time high priests. The disintegration of the royal power was accompanied by a religious disintegration. Religious syncretism had been set up at the same time as monarchical centralisation. All the local gods had been grouped in the solar theology into a system dominated by the one god, Ra. But the monotheist tendency which had been established under the IVth dynasty, at the same time as the royal absolutism, retreated as the oligarchy gained force. Under the Vth dynasty the theocracy restored to the local cults, now become the appanages of hereditary high priests, their former importance. Feudal dismemberment led each prince to consolidate his independence by referring the source of his power not to the ordination of the king but to the will of the god of his *nome*. The theory of the royal power fell to pieces; the princes invoked it to their own advantage and in the *nomes* the local gods became the source of princely power, even as Ra was the source of the royal power. Religion was dismembered at the same time as sovereignty.

Thus, under the VIth dynasty, the state of the country was similar to that which had existed in Upper Egypt before the unification of the country, that is to say a thousand years earlier; it is marked, from the political point of view, by the division of the country between sovereign princes, from the social point of view by the manorial system and the existence of hereditary and privileged classes, from the economic point of view by a closed economy in which every domain was organized to be sufficient to itself, and from the point of view of civil law by the principle of the collective responsibility of the group and the family, which took the place of the individualism of the classic law of the monarchy.

THE FEUDAL CRISIS IN LOWER EGYPT

The formation of a hereditary nobility and the introduction of a seigniorial and manorial system which resulted from it caused a serious economic crisis in Lower Egypt.

The manorial régime, by its tendency towards a closed economy, greatly hampered trade. At that time the economy of the Delta cities was based on grain export. A closed economy, by reducing opportunities for the purchase of grain, deprived the cities of their main return freights. On the other hand the collapse of the royal power led to the feudalization of the army and the security that had previously existed now disappeared. The nomads crossed the frontiers, brigandage was rampant and internal trade paralysed. The economic crisis led to unemployment and misery in the cities. There were no more sailings to Byblos. Raw materials no longer came from Syria. The cities, suffocated by the oppressive seigniorial régime, could no longer live. The economic crisis degenerated into social crisis. A violent popular insurrection broke out in all the cities and even in the capital, Memphis. The nobles and rich men were massacred, the offices of the land-survey—where the titles to land were deposited—

were destroyed and the old king, Pepi II, aged ninety-five, was kidnapped by the people in his palace. Throughout the Delta the nobles were in flight. The seigniorial régime was destroyed and the serfs recovered their liberty.

The cities, reverting to the autonomy they had known before the unification of the country, became independent republics under the rule of magistrates, the 'ten men', probably elected by the merchants and craftsmen who, outside the limits of seigniorial Egypt, continued to form a free population devoted to trade and industry.

Thus, after a thousand years of monarchical evolution, Egypt falls back into feudal dismemberment. In Upper Egypt she is divided into autonomous princedoms; in Lower Egypt, the free cities dominate the plains country. Royalty, however, has not disappeared. But the king, now only the first amongst the princes, is no more than a symbol of authority which, in fact, is divided among about forty states, feudal in the south, urban in the north. A period of insecurity and decadence sets in. The princes wage feudal wars against one another; seigniorial upper Egypt becomes completely detached from the north, withdrawn into a rigid and land-locked existence. The towns, as heretofore, turn towards the sea and live their own lives as independent cities.

The first cycle of Egyptian evolution has taken place.

CHAPTER IV

THE BABYLONIAN MONARCHY

REVIVAL OF THE SUMERIAN CITIES

AFTER the great floods that had destroyed some of the Sumerian cities, life soon returned to Sumeria. From the beginning of the XXXth century BC the ancient cities had been rebuilt and commenced their economic and maritime activity anew. In the third millenary they were to know a period of great prosperity, though disturbed by incessant struggles for leadership between Uruk, Ur and Lagash. Ur, at the beginning of the third millenary, was a great international mart; it was the trade centre for bitumen from Subartu, copper from the Caucasus, silver from Cilicia, gold from Elam and Cappadocia, bronze from Syria, calcareous stone from the upper valley of the Euphrates, diorite from Magan on the Persian Gulf, alabaster from the Iranian plateau and lapis-lazuli from Central Asia; and by way of Syria—whence came cedarwood—it traded with Egypt. Ur, therefore, became the central point for trade from India by way of Iran and the Persian Gulf, from Central Asia by the caravan routes, from the Caucasus down the Tigris, from Asia Minor down the Euphrates, from Egypt by way of Syria and from Arabia along the desert tracks. Its manufactured goods—which opened the way for its law and customs—reached as far as the Caspian Sea, were sold in the great market of Susa and were exported through Byblos to Egypt.

The traders of the Sumerian cities founded colonies along the rivers, at Assur and Agade on the Tigris, at Kish and later at Mari and Babylon on the Euphrates. From Assur, traders were to settle as far as Cappadocia where, at the close of the third millenary, real merchant 'communes' were established under the walls of the feudal cities and which obtained from the princes, by paying dues on the cloth that they imported, the right of free trading, of administering their own affairs and of living according to their own customs. Organized in guilds, which acted also as chambers of commerce and courts, the merchants of these communes helped one another and remained in constant touch with their own metropolis at Assur.

Map No. 3

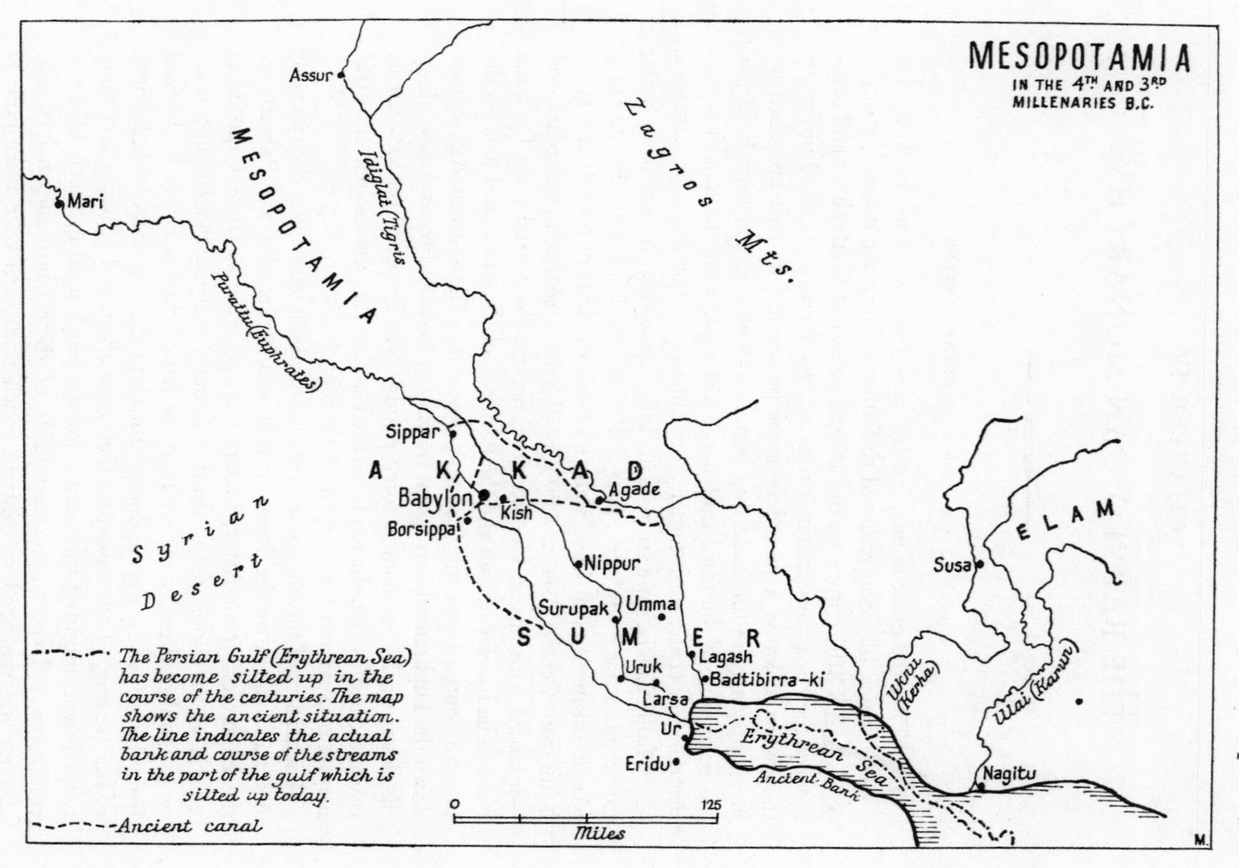
MESOPOTAMIA
IN THE 4TH AND 3RD MILLENARIES B.C.
Assur
Mari
MESOPOTAMIA
Idiglat (Tigris
Zagros Mts.
Puratu (Euphrates)
Sippar
AKKAD
Agade
Babylon
Kish
Borsippa
Syrian Desert
Nippur
Surupak
Umma
SUMER
Uruk
Lagash
Badtibirra-ki
Larsa
Ur
Eridu
Erythrean Sea
Ancient Bank
ELAM
Susa
Uknu (Kerha)
Ulai (Karun)
Nagitu
The Persian Gulf (Erythrean Sea) has become silted up in the course of the centuries. The map shows the ancient situation. The line indicates the actual bank and course of the streams in the part of the gulf which is silted up today.
Ancient canal
0
125
Miles
M.

In the cities of Sumeria, living under the rule of local kings, the ruling class was made up of the priests and the land-holding nobility. But the middle classes continued to increase in importance, and a financial and legal administration was formed about the king.

At the same time international relations between cities were organized about the holy city of Nippur which, situated in the centre of the Delta, played the role that had been played in Egypt, before the unification of the country, by Heliopolis. The power of the king who assumed leadership, after imposing his rule on the local kings, was made legitimate at Nippur by a ceremony of consecration conferred on him by Enlil, the god of the holy city. The priests of Nippur, thus invested with the mission of arbiters between the cities, laid the foundations of international law. From the third millenary the treaties concluded between the Sumerian sovereigns under the sanction of the god Enlil contained diplomatic formulae that are repeated, word for word, up to the XIIIth century BC in Babylonian, Hittite and Egyptian treaties.

THE COSMOGONY OF NIPPUR

The development of international law, making possible economic as well as political relations between cities, was closely tied up with the elaboration at Nippur of a cosmogony that grouped into a single system all the local cults of the Sumerian cities.

As in Egypt, so in Sumeria, political centralization developed side by side with religious syncretism.

At first, the local gods had no connection with one another; but under the influence of political circumstances, which were themselves due to economic needs, bonds of kinship were established between them. The supremacy of Ur made its moon-god Sin for a time the father of the sun-god Shamash, Lord of Larsa, and of Ishtar, the ancient mother-goddess, tutelary divinity of Uruk.

Similar groupings, confirmed at Nippur, ended by becoming united in a cosmogony.

In it the world is conceived as issuing from primordial liquid chaos made up of two elements, one male and creator, Apsu, the principle of life and therefore of good, the other female, Thiamat, matter, of which creatures are formed, the origin of created things and therefore finite, that is evil. The union of these two elements constitutes the world, symbolized by the heaven-god, Anshar, and the earth-goddess, Kishar. This world, born of good and evil, rests upon the ocean, Apsu, the creative principle that renews itself incessantly.

Thus creation takes place. And the created world, matter penetrated by the life-principle, is to develop by its own evolution, giving birth to a hierarchy ranging from the gods down to simple material beings. This creation is conceived, as in Egypt, in the form of a genealogy. To Anshar and Kishar are born three males, Anu, the god of heaven, Enlil, god of the earth and Ea, god of the primordial ocean. Then come the stars, pure spirits, the sun, Shamash, the moon, Sin, and the planets amongst which Ishtar or Venus is to have a leading place.

All creation obeys the three great gods of heaven, earth and sea. Anu is the supreme god, Ea the creator of men and Enlil, the god of Nippur, is the master of human beings and the dispenser of power; it was he who ordained the flood in order to punish the world for its impiety.

Such a cosmogony, which places the elements before the gods, is based on a pre-scientific idea of evolution: 'When the god Anu had created heaven, heaven created the earth and the earth created rivers, the rivers created the ditches, the ditches created marshes, and the marshes created worms'; then life appeared upon the earth.

Thus, whereas Egypt conceived the world as the manifestation of divine consciousness, making pure idea the first reality, Sumeria presented it as the product of an evolution inherent in matter, impregnated by the life principle. Under the symbols of the cosmogonies elaborated at Heliopolis and Nippur, there were thus outlined, before the XXXth century BC, the two systems between which human thought has never ceased to be divided: idealism and materialism.

Egyptian idealism regarded as the supreme goal of existence the search for God and the return of the soul to the divinity whence it had emanated, which led it to regard morality as the directing principle of individual and social life. Sumerian materialism regarded death as the end of human consciousness, as a return to material chaos, placing the aim of existence in this world as sensual satisfaction; it remained alien to moral preoccupations and turned entirely towards practical ends and material benefits, for the realization of which it was, from the third millenary onwards, to lay the foundations of commercial law, which were one day to be inherited by the West.

MONARCHICAL AND EGALITARIAN EVOLUTION

The development of trade and of personal property led to social conflicts between the middle classes and the privileged classes which, about 2400 BC, resulted in the great democratic reform by Urukagina, king of Lagash.

Class privileges were abolished and an individualist civil law was extended to all free men, under the jurisdiction of the king, which took the place of that of the priests. A first codification was established and the triumph of individualist civil law resulted in the coming into force of a liberal economic system by which foreigners were authorised to trade within the cities on equal terms with citizens.

The struggles for leadership among the cities led, in the XXIIIrd century BC, to the first unification of Mesopotamia under Sargon, the feudal king of Akkad, a region to the north of Sumeria, where the seigniorial régime was in force. But, though unified by a feudal king, Mesopotamia was compelled to follow the trend of the urban economic life of Sumeria, a phenomenon identical with that we have already noted at the time of the unification of Egypt by the feudal kings of Nekhen.

THE EMPIRE OF SARGON

Sargon's capital, Agade, became a commercial city and the centre of a policy of great economic expansion directly inspired by that of the Sumerian cities, but on a much larger scale, due to the power at the disposal of the new monarchy which at once aimed at the conquest of the trade routes and the commercial outlets by which the Sumerian cities lived.

The great trade routes to Subartu and Amurru, in the north of Mesopotamia, were seized and occupied. Sumerian influence was paramount at Susa, a caravan centre on the route to India, extended into Syria and even to the island of Cyprus. The political expansion of Mesopotamia towards the shores of the Mediterranean was the reason for the Palestine campaign of the Pharaoh, Pepi I. This was the first clash between Egypt, then in a state of decadence, and the Mesopotamian kings for the possession of the Syrian coast, which was to remain, through all the history of ancient times, the key to economic supremacy and, in consequence, political leadership.

THE SUMERIAN MONARCHY

The Empire created by Sargon did not last. An invasion of Ghutites, coming from the east, destroyed it and imposed the rule of a dynasty of barbarian princes on the Sumerian cities. One of the essential factors in the history of Mesopotamia was the constant series of barbarian invasions. The valley of the Nile was never an invasion route. Egypt could therefore

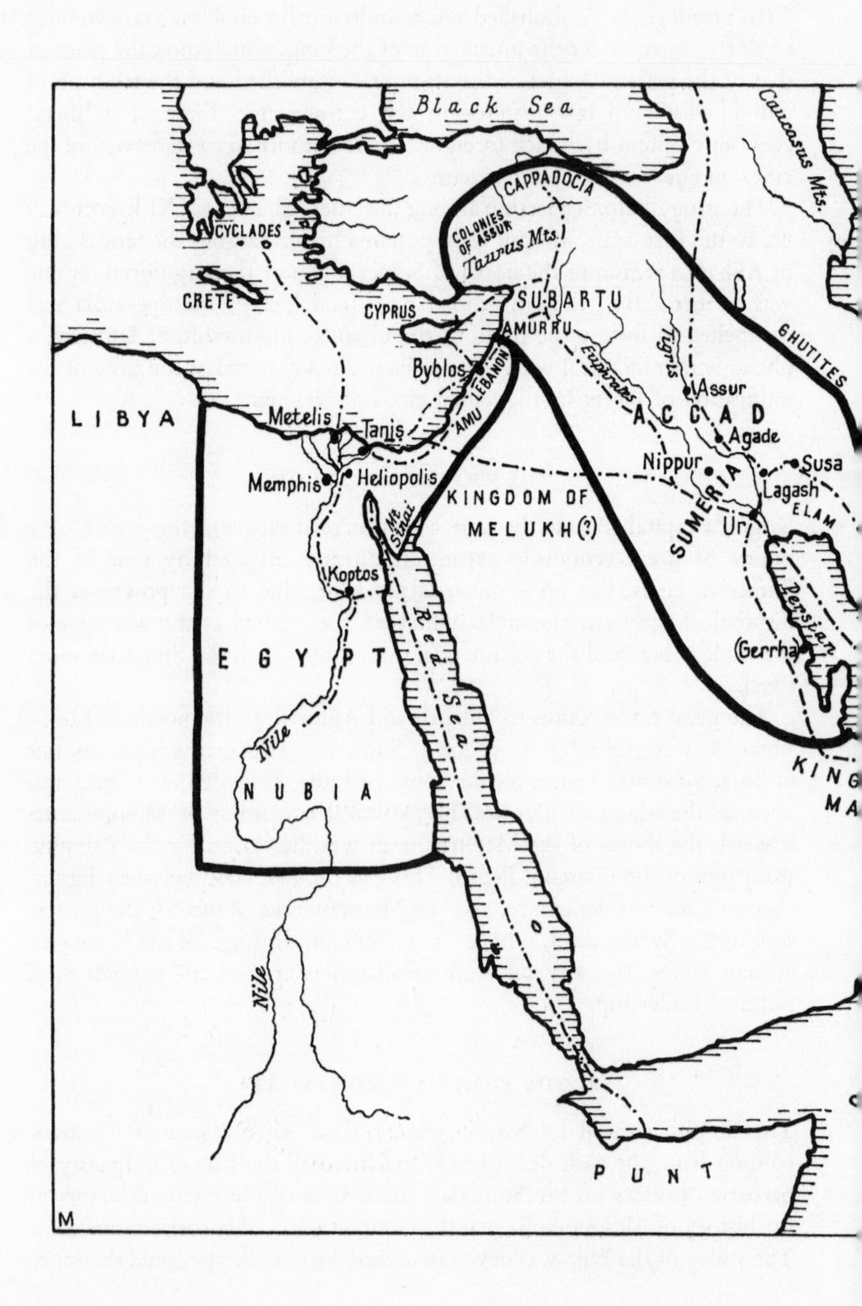
Black Sea
Caucasus Mts.
CAPPADOCIA
COLONIES OF ASSUR
Taurus Mts.
CYCLADES
CRETE
CYPRUS
SUBARTU
AMURRU
GHUTITES
Tigris
Euphrates
Assur
LEBANON
AMU
Byblos
LIBYA
Metelis
Tanis
ACCAD
Agade
Nippur
Susa
Memphis
Heliopolis
KINGDOM OF
MELUKH(?)
SUMERIA
Lagash
ELAM
Ur
Mt Sinai
Koptos
Red Sea
Persian
(Gerrha)
EGYPT
Nile
NUBIA
Nile
PUNT
M

Map No. 4

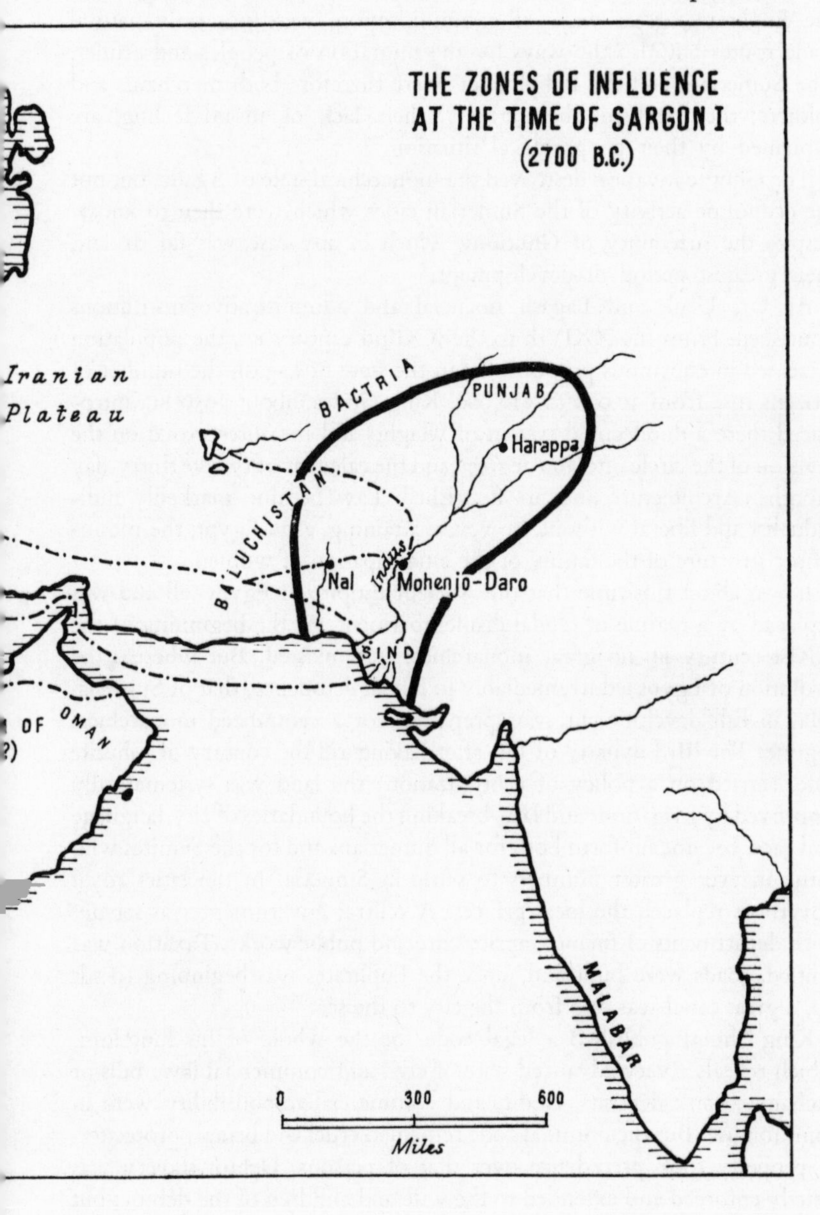
THE ZONES OF INFLUENCE
AT THE TIME OF SARGON I
(2700 B.C.)
Iranian
Plateau
BACTRIA
PUNJAB
Harappa
BALUCHISTAN
Indus
Nal
Mohenjo-Daro
SIND
OF
OMAN
MALABAR
0
300
600
Miles

develop her civilization sheltered from the continual wars to which, on the contrary, the Mesopotamian peoples were exposed. The Tigris and the Euphrates, great ways of communication, were not only natural trade routes but also the ways for the migration of peoples and armies. The Sumerians and the Babylonians were therefore both merchants and soldiers; their realism, their cruelty, their lack of moral feeling, are explained by their geographical situation.

The Ghutite invasion destroyed the monarchical state of Agade, but not the economic activity of the Sumerian cities which were then to know, despite the suzerainty of Ghutium, which in any case was far distant, their greatest period of development.

At Ur, Uruk and Lagash financial and administrative institutions flourished. From the XXIVth to the XXIInd century BC, the population increased in enormous proportions; in the state of Lagash the number of citizens rose from 36,000 to 216,000. King Gudea, about 2050 BC, introduced there a duodecimal system of weights and measures, based on the division of the circle into 360 degrees, and the calendar of twelve thirty-day months. Architecture and art flourished. Law became markedly individualist and liberal without, however, attaining, as in Egypt, the monogamic structure of the family or the emancipation of women.

It was about this time that the Ancient Empire of Egypt fell and was replaced by a regime of feudal dismemberment. At the beginning of the XXIst century BC no great monarchical state existed. But whereas the evolution of Egypt led irremediably to feudal decadence, that of Sumeria, then in full development, was preparing for a centralized monarchical régime. The IIIrd dynasty of Ur, after having rid the country of Ghutite rule, carried on a policy of centralization; the land was systematically improved by irrigation; and law, breaking the boundaries of city, language and race, became uniform both for all Sumerians and for the Semites who came in ever greater numbers to settle in Sumeria. In the cities royal governors replaced the local princes. A central government was set up, with departments of finance, agriculture and public works. Taxation was unified, roads were built and, since the Euphrates was beginning to silt up, a great canal was dug from the city to the sea.

King Shulgi published a legal code for the whole of his kingdom, which reveals a very advanced state of civil and commercial law; bills of exchange, bank deposits, credits and commercial responsibility were in common use. But the criminal code remained cruel and brutal; protection of property took precedence over that of persons. Debtor-slavery was strictly enforced and extended to the wife and children of the debtor; but the king was already trying to suppress it, by instituting a state credit system.

Schools for scribes were set up in the temples. Legal procedure, commercial accounts and contracts all show a very high level of civilization, confirmed by a literary activity mainly devoted to historical and religious subjects.

Despite the constant attempts at invasion by the Amorites on the west and the Elamites on the east, civilization found its way up the rivers; Mari became a powerful city and its kings carried on a diplomatic correspondence with all the rulers of the times; and already Babylon was rising to confront it as a rival.

But the Sumerian cities were threatened by an invincible enemy, the silting up of the Delta. The sea-coast retreated continually and the rivers became lost in the marshes that were formed at the estuaries. With indomitable energy the Sumerian cities struggled to preserve their access to the sea by digging canals.

But nature was the stronger and decadence set in despite all their efforts. This was to the benefit of Babylon, whose king, Hammurabi, restored Mesopotamian unity about 1800 BC.[1]

THE BABYLONIAN MONARCHY

HAMMURABI

Once again the country of Akkad, where the manorial system was in force, dominated Sumeria, despite the importance of a city like Babylon.

But, as in Egypt under the first two dynasties and as in Mesopotamia itself under Sargon, the monarchy founded on the manorial system was to be drawn onward by the civilization of the cities.

The work of Hammurabi was to unify the Sumerian cities and manorial Akkad under the authority of the king. He completed the evolution of power towards absolutism by liberating it from the guardianship of the holy city of Nippur; the god of Babylon, Marduk, who was originally a nature deity, was identified with the supreme god and replaced Enlil of Nippur as the royal god. Babylon became the religious centre of the kingdom. Theology, taken over in its entirety from the Sumerians, was adapted to the new monarchical idea. Here too centralization of the royal authority went hand in hand with a more and more syncretized organization of religion and justified the omnipotence of the king by presenting it as directly derived from the gods. Perhaps under the influence of the

[1] The chronology of the First Babylonian Dynasty is uncertain and much disputed.

Egyptian theory, the king was portrayed as the instrument of divine justice; the monarchy introduced the first moral preoccupations into religion. The problem of good and evil was thus placed before the theologians, but the attempt to introduce a moral code based on religious sentiment was fruitless. The cult continued to be no more than a means of propitiating the gods and acquiring a knowledge of the laws that govern the world. In contrast to the mystic and moral sentiment which in Egypt was the basis of religious conceptions the Babylonians held a strictly scientific and realistic view. The Sumerians, and the Babylonians after them, conceived the universe as generated from the evolution of matter. Divinity was no more than the force which presides over this evolution; gods like men, therefore, obey the laws of the universe. In the Egyptian theology Ra, the creator-god, is the conscience of the world; in the Babylonian theology Apsu, the life-principle, is its law. All the universe is one; all its manifestations are in harmony and interdependent. In order to determine the movements which it obeys, it is necessary to penetrate into the secret of our own lives. These movements are revealed to us by the stars. To the Babylonians the stars were not worlds but gods. Astrology, by studying the courses of the stars, tried to comprehend the laws that their movements obey in order to predict, thanks to the interdependence that exists between all beings, the future destinies of men and of human undertakings.[1] Such a conception of the interdependence of all beings led the Babylonians to believe that every man's life is determined by a spirit attached to him; an idea which, transplanted into mysticism, was to give rise one day to the idea of the guardian angel.

The king, who held his power from the creator-god Marduk, was the representative of authority and of law among men. The king's law was therefore the expression of universal law; the royal authority was at the same time divine and beneficent.

So indeed it was. Hammurabi carried out an immense task of unification. Akkadian became the only state language and the first Akkadian-Sumerian dictionaries were compiled. The country was divided into districts under the rule of royal governors. In the part of the country where seigniorial rule still existed, all hereditary powers were replaced by bureaucratic rule. The royal jurisdiction replaced the temple courts in Akkad and the city courts in Sumeria. Procedure was unified and a great task of codification of customs was undertaken, which led to the publica-

[1] On this idea of a universal law the Sumerians established their duodecimal system, the year of twelve thirty-day months and the circle of 360°, the laws of time, of numbers and of measures; all are dominated by a single principle.

tion of the famous Code of Hammurabi. It contained not only the codifications made earlier by the Sumerians but also the customary law of Akkad, only just freed from the manorial system which the royal legislation was doing its utmost to suppress.

In the crown lands especially it suppressed serfdom and replaced it by a system of direct cultivation undertaken with the aid of capitalists who leased the land. This social emancipation of the agricultural classes was accompanied, in the seigniorial country of Akkad, by the spread of Sumerian individualist institutions. These were spread both by the spontaneous influence of trade and by the systematic policy of unification practised by the monarchy.

THE CODE OF HAMMURABI

The code was one of the basic features of the monarchical policy of Hammurabi. It granted all his dominions a single law of contract which rapidly became the international basis of trade throughout all Asia Minor. In its wake, Babylonian law, brought by the merchants, penetrated even into Syria. It reached, at this time, a level not to be surpassed until the VIIth century BC.

It regulated all forms of contract. Sale, total or partial, for cash or credit, conditional or unconditional, acquired a flexibility—not yet in the code but in practice—that permitted a great expansion of trade. Loans, securities, guarantees and the pledging of real estate, permitting the use of revenue from land, foreshadowed the hitherto unknown idea of mortgage, thus continually enlarging the use of credit, the basis of all trade.[1]

Lending was made easier by the right granted to the debtor of paying off his loan by giving a bond for payment. In order to prevent the practice of usury, the state required the registration of all loan contracts; interest rates were fixed at 33%, and for commercial transactions at 20%, while loans were granted by the state itself at 12½%. The clause providing for payment to bearer led to the introduction of the sight draft. Commercial companies, as a result of loan contracts, drafts and goods on consignment, formed associations and partnerships. Fluctuating deposits led to banking; the current account combined with the draft introduced the use of the cheque which, endorsed to a third person, led to the bill of exchange.

The idea of commercial responsibility was extended so far as to introduce the principle that every action liable for damages gave a right to compensation. It even involved the public authorities themselves, who

[1] The idea of mortgage was to be introduced by the Athenians in the Vth century BC.

were forced to make good any damage caused by misdemeanours that they had been unable to prevent or to repress. This legislation, by making property fluid, favoured the expansion of business, and led to social services. Employment contracts were regulated by a law that fixed the reciprocal responsibilities of employer and employee; a minimum wage was fixed for all professions and all employers, whether commercial or agricultural, had to grant their workers three days paid holiday every month. Apprenticeship, the chartering of ships, and fees to doctors and architects were the subject of legal regulations sanctioned by a penal code whose archaism is astonishing when compared with the perfection of the juridical ideas that it was intended to safeguard.

Finally, the temples which, making use of the immense treasures that they possessed, acted as banks were compelled by the king to grant free loans to insolvent debtors to allow them to escape slavery for debt, and to sick persons whose families were freed from the necessity of repayment in the event of their death.

This legal task of Hammurabi was Babylon's great contribution to civilization. It was to survive the ruin of the state and to remain the foundation for every evolution of commercial law until the times of the Roman Empire.

CHAPTER V

THE TRADE ROUTES

TRADE ROUTES IN THE THIRD MILLENARY

THE Nile Valley, Mesopotamia, and the Indus Basin all owed their rapid cultural development to their commerce. But this was in its turn dependent on international trade. Thus, in the first centuries of civilization, the trade routes played a leading role.

Mesopotamia was the economic centre of the ancient world, since it lay on the main route from Asia Minor and Egypt to India.

The Euphrates linked the Persian Gulf to the Taurus region and the Tigris led to the Mosul area, whence came bitumen, and to Armenia. It was also by way of the Euphrates that the port of Byblos on the Syrian coast was reached from Sumeria and Babylon.

From Byblos it was possible to go to Egypt, either by the coastal route or by sea, and to the island of Cyprus, famous for its copper deposits.

For this reason Byblos, the exchange-mart of Asia, became an international centre of the greatest importance, and therefore Egypt—under the Vth dynasty—and later Mesopotamia, from the reign of Sargon of Agade, both tried to get control of it. The importance of Byblos was all the greater, since it was not only a staging-post on the route from the Nile to the Indus but also a great market for the metals of the Taurus and the timber of Lebanon.

Two routes, one by land through Elam and Baluchistan, and the other by sea through the Persian Gulf, led from Mesopotamia to India. Susa, on the caravan route, had become an important centre before the reign of Sargon of Agade (XXIIIrd century BC). At this time the Persian Gulf was entirely in the control of the fleets of Sumeria and the eastern coastlands of Arabia seem to have been forced to accept a protectorate.

The Red Sea was another trade route of primary importance to Egypt. Under the Ancient Empire, the Pharaoh was assured of a virtual monopoly of its trade. Royal expeditions regularly traded to the Arabian coast, which they reached somewhere near Aden, and the Somali coastline. The

Sumerians were at the same time in touch with the Arab kingdoms which, it seems, already existed in Southern Arabia; they also knew a Kingdom of Maloukh which can perhaps be identified with that of the Amalekites.

The Oman region, which was perhaps the Kingdom of Maan, seems to have known a great prosperity throughout ancient history, since it was an essential staging-post for trade between India and Egypt. This was carried on by coastwise shipping and even more by the land route which skirted the Arabian coast as far as the Persian Gulf where, from the times of Sargon, the coast of Oman was frequented by Sumerian and probably also Indian traders.

Between Egypt and Sumeria, the Byblos route was doubled by another route which reached Punt and the Red Sea by way of the Persian Gulf and Arabia. It is more than probable, moreover, that the route which stretched by way of Megiddo in Palestine to Egypt on the west, and to the eastern coasts of Arabia to the south, was also in use.

Finally, a very important trade route led from the Indus basin through Peshawar to the Central Asian oases. Beyond that point we know nothing.

From the third millenary BC, therefore, international trade seems to have exercised a decisive influence on the development of civilization. It is enough to look at the great routes that it made use of to see that it was essentially continental. Seagoing trade was, undoubtedly, an important factor; the seas and the rivers determined not only trade but also the areas where civilization developed and spread. But seagoing trade was turned entirely towards the continental area formed by Egypt, Nearer Asia and western India and was limited to sailing along their coasts.

Outside the three great river basins and the routes connecting them there was not yet any real civilization. In Cappadocia and Elam the peoples still lived under a seigniorial-feudal régime. In southern Syria they were still in the stage of tribal organization; while between Syria and Mesopotamia nomad peoples, like the Hebrews at the time of the patriarchs, still wandered.

EXTENSION OF NAVIGATION IN THE IIIRD MILLENARY

Until the 'Helladic' invasions, originating from Asia Minor and continuing in the Aegean Sea at the beginning of the IIIrd millenary, Crete seems to have been without communications with Egypt and Syria.

After these 'Helladic' invasions Crete passed through a period of feudal organization and also of maritime expansion which, some centuries later, was to be strengthened by the foundation of the Phoenician cities of the Syrian coast. The view has been expressed that the development of navigation in Phoenicia and Crete was due to Dravidians from the west coast of India. But this view has not been upheld. Today it seems certain that the Cretans were of the same origin as the Achaeans and that the Phoenicians were quite simply Canaanites who turned towards the sea and created a particularly advanced urban civilization.

By the end of the IIIrd millenary Crete had become a great economic centre. Ports like Palaiokastro and Zakro, industrial cities like Gournia, enriched by metal-work, formed centres of fresh attraction, stages between the eastern continent and unknown Europe. Cretan navigators went to northern Greece to look for tin which came to them from Saxony and Bohemia by way of the Danube. Sea-borne international trade began to spread outwards from northward-looking Knossos. This new economic development was to pave the way for one of the most brilliant and prosperous civilizations known to antiquity, while on the Syrian coast a chain of newly-founded ports, Ugarit, Tyre, Sidon, Arvad, in constant communication with Crete, were to deprive Byblos of her ancient maritime leadership and to give Mediterranean navigation an importance it had never before attained.

CHAPTER VI

FEUDALISM AND THE MONARCHICAL REVIVAL IN EGYPT

THE END OF CLOSED ECONOMY

AFTER five centuries of feudal slumber, Egypt again entered on a period of monarchical revival. In the course of this long period of dismemberment and constant wars between princes and free cities, under the nominal suzerainty of the kings of Heracleopolis who were no more than the first among the sovereigns of Egypt, power was slowly built up again within the local principalities. In Upper Egypt, in the little state of Thebes, the princes, real feudal lords, built up a military force which, as in the times of the Kings of Nekhen, they used to conquer the country. About 2130 BC they were able to subjugate all the princes of Upper Egypt and then began the struggle against the kings of Heracleopolis. A century later, they were masters of the entire country. The cities of Lower Egypt, which had been forced to accept their rule, brought, thanks to the financial resources that they got from them, a rapid increase of power, while the security restored to the country by monarchical unity gave a fresh impetus to trade all along the Nile which by breaking down the closed economies of the manorial system prepared its fall and the advent of a monarchical revival.

The kings of Thebes, now masters of the whole country, at once tried to reconstruct a central government. In addition to their feudal courts, they introduced a privy council which included traders and burghers who became the best representatives of their centralizing and economic policy. The law of the Ancient Empire, which had been more or less preserved in the merchant cities, served as a base for the revival of the royal administration, and the monarchy, driven by the economic interests of the burghers, returned to the policy of expansion formerly practised by the Pharaohs of the Ancient Empire. Royal expeditions once more took the Red Sea route to Arabia. The king found, in this state-commerce, the resources needed to re-establish an administration of officials; a new nobility of the robe which was to take a leading part in state affairs was created to counterbalance the ancient military and landowning nobility.

The revival of trade, the formation of a class of officials and the contact between the urban and agricultural population favoured a great movement of emancipation throughout the country, which was first expressed in the mysticism of the Osirian cult. The equality of all men before the god of eternal life encouraged in all classes a sense of piety, which was shown in the great pilgrimages to Abydos, where was the celebrated shrine of Osiris. The kings of Thebes, reverting to the monarchical formulas made use of two thousand years before by the kings of Busiris, did their best to rally their people around them in a frenzy of loyalty, by associating the monarchy with the Osirian mysticism.

The administrative nobility, amongst whom the kings recruited the viziers whose office they had revived, was to become so powerful that, when the XIth dynasty came to an end about 2000 BC, it was the descendant of a vizier and not of a feudal prince who founded the XIIth dynasty.

ECONOMIC EXPANSION AND MONARCHICAL CENTRALIZATION

It was at this time that Babylon was preparing to assume the leadership in Mesopotamia. Egypt, which looked towards Babylon economically, was certainly influenced by it. The development of the Fayyum, which was transformed into a vast royal domain by scientific irrigation and the introduction of direct exploitation methods which broke away from the earlier manorial organization, was evidently inspired by Babylonian practice. The favour shown by the king to private trading between the Egyptian cities and Byblos and Crete associated them more and more with the trend towards international trade. But at the same time the crown, by undertaking anew the colonization of Nubia, obtained gold, ebony and ivory, while the royal fleets went to Arabia to search for Eastern produce. The power that the king obtained from the results of his state-trading and the exploitation of his magnificent domain, together with the support he got from the cities, made it impossible for the feudal lords to resist any longer. Proclaiming himself feudal sovereign of the whole kingdom, he imposed his rule on his sub-vassals as well as his vassals, disposed of their fiefs, subjected them to his jurisdiction and the royal tax-system, and even went so far as to recruit troops in the formerly sovereign principalities.

Feudalism recoiled; trade developed. Individualist law, which had survived in the cities, expanded and won over the official classes, dislocated the seigniorial system and tempered the social hierarchy. Art, fertilized by renascent individualism, experienced a magnificent revival, directly inspired, as was also the case with law, by the classic antiquity of the Ancient Empire.

A new period of centralized monarchy began.

CHAPTER VII

THE FIRST ARYAN INVASIONS AND THE DESTRUCTION OF THE GREAT STATES

THE FIRST HELLADIC CIVILIZATIONS

It seems that it was only towards the VIth or Vth millenary BC that men made their first appearance in continental and insular Greece and also in Crete. The first Cretans lived for a score of centuries in caves or round huts. At the beginning of the IIIrd millenary a wave of invaders coming from Asia Minor seems to have spread bit by bit over the coasts and islands of the Aegean Sea. This was the opening of the Helladic or Minoan period. It was at this time that Troy, surrounded by powerful ramparts, was founded on the Hellespont. This cycladic civilization was essentially agricultural in character. But none the less the continental trade route that crossed the Straits, leading from Thessaly to Mesopotamia, was already sufficiently in use for Troy to wish to control it.

Even before the coming of the Helladic peoples, there were villages surrounded by walls in continental Greece. The most famous was Diminis in Thessaly, which had several ramparts. During the Helladic period there were fortified communities at Termi, Lesbos and Lemnos, little towns whose terraced houses formed streets that crossed at right angles. On the barren rocks of Aegina a town was built surrounded by ramparts—with towers similar to those of the second Troy—built about 2300 BC after the destruction of the first city of Troy which was founded after the invasion of Asia Minor by the Hittites.

About the middle of the third millenary the discovery of copper and tin deposits in Asia Minor was to lead to a rapid advancement in the life of the people of the Cyclades by making possible the smelting of bronze.

This primitive Hellenic civilization, which seems to have been peaceable, lasted until the opening of the IInd millenary.

Was Greece affected by the Helladic wave? The call of the sea seems, in any case, to have been felt about this time; it was then that the site of

Knossos was occupied. By 2400 BC Crete was covered with cities built along the sea-coast or at the foot of feudal keeps.

THE FIRST ARYAN INVASIONS

The Aryans, who came from the Russian and Central Asian steppes, crossed the Hellespont about the middle of the IIIrd millenary and destroyed the first city of Troy. They already possessed an advanced civilization. They had iron weapons and rode horses, which were then unknown to the eastern peoples. They advanced southward, invading Greece; they crossed the Hellespont, surmounted the barrier of the Caucasus, and made their way down the eastern shores of the Caspian.

In Asia Minor, the Hittites had settled in Cappadocia where, as a military aristocracy, they became merged into the feudal framework that they found there, and adopted as their own the shrines of Neriq, Zippalanda and Arinna. The Achaeans settled in Greece and on the coasts of Asia Minor. To the north of Mesopotamia, the Mitanni and the Hittites spread over Armenia and in the Mt Zagros region. To the east, the Medes and the Persians, a branch of the Scythian people, occupied the Iranian plateau. And in Turkestan other Aryan peoples—the Tokharians—settled in the oases which, some centuries later, were to be of such great importance in international commercial life.

RUIN OF THE BABYLONIAN EMPIRE

This great migration of peoples, drawn by the wealth of western Asia, was to have widespread repercussions on the course of history. They seem to have descended only very slowly—from the XXth to the XVIIth century BC—towards Mesopotamia. It was only after the reign of Hammurabi that the Kassites, who had been living a nomadic life on the Iranian uplands, were driven back by the invaders and descended into Mesopotamia where they were at first decimated by the Babylonian army. But Babylon was unable to halt their peaceful infiltration into the Tigris and Euphrates valleys, where they settled, disorganizing the administration of the empire and replacing the system of private property by a rudimentary system of tribal property, leaving the great temple estates as islands of civilization isolated in a sea of barbarism. They rapidly became transformed into self-sufficient lordships. To the west, under the pressure of the Hittites and the Mitanni, the Amorean nomads invaded the central valley of the Euphrates, while the country of Sumeria was overrun by very primitive peoples whose name history has preserved as 'the peoples of the sea'.

The great trade route that followed the course of the Euphrates and the Tigris was cut. Babylon, whose empire was crumbling, suffered a terrible economic crisis, soon made worse by the raids of the Hittite horsemen into the civilized lands in search of plunder. During the XVIIth century BC a dynasty of Kassite barbarians was seated on the throne of Babylon. The cities of Sumeria fell into total decay. Of the Babylonian Empire, now fallen and overrun by peoples scarcely more than nomads, there remained only one city, Babylon itself, which, without renouncing her trading activities which she was little by little to build up once more, ceased to be the capital of an Empire. She was no more than a great merchant city, isolated in a world of barbarians, set in the midst of a tribal or seigniorial economy.

CRETAN SEAPOWER

At the same time as Babylon, Syria felt the shock of the invasions. Not only had the Euphrates trade route been cut, but a combination of Aryan and Semite peoples was driving southward, disorganizing all economic life in its passage. The disappearance of the Sumerian merchant colonies in Cappadocia and the Cretan trading posts on the coast of Asia Minor, together with the decline of Byblos and the Phoenician ports, led to a crisis in Mediterranean sea-borne trade which was to have great consequences for Crete. It resulted in a social revolution, somewhat similar in origin to the one that had broken out in the cities of Lower Egypt at the time of the Ancient Empire. What remained of the feudal régime in Crete was swept away (1750 BC). Thus, while decadence was spreading slowly over Nearer Asia, re-establishing feudalism or nomadism everywhere, in Crete, on the other hand, the consequence of the Aryan invasions was finally to destroy the last vestiges of feudalism. The economic development resultant on this and the crisis of Syrian shipping allowed the Cretan sailors to assume maritime leadership. Relying upon Egypt, which alone remained unaffected by the invasions, they set out to win mastery of the seas and to create a real sea-power turned both towards Asia and towards Egypt. Knossos was to commence a period of enormous development and to become not only a brilliant centre of art and civilization but also the capital of a kingdom with wise institutions, whose cities were inhabited, thanks to their trade, by a rich and cultivated middle class.

Cretan trading posts were founded all around the Aegean Sea. In the

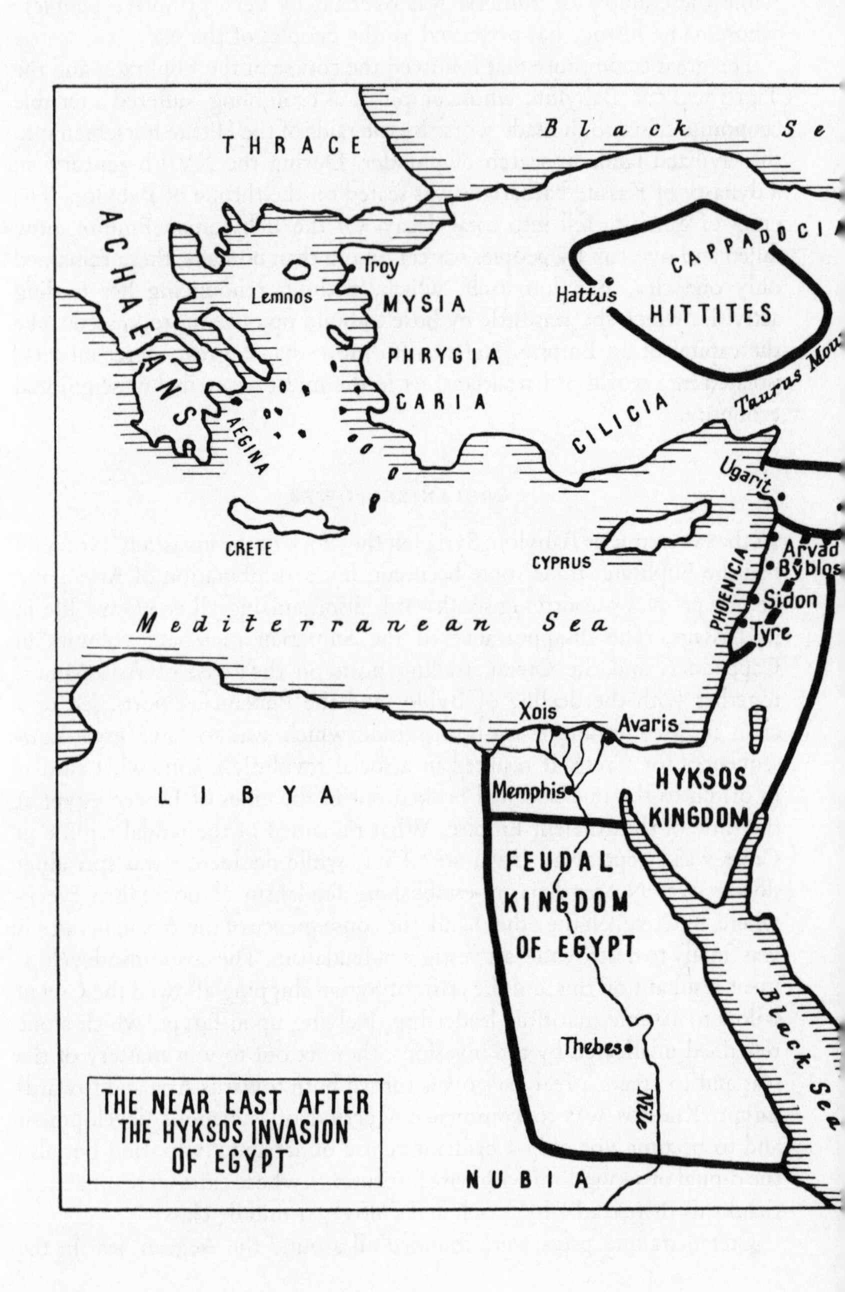

THE NEAR EAST AFTER THE HYKSOS INVASION OF EGYPT

Map No. 5

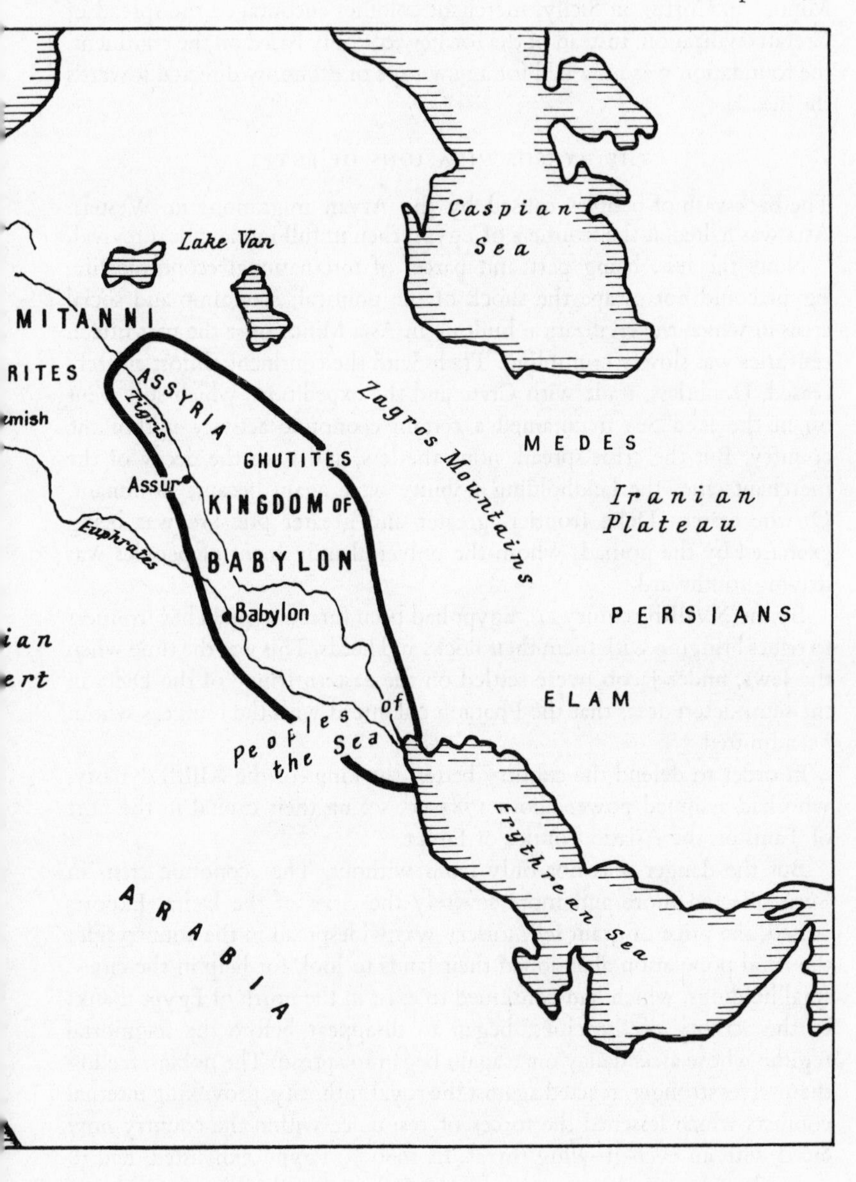
Caspian Sea
Lake Van
MITANNI
RITES
emish
ASSYRIA
Tigris
Zagros Mountains
MEDES
GHUTITES
Assur
KINGDOM OF BABYLON
Iranian Plateau
Euphrates
Babylon
PERSIANS
ian
ert
ELAM
peoples of the Sea
Erythrean Sea
ARABIA

Peloponnesus, Mycenae, Tiryns, Argos and Pylos were to become real maritime cities in the midst of Achaean feudalism. On the coasts of Asia Minor, on Corfu, on Sicily, merchant colonies encouraged the spread of Cretan civilization. Instead of the former economy based on the continent, the foundation was now laid for a new type of economy directed towards the sea.

THE HYKSOS INVASIONS OF EGYPT

The backwash of peoples caused by the Aryan migrations in Western Asia was halted at the frontiers of Egypt, then in full monarchical revival.

None the less, being part and parcel of international economic life, Egypt could not escape the shock of the political, economic and social crisis in which the civilization built up in Asia Minor over the past fifteen centuries was slowly crumbling. Trade with the continent almost entirely ceased. Doubtless, trade with Crete and the expeditions which still went on in the Red Sea maintained a certain economic activity within the country. But the crisis spread, none the less, and with the decay of the merchant cities the landholding nobility once again became dominant. On the eastern Delta frontier, greater and greater pressure was being exercised by the nomads whom the universal movement of peoples was driving southward.

By the XVIIIth century BC, Egypt had been forced to open her frontiers to tribes bringing with them their flocks and herds. This was the time when the Jews, under Jacob, were settled on the eastern fringe of the Delta in the semi-desert areas that the Pharaoh colonized with the refugees whom he admitted.

In order to defend the country better, the kings of the XIIIth dynasty, who had assumed power about 1785 BC, set up their capital in the port of Tanis on the Asiatic frontier of Egypt.

But the danger was not only from without. The economic crisis in Syria affected more and more severely the cities of the Delta. Exports ceased, the price of grain fell, misery was widespread in the countryside; the rural population abandoned their lands to look for help in the cities; smallholdings, which had continued to exist in the north of Egypt thanks to the activity of the cities, began to disappear before the seigniorial régime whose ascendancy once again began to spread. The nobles, feeling themselves stronger, reacted against the royal authority, provoking internal conflicts which lessened the forces of resistance within the country now faced with an ever-growing threat. In 1680 BC Egypt, exhausted, had to surrender; the invaders swept over the Delta. A multitude of peoples of varied race under a military aristocracy, Aryan or Syrian, rushed to plunder Egypt's wealth. For the first time since the reign of Menes, the Nile Valley felt the onrush of the barbarians.

For about a century, a number of states founded by the invaders, Mitanni or 'Hyksos', stretched from Middle Egypt to the Lake of Van. The most powerful amongst them, the kingdom of Mitanni, set up north of the Euphrates, was to know a period of greatness before being destroyed by the Hittites. As for the Hyksos kings of Egypt, installed at Avaris, they rapidly became Egyptianized.

THE HYKSOS KINGDOM OF AVARIS

The invasion of Egypt by the Hyksos was the final point of their expansion. They founded a kingdom in Lower Egypt, where they set up their capital in the great merchant city of Avaris, situated on the coast east of the Delta.[1] The attempt at monarchical revival was temporarily broken and the feudal régime favoured by the Hyksos kings was once again imposed upon all Egypt. A feudal dynasty reigned at Thebes, another at Xois in Lower Egypt, both vassals of Avaris. Under the rule of the feudal Hyksos, peace was none the less restored, and with it trade began to revive. The Phoenician cities, Babylon and the cities of the Nile Delta little by little recovered their prosperity. The invaders became merged into the peoples of higher civilization over whom they ruled. They had brought with them their gods, their heaven-god especially, who manifested his power in lightning and storm; he became identified with the Syrian Baal and the Egyptian Seth.[2] In Egypt and Syria, the Hyksos abandoned their own language, used the languages of their vassals and adapted themselves to their customs. Little by little the military structure set up by the Hyksos over Lower Egypt and southern Syria disintegrated. It finally collapsed in 1580 BC when the restored Egyptian monarchy rejected the suzerainty of the kings of Avaris and captured their capital. The Hyksos kingdom of Avaris was no more than a political framework; after the destruction of the dynasty which was the reason for its existence it rapidly disappeared.

THE ARYANS IN INDIA

Of all the states founded by the invaders in Asia Minor only the kingdom of Mitanni survived. Further east, the Aryan landslide slowly continued

[1] Perhaps the same city as Tanis.

[2] Seth, who had become the principle of evil in the Osirian myth, was still worshipped in Upper Egypt under his primitive form of the great god.

southward across the Iranian highlands, reached India and, in the XVIth century, penetrated into the Indus Valley.

The Aryan infiltration took place slowly. Aryan tribes, less civilized than those which had come into contact with the great oriental civilizations, filtered with their flocks for a whole century through the passes of the Hindu-Kush. By about 1500 BC their immigration ceased.

The great civilization that Sind and the Punjab had known in the times of Mohenjo-Daro and Harappa had for several centuries been sinking into irremediable decay, parallel to that of the cities of Sumeria. The Aryans gave it its death-blow by exterminating the Dravidian population. For a thousand years to come the Indus basin was not to play any economic role.

From the Indus valley the Aryans passed into the valley of the Ganges, where they became superimposed on the native peoples there, creating, in order to maintain their supremacy, a caste system which grew steadily stronger. In India, as in Nearer Asia, the Aryans formed a ruling military aristocracy. The kernel of their civilization was in the upper valley of the Ganges where, around the kingdom of Kuru, they created a feudal civilization based entirely on landholding without contact with the outer world. The Malabar coast and central India were only subject to the Aryan infiltration very much later, when they had already laid the foundations of a great civilization. Meanwhile, their economic activity remained entirely separate from that of northern India.

The Punjab was to become the centre of the Aryan civilization in India. The cult of Diaous, brought by the Aryans, became fused little by little into that of the great god Varuna, who sees everything, who rewards and who punishes. In contact with pre-Aryan beliefs, the Vedic religion was to centre around the belief in a future life. It was in the Punjab that between 1000 and 800 BC were written in their final form the sacred books of the Veda which bring down to us, mixed with Aryan ideas, an echo of the religious beliefs of the Dravidians, whose advanced civilization had been developed in the Indus between the IIIrd and IInd millenaries.

BOOK II

The Organization of International Life from the XVIth to the IXth Century BC

CHAPTER VIII
THE NEW EGYPTIAN EMPIRE

THE FALL OF THE HYKSOS

THE Hyksos invasion, though it had destroyed the monarchical unity of Egypt, had not halted social evolution. The kings of Avaris had merely subjected the country to a political control. In Lower Egypt peace had revived the economic life of the cities which found a fresh source of prosperity in their sea trade with Crete. And in Upper Egypt, despite Hyksos suzerainty which artificially maintained a feudal framework, the monarchy had again taken up its work of centralization. When it felt itself powerful enough it refused tribute to the kings of Avaris and began the struggle against them.

But the feudal lords feared the revival of the royal power, which was to mark their own decline, and made common cause with the foreign king against the Pharaohs. After Ahmosis I captured Avaris in 1580 BC, he had to turn on his own vassals and reconquer his kingdom from them. The defeated feudatories saw their fiefs confiscated for treason according to feudal law and the monarchy suddenly found itself re-established in its unity by force of arms.

The fall of Avaris led to the collapse of the political structure of the Hyksos kingdom. Ahmosis I, now master of Egypt, conquered Syria without difficulty and advanced the frontiers of the Egyptian Empire as far as the Upper Euphrates. To the south, Nubia was annexed. Egypt was not only reconstituted but was at the head of a magnificent empire. Her leadership, thenceforward, was asserted over all Nearer Asia. The reunion of Lower Egypt with the Theban monarchy brought resources which enabled the state to embark on a real imperial policy. The fall of the Hyksos kingdom opened up vast commercial opportunities for Syria and Babylon. Crete too was involved in the revival of international trade, in which Egypt, this time, was to be the main centre.

RESTORATION OF THE MONARCHY IN EGYPT AND RELIGIOUS SYNCRETISM

The return to monarchical unity in Egypt was accompanied by a revival of the public law of the Ancient Empire. The monarchical theory of divine right was restored to honour. The king, regarded as the son of Ammon, the ancient feudal god of Thebes, henceforward regarded as equivalent to the sun-god Ra, re-established his absolutism on a religious foundation. So, while the king took over all the powers of the former feudal princes, Ammon-Ra resumed the rank of great god, grouping around him all the local gods in a renewed version of the Heliopolis theology. But if Ra had been the centre of the Heliopolis system, the priests of Memphis had built up their theology about the god Ptah; in order to weld the cult, broken into fragments during the feudal period, into a single unity, the Theban theology assimilated Ammon both to Ptah and to Ra, creating a trinity, Ptah-Ammon-Ra, the body, the spirit and the conscience of the world, 'three gods but one'.

Once again political centralization was accompanied by religious centralization. None the less, the king of Thebes could not renounce the close union that the feudal monarchy had built up between the royal power and the mystic cult of Osiris, god of the dead and of good, which was the main object of the people's piety. The Theban theology therefore tried to combine the pantheist cult of the great creator-god and the mystic cult of the saviour-god.[1] Osiris was merged into the supreme god represented by the triad Ptah-Ammon-Ra. The creator principle was fused with the principle of good, and theology thenceforth developed towards a dualism; opposed to the creator, inseparable from good, there appeared a destroyer-god, the principle of evil, the snake Apophis.

The Osirian conception, in which the saviour-god dies and is born again, was extended to Ra himself who was conceived as daily destroyed by Apophis, to be born again by his own power alone. The course of the sun, which is seen to rise at dawn and set at night, was taken as the symbol of the creative life and death of the god; Ra, born every morning at sunrise, borrowed from Osiris his role of saviour-god. Mysticism was substituted for metaphysics and God drew nearer to man.[2]

The Egyptian religion penetrated even more deeply into the private lives of the people. In its practice, prayer and the love of God took an even greater part. Morals took on a more clearly religious character;

[1] A similar syncretism took place in Babylon in the times of Hammurabi between the nature-god Marduk and the creator-god Enlil.

[2] Egyptian texts often speak of God, *neter*, without giving him any other name.

not to repay evil for evil, to renounce violence, not to cause suffering, to submit to the divine mercy, became its essential rules, and the formula appeared· 'he who weeps shall be saved', thus introducing into religion God's predilection for the humble that was to be confirmed by Christianity.

In social affairs, religious mysticism favoured a democratic evolution which was in any case encouraged by the royal policy of hostility to class privilege; in political affairs the idea of the equality of all men before God was to lead, a century later, to the triumph of natural law.

During the reigns of Amenophis I, of Tutmes I and of Tutmes II (1557–1505 BC) the central authority and the official framework were again set up; courts of justice were created at Thebes, Memphis and Heliopolis and the army was reorganized on a conscript basis. Socially, the manorial régime was completely dissolved, serfdom disappeared and the nobility, though remaining the most important class within the state, lost its privileges. The equality of all men before the law was established. The manorial system of economy made way for an economy based on trade and personal property once more became fluid. This resulted in the breakdown of the laws of primogeniture and, in consequence, of family solidarity. Individualist law triumphed, as it had fifteen centuries earlier.

CONFLICT BETWEEN THE PRIESTHOOD AND THE ROYAL POWER

As the royal power waxed greater, so also did that of the priests, guardians of the cult upon which it was based. The two powers soon came into conflict, the king aiming at absolutism and the High Priest of Ammon trying to retain his tutelary authority over the monarchy, which reigned by divine right, and thus transform Egypt into a theocracy.

After the death of Tutmes II (1505 BC) the regency of the Queen Hatshepsut marked a period of priestly ascendancy. The High Priest of Ammon, invested with supreme authority over the religion and all the priests of Egypt, was also invested with the office of vizier, that is to say Chief of the Government and Lord High Justice. Karnak, where the High Priest lived, became a sort of 'Vatican'. The spiritual power asserted its supremacy in the state.

But the priesthood, devoted to their theocratic policy, neglected the empire. The cities of Syria, the princes of Palestine and Amurru, took this opportunity to throw off the Egyptian yoke. By the time Tutmes III came to the throne (1484 BC) Syria was lost. The empire had to be built up again.

THE EMPIRE UNDER TUTMES III

Tutmes III was the greatest warrior in the history of Egypt. He was also a great statesman. A series of campaigns, conducted in a spirit of conciliation for the conquered, restored Syria to Egypt. Reconquered Syria was again incorporated in the empire. With its three to four million inhabitants, its four hundred miles of coastline and its one hundred and ten autonomous states—merchant cities or feudal princedoms—it was one of the richest areas in the world, and meant for Egypt—which itself had six million inhabitants—an immense increase of wealth and power.

The main interest of Syria was the commercial activity of its free cities, urban republics like Tunip or Irkata, or principalities ruled by the burghers like Byblos, Tyre, Sidon or Arvad. They possessed large fleets and were international trade-marts between the Mediterranean, Egypt and Babylon. Incontestably, it was Babylonian influence that prevailed here. Babylon was not, at this time, an empire; it was a financial and commercial metropolis, a link uniting Nearer Asia and India. Though Egypt dominated Syria politically, Babylonian was the commercial language and Babylonian law was in force for all transactions. It was therefore economics and not politics that decided the trend of civilization.

The constitution of the empire, founded by conquest, was given a legal basis by a political theory based on religion; the god Ammon had created the world and was the master of all men; but the king of Egypt was Ammon incarnated. He therefore held, by virtue of his divine nature, universal sovereignty; to resist him was to rebel against the creator himself.

Under the supreme authority of the Pharaoh, to whom Ammon had entrusted the mission of reigning over all men, the states incorporated into the empire kept their own institutions and their own internal autonomy. The king represented them in external affairs and was the arbiter of conflicts which might arise between them. The subjects of the empire were not, like the Egyptians, subject to taxes on revenue but every state paid a tribute. Egyptian garrisons were stationed at strategic points. Babylonian and not Egyptian was adopted as the imperial language of 'the foreign service'. The sons of vassal princes were brought up at the Egyptian court together with the princes of the blood.

Nubia was not administered on these principles but was organized, under the rule of an all-powerful viceroy, as a colony to be exploited. Surrounded by an Egyptian administration and with a native army commanded by Egyptian officers at his beck and call, the main task of the viceroy was to watch over the exploitation of the goldmines and the reception of the tributes in kind imposed on the Nubian chiefs. Nubia was not, like Syria, a province of the empire; it was a colony.

The theory of universal sovereignty did not impel the Pharaohs to carry out a policy of territorial aggrandizement. What they were looking for was commercial hegemony. Once the Syrian ports had been occupied, conquest ceased and every effort was made to ensure the international *status quo*. Thenceforward, the Pharaohs were to practise a policy of peace and to consolidate their position by a system of alliances and treaties which were to usher the whole eastern world into a period of international organization.

The military power at his disposal and the resources that he was able to draw from the empire made the struggle between Tutmes III and the sacerdotal party an unequal one. But, on the other hand, the religious basis of the imperial theory assumed a more and more important place in religion throughout the empire. A balance was therefore struck between the power of the king and that of the priests. The High Priest of Ammon preserved the general control of the Egyptian cults, grouped into a regular 'church', whose dogmas were fixed at Thebes in official works of theology; but he was excluded from the civil administration, which was rigidly centralized in the hands of lay officials who derived their power from the king alone. The monarchy thenceforward rested on two pillars; the cult under the authority of the High Priest of Ammon, whom the king never ceased to load with rich donations, and the civil administration under the authority of the Vizier, united in their dependence on the all-powerful Pharaoh on whose will the nomination of both High Priest and Vizier depended.

With a splendid empire that assured it the control of all the trade routes of Nearer Asia and based on a wisely balanced internal system, the Egyptian monarchy, in the reigns of Amenophis II, Tutmes IV and Amenophis III (1450–1370 BC) knew a period of uncontested hegemony.

Map No. 6

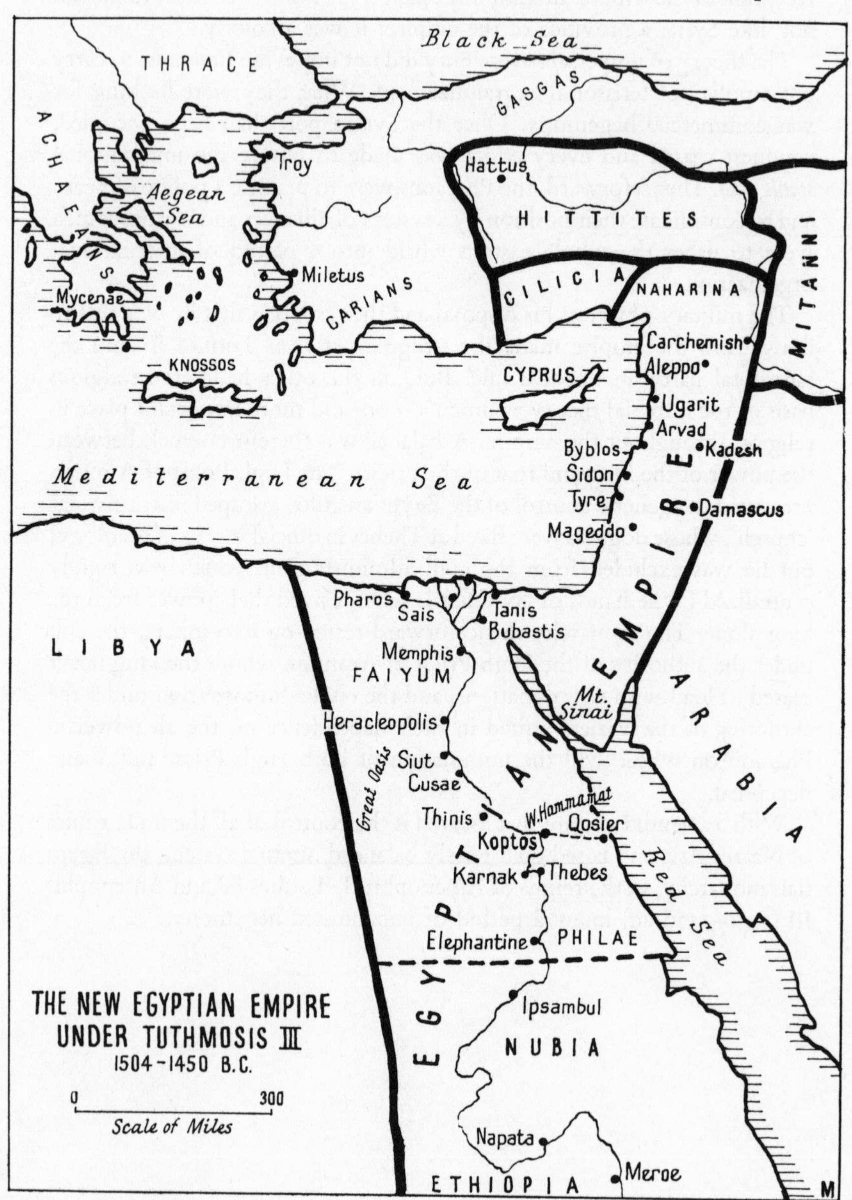

THE NEW EGYPTIAN EMPIRE UNDER TUTHMOSIS III 1504–1450 B.C.

CHAPTER IX

EGYPTIAN HEGEMONY

INTERNATIONAL POLITICAL AND ECONOMIC POLICY

IN the XVth century BC a new political balance was attained. Of the states that had been founded since the Aryan invasions only the kingdom of Mitanni, north of the Euphrates and Tigris, remained. It was made up of two distinct parts, Mitanni itself in northern Mesopotamia, and Hurri, east of the Tigris. It was a feudal monarchy, but it held the trade routes from Babylon to the Taurus and the Mediterranean. The stronghold of Carchemish, where these two routes joined, was the key. Mitanni also controlled the route from the Tigris to the Caucasus.

In Asia Minor, on the Cappadocian plateau, Hittite feudalism, after having been centred around the holy cities of Arinna, Nariq and Zippalanda, was unified in a feudal monarchy under the rule of the prince of Hattus. At first elected king by his peers, he made his royal title hereditary in the XVIIth century. About 1450 BC feudalism disappeared completely, to the advantage of the monarchy. The seigniorial régime also came to an end, and was replaced by free labour. Only the temples retained their archaic, manorial organization. Save for the temple estates, the Hittite code, published in the XVth century, did not recognize serfdom.

A dual development took place in the evolution of the Hittites similar to that we have already seen in Egypt and Mesopotamia; royal centralization, that is to say the suppression of class privilege, and social emancipation, that is to say the gradual abolition of collective group responsibility to the advantage of personal law, developed side by side.

Along the coasts of Asia Minor, commercial life and sea-borne trade advanced rapidly. Troy, on the Hellespont, became the seat of a great international fair and was an important centre, thanks to the tolls that it collected and to its own industries. Aegean colonies were founded on the sites of Miletus and Ephesus and in Caria. In Cilicia, where the passes of the Taurus form one of the gates of Nearer Asia, the call of the sea was also felt.

In the north, on the Black Sea, ships adventured to the iron deposits of Taurus and the gold of Colchis.

Routes were opened across Cappadocia, linking the Black Sea, Troy and Ephesus with the Hittite capital, Hattus, which, by encouraging trade, led to the dissolution of the seigniorial régime.

In order to assure her ways of communication, Babylon had re-established her rule over the course of the two rivers as far as the Persian Gulf. But she no longer, as in the XVIIIth century, presided over a great centralized monarchy. She was now a semi-feudal realm in which the ancient Sumerian cities, ruined by the silting up of the Delta, were dominated by the wealthy temples. Babylon herself, however, had preserved her urban structure, her individualist law and her royal institutions and, peace favouring trade, life revived in the whole Mediterranean basin, and Babylonian law, with the type of society that it represented, increased its ascendancy.

On the Tigris, between Babylon and the state of Mitanni, the Assyrian kingdom was being formed around the city of Assur. The Ghutites, after invading the country, ended by settling there. But the upheaval produced by the great Aryan invasions had almost annihilated the Sumerian civilization, which had been introduced at the close of the IIIrd millenary and which was now represented by the city of Assur. The capital of Assyria was still a merchant city where the burghers were important and where Babylonian law, although decadent, was still in force; but it formed an island in the midst of an essentially feudal countryside in the power of warrior-nobles whose domains were peopled by serfs.

In fact, the only great continental centres of civilization and activity were Egypt, the Syrian coastland and Babylon.

Egypt was the main artistic, intellectual and political centre. But while on the continent of Asia civilization flourished on the sea-coasts and along the great rivers, the Mediterranean was acquiring more and more importance.

Crete was a great sea-power. The city burghers, enriched by seaborne trade and industry, dominated it. About 1450 BC a revolution led to the final disappearance of the last vestiges of feudalism that still existed in the interior. The feudal castles were burnt down. This was the period of the great prosperity of Knossos under the dynasty of Minos. Civilization, though greatly influenced by Egypt, maintained its originality; life was cultured and luxury spread even among the middle classes; art was at a high level, especially fresco which produced masterpieces of elegance. Cretan ships diffused civilization along the coasts of Greece. An Aegean civilization was created which spread to the Achaean cities; a merchant class appeared into which the petty landowning nobility became more and more merged. Already the Achaeans of Thessaly were trying to penetrate into the Black Sea that Troy tried to keep closed against them. The story of Jason and the search for the Golden Fleece recalls the memory of their expeditions to the goldmines of Colchis.

The island of Cyprus, then divided into a number of petty kingdoms, also became, thanks to its copper deposits and its pine-resin, a naval and sea-trading power.

All this life of the sea was already looking westward. The Adriatic was opened up by Cretan ships. The Danube was known as a way by which to reach Central Europe, whence came the tin for which Crete was the great market.

But it was Egypt that was the magnetic pole for sea-borne commerce. The Delta ports were in constant touch with Byblos and the Phoenician ports which formed part of the Egyptian Empire. In order to centralize trade with Crete the kings of the XVIIIth dynasty founded the great port of Pharos on the site of present-day Alexandria.

The Cypriots concluded trade agreements with the Pharaohs, which granted them exemption from all customs dues.

Syrian, Aegean and Cypriot merchants settled in Egypt, where the international private law, developed by trade, gave them complete economic freedom and protected both their persons and their goods.

All Egyptian commerce with the Mediterranean was left to private enterprise; but eastward the State intervened. The port of Qoseir on the Red Sea was linked to Koptos on the Nile by a caravan route and, by way of the Mensaleh lakes, a canal linked the Red Sea to the city of Bubastis on the Nile. The isthmus of Suez was pierced and ships coming from Arabia as well as Phoenicia reached Memphis.

Fleets, equipped by the State and convoyed by warships, left regularly for the land of Punt, whence they returned laden with gold, ebony and spices. On the Arabian coasts ships undoubtedly carried Egyptian goods still farther, to India. The Indus, it is true, no longer played an important role. The Aryan invasion had not penetrated beyond the Indus and Ganges basins and the immense wealth of India now found its export harbours on the Malabar coast and probably also to the south of it.

On the Persian Gulf, the silting-up of the Mesopotamian Delta had stopped sea-borne trade; but the caravan routes to India by way of Susa and Baluchistan continued to be much used. It is impossible to understand the immense importance of Babylon without this economic hinterland

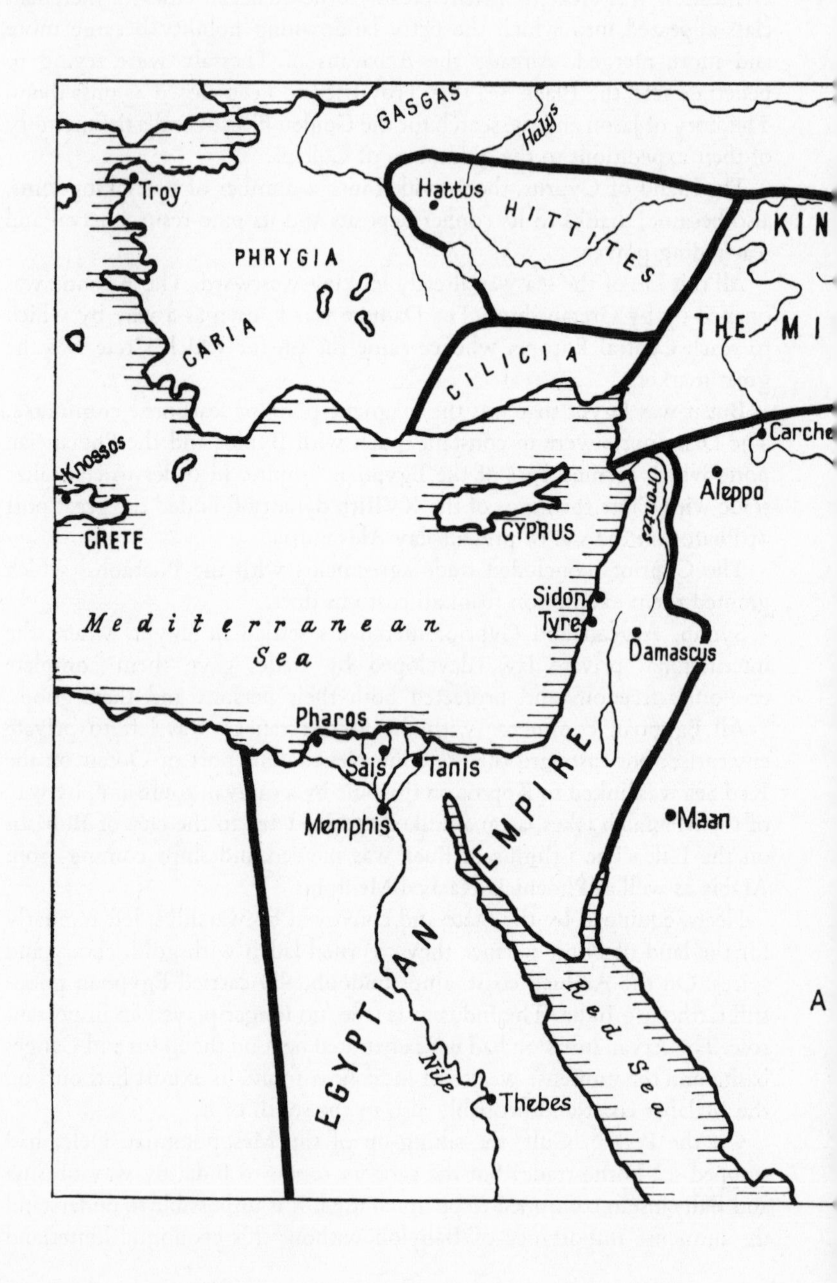
GASGAS
Halys
Troy
Hattus
HITTITES
KIN
PHRYGIA
THE MI
CARIA
CILICIA
Carche
Knossos
Aleppo
Oronte
CYPRUS
CRETE
Sidon
Tyre
Damascus
Mediterranean
Sea
Pharos
Sais
Tanis
Memphis
Maan
EMPIRE
EGYPTIAN
Red Sea
Nile
Thebes
A

Map No. 7

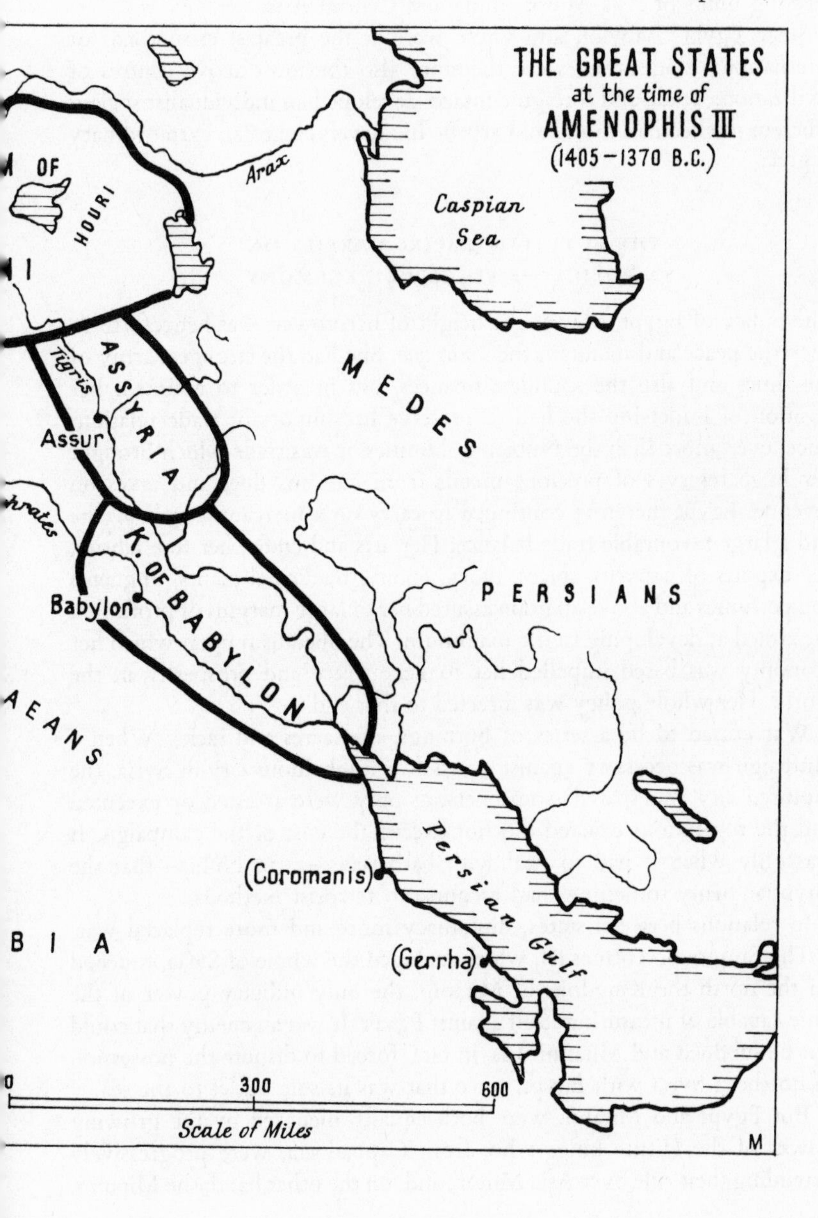
THE GREAT STATES
at the time of
AMENOPHIS III
(1405–1370 B.C.)
Arax
Caspian Sea
HOURI
Tigris
ASSYRIA
Assur
MEDES
K. OF BABYLON
Babylon
PERSIANS
Persian Gulf
(Coromanis)
(Gerrha)
B I A
0
300
600
Scale of Miles
M

of India and Central Asia. If Babylon was the main international centre of trade and finance, she owed this to her situation which made her the meeting point of Asia Minor, India and Central Asia.

Since Egypt, Babylon and Crete were at the greatest cross-roads of international trade, they were therefore also the most active centres of civilization. Trade and foreign contacts developed an individualist society wherein intellectual, moral and artistic life developed to an extraordinary degree.

THE EGYPTIAN EMPIRE CARRIES ON A POLICY OF PEACEFUL HEGEMONY

The policy of Egypt, now at the height of her power, was henceforth to keep the peace and maintain the *status quo*. She had the strongest army of the times and also the soundest finances, but in order to maintain her position of leadership she had to preserve her important trade relations since, even more than the Nubian goldmines, it was trade which brought her huge reserves of precious metals from customs dues and taxes on revenue. Egypt therefore continued to carry on a mercantile policy. She had a large favourable trade balance. Her arts and crafts, her fine fabrics, her exports of papyrus, spices, ivory, ebony, medicinal plants, unguents and perfumes and above all grain assured her of large margins of profit that she aimed at developing to the maximum. The liberalism upon which her economy was based impelled her to keep peace and prosperity in the world. Her whole policy was directed to that end.

War ceased to be a series of burnings, massacres and sacks. When a campaign was necessary against a vassal or a rebellious city in Syria, the captured city was spared; some persons only were arrested or executed and the reparations exacted did not exceed the cost of the campaign. It was only when it had to deal with barbarians—as in Nubia—that the Egyptian army sometimes had recourse to terrorist methods.

In relations between states, diplomacy more and more replaced war.

The Empire of Tutmes III, which included the whole of Syria, touched on the north the Kingdom of Mitanni, the only military power of the time capable of measuring itself against Egypt. It was an enemy that could not be subdued and Mitanni was, in fact, forced to dispute the possession of northern Syria with Egypt, since that was its sole outlet to the sea.

But Egypt and Mitanni were both equally menaced by the growing power of the Hittite kings who, from Cappadocia, were progressively extending their rule over Asia Minor; and, on the other hand, the Mitanni, bordered by the Hittites on the west, saw on their eastern frontier the growing power of the Assyrians.

Tutmes III, like a great statesman, instead of profiting by the situation, realized that the destruction of the Mitannian power, by exposing the northward flank of the Egyptian Empire, would have led it into fresh wars. He therefore decided to come to an agreement with the Mitanni, abandoning the northern part of the Syrian coastline to them. The Egyptian frontier was, therefore, withdrawn to the Orontes and thenceforward there was no further cause of dispute between the two kingdoms. Their interests became mutual and a policy of alliance allowed them, by joining forces, to assure the *status quo* in peace and to maintain an international balance favourable to both sides.

This was quite a new conception. The Pharaoh, without explicitly renouncing the monarchical theory that led him to aspire to universal sovereignty, began in fact to recognize other states as sovereign and equal. This attitude, taken on an international level, reacted also upon the internal policy of Egypt.

Until the times of Tutmes III the Pharaohs had married only Egyptian princesses, in whose veins flowed the divine blood.

From Tutmes IV onwards, in order to confirm treaties of alliance or friendship which were continually being signed with other states, the Pharaohs began to make political marriages. Tutmes IV took a Mitannian as his first wife, Amenophis III a Phoenician and Amenophis IV another Mitannian. In addition they married Babylonian and Cilician princesses.

There could no longer be any question of admitting the priestly theory that attributed the supremacy of the monarchy to the divine blood of the kings transmitted by the queens as the basis of their legitimacy. Amenophis III, master of the most powerful empire of his times, rejected this claim by formulating a new theory of theogamy. The king, by the sole fact of the power that he exercised, appeared as the divinity incarnate. When he conceived his heir, it was Ammon himself who gave life to the future king. The priesthood was no longer, therefore, the guardian of the divine nature of kings; that came directly from Ammon by whose wish they exercised sovereignty and whose spirit—the *ka*—resided in every sovereign. Power thenceforth found its justification in itself. The monarchy entered its absolutist phase.

THE ABSOLUTE MONARCHY

In internal affairs, the royal absolutism aimed at the suppression of the ascendency exercised in the state by the High Priests and the nobles who, though no longer possessing privileges, had in fact retained control of affairs.

Prosperity encouraged the expansion of smallholdings and individualist law triumphed. In conformity with the egalitarian ideas of the cult which conceived all men as equal before the god, the king introduced the lower classes into the legal framework of the state and called on new men to fill the highest offices. Individual merit replaced the prestige of birth.

Meanwhile trade led to the formation of great fortunes in fluid property and there was a great development of the law of contract. Private law, reverting to the classic formula of the Ancient Empire, sanctioned the civic equality of all Egyptians. Art flourished and the life of all classes became cultured. The dictates of fashion and elegance spread to the burghers. The cities were enriched with beautiful architecture in proto-doric or lotus-form style. It was at this time that the magnificent temple of Luxor was built. Science and literature were held in honour and were taught in schools, to which all classes of the population flocked. The state maintained high schools for the training of officials. Tutmes III created the first botanical garden at Karnak.

But international relations introduced slavery into Egypt. Prisoners of war captured in the campaigns, who had been formed into working brigades in the service of the state and more especially handed over to the temples, were now granted also to individuals; Syrian merchants circulated throughout the country selling slaves, mainly Syrian women. None the less, slavery was of little importance. The industrial workshops still employed only free workers. On the country estates slaves were employed only as house-servants. Only the state and the temples made great use of them and settled them on their estates. But the most unfortunate were those who worked in the copper-mines or in the quarries.

In international affairs, absolutism allowed the monarchy to carry on a strictly hegemonic policy. Egypt was the great financial power of the times. By the loans that she continually granted to the kings of Babylon, of Mitanni, of Assyria, she assured herself a dominant position with them, consolidated by diplomatic relations. However it was not Egyptian but Babylonian which, since it was the international language of trade, became also the international language of diplomacy. Diplomatic protocol, internationally agreed, controlled the correspondence of chancelleries. Ambassadors, protected by diplomatic immunity, travelled constantly between the great capitals, amongst which Thebes was recognized as the diplomatic centre. The development of personal law led to that of international private law. Between countries linked by treaties of friendship

—and such treaties were concluded with all states—a legal statute existed which protected the property of their respective subjects. Thus goods left by a Cypriot oil merchant who had died while on his way up the Nile in his ship were listed by Egyptian officials and the inventory sent to Cyprus by diplomatic messenger. Foreigners could contract legal marriages with Egyptian women. Syrians—they retained their separate nationality, although subjects of the Empire—became bankers or ship-chandlers in the Egyptian cities. Aegeans maintained important warehouses there.

This great international movement led to a profound transformation of political and religious ideas. The monarchical power had, since its formation, justified itself by its divine origin. The pantheist conception of divinity conceived the world as entirely penetrated by the divine spirit. It resided in all beings having a personality, in the Nile, in Egypt, in a mountain, a plant or an animal, as much as in man; though in varying degrees. It was in the person of the king that Ammon, the creator-god symbolized by the sun, manifested himself in all his power. The king was the repository of all the knowledge and power of Ammon. But the immense prestige that this conferred upon royalty only existed for the worshippers of Ammon; the Egyptian Empire extended into Syria, where the people venerated the Babylonian sun-god Shamash as the great creator-god. Thenceforward, in order to justify his power among the Syrians, Amenophis III assimilated Shamash to Ammon and in Syria declared himself the incarnation of the god Shamash.

Religious syncretism accompanied political expansion. Imperial absolutism tended towards an interpenetration of all the various solar cults in order to unite them under the omnipotence of a single god, of whom the king was the sole representative. But even as the Pharaoh derived his power from the solar god, so the vassal princes, the cities of the empire and even the Egyptian *nomes* had divine protectors who were the former local gods. Theology, parallel with the development of the monarchical power, presented these local gods as particular aspects of the Sun, the great creator-god incarnate in the Pharaoh. Absolute monarchy therefore tended towards a solar monotheism upon which it relied to legitimize its power, not only in Egypt but throughout the whole empire. It was a magnificent conception which, uniting in a single system religion, political power and morals, tended to extend more and more and to pass from the national to the universal plane. It asserted itself in this new form in the great reform of Amenophis IV. This was one of the most moving moments in the development of human consciousness.

AMARNIAN UNIVERSALISM (1370–1352 BC)

Extending the imperial theory to its ultimate consequences, Amenophis IV founded universal monarchy on universal religion. Himself deeply mystical, imbued with humanitarian and egalitarian ideas formed by the religious conception of the equality of man before God, he completely dissociated himself from nationalism. He himself, moreover, Egyptian on his father's side, Aryan by his mother and Semite by his grandmother, represented in his own person all the races of his empire. He conceived the world as an entity subject to a single god, who without doubt had created races and nations, and by whom all men were equally created. Freeing himself from the symbolism and the archaisms that encumbered the Egyptian religion, he proclaimed the absolute monotheism towards which it tended. Carrying out the greatest religious revolution ever attempted by a ruler, he abolished the cults of all the gods, to replace them by that of the one god Aton, creator of the world, whom he represented among men. Aton was not, however, a new god; he was the supreme God as conceived in the solar cosmogony, but reduced to his sole quality of creator. Represented by the solar disc that dispenses to man, by its rays, life and justice, he was free of all mythology and all symbolism; he was pure spirit. Worship given to him during great public functions was essentially an act of faith, hope and love.

God is good! The life created by him is good. On earth the creative divinity is represented by the couple; conjugal love is the symbol of divine love and the road that leads to it. It is not the fear, but the love, of God which must inspire and guide humanity.

Since God loves all men with an equal love, there can be no differences between them. The palace, the administration, are thrown open to men of all conditions and to foreigners. Only personal merit, love of God and loyalty to the king, come into question as standards.

In order that the love taught by God should reign amongst all men, Amenophis IV wanted to assure peace. He would maintain it at any price, despite the threats that menaced his empire. It was on Aton, and not on arms, that he counted to inspire in his subjects and throughout the entire world his tutelary absolutism.

Breaking with Pharaonic tradition, he does not seek glory in grandeur, but in the happiness that he will dispense to his peoples by showing them the road of truth and justice.

This new tendency was translated into all walks of life: socially, by the construction of new model workers' cities and the rapid raising of the living standards of the ordinary people; in personal relations, by intimacy, sincerity and the desire for comfort and in freedom of relations between the sexes; in art, by a realism that sought to express life as it was, but a life dominated by moral virtues alone.

The elegant and luxurious capital of El Amarna, centre of diplomatic and fashionable life, where all the wealth of the empire accumulated and the refinement of manners was combined with a simplicity full of charm and taste, was the expression of this luminous, but unhappily ephemeral, zenith of Egyptian civilization.

BREAKDOWN OF THE BALANCE OF POWER RISE OF THE HITTITES

It was ephemeral since, while Amenophis IV was dreaming of a universal state and a universal religion, the Egyptian Empire was involved in a very serious external crisis.

In the reign of Suppiluliuma (1380 BC) the Hittite monarchy had become a powerful military state. After the final disappearance of feudalism, monarchical unity had enabled the king to undertake a policy of centralization and expansion. Partly by force of arms and partly by diplomacy, the Hittite king had grouped under his rule all the petty states of Asia Minor, the Achaeans, the Phrygians, the Lycians of the western coast, the still primitive Gasgeans from the shores of Pontus, and the Cilicians who inhabited the southern coasts. A series of treaties had established between the king at Hattus and the bordering states a hierarchy of sovereignty which divided the latter into protected kings and vassal kings, all grouped under the tribunal of the 'Great Hittite'. Declaring himself their master and protector, he imposed peace upon them and associated them with his foreign policy. The vassals, his military allies, paid him tribute. The protected princes retained their sovereignty within their own dominions but in their foreign relations were bound by obligations which made them in fact 'clients' of the Hittite monarchy.

Having thus built up a solid political and military power, the Hittite state demanded its place in international life and quite naturally aimed above all at assuring itself an outlet to the sea through northern Syria and a means of access to Mesopotamia by claiming Aleppo. The district of Aleppo, like northern Syria, is a key spot, whose possession has been at all times one of the 'constants' of the policy of the states of Nearer Asia. The kingdom of Mitanni, by holding both of them, cut the two essential trade routes of Hatti, one to Mesopotamia and the other to Egypt by way of Syria.

Conflict between Hatti and Mitanni was therefore inevitable. Attacked by Suppiluliuma at the end of the reign of Amenophis III, Mitanni was overthrown. It had been considered a great military power and its rapid destruction by the Hittite army, before Egypt could come to its assistance, destroyed the balance of power. Suppiluliuma, victorious, installed himself at Aleppo and occupied Syria as far as the Orontes, thus controlling the access of Mitanni to the sea and becoming the immediate neighbour of the Egyptian Empire. Amenophis III, who was willing to go to any length to avoid a great international conflict, had made no move to support his Mitannian ally. Bowing before the *fait accompli*, he recognized the Hatti as masters of northern Syria. The international prestige of Egypt was greatly shaken, and she soon felt the reaction. Her default encouraged the Hatti to wage against her a diplomatic war, aimed at disintegrating the Empire before attacking it. Amenophis III, despite his desire for peace, had no other alternative than to abandon the neutrality he had tried to observe and to restore the Mitannian alliance.

It was at this moment of international crisis that Amenophis IV came to the throne. He too wished to preserve peace at all costs. He therefore tried to isolate the Hatti by diplomacy while avoiding an open break with them. He only succeeded in isolating himself. While Egypt was negotiating with the powers, the Hittite king was acting. Intervening in the internal dissensions of Mitanni, he succeeded in dividing the state by great dynastic quarrels that soon ranged the Hurri against the Mitanni proper, causing the break-up of the kingdom into two mutually hostile states.

Assyria, seizing the occasion, allied itself with Hurri against Mitanni which, attacked on the west by the Hittites, was entirely overrun and divided into Assyrian and Hittite protectorates. The Egyptian Empire, isolated in its neutrality, no longer had any allies. The situation was now very serious; for Syria, too distant from the Egyptian bases, could only be efficiently defended with the help of a northern ally. In order to restore the balance of power, Amenophis IV looked to Assyria which had just begun to appear as a military power. By granting a number of loans Egypt obtained her alliance. Treaties of friendship were renewed with Babylon and Cyprus. But the Egyptian Empire, riddled with Hittite propaganda, was disintegrating. Rebellions broke out among the Syrian princes, secretly supported by the Hittite king. The rich coastal cities, threatened by the forays of these petty robber-princes, appealed in vain to the Pharaoh for help. The prestige of Egypt dwindled and the provinces broke away from the Empire at the very moment when Amenophis IV was building a plan of universal empire on the idea of co-operation and peace. By the end of his reign he had to decide to take action. The Egyptian armies, under the command of General Horemheb, were about to intervene in Palestine when the king died.

CHAPTER X
THE PERIOD OF INTERNATIONAL BALANCE

THE CRISIS OF EGYPTIAN HEGEMONY AND THE SOCIAL POLICY OF HOREMHEB

THE reign of Amenophis IV ended at a time of great crisis both at home and abroad. Abroad, war broke out with the Hittites; at home, a violent Ammonian reaction, which restored the traditional cult, ushered in a period of anarchy. The re-established priesthood and the nobility again raised their heads and took over the control of the state in the colourless reigns of Tutankhamen and Ai, and pillaged the country. Only the army remained an organized force. Its leader, General Horemheb, held the real power. He was enthroned by the priests in 1339 BC.

But Horemheb, enthroned as the tool of reaction, was carried away by the spirit of the times. The cult of Ammon was restored to its former power, but in foreign and social affairs Horemheb adopted the policy of Amenophis IV. His reign marked the triumph of the principle of natural law which was expressed in a policy of extensive social reform. In order to defend taxpayers against the revenue officials he set up a State Council, prohibited the seizure of workers' tools or the harvest necessary for the existence of a farmer, introduced the presumption of good faith in favour of insolvent debtors and ordered monthly distribution of foodstuffs to those of the poor who asked for them, since, as he said: 'My Majesty makes laws to let the people prosper'. Civil equality was promoted to such a point that, having no heirs, Horemheb adopted as his successor a semi-Asiatic veteran who had risen to the highest ranks in the army, Rameses I. He was to inaugurate a military dynasty with an authoritarian, imperial and democratic policy.

Rameses I (1320–1318 BC) and his successors Seti I (1318–1298 BC) and Rameses II (1298–1232 BC) made their main aim the restoration of the Empire. Seti I organized the most powerful army that Egypt had ever known and commenced the struggle against the Hittite monarchy. The prize was the possession of Syria which meant political hegemony for the victor. The war lasted until 1278 BC without either side being able to destroy the forces of its adversary.

But while Egypt and the Hittite state were exhausting themselves in indecisive wars, Assyria completed her evolution from feudalism to military monarchy. The Mitanni, now crushed, were annexed to her empire, whose frontiers, advanced to the Euphrates, marched with those of Egypt and Hatti.

Peace between these powers, now both menaced, became imperative. In 1278 BC, in the reign of Rameses II, negotiations, commenced on Hittite initiative, ended in an Egyptian-Hittite understanding which marked a new era of international relations.

THE EGYPTO-HITTITE CONDOMINIUM

By this understanding, the first great international settlement known to history, the two powers renounced the policy of hegemony and concluded a close alliance by which they mutually guaranteed the integrity of their empires. The treaty of 1278 BC in reality established a joint hegemony of Egypt and Hatti; it was to give fifty years of peace to Nearer Asia.

STATE SOCIALISM IN EGYPT

During this half-century of peace Egypt became immensely prosperous and enjoyed incontestable international prestige. The absolute monarchy, continuing the social policy of Horemheb, little by little transformed the conception of natural law into a theory of state socialism. The state intervened more and more in social organization, fixed working conditions, promulgated laws on social hygiene, created workers' courts for the settlement of labour disputes, and exempted workers' houses from tax. The people lived in great comfort and the king tried to gain popularity among the working classes. The whole country became richer. Smallholdings increased in number. The middle classes made considerable fortunes in international sea-borne trade. Banking, in the hands of Syrians, developed greatly. Thebes, the religious capital, and the port of Tanis, which Rameses II made the capital of the empire, were the richest cities in the world.

In this individualist society, the state, however, played a larger and larger part. Bureaucracy was everywhere and paper-work became overpowering. The collection of the revenues became the essential basis of the unwieldy administrative machine. The more state socialism increased, the more the royal power had to make itself absolute in order to compete with it. As in the times of the Ancient Empire, it was through the cult that absolutism justified itself. The king was deified. But by linking its destinies with those of the cult, the royal absolutism by that very fact strengthened the priesthood. In the course of their great wars against the Hittites, Seti I and Rameses II had showered donations of lands and prisoners on the temples in order to keep intact the cohesion of the country under religious tutelage. The temples had thus become vast landholding communities. On their domains, as on those of the state, worked tens of thousands of prisoners of war and foreigners already settled in the country. A manorial economy was organized, based on slave-labour. This was the time when the Jews were subjected to forced labour, making bricks for the huge buildings erected at Tanis by Rameses II. The Theban temples possessed almost a hundred thousand acres of land and eighty thousand foreign slaves. These were not, however, the 'living tools' that the Greek and Roman slaves were later to become. They had a legal status and their marriages were legal.

This manorial servile economy was like a foreign body in the liberal economy of the country.

On the other hand, the power of the priests enabled them to wrest privileges from the king which transformed them into a caste of nobles. Under Seti I the great estates granted by the king to the temples in Nubia were given tax immunity. The goldmines too were soon to be handed over to the temple of Ammon. In the reign of Rameses II the priesthood obtained its own legal code, and a priestly court was set up at Thebes alongside the royal courts. Priestly families were granted the highest civil offices of the state. Immunity passed from Nubia into Egypt itself and the temples became states within the state. They were organized henceforth on the manorial system; those who lived on their lands were tied to the soil and were subject to their jurisdiction which abandoned the civil procedure in favour of jurisdiction by oracles.

The administrative system, dominated by an oligarchy, became entirely perverted. The priestly oligarchy became a real power opposed to the king. As its power increased, that of the crown diminished. Conscription was no longer possible on its estates because of the immunity and privileges that they enjoyed; the people, accustomed to a long period of peace since the reign of Amenophis II, in any case disliked the idea of military service. Rameses II found himself obliged to introduce the idea of a professional army made up of soldiers who had been granted fiefs in land; exempted from taxes, they too soon became a privileged class. Legal equality disappeared. Society became divided into classes, as at the close of the Ancient Empire. The unity of the state, once represented by the king, fell to pieces, divided into priesthood, administrative oligarchy and army. Individualism recoiled before the hierarchic principle.

The whole political and social structure of the state was cracking. Royal absolutism was no longer anything but a fiction. But the façade was maintained. The empire lived on the riches it possessed and the revenue it drew from the provinces. Civilization was at its height. It was at that time that the hypostyle hall was built at Karnak, the greatest monument in the world. No one paid any heed to the terrible internal crisis that was brewing.

In Egypt, at the end of the reign of Rameses II, there were two contradictory currents. One marked the height of individualism, linked to a sterile state socialism; the other, which was only just beginning to become apparent, was manorial and oligarchic; it was preparing the destruction of the centralized state and the creation of social classes which, under the rule of a hereditary nobility, were to stifle individualist civilization.

Religion was also subject to a double tendency, spiritual in that it tended towards a more and more purified monotheism, mystical because of the growing place that it gave to the practices of the cult but—and therein lay the stability of Egyptian civilization—the moral code was universally followed.

THE BALANCE OF POWER BROKEN BY ASSYRIA

After the Egypto-Hittite understanding of 1278 BC, Egypt, undermined by state socialism and by the serious crisis that weakened her, was doomed to decay. On the other hand, Hatti and Assyria, growing monarchical states, seemed like the great powers of the future. So that it was between these two that the struggle for the hegemony of Nearer Asia became inevitable. As to Babylon, devoted entirely to her commercial interests, she practised a policy of peace and tried, by her diplomacy, to impede the development of Assyria in order to prevent her gaining control of the great trade route linking the Euphrates and the Mediterranean.

Rameses II looked on impassively at the Assyrian victory over the Hittites. None the less, it overturned the balance of power, to safeguard which the Egypto-Hittite condominium had been established. But the

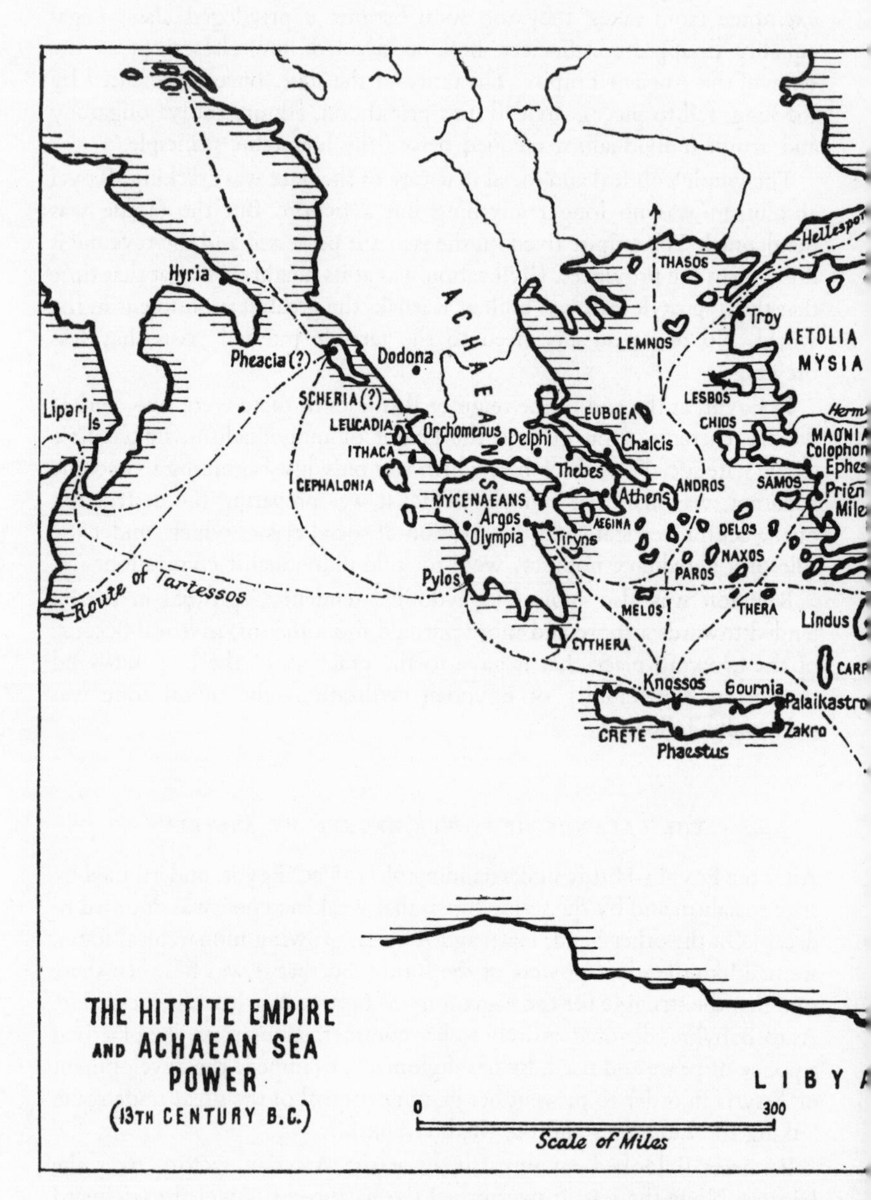

—·—·—·— Trade routes. ▬▬▬ Frontiers of the Er

Map No. 8

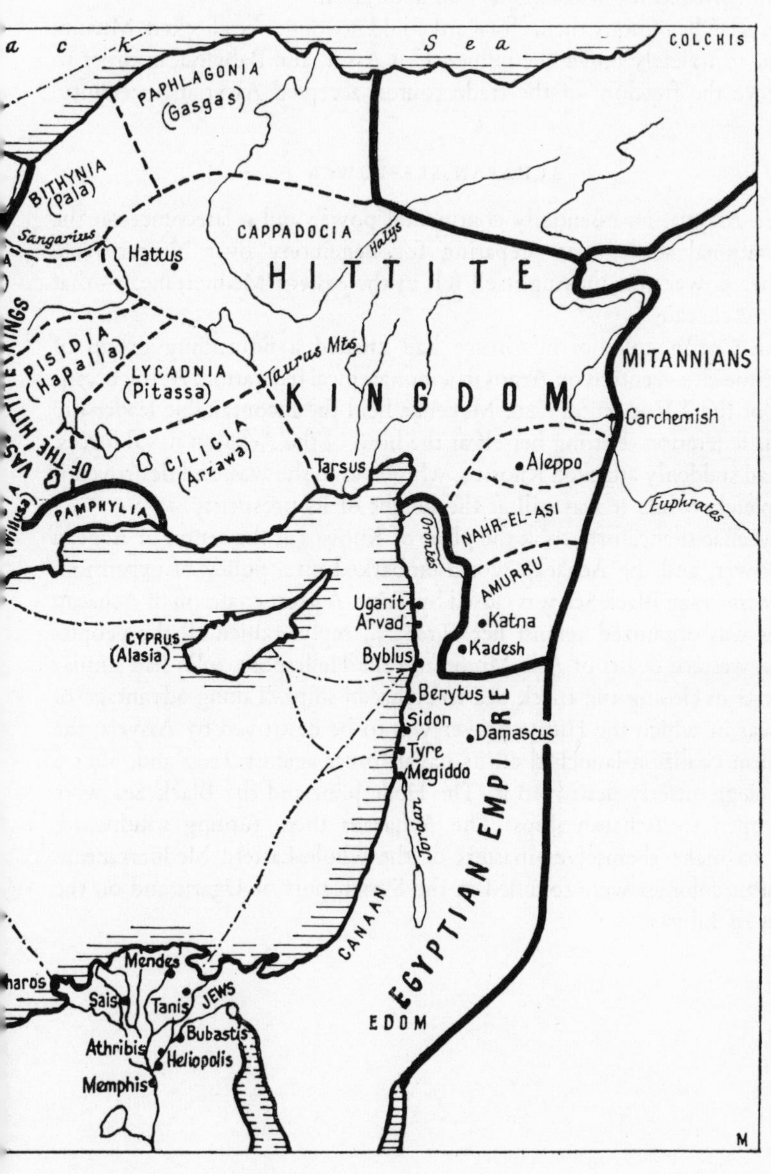

- - - - Frontiers of the Kingdom and Vassal States.

internal affairs of Egypt compelled her to withdraw into a neutrality which was understood for what it was—an abdication.

Assyrian hegemony thenceforward could no longer be checked. Mitanni passed completely under the influence of Assur, and Babylon, in order to preserve the freedom of the trade routes, accepted Assyrian suzerainty.

ACHAEAN SEA-POWER

While Assyria, an essentially continental power and a latecomer on the international scene, was preparing for hegemony over Nearer Asia, another power was making itself felt in the eastern Mediterranean—that of the Achaeans.

The Cretan colonies in Greece had created a flourishing group of maritime cities centred on Argos in a monarchical federation. At the beginning of the XVth century BC, Mycenae held the incontestable leadership in this federation. Putting herself at the head of the Achaean naval forces, she had suddenly attacked Knossos, whose vassal she was, and destroyed it completely while it was still at the height of its prosperity.

Mycenae thenceforth took the place of Knossos as the centre of Aegean sea-power, and the Achaean world embarked on a policy of expansion. Its access to the Black Sea was closed by Troy. A great coalition of Achaean forces was organized against her. Troy, in reply, rallied all the peoples of the western coasts of Asia Minor and the Hellespont, who had similar interests in closing the Black Sea to Achaean ships. Taking advantage of the war in which the Hittite power was to be destroyed by Assyria, the Achaean coalition launched all its naval forces against Troy and, after a long siege, utterly destroyed it. The Hellespont and the Black Sea were thus open to Achaean ships. The Achaeans then, turning southward, tried to make themselves masters of the whole Eastern Mediterranean. Achaean colonies were founded in the Syrian port of Ugarit and on the coasts of Libya.

CHAPTER XI

THE INVASION OF THE PEOPLES OF THE SEA AND THE DOWNFALL OF THE GREAT STATES

THE DORIAN INVASIONS AND THE EXODUS OF 'THE PEOPLES OF THE SEA'

THE migrations of the Aryan peoples which had caused the great waves of invasion at the beginning of the second millenary began again in the XIIIth century BC. Dorians coming from Illyria infiltrated into Greece and, after crossing the Hellespont, into Asia Minor. Even before the Trojan War Dorian bands had got as far as Pylos.

About the end of the XIIIth century BC the whole Dorian people moved into Greece. It was a terrible invasion. Organized on a basis of military feudalism, the Dorians destroyed everything in their way. Only Attica and the island of Euboea succeeded in holding back the tide that flowed into the Peloponnesus, where the great Achaean cities were destroyed. From Greece the Dorians passed into Crete where the work of destruction was continued, and tried to penetrate into Asia Minor by way of Rhodes, but the Carians, supported by the Hittites, checked them.

Other Aryan bands crossed the Hellespont and moved southward down the coast, massacring the populations of Mysia, Lydia and Phrygia who fled before them.

The entire Aegean sea-power was destroyed in a few years. The Achaeans of the Peloponnesus took their fleets to sea and emigrated, some to Attica and the island of Euboea, whence they went on to the colonies that they had founded on the coasts of Asia Minor, and others towards the new colonies recently founded in Libya, where they were joined by the sea-coast peoples fleeing from Asia Minor.

DOWNFALL OF THE HITTITE EMPIRE

Before the new Aryan wave neither the Hittite kings, Tuthalia IV and Arnawanda II, nor Rameses II of Egypt made any move. But the Hittite

Empire in Asia Minor crumbled away; one after the other the vassal states that bordered it on the south and west fell before the invaders. The Aryan raids, by destroying the harvests, threatened the Hittite population with famine. Merneptah, who succeeded Rameses II in 1232, aided his ally by sending grain, a proof that the Egyptian fleet still held control of the sea. However Egypt did not try to oppose the Aegean immigration into Libya which went on incessantly, composed of Achaeans from Greece, Etruscans from the island of Lesbos, Siculi from Pisidia, Shardans and Lycians from Asia Minor and the islands. Other emigrants, from the same regions, settled in Syria and Palestine, lands with which they had been in touch for centuries, or infiltrated into the Hittite kingdom. Assailed on the north by the Aryans, on the south by the Aegean peoples retreating before the invaders, and menaced by the rebellions of the vassal peoples who made common cause with its enemies, the Hittite Empire fell to pieces.

EGYPT LOSES HER EMPIRE

At the same time a great invasion of Egypt from Libya was being prepared. In 1227 BC the Achaeans, the Etruscans, the Siculi and the Shardans, together with the Libyan tribes, burst into the Delta. The Egyptian army threw them back. But Merneptah, realizing the danger that was pending in Syria, at once returned to Asia and reconquered Palestine in order to restore its natural bulwark to the Nile Valley.

Suddenly Egypt, surrounded by enemies, in Libya, in Syria and on the seas, was isolated. She withdrew into herself in a crisis of nationalism that naturally took a religious form. The fearful danger that threatened to overcome her from both east and west was averted, but her trade came to an end. The result was a serious economic crisis which dealt a terrible blow to the royal power. The resources that it drew from the empire were cut off and in the cities the taxes no longer produced anything. The king, unable to meet his commitments, could only give way to the demands of the priesthood who claimed fresh privileges which had the effect of transforming the temples into real territorial principalities. The fiscal crisis caused by the economic crisis hastened the feudal dismemberment of the country; and the stoppage of trade led quite naturally to the formation on the priestly estates of a system of closed economy suited to the principles of the manorial régime which had been gradually created since the reign of Rameses II.

The weakening of the royal power made it incapable of holding in check the foreigners and the masses of prisoners settled on the crown lands. After the Libyan invasion, rebellions among the enslaved peoples broke out over the whole country. Merneptah, in order to avoid this internal danger, expelled them. It was probably at this time that the Israelite tribes left Egypt.

In the midst of these multiple crises, the country people in Egypt naturally looked for protection to those social forces able to give it, the temples and the great landed estates. The Libyan invasions, driven back the first time, were constantly renewed and the whole country fell into anarchy. The cities, within their walls, were able to keep back the never-ending flood and became centres of refuge in Lower Egypt as the temples were in Upper Egypt. Their fleets protected the coasts. The Delta was divided amongst them.

In the midst of these disorders, accompanied by rapine and massacre, religion remained the only moral force intact, and the priests enjoyed an incontestable ascendancy. After the miserable reigns of the successors of Merneptah, which lasted thirty years, the priests enthroned Rameses III (1198–1166 BC). He was to restore a last period of glory to the monarchy.

SETTLEMENTS OF THE PHILISTINES AND HEBREWS IN PALESTINE: AND ETRUSCANS AND SICULI IN ITALY

Outside Egypt, the invasions were in full spate. The Philistines, coming from Caria and Crete, appeared in Syria and formed, around Aleppo, the nucleus of a coalition of Achaeans, Cilicians (Siculi, Etruscans and Shardans), Cretans, Lydians, Carians and Mysians, which systematically organized immigration, both by land and sea, and prepared, together with the Achaean and Asiatic refugees in Libya, a great invasion of Egypt. Cyprus, an important naval base, fell into their hands, and they concentrated their fleets there. Egypt was to be attacked simultaneously, by sea and by land, from Libya and Syria.

But, thanks to the resistance of the Delta cities, the Egyptian fleet remained intact. The Achaean and Aegean squadrons were destroyed in a great naval battle at the eastern mouth of the Nile, and the army of Rameses III cut the invading armies to pieces on the Syrian frontier. Defeated, they disintegrated. But the Philistines kept their hold on the Palestine coast—to which they gave their name—and in the cities of the Pentapolis where the Hebrews were to find them a few years later.

After wandering for forty years in the desert, the Hebrews entered Palestine about the beginning of the XIIth century. During their exodus they were closely united about the monotheistic cult of Jahve, a national god, though this had not caused the earlier cults of the various tribes to disappear completely.

The settlement of the Jews in the mountains of Palestine—the Philistines and the Canaanites prevented them from settling in the plains—broke the bonds which had united them in the desert. They scattered into villages and about this time were formed into twelve territorial tribes. This was the period of the Judges. More than a century was to pass before they attained a rudimentary political organization under elected tribal chiefs, to reach the stage of private property and to free themselves little by little from the primitive solidarity of the group, replacing it, under the influence of Hittite law, by a family organization in which the individual began to emerge.

At the time of the fall of the Ramesid dynasty in Egypt the Hebrews were entering a new phase in their history. After many attempts at federation, the tribes at last united to fight the Canaanites and Philistines. Their confederation ended by grouping them under a single elected chief, at first the High Priest Samuel (1075–1045 BC). The same phenomenon of the nation concentrating around a common cult was here repeated. Shiloh, where the Ark of the Covenant was preserved, played the role of Holy City. But by the time of Saul (1044–1029 BC) the monarchy became detached from the cult. With David (1029–974 BC) it became hereditary and military in character. The monarchical régime had been created. Jerusalem, captured from the Canaanites, became the royal residence and the transfer there of the Holy Ark made it the national capital of the Hebrew people who then began to take their place in international life.

While the Philistines and the Hebrews were settling in Palestine, the Etruscans and Siculi, renouncing any attempt to find a new home in Syria, again took to the sea. They left the shores of Asia Minor, where they had settled temporarily, to look for a new fatherland in the west. The Etruscans emigrated—the date is not known for certain—to central Italy where they founded the first cities and introduced an Aegean civilization; the Siculi went to the south of the Peninsula, whence they were later to cross over into Sicily.

Of the Hittites there remained only a few little feudal states in northern Syria where their law, which was to influence the Hebrews so deeply at the beginning of their evolution, was preserved. Two feudal kingdoms, Phrygia and Mysia, were founded in western Asia Minor on the ruins of the former Hittite Empire. They were to unite, three centuries later, to form the kingdom of Lydia.

PALESTINE AND SYRIA

Map No. 9

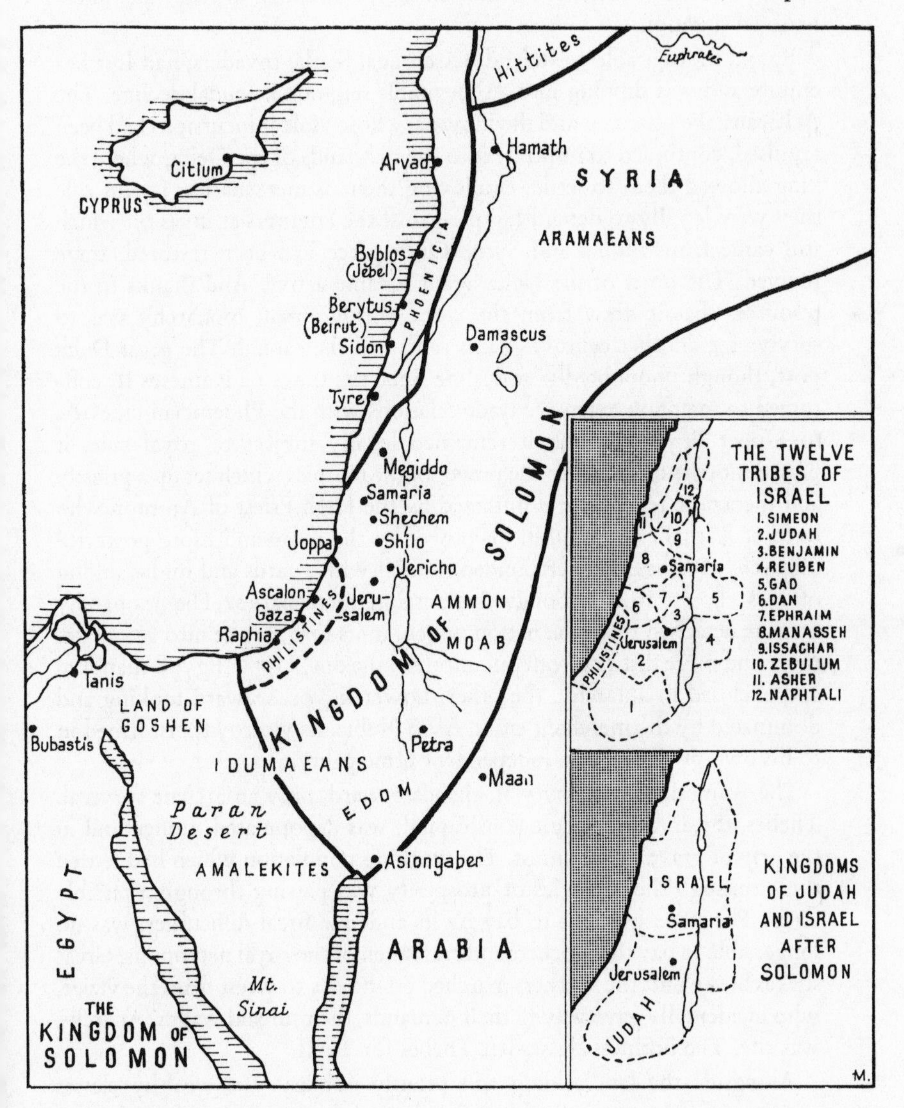

EGYPT BECOMES FEUDAL

The invasions and migrations which for almost fifty years had ravaged the countries of the eastern Mediterranean profoundly altered the international situation.

Egypt, though able to defend herself against the invaders, had lost her empire and was slipping into an inevitable seigniorial-feudal decline. The Achaeans, the Shardans and the Libyans, whose violent incursions had been repulsed, continued to infiltrate into the rich lands of the Delta, where the king allowed them to settle, employing them as mercenaries; in this role they were loyally to defend Egypt against the attempts at invasion which still came from Nubia and Syria. Once peace had been restored, trade revived. The ports of the Delta again became active. And thanks to the resources that it drew from the cities, the Egyptian monarchy was to survive for another century. Tanis remained the capital. The great Delta port, though undoubtedly in decline since the times of Rameses II, continued to maintain extensive trade relations with the Phoenician cities. As to Upper Egypt, though it remained legally subject to royal rule, it passed more and more into the power of the temples which set up a priestly and theocratic feudalism, dominated by the High Priest of Ammon who lived at Karnak. Menaced in his power by the more and more powerful oligarchy, Rameses III surrounded himself with guards and high-ranking officers chosen from amongst his foreign mercenaries. The monarchy became detached from the nation which, in its turn, broke into two states more and more distinct from one another; the one, Upper Egypt, manorial and enclosed in autarchy, the other, Lower Egypt, seaward-looking and dominated by the merchant cities. As to Nubia, its viceroy transformed it, to his own profit, into an independent principality.

The Ramesid monarchy was, thenceforward, only an archaic survival. Thebes, the ancient and glorious capital, was depopulated, ruined and in the grip of grave social unrest. The working population which had settled there through the centuries of prosperity was passing through a terrible crisis. The state, brought to bay by its endemic fiscal difficulties, was no longer able to pay the workers and craftsmen of the royal necropolis. Great strikes broke out; the workers marched on the city to wrest from the vizier, who incidentally gave way to their demands, their unpaid wages. Anarchy was rife. The business classes left Thebes for Tanis.

Alongside the landholding and priestly nobility, the wealthy classes were now solely represented by officials, mainly the scribes of the finance administration. Poverty led to the spread of corruption and demoralized the judges, who let themselves be bought; the workers, thrown into misery by unemployment, took to banditry.

In the Delta, though the cities maintained a certain economic prosperity, the royal power became weaker and weaker. The leaders of the mercenaries, Achaeans or Libyans, had the government of cities granted to them and thus became local princes. About 1100 BC a revolt in the city of Tanis forced the king, Rameses XI, to take refuge at Thebes under the protection of the High Priest of Ammon, Herihor, who thenceforward played the role of a Mayor of the Palace before proclaiming himself king in 1085 BC.

Egypt fell to pieces, engulfed in feudalism, after a social evolution parallel to that she had known at the end of the Ancient Empire.

She had passed through a second cycle of evolution which, in fifteen centuries, had made her pass from feudalism, through a period of monarchical revival, to centralized monarchy, only to be broken up, after a stage of absolutism, into a fresh feudalism. She had repeated, between 2500 BC and 1000 BC, the same political, economic and social stages that she had passed through between the IVth millenary and 2500 BC.

THE DECLINE OF BABYLON AND THE RECOIL OF ASSYRIAN EXPANSION

The migrations of the Peoples of the Sea had led to great movements among the Aramean tribes that had settled between Syria and Mesopotamia. The invasions of the Euphrates and Tigris basins and the insecurity of the trade routes had caused a grave economic and social crisis throughout all Mesopotamia. In Babylon, the Kassite dynasty which had been reigning there for six centuries came to an end and was replaced by the petty kings of Susa, who descended in 1170 BC from the Elamite highlands. They were in their turn succeeded, in 1038, by semi-barbarous princes from 'The Country of the Sea'—in other words Sumeria, which had been invaded by land-hungry nomads—only to be themselves supplanted by the Elamites in 996 BC.

Around Babylon, however, the temples still remained and were respected by the invaders. Quite naturally they became centres of attraction and transformed themselves into seigniorial principalities by a process similar to that which, at the same time, brought Egypt and Hittite Cappadocia to the feudal régime of closed economy and servile social structure. These great priestly estates obtained privileges of immunity from the kings of Babylon. The country was broken up into petty seigniorial or priestly principalities. In Sumeria, the ancient cities, formerly so rich and powerful, were completely in decline since the silting-up of the Delta had cut them off from the sea. They were no longer anything save priestly cities over which the High Priests exercised a princely authority.

Babylon alone, with its numerous middle-class population, preserved its urban institutions. Isolated in the midst of a feudal world, she attempted under Nebuchadnezzar I (1146–1123 BC) to regain control of the great commercial artery of the Upper Euphrates; but she was militarily incapable of keeping possession of distant territories and had to withdraw into herself. She was to remain for three centuries an island of individualist law, despite the dynastic disorders she was to know under the rule of Aramean and Elamite princes, semi-barbarians, who, drawn by her wealth, succeeded in making themselves her masters. Despite the pillage of the Arameans, the forays of the Assyrians and the rule of foreign dynasties that they endured to keep the peace as far as was possible, the Babylonian middle classes persevered in their trade activities. Fed by the Phoenician ports of the Syrian coasts and by the caravans that reached her from the shores of the Mediterranean, Babylon continued to be the great market where western merchants met those who came by the caravan routes from Arabia, India and Central Asia.

As to Assyria, after having carried her arms as far as Arvad on the Syrian coast under Tiglath-Pileser I (1116–1090 BC), she dared not confront the powerful Phoenician cities and withdrew within her national frontiers where she was to remain on the defensive until the beginning of the IXth century BC.

CHAPTER XII

THE PHOENICIANS DISCOVER THE WEST

FEUDALISM AND THE MERCHANT CITIES

THE period that follows the invasions of the Peoples of the Sea marks the second period of decline of the great states. Everywhere, the monarchies made way for feudal states. International life, which had attained so high a level between the XVth and XIIIth centuries BC, fell into complete confusion. Civilization in all its forms declined rapidly, even as it later did in the west after the ruin of the Roman Empire. But international trade, even though slowed down, did not disappear. In its reduced state, it was concentrated in the cities, which henceforth lived on their own resources; Babylon, the Phoenician cities, Aleppo, Damascus and the cities of the Egyptian Delta. They were the only centres of artistic and intellectual development, since they alone had preserved contact with foreign lands and the individualist system of law which permitted the development of the individual. The classic law of the Egyptian Empire was still in force in the cities of the Delta, as the Code of Hammurabi at Babylon. In the cities that lived only by trade, private international law assured foreigners a very favourable civil status.

But outside the cities, in the stagnant marsh of feudalism which had spread over almost all of Nearer Asia, there was constant war. Complete insecurity reigned and continental trade was ruined. Mesopotamia was overrun by the Arameans and was deserted by the traders who had at one time passed through it. Trade was carried on, as far as possible, by sea.

The Indian trade route had been deflected from Babylon and now followed the sea-route by Arabia and the Red Sea. In Arabia the little coastal kingdoms became important transit centres, while between the Red Sea and the Jordan the Elamite cities developed rapidly.

JERUSALEM, COMMERCIAL METROPOLIS UNDER SOLOMON

The Jordan route linking Tyre with the Red Sea was controlled by Jerusalem, which since the time of David had become the capital of the

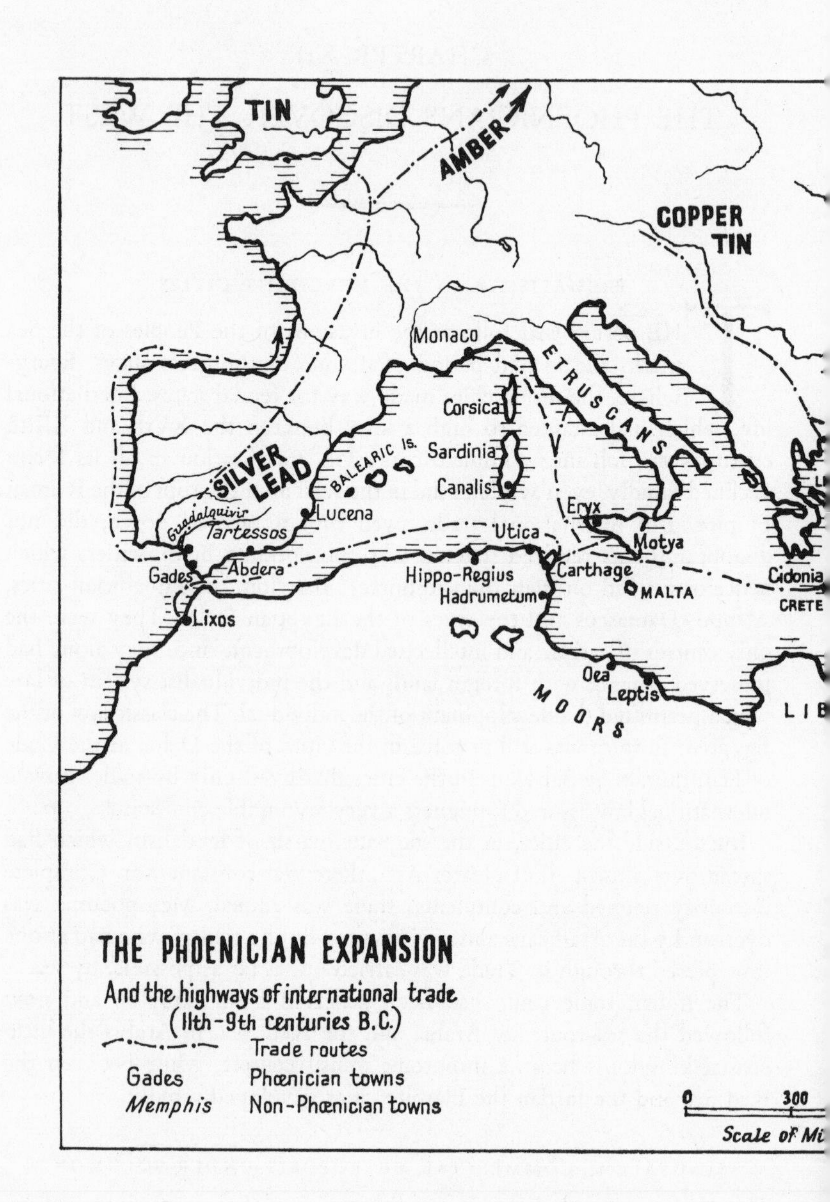
TIN
AMBER
COPPER
TIN
Monaco
ETRUSCANS
Corsica
Sardinia
Canalis
SILVER
LEAD
BALEARIC IS.
Lucena
Guadalquivir
Tartessos
Eryx
Utica
Motya
Gades
Abdera
Hippo-Regius
Carthage
MALTA
Cidonia
CRETE
Hadrumetum
Lixos
Oea
Leptis
MOORS
THE PHOENICIAN EXPANSION
And the highways of international trade
(11th-9th centuries B.C.)
Trade routes
Gades Phœnician towns
Memphis Non-Phœnician towns
0
300
Scale of Mi

Map No. 10

Black Sea
Caucasus
Caspian Sea
IRON
GOLD
COLCHIS
Taurus
SILVER
IRON
GOLD
CARIA
Miletus
CILICIA
ODES
Citium
CYPRUS
Ugarit
Arvad
Byblos
Berytus
Sidon
Tyre
Jerusalem
Tanis
COPPER
Asiongaber
mphis
PT
Thebes
GOLD
N U B I A
Nile
Assur
Babylon
Susa
Ur
Persian Gulf
Red Sea
YEMEN
KINGDOM
OF
SHEBA?
M.

Hebrew people. Solomon (973–936 BC) was to profit by this dislocation of the international trade routes to carry out a large-scale economic policy. He made himself master of the Edomite cities and, now having control of the access to the Red Sea, made an alliance with the powerful city of Tyre, which was rapidly becoming the largest port on the Syrian coast. The control of the route to India, and the tolls he levied on it, was of immense value to Solomon. The declining Egyptian monarchy no longer sent the fleets to the land of Punt which, in Imperial times, had left regularly to bring back the produce of Arabia. Jerusalem took, on the Red Sea route, the place of enfeebled Egypt. Solomon had a port constructed by the Tyrians at Asiongaber, and there launched a fleet manned by Phoenician sailors. Every three years his ships left for Arabia, where they came into contact with Hindu traders. The commerce of Jerusalem in Solomon's times was essentially a state monopoly. The maritime expeditions were the work of the king and not of private traders. But the produce that they brought back to Jerusalem made foreign merchants flock there. Suddenly, this peasant people, as the Hebrews were then, found its capital had become one of the most active commercial centres of the eastern world.

Solomon, ally of King Hiram of Tyre, also tried to maintain friendly relations with the great Egyptian port of Tanis, and married Psusennes, daughter of the Pharaoh. But Jerusalem, because of the tolls imposed on the Arabian trade, was of necessity a competitor of the Egyptian cities of the Delta.

The struggle between Palestine and Egypt for the control of the Red Sea trade became inevitable at the moment when the death of Solomon led to the division of Israel. The northern tribes, under the influence of prophets who feared contacts with foreigners for religious reasons, broke away; only Jerusalem and Judah, which had become wealthy through trade and where a middle-class was being formed, remained loyal to the house of David.

At this time, a new dynasty ruled in Egypt. In 950 BC Sheshonq, chief of the Libyan mercenaries who had settled in the Delta, had himself crowned king and fixed his capital at Bubastis. Entirely egyptianized, he continued the traditional policy of the country and, supported by the cities which wanted to recover control of the Red Sea route, marched upon Palestine which was weakened by civil war. He captured Jerusalem, laid his hands on Solomon's treasure, and imposed his protectorate on the Kingdom of Judah.

The Phoenician cities, which for the past two centuries had freed themselves from Egyptian protection, immediately got into touch with the King of Egypt, since he now had the Red Sea route in his power, and paid him a tribute to ensure their freedom of trade. Egypt once again dominated the Arabian trade and the Libyan kings of Bubastis acquired great wealth. A real economic renascence took place in the Delta. In order to provide return freights for the Egyptian ships, which were hampered by the system of closed economy that existed in Upper Egypt, Sheshonq occupied the great Libyan oasis, an important grain-producing area.

MARITIME EXPANSION OF THE PHOENICIANS IN THE WEST

The Egyptian fleet, however, was no longer what it had once been. The shipowners of Tyre and Sidon had the major part of the sea-borne trade of the Delta in their hands. The total ruin of the Achaean sea-power had, moreover, delivered the Phoenicians from their most formidable rivals. The Aegean Sea, it is true, was almost closed to navigation, being infested with Carian and Cilician pirates, since no great power guaranteed its security. But the sea-going Phoenicians found compensation in their relations with the Etruscans and Siculi who had settled in Italy. As continental trade, for which the Phoenician cities had been the ports of entry, had greatly diminished because of the feudalization of the states of Nearer Asia, the Phoenician sailors and merchants looked for new outlets to the west. Tyre and Sidon made themselves masters of Cyprus, Cilicia and Crete, occupied Malta and founded trading posts in Sicily and at Miletus. Then they struck out into the western Mediterranean. About 1000 BC they reached Gibraltar, passed through the Straits and had their warehouses at Gades (Cadiz) where they came into contact with the kingdom of Tartessos which occupied the basin of the Guadalquivir. Its peaceful and industrious population was devoted to the exploitation of silver, copper and lead mines and had trade relations, by way of France and Spain, with England whence it obtained tin, and with Scandinavia which provided amber.

Pushing onward still farther, the Tyrian sailors founded a trading post at Lixos on the Moroccan coast where they came into contact with the native peoples. In less than a century a new and immense world, with unlimited potentialities, was opened in the west. The Phoenician cities became the great exchange marts for silver, copper and tin for the whole Mediterranean, trafficked in slaves captured on the coast, and exported the manufactured goods of Egypt and the spices of India to the new countries of the west.

After the discovery of Tartessos, the abundance of silver was such that the relation of gold to silver, which in Egypt had been one to two, fell to one to thirteen. This great trade of the Phoenician cities was as much the work of private individuals as of the local city kings. At Byblos, King Zikarbal was a business man who kept a strict account of his sales.

These cities, in which as the Bible says 'the merchants are princes, and the traffickers are the honourable of the earth', were governed by ship-owning and commercial oligarchies, from whom, when he was not chosen from amongst the priests, the king was elected. Their enormous prosperity in the Xth century gave rise to social movements which, in Tyre, resulted in replacing the king by annual magistrates, the *suffetes*. The Republic of Tyre became almost a maritime empire. In 814 BC it founded the colony of Carthage which, in less than a century, was to dominate the navigation of the western Mediterranean. All the trading posts founded on the African coast, in Sicily, in Sardinia and in Spain, remained grouped around the metropolis, to which they sent a tithe levied on all commercial transactions. Already a great maritime and commercial power, Tyre thus became a great financial centre.

In order to preserve their sea-power and the profits of their expansion, the Phoenician cities inaugurated a monopolistic policy that no other power was able to contest.

The discovery of the West by the Phoenicians in the XIth century BC opened a new era in the history of the ancient world, even as the discovery of America at the end of the 15th century AD was to mark the beginning of the modern era in the history of Europe.

BOOK III

The Continental Empires and the Attraction of the Sea: From the IXth to the VIth Century BC

CHAPTER XIII

THE ASSYRIAN EMPIRE

CONQUEST BY TERROR

FROM the XIIth to the IXth century, feudal Assyria, which made war the reason for existence, unceasingly raided beyond its frontiers. At the beginning of the IXth century, when the monarchy had given greater cohesion to the country, these forays became conquests and Assyria resumed the role of a great military power that it had played before the invasions of the Peoples of the Sea. Under Adadnarari II (911–891 BC) Assyria became master of Babylon. Assurbanipal II (884–859) reached the Mediterranean and turned the Phoenician cities into Assyrian protectorates.

The immense state founded by Assyria, whose military power no people was able to resist, was not an empire in the sense that those of Egypt and Babylon had been. It was a conquest whose aim was pillage. War, for Assyria, was not a means, it was an end. It carried on war as Babylon carried on trade. War, at the great period of the development of international law between the XVth and the XIIth century BC, had had definite rules which had lessened to a great extent its disastrous consequences. From the times of Tutmes III, captured cities had no longer been destroyed, vanquished peoples no longer massacred and sack had been replaced by a tribute of war. In the course of the terrible wars between Egypt and Hatti there had been, it is true, a reversion to more brutal methods. The disappearance of the Egyptian hegemony, the disastrous invasions of the Peoples of the Sea, had brought back ancient precedents of massacre and the enslavement of peoples.

The period of decadence which, from the XIIth to the IXth century BC, had plunged all Nearer Asia into feudalism had caused the former practice of constant diplomatic relations to be forgotten. Everything had to be done again, in order to re-establish legal relations between peoples.

The kings of Assyria, far from concerning themselves with this, inaugurated the principle of total war in order to build up their empire.

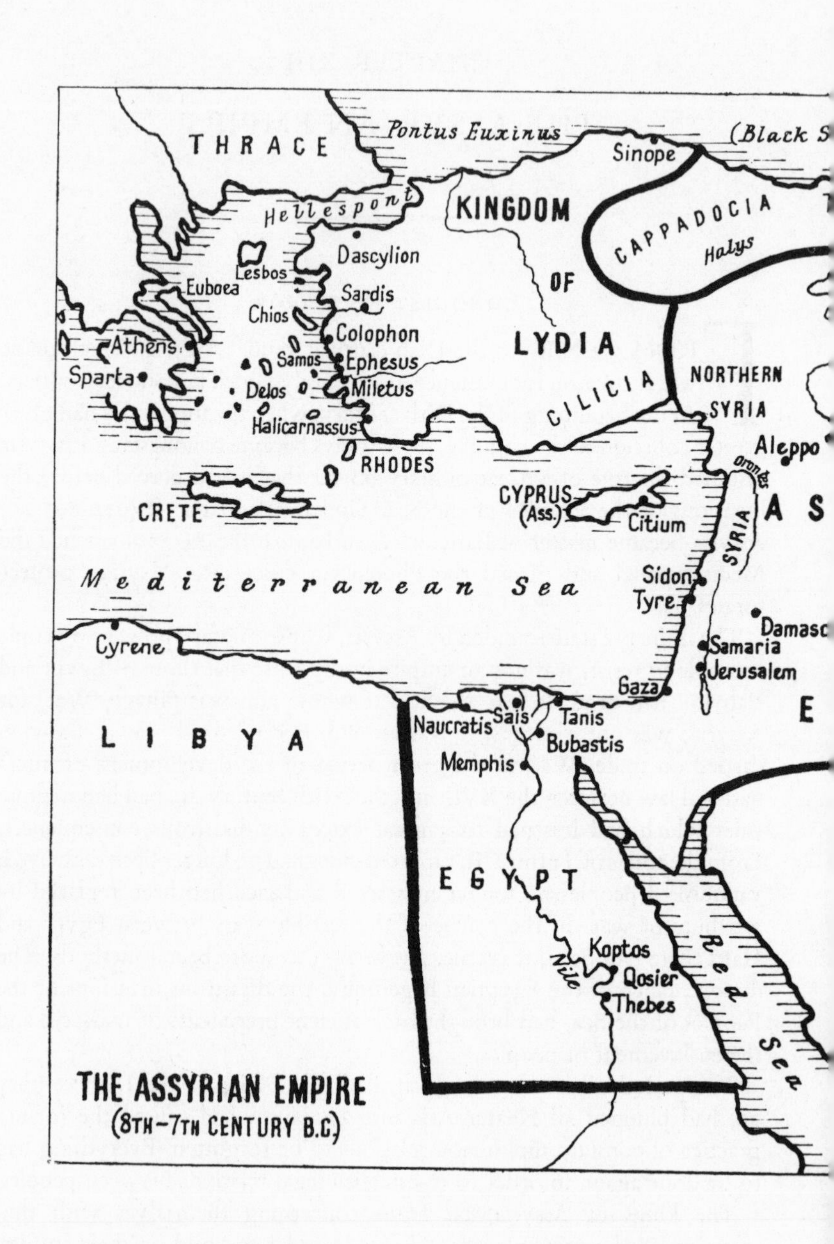

THE ASSYRIAN EMPIRE
(8TH–7TH CENTURY B.C.)

Map No. 11

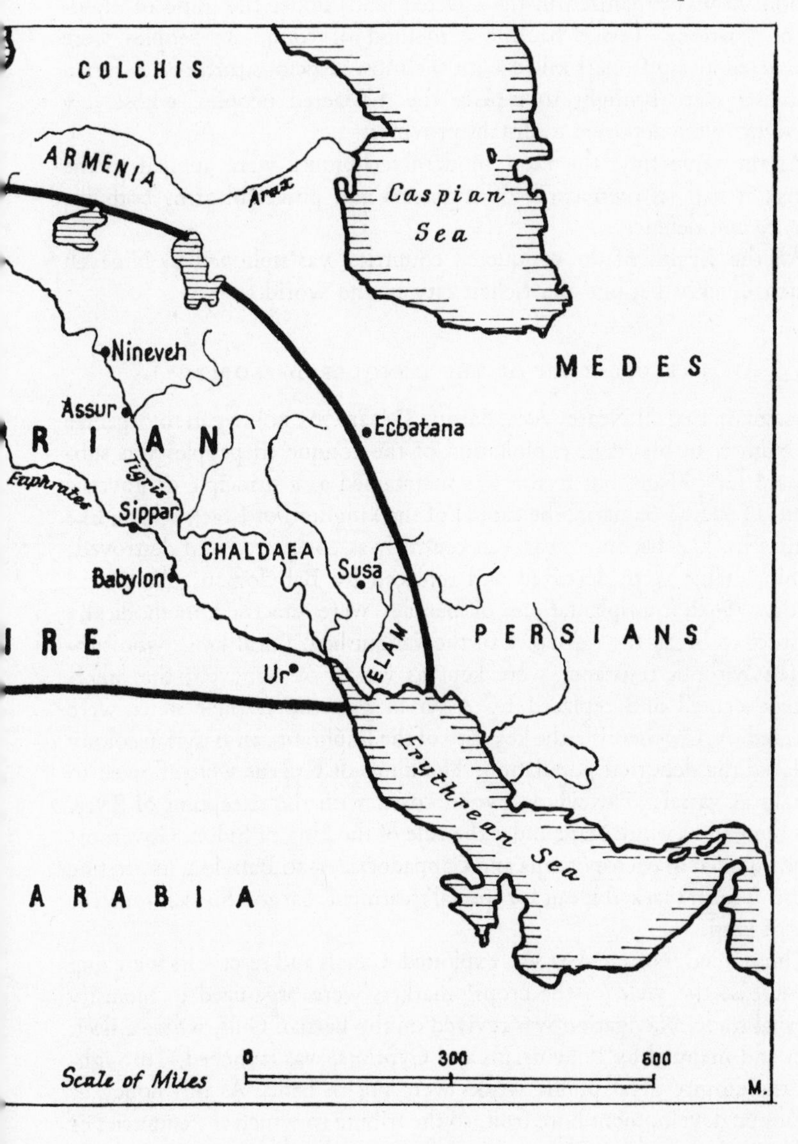
COLCHIS
ARMENIA
Arax
Caspian Sea
Nineveh
MEDES
Assur
Ecbatana
RIAN
Tigris
Euphrates
Sippar
CHALDAEA
Susa
Babylon
ELAM
PERSIANS
IRE
Ur
Erythrean Sea
ARABIA
0
300
600
Scale of Miles
M.

Declarations of war which had till then been customary were done away with, and Assyria took every advantage of surprise attack. Systematic espionage was organized in the coveted lands under the guise of diplomatic relations. Terror became a method of conquest; peoples were massacred and prisoners killed with the most atrocious tortures. Assyrian colonists were brought to replace the massacred peoples, whose few survivors were deported to distant provinces.

At the same time the most modern techniques were applied to the army; it had its own corps of engineers and powerful arms both for offence and defence.

All the wealth of the conquered countries was siphoned to Nineveh which quickly became the richest city in the world.

EXPLOITATION OF THE CONQUERED PEOPLES

Once master of all Nearer Asia, Sargon II (722–705 BC) began to organize his empire. In his reign exploitation of the conquered peoples was substituted for pillage, but terror was maintained as a principle of government. In 722 BC Samaria, the capital of the kingdom of Israel, which, like Damascus, had become a caravan centre, was conquered and destroyed; its inhabitants were deported and replaced by Babylonians, Arabs and Hittites. Such transplantations of peoples were practised methodically in order to break the resistance of the vanquished. Local kings who submitted without resistance were kept as vassals of Nineveh; the others were executed and replaced by Assyrian governors; their states were annexed. At Carchemish, the key-city of the Euphrates, an Assyrian colony replaced the deported population. The kings of Cyprus were allowed to remain as vassals. The whole Syrian coast, with the exception of Tyre, was united in a single state under the rule of the king of Sidon. Governors were installed in Mesopotamia and Cappadocia. As to Babylon, its prestige and its wealth marked it out for special treatment. Sargon himself took the title of king.

Thus tamed, Nearer Asia was exploited. Canals and reservoirs were dug to increase the yield of the crops; markets were organized to intensify internal trade. Navigation was revived on the Persian Gulf, where a fleet, built and manned by Phoenicians and Cypriots, was launched. Throughout the empire great public works were put in hand. As this policy of economic development bore fruit, so the tribute to which the countries of the empire were subject was reduced.

At Nineveh, which had now become a great capital, botanical and zoological gardens were created, and an enormous library which housed all the Babylonian works that Sargon ordered to be collected. The royal palace was built in Babylonian style and the administration was confided to Babylonian scribes. From Babylon Sargon took his calendar, his system of weights and measures, his science and his law.

So an immense territorial Empire of an entirely new type was founded and organized in less than a century. Nineveh, which was its centre, was not in any way responsible for its creation. It was the imperial residence, not the centre of culture or even of trade. Mistress of the Empire, Assyria had been the tool of conquest; the army remained the essential institution, thanks to which Nineveh exploited the provinces by making all their wealth converge on her. But the Empire did not correspond to any economic necessity; the role of Assyria was not to make economic life and international policy regular and normal, but on the other hand to impress on them an artificial character that allowed Nineveh to gain every benefit from them.

In Assyria the king was a feudal sovereign obliged to associate the great feudal lords, who commanded the army, with his power. But in the conquered countries, he was an absolute monarch. His power, created by force of arms, was imposed upon peoples to whom he himself remained a foreigner; it did not justify itself either by slow social evolution or by religious concept; it knew no limits; it was the first appearance of *bon plaisir*, free of any contact with the culture of the subject peoples.

The nucleus of the Empire was not, therefore, Assyria but the king. His power had only one base and one justification—force, that is to say the Assyrian army. The king, in order to keep power in his hands, was obliged to carry out a policy of exploitation for the benefit of the Assyrian feudal lords, for whom the empire only existed to provide them with booty, either in the form of pillage or in a regular and legal form. The empire could not, therefore, be anything but a military and political framework. National resistance of the subject peoples had to be destroyed by breaking their unity and their national consciousness, by deportations and by the destruction of the national cults.

Sargon, none the less, tried to give the empire an economic unity that made it capable of enduring and which he conceived as organized around the axis: Persian Gulf-Mesopotamia-Syria, that is to say essentially continental. But such an economy could not exist by itself alone. Its prosperity depended on international trade with India on the one hand and the western world on the other, both of which were outside the authority of the kings of Nineveh.

Thus a double obstacle hindered the imperial policy of Sargon. Firstly, a moral obstacle; the empire, having the king as its centre, could only be built up on a sentiment of loyalty to the person of the sovereign. But the régime of force based on terror, carried out in order to satisfy the Assyrian feudal lords, created universal hostility to the conquering dynasty. Secondly, a material obstacle; only economic unity could create a unity of interest among the conquered peoples. But Nearer Asia did not form a complete economic unit; to isolate it in a continental economy was to ruin it. Wealth came from the sea, but the sea was not subject to the power of the Empire.

CHAPTER XIV

GREEK EXPANSION AND THE BEGINNINGS OF INTERCONTINENTAL SEA-BORNE TRADE

WHILE the Assyrian Empire was unifying Nearer Asia by conquest, the Mediterranean was becoming of ever growing economic and cultural importance.

From the XIIth century onward, after the wave of invasions had passed, contact was resumed on the coasts of Asia Minor between the Asiatic peoples and the Achaeans who continued to infiltrate into Aeolia and the future Ionia.

THE GREEK CONCEPT OF THE WORLD AND THE HOMERIC EPIC ARE CREATED IN AEOLIA

In Aeolia, in the ancient Troad, between the XIIth and the VIIIth centuries BC, a half-Greek, half-Asiatic culture was being formed, which was reflected in Greek mythology. Created on a basis of Cretan ideas, with extensive Egyptian influence brought there by the Achaeans, it had, in Asia Minor, assimilated Phrygian and Lydian beliefs which were themselves formed by the influence of the Babylonian cosmogony. In it the mother-goddess of Knossos, Aphrodite, merges with the Asiatic Artemis, who was herself analagous to the Babylonian Ishtar; Zeus, of Cretan origin, the god of fertility who became a solar god, was related to the Trojan Apollo; Themis, goddess of Justice, is daughter of Ouranos, the Greek god of the heavens, even as in Egypt Maat was the daughter of Ra; and Atlas who 'stands erect, supporting the vast sky with his head and his indefatigable shoulders', separates it from the Earth, its wife, as in Egypt Shou, god of the air, keeps the heaven-goddess separated from her husband, the earth.

From all these various and diverse elements, a Greek theology was formed, which closely recalls that of the Sumero-Babylonian religion. Even as in the Sumerian cosmogony Anshar, the heavens, and Kishar, the earth, procreate a triad of male gods (Anu, king of heaven, Enlil, king of the earth and Ea, king of the sea), so also in Greek mythology Ouranos, heaven, and Gaia, earth, give birth to Chronos, time, father of Zeus, king of heaven, Poseidon, king of the sea and Hades, god of the underworld, only differing from the Babylonian tradition in that earth in the Greek system is the common heritage of all three gods.

Like their concept of the world, so also the great national epic of the Greeks, the Homeric poems, took its classic form in Aeolia, by the fusion in a single work of ancient Achaean and Trojan traditions. The result was an entirely new conception of literature. In the Iliad and the Odyssey, the evocation of life has a richness, a charm and an artistic value that neither the Egyptians nor the Babylonians had attained. Homer paints with words, as the Egyptians had with brush and chisel. The art of literature was born, or at least is first known to us, in these two immortal masterpieces which were clearly based on some earlier literature, Achaean or Cretan, now totally lost. The Homeric epic is not an isolated phenomenon. It developed step by step with the so-called 'Homeric' hymns which, written under Asiatic influences, extolled the glory of the great mother-goddesses. They belong to the same tradition as the Babylonian hymns and the magnificent poems written in Egypt to celebrate the solar god.

THE DEVELOPMENT OF URBAN AND MARITIME CIVILIZATION IN IONIA AND THE AEGEAN

At the same time as Greek religion and literature appeared in Aeolia as the product of an Achaean-Asiatic syncretism, the Ionian immigration, which had been going on continually from Attica and Euboea to the ancient Cretan and Mycenaean centres of Asia Minor, revived, about the Xth century, the former urban and maritime civilization around the Aegean Sea. Cities were founded, peopled by Carians, Phoenicians and Achaeans, which were soon to be ruled by an Ionian aristocracy.

Miletus, Priene, Ephesus, Samos, Colophon, Teos, Clazomene, Erythrea, formed an Ionian federation which, from the IXth century BC onward, took the place formerly held by the Cretans. The Ionians and the Carians soon won mastery in the Aegean and Black Seas. And, parallel with this revival of navigation, economic life began to revive in Asia Minor, helped by the peace assured by the Assyrian Empire. Miletus, where the trade route to the Euphrates starts across Lydia and Cappadocia, became a great trading centre. Its ships dominated the Black Sea where, from the VIIIth century onwards, Miletus possessed ninety trading posts, amongst them Sinope and Trebizond which were soon to become famous, the first as a city of shipbuilders and the second as the principal market for iron from the Caucasus. Milesian colonists also founded Cherson (Sebastopol) in the Crimea, Theodosia, Pantacapea (Kerch) and, at the mouths of the great Russian rivers, Olbia (Odessa) and Tanais (Azov), which exported the grain and dried fish of Scythia.

In the VIIIth century BC Miletus became the great port of Asia Minor and Ephesus became the financial centre. As at Babylon, the temple, dedicated to Aphrodite, acted as a bank, and the Ephesian bankers, in the Babylonian tradition, became so powerful that they played a political role of the greatest importance in international affairs.

Euboea, with its valuable copper mines, was a magnet for Milesian shipping. Taking up once more the role played by Crete, Euboea became a great metal-market, and tried to reserve for herself the monopoly of the iron mines in Thrace, whence she also obtained gold, silver, resin, wood, wine and grain. Chalcis, the principal town of Euboea—so called after the bronze that was the basis of her prosperity—founded a series of colonies on the coast of Thrace which enabled her to hold her monopoly.

The trade in bronze made Euboea look westward, whence came her supplies of tin. Erythrea founded a trading post on Corfu which controlled the Adriatic Sea and came into contact with southern Italy, establishing relations with the Etruscans.

Thus a great sea-route was created by the Milesians, which led via the island of Euboea to Italy and Sicily. This route led to the foundation of Corinth, Megara and Sicyon, as well as Aegina where an export industry of household implements and pottery was established. Corinth, looking to the west, in her turn founded Syracuse in 743 BC. In southern Italy, Sybaris, Croton, Metapontum, founded by Achaean emigrés from Greece, formed a league to assure the economic mastery of Magna Graecia. From the VIIth century onward Greek ships began to rival those of Carthage in the central Mediterranean.

Quite naturally, Miletus renewed contact with the cities of the Egyptian Delta, and set up, on the Bolbitic mouth of the Nile, a trading post where the Greeks soon became the middlemen of Sais, which was then rapidly becoming one of the principal ports of Egypt.

Miletus, the junction of three very important trade routes—to the Black Sea by the Hellespont, to Egypt by Rhodes and Cyprus and to the west by Euboea and Corinth—thus became one of the main centres of international trade.

All the peoples which took part in this great maritime movement, Egyptians, Phoenicians, Etruscans, Ionians, Achaeans and Carians, developed under the influence of similar economic forces. Their civilizations quite naturally influenced one another. Their nature cults were strongly influenced by the Osirian cult; and the sea-borne trade that unified them, though not always friendly—there was always a lively rivalry between Greeks and Phoenicians—led them to adopt similar trade usages.

The merchants became of great importance, because of their great wealth. At Ephesus, the banking family of Melas was to play a leading role in the history of Asia Minor by granting to the Lydian kings the credits that they needed to carry out their monarchic policy. At Miletus, the shipowners introduced a new form of coinage by putting into circulation silver ingots stamped with their seal.

Thus, from the IXth century BC onward, two economic, political and social movements were developing in sharp contradiction to one another; on the continent, the Assyrians were uniting under their rule a great empire founded on absolutism and military force; on the coasts of the eastern and central Mediterranean a group of autonomous cities, devoted essentially to trade, were the origin of an urban civilization in which social ferment already foreshadowed their democratic evolution.

The Assyrian Empire unified the continent politically without giving it any cultural unity. On the sea-coasts international trade created a cultural unity in the midst of political diversity.

Up to the XIth century BC, the economy of the ancient world had been decided by continental factors; Mesopotamia was its centre. The great capitals, Babylon, Memphis, Thebes, Nineveh, Hattus, were continental cities. The aim of navigation was to link the sea-coasts of a single continent. In the XVth century, Cretan sea-power had introduced the Aegean into the sphere of eastern trade, and thenceforward the sea had played a more and more important role in international commercial life. Egypt, drawn towards the sea, had created the port of Pharos for the Cretan trade, and later Rameses II had made the sea-port of Tanis the capital of his empire. The invasion of the Peoples of the Sea had suddenly cut short this expansion of sea-borne trade. But it had been revived with even greater vigour in the XIth century when the Phoenicians had discovered the west.

The Phoenicians, soon to be followed by the Greeks, had thus created an entirely new maritime economy which linked worlds hitherto unknown to one another. From then on, the sea, instead of being the boundary of the known world, became a centre of attraction. A new phase was opening in the history of the ancient world.

CHAPTER XV

THE CALL OF THE SEA

DEMOCRATIC EVOLUTION OF THE EGYPTIAN CITIES

THE economic revival set in motion by the widening extent of the Phoenician and Greek voyages was reflected in a democratic evolution first apparent in Egypt.

For about three centuries, feudalism, sacerdotal in the south, princely and military in the Delta, had sub-divided the country more and more. Upper Egypt was moribund, cut off from the world, with a seigniorial régime of closed economy which had enslaved the people on the priestly estates. In Nubia, the priests of Ammon had organized a theocratic monarchy in which the king, the High Priest nominated by the priests of Napata, was merely an instrument in their hands.

In the Delta, after the time of the Libyan kings, the monarchy had lost all power. The country was split up into virtually independent principalities in which, outside the cities which had maintained their activity and their autonomous social organizations, the petty landowning nobles, descended from the former mercenary armies, lived a like feudal-chivalry caste, always involved in local wars. These feudal lords and knights were descendants of the Achaeans, the Asiatics and the Libyans who had settled in Egypt after the invasions of the Peoples of the Sea; the echo of their martial exploits has come down to us in the military epics which, written in the Egyptian language in the Xth century BC, show a strange kinship with the *Iliad* which was also an Achaean epic.

The feudal tutelage exercised over the Delta cities, the seigniorial régime which had been imposed on the petty military fiefs and on the temple estates and which extended to the outskirts of the merchant cities, hindered the economic activity of the urban middle classes made up of traders and free artisans.

In the IXth and VIIIth centuries BC the development of trade and the diffusion of money had increased the cost of living without allowing the farmers, hampered by the régime of perpetual tenures, to increase their resources, and forced them into debt—the interest on loans granted by the temples was 120%—and reduced them little by little into debt-slavery. Smallholdings disappeared, absorbed into the great sacerdotal estates and, as at the end of the Ancient Empire, the cities, hemmed in by a régime incompatible with the commerce on which they lived, were threatened with suffocation.

The economic and social crisis which resulted caused a reaction of the urban population against the privileged classes, priests and nobles. It was at Sais, where the Milesian trading post created at the mouth of the Nile had led to a rapid expansion of sea-borne trade, that the movement took shape.

In 730 BC a local ruler, Tefnekht, put himself at the head of the city party. His successor, Bocchoris, in 720 BC began a democratic, anti-feudal policy which foreshadowed that of the Greek tyrants a century later.

A great wind of liberty was blowing over the Delta.

Bocchoris cancelled all debts not sanctioned by a written contract, freed the debt-burdened properties and the persons enslaved for debt, abolished arrest for debt and instituted *habeas corpus*. The rural population was thus freed from their servitude to the temples.

To encourage and organize business, he published at the same time a law of contract, reduced interest rates to 33% and limited back interest to 100% of the capital lent. The new law regarded movable and immovable property on the same basis and thus restored the alienability of land which the manorial system had abolished. This reduced inherited privilege which had served as the basis of collective family responsibility and did away with perpetual tenure.

This far-reaching social reform, which meant the revival of individualist law, led to a policy in sharp opposition to feudal privilege and encouraged the unification of the Delta under a single monarchical authority.

The priests of Ammon reacted immediately. From Nubia, where theocracy had been developed to its greatest extent, the army of King Shabaka (716–701 BC) marched to crush the democratic revolution of the cities. These had nothing to oppose the semi-barbarous but well-commanded Nubian troops of the king of Napata except the town bands. Sais fell and Bocchoris was burnt alive. Shabaka, the descendant of former Libyan mercenaries whom the priests of Ammon had made king of Nubia, suddenly found that he had restored the unity of Pharaonic power to his own advantage.

Once master of Egypt, Shabaka forgot the origin of his power and adopted the policy of the cities, under the influence of their wealth. He did not hesitate between the Theban priests representing seigniorial feudalism, and the liberal and anti-feudal merchant cities. He set up his capital in the seaport of Tanis, once the residence of Rameses II, and thanks to the financial resources that he got from the Delta, he began to carry out a monarchical policy directly inspired by the commercial interests of the cities.

The key to the commercial prosperity of Egypt, which was dependent on its trade with Nearer Asia, was the possession of the Syrian ports. These were at that time incorporated in the Assyrian Empire. Shabaka therefore established friendly relations with Sargon II. But not realizing the disproportion of force between Egypt and Assyria, he allowed himself to become involved in a policy of hostility to Nineveh by supporting the revolt of the king of Jerusalem, Hezekiah (727–699 BC), against Sennacherib. Though aided by the powerful city of Tyre and by the king of Sidon, Jerusalem fell and was compelled to pay an enormous sum in reparations. The king of Sidon was put to death and the people of that wealthy metropolis were deported. Tyre immediately fell into line and offered Sennacherib the co-operation of its fleets.

Egypt, suddenly isolated, found herself obliged to face the powerful Assyrian army at the moment when she was going through a serious internal crisis. In order to restore monarchical unity, Shabaka had boldly undertaken a policy that aimed at nothing less than the suppression of the military fiefs. When, faced with the threat from Assyria, he summoned his vassals and their retainers to support him they refused him any assistance, counting on the defeat of Egypt to restore their feudal privileges. The city militias alone responded to his appeal and it was an improvised army of burghers and artisans that halted the Assyrian invasion at the frontiers of the Delta.

Egypt was, however, in no state to measure her forces with the military power of the king of Nineveh. In 671 BC Assarhaddon invaded the country. The Pharaoh Taharqa, abandoned by the feudal lords who rallied to the invader, fled to Thebes, and Lower Egypt was incorporated into the Assyrian Empire.

EGYPT A PROVINCE OF ASSYRIA

The policy of terror practised by Nineveh, and also the advantages of collaboration, gained the king of Assyria not only vassals but clients. In Egypt the feudal lords rallied to him loyally. As to the cities, whose activities, far from being hampered by annexation to the empire, found fresh opportunities for expansion, they no longer resisted and accepted, as Tyre had done before them, a collaboration favourable to their business interests.

Thus when King Taharqa, after raising an army in Nubia, tried to reconquer the country (669 BC) they closed their gates to him and the feudal lords banded together to resist him. However the tardiness of the Assyrian counter-offensive soon induced the local princes to offer their alliance to the Pharaoh on condition that he agreed that Egypt be parcelled out under their rule. But the arrival of Assurbanipal, whose army marched up the Nile as far as Thebes, did not allow these plans to be put into operation. Determined to break Egyptian resistance, the Assyrian king introduced a policy which, by destroying her prestige, her religion and her traditions, would finally denationalize her. The cities were given new Assyrian names, the autonomist tendencies of the cities and the princes were cleverly exploited, garrisons were billeted in the country and an all-powerful governor took possession of the Royal Palace at Memphis. The Pharaoh Tanutamon, who had taken refuge at Napata, made a last attempt to reconquer the kingdom (664 BC). Received in triumph by the priests, he was able to assert his power for a brief period over the feudal lords, but in 661 BC the capture and sack of Thebes set the seal on the final annexation of Egypt. Assurbanipal, now undisputed master, confirmed the twelve princes of the Delta in their sovereignty.

This feudal dismemberment was the best proof of the submission of the country. By the conquest of Egypt the Assyrian Empire now controlled the Red Sea, and the trade route to India was completely in its power. But now it had to face a new problem, that of its relations with the Mediterranean on which the economic life of Asia Minor depended more and more.

ASIA MINOR LOOKS SEAWARD

At the time when Egypt had become an Assyrian province, a new economic power was growing in Asia Minor. The development of Greek sea-borne trade in the Aegean and Black Seas had given essential importance in international trade to the routes from Ephesus and Sinope to Babylon, which met at Sardes.

Sardes, capital of the Lydian kingdom which had arisen on the ruins of the former Hittite state, had since the reign of Gyges (687 BC) held a leading place in transit trade. The rapid prosperity of the city of Sardes under Gyges recalls that of Jerusalem under Solomon. Born of international trade, its power rested on a cosmopolitan merchant class, looking both towards the sea and towards Babylon. The kings of Sardes did not seek for alliances among the feudal princes of Asia Minor but with the powerful banking family of Melas of Ephesus, with which they were several times united by marriage. Their policy was less concerned with getting more lands than with imposing their protection on the Ionian ports and entering into relations with the Greek world. The fabulous donations that they made for this purpose to the shrine of Delphi have remained famous.

At this time the merchant class of Miletus which assumed power in the city about 650 BC was a real force, as were the bankers of Ephesus. Miletus was the great gateway of Asia upon which Greek shipping, which was steadily growing in importance, converged. The island of Naxos, where the Greek alphabet was formed, the island of Rhodes, and Corinth, stages in the Asiatic trade with the west, Syracuse, where an important industrial centre developed, Sybaris, the warehouse of Miletus in the central Mediterranean with its advance port of Paestum looking towards Etruria, became great business centres.

But they were already divided by trade rivalries. Miletus aimed at dominating the Dardanelles and Corinth the straits of Messina. Carthage tried to reserve the West and Sicily for herself, while the Phoenicians disputed Cyprus with the Greek sailors. Phoenician expansion, however, was hampered by Assyrian domination. Sidon revolted once more and was destroyed by Assarhaddon (677 BC) while the Greeks founded new colonies on all the coasts.

The Caucasus, Thrace and its European hinterland, Italy, Sicily, Spain and the tin-mining countries with which it was in constant touch, were just as important to all this seafaring world as were Asia and Babylon. Phoenician and more especially Greek shipping drew Sardes and the cities of the Egyptian Delta more and more into an economy based on the Mediterranean. But while Phoenicia remained the main port of entry for Babylon, Egypt became the great transit route of the West to Arabia and, farther, to India, while Sardes became the market where East and West met.

The call of the sea tended to shift the axis of trade from Mesopotamia to the Mediterranean. Sea-borne trade had become the rival of continental trade. In those countries which, like Lydia and Egypt, were subject to both influences, the feudal and landowning classes looked towards Assyria while the people and the merchants of the cities looked fixedly towards the sea and the Greek world.

EGYPT LOOKS SEAWARD AND RECOVERS HER INDEPENDENCE

While the civilized world was following the sea-routes westward, the whirlpool of the nomadic peoples of the great European and Asiatic steppes was once again to shake the foundations of the international balance of power.

The Dorian invasions which had devastated Greece in the XIIIth century BC had been the result of a great migration of the Cimmerians, an Aryan people from Hungary who were moving towards the great plains of Russia. They had remained there ever since. But between 750 and 700 BC the Scythians, followed by the Sarmatians, a branch of the Iranian race, had begun to move westward from Russian Turkestan, driving the Cimmerians before them towards Thrace. The Cimmerian hordes crossed the Hellespont, burnt Sardes and appeared before the walls of Miletus, destroying on their way the trading posts which the Milesians had founded all around the Black Sea. In order to repulse them, Gyges was forced to appeal for Assyrian protection and had to accept the suzerainty of Nineveh.

But at this time Psammetichus, one of the greater Egyptian feudal lords whom Assurbanipal had made King of Sais regarding him as a docile instrument of Assyrian policy, who had been won over by the interests of that great merchant city turned his eyes to the sea and tried to free himself of Assyrian tutelage.

Since they had similar interests, it was quite natural that the kings of Sardes and Sais should conclude a close alliance. Both were carrying out a policy of economic expansion supported by the merchant classes in their cities and both had the same enemies, the feudal princes and the king of Assyria.

Gyges sent to Psammetichus gold and mercenaries levied in Ionia and Caria, which enabled him easily to conquer the other feudal lords of the Delta and expel the Assyrian garrisons in Egypt. Feudalism, which was no more than an archaism artificially maintained by the Kings of Nineveh to prevent the re-building of Egyptian unity, completely collapsed and was replaced by a swift monarchical revival energetically undertaken by the Saite dynasty (655 BC).

Paralyzed by dynastic quarrels which the subject provinces, from Elam to Sinai, had taken advantage of, in order to unite and rise in a formidable rebellion, the Assyrian Empire was in no position to react. Thus both Ardys at Sardes (625–615 BC) and Psammetichus I at Sais (655–609 BC) were able to carry out freely a monarchical policy which allowed the first to create a unified and powerful Lydian kingdom by the subjection of Phrygia and Caria, and the second to unify Egypt by asserting his authority over the priestly feudalism of the south, which soon began to disintegrate.

The policy of the kings of Sais aimed at restoring the Egyptian protectorate over Syria and the Phoenician ports in order to control both the route to India by way of the Red Sea and that to Babylon by the caravan routes.

The policy of the kings of Sardes aimed at establishing authority over the cities of Ionia and the Hellespont, to assure themselves control of the Greek trade with Asia and the countries of the Black Sea.

The alliance of Egypt and Lydia meant that the Assyrian Empire was thrust back to the continent. Egyptian independence took from it control of the sea route to India and Lydian independence prevented it from imposing its authority over the Greek trade. The only access to the Mediterranean that remained to it was Phoenicia. But the destruction of Sidon by Assarhaddon, and the protectorate forced upon Tyre, had broken the bonds that united the Phoenician colonies to their metropolis. Carthage had become the centre of an independent maritime empire. Reduced to a purely continental role, the Phoenician cities of Syria were to lose the mastery of the sea to the Greeks.

CHAPTER XVI

THE RUIN OF THE ASSYRIAN EMPIRE

THE SAITE REVIVAL IN EGYPT

THE advent of the Saite dynasty in Egypt (655 BC) marks a turning point in the history of the ancient East. Egypt divorces herself from the continent and turns definitely to sea-borne trade.

In internal affairs, the Saite Pharaohs were essentially the Kings of the Delta. The ancient Pharaonic tradition was broken. A quite new monarchical policy was inaugurated, wholly devoted to the economic development of the country and no longer relying on the priests but on the urban middle classes. The holy city of Thebes was no longer of any importance. The High Priest of Ammon, already suppressed by the Nubian king Shabaka who had himself assumed that rank at Napata, had not been reinstated. He had been replaced by a virgin, the 'divine worshipper of Ammon', assisted by a second priest who administered the affairs of the cult. Memphis had again become the religious metropolis of Egypt, as it had been under the Ancient Empire. After the disappearance of the seigniorial régime which the reforms of the Saite kings had finally managed to suppress, the temples of Upper Egypt had lost their social importance. On the other hand, the temples of Lower Egypt, which had no great estates but possessed immense quantities of precious metals, became involved in the mercantile evolution of the country. Like the temples of Babylon and Ephesus, they put their treasures on the money-market and played the role of bankers; in imitation of the Milesian shipowners they issued controlled ingots of silver stamped with their mark. Egypt, entirely dominated by the Delta, entered a phase of capitalism.

This economic revival went hand in hand with a centralized monarchical policy. The state, reorganized on the principles of the ancient law, experienced a renascence both in public and private affairs. Bureaucracy, income-tax, registration, the land-survey, all reappeared. Individualism reached a degree hitherto unknown. Women had a status in every way equal to men; polygamy, which had been widespread among the upper classes in feudal times, was abolished and replaced by a strict monogamy tempered by divorce which a wife could obtain for the same reasons as a husband. Marriage, up till then a religious function, became a civil contract. Contract law, influenced by Babylonian example, developed greatly.

Legal equality wiped out the last traces of seigniorial rights. The priesthood lost its privileges and the immunity of the temples was abolished. But this magnificent renascence of classical antiquity in Egypt, which was evident in art and science as well as in law, did not give the country the cohesion it had had in the times of the Ancient or the New Empires. The balance which had then existed between town and country dwellers was broken to the advantage of the former, since Egypt, instead of being the centre of a political and economic system, was now no more than a factor —though an important factor—of international economy. All her policy aimed at getting control of the route from the West to India in order to become the meeting place of Mediterranean and Oriental trade.

For that reason she aimed at mastery of the seas. Such an economic policy pre-supposed of necessity a great military force. But the business classes in the cities and the petty artisans were unwilling to be conscripted. Like Carthage, the Egyptian cities preferred to pay mercenaries. That was to be the weakness of the Saite monarchy.

COLLAPSE OF THE ASSYRIAN EMPIRE

At first this weakness was not apparent because the Assyrian Empire was on the point of collapse. It had been founded on force and maintained in existence by its national army. But the very extent of its expansion had compelled it to levy armies in the provinces. Consequently it could no longer impose its authority as it had done when the Assyrian lords had themselves assumed the defence of the Empire in order to exploit it for their own profit.

On the other hand the régime of *bon plaisir* which made the monarchy a family possession had delivered it over to constant dynastic crises, which had become endemic since the death of Sargon II.

The loss of Egypt had been the death-blow of the Empire. Sargon had conceived it around the axis: Persian Gulf–Mediterranean. This plan could not be realized without Egypt. From then on the Empire began to disintegrate, dismembered by countless rebellions. In order to repress them, Assurbanipal had destroyed Babylon with the greatest ferocity (648 BC) and had razed Susa to the ground (640 BC). But in destroying them, he had destroyed his own empire.

In the midst of all these internal troubles, the Scythian tribes that had reached the northern confines of the empire poured like a torrent across Nearer Asia. They devastated Syria and dealt a terrible blow to the Phoenician cities, but were halted at the border of Egypt by the gold of the Saite kings.

In 626 BC, at the death of Assurbanipal, the Assyrian Empire was in full decline. Nabopolassar proclaimed himself King of Babylon (626–605 BC), and Psammetichus invaded Syria, still gasping after the Scythian invasions, and advanced the Egyptian frontier once again to the Euphrates. The military power of Assyria was destroyed. Thenceforth the Empire, deprived of its force, represented nothing and collapsed.

But in order to keep Syria which he had just conquered Psammetichus had at all costs to prevent Babylon from taking the place of Assyria. He therefore reversed his system of alliances and gave every help to Nineveh, in order to keep it as a counterweight to the growing power of Babylon. Nabopolassar replied to the Egypto-Assyrian coalition by allying himself with the King of the Medes, Cyaxares, who was building up a powerful feudal and military monarchy on the Iranian plateau.

In 612 BC Nineveh fell to the Babylonian and Median armies. Its destruction, carried out with the utmost ferocity, was welcomed by the whole Eastern world with an immense cry of joy and deliverance of which we hear the echo in the Bible. In order to bar the Babylonians from Syria, Psammetichus joined up with the remnants of the Assyrian army of Assurutballit, but was unable to save it from annihilation (609 BC).

The role of Assyria was ended for ever. After the immense effort that she had made to found an empire upon military force, which was to be no more than a field of exploitation for the benefit of the Assyrian people, she fell back exhausted and hated. Of the huge artificial edifice that she had built upon terror, nothing remained. Thenceforward, Assyria was to take up once more the obscure role of a petty landlocked state under the suzerainty of Babylon.

CHAPTER XVII

THE NEO-BABYLONIAN EMPIRE AND THE NEW BALANCE OF POWER

PARTITION OF THE ASSYRIAN EMPIRE

THE downfall of the Assyrian Empire created an entirely new state of affairs. All the national states had disappeared and rebellions had broken out everywhere. None the less, the union imposed upon Nearer Asia by Assyria provided an economic common interest which it was impossible to ignore.

Nabopolassar and Cyaxares kept those parts of the empire which they held in their power or at their mercy.

Babylon obtained Mesopotamia, with the exception of the upper reaches of the Tigris, together with all the Aramean countries. All Nearer Asia was within her sphere of influence.

The Medes kept for themselves the vast territories stretching from the Persian Gulf to the Caspian Sea and the Lake of Van, as well as the upper Tigris. Only one city belonged to them—Susa, the capital of Elam—but by holding it they dominated the caravan route to India. By abandoning Susa Babylon committed a serious political error, for not only had she handed over to the Medes the control of the Indian trade but, by allowing them to occupy so important a post on the international trade routes, she forced them of necessity to carry out an economic policy that was bound in the end to compete with her own.

On the other hand, even if Babylon had won Nearer Asia by the partition, she still had to conquer it, for Psammetichus I had occupied all Syria as far as the upper Euphrates and thus cut Mesopotamia off from the Mediterranean, even as the Medes had cut her off from India.

Because of her alliance, Babylon had no need to fear any immediate threat from the Median Empire. Moreover, the Medes did not appear to be trying to expand westward. Coming from the steppes where their kinsmen the Scythians were still roaming as nomads, they had an exclusively land-owning civilization to which the great spaces of Central Asia opened unlimited possibilities for expansion eastward.

THE MEDIAN EMPIRE
ZOROASTER

The Medes had settled on the Iranian highlands about the beginning of the second millenary. They had evolved slowly, passing from a tribal régime to a village system and grouping themselves little by little into federations under 'judges', to unite in the VIIth century BC under the rule of a king, at first elected, but soon to become hereditary.

The Median dynasty had set up its fortified capital at Ecbatana and asserted its authority over the aristocratic Persian tribes, half-nomad and half-sedentary. The continual war against the kings of Nineveh had forced the Medes to organize an army on the Assyrian model and their victory over Nineveh, which was to make Media a great power, established the monarchy on a sound foundation. The power of the aristocracy diminished and the aspirations of the people towards greater political equality found expression in the mystical ideas of Zoroaster, which triumphed at this time. Zoroaster did not found a new religion, but he introduced a moral system into the Mazdaism professed by the Iranians which was directed towards a great heaven-god, a mother-goddess and a creator-god. Zoroaster taught that the world is dominated by the struggle of the creator, Ahura-Mazda, the principle of good, against Ahriman, the spirit of destruction and of evil.[1] Men are called to play their part in this struggle; defenders of the good will win eternal life in the paradise of Ahura-Mazda. For the present world is only transient. It will end in its own dissolution which will mark the final victory of good over evil, of spirit over matter, of life over death. When the time of the final triumph of good is at hand, a saviour will appear, a descendant of Zoroaster, who will announce the coming of his reign. This will be the end of the world. All men will be resurrected in their own bodies. At the Last Judgment, Ahura-Mazda will separate the good from the evil and life eternal will begin.

The spiritual idealism of the Egyptians was henceforth to exist side by side with the spiritual idealism of the Iranians which was to have so great an influence on human thought.

Between the Medes and Persians, who knew nothing of business, and the Babylonians, whose policy was essentially mercantile, it seemed that no conflict could ever arise.

[1] In the form of a serpent like Apophis, the god of evil in Egypt.

EGYPT UNDER THE SAITE DYNASTY

But war immediately began against Egypt for the possession of Syria, the natural outlet of Mesopotamia to the Mediterranean. In 605 BC Nebuchadnezzar had driven the Pharaoh Necho out of Asia and had installed himself on the Phoenician coast. In 586 BC, after the revolt of Jerusalem under Zedekiah, which was supported by Egypt, Nebuchadnezzar annexed the Kingdom of Judah and, reverting to Assyrian methods, deported a part of its population to Mesopotamia where, however, it was to prosper and learn the practice of business. Necho resigned himself to the loss of Syria and Palestine. But, since with his small mercenary armies he was unable to defeat Babylon on land, he undertook a policy of naval hegemony which demanded an immense effort from Egypt. Egypt rose to the occasion and created a powerful navy, partly built and manned by Greeks.

Unable to retain his hold over Syria, Necho resolved to make himself master of the Indian trade-route by rebuilding the canal that had formerly existed between the Red Sea and the Nile, but this time conceived as a major waterway. Work was immediately put in hand, but it was only to be completed under the reign of Darius. At the same time Necho searched for fresh outlets and, following the example of the Phoenicians and the Greeks who had created maritime empires in the Mediterranean and the Black Sea, he sent a Phoenician fleet to conquer unknown Africa. This fleet accomplished the circumnavigation of the continent, starting from the Red Sea and returning to Egypt through the Straits of Gibraltar. This great expedition which revealed to the civilized world the extent of the African continent had, however, no economic consequences. The Saite dynasty limited its activities to the Red Sea—it seems that about this time, by the mediation of Egypt, the Greeks entered into relations with southern Arabia—and the central Mediterranean where, under Apries, it tried in vain to take possession of Cyrene.

The commercial expansion of the Saites, based on a liberal-economic policy, was balanced by a democratic trend in social affairs and a policy of peace abroad. It seemed that an era of peace must now begin for the eastern world.

THE NEO-BABYLONIAN EMPIRE

In contrast to seaward-looking Egypt, Babylon, the mistress of Mesopotamia, Syria and Palestine, of the access to the Red Sea at Asiongaber, and of the caravan routes of Nearer Asia and the Arabian frontiers, dominated the whole continental trade.

Her policy, like that of the kings of Sais and Sardes, was determined by

THE GREAT STATES AT THE TIME OF

BABYLONIAN EMPIRE (6th Century B.C.)

Map No. 12

economic factors. Trade took pride of place over politics in international affairs.

But what distinguished Babylonian from Egyptian and Lydian policy was that, instead of being attracted by the sea, it was essentially continental. Mastery of the seaways forced Egypt to build a powerful navy. Possession of the continental trade-routes, which linked Syria to the Red Sea, to the Caucasus and to the Persian Gulf, forced on Babylon the necessity of becoming a military power. To assure safety and freedom of trade for her caravans, Babylon was compelled to assure her rule over the countries of Nearer Asia. Her policy had therefore to be territorial, not for imperialist political reasons, but to assure her economic expansion.

In order to maintain her authority over the diverse lands she had annexed, Babylon, like Nineveh, had recourse when need arose to terrorist methods and deportations, but her policy was, on the whole, pacific and liberal.

Babylonian trade was based on private initiative. She neither practised monopoly nor state socialism. Her wealth depended on that of her merchants, her financiers and of the commercial groups composed of all the subjects of her empire, all of whom, therefore, availed themselves of the Babylonian law. A deported Jew could just as easily become a tax-farmer as a Babylonian could. In this way Babylonian law spread throughout all Nearer Asia. It was adopted word for word by the Phoenician cities, followed the Babylonian merchants into Lydia and everywhere determined the conduct of international high finance. The economic liberalism of Babylon favoured the economic prosperity of Syria which in its turn reacted upon the Babylonian law, giving it an ever greater individualism and suppleness. The principle of sureties and guarantees, the idea of collective responsibility, the rules of credit and of commercial association reached a pitch of perfection not to be surpassed before the 19th century AD. Babylon, the economic and financial centre of the continent, where flowed the trade of India from the East, of the Mediterranean from the West and the Caucasus from the North, was soon the greatest and most luxurious city in the world; a Syro-Babylonian cosmopolitanism developed there and national individualities began to disappear. A Syriac dialect, Aramean, became a veritable *lingua franca* spoken throughout all Nearer Asia.

THE KINGDOM OF LYDIA

The prosperity of Babylon was the direct cause of the prosperity of Sardes which became, because of its position, one of the greatest markets of its time where, in the footsteps of the Babylonian, Lydian and Ionian traders, the Mediterranean and Asiatic worlds met.

After the time of Gyges, the kings of Sardes competed with the Phoenician ports for the traffic between Asia and the West. They could only become its masters by controlling the Ionian ports. Ephesus, where a financial oligarchy looking entirely to Asia was in power, fully supported them, but Miletus, which had founded a great maritime empire on the Black Sea and whose interests were as much at Sybaris as at Sardes, resisted.

However the wealth of Sardes and the Ionian cities was firmly based, dependent both on Babylon and on Greek sea-borne trade.

Quite naturally Sardes, a transit centre like Babylon itself, pursued a free-trade liberal policy. The business classes dominated the policy of the king. A Greek party competed for influence, both in the city and at the court, with a national party which, supported by the former Lydian aristocracy, tried to react against the tide of democracy and cosmopolitanism.

Sardes had become as necessary to Babylonian prosperity as Babylon was to Sardes. It was through Sardes that the produce of Mesopotamia was exported to the Greek world, then in full expansion. The traffic between the Black Sea, the Aegean Sea, Sardes and the Euphrates was so intense in the VIIth century BC that the Lydian kings were the first to organize a road network, with posting inns and guardposts, provided with pontoon bridges to make easier the circulation of the caravans between Babylon and their lands.

None the less, Babylon does not seem to have realized the vital importance of Asia Minor. Absorbed by the sole preoccupation of fostering her business interests, she tried to keep peace at any price. This made her commit the folly of allowing the Median Empire to expand westward without opposition and to occupy Asia Minor up to the Halys, the frontier of the Lydian kingdom, and set foot on the Black Sea coast. The attraction of the sea was bound to influence this immense empire which bordered on the Persian Gulf, the Caspian and the Black Sea. War for the possession of the great Greek port of Sinope, in the immediate vicinity of the Halys, was soon to break out between Cyaxares and the king of Lydia, Alyate, who, wiser than Nebuchadnezzar, realized how dangerous the presence of the Medes on the Pontic shore could be. Nabuchadnezzar, who had friendly relations both with Lydia and with the Medes, intervened, and thanks to his diplomacy was able to end the conflict by an arbitration, confided to a Babylonian and a Cilician. Peace was saved

THE GREEK EXPANSION
AT THE MIDDLE OF THE 6TH. CENTURY B.C.
Phoenician zone
Greek zone
Etruscan zone
STATE OF
TARTESSOS
IBERIANS
LIGURIANS
Ebro
Rhône
Po
Tiber
Emporia
Port Vendres
Marseilles
Nice
Monaco
ETRURIA
VENETI
Lucca
Florence
Pisa
Populonia
Tarquin
LATI
Rome
Cumae
Naples
Paest
CORSICA
Alalia
SARDINIA
Caralis
Tyrrhenian Sea
BALEARIC IS.
Saguntum
Tartesso
Gades
Abdera
Lucena
Caine
Pillars
of Hercules
Abyla
Lixos
Utique
Hippo-Regius
Carthage
Hadrumetum
Leptis
Thapsos
Palermo
Eryx
Motya
Selinonte
Agrigentum
Gela
SICIL
MOORS
Oea
Leptis-Mag

Map No. 13

SCYTHIANS
Tanais
Borysthenes
Olbia
Panticapea (Kertch)
Phanagoria
Chersonesus
Taurica
Theodosia
Cherson
(Sebastopol)
Istros
Ister (Danube)
Callatis
Black Sea
Dioscurias
COLCHIS
Mesembria
Apollonia
Sinope
Kytoros
Heraclea
Trebizond
ILLYRIANS
Sea
Epidamnos
THRACE
Strimon
Abdera
Chalcedon
Halys
KINGDOM
OF THE PERSIANS
Tarentum
Apollonia
MACEDONIA
Sestos
Metapontum
Cyzicus
KINGDOM
OF LYDIA
Sybaris
Croton
Potidea
Phocaea
Clazomene
Sardis
CORCYRA
Dodona
LESBOS
Delphi
Chalcis
CHIOS
Locri
Rhegion
Megara
Colophon
Euphrates
SAMOS
Ephesus
Miletus
CILICIA
Soli
Aleppo
Sicyon
Athens
Olympia
Corinth
Aegina
Halicarnassus
Sparta
Phaselis
Calendria
NEW
SYRIA
Cnidus
RHODES
CYPRUS
Salamis
Arvad
Ionian Sea
Paphos
Citium
Byblos
Berytus (Beirut)
Damascus
CRETE
Gortyne
Sidon
Tyre
BABYLONIAN
Phoenicia
Palestine
Samaria
Jerusalem
Cyrenaica
Apollonia
Milesians' Wall
PHILISTINES
Gaza
EMPIRE
Barka
Hesperis
Naucratis
CYRENAICA
Sais
Tanis
Bubastis
LIBYA
Memphis
ARABIA
SAITE
KINGDOM
OF EGYPT
Red Sea
300
of Miles
Koptos
Qosier
Thebes
M.

without Babylon having to depart from her policy of neutrality. But that neutrality, equivalent to abstention, was, twenty-five years later, to lead to her final downfall.

THE APPROACHING CONFLICT BETWEEN THE MEDITERRANEAN AND CONTINENTAL INFLUENCES

If the prosperity of Sardes was dependent on that of Babylon, this was no less true for Egypt. Since Babylon had laid hands on Syria, the trade of Egypt had been decisively cut off from the continent. Even as Sardes owed her wealth to her role as intermediary between Nearer Asia and the Mediterranean, so Egypt tended to become the great transit centre between the Mediterranean and India. The interests of Egypt thus became clearly competitive with those of Babylon. The struggle was inevitable—it was to go on until the advent of the Roman Empire—between the land and sea routes from the West to India, the first represented by Babylon and the second by Egypt.

CHAPTER XVIII

GREECE AND EGYPT IN THE VIIth AND VIth CENTURIES BC

DEMOCRATIC EVOLUTION OF THE GREEK CITIES

THE Babylonian Empire was continental and unified, and individualism developed there within a framework of egalitarian absolutism.

The sea-going peoples of the Eastern Mediterranean, on the other hand, lived under an urban decentralised régime and were in the main flood of the democratic movement. This first became evident in Egypt about 715 BC, with the reforms of Bocchoris, and then at Sardes where, during the reign of Gyges, the rich burghers assumed the leadership. At Miletus, the royal family of the Neleids was obliged to hand over power to the influential corporation of shipowners. At Ephesus it was the financial oligarchy, dominated by the Melas family, that took over the control of affairs. At Colophon and Samos in Ionia, at Sybaris in Magna Graecia and in the Black Sea cities, oligarchies of rich burghers ruled.

In Greece, where up till the VIIth century the Dorian aristocracy had maintained a lawless seigniorial system in sharp contrast to the development of the cities, a popular movement brought to power tyrants who destroyed the great estates and overthrew the rule of the nobles. In 670 BC at Sicyon, Orthagoras expelled the city aristocrats, emancipated the tenant-farmers and abolished class distinctions. At Corinth, Clypselos in 657 BC expropriated the estates of the nobles which he transformed into villages with a municipal organization, inaugurated a mercantile and democratic policy and made laws against the indolent. Periander in 627 BC undertook large-scale public works to lessen unemployment, endowed the city with drinking water and built a port. At Megara in 640 BC, Theagenes confiscated the great estates and divided them amongst the people.

In Magna Graecia in the new colonies where there was no nobility, the cities commissioned their law-givers to draw up constitutions for them.

In 663 BC Zaleucos at Locri introduced equality of citizenship and confided the government to a rich oligarchy; thirty years later, Charondas at Catania gave the power to a popular assembly, replaced class jurisdiction by popular jurisdiction and broke up family privilege. At Athens, the Code of Draco in 621 BC put an end to the privileges of the nobles, and Solon in 594 BC, inspired by the laws of Bocchoris, whom he had known in Egypt where he went to sell oil, introduced a tempered democracy and civic equality, abolished arrest and slavery for debt, restored to their owners lands confiscated for debt and put an end to the aristocratic régime. Wealth and not birth became the basis of the social hierarchy. The control of public affairs passed to the rich oligarchy, alone capable of carrying out the duties of *archons* and treasurers. But all the Athenians took part in the government by electing in the popular assembly the hundred candidates from whom the *archons* were chosen, setting up popular courts and electing the members of the council of Four Hundred which, together with the Areopagus formed by *archons* no longer in office, exercised sovereign power.

Thus appeared the principle of representation of the people by elected assemblies—applied for the first time at Chios in Ionia—which was to create an essential innovation in the history of public law.

The constitution of Solon, promulgated in the midst of social unrest of the utmost violence, pleased nobody. The aristocratic party denounced it for having handed over the government of the city to the people, and the popular party for not having expropriated the lands of the nobles. The social conflict, stilled for a moment, broke out again with renewed violence until Pisistratus in 561 BC, brought to power by civil commotion, set up a tyranny at Athens which was to lead to the total triumph of democracy and to cause the city, once and for all, to turn towards sea-borne trade.

On all the coasts of the Eastern Mediterranean, in Egypt, in Lydia, in Ionia, in Greece, in Magna Graecia and in Sicily, a great movement of social emancipation went hand in hand with economic development.

But whereas in Egypt the reforms were the work of the king, supported by public opinion in the cities, in the autonomous Greek cities they were due to the democratic parties struggling for power.

It was the Egyptian cities that represented the highest degree of civilization, which explains the influence that the reforms carried out by Bocchoris at Sais had on the Greek world. Amongst the Greek cities by far the richest, the largest and the most civilized were the Ionian cities of Asia Minor. It must not be forgotten that trust deeds existed at Miletus at a time when wills were not even yet in use in Athens, and that Ephesus was an international centre of bankers powerful enough to grant loans to the King of Lydia while the cities of Greece proper were still ignorant of the first principles of banking.

But though more advanced in Egypt and Ionia than in Greece, the civilization that was developing in the VIIth and VIth centuries BC along the whole eastern Mediterranean coast possessed common features which established intellectual, religious and moral, as well as economic, bonds between Egypt, Lydia, Greece and the Phoenician cities. This is shown by the fact that the great Asiatic sanctuaries of Didymos at Miletus, of Clarion at Colophon, of Artemision at Ephesus, like the Greek sanctuary at Delphi and the Egyptian temple at Butos, enjoyed a universal prestige amongst all these sea-going peoples. Among them nature-worship also assumed a similar form. From the times of the Ancient Empire, the Osirian cult, which originated in Egypt, was so merged with the Adonis cult of the Syrian coast as to be almost identical with it. The Mysteries which penetrated into Greece with the Orphic doctrine, and of which Eleusis was to become the most important sanctuary, were also directly influenced by Osirian ideas. The Greek cosmogony was permeated with Babylonian, Cretan and Egyptian elements. The Homeric epic contained a substratum of mingled Achaean and Trojan traditions.

The idea of the immortality of the soul, of the redemption of the world by the death of the god—Osiris, Anubis or Dionysus—the belief in a moral code upon which the destiny of man in another world depends, represented the greatest contribution made by Egyptian to Greek thought. It gave life to the mystical element which everywhere accompanied the democratic movement and prepared, six centuries before the birth of Jesus, for the advent of Christianity.

THE DEMOCRATIC REFORMS OF AMASIS IN EGYPT AND GRECO-EGYPTIAN CONTACTS

This commercial, democratic and cosmopolitan evolution led to a serious crisis in Egypt. The priests, devoted to tradition and large landholding, defended their privileges which were attacked by the people of the cities. At the same time a feeling of hostility against the Greeks, who penetrated everywhere and competed with the Egyptians even in their own cities, was widespread in Egypt. King Apries, relying on his Greek mercenaries, resisted the social claims of the urban population, but a rebellion broke out against him among the Egyptian militia sent to conquer Cyrene. Amasis, a general of popular origin, was proclaimed king by the troops. Apries was murdered by the crowd during the revolt. An era of great social reforms was about to begin.

During the reign of Amasis (568–525 BC) Egypt was enormously prosperous. This king, placed on the throne by revolution, was both a great social reformer and an astute politician. The first question to be solved was that of the relations between Greeks and Egyptians. Amasis collected all the Greeks into the town of Naucratis, near the port of Pharos formerly created for the Aegeans and where the Milesians had already set up a trading post. The Greeks, amongst whom the Ionians were the most important, obtained the right to govern themselves according to their native institutions while paying taxes to the Pharaoh. Naucratis rapidly became one of the principal ports of the Mediterranean. It was there that the Greeks came into contact with Indian and Arabian traders. A Greek city of business and pleasure, set in the heart of Egypt, Naucratis was one of the most important meeting places of the two great Mediterranean civilizations. Through Naucratis, Amasis brought Egypt into close touch with Greek trade. Furthermore, he proclaimed himself a friend of the Greeks, sent his statue to Sparta and to Rhodes and married a Greek princess of Cyrene; he established a foothold on Cyprus where he set himself up as protector of the petty Greek kings against their rivals the Phoenician colonies. At the end of his reign he was to try to become master of the seas by his alliance with the tyrant Polycrates of Samos, who had one of the most powerful fleets of the age. But at the same time he formed a close alliance with Croesus who was about to mount the throne of Sardes (561 BC) and who also was more and more drawn to Greece by his mercantile policy. Even as Amasis had the Greek port of Naucratis at his disposal, so Croesus incorporated the Ionian cities into his kingdom, though leaving them their autonomy. Both made sumptuous gifts to Delphi.

There were constant comings and goings between Greece and the courts of Sais and of Sardes. The famous Milesian philosopher, Thales, entered the service of Croesus as a military engineer. Croesus also invited to his court the philosopher Bias, granted a pension to Aesop, ordered jewels from Theodoros of Samos, heaped gold upon Alcmaeon of Athens, and gave aid to Miltiades, held prisoner by the natives of Pontus. He underwrote loans with the Ephesian bankers and inaugurated the minting of royal coinage, a practice soon to be imitated by all the Greek cities.

Contact between Egypt and the Greeks was no less constant. Solon, Thales, Pythagoras, all visited Egypt for the purpose of study; at Naucratis, as at Sardes, the Greeks learnt the practice of international affairs, while mercenaries, merchants and mariners got to know there the great democratic reforms that Amasis was at this time putting into force.

Amasis, brought to the throne by revolution, was more like a Greek tyrant than a Pharaoh. His reign inaugurated a new regime in the history of Egypt. Extending to a national scale the political ideas of the Greek cities, Amasis convoked an assembly of notables amongst whom—most remarkable for Egypt—there was not a single priest. With the help of this assembly he carried out a thorough reorganization of Egyptian institutions. The privileges of the clergy were suppressed, the temples placed under royal administration and the last vestiges of the seigniorial régime that had survived in Upper Egypt were abolished; all the dues that the temples levied on the people as a sort of tithe were revoked. The revenues from the temple domains went to the State which, in compensation, reserved a special budget for the cult.

This reform, comparable in scale and principles with that effected in France by the National Assembly in 1789, was accompanied by a fiscal reorganization; the land-survey, now re-introduced, became the basis of all taxation, which was henceforward reckoned only in money and was calculated according to the means of the taxpayer.

By freeing the purchase and sale of land, the reforms of Amasis led to an increase in capitalist economy. The temples, whose properties were administered by the State, organized industrial workshops on their domains. Leasehold spread, taking the place of hereditary tenure, and interest rates continued to rise steadily following the rise in prices for agricultural produce. Land became the object of commercial speculation. The individualism evident in private law encouraged business development. Free trade triumphed and with it free labour. For, contrary to the case in Greece where the industrial workers were for the most part slaves, the workers in Egypt were recruited from the free population. Even the state no longer made use of slaves, since the pacific policy of the Saite kings did not provide prisoners of war.

In Greece the development of social democracy went hand in hand with that of political democracy. In Egypt, on the other hand, it coincided with the strengthening of monarchical power. The cities ended by losing their autonomy, and social equality prevailed throughout the entire country. In Greece every democratic city lived by the exploitation of a numerous proletariat of slaves; in Egypt there were no slaves. The Greek cities recognized the rights of their own citizens only; passing from one city to another, the Greek became a foreigner, unable to own fixed property. In

THE WORLD ACCORDING TO HECATAEUS
(about 500 B.C.)

Map No. 14

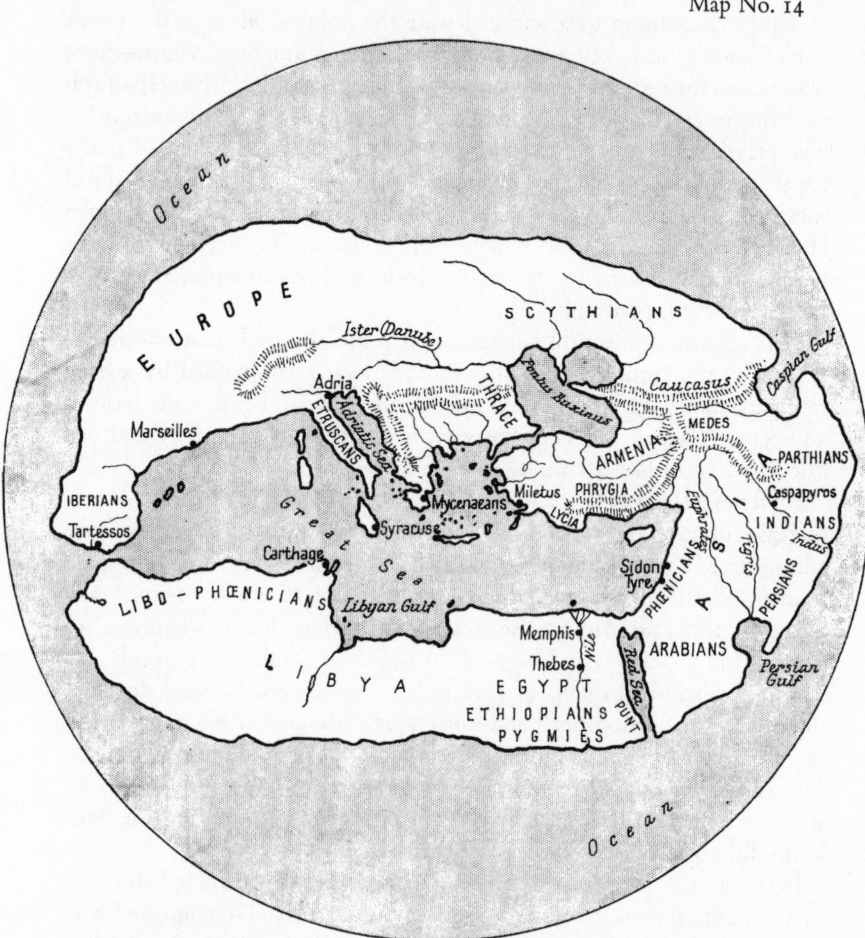

Hecataeus regards the world as a flat disc. The earth is made up of three parts—Asia, Libya and Europe—surrounded by the primeval ocean.

Egypt, throughout the whole kingdom, there were only Egyptians, all equal before the law. In Greece, each city was a little state, tightly grouped about a strictly national cult; in Egypt, religion united all the inhabitants in a single mystical faith obeying a single code of conduct.

FORMATION OF THE MEDITERRANEAN CIVILIZATION

Egypt, now on the flood-tide of an artistic and spiritual renascence, exercised during the Saite period a considerable influence on Greek thought, of which the great Ionian cities, so closely in touch with the cities of the Delta, were the birthplace.

From the VIIth century BC, a remarkable intellectual movement accompanied the economic and social progress of the Greek peoples of Asia Minor. In religion the ancient tradition represented by the Homeric hymns assumed a new character; under the influence of Osirian mysticism an Orphic literature developed which penetrated into Greece with the great Ionian gods Apollo and Demeter, of whom Delphi and Eleusis were to become the classic shrines. Hesiod attempted a synthesis of the different cosmogonies and gave to the Greek theogony a final form, presenting its genesis, according to Oriental tradition, as a genealogy of the gods.

The great expansion of the Mysteries led in Greece to the spread of the musical art of Phrygia and in Ionia and Magna Graecia to a magnificent upsurge of choral poetry.

The threat of the Cimmerian invasions and the struggle of the Ionian cities against Gyges produced the political poems of Callinos of Ephesus and Mimnermus of Colophon, while the rich and easy life, permeated by the voluptuous softness of Asia, that commercial prosperity had diffused through the merchant cities produced the erotic poetry of the odes of Mimnermus, of Alcaeus of Mitylene and Sappho of Lesbos.

But alongside the wealthy classes the people were in ferment; social struggle degenerated into civil war. Archilochus of Paros insulted the aristocrats in his satiric iambics, while Mimnermus and Alcaeus breathed their hatred of democracy and Xenophanes jeered at the youthful and effeminate scions of the wealthy classes who paraded their waved hair and anointed and perfumed themselves like women. All the fervent life of Greece was translated into an entirely new poetic outburst.

But however interesting this Ionian literary movement, it paled into insignificance before the vast horizons opened suddenly to human thought in the VIIth century BC with the Ionian philosophy, inspired at Sardes and Naucratis by the thousand-year-old civilization of the ancient East.

It flowered first in Miletus at a moment when individualism was expanding in an onrush of social and economic unrest, coupled with great material prosperity and an extraordinary development of human personality.

The Ionian School of philosophers, founded by Thales, a shrewd business man and an encyclopaedic spirit, was to initiate the Greeks into Egyptian and Asiatic thought and enable them to assimilate all that had been acquired in thirty centuries of Oriental civilization.

The thinking of Thales was directly inspired by the Egyptian solar cosmogony whence it took the conception of a universe formed of both spirit and matter, but transferring this conception into philosophy and physics.

The pantheism of Anaximander, which went so far as to formulate a moral code closely related to the Ammonian theology, led him to deduce from the primordial chaos conceived by the oriental religions the notion of the infinite, which he made the principle of all things. He substituted for the idea of the perpetual creation of the world by divinity, that of eternal movement and the evolution of matter, an idea inspired by Babylonian evolutionism. Anaximenes was only adapting the idea of the Egyptian *ka* to philosophy when he wrote: 'Our soul, being of air, is a principle of union within each one of us, even as the breath, or the air, contains in its entirety the whole world'.

As well as their theological opinions, the Milesians borrowed from Chaldea and Egypt their scientific, astronomical and mathematical ideas.

Pythagoras of Samos introduced into Greece mystical conceptions of the after-life directly inspired by 'The Book of the Dead'. Xenophanes of Colophon, founder of the school of Elea, in expressing the conception of a single god conceived in terms of pure spirit, was doing no more than paraphrase the famous solar hymns written in Egypt at the time of the New Empire. Heraclitus of Ephesus, it is true, departs from the idea of creation when he writes: 'This world, which is the same for all, has not been created either by gods or men, but has always been, still is and always will be, a fire eternally living, kindled and extinguished in a regular manner'; but, far closer to Egyptian thought than he believed, he came back once more to it when he made the identity of opposites the very principle of the world, even as the Egyptians had united them in the absolute of the divinity. Not only Greek thought but also Greek art was fertilized by Egyptian example; the protodoric style which had reappeared under the Saite monarchy directly inspired both the Doric and Ionic styles which were the bases of all Greek architecture.

Greece, nourished by the ancient religious, scientific and artistic heritage of the East, refashioned it to extract an entirely fresh conception of the world. Comparing the conclusions reached by Egyptian and Babylonian thinkers, Greece created the logic whence emerged both philosophy and the scientific method that replaced the theology and empiricism of the ancient civilizations. The extraordinary literary talent of the Greeks, the new sense of measure that they introduced into their less mystic and more realist conception of art, brought a hitherto unknown way of thinking to the civilized world: rationalism. Egyptian mysticism and Greek rationalism were henceforth to be the two poles between which a new civilization, the civilization of the Mediterranean, was to evolve, born of the contacts that the sea had established between the East, Egypt and Greece.

It is very striking to note that the Greeks, from the VIth century BC onward, took account of the continuity and unity of the civilizations to which they owed their own, and it was to study them that Hecataeus of Miletus, struck by what divided but also what brought together the peoples, created historical criticism, which was later to inspite the brilliant Ionian school of historians and geographers. The philosopher Anaximander published the first treatise on geography. Scylax of Carianda, later to become admiral of the Persian fleet of India, wrote a *Description of the World*. Cadmus of Miletus studied the origins of his own city. But Hecataeus outshone them all; as a geographer he based his *Voyage around the World* on his own travels in Persia, in Egypt and as far as Spain; as a historian he tried, in his *Genealogies*, to establish a concordance between the histories of Ionia and Egypt,

Oriental civilization attracted the Greeks to such an extent that the successors of Hecataeus, Charon of Lampsacus, Xanthos of Lydia and Dionysus of Miletus, were to devote their works only to the history of the East, until the day when Herodotus, born about 485 BC at Halicarnassus, was to give Greece her place in his magnificent précis of the known world of his time, that great work conceived, perhaps without his being aware of it, as a real essay in universal history.

THE WORLD ACCORDING TO HERODOTUS (about 450 B.C.) — Map No. 15

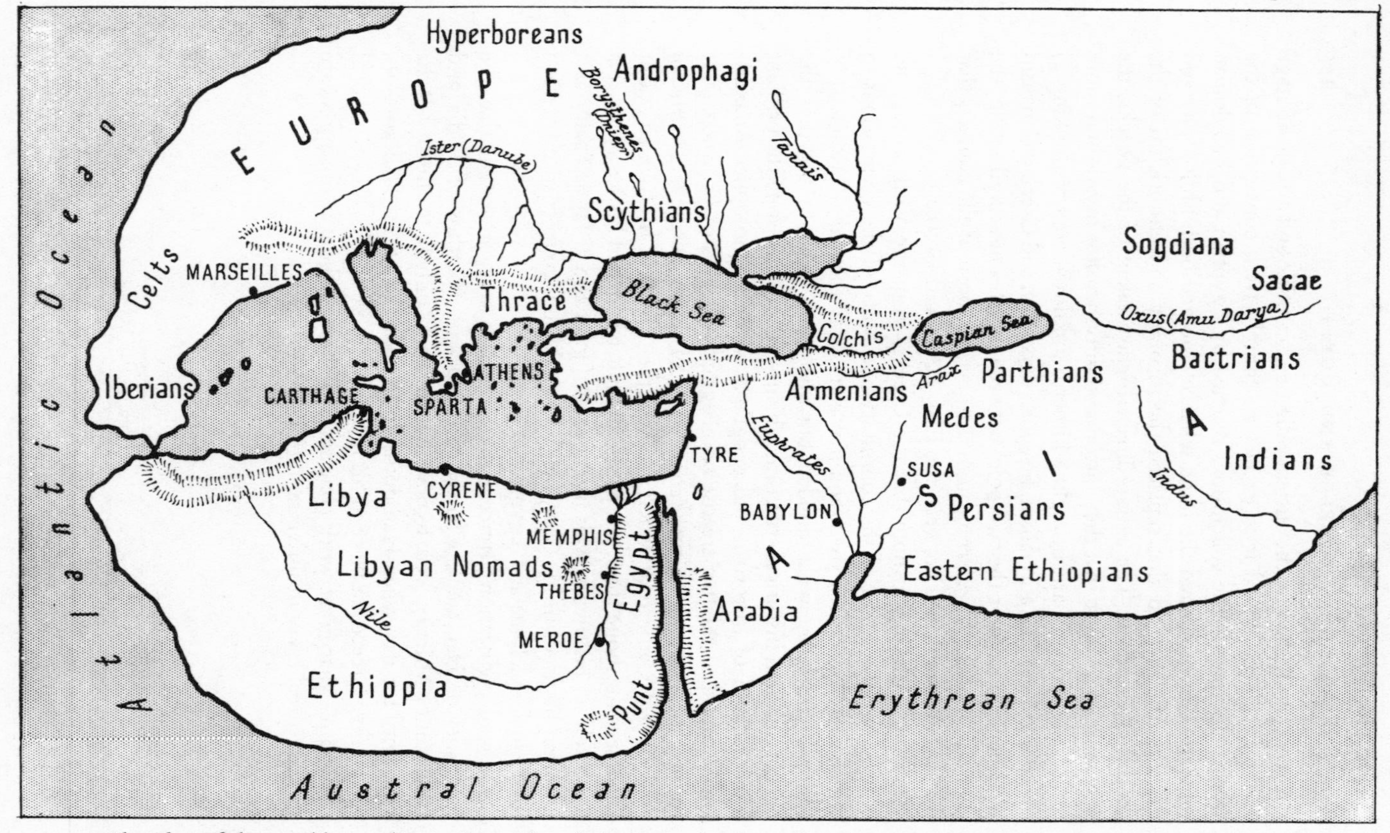

The idea of the world as a disc in the midst of the Ocean has been abandoned. Herodotus believes that the shape and

BOOK IV

The Persian Empire opens an Era of Universal Trade from the VIth to the Vth Century BC

CHAPTER XIX

THE FORMATION OF THE PERSIAN EMPIRE

THE CONQUEST

IN the VIth century BC the evolution of the Eastern world created a close interdependence between its peoples. Great events, wherever they occurred, had an immediate international repercussion.

The Median Empire, which encircled the Babylonian Empire on the east and north and which extended from India to Lydia, had not, like Egypt, a national basis nor, like Babylon, a commercial one; it was a feudal amalgam. It had no other bond than the dynasty which took a leading place in international affairs since both Babylon and Sardes sought its alliance. The extent of its territory, its army, its control of the trade routes from the Black Sea to India, its immense potentialities, made of it, thanks to its size, a sort of international arbiter.

But this immense empire was dependent upon the little Medo-Persian state which, in the VIth century BC, was rent by an internal crisis which ranged the Persian feudal lords against the monarchical policy of their Median suzerain. Cyrus, having effected the monarchical unity of feudal Persia in 555 BC, then rejected the suzerainty of the King of Ecbatana. Nabonides, then King of Babylon, hoping in this way to promote the dissolution of the Median Empire, supported Cyrus against his suzerain Astyages. But Cyrus, instead of liberating him from the tutelage of Astyages, took Astyages' place and the Achaemenid dynasty replaced the Median dynasty (549 BC). The Empire remained intact.

Nabonides, fearing a conflict, made no move. On the other hand Croesus, King of Sardes, who hoped to profit by these dynastic quarrels to drive the Medes and Persians out of Asia Minor, took the side of Astyages, who was in any case his ally, and crossed the Halys; he appealed for aid to Egypt, to Babylon, and to Sparta which was beginning to emerge as the principal military force in Greece. Neither Babylon nor Sparta responded. Only Amasis, realizing the serious danger from the Persian Empire, sent an army by sea to assist Croesus. But it arrived too late. The famous Lydian cavalry was wiped out by the Persian camel corps. Croesus shut himself up in Sardes which was taken in 546 BC. The Ionian cities, divided amongst themselves and hostile to Croesus whose protectorate they submitted to with impatience, refused to help him. They fell one after another to the Persian army, after Cyrus had neutralized the most powerful of them, Miletus, by a treaty of friendship.

Cyrus magnanimously spared Croesus and granted him an appanage in Media. In the Ionian cities Croesus had supported the democratic parties, but Cyrus, relying on the oligarchies, set up tyrants who, unable to maintain themselves without his aid, were to become docile instruments in his hands.

A few months' campaign had altered the balance of power in the world. The Egypt-Lydia-Greece bloc, then in process of formation, was smashed. Persia, master of all Asia Minor, became a maritime state.

Cyrus, however, did not push his conquests farther towards the Mediterranean, but, returning eastward, extended his rule to the Indus and as far as the Jaxartes on which he founded the city of Cyropolis, a starting-point for the trade route which, by way of the great oases of Central Asia, led to China (545–539 BC).

Nabonides had watched without reaction this threatening expansion of the Persian Empire which had now become master of all the continental trade of Asia Minor, from the Black Sea and the Caucasus to the Mediterranean, from Central Asia and China to the West and from India to the Euphrates.

Babylon henceforth was at the mercy of Cyrus. He entered it almost without resistance in 539 BC, despatched Nabonides to govern the satrapy of Carmania and made his own son, Cambyses, King of Babylon.

It only remained for the Phoenician cities to make their submission. They did so. In seven years all Asia, from the Mediterranean to Turkestan, had been occupied almost without war.

EGYPT AND GREECE AGAINST PERSIA

Only the maritime states—Egypt and the Greek cities—remained to face the Persian Empire. Greece was at this time in the flood-tide of development. Ionia, the wealthiest and most civilized part of the Greek world, was in Persian hands. But European Greece was developing rapidly. In 561 BC, a few years after the democratic revolution which had placed Amasis on the throne of Egypt, and in the same year as Croesus became king of Sardes, Peisistratus, at the head of a rising of the people, set up a tyranny in Athens and completed her democratic evolution by promoting smallholding and establishing an Agrarian Credit. From then on, Athens looked definitely seaward. The conquest of Ionia by Cyrus, which caused a great influx of Ionians into Athens, led to a sudden renascence. Meanwhile the exile of Pythagoras and Xenophanes, who left Ionia for Magna Graecia, shifted thither the centre of Greek thought.

In 535 BC a democratic tyranny was set up at Naxos under Lygdamis and at Samos under Polycrates. Immediately an alliance was formed between the tyrants of Athens, Naxos and Samos, who had a similar social and economic policy.

Under the firm and energetic guidance of Polycrates, a former cloth merchant, Samos soon became a great naval power. Amasis, realizing that he must have a powerful navy in order to resist the Persian threat, allied himself with Polycrates, and their united fleets soon gained mastery of the seas.

Driven from the continent, Egypt formed a block with Greece. The duel between land and sea power was being prepared.

Asia, however, accepted the Persian conquest, since the absolutism of Cyrus in no way resembled the former Assyrian absolutism. Conquered without violence, fortunate in having found peace under a firm but liberal rule, Asia surrendered. Everywhere the peoples formerly deported by Nineveh or Babylon returned to their homelands. Palestine was restored to the Jews (549 BC) and Cyrus granted them large donations for the rebuilding of their temple. The statues of the gods, which had been taken from the conquered peoples, were now restored with marks of the highest respect. After the Assyrian and Babylonian rulers, Cyrus appeared as a liberator.

In contrast to the unified continent, Greece was wearing herself out in internecine quarrels. The cities were constantly fighting among themselves, while within their own walls they were tearing themselves to pieces in terrible social conflicts. Meanwhile Egypt, relying on the power of her fleet, neglected to build up a land army and devoted all her energies to her social reconstruction, which was sullenly opposed by certain classes of the population, notably the priests and the aristocrats.

Before beginning the war, Persia prepared for it by diplomatic action. In order to conciliate the aristocratic party in Egypt, Cyrus married the daughter of Apries; and by his goodwill towards the Ionian cities did his best to wean his Ionian and Carian mercenaries from Amasis.

In 529 BC Cambyses succeeded Cyrus, and in 526 BC Persian diplomacy won a decisive victory. It broke the alliance of Polycrates with Amasis and obtained the collaboration of the Samian fleet. Egypt, from then on, was lost. Without a national army and with all classes, even up to the direct advisers of the king, politically divided, she was to collapse at the first assault of the Persian army. The death of Amasis was the moment awaited by Cambyses to undertake the invasion of the Delta. Egypt, undermined by enemy agents, disintegrated. Phanes, who commanded the mercenary army, betrayed the king, Psammetichus III, causing the defeat of the Egyptian army at Pelusium. The admiral of the fleet, Udjahorresent, at once opened negotiations and offered his co-operation to the enemy. The king, meanwhile, shut himself up in Memphis. But the city was taken by storm (525 BC) and despite the horrible cruelties and the shameful pillage ordered by Cambyses, the country as a whole surrendered without a struggle. Cambyses made the admiral, to whose frailty he owed his rapid victory, Chancellor of the conquered country. Egypt, suddenly vanquished at the height of her prosperity, collapsed morally, internally divided and betrayed, not by the king but by the leaders who should have defended her.

CHAPTER XX

GREECE BEFORE THE PERSIAN WARS

POLITICAL AND SOCIAL STRUGGLES

AT the time when Egypt fell, conquered by Persia, the Greek world, which alone had escaped Persian ascendancy, was in ferment.

In Magna Graecia the Achaean League—Sybaris, Locri and Croton—which was a real power in that area, was torn by internal strife. The democratic party triumphed at Sybaris, then the richest of the Greek cities of the West; while at Croton, where the religious associations founded by Pythagoras preached a régime controlled by a moral élite, the aristocracy ruled. These political divergencies masked an implacable commercial rivalry; Croton wished to wrest from Sybaris control of the trade-route which, by way of Paestum, assured her a monopoly of trade with the Etruscans. In 510 BC Sybaris was vanquished and razed to the ground. The Achaean League had committed suicide. Tarentum, governed by the aristocratic party, assumed the leadership in Magna Graecia. But triumphant democracy was soon to gain power at Tarentum (475 BC) and to overthrow at Croton the government of the Pythagoreans, whom the people exterminated by burning them in the convent where they had been organized as a religious community.

In Sicily, Syracuse, Agrigentum, Leontini, Megara Hyblaea, ravaged by terrible social crises, were fighting one another to the death. At Megara Hyblaea (608 BC) and at Agrigentum (570 BC) the plebeians had brought to power tyrants who behaved like military leaders because of the struggle that the Greek cities were forced to wage against the double hostility of the Carthaginians and Etruscans. A similar struggle had broken out in Marseilles, the powerful city founded by the Ionians in the VIth century BC in their search for Spanish silver, and which had become the centre of a wealthy sea-power that dominated the whole coast of Provence and the course of the Rhône. Carthage, which laid claim to a monopoly of the trade with Spain whose coast she had occupied, and the Etruscans settled in Corsica and Sardinia united against Marseilles in 535 BC. But far from combining against this double threat the Greek cities were ferociously hostile to one another, so entirely preoccupied by their immediate commercial interests that the conquest of the Ionian cities by Persia in 546 BC had passed unheeded, since it had not checked their trade with Asia Minor.

At the close of the VIth century BC social evolution in Sicily developed very rapidly as material prosperity increased. The régime of popular tyrannies spread to Gela, Himera and Rhegion.

In continental Greece, on the other hand, Corinth, Megara and Sicyon had by this time passed the crisis of dictatorship. Moderate democratic régimes, dominated by oligarchies of business men, had replaced the tyrants. Only Aegina had never had tyrants because, founded on a barren rock, she had never had a landowning aristocracy. Her social evolution had therefore gone on without opposition, and she lived under an openly democratic government, organ of the mass of small producers who made up her industrial power. Industry in Greece, born out of the needs of trade, was a recent phenomenon. As it had developed so rapidly, it lacked workers. The Greek sailors were merchant-adventurers. They traded, but they also were pirates when occasion offered. They were traders in wine, grain, oil, metals, cloth, hardware and pottery, but they were also dealers in slaves whom they kidnapped in Scythia and Thrace. Chios had become the principal market where Greek industry went to recruit its workers. At Aegina countless slaves, perhaps a hundred thousand, toiled in the workshops.

This was a new feature in economic organization. The East had never known industrial slavery. In Egypt, in Phoenicia, at Sardes, and perhaps also in Ionia, free men toiled in the workshops. The East had known agricultural slavery, it had tied whole populations to the land and had made use of household slaves, but it had never employed large numbers of industrial slaves. This was a Greek innovation. Industrial slavery, the tool of capitalism, was born in Greece.

At the time when Cambyses captured Memphis, Athens was living under the rule of the sons of Peisistratus, Hippias and Hipparchus. They had abandoned the policy of their father and, in imitation of the tyrants whom Cyrus had set up in the Ionian cities, had tried to transform themselves into sovereigns, thus breaking their ties with the democratic party. The aristocrats were no better disposed towards them. Threatened by the democrats, made up of the merchant classes and the proletariat, they were to try to defend their interests by allying themselves, outside Athens, with the class of landed proprietors which ruled in the Peloponnesus and was mainly identified with Sparta. Thus the party struggle extended beyond the city walls; class interests, especially those of the aristocratic party, took precedence over the interests of the national community. Democrats and aristocrats made agreements among themselves from one city to another. Sparta, whose constitution made her the champion of oligarchic government, was to attract all the elements at odds with democracy. To understand the deep division which was at this time to rend continental Greece, it is important to know what Sparta really represented.

SPARTA

The origin of Sparta goes back to the Dorian invasion which, after destroying the Mycenaean civilization, set up colonies in the Peloponnesus, which soon became landholding aristocracies. On the coasts, at Corinth, Sicyon, Megara, Argos, these aristocracies were absorbed or destroyed as a result of the social evolution produced by the renascence of sea-borne trade. But at Sparta, a group of villages isolated from the sea, the Dorian aristocracy held its own and even extended its rule into Messenia, occupied by former Achaean peoples. By contact with them, and under the influence of external trade that penetrated into the Peloponnesus, Sparta too had evolved. United in a single city under two dynasties, the one Dorian and the other Achaean, she had her assembly of citizens, formed by the landholding proprietors, and her *Gerusia*, a sort of senate where the more important nobles had seats. At the beginning of the VIth century, Sparta took the form of a military territorial state. Sardes and Egypt sought for her alliance.

About 550 BC an aristocratic reaction, led by Chilon, took place in Sparta.

The 25,000 Spartans—upon whom depended 100,000 helots or serfs and 250,000 *perioikoi*, Messenians who had no political rights but enjoyed complete economic and social liberty—were in danger of being submerged by their own subjects. Chilon, in order to save the leadership of his class, was to halt the development of Sparta. To enlarge her conquests still further would mean to condemn the domination of the Dorian minority to disappearance; Sparta must therefore stop increasing her territory. To permit the economic development of the city would mean to drown the aristocracy in a rich trading middle class, with whom it would inevitably have to share its power; to preserve that power the Spartan aristocracy, landowning and military, was to refuse all activity save that of arms.

Thenceforward the Spartan State became a sort of military community.

All its citizens, each allotted an inalienable property cultivated for them by helot serfs, were to be conscripted to the exclusive service of the state. From the age of seven to twenty, their social education was carried on in youth camps where, all brought up in a similar manner, they would receive no intellectual or moral training, but only military and sporting instruction. In these camps they were inculcated with the idea that the individual is of no account independently of the group; only the state, that is to say the community of Spartans who made up the ruling class, existed. Individual conscience was replaced by passive obedience to the law which, moreover, was never written down. From twenty to sixty, every Spartan was enrolled in a military company which was always in a state of mobilization. In order to ensure the continuity of the state, every Spartan was obliged to marry; but to prevent the state from having unhealthy citizens, every weakly child was put to death. As there could be no poor citizens in Sparta, the inalienable patrimonial lot must remain indivisible and was transmitted by strict primogeniture; if a child of citizens had not the means of living, then he was expelled from the civic body, to be ranked with the *perioikoi*. Whereas the helots were simple serfs, the *perioikoi*, though deprived of political rights, possessed civil rights and were free to devote themselves to all the economic activities necessary for the life of the city. They thus constituted a real bourgeoisie. In this way the Spartan state was made up of two classes of inhabitants, but only the citizens, all of whom were landowners and soldiers, governed it. They alone formed the Assembly which represented the civic body of the state and which held, in law, the sovereignty. In fact, however, this belonged to the *Gerusia*, the senate, formed, in addition to the two kings, of twenty-eight members who co-opted one another, and which proposed to the Assembly the candidature of five annual *ephors*, charged with carrying out the executive power. The two kings acted as leaders of the army, the *ephors* administered the state and the *gerontes* formed a close oligarchy which governed and which formed the High Court of Justice.

Chilon wished to make all Spartans 'equal'; that was why each one of them was provided with an equivalent grant of land. But, in fact, certain of them—they must have made up the oligarchy of the *gerontes*—possessed immense domains in Messenia; and though the Spartans could not trade or possess precious metals in order to preserve a simplicity of manners which made them soldiers only, their wives possessed it in their name and the temples of Achaea soon found themselves stuffed with treasures that the governors of Sparta had won by war or by clandestine trade.

Sparta was therefore the exact opposite of a trading city. It was a landowning aristocracy, but halted in its evolution because it wished to remain a privileged oligarchy so as to keep under its sway, without soiling itself by contact with them, the peoples over whom it ruled. It could not become a centre of a united Greece, because to do that it would have to extend (as Rome was to do) the rights of citizenship; nor could it maintain a landowning régime based on a social heirarchy because, in fact if not in law, its ruling class allowed itself to become absorbed by the economic organization of Greece in order to acquire wealth.

Sparta represented the oligarchy of a race of invaders that strove to perpetuate its rule by force. Its solid military structure was to assure its existence for two centuries as a real power and allow it to form under its authority the Peloponnesian League, the instrument of its territorial hegemony in continental Greece.

ATHENS

Chilon's reforms made Sparta attractive to the Athenian aristocratic party. Equally hostile to the monarchical policy of Hippias as to the policy of the democratic party, it appealed to the Spartan army, which conquered Athens. Hippias fled to the Persian court, and an oligarchical régime was set up in the city. The Constitution of Solon was abolished and a tribunal of three hundred aristocrats inaugurated a reign of terror, which soon collapsed when faced by a popular rising. The democrats assumed power and Cleisthenes (508 BC), their leader, gave Athens a constitution which marked the triumph of democracy. Attica was divided into a hundred *demes*, a sort of commune each having its own assembly, its elected *demarch*, who attended to its budget, its land-survey and its registration. The hundred *demes* were grouped into ten administrative tribes, made up of urban, rural and maritime *demes*, in order to unite in each elements belonging to all social classes and all professions. Each tribe must raise a regiment. Athens was henceforth to be governed by ten *archons*[1], drawn by lot from amongst forty candidates of the first class of the census, elected in the assemblies of the *demes*.

The former council of the 'Four Hundred' created by Solon became the council of the 'Five Hundred' made up of fifty members of each tribe, they too drawn by lot from candidates elected in the *demes*. The council was divided into ten sections which sat permanently in rotation to administer current affairs. Every day the president of the council was designated by lot. He was the Head of the State.

[1] To make up the number a secretary was added to the College of the Nine Archons which represented the ten tribes.

Alongside the council of the Five Hundred, the Areopagus, made up of *archons* who had formerly held office, continued to exist as a Supreme Court, the guardian of the constitution.

The administration of the city finances was confided to ten receivers-general and ten treasurers, chosen like the *archons* from the first class of citizens in the census.

As to the popular assembly, the *ecclesia*, which had till then been of little importance, it was granted very extended powers, controlling the administration of the magistrates, deliberating on peace and war, and voting laws previously prepared by the council.

In this constitution the *archons* and the Areopagus represented the wealthy classes, the *ecclesia* and the council of the Five Hundred the whole population. There still remained, however, the privilege of wealth; but already the struggle to deprive the wealthy classes of this last privilege had become inevitable.

Sparta and Athens represented the two opposite poles of Greek political life. After combining momentarily in a common front against Persia, they were to compete for leadership and finally to destroy one another after a merciless struggle.

CHAPTER XXI

THE EMPIRE OF DARIUS

THE IDEA OF UNIVERSAL EMPIRE

LIKE the Assyrian Empire, the Persian Empire was an immense amalgam created by a feudal king who, in the conquered countries, became an absolute sovereign. Persian policy, however, differed markedly from that practised by Assyria; instead of the exploitation of the empire to the advantage of the conquerors, the Persians conceived the idea of a great imperial commonwealth. But this necessarily led to conflict between the king and the Persian feudal lords who, on the death of Cambyses, rebelled against the monarchical policy and brought to the throne one of their own representatives, the Achaemenid Darius I (521–486 BC). Although the tool of feudal reaction, Darius at once became absorbed in the administration of his Empire, and was to become an organizer of genius. The Persian feudal lords continued to figure in his council, to provide satraps for the provinces and to preserve their privileges within Persia itself, while at the same time becoming simple courtiers; they could not prevent the king whom they had elected from becoming—thanks to the power given him by the empire—an absolute sovereign whose policy was to aim at the creation of a universal state.

The Persian Empire was the most extensive hitherto known. It included Asia from the Mediterranean to the Jaxartes and the Hindu-Kush. It took Darius only a few years to give it unity. An Empire so diverse could only have monarchical power as a basis. Darius, who had come to the throne as a feudal king, became a hereditary emperor, claiming to hold his power only by the will of the gods. In Persia he claimed descent from Ahura-Mazda, in Babylon from Marduk and in Egypt from Ammon. He was not therefore a conqueror imposing his will by force, but the legitimate holder of sovereignty granted him by the gods; in the other parts of the Empire, where no dynastic theory existed, he tried to introduce with the aid of the Persian Magi a religion which was both monarchic and universal in tendency. The great temples of Ephesus, of Sardes, of Pessinonte, were

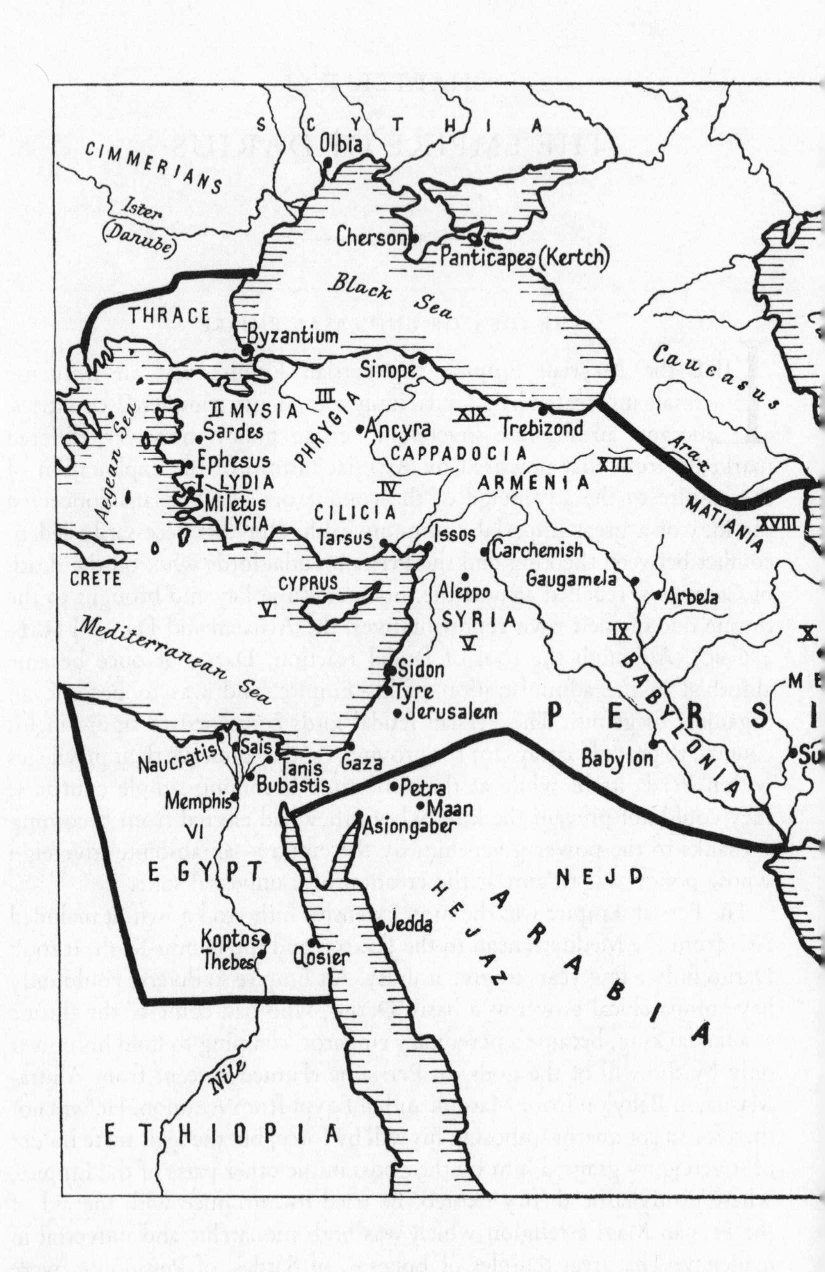
SCYTHIA
Olbia
CIMMERIANS
Ister (Danube)
Cherson
Panticapea (Kertch)
Black Sea
THRACE
Byzantium
Caucasus
Sinope
III
II MYSIA
PHRYGIA
XIX
Trebizond
Sardes
Ancyra
Araz
Aegean Sea
CAPPADOCIA
Ephesus
XIII
I LYDIA
IV
ARMENIA
Miletus
MATIANIA
LYCIA
CILICIA
XVIII
Tarsus
Issos
Carchemish
CRETE
CYPRUS
Gaugamela
Aleppo
Arbela
V
SYRIA
X
Mediterranean Sea
V
IX
Sidon
BABYLONIA
ME
Tyre
Jerusalem
PERSI
Naucratis
Sais
Tanis
Gaza
Babylon
Su
Bubastis
Memphis
Petra
Maan
VI
Asiongaber
EGYPT
NEJD
HEJAZ
ARABIA
Jedda
Koptos
Thebes
Qosier
Nile
ETHIOPIA

Map No. 16

THE EMPIRE OF DARIUS (521-486 B.C.)
THE ROMAN FIGURES ARE THE NUMBERS OF SATRAPIES ACCORDING TO HERODOTUS
Aral Sea
Jaxartes (Syr Darya)
SACAE
Cyropolis
CHORASMIA
XVI
SOGDIANA
Oxus
XV
SCYTHIANS
Bactra (Balkh)
XII
BACTRIA
Hindu-Kush Mts
GANDHARA
PARTHIA
SAGARTIA
XIV
N
EMPIRE
XX
INDIA
VII
ARACHOSIA
Carmana
Pasargada
Persepolis
Indus
XVII
GEDROSIA
OMAN
0
300
600
Scale of Miles
M.

manned by Persian priests who introduced, together with Mazdaist ideas, the moral code of Zoroaster, associating with its ideas of the after-life the mystery cults then prevalent in all the Mediterranean countries. These temples were to become not only religious and political, but also economic, centres; the King of Persia, turning them into great treasuries, was to permit them to enlarge the role as bankers which they had carried on since the VIIth century, and therefore to acquire an immense ascendancy, to the detriment of those shrines which remained alien to the cult of the Achaemenids, such as the famous shrine of Didymus at Miletus, which declined both in religious prestige and economic power.

King by Divine Right, Darius was not, like the Assyrian kings, a despot whose absolutism was derived only from his national gods. As representative of all the gods of his subjects, he was responsible before them. Thus he took over from the Egyptian Pharaohs and the kings of Babylon the notion of monarchic power identified with justice. He would be the protector of the weak, the representative of order and the guardian of the good.

THE IMPERIAL INSTITUTIONS

As universal sovereign, he surrounded himself with a council in which, alongside the Persian feudal lords, Greeks, Jews, Babylonians and Egyptians took their seats. Like his councillors, his collaborators—architects, engineers, doctors, generals and admirals—were chosen from all the peoples of the empire. Babylonian scribes manned the offices of the financial administration and of the chancellery where Iranian, which had no written form, was adapted to cuneiform characters. Babylonian and Aramean became, alongside Iranian, official languages of the empire. In all the satrapies royal edicts were issued bilingually, in the local language and in one of the official languages. Schools for scribes were set up in the three capitals of Susa, Babylon and Ecbatana, as well as at the seat of government of every satrapy.

The empire was divided into twenty satrapies, not drawn according to former national frontiers, but conceived as cultural or economic units. Thus it was that Asia Minor was made up of four satrapies, while Egypt and Cyrene were grouped in a single one; Mesopotamia, as well as Syria, was unified.

A viceroy was appointed in each satrapy, alongside whom a chancellor controlled the police and a general commanded the army. These three high officials, whose offices were independent of one another, depended directly on the king. Travelling agents of the king had the duty of controlling the administration of the satrapies; on the basis of their reports the king passed judgment without hearing any defence from the incriminated satraps.

Each satrap governed by superimposing his authority on existing local institutions. In Egypt and in Babylon nothing was changed in the administration save that some local governors were replaced by Iranians. The satrap represented the king and received tribute in his name. This tribute was fixed in a uniform manner for the whole empire at ten per cent of the land tax and was payable in precious metals. This basis for the royal tax system favoured the middle classes in the cities, since income from trade was not reckoned in the calculation of the tribute. On the other hand, it had the advantage of assuring a stable and regular yield, which enabled the Persian kings to avoid fiscal crises and to accumulate immense reserves of metal; Alexander was to find at Susa a treasure of 180,000 talents of silver.[1] The land tax made the great agrarian regions of the East the basis of the Empire. They furnished an annual tribute of 3,320 talents, while Egypt, Syria and Asia Minor together only paid 2,810 talents and Mesopotamia 1,600 talents. Only the Indus, a gold-producing region, incorporated by Darius in his empire, paid a tribute which was not calculated on land; its part, paid in gold dust, represented the enormous sum of 4,071 talents.

The tribute paid by the satrapies served to cover the imperial expenses; those of the court, the army, and public works, mainly the construction of roads built according to the precedent of the kings of Sardes. The vital artery of the empire was the Susa-Sardes road, nearly fifteen hundred miles long, which the royal couriers covered in a week.

ECONOMIC AND SOCIAL POLICY

Fiscal organization was complemented by monetary policy. Darius minted gold '*darics*' of 8.41 gr, the first coins to bear a royal effigy, and silver drachmas, which became the only coins to have currency throughout the empire. This enormous work, the stabilization of monetary unity throughout all Nearer Asia, was supplemented by the unification of the system of weights and measures on the Babylonian model. Trade and banking thus received a considerable stimulus. Capitalism developed to such an extent that a Lydian business man could possess, in ready cash, two thousand talents of silver and four million gold *darics*.[2] Credit developed and interest rates fell to 12%.[3]

[1] The Alexandrian talent weighed just over 57·5 lb.
[2] The Babylonian talent weighed about 66 lbs.
[3] About 715 BC Bocchoris had fixed interest rates in Egypt as 33% and in Babylon, at the same period, the interest rate was 20%.

Save for these great imperial reforms, Darius continued, in the various countries over which he reigned, to carry on a policy in accordance with their traditions. In Egypt he accentuated the lay character of the Saite policy; the temples remained under civil administration and their revenues were handed over to the treasury; marriage remained a civil contract rather than a religious rite.

But in social matters, relying upon the conservative parties, he reacted against the democratic tendencies of the reign of Amasis. Certain measures considered too radical were repealed, such as that which had granted scholarships to young men of slender means to allow them to attend the medical school at Sais.

This trend towards a policy of tempered democracy—which was to be continued by Alexander and also by the Roman Empire—led Darius to re-examine all the laws promulgated since the advent of Amasis and to publish a Code of Egyptian Law. This was the first great legislative undertaking since Hammurabi. Its completion was entrusted to a commission of notables in which, this time, members of the priesthood took part. It sat from 519 to 503 BC. The Code of Darius gave the Egyptian Law of Contract the form it was to preserve intact throughout the whole Ptolemean period until the times of the Roman Empire. It was published in Egyptian, Aramean and Iranian. It is interesting to note that in Egypt this great juridical development coincided with a moral movement of purely religious inspiration which foreshadows the Christian moral code.

In the economic field Darius continued the policy of improving agriculture and encouraging the development of private trade that the Saite kings had practised with such success. Liberal economy, both in Egypt and throughout the whole empire, then reached its highest point, thanks to the advantages granted to trade by the unity of the Persian Empire.

Necho had undertaken the construction of a great navigable canal across the Isthmus of Suez; Darius was to complete it.

This was the greatest achievement of his reign. By putting the Mediterranean into direct contact with the Red Sea and the Indian Ocean, Darius was pursuing a vast design, that of uniting in a single economic system Egypt, Mesopotamia and India, now for the first time all united in a single state.

CHAPTER XXII

THE PERSIAN EMPIRE AND ASIA

EXPANSION OF THE EMPIRE TOWARDS INDIA AND CHINA

THE annexation of the Indus basin by the Persian Empire was a historical event of the greatest importance. The economic policy of Darius was clearly aimed at establishing a link between the economies of the Mediterranean and Central Asia and the Far East. By founding Cyropolis on the Jaxartes, Cyrus had already been looking toward the caravan routes which led through Central Asia to China. Darius, installed on the Indus, immediately undertook a policy intended to include India within the economics of the Empire.

INDIA IN THE VIth CENTURY

For many centuries now, certainly since the times of the Aryan invasion, the Indus basin had fallen into decadence. It was in the Ganges basin that the Aryan civilization had developed, in the form of a feudal society which, after a long evolution, had reached, by the times of Darius, the monarchical stage. Cities created by trade had sprung up along the river, and the middle classes in them had already acquired such prosperity that they equalled in importance the large landowners. Organized in trade guilds, they showed a great spirit of initiative. Caravans of traders set out regularly for the western sea-coast where they reached the great Dravidian port of Barygaza (Baroch), which looked westward. On the Gulf of Bengal another port, Tamralipti, formed a link between the Ganges area and southern India, Ceylon, Indo-China and the Malay archipelago.

The Ganges basin was not only an important commercial centre, but it also became the centre of a moral and religious movement which was to play a major role throughout the whole history of Asia.

BUDDHISM

The cult of Vishnu—at first symbolized by the phallus, like the cult of Osiris—had little by little become transformed into a mystical religion striving towards the search for perfection, whence had emerged the conception of asceticism. Orders of religious mendicants tried by inner contemplation to draw nearer to the great god Brahma, master of everything. As in Egypt, the creator-god was conceived as a pure spirit, made evident in creation. The essence of man was therefore spiritual; salvation consisted in taking cognisance of man's relation with the 'Great All', that is God himself. This idealistic and pantheist conception of the world, which so closely recalls the solar theology elaborated at Memphis, markedly departed from it, however, in the effect that it exercised upon the faithful. In Egypt the spiritual pantheism, considering tangible things as material realizations of the divine thought, resulted in an optimistic conception of the world that impelled men to action. In India, on the contrary, by assimilating the spirit to good and matter to evil, Brahmanism resulted in a scorn for terrestial life and a search for the supreme good in Nirvana which, by dissociating man from the world, integrates him with God. This tendency had, about 750 BC, taken the form of Jainism which preached in order to avoid all evil, a penitence that went so far as death by wasting away.

The Buddha, Sakyamuni (560–483 BC), who lived in the times of Darius, was one of the seekers after Nirvana. He taught asceticism and renunciation of worldly possessions but also, for those who did not feel themselves capable of this, the practice of goodness, modesty and tolerance. Male and female convents were founded to practise the total passivity preached by the Buddha.

India thus presented a double and contradictory aspect, that of a people amongst whom trade had developed to an exceptional degree and at the same time a mysticism that was pushing its moral élite towards an absolute nihilism.

TRADE BETWEEN INDIA AND THE WEST

Darius, master of the Indus, tried to restore its economic life. The decay was so great in the Punjab that navigation on the river had ceased. Darius sent the Greek admiral Scylax to discover into which sea it ran. He founded a port at its mouth, launched a fleet on the Persian Gulf and sent it, sailing along the coasts of Arabia, to reach Egypt by way of the Red Sea. After thirty months sail Scylax arrived at his destination. Darius went to Egypt to await him there. The arrival of the Indian fleet decided the Great King to order the completion of the canal, fifty yards across, that was to pierce the isthmus of Suez.

At the moment of its inauguration a fleet left the Mediterranean in the presence of the king to reach Persia by way of India.

The opening of the Suez canal was to have a decisive influence on the history of Nearer Asia and of Egypt. Henceforward, Mesopotamia was no longer the great trade-route of the West to India. The sea was to dethrone the land. Egypt was to find herself called upon to play the role which had up till then given such great prosperity to Babylon. The destinies of Egypt were now assured: she was to become the meeting place of East and West. Two centuries were enough to effect this profound change in the economic life of the world; it was to result in the decline of Mesopotamia and the advent of the Roman Empire.

India, because of the Suez canal, was to become part of the economic life of the West.

Cyropolis was to play a similar role with regard to China.

China, which had hitherto existed outside all direct contact with the world of Nearer Asia, was little by little to come closer to western economy.

CHINA

While in the third millenary BC Egypt and Mesopotamia had reached the peak of their development in the first period of their history, the first elements of Chinese civilization appeared in the valley of the Huang-Ho. By the second millenary it made its way up the valley of the Wei westwards, reached Shantung on the east and moved southward towards the Han and the Huai-Ho. Writing, in a still archaic form, appeared in the XIIth century BC. At this time Chinese civilization, still entirely feudal, had already reached a high level, as is proved by the beauty of its bronzes. Trade relations began to be established westwards; the caravan route was opened by way of the great oases inhabited by the Aryan Tokharians, a people apparently akin to the Iranians.

THE MANORIAL CHOU EMPIRE

All this time China remained predominantly agricultural. She possessed no real urban centres and the sea played no part in her economy. Her religion, which still included human sacrifices during funeral rites, had no moral code. The gods intervened in human affairs by oracles.

In the twelfth century, therefore, the Chinese monarchy represented a society far less developed than Egypt, Sumeria or the Indus in the third millenary. The social unit was the hereditary fief; the population on it were slaves and tied to the soil; but there already existed, in every domain, at least in the basin of the Huang-Ho, a princely governor who acted as leader of the cult and its rites, who organized instruction and fixed the tasks of cultivation according to an astrological calendar, a leader of the army which was conscripted, a judge who apprehended criminals and an industrial leader who presided over arts and crafts.

In this society, founded on a feudal and aristocratic basis, a code of morals developed which was based on the 'five social relations'; of sovereign to subject, father to son, husband to wife, friend to friend, and young to old.

For centuries, under the Chou dynasty which gave it its first unity, China went on living in this state of social equilibrium which had been given it by the manorial system, a mosaic of fiefs under the authority of a king who alone acted as a bond in this vast territorial state.

But little by little a literate class was formed around the princes, whose power continued to increase. Local wars gave rise to federations between lordships. Sovereign principalities were created among the fiefs and the vast empire disintegrated in the VIIth century into a feudalism rent by intestine wars.

At the same time a social movement began which aimed at the emancipation of the serfs, and a number of local lords were murdered by their tenants.

Social and political evolution advanced rapidly.

In the VIth century BC feudal kingdoms appeared, the more powerful states absorbing the others. Among these states that of Tsin, a fief constituted in the IXth century for a court official, became the most important. It was situated in the east of China, in the area where the caravan routes from Central Asia and India ended. In China the desert played the role that the sea had played in Egypt.

LAO-TSE AND CONFUCIUS

At the beginning of the VIth century BC China entered a fresh period of her history, marked by a great intellectual and moral development. Two great philosophers, Lao-Tse (born in 604 BC) and Kong-fu-Tse (Confucius: born in 552 BC), were to leave on China the definite imprint of their thought. Lao-Tse, the Chinese Plato, formulated an idealist philosophy which saw true reality in pure thought. Nothing exists save thought. The material world is therefore only an illusion of the senses, and wisdom consists of inaction, since thought alone is free. From the doctrine of Lao-Tse—which one cannot avoid associating with Brahmanism—arose the mysticism which had so profound an effect on the history of China and was a preparation for the success that Buddhism was to have there.

As in all the great religions of the ancient world the doctrine of Lao-Tse was pantheist; the aim of man was to merge himself, by way of thought, with God, the Great All.

In direct contrast to the doctrine of Lao-Tse, idealist but pessimist like that of Buddha, Confucius taught a code of morals based on tangible reality which, he said, must be made use of in the best manner possible. His method is scientific; his aim is action, the reform of civilization, the search for the general happiness of the people. The gentleman must transform society by his example. Power must be based on order and justice.

The moral code of Confucius was to become the basis of political order in China.

MONARCHICAL EVOLUTION

These two divergent philosophical currents reflect exactly the crisis through which China was passing in the VIth century BC. The monarchical idea was opposed to feudalism and tended towards the emancipation of the poverty-stricken people by the destruction of the rich feudal lords.

In the state of Tsin great reforms were carried out, human sacrifices were abolished and a tax on grain replaced the feudal dues (which was equivalent to an emancipation of the serfs), and the system of weights and measures was unified as in Persia. The closed economy, which had existed in the manorial period, broke down before the economy of trade. Exchanges multiplied and contacts with India by the caravan routes continued to increase.

It was at this time, when China was beginning her monarchical evolution, emancipating the serfs and developing her trade, that Darius first entered into trade relations with her. International trade was now to expand rapidly over Asia.

The Phoenicians in the XIth century BC had opened to the West the vast domain of Mediterrranean trade. In the VIth century BC the continent of Asia—India and China—revealed unsuspected opportunities to the Western peoples.

The Persian Empire, situated between the Mediterranean and Asia, appeared as a possible centre for a universal empire.

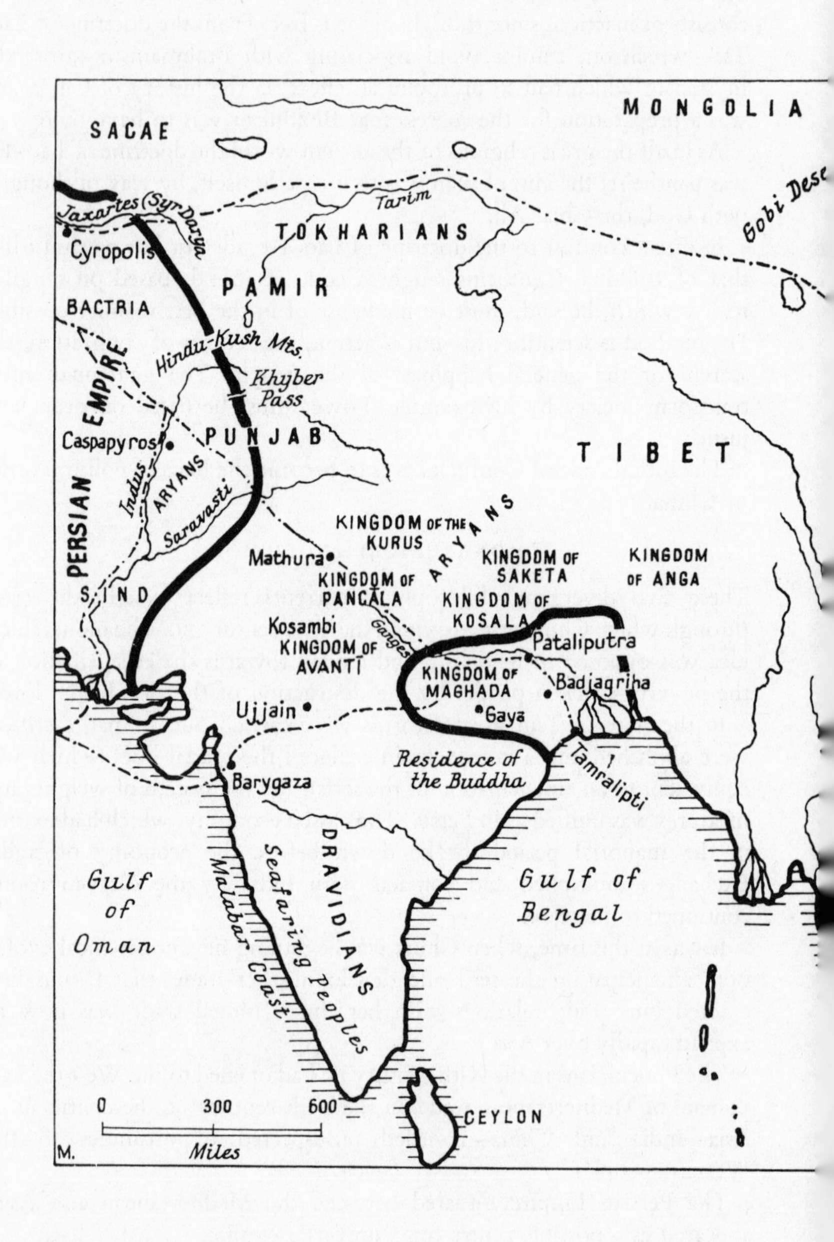
MONGOLIA
SACAE
Gobi Desert
Jaxartes (Syr Darya)
Tarim
TOKHARIANS
Cyropolis
PAMIR
BACTRIA
Hindu-Kush Mts.
PERSIAN EMPIRE
Khyber Pass
Caspapyros
PUNJAB
TIBET
Indus
ARYANS
Saravasti
ARYANS
KINGDOM OF THE KURUS
Mathura
KINGDOM OF SAKETA
KINGDOM OF ANGA
SIND
KINGDOM OF PANCALA
KINGDOM OF KOSALA
Kosambi
KINGDOM OF AVANTI
Ganges
Pataliputra
KINGDOM OF MAGHADA
Badjagriha
Gaya
Ujjain
Residence of the Buddha
Tamralipti
Barygaza
DRAVIDIANS
Seafaring Peoples
Malabar Coast
Gulf of Oman
Gulf of Bengal
0
300
600
Miles
CEYLON
M.

Map No. 17

Huang-ho
PTY. OF CH'AO
PTY. OF WEI
PTY. OF CH'I
MONIC
PALITY OF
CH'IN WEI
Yong
KINGDOM
Wang-Cheng
OF CHOU
Huai-ho
BARBARIAN STATE
OF CH'U
BARBARIAN STATE
OF WU
Yang-tze Kiang
China Sea
INDIA AND CHINA at the time of
Darius (521-486 B.C.)
Trade Routes

CHAPTER XXIII

THE PERSIAN EMPIRE AND EUROPE THE PERSIAN WARS

THE SCYTHIAN CAMPAIGN

THE organization of imperial trade at which Darius was aiming could not be conceived without the Mediterranean. In order to integrate the Mediterranean into the Empire, Cambyses had already undertaken an expedition against Carthage. It failed. Darius, however, adopted a policy of alliance with Carthage. But, before trying to subjugate the Greek world, he turned northward.

The Scythians, who formed a branch of the Iranian race, had settled on the steppes of the Black Sea and central Russia as far as Turkestan. Though they had become settled cultivators in the basins of the great Russian rivers, in the areas around the Caspian and on the European steppes they had remained nomads. By conquering their vast territories, Darius would have saved the Empire from their terrible forays which, at the close of the VIIth century, had led to the downfall of Nineveh; he would also have assured himself vast reserves of grain, the mastery of the Black Sea and the mines of the Caucasus, and control of the trade-routes for tin and amber.

In order to obtain the alliance of Carthage, Darius had carried out a policy favourable to the Phoenician cities. But this had resulted in a crisis for the Ionian ports. By extending his rule into Europe he would have opened vast possibilities for trade expansion to the Ionian cities which the Greek trading posts, founded on the northern shores of the Black Sea, had already begun to exploit in their expeditions up the Russian rivers.

The Ionian cities therefore took part with enthusiasm in the campaign against the Scythians. It failed. But it was not without result. It allowed Darius to create the satrapy of Thrace and impose his protectorate on feudal Macedonia; but the Danubian regions and the northern coasts of the Black Sea remained free.

REVOLT OF THE IONIAN CITIES

The failure of the Scythian campaign was a great disappointment for the Ionian cities and the Greek colonies on the Black Sea. Their position was made all the worse since not only did the Phoenician ships bar their way to the Eastern Mediterranean, but the destruction of Sybaris by Croton, depriving them of their principal market in the west, had caused a serious crisis in their export trade. The cities of the Hellespont revolted and were soon joined by those of Ionia. An Ionian Congress met. It decided that the combined fleet of the Ionian cities should try to take Byzantium in order to control the Black Sea and to conquer Cyprus and drive out the Phoenician trading posts there. A common currency was introduced for all the Ionian cities. Only Ephesus and Colophon, whose temples were under the influence of the Persian magi, refused to take part in the revolt. The tyrants set up by the Persian kings were driven out and democracy re-established. Athens and Sparta were appealed to for aid. Sparta, hostile to the democrats, refused. Athens, where the popular party had triumphed under Cleisthenes, sent a fleet and a military contingent. The struggle with the Persian Empire for the mastery of the seas began. At the same time it assumed the form of a crusade for democracy.

In 499 BC an army composed of Milesians and Athenians took and burnt Sardes.

Darius made no move. He tried at first to find a peaceful outcome to the conflict. But not being able to find one, he took the field with his army in 494 BC. The Persian Wars had begun.

THE FIRST PERSIAN WAR

The Ionian cities were sea-powers. It was therefore at sea that they must be defeated. A great Persian fleet of six hundred Egyptian, Phoenician and Cypriot vessels destroyed the three hundred and fifty ships of the Ionian fleet. Miletus, which had been at the head of the revolt, was razed to the ground and its people deported to the banks of the Tigris (494 BC).

But it was not enough to conquer Ionia alone; Persia had to win command of the sea, because of the sea-borne activities of the Ionian cities. It was not possible to separate the cities of Asia Minor from the Greek economy without ruining them. Asia Minor owed its wealth to the sea alone. It was therefore necessary either to assure Persian control of the sea-borne trade, of which the cities of Asia Minor were an essential part, or to conquer Greece. This alternative was the more pressing inasmuch as, since the opening of the Suez canal, the wealth of Egypt, which was an essential factor in the economy of the Empire, no longer depended on the prosperity of Nearer Asia, but essentially on sea-borne trade.

The Persian Empire had therefore either to resign itself to becoming a continental and Asiatic empire and accept the loss of its richest provinces, Ionia and Egypt, or to obtain control of the Mediterranean trade by subduing Greece.

Darius at first tried to take possession of Greece peacefully, by conciliating the Ionians and seeking an alliance with Carthage.

In 492 BC he summoned the delegates of the Ionian cities to Sardes to tell them of their new status. The system of tyrannies set up by Cyrus was abandoned and democratic governments restored in all the cities; they were allowed to keep their autonomy in all internal affairs and granted the right to maintain diplomatic relations among themselves and even abroad, but they were not given the right to make war. Darius insisted on becoming the mediator in all conflicts which might arise between them; and finally a new land-survey, on a rigorous and exact basis, was introduced to stabilize the tribute, a very moderate one, to which they were subject.

These wise measures, which restored the internal security of the Ionian cities and assured peace amongst them, were so well received that the cities renounced the close alliance that had been formed between the democratic parties of Ionia and Athens. The democratic alliance fell to pieces.

All that now remained to Darius was to extend his rule over Greece proper and he set himself to the task by clever diplomatic action aimed at dividing the Greek states, blind to everything save their own special interests.

Corinth, a maritime and trading power, did not concern herself with the Persian conquests; her interests were in the West and the ruin of her rival, Miletus, favoured her expansion. Argos, a land state threatened by Sparta, was ready to rely upon Persia to defend her. Aegina could conceive of no policy save one that could lead, even with the aid of Darius, to the downfall of Athens, her most dangerous commercial rival. The Thessalian and Phocaean feudal lords were constantly at war with one another and the Thessalians were already thinking of turning to Darius as an ally. As to the smaller cities, they remained totally indifferent to international politics, being entirely preoccupied with their local and immediate interests. Only Sparta, hoping for territorial hegemony in Greece, and Athens, aiming at mastery of the Aegean Sea and the straits of the Hellespont, were resolved to defend themselves against Persian ascendancy. But their internal politics were troubled. At Sparta, the two kings, Demarates and

Cleomenes, one advocating the strictly aristocratic policy and the other a policy of hegemony, had each formed their own party and the loser, Demarates, had fled to the court of Darius. At Athens, Hippias, driven from power, had also taken refuge at the court of the Great King and asked for his help. Persian agents travelled through Greece, Sicily and southern Italy to learn what they could about the chances of an invasion and to form parties favourable to Darius. Already the king's agents had obtained assurances of submission from all sides, when Sparta and Athens, refusing to concede 'the earth and the sea' as Persia demanded, concluded a close alliance to resist the formidable and hitherto unconquered Persian army which had begun to march against them. In 490 BC, on the plains of Marathon, at the moment when the oligarchic party in Athens was already preparing to recover power by handing the city over to the enemy, the little army of Athenian democracy crushed the mighty military machine of the great Persian Empire. Darius' dream of universal empire vanished.

CRISIS OF THE PERSIAN EMPIRE UNDER XERXES (485–464 BC)

The defeat of Darius at Marathon had immense repercussions throughout the Empire. At his death (485 BC) Egypt rebelled. Babylon, going through a serious economic crisis because of the deviation of traffic through the Suez canal and the decline of Phoenician sea-borne trade due to the blockade by Greek ships, in her turn rebelled. In order to reduce the city, Xerxes sacked it in so terrible a manner than it was never afterwards to recover its ancient splendour. But by destroying Babylon, he diminished still more the importance of the continental trade-routes to the advantage of sea-borne trade, and consequently of Egypt. This incredible error was to have fatal consequences for the Persian Empire. Nearer Asia, finding itself faced by the sea-borne economy dominated by Greece and Egypt, was to become more and more attracted by the vast feudal provinces of the Empire and Central Asia, while the Phoenician cities, involved in the decline of Babylon, were no longer able to compete with the maritime supremacy of the Greek cities.

The struggle between the continent and Greece was imminent. Xerxes declared himself the champion of Asia. He tried to create an Asian unity against Greece, recalling the Greek provocation to Asia in the sack of Troy and evoking the Asian origin of Pelops—to whom the Peloponnesus owed its name—to justify the domination of Asia over Greece. To realize his plans, Xerxes did not invoke, as had the Pharaohs, a theory of sovereignty based on divine right, but relied on the unity of the Asian continent, which, however, did not exist. This Asiatic policy, which abandoned the universalism professed by Darius, was associated with a real Persian nationalism. Xerxes declared himself a Persian king, inspired by Ahura-Mazda and no longer by Marduk or Ammon; his council was no longer cosmopolitan but Persian. In his empire the 'non-Asiatics' would have only the inferior status of 'subject peoples'. To justify the war that he was preparing, the king announced that the submission of Greece would imply the submission of Europe to Asia.

A great imperial army was levied, which marched under the lash, made up, if Herodotus is to be believed, of several hundreds of thousands of men. Twenty-four thousand Persians formed the shock-troops. The fleet, which numbered twelve hundred ships, included Phoenician, Ionian, Egyptian and Cypriot squadrons. Such great forces had never before been assembled.

While he was preparing to attack continental Greece, Xerxes sought for an alliance with Carthage against the Greeks of Sicily, who were deeply divided amongst themselves. Gela and Agrigentum were united against Selinonte and Syracuse, which had not hesitated to ask for aid from Carthage. But in 482 BC Gelon, tyrant of Gela, captured Syracuse. Thenceforward, governing Sicily as a monarch, he set himself up as the champion of Hellenism and rallied all the Greek cities against the Carthaginian threat.

In Greece, too, Athens and Sparta had set themselves at the head of a national movement by forming the Panhellenic League which was made up of thirty-five cities and opposed seventy-five thousand men and three hundred and seventy-eight ships to the Persian menace.

The Greek world faced up to the onslaught of Asia, which was ready to encircle it from east and west.

In 480 BC Xerxes, after breaking through the pass of Thermopylae and taking Athens, was beaten by Themistocles, the leader of the Athenian democratic party, at the great naval battle of Salamis, while powerful Carthaginian forces, commanded by Hamilcar, were destroyed by Gelon before Himera.

Victorious on both fronts, Greece took the offensive. In 479 BC she defeated the Persian army at Plataea and the Athenian fleet defeated the naval forces of Xerxes off Cape Mycale. Definitely beaten at sea, the Great King lost Ionia which again took its place in the Greek world.

MARITIME AND SPIRITUAL SUPREMACY OF ATHENS

All the Greek maritime cities rallied around victorious Athens which, at the head of the Delian League founded in 477 BC, assured herself within a few years an uncontested naval supremacy. A little later, the triumph of the democratic party under Pericles made Athens the centre of the great movement of social emancipation which was then felt in all the maritime cities. After Ionia and Magna Graecia, it was now the turn of Athens to become the centre of Greek civilization. Callicrates and Ictinus built the Parthenon and Mnesicles the Propylaea; Phidias, surrounded by a magnificent school of sculptors who came from every part of the Greek world, and the Ionian painters gave Athens an incomparable artistic splendour. The greatest of the Greek thinkers were to settle within her walls. By breaking down the narrow framework of Athenian thought, limited to the cult and the interests of the city, they were to prepare Athens for her great role, both intellectual and economic. Naturally this did not take place without crises. The Ionian Anaxagoras, by professing a philosophy of nature which conceived the sun as a mass of incandescent matter and the moon as a material body, deeply offended the beliefs of the devout middle classes who formed the majority of the Athenian civic body. They reacted by condemning him to death for having denied the divinity of the sun. But the Ionian trend was to overwhelm even them. Herodotus, by revealing to his readers the manners of all the peoples of his time, civilized and barbarian, was to make them aware of the world around them.

It was at Athens too that the drama, the glory of classic Greek literature, was to reach its height. Born out of the Dionysiac chorus brought to Corinth by Arion of Methymna in the time of Periander, the art of the theatre found its first real expression in Athens when Phrynichus in 493 BC staged the taking of Miletus. But it was really only with Aeschylus that tragedy first made its appearance.

Aeschylus, a former aristocrat of Eleusis, still restricted himself to religious dramas; but they already served only as a framework for the study of moral problems. With *The Persians*, which displays the author's admiration for the genius of Darius, the breath of a universalist way of thinking was felt in Athens.

A few years later Sophocles, the son of an industrialist, who had attended the lectures of the Ionian philosophers abandoned theology to devote himself to human nature, while Euripides, representing the intellectual middle classes, showed himself a freethinker, who, above all else, searched for moral truth.

In contrast to Oriental civilization, Greek thought, now fully mature, laid the foundations of a new world.

THE PERSIAN EMPIRE DRIVEN BACK TO ASIA

The victory of Themistocles, while it gave Athens the mastery of the seas and grouped around her all the vital forces of Greece, ruined for ever the plan for a universal Persian Empire. Reduced to becoming no more than an immense land state, Persia was to restrict herself to a continental policy which was to lead her kings to exercise a more and more despotic power. A prisoner of the land, which it was to consider more and more as its inherited patrimony, the Achaemenid dynasty was to become involved in interminable family quarrels, while the isolation of the provinces, left to their own devices, was to drive the Empire towards feudal dismemberment. Thrown back from the sea, landlocked and absolutist, Persia turned eastward and withdrew into a continental economy. Mesopotamia, formerly the great international artery, was dethroned by the seaways and gradually became a route of secondary importance. The Achaemenids amassed in their luxurious palace at Persepolis the fabulous treasures that the land-tax created by Darius still poured into their coffers, but economic activity, moving more and more coastward, was to detach the maritime provinces of the Empire one after the other and to group them into a new economy dominated by Greece and Egypt.

Thus two economies opposed one another, the one continental, the other Mediterranean. They corresponded to two divergent political and social systems, the first absolutist, manorial and aristocratic, the other democratic, commercial and individualist.

This was doubtless not a conscious political divergence; Xerxes did not deliberately pursue a continental policy. Repulsed from the Mediterranean, he seems to have wanted to look for compensation on more distant seas. He ordered a circumnavigation of Africa, which failed. In fact the continental policy was forced upon him because the land, and the aristocratic system that it presupposed, became the preponderant influence. The nobility, therefore, dominated the Empire. Xerxes was assassinated, victim of a reaction of the Persian aristocracy against the policy of royal centralization. The monarchy, restored by Artaxerxes I (464–424 BC), was constantly to struggle against the movement of feudal dismemberment which was finally to cause its ruin.

BOOK V

The Predominance of Maritime Economy and the Formation of Hellenistic Civilization. Vth to IVth Centuries BC

CHAPTER XXIV

THE MARITIME EMPIRE OF ATHENS

THE DELIAN LEAGUE

AFTER the victory at Mycale, Athens had become a great naval and economic power. Adopting a strictly mercantile policy, she made the Piraeus one of the finest ports on the Mediterranean, open to foreigners who were exempted from taxes, and established herself on the Hellespont so as to ensure commercial supremacy in the Black Sea.

In 477 BC the Panhellenic League, formed against Persia, broke up. In 476 BC Athens convoked a great congress of maritime cities, which resulted in the formation of the Delian League. This was soon to number two hundred member-cities spread throughout the whole Aegean and Black Sea region.

The League, grouped around the ancient sanctuary of Delos and under the presidency of Athens, was formed to organize the defence of the Greek world against Persia. The Federal Council, in which every city had a vote, fixed the share of each of the allies in the expenses of maintaining the fleet—which had a strength of two hundred ships, manned by forty thousand sailors—and acted as arbitrator in any disputes which might arise between members.

As centre of this vast maritime federation, Athens became an international market of the first order. Its population increased rapidly; besides 47,000 citizens, representing 188,000 souls, it soon counted 30,000 *metoikoi* (resident foreigners) and 200,000 slaves. Personal wealth increased so rapidly that from 490 to 431 BC it rose from 2,000 to 25,000 talents; interest rates fell to 12%. The land—thanks to the system of mortgages introduced at this time in Athens—became a source of credit. Banking, in the hands of foreigners, expanded rapidly and great fortunes were made in the exploitation of the silver mines of Laurion. A class of capitalists was created which soon acquired enormous influence in the city.

Athens was therefore passing through a brilliant period of economic liberalism. The theory of *laissez faire* gave foreigners, in business matters,

ILLYRIA
Epidamnus
Strymon
T H R
Apollonia
Aigai
Pella
Amphipolis
MACEDONIA
CHALCIDICE
Pydna
Olynthus
Mt. Olympus
Potidea
Larissa
Corcyra
EPIRUS
THESSALY
PROVIN
II
Dodona
Pharsalus
Ambracia
Thermopylae
LEUCADIA
ACARNANIA
AETOLIA
PHOCIS
Naupactus
Delphi
BOEOTIA
Chalc
CEPHALONIA
Thebes
Aiyon
Leuctres
Plataea
Eleusis
ACHAIA
Megara
Sicyon
Corinth
Ath
ZACYNTHUS
Olympia
SALAMIS
Aegina
PIRAEUS
LAUR
PELOPONNESIAN
Argos
MESSENIA
Mantinea
LEAGUE
Sparta
LACONIA
THE MARITIME EMPIRE OF ATHENS
DIVIDED INTO FIVE FISCAL PROVINCES
AND THE PELOPONNESIAN LEAGUE
(5TH. CENTURY B.C.)

Map No. 18

E
Abdera
Mesembria
Selymbria
Byzantium
Chalcedon
PROVINCE OF THE HELLESPONT
III
SAMOTHRACE
THRACE
Sestos
Lampsacus
Cyzicus
Dascylium
IMBROS
Abydos
LEMNOS
HELLESPONT
AEOLIS
MYSIA
I
IV
VINCE
Methymna
Mitylene
LYDIA
PROVINCE OF IONIA
Phocoea
Cyme
PERSIAN EMPIRE
Sardes
OF THE
Erythrae
Clazomene
CHIOS
Teos
ISLES
Colophon
Lebedos
ANDROS
Ephesus
SAMOS
IONIA
TENOS
Priene
Cape Mycale
Miletus
DELOS
PROVINCE OF CARIA
PAROS
NAXOS
Myndus
Ceramus
V
LEROS
Halicarnassus
CARIA
COS
AMORGOS
MELOS
Cnidus
Telmissus
Lorima
THERA
RHODES

a status equal to citizens, and the moderate customs duties which never exceeded 2·5% attracted an immense traffic to the Pireaus.

PERICLES AND ATHENIAN DEMOCRACY

With economic freedom and free-trade, democracy also triumphed; it was to give Athens her period of greatness under the wise direction of Pericles (462–429 BC). Thucydides attributes to him this fine definition: 'The democratic state must strive to serve the greatest number of its citizens, to preserve the equality of all before the law and to work in such a way that the liberty of the citizens derives from the liberty of the state. It must give aid to the weak and call men of merit to the highest posts. The harmonious balance between the interests of the state and the interests of the individuals who compose it ensures the political, economic, intellectual and artistic advancement of the city, protecting the state against the egotism of individuals and protecting the individual, thanks to the constitution, against the arbitrary action of the state'.

The state, in the democratic conception, rested on a real social contract defined by Demosthenes as a 'universal contract to which all in the city must conform in their way of life'.

From all sides the democratic parties, not only in the Greek cities but also in Egypt, turned to Athens which declared herself their protector. In 464 BC, after the assassination of Xerxes, the national and democratic party in Egypt rose in revolt and appealed to Pericles who, without hesitation, sent all the forces of the League to its aid. In 459 BC the Athenian fleet sailed up the Nile, drove the Persian garrison out of Memphis and restored Egyptian independence. But, profiting by this expedition so far afield, Sparta—whose landowning aristocracy looked with hostility on the military and economic power of democratic Athens—threw herself on her rival. Athens was forced to recall a part of her army. She triumphed over Sparta, but the squadron and the contingents left in Egypt were overwhelmed by the Persian army sent to the rescue. Egypt fell once more under the yoke and the loss of almost half its fleet placed the Delian League, and with it Athens, within a hairsbreadth of ruin.

THE IMPERIALIST POLICY OF ATHENS

Pericles saved the situation by strongly centralizing the League under the authority of Athens and making the cause of democracy rather than the feeling for Greek patriotism the cement of the alliance. The Athenian democratic constitution was imposed upon all the cities of the League. The treasury was moved to Athens. The Federal Council was replaced by the Athenian Assembly and the powers of arbitration that it had held were transferred to the Athenian courts, whose competence was extended not only to public disputes between cities but also to criminal cases and to all commercial litigation arising out of contracts concluded at Athens.

This reform which unified democratic institutions, commercial and criminal law on the basis of absolute equality of the citizens, whether of Athens or of her allies, turned the League into a real state under Athenian leadership. Trade agreements concluded with all the cities in identical terms assured them the freedom of the seas and of trade. The famous Athenian 'owls'—which became the most sought-after coinage of the time—were imposed on the whole League and, save for Ephesus which retained the right to issue her own coins, Athens reserved the monopoly of minting. The system of weights and measures was also unified.

This great attempt to collect in a single unit the whole economic life of the Greek cities involved a policy of peace. In 449 BC Athens concluded a treaty with Artaxerxes, by which Persia entirely abandoned the Aegean Sea whereas Athens renounced any intervention in Asia. In 446 BC another agreement, concluded with Sparta, divided hegemony between the two cities; the Peloponnesus went to Sparta and the sea to Athens.

Athens immediately set out to create, under her own leadership, a general agreement between all the Greeks. In 446 BC she summoned a Panhellenic Congress, but Spartan hostility caused it to fail. Athens was forced to fall back upon her maritime league alone, which she tried to unite closely on the basis of the mystical cult of Demeter and Dionysus, exactly corresponding to the Egyptian cult of Isis and Osiris. As in Egypt, democracy was accompanied by a mystical movement.

The Athenian policy, however, was destined to failure for two reasons; one within Athens herself and the other external.

Within Athens because, although democratic, Athens had never been liberal in her policy. Her narrow nationalism always prevented her from extending the privileges of the city to foreigners, even those who had been resident for several generations and who, by their commercial, industrial and financial activities, had made her wealthy. The majority in the assembly of the people were petty landed proprietors, artisans and sailors, jealous of the privileges that their status as citizens gave them. Though a great international metropolis and mistress of a maritime empire, Athens was ruled by an electoral body of petty bourgeois, patriotic and capable of great enthusiasms but grasping and superstitious. They acclaimed the works of Sophocles but they condemned to death Anaxagoras—whose life Pericles was barely able to save—because he had taught that the sun was not a god.

Between the élite—composed in great part of *metoikoi*, intellectuals and artists as well as business men—and the popular masses, masters of the *ecclesia*, a lack of concord always existed which prevented Athens from freeing herself from the viewpoint of a policy limited to the immediate interests of the city.

City nationalism was not, however, limited to Athenian democracy. It showed itself even more impervious at Corinth, which was governed by an oligarchy of business men, and in aristocratic and landowning Sparta.

These nationalisms embittered the economic and political rivalries that ranged the little Greek states against one another. Corinth dominated the Adriatic and aimed at hegemony in the West, as Athens dominated the Aegean and the Black Seas. No agreement could ever be concluded between the two rivals. Sparta, whose policy of hegemony on land was threatened by the democratic influence of Athens in Boeotia, in Locris and in Phocis, was to remain implacably hostile.

Between Sparta, landlocked and aristocratic, and Corinth, maritime and oligarchic, an alliance was concluded against Athens.

Thus the Greek world destroyed itself. Not only did leadership on sea conflict with leadership on land, but on the sea itself the rivalry between Athens and Corinth prevented Greek economic life from finding a stable balance. Athens alone tried to consolidate Greece, but by imposing a supremacy which neither Corinth nor the great western cities like Syracuse and Tarentum could accept. For this reason she failed.

Obliged to renounce his policy of consolidation and leadership, Pericles took up an openly aggressive attitude towards Corinth. Not being able to subject it to his protectorate, he tried to overthrow it by restricting free trade and commercial liberty to the allies of Athens. Thenceforward, war was inevitable. In 431 BC, as a result of the closure of the League markets to the traders of Megara, Corinth took up their cause and appealed to Sparta. The Peloponnesian wars, which were to lead to the ruin of Greek maritime supremacy, began.

CHAPTER XXV

THE POLITICAL DISINTEGRATION OF THE EAST

THE PERSIAN EMPIRE AFTER XERXES

THE loss of Ionia, the insurrections in Egypt after the death of Xerxes and the Egypto-Athenian alliance in 460 BC which resulted from them created an ever clearer separation between the continental part of the Persian Empire and its maritime provinces. Artaxerxes, it is true, restored Persian authority in Egypt. Although, thanks to the treaty concluded with Athens in 449 BC, Persia recovered Egypt the resultant period of unbroken peace made Egyptian trade relations with the Greek world easier and drew Egypt more and more into the Mediterranean economy. After the opening of the Suez canal Egypt took a greater and greater share in the trade between the West and India and assumed the role formerly played by Babylon.

For Persia the peace of 449 BC thus meant the beginning of her political disintegration. Driven back into Asia, where since the downfall of Babylon the landed aristocracy prevailed, the Persian Empire was to break up among the satraps who, in accordance with the feudal ideas of Persia, considered themselves the equals of the king and took a more and more independent stand. At the death of Artaxerxes in 424 BC the king's relatives tried, amid palace tragedies, to carve out princely appanages for themselves and plunged the Empire into a governmental crisis.

THE PELOPONNESIAN WAR AND THE RETURN OF PERSIA

While Persia was disintegrating, Greece became divided into two hostile camps. In 431 BC war broke out between Sparta, leader of the Peloponnesian League allied with Corinth, and Athens and her maritime empire. The pretext was a rivalry of economic interests between Megara and Athens, but it was soon to become clear where the real contest lay; it was a struggle between two hegemonies, one military, the other naval, and between two ideologies, one oligarchic, the other democratic, and two systems, one—that of Sparta—aiming at splitting Greece among autonomous cities, and the other—that of Athens—aiming at Greek unity under a single control.

Athens possessed, at this time, both wealth and prestige. But she was to become divided within herself. In 429 BC the death of Pericles delivered the city over to party strife. The smallholders and the property-owning bourgeois under Nicias were for peace, while the common people and the arms manufacturers under Cleon were for war. The war party won, and democratic reforms placed the financial burden of the conflict on the rich and on the cities of the League. Ten years of war resulted in the exhaustion of both Sparta and Athens. In 421 BC Nicias signed a peace that restored the *status quo* of 431 BC and made provision for arbitration in the event of further conflict.

But peace also revived the ancient rivalry between Corinth and Athens. Athens, led on by Alcibiades, thought the moment propitious to carry out a policy of large scale hegemony extending as far as the Central Mediterranean. A great military expedition was prepared with the intention of overthrowing the power of Syracuse and so ruining Corinth and at the same time uniting Greek economic life under Athenian supremacy.

After the victory of Gelon over Hamilcar in 480 BC, Syracuse had known a period of prosperity and, under the military tyranny of Hieron, it had at one time seemed possible that she could achieve the unity of Sicily. But after 445 BC the island was divided between the cities, and internal strife had broken out again. Athens hoped to profit by this.

However, as soon as Athens revealed her intention of intervening in Sicily, a congress, at which most of the Sicilian cities were represented, expressed its will to resist her (424 BC), proclaiming the principle of 'Sicily for the Sicilians'. Athens paid no heed and in 415 BC, with Leontini and Segesta, sent powerful forces against Syracuse. It was a terrible disaster (413 BC). The whole Athenian army was lost. Sparta at once took advantage of this defeat to deal Athens the deathblow. Athens was saved only by the internal dissensions of her enemies. The democratic riots which broke out in Syracuse after her victory prevented her from carrying on the war efficiently, and Sparta, which had counted on the resources of Syracuse, did not hesitate to turn to the Persian king, whose financial resources were inexhaustible, for the money and ships she lacked. In 412 BC Sparta solicited the alliance of the Great King, ceding him, in return for subsidies, the Ionian cities, allies of Athens.

The Sicilian disaster had shaken the democratic government in Athens. Ten commissars, entrusted with full powers, were nominated to assess the responsibility. The aristocratic party, controlled from afar by Alcibiades who had taken refuge at the Persian court, carried on the struggle against democracy; Alcibiades let it be understood that the abolition of the Laws of Solon and Pericles would be the price of Persian alliance with Athens against Sparta.

The war between the Greeks gave Persian diplomacy the unhoped for chance of reviving the imperial policy. Persian garrisons occupied Ionia. The Athenian League hesitated. Athens, confronted by this danger, mobilized all her forces. But the aristocratic party, profiting by the absence of the great majority of the citizens who were with the fleet, succeeded in staging a *coup d'état* which overthrew democracy; power was entrusted to an oligarchic council of four hundred members charged with designating five thousand active citizens; all other Athenians lost their political rights (411 BC).

Faced with this betrayal, the Athenian fleet, which had just restored democracy to Samos, established the headquarters of the democratic party there, in opposition to the oligarchic government at Athens. The council of the Four Hundred appealed to Sparta. But Sparta was defeated at sea and, in 410 BC, democracy was restored in Athens.

Sparta, relying more and more upon the Persian alliance, built a fleet with the gold of the Achaemenids and, in 405 BC, defeated the Athenian squadrons at Aegospotami. Athens, blockaded and reduced to famine, capitulated (404 BC). The Athenian empire and democracy fell and, on the ruins of their greatness, the aristocratic party assumed power. The government was handed over to thirty tyrants and the courts to five hundred oligarchs. The reaction initiated a policy of terror and proscriptions; democrats and *metoikoi* were hunted down and their goods confiscated while, supported by Sparta which thus completed the downfall of Athens, the masters of the moment limited to three thousand the number of citizens entitled to bear arms. The aristocracy built their triumph on the ruin of their country.

The hegemony of Athens was to be succeeded by the hegemony of Sparta.

RESTORATION OF EGYPTIAN INDEPENDENCE AND THE POLITICAL COLLAPSE OF GREECE

The capitulation of Athens in 404 BC gave Persia supremacy in the Aegean. But this success did not compensate for the disaster she was to undergo by losing Egypt. In 410 BC, while democracy was being restored in Athens, an insurrection broke out throughout the Delta, which culminated in the coronation of Amyrtaeus at Mendes and in 404 BC Darius II, unable to undertake a great expedition against Egypt, recognized her independence.

The Eastern Mediterranean was then entering a period of political confusion. In 403 BC the Thirty Tyrants were overthrown at Athens and democracy restored. Sparta, allied to the King of Persia, found herself involved in the dynastic struggles that followed the death of Darius II (404 BC) and was dragged into the war against King Artaxerxes II (404–358 BC).[1] Egypt rebuilt her navy and tried to make an alliance with Greece against Persia. It was therefore to Sparta—and no longer to Athens, her ancient ally—that she turned, hoping thus to gain the support of Syracuse which had remained the ally of Sparta since 415 BC. The system of alliances was, from now on, reversed. Persian diplomacy, no longer in fear of Athens, supported her against Sparta, now the ally of Egypt. Athens entered a League created by Corinth, her former rival, and both allied themselves with Thebes which, mistress of Boeotia, aimed at disputing territorial hegemony with Sparta.

This time it was Athens which, supported by Persian gold, destroyed the Spartiate fleet (394 BC). The victory aroused a wave of enthusiasm in Athens. The democrats dreamed of restoring Athenian power and, imputing the cause of its downfall to the abandonment of the ideal of the city, energetically pursued a nationalist policy.

Athens was at this time in the midst of crisis, not only political but moral. The Milesian philosophers had ended by formulating, with Leucippus and Democritus, the materialist theory of atoms. Scientific thought became dissociated from religion as represented by the mystery cults. The sophists undertook the examination of all accepted values, but they only ended in total scepticism. It was then that Socrates, a man of the people, posed the problem in its moral aspect; he brought to Athens the humanist code of morals which had triumphed in Egypt and which, built on universal principles—self-control, the golden mean, respect for others—did not fit in with Athenian civic ideas, which were confined to the narrow limits of the city. The moral code of Socrates, derived from natural law which regarded all men, citizens or not, as equal, and from the idea of divinity conceived as the universal conscience, was considered a crime by the Athenian nationalists; the Assembly of the People sentenced him to drink hemlock (399 BC).

[1] After the 'anabasis' of the Ten Thousand sent to Asia by Sparta to support the claims of Cyrus the Younger against his brother, Artaxerxes II.

At this time the economic prosperity of Athens, as a result of the flourishing state of international trade, revived rapidly. Banking, mining, shipbuilding—in great part in the hands of foreigners—created great capitalist fortunes. Corinth and Syracuse had become great industrial powers. Rhodes had taken her place among the more important transit centres. But international trade, which had enriched the Greek cities, was no longer compatible with the restricted framework of the city-state. The nationalism of Athens was an archaism that could only lead to fresh crises.

Egypt, enjoying great prosperity under the reign of Achoris (392–380 BC), tried to force Athens and the island of Cyprus into a naval alliance against Persia. Athens adhered to the alliance, rebuilt her fleet and prepared to restore her empire.

But Sparta was on the alert. At all costs she wanted to prevent Athens from forming a Greek maritime bloc. In 392 BC, in order to forestall her, Sparta convoked a congress at which she proposed a universal peace on the basis of the autonomy of all the cities. It was to ensure, by the parcelling out of Greece, her inevitable decline, but it meant also the domination of the Peloponnesian League and the hegemony of Sparta. Athens refused. Sparta, once again, offered alliance to Persia, promising her, as well as Ionia, the islands of Cyprus and Chios, on condition that she imposed on Greece perpetual peace based on the autonomy of the cities. The Greeks therefore placed themselves under Persian protectorate and the Satrap of Sardes in 392 BC summoned the Greek ambassadors in the King's name in order to propose to them the plan elaborated by Sparta. But Athens refused to sanction the abandonment of Ionia to Persia. The court of Susa avoided war and limited itself to economic sanctions, closing the Straits (387 BC). A serious crisis resulted. Syracuse, allied to Sparta and fearing the renascence of Athens, offered her co-operation to restore 'the King's peace'. Faced with mounting threats and impelled by the trade crisis resulting from the closing of the Black Sea, the delegates of all the Greek cities met at Sardes to hear the Satrap, in the King's name, dictate to them a peace which fixed their status (386 BC). Never before had diplomacy spoken in this tone. Persia restated the theory of universal sovereignty. The Greek cities became petty states and the instrument of their decline was their own autonomy which reduced them to impotence and obliged them to accept the protection of the Great King, under whom, for the first time, the unity of Greece was attained.

To return to the great imperial policy of Darius, it only remained for Artaxerxes II to reconquer Egypt.

POLITICAL COLLAPSE OF EGYPT

Egypt, which had just recovered its independence, was enjoying unparalleled prosperity. But, like Greece, it was undermined by party strife in which the urban bourgeoisie and the sacerdotal oligarchy were the opposite poles. To the Mendes dynasty, enthroned after the rebellion of the cities, the priestly party opposed the governor of Sebennytos, Nectanebo. He seized the throne and, in 378 BC, founded a new dynasty (378–360 BC). Obliged to rely upon the priests, the throne abandoned the lay policy of the Saite kings and of the Persian government, restored the administration of their properties to the temples and made magnificent donations to them. But the priests were not satisfied; they wished to have their class privileges restored. In the midst of these internal troubles Egypt neglected to build up her army. In 373 BC a large Persian army invaded the country, but was halted by the Nile floods.

This check to the campaign against Egypt had immediate and far-reaching repercussions in Persia. In Phrygia and in Pontus the satraps proclaimed their independence and returned to the policy formerly pursued by Croesus, looking towards the Egypto-Athenian alliance. The cleavage between the continent and the sea was once more evident, since the trade of Asia Minor, of Greece and of Egypt was interdependent.

Athens, freed from the Persian menace, continued her new imperial policy with brilliant success. Seventy-five cities rallied around her reconstituted naval power. But she was no longer financially capable of meeting the costs of a great navy. Economic conditions had changed since the time of the Delian League. The political impotence of the system of city-states was only too evident. In 371 BC Athens, no longer able to hold out against Sparta which had Persian gold at its disposal, signed a peace which to all intents and purposes restored the 'King's peace' of 386 BC. For several years more she was to struggle to maintain her naval power, this time with the help of Syracuse, but she was no longer of a stature to sustain such an effort. Athens was now finally out of the running as a political force. She could not exist without the financial support of Egypt. Nectanebo, hostile to the democratic party which he did not want to strengthen by aiding Athens, committed the serious error of not granting her such support.

After the peace of 371 BC Egypt faced Persia alone. The policy of Nectanebo had utterly failed. All that remained for him to do was to abdicate in favour of his son Teos who feverishly made ready for war.

It was urgently necessary to reorganize the army. But the priests refused to make any sacrifices. The king turned to the cities, reintroduced conscription and raised 80,000 men and built a fleet of 250 triremes. But he needed allies. Reverting once more to the traditional policy of Egypt, he sought them in Greece.

Greece was now emerging from yet another civil war. By her victory at Leuctra (371 BC) Thebes had destroyed the military power of Sparta and for several years had claimed hegemony. Athens was brought closer to Sparta and Syracuse in opposition to her. Teos asked for their alliance and engaged the Spartan army as mercenaries under its king, Agesilaus, now reduced to the profession of *condottiere*.

Egypt, only recently restored to freedom, had not the reserves of precious metals to finance so great an effort. Fresh taxes were levied; on houses and on manufactured goods. Customs duties were raised to 10% *ad valorem*, and a forced loan was decreed that compelled all Egyptians to hand over their objects of gold and silver to the state. The loan was repayable by annual instalments and guaranteed by the poll-tax. It was the first State Loan of which we know.

The temples resisted. The King paid no heed and impounded 90% of their revenues.

From the precious metals that he had collected he struck silver coins bearing the Egyptian papyrus and the Athenian owl, symbols of the alliance of Egypt and Greece.

Teos understood that to defeat Persia he must first cut her off from the sea. He marched on Syria and gave financial support to the Satrap of Armenia who had revolted. Phoenicia was quickly conquered. But at this moment the priestly party betrayed him and proclaimed his nephew, Nectanebo II, as king, with the complicity of the king of Sparta, Agesilaus, who, although a general of mercenaries in Teos' service, had remained inclined to the oligarchic party which was represented in Egypt by the priests.

To satisfy a policy of social reaction the priestly party was to give the death blow to Egypt, even as fifty years earlier the Spartan oligarchy had sacrificed Greece.

Teos fled to the Persian court. Nectanebo II (359–342 BC), enthroned by the priests, restored to them the administration of their revenues and even granted them the customs dues and taxes on manufactures of the city of Naucratis. The people of the cities, called upon to support alone the burdens of the war, revolted. Without resources, Nectanebo sacrificed his fleet rather than see civil war break out again. To calm public opinion, he renounced conscription and returned to the policy of hiring a mercenary army.

Thus Egypt, more and more defenceless and undermined by civil strife, abandoned herself to the Persian menace.

Persia, it is true, was no longer a great power. The end of the reign of Artaxerxes II was marked by fresh palace dramas and the revolts of satraps. But there was no other country able to stand up to her. Greece, torn by a fresh struggle for hegemony between Thebes and Sparta, could no longer make war save with the aid of the Persian gold that the land-tax continued to pour into the treasuries of Susa. The huge feudal satrapies of Eastern Persia were inexhaustible sources of men and money. Artaxerxes III in 343 BC mustered all his forces against Egypt which, betrayed by the highest representatives of the ruling classes and abandoned by her Greek mercenaries, immediately collapsed.

Now master of Egypt, Artaxerxes III, by taking the Greek mercenaries of the Pharaohs into his pay, easily reconquered the revolted satrapies of Asia Minor. Nothing, it seemed, stood in the way of the realization of universal empire.

CHAPTER XXVI

THE GROWING IMPORTANCE OF THE WEST IN INTERNATIONAL TRADE

THE EMPIRE OF CARTHAGE

WHILE Athens at the head of the Delian League was dominating the shipping of the Aegean, Greeks and Phoenicians were fighting for leadership in the Central Mediterranean. Carthage, founded by Tyre about 800 BC, had rapidly become a powerful commercial metropolis. Her real greatness, however, dated only from the VIth century BC, when the sea-borne trade of Tyre in the West declined after the conquest of Phoenicia by Persia. It was Carthage that reaped the benefit of the great trade in silver and tin that Tyre had formerly carried on with Tartessos through Gades.

Since the VIIth century BC the Greeks had held control of the Straits of Messina. In the VIth, Marseilles had tried to extend her empire over the Tyrrhenian Sea, and, to prevent this expansion, Carthage had concluded an alliance with the Etruscans.

The Etruscans were not great seafarers. They had come to Italy from Lycia in Asia Minor and had settled in 'Etruria', where they had founded a number of cities, soon to be grouped into leagues. The port of Populonia made them look seaward, but their activities were mainly industrial. In the VIth century the Etruscan cities became very prosperous thanks to Greek and Carthaginian trade. Sybaris was the exchange mart for Milesian and Etruscan products. They came there by way of Paestum which served as a port of entry on the Tyrrhenian Sea. From that time the Etruscans entered on a period of great territorial and industrial development. In the north they had settled in the valley of the Po, and in the south had founded colonies as far as Capua and Salerno. The highway that linked the Etruscan cities of the north and south crossed the Tiber at Rome, a little township founded in the VIIth century BC where momentarily Etruscan tyrants were in power.

The Etruscan civilization, which had been greatly influenced by Crete, had a very advanced urban development and carried on an extensive trade. At the end of the VIth century BC their alliance with the Carthaginians drove the Massilians out of Corsica and Sardinia where they had founded trading posts.

The protection given by the Persian Kings to Tyrian shipping led, at the beginning of the Vth century BC, to an alliance between King Darius I, who was trying to obtain a foothold in the West, and Carthage. The Greeks thus found themselves encircled; in 480 BC Sicily had been attacked by a Carthaginian army under the command of Hamilcar at the very moment when Athens had been assailed by the army and fleet of Xerxes. But Hamilcar had been defeated at Himera and in 474 BC Syracuse had crushed the combined Carthaginian and Etruscan fleet at Cumae. From then on, Syracuse became a great naval power.

Carthage was at this time, however, mistress of a magnificent empire whose trading posts extended over all the shores of the western Mediterranean and even beyond the Pillars of Hercules, along the Spanish and Moroccan coasts.

The naval empires of Athens and Carthage were contemporaneous. But whereas democracy was triumphant in Athens, Carthage, like Tyre, was a royal city, ruled by the powerful Magon family which had become wealthy through trade. About 450 BC, at the same time as Tyre, Carthage had transformed herself into an aristocratic republic. Its institutions thenceforward were very similar to those of the Greek oligarchic cities. The assembly, made up of the property-owning middle class, elected the generals and the *suffetes*, and money played a predominant part in the elections. The people were excluded from political rights. The senate—it is not known how it was recruited—represented the oligarchy of traders. The *suffetes* were chosen from amongst the richest citizens. Justice was administered by a hundred judges chosen from the senators. The government, therefore, belonged to an aristocracy of money grouped around a few powerful families who competed with one another. As in the Greek cities, there were countless slaves who were employed in the industrial work-shops, the trading firms and the state administration.

The advent of the oligarchic régime in Carthage coincided with the greatest development of her wealth. In order to assure the provisioning of the city, Carthage at this time had taken possession of a vast hinterland, where the rich men carved out immense estates on which the natives were reduced to slavery. At the same time she was trying to find fresh trade outlets. Necho and Darius had set the example of great maritime enterprises, and about 450 BC Carthage in her turn sent exploring expeditions out into the ocean. Southward, her sailors explored the coasts of Africa as far as the Gulf of Guinea, set up trading posts in Morocco and Senegal and occupied the Canary Islands; northward, they reached the English Channel, in an endeavour to establish direct relations with Britain, the source of tin.

The Carthaginian Empire was organized in a manner similar to the Athenian. The cities which comprised it were autonomous, but Carthage alone kept control of the fleet of two hundred triremes and the army of mercenaries, which was maintained by the yield of the customs dues levied in all the cities. Furthermore, Carthage exploited the mines of Cartagena as a state monopoly. Trade was completely free in Carthage and Gades but, in the other cities of the Empire, Carthaginian shipowners had a monopoly of transport. Foreigners were excluded; Carthage aimed at preserving a monopoly of navigation over the whole African coast and as far as Sardinia and Corsica, at Cyrene and at Malta, and in all the Spanish ports with the exception of Gades, which remained open to the Greeks. The policy of democratic Athens was liberal; that of aristocratic Carthage was based on monopoly. Thus the rivalry between Greeks and Carthaginians was intensified by the contrast between two conflicting economic systems.

Carthage disposed of resources far greater than those of Athens and Syracuse. None the less, she did not issue coins before the close of the Vth century BC. Her first coins were minted to pay her mercenaries. The system was similar to that in force in Egypt. The Greeks were the first to introduce money in the West, as Darius had been in the East. But monetary economy was far more active in Greece than in Asia or Egypt, where it played only a subsidiary role until the times of the Ptolemies.

From 480 BC the rivalry between Carthage and Syracuse had become intense. The two great cities were constantly at war. Carthage had one great advantage in the struggle for no conflict ever broke out between the Phoenician colonies, while the Greek cities were continually at odds with one another.

THE EMPIRES OF SYRACUSE AND TARENTUM

The collapse of the Athenian Empire did not mean the end of Greek maritime power, but only that it moved westward.

Athens had attempted to form a Panhellenic Empire by imposing her rule on Sicily. This ended in a terrible disaster (413 BC). But once Athens had been vanquished, the democratic party at Syracuse was able to overthrow the military tyranny and take over the government. Carthage profited by these disorders to invade Sicily. On the pretext of coming to the aid of Segesta, Hannibal in 406 BC destroyed Selinonte and Himera and annexed Agrigentum. Thus, at the very moment when the downfall of Athens gave Persia control of continental Greece, Sicily was being seriously threatened by Carthage.

It was then that Dionysus, elected general by the people of Syracuse (406 BC), re-established the tyranny and, after crushing the aristocratic party, prepared for the struggle against Carthage by building a fleet of two hundred ships and raising a mercenary army of fifty thousand men. All methods were good enough to raise the necessary funds; taxes, customs dues, confiscation of the property of political opponents, a 20% capital levy and debasement of the coinage, the first example of this known to history.

To create a common front against Carthage, he unified Sicily by force under his personal rule and had all the Semitic merchants massacred. His luxurious court attracted philosophers and historians from all parts of the Greek world, who grouped themselves around Plato.

Like Sicily, Magna Graecia was at this time concentrated in a confederation around Croton (392 BC).

In Greece, on the other hand, Sparta, allied to Syracuse which helped her to impose the King's Peace on Athens (386 BC), remained the only major power among a galaxy of autonomous cities.

It seemed as if the Greek world were tending towards two hegemonies, the one maritime under Syracuse, the other territorial under Sparta. But in fact the hegemony of Sparta was only an illusion which concealed the decline of Greece and her submission to Persia. Syracuse, on the other hand, was extending rapidly over Magna Graecia. She annexed Croton in 379 BC and was only halted by Tarentum.

Tarentum was at that time governed by a tyrant who was none other than the philosopher Archytas, the friend of Plato. He had endowed his city with an army and navy, equipped, thanks to his mathematical discoveries, with a real artillery-train of catapults. Commerce, art, philosophical enlightenment, all flourished equally under his wise and humane government.

Syracuse shared the hegemony with Tarentum; she kept for herself Sicily with Rhegion, Locri and the Straits of Messina, leaving to Tarentum the rest of Magna Graecia as far as Naples. To protect their possessions, the two Greek empires combined against the barbarians of the interior.

Two great Greek maritime cities had tried to rally around them the whole of the Greek world. In 371 BC Athens had seen the collapse of her attempt, at one time so brilliant, to reconstitute her empire; of her former possessions she now kept only the Straits of the Hellespont. Dionysus tried to come to terms with her in 367 BC, whereas Tarentum was closely associated with Cyrene, the only great Greek city on the African coast.

The alliance of three great Greek cities, Syracuse, Tarentum and Athens, should have been able to exercise an incontestable mastery in the Mediterranean, but the death of Dionysus brought back the scourge of civil war. In a few years the struggle between the popular party and the party of the landowners and merchants led to the collapse of the empires of Syracuse and Tarentum, and the natives of the peninsula were seething with unrest. Rome, intervening for the first time in Greek politics, made an alliance with the Samnites against Tarentum, and the Carthaginians disembarked in Sicily. Exhausted by civil war, Syracuse called on Corinth for aid. Corinth sent her Timoleon, who restored peace and gave the city a government based on the middle classes. On this basis, peace was established throughout all Sicily. Carthage, which attacked at this moment, was defeated (341 BC). Timoleon had saved Hellenism. His task accomplished, he retired to the country, to an estate voted him by the people.

The democratic régime based on the census set up by Timoleon did not disappear with his death. Social peace was maintained and foreigners from all sides flowed into peaceful Sicily. The cities destroyed by Carthage were rebuilt. The last tyrannies disappeared. Peace was concluded with Carthage (339 BC) and Sicily became immensely prosperous. The system of government by the middle classes, which was inaugurated there, was to have an enormous influence in the whole Mediterranean and was to be adopted, a few years later, by Alexander the Great. It was to become the normal régime for cities in the Hellenistic period.

At this time, continental Greece was politically stagnant. Egypt, reconquered by Persia, was in eclipse. Sicily appeared as the centre of Greek economic life.

Only two sea-powers remained to face Persia and escaped her rule; Greek Sicily and the sea-power of Carthage. The centre of sea-borne trade had shifted westward. The central Mediterranean would henceforward be an essential element of international life in the maritime and economic, and very soon also in the political, field.

CHAPTER XXVII

THE BEGINNINGS OF ROME

THE ORIGINS OF ROME

THE expansion of the Carthaginians, the Etruscans and the Greeks had brought into the international arena the coasts of Africa, Sicily, Magna Graecia, Campania, Etruria, Provence and the western and southern coasts of Spain; but central Italy, less suitable for maritime expansion, for a long time went on living on the outskirts, sufficient unto itself.

In the Xth and IXth centuries BC the Latins had settled in Latium. In about the VIIth century BC a group of villages, Alban, Sabine and Latin, of differing races, languages and religions, peopled by immigrants and natives, formed a little League, the League of Septimontium, or the Seven Hills. It was a purely agricultural community ruled by landholding nobles under whose patriarchal authority lived a population of tenants. The nobles were grouped into *curiae*, until a federation of these *curiae* led to a political organization under a Council of Elders, the Senate, which nominated a king.

THE ETRUSCAN TYRANNY

Etruscan influence had made itself felt in this little primitive community since the VIth century BC. Rome was situated on the highway that linked the Greek cities of the south with Etruria; the Etruscans, spreading southward, had gained a foothold in Rome where they built a wooden bridge, and set up as tyrant Tarquin, the son of an emigré aristocrat from Corinth and an Etruscan woman. He introduced the first institutions of the city and superimposed on the ancient religion of the mother-goddess Ceres and the fertility god Jupiter a national cult devoted to the Capitoline Trinity—Jupiter, Venus and Juno. A small commercial enterprise exploited the salt-pans of the Tiber estuary. Tarquin was succeeded by a king, apparently a Latin named Servius, who enclosed the citadel with walls. But a new Etruscan tyrant appeared, a descendant of Tarquin, who governed in a manner similar to the Greek tyrants, then in their full glory. He undertook an extensive programme of public works, broke the power of the large landholders and admitted into the army the small property-owners, liberated from the power of the nobles.

THE ARISTOCRATIC PERIOD

About the time of the fall of the Peisistratids in Athens, Tarquin the Proud was overthrown by an aristocratic revolt.[1] It was then that the Roman *gentes* appeared in the form in which we know them. Like the Greek *genè*, these were derived from the families of the former landholding lords dispossessed of the sovereign rights which they had once held over their lands. They became the seventeen rustic tribes which formed a nobility that entrusted its powers to two consuls chosen from amongst its members.

Roman society thenceforward was divided into nobles (patricians) and plebeians. The nobles lived under a patriarchal law, had their own family cults, considered their properties as inalienable, practised communal responsibility and waged private wars. The tenants on their lands were clients, entirely under their authority. The plebeians were either smallholders who had formerly been dependent on the nobles, or newcomers to the city who had, since the time of Tarquin, become Roman citizens. They had a more individualist law than the nobles, did not recognize the inalienability of family possessions or communal responsibility; but were dependent for justice on the nobles who retained this prerogative of their former authority as sovereign lords. In the city, the plebs were grouped about the nature-worship cult, symbolized by the mother-goddess Ceres; the nobles celebrated the cult of the god of Heaven, Jupiter, who, like Zeus in Greece, was the royal god.

Although citizens, the plebeians had no part in the political life of the city. Their military leaders were the tribunes and they made these tribunes and the *aediles*, who were guardians of the temple of Ceres, their political leaders. It was under their protection that they made their first social claims.

Deprived of land, for the nobles possessed almost the entire territory of the city, the plebeians revolted; but on their threat to emigrate, they were granted parcels of land taken from the *ager publicus* (commonland)[2] and

[1] The classic date is 509 BC. But right up to the IVth century BC the greater number of the traditional dates of Roman history are based on calculations made much later and quite certainly are mostly incorrect.

[2] Public lands conquered from neighbouring peoples.

were allowed a share in the political life of the State, being granted the right of electing their own tribunes and of meeting legally under their presidency.

The distribution of land to the plebeians settled the social problem. But, once introduced into the active life of the city, the plebeians did not delay in demanding the codification of the laws under which they lived. A ten-member commission, the Decemviri, was set up which, like the *aesymnetes* in the Greek cities, was charged with codifying the law. This resulted in the Law of the Twelve Tables (about 450 BC) which shows evident analogies with the first forms of Greek law. It corresponds, in the evolution of Rome, to the Draconian Laws in Athens. It recognized a single and uniform private law for both nobles and plebeians which was none other than the plebeian custom; it declared land to be alienable, even for the patrimonies of the nobles, abolished communal responsibility, only retaining the authority of the *paterfamilias*, and substituted for the former practice of private war a criminal code enforced by an obligatory arbitration tribunal for all citizens.

Legal equality once established between nobles and plebeians, it was naturally only a question of time before the privileges of the nobles disappeared. The system of nobility, which made political status depend upon birth, was replaced by a system based upon the census; citizens were henceforth graded according to their wealth. Rome followed step by step, but only after a delay of two centuries, the evolution of Athens.

The army was organized according to the census classes and divided into *centuries* which, transferred to the political field, little by little took the place of the ancient and aristocratic framework of the assembly of *curiae*, substituting for it the assembly of centuries. Thereafter nobles and plebeians were merged into the same political groups. Socially, the contrast between rich and poor began to be of greater importance than that between patricians and plebeians.

At this time, Rome together with the other Latin cities formed part of a religious confederation of the type we have already noted, in the dawn of their history, among the Egyptians, the Sumerians, the Hittites and the Greeks.

This confederation waged petty local wars against the neighbouring mountain peoples, the Volscians, the Aequi and the Etruscans. But at the same time contact with the Etruscans civilized Rome and made her responsive to Greek influence.

During the Vth century BC Rome passed through a period of stagnation. This was a reaction to the events of Greek history. The downfall of

Sybaris in 510 BC, and the defeat of the combined fleets of the Carthaginians and Etruscans by Syracuse near Cumae in 474 BC, led to the decline of the Etruscan cities in the north and the Greek cities of southern Italy. This meant the isolation of Rome.

Little by little, however, Greek merchants began to appear again in the Aventine markets and, by the balance established between the values of livestock and of copper, metal ingots began to be used as means of payment. A foreign class of plebeians infiltrated into Rome and brought with them the first specialized crafts known there, thus creating an urban proletariat.

At the same time Rome was expanding, through conquests in her immediate vicinity carried out by the most primitive methods. The lands of the conquered villages were confiscated, save those of a few great families, and the populations taken to Rome where they swelled the number of plebeians.

It was at this stage in her evolution that Rome fell, about 382 BC, to a raiding party of Gauls who, coming from the Danube valley, had invaded the valley of the Po and thence pushed southward.

This invasion had a decisive influence on the history of the Mediterranean. The Po was permanently occupied by the Gauls, and the Etruscan expansion, which might eventually have been enforced on Rome, was halted.

DEMOCRATIC EVOLUTION

In Rome the invasion was followed by a period of anarchy and social unrest. The government was confided to officials (military tribunes), whose office was open to the plebeians. The social crisis was ended in 366 BC by a series of reforms that reduced debts, regulated the use of the public lands in such a way as to allow the plebeians to reap greater advantage from them, and divided the consulship between patricians and plebeians.

Once again the social question was solved by the extension of smallholding. And the plebs, or at least the richer amongst them, saw the way to political power open before them.

The reform carried out in Rome after the invasion of 382 BC seems like an echo, albeit on a lower plane of civilization, of the reforms of Solon in Athens in 594 BC.

This democratic evolution was forced upon Rome by the need to struggle against neighbouring peoples who threatened her independence. She needed soldiers and, consequently, citizens. Faced with the danger from without, the Roman patricians had the wisdom to understand that they could not strengthen the position of Rome without making concessions to the plebeians.

To ensure her defence Rome finally took possession of the Tiber estuary where Tarquin had already built a small port. A Roman colony was settled there. By setting foot on the seacoast, Rome entered a new phase of her history.

As at Athens under Solon, so democratic evolution at Rome coincided with more stable relations with the outside world. Rome began to take her place in international life. She stabilized her position by treaties with the Aequi, the Samnites and the Etruscans. In 348 BC she signed a treaty of friendship with Carthage by which the Phoenician metropolis undertook not to set up trading posts in Latium while, in exchange, Rome allowed her every latitude outside those frontiers.

The control of the mouth of the Tiber by Rome led to a rapid increase in her population and gave her an evident supremacy over the other cities of the Latin confederation, which she ended by annexing after a three years war (338–335 BC).

A LIBERAL POLICY MAKES ROME THE CENTRE OF A REPUBLICAN STATE

Rome thenceforward was a territorial state. It was at this stage of her history that her evolution begins to differ from that of the Greek cities.

Sparta, once she had become a territorial state, had tried to maintain the supremacy of her citizens by transforming them into a military nobility which alone had political rights; by doing so, she cut short her own evolution.

Rome, on the other hand, after having annexed Latium, conferred individually on many of the Latins the right of Roman citizenship. She renounced, generally speaking, her former methods of confiscation of conquered lands and left the Latin owners in possession. The new Latin citizens were grouped into 'tribes' which joined the seventeen rustic tribes formerly made up of the Roman landholding nobility and the four urban tribes into which the plebeians of the city had been divided and formed with them the framework of the city administration. By making the Latins Roman citizens and accepting into her body politic, with remarkable liberalism, all the foreigners and even the freedmen who had swelled the Roman plebs, she ceased to be a city and became a state. Doing what no Greek city had ever thought of doing, she was, henceforward, and as her conquests extended, to grant progressively to the conquered peoples the private rights of her own citizens and even their political rights. By enlarging the framework of the city, she was to strengthen her army which she could thus continue to recruit from Roman citizens.

This liberal—and entirely novel—idea of the extension of the rights of citizenship to the annexed populations allowed Rome to become a real state without relinquishing her republican institutions. Alone among the democracies she was to succeed in founding a territorial empire, because she alone had the wisdom to bind the conquered peoples to her and make them a part of the republic by practising a liberal policy towards them.

Certainly the number of plebs who were flocking into Rome was also increasing, but as Rome expanded she assimilated them by reforms. A half-century after the conquest of Latium she underwent a great democratic reorganization by which the Assembly of Centuries which had become the real political assembly of the republic was freed from the tutelage of the Senate which was compelled to ratify all its decisions in advance. The Senate, moreover, was made up of officers of state who had completed their term of office and thus lost little by little, as the plebeians were admitted to the consulship, its aristocratic character. The people became sovereign. However, the accession of the people to power was only to take place gradually. Rich and poor were, it is true, all included within the centuries. But in the centurial assemblies, voting was by centuries and the richer classes held more than a half of the centuries while the proletariat, who were not liable to military service, were all inscribed in a single one.[1] No Roman was excluded from political rights, but only property owners made the laws and elected the magistrates.

However, the poor plebs, whose number was continually increasing, claimed a more effective participation in power. In 337 BC Rome conceded this by permitting them, united in *concilia plebis* (peoples' committees), to vote plebiscites which were obligatory for every citizen. About the same time, a reform inspired by Egypt and Athens proclaiming the principle of *habeas corpus* was to open a new phase for Rome. In 326 BC, surpassing by her liberalism all the Greek cities, Athens excepted, Rome suppressed slavery for debt, thus opening for the people, as Cicero was to say later, a new era of liberty.

A democratic and territorial state, with an army of free citizens, Rome was making ready to take her place in international life.

[1] The seven census classes amounted in all to 193 centuries. The *equites* (those who possessed a horse) formed 18 centuries, the rich landowners 80 centuries, the middle and small owners 90 centuries; the craftsmen had only four. Finally, the proletarians, that is to say those whose only fortune was their children, were all united in a single century.

CHAPTER XXVIII

INDIVIDUALISM IN EGYPT PAVES THE WAY TO HELLENISTIC CIVILIZATION

POLITICAL, ECONOMIC AND SOCIAL FACTORS

THE main feature of the history of the Mediterranean area, from the time of the Persian wars up till Alexander the Great, was the formation, by the rapprochement of Egypt and Greece, of a common civilization.

This community of interest was first shown in the form of trade which united the maritime countries of the eastern Mediterranean and extended more and more westwards. Doubtless there was a considerable difference between the economy of the seacoast lands of the Near East and that of Greece. The former was created slowly, by the exploitation of agricultural products and the creation of an industry born of the needs of the countries themselves, and which was the work of free men. Commerce, which arose out of the need for basic necessities, slowly became transit trade and later export industry. Greece, on the other hand, developed during a period when trade was already organized, and devoted herself—as formerly the people of Byblos and the Phoenicians had done—to transit trade. The Greeks were above all middlemen; export industry was only developed in Greece to supply return freights for their ships. As Greece lacked manual workers, she created an industry based on slave-labour, and slave-trading became a very profitable industry.

The Greek economy was mainly one of middlemen and therefore the use of money developed much more rapidly in Greece than in Egypt. There was a similar phenomenon at Babylon. If banking developed there so extensively before the XXth century BC, this was because transit trade was the essential basis of Mesopotamian economy.

In Egypt where trade was mainly based on barter, finance and money only played a subsidiary role until the times when, under the Ptolemies, Alexandria became the busiest centre of international transit trade.

But precisely because its role was that of a middleman, Greek trade became complementary to Egyptian trade. After the opening of the Suez canal, the two became inseparable.

That is why it was essentially liberal. In Greece, customs duties never exceeded 2·5%. Egypt, also liberal in principle, none the less taxed Greek imports with a duty of 10% at the beginning of the IVth century BC in order to protect her home industries.

The interpenetration of Mediterranean trade introduced in all the sea-coast countries, not only in Greece and Egypt but also in Asia Minor and Syria, a similar social system, marked by the development of the cities and the urban middle classes. Here too, it is true, there were marked differences. In Egypt, the cities were very old, wealthy and well built; they had taken their place in the monarchical state. Local politics played only a small part in city life. Slavery did not exist, or hardly existed, among the urban population. In Greece as well as in Phoenicia the cities were autonomous and dominated by their local politics. Socially, it was mainly the existence of a great slave-proletariat which distinguished the Greek cities from those of the Egyptian Delta.

But however different they might be, all these cities were subject to a similar social evolution, due to the growing importance of the wealthy middle classes and the popular movements that were a result of this. This evolution appeared, however, in a different form in Egypt and in Greece. The Egyptians, civilized for many ages past, courteous, individualist, accustomed to the legal equality of the sexes as well as to the political equality of all classes of society, possessed a great stability inherent in their moral ideas which made them respect things as they were; thus popular revolts occurred very seldom in Egyptian history and only when great crises threatened the very foundations of urban economy. There were, doubtless, local movements and social revolts in great cities like Sais, Bubastis, Mendes and Tanis, like the one that brought Amasis to power. But in the Greek cities, which were of recent formation and where social problems appeared as something new—by that time they had been long solved in Egypt—social unrest was endemic and often ended in bloodshed. Local democracy, by giving the people a power that no force outside the city could counterbalance, tended towards demagogy. The Greek cities had not got the social stability of the Egyptian cities and were not, like them, integral parts of a great state. In Egypt problems appeared in a national framework, in Greece in a local one. But both Greeks and Egyptians were dominated by the same tendency towards individualism.

In Greece the struggle, on the local plane, was between rich and poor.

In Egypt there were certainly echoes of a similar struggle, but the conflict went beyond the framework of any individual city; it was between the peoples of the cities as a whole and the priesthood, between the individualist and liberal conception of social and economic life and the aristocratic and manorial policy to which the temples constantly reverted. The conflict that we have seen in Greece between the commercial and the landholding classes, which found its expression in the constant wars between Athens and Sparta, was also to be found in Egypt, but within the state itself, between the urban population and the priests.

But despite these profound divergencies, the main lines of social and economic evolution were similar. They developed in a similar atmosphere of cosmopolitanism, which stifles nationalism, however narrow it may be. The Egyptians were more home-loving, and settled abroad less willingly than the Greeks and Phoenicians. It was because the Greeks were travelling merchants that they diffused their language everywhere and made it, from the VIth century BC onward, a *lingua franca* which was especially widespread in Egypt.

In the IVth century BC individualism led to a development of capitalism. Personal wealth increased. Banking played a more and more international role and even interfered in politics. The second maritime Empire of Athens was much more an enterprise of bankers and shipowners than a political plan. Commercial associations were common. Common interests brought the Greeks together, not only economic interests but also social interests. The property-owning classes and the proletariat had each a policy which was not limited by the bounds of the city. The middle-class democrats remained attached to it but, from the time of Socrates onward, the intellectuals were searching for a new formula. Neither from the economic, nor from the moral, viewpoint was the city any longer a sufficient framework. The complexity of trade, more and more international, caused class interests to predominate over political preoccupations. Both in Egypt and in Greece national sentiment weakened and this slackening of national bonds advanced hand in hand with the advent of new moral ideas.

The individual, rather than the city or the social group, became more and more the centre of society. Individualism triumphed in law by the appearance of theories of natural law, in economics by free trade and in art by portraiture.

THE MORAL AND RELIGIOUS PROBLEM

In Egypt the moral code had attained a high degree of humanism; it was essentially individualistic in the respect it paid to the human individual;

it was universalist also by the very fact that it considered man as an entity; to know oneself, control oneself, observe measure in all things, practise charity, mutual aid and courtesy; it was the Egyptian moral code that Socrates, no doubt unconsciously, brought to Greece. The Egyptian moral code was religious. For thirty centuries the Egyptian religion had been turned towards the beyond. It tended towards a monotheist pantheism. But at the same time democracy had developed mysticism which had shown itself in individual piety as well as in the processions and popular ceremonies of the cult. The local cults, turning to the gods and their symbols, were manifestations of love for all the aspects in which divinity was apparent. They must not be looked upon as a rudimentary zoolatry nor as a magic alien to religious ideas, but as a great outburst of piety. Magic, in the true sense of the word, doubtless existed, but it was not common in Egypt. Thus in reality the cult took the most varied forms and did not address itself solely to the gods but also to the sages who had known how to approach the divine, thus foreshadowing the cult of saints.

Alongside these popular manifestations of the cult, personal and individual piety assumed the most exalted forms.

But whatever its mode of expression, piety leads to the belief that religion possesses truth. The moral code becomes more and more dominated by religion. Since God is supreme justice, wisdom consists in submitting to him, of accepting his will even if sometimes it seems incomprehensible. Everything comes from God, evil as well as good. One must therefore refrain from judging one's neighbour, since God alone can do that. Already the problem is posed of how to reconcile individual liberty with divine omnipotence.

The religious influence of Egypt on the Mediterranean countries was enormous between the VIth and IVth centuries BC. A closer and closer syncretism was evident between the solar cults, which tended towards monotheism, and the nature cults which, conceived from a mystical vision, turned towards the world to come. Everywhere, as in Egypt, the solar religion and the nature cults began to merge; only the Jews escaped this mystical evolution despite the ascendancy that the Egyptian wisdom literature exercised on Biblical thought.

But elsewhere the cults became interpenetrated. In the Vth century BC Herodotus had already assimilated the Greek to the Egyptian gods from whom, he states, the Greek gods were derived. The cult of Osiris, associated for centuries in Syria with that of Adonis, is also associated with that of Dionysus. The mysteries of Eleusis, which also looked towards the future life, are entirely Egyptianized, and the initiation that the adepts received there seems clearly derived from the rites of priestly initiation practised in Egypt which aimed at 'liberating' the souls of the priests in a manner similar to the 'liberating' of the souls of the dead.

GREEK THOUGHT IN THE VTH AND IVTH CENTURIES BC

Greek philosophy, so deeply influenced by Egypt and the East during its Ionian period, remained throughout the Vth and IVth centuries BC in close contact with Egyptian thought. The Greeks never regarded the Egyptians as barbarians. They went to Egypt to be initiated into the religion and to learn Egyptian sciences. But Egyptian influence, which was direct on the scientific conclusions of the Milesians, on the spiritual concepts of Xenophanes and on the mysticism of Pythagoras, was only indirect on Heraclitus and his successors. Heraclitus retained the Egyptian idea of divinity, in which the absolute resolves all contraries; he also retained the doctrine according to which individual souls are only a part of the universal soul, but he diverged from the religious plane by rejecting the ideas of the creator-god and of individual survival. Empedocles combined Egyptian and Zoroastrian conceptions, but nothing is more foreign to Egyptian thought than the pessimism to which his idealism led him. Beginning, as in Egyptian theology, with the primacy of the spiritual over the material, he arrives at pessimism because, instead of assimilating, as did the Egyptians, the good to life since life is only the manifestation of the divine will, he ends up, by a reasoning analogous to that of Buddha or Lao-Tse, by considering life as an evil.

Egyptian influence, so strong in Ionia which had maintained close trade relations with Egypt, was scarcely felt in Magna Graecia, where commercial activity was mainly concerned with Carthage and the West. At the time when the Greek philosophers were moving away from Egyptian thought, the thinkers of Magna Graecia were turning towards materialism. Parmenides of Elea accepted it totally. Anaxagoras, on the other hand, being an Ionian from Clazomene, though like Parmenides he included scientific factors in his philosophy, kept the idea of God under the form of *nous*, the mind of the world, thereby returning to the Egyptian theology which conceived Ra, the great creator-god, as the *ka*, that is to say the mind, of the created universe.

With Leucippus and Democritus, Greek thought, departing more and more from Egyptian idealism, abandoned spiritual concepts for atomism. In consequence there was a more and more marked trend towards the materialism and scepticism of the Sophists which was to result in the subjectivism of Protagoras.

Thenceforward there was a clean break between the religious conceptions of Egypt and the philosophic attitude of Greece. Egyptian religion was sure that it possessed the truth. Greek philosophy, also searching for the truth, ended by denying the possibility of attaining it.

This crisis in Greek thought, which is evident in the attempt undertaken by the Sophists to revise all values, coincided with the crisis in democracy towards the end of the Vth century BC.

At this time the Sophists played a considerable role; they won the battle for freedom of thought and transferred to the universal plane the examination of political and philosophical problems. This was also the plane upon which Socrates had wished to place moral problems, and consequently law, which led to his condemnation to death.

The spiritual freedom, critical sense and universalism of the Sophists was to be found in various forms, but in characteristic manner, in all domains of Greek thought.

Euripides, in his tragedies which shocked the Athenian people even as the ideas of Socrates had shocked them, dissociates himself from the national plane and envisages moral problems under the universal aspect. Aristophanes, on the other hand, remains purely Athenian in his comedies,[1] but scourges the men and the institutions of his time with a freedom that stopped at nothing; even when he defends the traditional religion it is in such a tone that we cannot be sure if he is mocking or speaking seriously.

Thucydides, the great historian of the Peloponnesian war, applies to history the same methods as Socrates applied to morality. In searching for the origins of the Greek people he consigns the fables of mythology to oblivion, and while studying the distant causes of facts he probes into society even as Socrates tried to probe into the nature of man. The Athenian horizon continues to grow wider. Xenophon writes the *Cyropaedia* and Ctesias, who had been a doctor at the court of Susa, tells his readers about Asia with which the economic and intellectual bonds of Greece were becoming closer and closer. To crown this attitude of mind, Ephores writes a universal history.

Universalism, triumphant among the intellectual élite of Athens, was still far in advance of the opinions of the mass of the people. The condemnation of Socrates, by revealing the abyss that separated them, showed that the rationalism of the cultured classes was unable to have any effects on popular sentiment, which was more and more attached to mysticism.

[1] Comedy, created by the Greeks, first appeared at Syracuse with Epicharmis in 488 BC.

PLATO

It fell to Plato to reconcile these two poles of Greek civilization: rationalism and mysticism. On the death of Socrates, his disciples left Athens and Plato himself went to Egypt. On his return, he united in a single synthesis the conclusions of Egyptian religious thought and rationalism, that is to say Greek materialism.

Taking over from Egyptian theology its idealist metaphysics which envisaged God as the conscience of the world and considered his ideas as true reality, Plato in his 'theory of ideas' identifies God with knowledge, with good and with life and makes divine goodness the bridge between God—the supreme reality—and the created world in which it is expressed. One finds again in Platonism the Egyptian conception of creation according to which matter is not created but fashioned by the divine thought, and also the conception of the soul formed simultaneously of intelligence, an emanation of the divine, and of will, the personal element in every human creature. Conceiving the life of the other world as the return of the soul to God, and morality as the practice of harmony, that is to say of justice, Plato did no more than translate into philosophical terms the religious ideas of Egypt. For that reason he, in accordance with these ideas, attained that optimistic viewpoint on the world which alone allows mysticism to be reconciled with reason, that is to say with science, and with morality, that is to say with action.

But in order to explain the nature of matter Plato adapts the atomism of Leucippus and Democritus to Egyptian mysticism, thus uniting in a single system Egyptian mysticism and Greek rationalism.

Plato thus appears as the synthesis of all ancient thought rather than as an innovator. By introducing into Greek philosophy Egyptian religion purged of the archaic claptrap that encumbered it, he made it intelligible to Hellenism. Expressed in the wonderful Greek language with the art and poetry of a Plato, it became accessible to all.

Plato marks the end of a world. In politics, he looked back toward the past and saw the solution of the crisis in the city system reduced to even more restricted proportions and organized on a rigid basis, aristocratic and communal at the same time, that recalls the institutions of Sparta. An aristocrat attached to the soil, Plato, who had nothing of the realist in him, did not realize either the importance of economics or the evolution of his own times. There is a radical contradiction between his philosophical thought, widely open to universalism, and his political and social ideas. The fact was that Plato, the Greek aristocrat, remained socially a man of his own country. He looked to the past and not to the future. But, spiritually emancipated by his philosophic and religious theories, he was the first to unite in a single system all that was most exalted in Egyptian and Greek thought and, thereby, foreshadowed the Hellenistic civilization, that is to say the common civilization which had been developing in both Egypt and Greece ever since the VIth century BC.

Its varied origins were to allow Greek thought, as synthesized and harmonized by Plato, to conquer the Empire that Alexander was about to create.

PART TWO

THE SEA AND THE CONTINENT

BOOK VI

The Empire of Alexander and the Formation of the Great Monarchies

CHAPTER XXIX

PHILIP OF MACEDON UNIFIES GREECE

MACEDONIA

FROM the time of the Achaean invasions, Macedonia, landlocked and feudal, had passed slowly from a seigniorial régime to a system of local confederations. In the VIIIth century BC it had its first contact with the sea. Corcyra, a Coronthian colony, sent merchants into Epirus. In the VIIth century BC Corinth set up a trading post on the island of Leucadia and another one at Apollonia (Valona), whence it dominated the whole trade of Epirus, while from Epidamnus (Durazzo) it penetrated into Illyria. In Chalcidia, among a number of colonies founded by Chalcis from the VIIIth century BC onward, Corinth founded the important market of Potidea. Thenceforward Greek influence, coming from the east and south, was more and more felt in Macedonia.

By setting up a protectorate over Macedonia at the end of the Vth century BC, Darius had brought the country into touch with Persia. But after the Persian wars Macedonian sympathies were definitely with Greece.

In the Vth century BC feudalism in Macedonia was centralized under the royal authority. Perdiccas II founded his capital at Aigai in the mountains and tried meanwhile to find an outlet to the sea down the valley of the Strymon. In 436 BC Athens, then at the height of her power, founded a colony at Amphipolis, in order to open a way to the mines of Pangea. The Macedonian monarchy quickly fell under its influence, became Hellenized and hereditary. A royal army was formed and the capital was transferred to Pella in the lowlands. Archelaus, with Greek mercenaries in his pay, laid the foundations for a centralized administration, built roads, coined money and organized local markets in the interior. His court was similar to that of a Greek tyrant; Zeuxis was often there, and Euripides settled there, after leaving Athens where he had not been understood.

The royal policy became anti-feudal and turned definitely towards Greece and the sea. The king aimed at conquering Thessaly and Chalcidia.

Map No. 19

ILLYRIA
THRACE
Epidamnus
Stobia
Axios
Strymon
KINGDOM OF MACEDONIA
EDONIA
Philippi
Pangaion Mts.
Apollonia
Aigai
PELLA
EMATHIA
Amphipolis
Eion
Stagyra
THASOS
ORESTIDE
Methóni
Pydna
CHALCIDICE
Olynthus
EPIRUS
PIERIA
ELYMIA
Potidea
Mt. Athos
MOLOSSIA
Mt. Olympus
Mende
Thermal Gulf
THESSALY
Aegean Sea
CORCYRA
Dodona
Tricca
Larissa
Pharsalus
Ambracia
AETOLIA
LEAGUE
LEUCADIA
ARCANANIA
PHOCIS
EUBOEA
BOEOTIA
Naupactus
Delphi
Chalcis
CEPHALONIA
ATTICA
Thebes
Aíyion
ACHAIA
Megara
Eleusis
CORINTHIAN
Sicyon
ZACYNTHUS
Athens
Corinth
Olympia
Argos
AEGINA
MESSENIA
Sparta
LACONIA
MACEDONIA
UNDER THE REIGN OF PHILIP
(359-336 B.C.)
Limits of the kingdom
Vassal States
M.

Under Philip II (359–336 BC) the feudal lords were finally overcome. Greek economic penetration led to the rise of cities, not autonomous like the Greek cities but placed under the rule of royal governors. Supported by the king, they were able to destroy the political influence of the nobles. The seigniorial system disappeared. Thenceforward the country was composed of small freeholders, landowning nobles who formed a solid social and military backbone, and the cities in which trade was concentrated. By the exploitation of the silver mines of Dysoron and the gold-mines of Pangea, the king was able to dispose of large reserves of precious metals which enabled him to mint his famous 'Philips', which were correlated with the Persian and Athenian currencies. With these resources he organized a national army, based on conscription and equipped in the Greek manner. The court at Pella became a centre of Greek thought. Aristotle, son of a doctor from Stagira, was hired to act as tutor to the young crown-prince, Alexander.

Athens, whose second maritime league had just dissolved, was at this time in full decline. Philip profited by this to take possession of Amphipolis and thus freed himself from Athenian economic control; he then invaded Thessaly and, advancing towards Chalcidia, captured Potidea, at that time under Athenian rule, and razed it to the ground. The mines which Athens possessed in Thrace also fell into his hands. Macedonia became a great territorial state with a coastline on the Aegean, and Epirus, which held the Adriatic coast, was compelled to acknowledge her suzerainty. Her army assured her an incontestable military superiority over Greece, which Sparta had succeeded in keeping broken up into autonomous cities. The fate of Greece, from then on, was sealed. Her unity was to be achieved by the King of Macedonia, even as formerly the unity of Egypt had been imposed on the cities of the Delta by the Kings of Nekhen.

GREECE UNIFIED

Faced by this Macedonian kingdom which had now become a Greek kingdom, the Greek cities were less united than ever before. Everywhere there were pitiless political faction fights; twenty thousand Greek exiles were wandering through the Eastern world. The party of the wealthy and the business men turned to Macedonia. The democratic party, on the other hand, stood for independence and patriotism. At Athens, its chief was Demosthenes. But he was unable to see beyond the ideal of the city. A prisoner of archaic formulae, his cause was lost in advance. Although Athens had ready the largest fleet that she had ever possessed—three hundred triremes—she was unable to service it for lack of money.

By comparison with the cities, the Greek territorial states had become of greater importance. The seigniorial régime was dying in Thessaly, Boeotia and Phocis. Thebes had become an urban centre. The diffusion of individualist law in these previously self-sufficient regions had led, together with the increase in small freeholdings, to the possibility of free trade. The role of the cities, formerly islands of individualist law created by economic needs, had come to an end. Greece was to find herself included in the complex of monarchical states, such as had existed in the East for centuries past. At that time she was undergoing an evolution exactly analagous to that we have already followed in the Nile Valley at the end of the IVth millenary, and in Mesopotamia at the time of the unification of the country under the Babylonian kings in the XIXth century BC. In Greece, as in Egypt and Mesopotamia, it was a territorial state that was to achieve the unity of the country, but it was the cities that were to give it their civilization. It was at this moment that Philip, by the taking of Potidea, entered into hostilities against Athens, crushed her at the battle of Chaeronea (338 BC) and made himself the uncontested master of Greece.

Philip, however, did not exactly conquer the country; by uniting all the Greeks in a confederation, the Panhellenic Corinthian League, he took up once again the policy previously employed by Darius towards the Ionian cities; he forced the Greek states to accept a statute establishing a permanent peace between them, and obliged them to refer all disputes to the arbitration of the League, while guaranteeing freedom of trade and navigation. All the members of the League were represented on his Council by delegates whose number was proportional to their military contingents. This system reversed the ancient order of supremacy; it gave predominance to Thessaly. The cities were grouped into districts, and Sparta, which had refused to belong to the League, had her territory taken from her. Henceforward she was to be no more than a city, isolated and powerless.

Within the Corinthian League the cities kept their autonomy but lost their independence. Philip intervened even in their internal politics and forbade them to pronounce the penalties of death or confiscation of goods for political reasons. He set himself up as the protector of property against the claims of the masses and favoured the system of government by the middle classes that had yielded such good results at Syracuse and Tarentum.

While Macedonia was unifying Greece, the cities of Magna Graecia, grouped under the leadership of Tarentum, felt menaced by Rome, then allied to the Samnites. After the defeat of Athens at Chaeronea, Tarentum realized that the Greek cities could no longer be of any assistance and appealed to Alexander of Epirus, a vassal of Philip of Macedon, for aid against the Samnites and furnished him with ships to transport his troops. Alexander's army crossed into Italy and defeated the Samnites but, taking over the role that Philip had played in Greece, he made himself president of a Panhellenic League (332 BC). But he was killed while fighting the Bruttians in 331 BC and Tarentum again assumed the leadership. The struggle against Rome now appeared inevitable.

Master of Greece, Philip immediately declared himself the champion of Hellenism against the Persian Empire. Even as Xerxes had earlier called on the solidarity of Asia against Greece, so Philip tried to rally the whole Hellenic world in a campaign of liberation of the Ionian Greeks. By 336 BC he had already crossed into Asia Minor, defeated Memnon of Rhodes sent against him at the head of the Greek mercenaries, and taken Ephesus. A little later he was killed by a dagger thrust.

CHAPTER XXX

THE EMPIRE OF ALEXANDER

UNION OF GREECE AND EGYPT

WHEN Alexander came to the throne in 336 BC, the ancient East had disintegrated. In Greece the régime of the cities was bankrupt. The Persian Empire was falling to pieces in the midst of dynastic crises. Artaxerxes III, after having disposed of almost all the royal princes, was himself assassinated in 338 BC. The usurper who succeeded him was also assassinated. Finally, Darius III Codomanes was able to maintain himself in power (336 BC); but the Empire, torn between the continental claims of the East and the call of the sea in the West, lost all cohesion. But it still remained a real power, thanks to the treasures that the land tax and a wise financial administration had piled up at Susa. Egypt, weary of the severe occupation régime of the Achaemenids which had gone on since 341 BC, dreamed of independence without being able to recover it by her own unaided efforts.

The death of Philip left his work unfinished. Athens, whose political leaders, dominated by the strong personality of Demosthenes, were only local politicians, was ready to join Persia in her war against Alexander. He did not give her time. After offering a sacrifice to the shade of the first Greek hero fallen before Troy, he won the victories of the Granica and Issus, one after the other (334–333 BC). As soon as his success was known the Egyptian national party sent an embassy to offer him their alliance.

Once Asia Minor had been conquered, the satraps were replaced by Macedonians, but the cities retained their local institutions, and their gods were treated with the greatest respect; Alexander was making war on the King of Persia, not on his peoples. Soon the Syrian cities opened their gates to his victorious armies. Tyre alone, ancient rival of the Greeks, resisted desperately. It was razed to the ground, and those of its inhabitants who escaped massacre were sold as slaves. The old hatred of the Hellenes for the Tyrians was sated ferociously. The Philistine city of Gaza, which refused passage to Alexander, suffered the same fate. Asia and Egypt were now open to the Macedonian army. Alexander did not hesitate; he penetrated into Egypt, where he was hailed as a liberator. His presence sealed the alliance which, since Marathon, had united the Greeks and the Egyptians of the party of independence. The 'Greek King' bowed before the god Apis at Memphis and assumed the double crown of Egypt (332 BC).

King of the Macedonians and *hegemon* of the Greeks, Alexander was not for a moment thought of by Egypt as a conqueror, but as the legitimate successor of the Pharaohs and the restorer of her independence, of which Asia, since the times of the Assyrian Empire, had been regarded as the traditional enemy.

The idea of universal monarchy that had dominated Eastern policy for centuries past, the close community of Greek and Egyptian interests, made the union of Pharaonic and Greek sovereignty in the same hands seem quite natural. In Alexander, recognized by Ammon as his son at the oasis of Siwah, Egypt again found a legitimate sovereign.

After restoring the unity of the Greek world by the conquest of the Ionian cities, which were immediately incorporated into the Corinthian League, and completing the occupation of Syria, Alexander restored the Egyptian Empire within the frontiers formerly given it by Tutmes III, and united Greece and Egypt for the first time under the same sovereignty. Before taking the road again to Asia, he wished to trace upon the sands the site of the city of Alexandria, which was to transport the centre of the Hellenistic world to Egyptian soil, at the very spot where the kings of the XVIIIth dynasty had created the port of Pharos for the Aegeans.

A new era opened in the history of Egypt and Greece. Alexandria was to confer on Egypt the mastery of the Mediterranean and to fuse into a single whole the two civilizations, Greek and Egyptian, which, closely united, were to create Hellenistic culture.

CONQUEST OF THE PERSIAN EMPIRE

Alexander then left Egypt to conquer the Persian Empire. It collapsed at the battle of Arbela, where its immense and heterogeneous army was broken by the Macedonian phalanx (331 BC). On his way to Persepolis, Alexander set fire to the famous palace of the Achaemenids and reached Susa, where he laid hands on the immense reserves of precious metals of the Empire. Darius III fled, and was assassinated by his courtiers.

Five years campaigning brought the arms of Alexander as far as the Jaxartes in the north and beyond the Indus in the east. He was about to pass into the Ganges valley and set foot on the shores of the Bay of Bengal, looking towards the East, when his troops refused to follow him any longer. Two years later he died at Babylon (323 BC) on his way back.

ORGANIZATION OF THE EMPIRE

As his conquests extended, Alexander organized the Empire, while retaining the framework of the Persian state. Save in the sea-coast districts the system of satrapies was, on the whole, maintained. The Greek cities of Asia Minor were detached and united to the Corinthian League. Asia Minor, because of its growing importance, was divided into seven provinces. In Syria, the sea-coast cities were also detached from the territorial satrapies and reconstituted as little autonomous states, but were placed under the rule of royal governors. Egypt, ceasing to be a province, once again became, under Alexander, a sovereign kingdom. Cyprus, as under the Achaemenid régime, kept her local dynasties. In all the continental provinces, the borders of the satrapies remained unchanged. In India, Kashmir and the states of King Porus on the Indus became vassal kingdoms. Alexander no doubt wished to keep there a sufficient autonomous power to serve as a means of penetration towards the Bay of Bengal and the Far East.

This immense Empire was not, like the Persian Empire, a unified monarchical state, but a federation of states under a single sovereign. Alexander himself was the bond that united the Greco-Macedonian kingdom, the Egyptian monarchy, Persia and the Hindu kingdoms, all of which retained their own institutions. The central government was, in fact, reduced to the king's privy council, to which was added a chancellor and a sort of vizier.

Nothing, it seemed, had been changed in the political and economic structure of the various parts of the Empire, save that the authority of Alexander had replaced that of the King of Persia. In reality, these twelve years of campaigning were decisively to transform the balance of the Eastern and Mediterranean worlds. The Achaemenids had ruled it from Susa, a distant continental capital, situated at the meeting place of India and Nearer Asia; Alexander, champion of the new world which had been in process of creation since the VIth century BC, fixed its centre at Alexandria. Leadership had left the continent for the sea.

WORLD TRADE TURNS SEAWARD

By uniting the Persian Empire, Egypt and the Greek world in a single whole and by setting foot in India and Central Asia, Alexander was to make possible the organization of world trade with its axis in the Eastern Mediterranean. There all the great trade-routes converged. Wide open to the West, it communicated with Europe through the Aegean and Black Seas; the Red Sea brought it the produce of Africa, Arabia and India; Syria linked it to Central Asia and China by the eastward caravan routes.

Alexander was the first man, after Darius, with the genius to conceive the idea of making the international trade routes the framework of a universal empire by founding cities along them. In a few years, seventy Alexandrias were founded; the first, which was to become the economic mistress of the world, was Alexandria of Egypt, the heir of Pharos; in Northern Syria, at the end of the Euphrates route, there was Alexandretta; on the Persian Gulf, Alexandria-on-Tigris; on the Indus delta, Port Alexandria; on the caravan route between Susa and India, Alexandria of the Paricanians in Baluchistan; at the point where the great tributaries of the Indus met was Alexandria on the Indus; in Central Asia, a whole series of key cities were founded, which were to become great caravan markets, Herat in Asia, Kandahar in Arachosia, Khodjend on the Oxus and, finally, two more Alexandrias on the outermost frontiers of the Empire, one, Alexandria-Oxiana, on the route from Peshawar which commands the passes of the Hindu-Kush, and the other, Alexandria-Eschata, on the Jaxartes, which looked towards distant China.

The great trade routes of Central Asia were from now on fixed for all time; one led across the passes of the Hindu-Kush, and reached the Persian Gulf through Kandahar and the Caspian regions through Herat; two others linked China with the West; a southern route ended at Khodjend, a northern at Alexandria-Eschata.

But the main artery of the empire was the sea and all the great trade-centres were to be founded on its shores.

The cities destined to serve as framework for this system were not to be like the Greek cities, independent states; they were to be royal cities, administratively autonomous, but an integral part of the Empire. Citadels, in whose shadow markets were organized, would complete the urban system conceived by Alexander as the backbone of the new world.

Trade which, by circulating through the vital arteries of the Empire, would give it vigour must be balanced by a flourishing agriculture, the basis of all stable economic life. So Alexander took up again the policy of land improvement formerly carried on by the kings of Babylon, Egypt and Persia. The improvement of water-courses, the digging of canals, irrigation, and intensification of cultivation were to be systematically undertaken by his successors in all regions, especially in Western Asia. This policy broke down the seigniorial structure of the land. In all nearer Asia the social evolution, which since the VIIth century BC had affected first Egypt and then Greece, was quickened. Everywhere the urban movement created a class of individualist middle-class business men and led to the disappearance of the seigniorial régime, thanks to the spread of the economic principle: grow for sale. The creation of cities, the break down of closed economies, the emancipation of the rural population were the social tendencies of the empire built by Alexander according to a plan based on sea-borne trade.

The Achaemenids had tried in vain to associate the maritime cities with their continental empire. The policy of Alexander substituted the sea for the continent as the centre of attraction.

THE POLICY OF IMPERIAL COSMOPOLITANISM

The union of the world into a single economic system led to an imperial policy of cosmopolitanism. Philip had begun his conquests by proclaiming himself the champion of the Greeks. Alexander, while making himself the instrument of Hellenism, let himself be seduced by Egypt and the East. His whole policy tended to create a new 'climate' by the destruction of the nationalist sentiments which, since the Assyrian, Babylonian and Persian conquests, had already been greatly weakened in Asia. That was why he favoured the mixture of races. He himself set the example by marrying Statira, daughter of Darius III, and Parysatis, daughter of Artaxerxes III, thus allying himself to the dynasty of the Achaemenids. He offered rewards to the Macedonian soldiers who married Asiatic women, and practised a policy of religious toleration and respect for local institutions. Trade had made Greek an international language in Egypt and in Asia Minor; Alexander made it the official language of the empire. It was to penetrate, in the wake of the Greek soldiers, colonists and merchants, as far as Central Asia. The Greek language was to become one of the bonds to unite all parts of the Empire, bonds that Alexander wished should be both intimate and spontaneous. Economic interpenetration must be accompanied by moral interpenetration, which would be shown in a double form; the Egyptian theory of monarchy by divine right was to spread over the Greek world, while Greek philosophical conceptions would spread rapidly throughout the whole Mediterranean East.

Under the influence of Egypt, Alexander wished to give to his universal Empire the mystical idea of monarchy by divine right as the formula for legitimate power. Son of Ammon-Ra in Egypt, he wanted to be recognized as a man-god by the Greeks also; by a decree signed at Susa he ordered all the Greek cities to rank him among the gods of their Pantheons.

But the monarchy of Alexander also adapted itself to Greek democratic principles which were applied to all the new cities endowed with governments elected by the middle classes. Thus was prepared the fusion, in a single political system, of the oriental type of monarchy and Greek democracy, creating a new political formula which marked the end of the era of independent cities and at the same time announced the expansion of Hellenism. Up to the IVth century BC Greece had only had a slight influence, save for the diffusion of the Greek language by trade, on the countries around her. From the times of Alexander, Greek culture set out to conquer the world and to become, side by side with Egyptian mysticism which spread more and more with the diffusion of the mystery cults, the moral bond which was to unite the Mediterranean peoples in a single civilization.

If Greek thought was now ready to conquer the eastern world, it was because, as we have seen, it had originated there. The East was to find again its own ideas, but freed from the dross which had sullied them. Greece was to break the yoke of national prejudice and religious formalism which had hampered Eastern thought, then at its greatest, and threatened to make it sterile. This was to result in an intellectual renaissance, expressed in Greek which had now become the international language of philosophy and science. But just when Greek thought was to assert its influence over the entire world, it was itself to enter a new phase inaugurated by Aristotle.

THE REALIST PHILOSOPHY OF ARISTOTLE

Aristotle broke away both from the scepticism of the Sophists and the idealism of Plato. Like Plato, he admits that human reason has in it a part of God; he also affirms the possibility of reason attaining knowledge, and repudiates the sterile attitude of the sceptics and the subjectivists. But he deviates from Plato by professing that realities are not absolute concepts, but concepts realized in the things that our senses make known to us. By affirming the identity between the perceptible aspect of things and the conception that we have of them, he creates the scientific method and also logic, whose principles he, first of all thinkers, established.

Aristotle's metaphysics led him to an optimistic view of the world. A monotheist, he assimilates divinity to perfection, that is the absolute. God did not create the world, but he is the supreme intelligence within it, the end towards which all matter tends; nature therefore tends towards the good. But even if intelligence, being divine, is immortal, man, a momentary form in the universe, cannot have an immortal personality. The aim of intelligence is to know the eternal universe and the method of knowing it is science. Aristotle, an encyclopaedist, studied all the sciences and divided them into theoretical sciences—mathematics, physics, theology—which lead to a knowledge of the primal verities; practical sciences—ethics and politics—whose aim is utility, and the poetic sciences which aim at the beautiful. Morals, that is the happiness given by virtue, reside in the golden mean, equally distant from all excess. Politics is the science of society, an essentially practical science, for there is no régime that is good of itself. Régimes must vary according to peoples and periods. The best régime is that which realizes harmony. In his own times, Aristotle sees this harmony in government by the middle classes, corresponding to the golden mean, and in monarchy, the image of the government of the universe by God.

Plato crowns the thought of classical Greece. With Aristotle appears the realist thought of the Hellenistic period; science becomes detached from religion. Henceforward scientific thought and mystical thought will develop on different planes. The realist system of Aristotle fitted his own times perfectly, when trade dominated social and political relations; his thesis, according to which political régimes have only a relative value, justified the disappearance of the independent cities and the advent of the Hellenistic monarchies. Avoiding both materialism and scepticism, his optimistic realism led to action and scientific research.

Aristotelian philosophy responded to the intellectual and moral sentiment of the new era that was beginning. By endowing it with scientific method and giving it faith in reason, it was to permit human thought, during the IIIrd and IInd centuries BC, to rise to heights greater than it was not again to know until the 19th century of our era.

CHAPTER XXXI

THE HELLENISTIC MONARCHIES

THE EMPIRE BREAKS UP

ALEXANDER left no heir capable of succeeding him. His Empire was even less solid than the Persian Empire, which had Persia and its dynasty as a foundation. The only political bond that united the immense conquests of Alexander was the royal power. The only means of saving the Empire was, therefore, to save the dynasty founded by Alexander by preserving it for the son whom Roxana, one of his wives, was about to bear.

The generals therefore organized a regency, entrusted to Perdiccas, and divided the Empire into huge governorships under their rule.

EGYPT REVERTS TO HER HISTORICAL TRADITION

In Egypt, one of the generals, Ptolemy, became regent. He had Alexander buried at Alexandria, thus both proclaiming Alexander the legitimate Pharaoh of Egypt and Alexandria as the capital of his Empire. The country loyally rallied around Ptolemy. At Memphis, the administrative capital, the Egyptian government was preserved with its national institutions, while Ptolemy himself lived at Alexandria, which quickly became a great port and a sumptuous royal residence. Reverting exactly to the policy of the Saite kings, Ptolemy prepared for the maritime supremacy of Egypt by reorganizing the fleet, and created an army of mercenaries by enrolling the Greeks who were offering their services to any who required them. Showing no interest in the Empire, he limited himself to a purely Egyptian policy aimed at the domination of the trade centres of the Eastern Mediterranean. In a few years he occupied Cyrene on the African coast, the island of Cyprus, Delos, Tyre and Sidon.

In the midst of the wars which broke out among the generals from 321 BC onwards Ptolemy kept to himself, only intervening when Egyptian interests were involved, and trying to recreate the traditional Egyptian

Map No. 20

alliance with the Greek cities, those of continental Greece and those of Asia Minor and Sicily.

In 321 BC, after the assassination of Perdiccas, Ptolemy refused to accept the regency of the Empire; and when Cassander, one of the generals scheming to obtain control of the Empire, had Roxana and her son murdered about 310 BC, and when the last bastard (309 BC) and the sister (308 BC) of Alexander had mysteriously disappeared, Ptolemy, in the absence of any legitimate heir, had himself crowned Pharaoh in 305 BC.

In 285 BC, in order to assure the succession, he made his son co-sovereign. The dynasty of the Lagidi, thus legitimized, once more took up the traditional policy of Egypt.

But the case of Egypt, which reverted to her historical tradition, thanks to the strong national and moral cohesion of the country, was unique in this period.

MACEDONIA TRIES IN VAIN TO UNITE WITH GREECE

After various partitions and endless wars, in the course of which the Greek cities, changing masters several times, tried in vain to recover their independence and experienced constant internal revolts resulting in a succession of régimes, democratic, aristocratic, oligarchic or tyrannical, Greece and Macedonia fell finally under the rule of the Antigonids (277 BC) shortly after the terrible panic caused by an attempt of the Gauls who descended from the Danube to invade Greece (279 BC). Fifty years of war had resulted neither in unifying the Greek world of the Aegean under a single rule, nor in integrating the Greek cities into the Kingdom of Macedonia.

Athens had lost her commercial prosperity. But, in recompense, she had become more than ever the intellectual capital of Hellas, the University City *par excellence*.

The ancient cities, persisting in their political squabbles, slid into irremediable decline, save for Corinth which remained a great commercial centre. But other cities came to the fore; Byzantium, Chios and Rhodes. The cities, however, no longer represented the political life of the Greek world. A national feeling was taking shape, no longer in the cities but in parts of the countryside where democracy had penetrated slowly, and which had become, in the form of Leagues, the territorial states of Aetolia and Achaea.

THE AETOLIAN AND ACHAEAN LEAGUES

The Greeks of classical times had regarded the Aetolians as barbarians. But, since Philip, Aetolia had had a port, Naupactus, and trade had hastened the evolution which led her towards smallholding. About 275 BC she was given a democratic constitution. By it, power was vested in an Assembly in which all citizens took part and which met twice a year to pass laws drawn up by a College of Nomographs (legislators); it elected a general (*strategos*) with executive power, assisted by a Master of the Horse (*hipparchos*), a chancellor, and an *agonothete* and seven magistrates in charge of financial affairs, all of whom were elected. Besides the *strategos* there was a *synhedrion*, which was both a state council and a supreme court, made up of a thousand delegates from different regions, whose numbers were in proportion to the importance of their military contingents and to the taxes which they paid to the League; a permanent commission of thirty members, chosen from it, directed foreign affairs.

As for the Achaean League it was born in the Vth century BC out of a federation of a dozen villages formed on a religious basis, and which ended by including Achaea, Argolis and a part of Arcadia. In 281 BC sixty states were members. They were represented by two assemblies; the *synod*, made up of several thousand delegates sent by all the states proportionately to the total of their contributions, and the *ecclesia*, open to all Achaeans over the age of thirty. The two assemblies shared legislative power. The synod, which met in the capital, Aigion, dealt with current affairs. The executive power was granted to two *strategoi*, assisted by *demiurgoi*, a chancellor, a *hipparchos*, a *hypostrategos* and a treasurer. The League encroached on the autonomy of the member-states in order to assure economic unity and a unified system of coinage, weights and measures.

Later, Megara, Corinth and Sicyon were to join the League. It was to become a real Greek democratic state that was to affirm Hellenic independence against Macedonia and, still later, courageously against Rome.

Macedonia, because of her outlets on the Adriatic on one side and the Straits on the other, should have been able to play an important economic role. But the constant opposition of the Greeks prevented this. Though well governed by kings who looked on the monarchy as a magistrature, she saw herself little by little reduced to the status of a minor power. In 289 BC Epirus broke away; under Pyrrhus—a real Greek—it knew a short moment of glory without morrow, but of considerable historical importance because of the repercussions it was to have on Roman policy.

SELEUCUS TRIES TO RESTORE THE PERSIAN EMPIRE

Thus, with Egypt restored and Greece a prey to anarchy, it was quite natural that the wars between the successors of Alexander should end in an attempt to restore the Persian Empire.

But Seleucus I, who tried to carry this out, found himself faced by the same problem that had faced the Achaemenids; was the axis of the Empire to be the continent or the sea?

At first Seleucus was attracted by the continental policy. He fixed his capital at Babylon, centre of the economic life of Nearer Asia, and tried to reconquer the eastern and Indian provinces of Alexander's Empire.

The result was that the maritime satrapies seceded, since they were an integral part of Mediterranean economy. One after the other, the provinces of the Black Sea coast proclaimed themselves independent; Bithynia, in 315 BC, fell into the hands of a local chieftain who assumed the title of King in 297 BC and set up his capital at Nicomedia, founded by him on the Sea of Marmara; about the middle of the IIIrd century Cappadocia became a sovereign state and, soon afterwards, Pontus, with the two great ports of Sinope and Trebizond.

These new kingdoms had no links with earlier traditions; they had been formed by contact with the sea. All their economic activity remained in the hands of the Greek cities which, because of the primitive social conditions of the countryside, retained their role and, consequently, their political autonomy.

The régime of the city-state, which had collapsed in the Aegean, continued to exist in the Black Sea area for a long time to come. On the northern shore, Olbia on the estuary of the Borysthenes (Dniepr), Cherson (Sebastopol), Theodosia and Panticapea (Kertch) in the Crimea, situated in a purely Scythian countryside, were to remain sovereign republics for centuries to come.

Ionia and Phoenicia were drawn into the orbit of Egypt and annexed to her Empire, for which Rhodes, a republic allied to the Ptolemies, became the great transit centre.

Thus the Empire of the Seleucids, like that of the Achaemenids, was torn asunder by the double attraction of the sea and the continent. The continental provinces themselves, moreover, had nothing in common, neither race nor language, tradition nor religion. Nor did they form an economic unit. Only dynastic feeling could have kept them united. But Seleucus could not invoke it since his power was not derived from any legitimate source. Thus the continental kernel of the Empire was also destined to fall rapidly to pieces. Armenia, which had already broken away under the Achaemenids and which Alexander had not reconquered, became an independent kingdom. In Media a national reaction began under Prince Atropates, and in the Median kingdom of Atropatene (Azerbaidjan) which he founded Zoroastrianism enjoyed a renascence which was to spread to the whole of Iran and make it impervious to any form of Greek influence.

As to the satrapies of the East which were strongly influenced by India, Seleucus, halted by the power of King Chandragupta who had extended his rule over the Ganges and Indus basins, renounced their reconquest. Gedrosia was annexed by India; with it, Seleucus lost control of the caravan route in Baluchistan. He had the wisdom to recover the use of it by negotiating a treaty of alliance with the Indian king. But in consequence of these reverses, it seems that Seleucus understood that his Empire, now cut off from the sea, could only disintegrate. After his defeat in India (305 BC) he returned to the West resolved to re-establish his authority in Asia Minor and extend it to Greece. It was a complete reversal of policy. In 301 BC he defeated Antigonus at Ipsus, thanks to the five hundred war-elephants that his alliance with Chandragupta had brought him. Then, having reconquered northern Syria and thereby an outlet on the Mediterranean, he carried on a purely western policy. He abandoned Babylon and made Antioch his capital in that key-position of Northern Syria which he had just recovered. In order to restore life to the great continental trade-route to India, he deported the population of the ancient metropolis to settle it in Seleucia-on-the-Tigris, whose population reached six hundred thousand within fifty years.

The Antioch-Seleucia route was to be the vital artery of his empire, as the Sardes-Babylon-Susa route had been that of the Empire of Darius. But under Darius, Babylon had been at the centre, a stage towards Susa and India. Under Seleucus I, Seleucia was the end; it was Antioch that should have been the centre, which presumes that the other end should have been Greece. To realize this policy, looking both towards the Mediterranean and the Persian Gulf, Seleucus came too late. Ptolemy was installed in the island of Cyprus, in Ionia and in Phoenicia and had revived the traditional alliance of Egypt with the Greek lands. The Egyptian policy of maritime supremacy was opposed to the formation of an Asiatic kingdom which looked seaward. Their economic policies made it inevitable that war would break out between the kings of Antioch and Alexandria for the possession of the Syrian coast, the Greek islands and the cities of Ionia.

In this struggle it was not territorial aggrandizement that the two kings were looking for, but control of the trade-routes. The duel was to be waged for control of the route to India. The Seleucids dominated it on the continent, by Mesopotamia, and the Ptolemies on the sea, by the Red Sea. Victory was to go to whichever side could assure itself of the possession of Syria and the mastery of the sea.

CHAPTER XXXII

THE GREAT MONARCHIES OF INDIA AND CHINA

THE struggle for the Indian trade-route, which dominated the whole policy of the Hellenistic kingdoms, can be explained by the ever-growing importance that trade with India and the Far East had assumed in international affairs since the VIth century BC.

THE INFLUENCE OF THE MEDITERRANEAN ON INDIA

Darius had given fresh impetus to navigation on the Indus by re-establishing maritime communications between Sind and Egypt. Alexander, by founding cities on the river delta and in the Punjab, had turned Hindu trade westward. But instead of going by way of Mesopotamia, it had at once chosen the sea route from India to the Mediterranean through the Red Sea.

On the death of Alexander, the influence of the Mediterranean on India was so powerful that it was felt even as far as the Ganges basin.

Since the VIth century BC Aryan feudalism in the Ganges basin had rapidly evolved towards a monarchical system. In 321 BC, the very year when war broke out between Alexander's generals, the feudal sovereign of the Ganges kingdom of Maghada had been overthrown by a general, Chandragupta, who founded the dynasty of the Mauryas. Chandragupta, drawn into the great struggle for supremacy that had just broken out over the whole East, at once undertook a policy of imperialist expansion towards the Indus.

THE FORMATION OF THE MAURYA EMPIRE

The Punjab was at this moment defenceless. The satrap, Eudamos, who had governed the whole Indus basin after murdering Porus whom Alexander had kept there as a vassal king, had just left westward at the head of an army, formidable because of its war-elephants, to try his luck in the war between the *diadokoi*.

Chandragupta took advantage of this to invade the Macedonian provinces of Kabul, Punjab and Sind. He thus became the master of a great Indian Empire which, since it included both the Indus and Ganges basins, was open to two seas, one of which gave access to the west by Arabia and Egypt and the other to the Malay Archipelago.

For the first time a great state, monarchical, absolutist and centralized, appeared in India. Built up on principles analogous to those that had been successful in the Empire of Alexander, the monarchy of the Mauryas claimed divine right and, relying upon a bureaucratic administration, based the royal policy on its mission of justice.

In 305 BC Seleucus, who had received as his share in the partition all the Asiatic part of the Empire, tried in vain to recover the Indian satrapies. Halted by Chandragupta, he renounced his plans in order to sign a treaty of alliance with the Indian king which seems to have been confirmed by a political marriage. The Maurya king ceded him five hundred war-elephants, but made him recognize the Indian possession of Gedrosia (Baluchistan). Thenceforward, the Indian Empire controlled the whole coast of the Indus Delta and as far as the Persian Gulf.

India thus became one of the great international powers of the time. She at once devoted herself to building up her trade with the West. The sea-route from Alexandria, through the Red Sea, to the Indus and Malabar ports became the essential axis of economic life. For two centuries the Ptolemies and the Seleucids were to be incessantly at war for its control. Pataliputra, the Ganges capital of Chandragupta, was to rival the wealth and luxury of Alexandria; the royal palace, built on the model of the palance at Persepolis, was to become one of the most important diplomatic centres of the Hellenistic era.

THE CENTRAL ASIAN TRADE ROUTES

The great role played for centuries by India in Mediterranean trade was not due solely to her own wealth, immense though it was, but to the fact that she was in direct communication with the Far East.

The Central Asian trade routes, whose importance Alexander had understood when he founded the caravan cities of Herat, Kandahar and Khodjend, linked China by the northern oases to the regions around the Caspian Sea and thence to Syria; by the Peshawar Pass and Baluchistan, they reached India and thence the Red Sea and Egypt. In the IVth century BC these routes became of even greater importance because of the evolution of China.

THE MONARCHICAL EVOLUTION OF CHINA

As in India, so also in China, the IVth century BC marked the advent of a centralized monarchical régime. After a long manorial development, which had for centuries given her social, economic and political stability, thanks to which a brilliant intellectual and artistic culture had flourished, China entered a new era in her history. Feudal coalitions were formed which destroyed the authority of the feudal dynasty of the Chou and replaced it by a series of kingdoms, all fighting amongst themselves, which paved the way for a centralized monarchy.

THE REALIST PHILOSOPHY OF MENCIUS

In ancient times China had found in the idealist philosophy of Lao-Tse—as Greece had found in the idealist philosophy of Plato—the highest expression of her thought. But, like Plato, Lao-Tse represented the past. It was to be the realist doctrines of Confucius, revised in the IVth century BC by Mencius, which, like Aristotelian realism in the Hellenistic world, were to serve as a basis for the monarchical period which was then beginning in China.

Mencius (Mong-Tse, born 372 BC) gave the monarchy a new moral and juridical system which, less scientific than that of Confucius but more realistic and more human, exactly represented the political evolution towards the centralization of power and the social evolution towards individual emancipation which was going on in China. The jurists became the dominant influence; they were the protagonists of the monarchy and the servants of the princes; to assure their triumph they drew up a juridical theory that transformed the realism of Mencius into an opportunism similar to that which would one day be professed by Machiavelli.

The nobles, excluded from the government, were replaced by the jurists, docile instruments of the absolutist policy of the kings whose imperialism was kept alive by war. It was at this time that war in China adopted those measures of terror and extermination that China was to retain throughout her history and which offer so strange a contrast to the humanity and highmindedness of her moral and political philosophy.

At the very moment when the armies of Alexander were penetrating into Central Asia, the armies of the Kings of Tsin—the most western of the Chinese kingdoms—were undertaking the conquest of all the ancient empire of the Chou.

THE TSIN EMPIRE

The Tsin Kingdom was called upon to create the monarchical unity of China because it was the most commercially developed, and incidentally the wealthiest and most powerful, of the Chinese states. Its capital, Hien-Yang, situated on the Huang-Ho, was at the end of the caravan route which linked China to India, Mesopotamia and thence to the West. Brahmanic idealism, whence had come the philosophy of Lao-Tse, had penetrated into China along this international trade route. At this time, the China Sea had no influence on Asia because, instead of being a route leading to other lands, it was then only a frontier, the limit of a world. The maritime countries in the south of China, one day to become the centre of the most highly developed Asiatic civilizations, were then still wrapped in semi-barbarism.

Shut off from the sea, China remained open to the outer world through the Central Asian oases. The cities of Khodjend and Kandahar were for China like distant ports, far across the deserts, whose influence awakened China to international trade.

The extension of trade relations to Central Asia and India in the times of Darius had had a decisive influence on the internal development of China, and the formation of the Chinese monarchy in the IVth century BC was certainly associated with the current that had been evident in western Asia from the VIth century onward and which drew China into the orbit of international trade.

In the VIth century BC a great wave of idealism had permeated the Asiatic world. It was at that time that the Zoroastrian religion triumphed in Persia, Buddhism appeared in the Ganges valley and the philosophy of Lao-Tse in the feudal China of the Chou.

It was from Persia that this wave had started, doubtless influenced by the moral ideas of Egypt, which were widespread in the eastern Mediterranean.

In the IVth century BC it was once again from western Asia that the wave of monarchical imperialism and political realism that passed over the whole Asiatic continent had started. In India it had presided at the foundation of the Maurya Empire and in China at that of the Tsin monarchy.

The world entered a new phase of its history, marked by the development of international trade and by the formation of large monarchical states.

BOOK VII

The Wars for Mastery of the Seas IIIrd and IInd Centuries BC

CHAPTER XXXIII

GROWTH OF THE ROMAN POWER

INTERNATIONAL TRADE

DURING the IIIrd century BC international trade spread mainly eastward but was also of growing importance in the central Mediterranean. Tarentum and Syracuse were at that time the great centres of Greek trade. Tarentum was in contact with Rome and Syracuse with Carthage.

But while Rome was extending her territorial conquests and Carthage was keeping a firm hold on her maritime empire, Tarentum and Syracuse were exhausting themselves in internal conflicts.

At Syracuse, after the wise government of Timoleon, a period of anarchy led to the tyranny of Agathocles, who seized power by promising the people remission of debts and distribution of public lands. Supported by a democratic movement of clearly revolutionary nature, he succeeded in uniting the whole of Sicily under his rule and, carried away by the trend of the times, assumed the title of King (306 BC). But at his death his ephemeral kingdom dissolved into anarchy and party strife.

In Italy, Tarentum held all the south of the country under her rule. Rome was expanding towards Campania. To halt her, Tarentum made an alliance with the Greek city of Naples. Rome replied by signing a treaty of friendship with Carthage (306 BC), which reserved Italy for Rome and abandoned Sicily to the Carthaginians as a sphere of influence and expansion.

At this time Rome was clearly looking seaward; she built a fleet, concluded a commercial treaty with Rhodes (306 BC) and made an agreement with Tarentum to share the whole Italian coast, which was divided into two spheres of influence separated by the Lacinian Promontory.

A little later, Naples was forced to accept Roman rule (304 BC). But, as soon as she had been conquered, Naples imposed a mercantile policy on Rome and forced her to coin silver money for commercial use. Greek and Syrian merchants settled in Rome, where freely available capital became of growing importance. In 312 BC it had become the basis of the census, which meant that business men enriched by trade could join the first classes of citizens; and the Senate, made up of magistrates who had completed their term of office, lost its former character of a patrician assembly now that plebeians were able to become consuls. There was thus formed a new nobility, recruited both from patricians and rich plebeians, the senatorial party, made up of families some member of which had sat in the Senate. From these most of the magistrates were chosen.

ECONOMIC EVOLUTION HASTENS SOCIAL EVOLUTION

Thus democracy advanced with the increase in liquid capital. The plebs saw their way free to all offices of state, even those of the pontificate (296 BC); and legal procedure, which had until then remained the monopoly of the patrician pontiffs, was put in writing and the first rudiments of a science of law were introduced in Rome.

By becoming more democratic, public affairs became more and more involved with party politics. The assemblies of the centuriate committees, where the wealthy classes predominated, gave ground before the tribal *comitia*, in which the citizens voted according to their tribes. Democratic evolution had completed its cycle. The right to vote, at first determined by nobility, then by wealth, now depended only on domicile. The plebs, it is true, had only the four urban tribes, but in the countryside a class of peasant plebeians had been formed, so that the democratic movement soon penetrated all the rustic tribes, formerly composed only of patrician landowners. Like the centuriate assemblies, the tribal assemblies made themselves independent of the Senate by ensuring that their decisions were ratified in advance. The Roman government, thenceforward, depended on the parties. The party of the nobles (*nobilitas*) was in reality the party of the rich, opposed to the popular party made up of the city plebs; between the two, the smallholders constituted a middle class, on which the *nobilitas* relied to resist the pressure of the populace. This coalition of property-owners was to hold uncontested power till the IIIrd century, mainly thanks to its firmly democratic policy. In the conquered lands Roman colonies were set up, formed of plebeians who had been granted land. Thus the plebeians were gradually transformed into a peasant petty bourgeoisie which gave a solid military backbone to the state; in the north, the colonies included Gauls settled in the Po valley, who tried, once again, but this time in vain, to invade Italy in 299 BC; in the south, they maintained the authority of Rome over Campania and Apulia.

While extending her territory and increasing the number of her citizens, Rome continued to develop her constitutional structure; she introduced a tax system of Egyptian and Greek type, calculated on the total value of individual wealth, and the first administrative offices were founded. Their personnel was recruited from slaves and freedmen, often of Greek origin. Slavery spread and moral preoccupations were introduced into political life with the patrician democratic censor, Appius Claudius, as formerly in Athens under Solon.

Rome ceased to be a rural republic; she was now a powerful state, receptive to influences from the outside world.

THE CONQUEST OF TARENTUM

It was at this time that she came into conflict with Tarentum. The Roman army of citizens was faced on the battlefield by Tarentine mercenaries. The Spartans, whom Tarentum first of all hired, proved themselves unreliable, so, for the second time, she turned to Epirus and appealed to Pyrrhus, whose army, strengthened by elephants, defeated the Romans in 280 BC. But Pyrrhus, dreaming of carving out an empire for himself, crossed into Sicily. This political error roused both Rome and Carthage against him and he was forced to retreat to Epirus. It is known that he tried later to conquer Greece and was killed in street fighting at Argos.

The campaign of Pyrrhus was to have important consequences. For the first time Rome had entered into war with a Hellenistic state. She was soon to become involved in the whirlpool of international politics. Pyrrhus had shown her the way to Magna Graecia, which she lost no time in following. But fearing lest Rome might become a dangerous rival by conquering the cities of Magna Graecia, Carthage, reversing her system of alliances, joined with Locri against her. Rome paid no heed. She accepted the gage and captured Locri and, a little later, Tarentum (272 BC). By 265 BC all Italy south of the Po was Roman. Tarentum, promoted to the rank of an ally, became a great naval base which caused Rome to look eastward. Between the Roman Republic, now a great naval power after the capture of Tarentum, and Carthage, determined to defend her mastery of the seas, war was inevitable.

CHAPTER XXXIV
EGYPT AND ROME SHARE THE MASTERY OF THE SEAS

THE STRUCTURE OF WORLD TRADE

IN less than fifty years the balance of the world had greatly changed. In the ancient East the sea had triumphed over the continent. The great capitals of the ancient world had been continental: Memphis, Thebes, Babylon, Nineveh, Susa. Their role was ended. Henceforward, the capitals were all situated by the sea-coast: Alexandria, Antioch, Carthage, Rome.

The axis of the economic life of the East was no longer continental but maritime. It passed through the Mediterranean, reached India by the Suez canal and the Black Sea through the Straits. It was around this double route that political and commercial leadership was to be concentrated, as formerly around Mesopotamia. That was why, when Babylon disappeared from the scene, Rome came to the fore. Nearer Asia ceased to be the centre of the civilized world. All attempts to make it a centre for the Mediterranean, Central Asia and India had failed. The extension of trade both to the western Mediterranean and to the Far East had shifted the balance. Two irresistible forces now made themselves felt; the sea which three centuries later was to lead to the formation of the Mediterranean Empire of Rome, and the Asiatic continent dominated by the vast landmass of China which was to give rise, at the same time as Rome, to a great empire. Between the maritime empire of Rome and the continental empire of China, Nearer Asia, formerly the point of convergence, was to become a point of transit; a transit point of essential importance, without doubt, as was shown by the development that Seleucia-on-Tigris, the successor of Babylon, was to show, but a point of transit just the same. But, however busy the continental route through Mesopotamia, one branch of which led through Baluchistan to India and the other by the Central Asian routes and cities to China, it could not compete with the great sea-route, whose importance increased continually throughout the whole

Hellenistic period. This explains the remarkable prosperity of Alexandria and India. Egypt was the point of contact between the West, where Roman power was growing, and the Asiatic world. India was the point of contact between the Far East, where the Chinese Empire was being formed, and the western world. This was the pattern of the history of the three centuries that preceded the Christian era.

MEDITERRANEAN TRADE

A new economic unit was being formed around the Mediterranean. Three great trade-routes converged there; the Indian route, which put it in contact with the Far East, the Pontus route to the Russian plains and the Caucasus on the one hand and the Danubian region on the other, and finally the route which, through the Pillars of Hercules, led to the Ocean where a new world had been revealed since the Phoenicians had founded their colonies on the Atlantic coasts of Africa, and the sailors of Tartessos had found their way to the British Isles. About 320 BC Pytheas of Marseilles reached the coasts of Scandinavia. Marseilles, which dominated the Rhone valley, brought the rich territories of Gaul into the orbit of Mediterranean trade. Hellenism, which had reached the Gauls settled in the valley of the Danube, began to have an influence on Gaul itself. Continental Europe entered history.

THE STRUGGLE FOR SEA-POWER

The IIIrd century BC marks the end of the sea-power of the cities and the triumph of the territorial states. The sea-power of the great Greek cities had declined and that of Carthage was menaced. The first had passed to Egypt and the second was contested by Rome since her conquest of Tarentum. This double trend towards supremacy, Egyptian in the eastern Mediterranean, Roman in the central Mediterranean, was the basic fact that explains all the great wars of the IIIrd century BC.

THE SYRIAN WARS AND EGYPTIAN SEA-POWER IN THE EASTERN MEDITERRANEAN

Egypt was only able to assert her leadership after a series of wars against the Seleucid Empire. Mastery of the seas depended on the possession of Ionia, the Aegean islands and Syria. It was to ensure this that Ptolemy I installed himself at Tyre and Sidon and took possession of the islands of

Cyprus and Delos. Continuing the traditional policy of Egypt, he inclined towards an alliance with Greece, then represented on the continent by the kings of Macedonia and in Sicily by Agathocles of Syracuse. The Ptolemies aimed at mastery of the seas by carrying on a policy of Egyptian-Greek alliance.

But the kings of Antioch, whose policy of a continental empire had failed, determined to contest the Egyptian economic supremacy. This they could only do by gaining control of the seas. An armament race began with the building of powerful fleets which were to decide the victory.

Three wars ended with the indisputable victory of Egypt. All three had for object the possession of the eastern shores of the Mediterranean. The first (279–271 BC) was waged between Ptolemy II (285–246 BC) and Antiochus I (281–261 BC). It ended with the decisive victory of Egypt, who occupied Cilicia, Pamphylia, the coasts of Lycia, Cnidus and Halicarnassus, Miletus, the Cyclades, Samos, Itamos, then the great port of Crete, Arvad and the Phoenician cities; furthermore, firmly entrenched at Samothrace, Egypt controlled the Straits. The whole Greek world was drawn into her orbit. Her influence was the deciding factor at Athens and at Corinth.

Shipping, thenceforth, streamed into Alexandria which became the busiest port on the Mediterranean.

But at this time Rome had just thrown Pyrrhus out of Italy and was preparing to occupy Tarentum. She wanted, therefore, to make herself secure by being on good terms with Egypt. In 272 BC a Roman embassy went to Alexandria to negotiate a treaty of alliance with Ptolemy II. The Egyptian policy of alliance with Greece was extended to Rome and a coalition was formed between Rome and Alexandria.

Antiochus, driven out of the Mediterranean, which his empire no longer touched save at Antioch and in northern Syria, reverted to his continental policy; he founded a temple at Babylon and new cities in Mesopotamia.

Unable to hold his own in the north of Asia Minor, which he still held as far as Miletus, he was forced to allow the secession of the governor of Pergamon and recognize his title of King (262 BC). Pergamon, thenceforward, was to dominate the north of the Aegean Sea, even as Egypt controlled the south.

But the continental policy of Antiochus I failed. His Empire, lacking unity, disintegrated. Central Asia was more and more drawn towards the East. The Persian nationalist movement that had developed around the religion of Zoroaster spread, extending from Atropatene to the south and west. About 250 BC Arsaces founded, south of the Caspian, the kingdom of Parthia, whose capital, Zadracarte, on the eastern shores of the Caspian, clearly looked towards the caravan routes of Central Asia.

Thenceforward, Antioch was cut from the provinces of Bactriana and Sogdiana, which had kept her in touch with the continental trade of China and India. The governor of Bactriana, Diodotus I, united them under his rule and made them an independent Greek kingdom.

Driven back towards the sea, Antiochus II (261–246 BC) again found himself forced to wage war for the recovery of the Syrian coast. Profiting by a revolt among the Gaulish mercenaries of Ptolemy II, he obtained advantages that allowed him to conclude a favourable peace (253 BC), which was confirmed by a treaty of friendship.

Egypt, mistress of the seas, wished, as formerly under Amenophis III, to carry on a policy of peace and maintenance of the *status quo*. An alliance was concluded between Alexandria and Antioch, confirmed by the marriage of Antiochus II with Berenice, daughter of Ptolemy II. She brought with her as dowry Ionia, which was however in the occupation of the King of Pergamon, the southern coasts of Asia Minor, Cilicia, Pamphylia and an extension of frontiers on the Syrian coast.

A balance could doubtless have been struck on these conditions. But the murder of Antiochus II and Berenice, after a series of palace plots (246 BC), revived the war between Ptolemy III (246–221 BC) and Seleucus II (246–223 BC).

The result of the third Syrian war was disastrous for Seleucus II. Ptolemy III advanced to the Tigris. Seleucus, totally defeated, lost Syria together with the great naval port of Seleucia-of-Pieria, which he had founded, and all the southern coasts of Asia Minor as far as Ephesus; furthermore, Egypt laid hands on the Thracian Chersonese which assured her control of navigation in the Black Sea.

This terrible defeat resulted in a serious internal crisis in the Seleucid Empire. Seleucus II was obliged to cede all Asia Minor, as far south as the Taurus Mountains, to his brother, Antiochus Hierax, who, unable to defend his lands, saw them annexed by Attalus I, King of Pergamon, supported by an Egyptian alliance. Pergamon, now mistress of the southern shore of the Straits while Egypt controlled the northern, became the principal Greek naval power and a great capital of Hellenism, while continuing to gravitate within the Egyptian sphere of influence.

Ptolemy III now possessed an indisputable mastery of the seas. He called himself 'Master of the Mediterranean and the Indian Sea'. His coins, which dominated international trade, bore a trident, symbol of the King-

Map No. 21

THE ROMAN REPUBLIC
and its Empire, about 230 B.C.

dom of the Sea, and a crown with rays, the symbol of universal sovereignty.

Egypt was then at the height of her wealth and power and the fascination of Alexandria drew thither all the intellectual forces of the time.

THE FIRST PUNIC WAR AND ROMAN SEA-POWER IN THE CENTRAL MEDITERRANEAN

While Egypt was triumphing over Asia, the duel between Rome and Carthage was about to begin. Now in possession of Tarentum, Rome aimed at the mastery of the central Mediterranean. This depended on the Straits of Messina upon which Syracuse, then enjoying a period of great prosperity under the royal government of Hieron II, had also cast her eye. But Carthage, at that time all-powerful in the Tyrrhenian Sea, had no intention of abandoning her dominant position. To assure this, she occupied Messina. Rome obviously could not tolerate Carthage having control of all trade on the Italian coasts. The first Punic War (264–241 BC) broke out. Syracuse which, since the capture of Tarentum by Rome, had been allied with Carthage, hastened to proclaim her neutrality, but at the same time undertook to give supplies to the Roman army which, thanks to this aid, was able to carry on the campaign in Sicily, using squadrons built in the Tarentum shipyards and in the cities of Magna Graecia. The Roman 'quinquiremes' triumphed at first in the naval battles of Mylae and Ecnomos, but the defeat of the Roman fleet in 254 BC saved Carthage. It was only after recovering the mastery of the seas that Rome, at the price of fourteen years of war, could triumph over her powerful rival (241 BC). The war cost Rome seven hundred ships of war, and Carthage four hundred.

Vanquished Carthage lost Sicily. All the Greek cities which, save for Syracuse, had made common cause with Carthage, were annexed by Rome. Syracuse became an ally.

Sea-power was to make Rome an empire: the first stage was the reduction of Sicily to the status of a province.

Carthage, on the contrary, thrown by defeat into civil war and a prey to her mercenaries who were in revolt, was obliged to buy the neutrality of Rome a few years later by ceding Corsica and Sardinia (237 BC), which in their turn became a Roman province.

The hegemony in the Tyrrhenian Sea passed from Carthage to Rome.

Carthage, however, did not give up. After restoring internal peace, she tried to recompense herself for her losses by undertaking the conquest of Spain (237 BC). Tartessos and its rich silver mines were annexed and

Hamilcar founded the naval base of Cartagena to protect them (225 BC). Rome based her power on Italy, a great territorial state; Carthage, in reply, conquered Spain.

But Marseilles, the ancient enemy of Carthage, feeling her possessions in Provence menaced by the Punic expansion, appealed to Rome. A treaty was concluded which fixed the Ebro as the limit of navigation, which was reserved to Rome on the north and Carthage on the south. Peace, however, was only a fiction. A trade war at once broke out; Rome introduced a maritime economic policy of monopoly against Carthage, similar to that which Carthage herself practised in Spain.

THE FORMATION OF THE BLOCS: EGYPT-ROME-PERGAMON AND ASIA-MACEDONIA-CARTHAGE

The Mediterranean was thus divided between three sea-powers; Egypt in the east, Rome in the centre and Carthage in the west. Relying upon powerful battle fleets, each was backed by a great territorial state: Egypt, Italy, Spain. Rome, linked to Egypt by a policy of friendship, the ally of Syracuse, and mistress of the great Greek cities of Italy and Sicily, was led to adopt the policy of a protecting power over continental Greece. The rich colonies of Corinth in the Adriatic, Epidamnus, Apollonia, Corcyra, victims of the Illyrian pirates, turned to Rome for aid, since she had taken the place of Tarentum. A Roman fleet of two hundred ships took part in the war against the pirates and, in order to assure the safety of the seas, a state, vassal of Rome, was created on the Dalmatian coast whose ships were forbidden to round the cape of Alessio (225 BC). Rome became the successor of Corinth in the Adriatic. The eastern Mediterranean was now open to her influence.

Rome was allied to Egypt, which in turn was allied to Pergamon. The ancient policy of Greco-Egyptian alliance, that is to say an alliance of the maritime lands against the Asiatic continent, was thus continued.

Shut in between Rome, now installed on the Dalmatian coast, and Egypt, which occupied the northern shores of the Hellespont and drew the Greek cities into her orbit, Macedonia, cut off from the sea, approached the Seleucids.

Asia, Macedonia and Carthage prepared to form a coalition against Egypt, Pergamon and Rome to dispute with them the mastery of the seas.

A world war was about to break out, and on its issue the destinies of Rome were to depend.

CHAPTER XXXV

ECONOMIC AND SOCIAL EVOLUTION IN THE IIIRD CENTURY BC

INTERNATIONAL ECONOMIC EVOLUTION

IN the IIIrd century BC trade was a determining influence in the evolution of civilization. Sea-borne commerce led to an expansion of capitalism. Great industrial centres were formed where, except in Egypt, the workers were mainly slaves. Fluid wealth increased, as well as monetary circulation. Banking, in the hands of powerful financial combines, expanded enormously. The abundance of money eased credits. Interest, which was 12% in the time of Alexander, fell to 10% about 250 BC and then to 6% about 200 BC, except in Egypt where it was kept steady by the operations of the National Bank at the high rate of 24%.

Private wealth increased considerably. Rich men invested their money in land and formed great estates, a phenomenon as evident in Italy as in Greece, in Asia as in Egypt. The great capitalist estates led to a decrease in small free-holdings, so much so that while slavery disappeared in those countries where it still existed, smallholdings gave way to capitalism in those areas which had long been exploited and the large landowners began to settle agricultural slaves on their estates.

On the other hand, the circulation of coined money led to a rise in living costs, while the influx of slaves captured in war competed with free labour to a distastrous extent and led to a continual fall in wages.

Thus, while landowners rapidly became rich, the middle classes were burdened with debt and sank gradually into the proletariat, whose situation continued to worsen. The artisans, in order to resist this lowering of living standards, grouped themselves in guilds which were sometimes united into confederations between one city and another and put forward social claims, especially in the Aegean cities where a serious crisis resulted from the exhaustion of the silver mines of Laurion and the gold mines of Pangea and also from the disappearance of smallholdings and the decay of the ancient cities which could no longer provide a living for their population.

The peoples rebelled, demanded land reform and the abolition of debts; social troubles broke out; the slaves too rebelled and their number, in the Greek lands, became a social danger which, however, did not prevent them from continually increasing. Delos, the main centre of the slave trade, became very wealthy.

International trade led to specialization in production. Alexandria exported grain, Aeolia and Judaea hemp, Pontus nuts, Babylon dates, Antioch figs, Syria and Ionia horsehair, Beirut currants, Damascus plums and Assyria cotton. Alexandria was the great market for Indian and Arabian products and the Phoenician cities were the export centres for Chinese goods which reached them through Bactriana. Miletus, Ephesus, Smyrna and Priene, supplied by the trade routes from Central Asia, enjoyed an immense industrial revival; silk was woven at Cos and Milesian cloth competed with Syrian industry; Alexandria manufactured textiles and paper, Pergamon luxury stuffs and parchment; Tyre and Sidon purple.

New centres sprang up and became very prosperous. Over-exploitation of silver in Attica and Thrace gave the Spanish mines a leading place in international trade; the copper mines of Euboea and Cyprus were exhausted; copper from Sinai replaced them, a fresh source of wealth for Egypt.

Specialization, made easier, quicker and more regular by new methods of navigation, led to a standardization of prices throughout the whole Mediterranean basin.

The possession of international trade-routes became a vital necessity for the great states. Because of the Suez canal, Egypt controlled the route to India, which made her the wealthiest country of the Mediterranean; Antioch owed a great part of her wealth to the caravan routes which stretched far into Asia towards China and India; Pergamon, which controlled the Straits, was enriched by the trade of the Black Sea and the Aegean; Rhodes had become a great financial centre because of her transit trade, and it was due to her position in the central Mediterranean that Rome controlled the extensive trade in silver, tin and lead extracted from the Spanish mines which were in Carthaginian hands.

These great international currents were the origin of all the wars of the IIIrd and IInd centuries BC. It was these too which determined the social evolution of all the countries through which they passed.

THE URBAN POLICY OF THE SELEUCIDS

The development of international trade led to city life and to liberty. It was the merit of the Seleucids to have understood—following the example of Alexander—the role which the urban middle classes were called upon to play in this new economy. It was the great merit of their policy to have fostered the formation of cities and the emancipation of the rural population. In all Nearer Asia, which Seleucid policy had now made a part of this economy, new cities were established. They were not, like the Egyptian cities, bound closely to the central administration or integrated with the provinces; the organization of Asia, made up of diverse peoples and lacking social and political unity, would not have allowed this. The new cities of the Seleucids were envisaged as autonomous but under the control of the king. They each had a citizens' assembly, whose function was to discuss the laws and vote the municipal budget, they elected their magistrates and they had a senate composed of those magistrates who had completed their term of office; they were presided over by a mayor, nominated by the king from among the citizens. Like the Greek cities they had a right of citizenship, that is to say a nationality of their own. They were free to maintain diplomatic relations with other cities regarding questions of mutual interest, but in political and financial matters they were subject to the royal tutelage which made them the principal economic and strategic centres of the state as well as centres of Hellenism, upon which the Seleucids tried to build the unity of their lands.

Some of these cities were military strongholds, others administrative capitals; most important among them were the trading cities established along the trade-routes, on the seacoast or in the mining areas that the king wished to exploit; there were also some which arose in the purely agricultural provinces to act as local markets and serve as a framework for the new administrative division of the country. A number of townships became cities, new towns were formed by the grouping of villages, and the villages themselves were granted elected magistrates who collected the taxes, controlled their use and administered justice.

Every city became the centre of an area which it administered, leaving the villages to decide their own internal affairs. Entire provinces of the empire were subdivided into regions under the control of cities whose government was handed over to the citizens, that is to say the property-owning middle class.

The middle classes of these new cities were built up from scratch. In order to people them, the king granted the colonists—for preference Macedonians and Greeks, but sometimes Syrians—lands taken from the crown estates, not so much that they should occupy them but that the revenue from these lands on which they were settled as free tenant-farmers might allow them to form a property-owning urban class on which the royal policy could rely. Antioch was created in this way and its population made up of ten thousand families of colonists who had been granted lands.

As for the ancient cities, they were either transformed into royal towns or were surpassed by their younger rivals. Thus Babylon, whose thousand-year-old prestige might have become an obstacle to the new policy, was finally depopulated to people the new Mesopotamian metropolis of Seleucia-on-Tigris. The ancient Phoenician and Syrian cities were eclipsed by the capital Antioch, the great port of Seleucia-of-Pieria, Laodicea-on-Sea, Apamea, Seleucia-on-Tigris, Dura Europos and many others. Tarsus became the university city of the Seleucids. And though Miletus, Ephesus and Colophon retained their prosperity, it was a new city, Pergamon, which, heir both of Troy and of Sardes, became the metropolis of Asia Minor.

Following the principles of town-planning inherited from the Babylonians and Greeks, the Seleucid cities were built according to a regular plan, both rational and grandiose, which was to serve, in the 2nd century AD, as a model for the urbanistic policy of Rome. Throughout the whole Hellenistic world, cities took on a new appearance. Each one had a theatre and a sumptuous city centre. The luxury and comfort of private houses increased greatly. Capitalists built several-storey houses to let or sell as flats.

While these cities were rising, the ancient seigniorial régime was losing ground to democracy based upon the census. The kings suppressed the last vestiges of slavery on their estates and transformed perpetual tenures into leases based on Greek law.

The great priestly estates passed gradually under state administration; the archaic seigniorial régime was suppressed, the serf villages transformed into municipalities and the priestly towns into autonomous cities. This was not, however, a systematic but a gradual reform. Immense priestly estates continued to exist in Asia Minor, in Syria and in Mesopotamia, which formed, like Jerusalem, vast sacerdotal principalities that were only to disappear in the time of the Roman Empire. But the greater number of the big temples, notably those of Ephesus and Colophon, lost their privileges and their autonomous social status.

This deep-rooted reform of social organization was accompanied by a powerful movement for the unification of law. The ancient national laws were not abolished, but the development of trade led everywhere to the adoption of a uniform system of contract, which had for a long time past been in force in the great international trade centres under the influence of

Babylon; the royal taxes, conceived in the form of a levy on landed property such as had been introduced by Darius, became general; the registry of deeds, the land-survey, were organized in the cities according to the methods, still imperfect though they were, that the Greek cities had adopted under the influence of Egyptian law. Mixed marriages spread the Greek system of marriage contract.

On the royal estates the Greek system of leases was the only system in force; the Athenian type of mortgage became a normal source of credit. Royal legislation unified banking and commercial institutions.

SOCIAL CRISIS IN THE GREEK WORLD

An analogous evolution was taking place in the kingdom of Macedonia. The capital, Pella, and the new cities of Salonica and Cassandraea were granted similar institutions to the Seleucid cities.

In the ancient Greek cities, where political life was moribund and the parties had become groups devoted to class interests, the royal authority became more and more apparent in financial and legal affairs. Courts, giving judgment according to a unified procedure, replaced popular jurisdiction. Law became a science, and the *Studies in Jurisprudence* by Theophrastus, which was to have so great an influence on the Roman jurists, is still existent to remind us of this.

Despite their economic decline, intellectual life remained intense in the ancient cities. The problem of education took, alongside that of food-supply, a leading place in internal politics. Miletus organized a state school system; in many cities elementary schools were opened and education was continued in secondary schools. Girls' schools were created. This was only one of the aspects of the emancipation of the individual which became more and more apparent; one of its characteristic features was the astonishing efflorescence of religious, funerary and scientific associations where Greeks and foreigners, free men and slaves, met. Women's clubs began to appear in Athens in imitation of those of Alexandria. The influence of women increased in all fields; they interested themselves in politics, literature and sport. In the Ist century BC they ended by holding city office.

This emancipation was accompanied by the diffusion of new philosophical ideas. The old conceptions were abandoned. Zeno, a Semite merchant, created a new social ideal in harmony with the economic evolution of the times. In the *Republic* he dreams of an egalitarian and international world where there will no longer be distinct states and where brotherhood will reign amongst all men. His influence was enormous; it penetrated the cultivated classes and the mass of the people alike and served as the doctrine of the democratic party. The diffusion of oriental ideas, on the other hand, transformed the Greek notion of slavery. Slaves were no longer regarded as 'living tools' though, in the great mining enterprises, the capitalists continued to exploit them in a horrible manner.

But while philosophy and law were smoothing out the legal differences between men, the gap between rich and poor continued to grow wider. Pauperism and unemployment were endemic in the Greek cities and led to social legislation. Doles were given to the unemployed and the infirm, and charitable funds were set up by levies on great fortunes; the public authorities made free distributions of grain. The idea spread of a human solidarity which required society to grant to all men the minimum necessary for existence. The philosophers and political writers claimed a share of the wealth of the property-owners for the disinherited. The people demanded, with threats, the abolition of debts and a land reform; the intellectuals demanded the liberation of the slaves and the suppression of private property. Insurrections broke out among the proletariat and the slaves. At Sparta, where some seven hundred families monopolized the land, there were continual revolts. In 242 BC the king, Agis IV, attempted a great reform; he cancelled debts, abolished the mortgages and divided the lands into 19,500 lots. The aristocrats rose against him. Throughout Greece conservative ideology was ranged against revolutionary ideology. The Achaean League, dominated by small property-holders, made itself the champion of the landowners, thus serving, without being aware of it, only the interests of the capitalists who were destroying the middle classes. It intervened in Sparta; Agis was condemned to death and his reforms annulled. In 237 BC Cleomenes made a fresh effort to re-establish a middle class and to reduce the too flagrant social inequalities; he gave citizen rights to the *perioikoi*, allowed six thousand helots to buy their freedom and distributed four thousand parcels of land. Once again the conservative party resisted; the Achaean League intervened and annulled the laws of Cleomenes, who was forced to flee. Thenceforward, social agitation was never to cease in Sparta, and in all the cities the party of social claims was to assume an openly revolutionary and extremist attitude.

THE SEACOAST CITIES REMAIN NEUTRAL

Despite all these troubles trade went on; but the naval wars between

Egypt and Asia curtailed it considerably. The great Greek cities, which were the stake of these wars, took no interest whatever in international affairs. They were preoccupied only with business and were drawn into armed conflict only against their will. Their merchant ships were intercepted by privateering and blockading fleets and their goods and traders were seized at sea and in port.

The seacoast cities also tried to dissociate themselves from the war by making the great states—of which they were often a part—recognize their neutral status. Miletus first, in 245 BC, managed to obtain from the powers the status of 'a city holy and inviolate', that is to say non-belligerent, which protected its citizens and its goods from the hazards of war. During the course of the IIIrd and IInd centuries BC a number of Greek, Phoenician and Syrian cities had a similar neutrality guaranteed them.

But the largest of the great merchant cities tried to avoid war by preserving their economic and political autonomy.

Rhodes, a staging-post of international trade, a grain market and a financial centre, Byzantium and Heraclea of Pontus, which held the control of the Straits, managed to remain independent republics, thanks to their fleets, as did also the cities of the northern shores of the Black Sea, whose isolation, in the midst of barbarian lands, made them of necessity autonomous states.

THE FREE TRADE POLICY OF RHODES

Rhodes was the most powerful of all these free cities. Enriched by transit trade, she practised a policy of free trade and freedom of the seas, which explains her close friendship with Byzantium, upon which the freedom of the Straits depended. Ruled by an oligarchy of traders, shipowners and bankers, Rhodes was able, thanks to her fleet, to stand up to the greatest of the states. She became a rival to Alexandria. Profiting by the wars in Syria, she tried to monopolize the trade of the Syrian cities against which Egypt was waging a tariff war. When Alexandria was imposing high customs dues on Syrian imports, Rhodes declared herself a free port, and while the royal bank of Alexandria was keeping interest rates at 24%, the Rhodian bankers offered large credits to business men at 8%.

In the IIIrd century BC Rhodes was not only a powerful economic and financial centre, but also an intellectual centre. Her university rivalled those of Tarsus and Alexandria. Her jurists, by codifying the usages of sea-law, carried out one of the greatest tasks that antiquity has bequeathed to us. After dominating the Hellenistic era, the Rhodian law of the sea was to be accepted by Rome and confirmed by Justinian; surviving the ruin of the Roman Empire, it continued to be in use at Venice, whence it passed to the cities of southern France, to Bordeaux, and then to Bruges with the wine carracks, there to become the law of Damme, and was once again adopted by Colbert in his Marine Ordinances, which remained in force until well into the 20th century.

The policy of Rhodes was diametrically opposed to that of Carthage, which monopolized the freight trade between the numerous cities of her empire. But that was precisely because Carthage was an empire and wished to preserve the huge profits of the silver mines which she possessed in Spain. Rhodes was only a staging-post without hinterland, living by international trade alone.

STATE SOCIALISM AT PERGAMON

The policy of Pergamon was quite different. From 262 BC she had been the capital of a kingdom which enjoyed an immense prosperity during the IIIrd and IInd centuries. In the Hellenistic era Pergamon took up once again the role that Lydia had played under the kings of Sardes in the VIIth and VIth centuries. She was a mercantile state whose reason for existence was trade and industry, the great international market where the trade-routes from the Mediterranean, the Black Sea and the Aegean met; she was the gate of Asia looking towards Europe. Like Lydia in earlier times, Pergamon remained strictly loyal to Egypt, upon which she relied to escape the ascendancy of the continental empire of the Seleucids. Thus she was strongly under Egyptian influence. Differing from Rhodes, which lived entirely from transit trade, Pergamon, like Alexandria, tried to obtain return freights from her own territories. Her kings therefore, following capitalist methods, practised a systematic exploitation of their crown lands, into which the vast expropriated estates of the temples were incorporated. But, contrary to Egypt, Pergamon, a Greek city, practised the exploitation of slave labour; the crown lands were confided to bailiffs who controlled the slaves and the wage-earners who were little better than slaves; in the state workshops all the workers were slaves. Parchment, the manufacture of which Pergamon introduced when the protectionist policy of the Ptolemies had made the price of Egyptian papyrus too high, was a state monopoly.

Wealth flowed into Pergamon; magnificently built, she became one of the most beautiful cities of the Hellenistic world. Her library was second only to that of Alexandria. A three-stage educational programme was organized by the state. A bold legislation on public health and hygiene was promulgated. Individualism vied with state socialism.

THE ECONOMIC POLICY OF EGYPT

In Egypt the influence of the current of cosmopolitanism took quite a different form. Egyptian economy was dominated by the Delta, the region of the cities; slavery had completely disappeared since the Vth century BC, and the aims that the policy of the Seleucids had set in Nearer Asia had already been long fulfilled in Egypt which was by far the most advanced state of the times. The bond between Egyptians and Greeks, which had grown closer and closer since Saite times, brought to Egypt the language and, with it, the culture of the Greeks. Since Alexander, Greek had become the official language not only of the empire but also of the internal administration, as in the Seleucid kingdom.

Greek law, under which the Greeks settled in Egypt had continued to live, had, however, little or no influence on Egyptian law, save that the mixed marriages between Greeks and Egyptians, which were frequent in the IIIrd century, led to a setback to Egyptian individualism because of the introduction of guardianship over women which was sanctioned by a decree of the Ptolemies in the IIIrd century.

But, over and above this system which created a new conception of legal personality, a new usage was created which introduced simplified legal forms, among which was the contract of 'homologation' which was substituted for sale, rent or loan and which was to pass into Roman law in the times of Justinian; as also the Egyptian accounting method which introduced new usages into commercial law, such as the need for a trader to prove his credits by producing his ledgers. The diffusion of international commercial usages was only one aspect of the economic cosmopolitanism which was expressed in characteristic fashion in the importance assumed by banking. In all the Greek world, in Syria and Rome, banking was in the hands of private companies. But in Egypt, where the administration was strongly centralized, the Ptolemies made it a part of the state institutions. A royal bank which was set up at Alexandria had a monopoly of banking operations throughout the whole country. Placed under the supervision of the Ministry of Finance, which was controlled by the capitalists, it had agencies even in the smaller towns. The state empowered it to centralize all its treasury operations, in order to make use of its reserves of precious metals by lending them at the rate fixed by law at 24%. The result was a great extension of credit possibilities. But the lack of initiative due to an official monopoly soon showed that it was incapable of competing with the private banks which continued to reduce their interest rates. In the IInd century Alexandria saw herself surpassed as the centre of international finance by Rhodes, where interest rates were to fall to 8%.

The economic policy of Egypt was not based on the same premises as those of the Greek states, more especially Rhodes. Egypt was an import and an export centre. Commerce was kept alive by the exploitation of products cultivated and manufactured within the country. Rhodes lived from the transport of goods, from her role as middleman and from finance. Egypt lived from the sale of her own products and those which she imported from Nubia, Arabia and India. She possessed a prosperous agriculture and industry. Alexandria was not a city of shipowners and bankers like Rhodes; it was a city of merchants. The policy of Egypt was to assure a favourable trade balance and, to do that, she must produce what she sold.

That is one of the reasons which explains why Egypt had not given monetary economy so large a place as it occupied in the Greek cities of traffickers and shipowners.

Taxes and even rents were often paid in kind, at least partially. The state thus amassed enormous reserves of grain and raw materials. Formerly, it had used these to pay its officials and its workers. But the extension of international monetary economy compelled her in the IIIrd century to cash in on her stocks, that is to say to manufacture them and sell them either within the country or abroad. The Ptolemies thus became the greatest grain merchants of the world and the crown lands played a more and more important industrial role in the economy of the country.

Continuing the policy of exploitation already undertaken by the Saite kings, the Ptolemies did their best to improve the yield from their domains; they acclimatized the famous Milesian breed of sheep, which allowed them to introduce a textile industry into Egypt, had selected seed reserved for their tenants and inaugurated a system of production bonuses in the estate workshops where only wage-earning labour was employed.

Since the mines and quarries had always been a state monopoly in Egypt, it is possible to estimate the importance of the business that depended directly on the king, though the commercial policy of the Ptolemies was, to begin with, frankly liberal; it aimed at enriching the country through the prosperity of business and making Alexandria the leading trade metropolis of the world. The wars waged with the Seleucids had no other aim than to assure to Egyptian merchants mastery of the India trade-route and the traffic of the Aegean. In the IIIrd century trade with India was mainly by way of the Red Sea, where, thanks to the Suez canal, Berenice and Arsinoe became important ports. The Egyptian squadron which was moored at Samothrace controlled the traffic with the Pontic Euxine, and the Phoenician cities, which formed part of the empire of the Ptolemies, dominated the Asiatic hinterland.

Alexandria, centre of distribution for spices, luxury goods, grain exports, papyrus, textiles, Sinai copper, gold, ebony and ivory from Arabia and Nubia, was the richest city in the world. The Ptolemaic gold *stater* played in the IIIrd century BC the same role in international trade as the pound sterling in the 19th century of our era.

Alexandria was also the principal centre of scientific knowledge, which greatly extended its influence. Missions, both scientific and economic, were sent to India, Eritrea and Arabia. The discovery of the periodicity of the monsoons enabled Egyptian shipowners to develop regular trade relations with India.

But Egypt, though she practised a liberal policy, was not absolutely a free trade state. She wished to reserve her home market for her own products. So, in the IIIrd century BC, she found herself faced by a formidable problem. In Egypt, industry and agriculture did not use slave labour, while throughout the Hellenistic world slavery became more and more widespread and wages fell. Egyptian industry was therefore dangerously threatened by foreign competition, where manufacturing costs were lower, and more especially by imports carried by Phoenician and Syrian ships. Egypt therefore took customs measures against them. From the middle of the IIIrd century she carried out an openly protectionist policy. Syrian wines paid from 33⅓% to 50% entry duties *ad valorem*, honey 25%, salted meats 25% and oil 50%. It was the first example of a policy of customs protection. Undertaken at first to favour national production, it was influenced, from 259 BC onward, by fiscal needs. The expenses of the wars and the maintenance of the armed forces were heavy. The state tried to increase the production of the crown lands; it developed its industrial activity and thus found itself drawn into monopolies, at least a monopoly of oil which was indispensable for food and light and whose sale it reserved to itself; it was a form of indirect taxation. But Egypt only produced sesame oil of low quality. Imports of olive oil were therefore necessary; it was admitted, but subjected to a 50% duty and restricted to a quota. At first oil was the only monopoly introduced, but monopolies of salt and nitre were to follow. It is true that the customs duties only affected certain goods and that imports from Asia and Arabia were exempted. The economic policy of the Ptolemies was based on a mercantilism which aimed at increasing national production and assuring a favourable trade balance. That explains the state bank monopoly and the high money rates; Egypt was not trying to attract traders, bankers and speculators. She produced, imported and sold.

THE IMPERIAL POLICY OF ROME

Rome, in the IIIrd century BC, had become the centre of a great state and had under her rule great democratic merchant cities like Naples, Tarentum and the cities of Sicily, as well as landowning peoples in the most diverse stages of evolution. She could no longer dream of integrating her conquests purely and simply into the Roman state; they would have swamped it.

The Republic became, after the annexation of Sicily, Corsica and Sardinia, an empire, which included territories with differing degrees of legal development; the Roman territory, divided among thirty-five citizen states, extended over central Italy, from Cerea to Cumae on the Tyrrhenian Sea, from Pisaurum to Hadria on the Adriatic. It was a national state, of which Rome was the centre, and all of whose inhabitants lived according to the same private law and possessed, if they settled in Rome, the same public rights. The rest of Italy formed the allied territory. It was divided into 'Latin colonies' whose constitution was similar to that of Rome and whose inhabitants lived under Roman law, though they were not citizens, and allied or federated cities whose status varied and which did not form part of the Roman state. Finally, the two provinces, Sicily and Corsica-Sardinia, were put under the rule of magistrates, annually nominated at Rome and given the power of viceroys. It was the first time that a republic applied in its provinces a policy similar to that of the monarchies.

Even outside her national territory Rome practised a policy of assimilation with supreme skill. Colonies of Roman citizens were settled throughout the country and formed part of the national state. Certain peoples were integrated with the Roman state and obtained the right of citizenship. Furthermore, Rome everywhere accorded Roman citizenship individually to members of the ruling class and to local magistrates in the conquered countries. Roman democracy was thus projected outwards in a gradation that conferred first the lesser and then the greater rights of naturalization, thus gradually assimilating the subject peoples and practising a liberalism that the Greeks never knew and of which, about 200 BC, Philip V of Macedon had given them an example in vain.

However the problem soon arose of the relations between Roman citizens and the *peregrini* (foreigners) who remained outside the scope of Roman law. The annexation of Sicily, reduced to a province in 241 BC, gave Rome one of the richest and most civilized countries in the Greek world. Quite naturally, the *peregrini*, especially the Greeks, who came to settle in Rome took a more important part in economic life from day to day. Rome was drawn, by the Greek cities which she had conquered, into the orbit of international trade. The annexation of Naples forced her to mint a silver coinage, whereas in her relations with Illyria she limited herself to issuing stamped bronze tokens. The capture of Tarentum and her victories over Carthage made her a great naval power. Commerce and capitalism at once appeared. Senators placed their fortunes at sea and owned ships; a middle class of business men was rapidly created, among which were numerous *peregrini* and foreign freedmen who had been admitted to Roman citizenship. As formerly at Athens under Pericles, Roman commerce was mainly in the hands of non-citizens, amongst whom the Hellenized peoples took the lead. Transactions between Romans and *peregrini* necessarily created legal complications which Roman law, still very archaic, did not foresee. Rome did not hesitate. With a liberalism which recalls that of the Saite kings, who authorized the Greeks to have recourse to their own courts at Naucratis, Rome accorded a legal status to foreigners. In 366 BC the administration of justice was taken from the consuls and handed over to a special magistrate, the praetor. In 241 BC, the same year as Sicily became a Roman province, a praetor was instituted known as the peregrine praetor; his duty was to render justice in cases where *peregrini* were involved and he was not compelled to apply the rules of Roman law. He was quite naturally inspired by their national laws and a procedure was created with astonishing speed which was to adapt Roman law to new requirements, leading to a greater and greater emancipation of the individual. Women were freed from marital authority; in the IInd century a woman was able to sue for divorce; marriage, as in Greece and Egypt, became a simple civil contract; the power of the *paterfamilias*, always so tenaciously maintained at Rome, began to be restricted. Contract law became more supple, permitting an even greater fluidity of both movable and immovable goods. The usages of international commercial law became current at Rome. Banks and business companies made their appearance. At the same time Hellenic culture was revealed to the Romans. A Greek, Livius Andronicus, brought as a captive from Tarentum, introduced the works of Homer; he translated them into Latin (240 BC) and wrote the first Latin tragedies; while Naevius the Campanian staged political comedies inspired by Aristophanes (235 BC). The breeze from the outer world came from Alexandria, where the university founded by Ptolemy I had become the centre of Hellenism which now forced its way into the Roman spirit of nationalism. The moral ideas of the east and the oriental religions spread. Rome was conquered by the great cosmopolitan movement that had already traversed the Greco-Oriental world.

CHAPTER XXXVI
HELLENISTIC CIVILIZATION

CIVILIZATION BECOMES UNIVERSAL IN CHARACTER

As international trade was profoundly changing social ideas, so intellectual life was also being transformed. Cosmopolitanism and conceptions of natural law led to the disappearance of the former nationalisms. In all the Mediterranean countries, philosophical thought, science and literature expressed in a common international language, Greek, acquired a universal character. Civilization became a value common to all men. Even religions were subjected to this great movement of syncretism. It was in Alexandria that the movement was at its most vigorous. This international city was open to all cults. All the nature gods, Osiris, Adonis, Dionysus, Attis, Tammuz, all the solar gods, Ammon-Ra, Shamash, Zeus, attracted the piety of the masses who treated a number of them as identical. At the beginning of the IIIrd century BC a doctrinal essay at synthesis was attempted there by two theologians, the Greek, Timotheos of Eleusis, and the Egyptian, Manetho, who united all the solar and nature gods in the single cult of the great god Serapis, who was both a creator-god and a saviour-god.

Basically conceived as a syncretism of the creator-god, Ammon-Ra, and the saviour-god, dead and resurrected for men, Serapis was, following Egyptian tradition, a trinity. But the triune character of the divinity had been considerably modified since the times when the Egyptian New Empire had conceived it in the form Ptah-Ammon-Ra, the body, the spirit and the conscience of the world.

The new trinity, Ammon-Ra-Osiris, which was manifested in Serapis no longer included the notion of the 'body' of the universe. In compensation, it combined solar spirituality with the mysticism of the Osirian cult. Serapis was no longer the image of the universe; he was, in a single godhead, the creator of the world, its conscience and the saviour of men.

Alongside the cult of Serapis, that of Isis, wife of Osiris, who presided over the Isiac mysteries, became more and more important. Uniting in herself all the ancient mother-goddesses she became a divine pantheon of love, abundance, truth and wisdom: 'Our Lady of Perpetual Help'. Curiously enough, she lost her role as wife to Osiris, and was adored under the double aspect of goddess-queen and goddess-mother of Horus, the god-infant, the conqueror of evil, born miraculously of Isis after the death of his father, Osiris. The role of saviour-god was handed on by Osiris to his son Horus, the son of god, whose weakness, by triumphing over evil, saved mankind.

The cult of Serapis, symbolized at Memphis by the bull Apis, was to spread very widely and, in its solar aspect, was later to be adopted as the official religion of the Roman Empire.

ZENO AND STOICISM

The religion of the mystery cults broke away from philosophy which, however, no longer occupied, as in the times of classical Greece, the leading place in intellectual speculation. Since Aristotle, metaphysical speculation had receded into the background. The contradictory systems proposed by the idealist and materialist schools had ended in scepticism.

In opposition to the religious sentiment, more and more disposed to mysticism and faith, Epicurus professed the most absolute materialism. He proposed a moral system based on the search for a happiness made up of moderated and wise pleasures, avoiding ambition and excessive desires. Scepticism thus found its conclusion in a resigned pessimism.

It was a Semite, Zeno of Citium (died 260 BC), an insolvent Cypriot merchant, who restored to Greek thought confidence in its possibilities. Since philosophy was bankrupt, Zeno proposed to turn to knowledge; not towards a speculative and theoretical knowledge, but to a living knowledge devoted to practical research, and on this search for scientific truth he constructed a code of morals. Regarding God, like the Egyptians, as the conscience of the world, Zeno took from the Heliopolitan theology its magnificent and fruitful optimism. While conceiving the soul as a particle of divinity, which after death would return to and become merged in it, he denied individual immortality. He therefore expected no other reward from virtue than the joy of doing good; man will attain his highest moral development by devoting himself to knowledge, since knowledge is the law of the world, ordained by the divine conscience to perpetual progress.

Not only religion, but also the Stoic philosophy which was to become almost a religion for the intellectual élite was a synthesis of all the trends of the time. Though realist, it remained attached to spirituality by affirming its faith in a pantheist monotheism. By regarding the soul as a particle of divinity, it proclaimed the equality of all men, as well as the close bond that united them; it made itself the champion of the ideas of natural law and, in consequence, of democracy which it wished to base both on respect for human individuality and on a close social unity, in the name of which it advocated extensive humanitarian reforms.

FREEDOM OF THOUGHT AND SCIENTIFIC DEVELOPMENT

The Stoic philosophy of the democratic movement led to a remarkable diffusion of culture. Great libraries were collected at Alexandria, which had seven hundred thousand volumes, Antioch, Pergamon, Rhodes and Smyrna. Near their palace the Ptolemies founded the 'Museum' where savants subsidized by the royal treasury were devoted solely to the search for knowledge. All the sovereigns of the time surrounded themselves with historians and learned men. Many of them, like Ptolemy I and Pyrrhus, published their memoirs.

Athens remained the centre of the philosophic schools where the great systems were taught; Platonism at the Academy, Aristotelianism at the Lyceum, Stoicism in the Porch and Epicureanism in the Garden of Epicurus. They attracted many students from all countries. Tarsus was the principal university city of Asia. A school of medicine, soon to become famous, was opened in Alexandria; and the lectures of Euclid made it the centre of mathematical studies.

There were continual scientific exchanges between all countries, encouraged by a freedom of opinion not to be found again before the 19th century of our era. Despite the triumph of mysticism, freedom of thought prevailed throughout the East unhampered by the slightest political or religious censorship, except at Jerusalem where the priests tried to impose their official doctrine under pain of death.

Greek literature, by becoming international, changed profoundly. Writers and public alike avoided traditional subjects and classical tragedy. The comedy of manners triumphed with Menander, and didactic poems, works of imagination and picturesque idylls—like the *Pastorals* of Theocritus—had an enormous vogue. The study of human personality, which made portraiture the artistic fashion of the times, was represented in literature by the *Characters* of Theophrastus. Romances were all the rage. The *Romance of Alexander* was read from India to Gaul. Books were written on every conceivable subject; gastronomy, stock-breeding, gardening, to say nothing of licentious tales of the demi-monde and scandal about men in the public eye. The public crowded to lectures and concerts, were interested in learned publications which daily became more numerous. As a result of this erudition, history, from the time of Aristotle, entered a new phase. Dicearchus sketched out a history of Greek civilization. Histories of art, poetry and the sciences were published. Philology and grammar were the subject of learned studies. Science, in the real sense of the word, developed extraordinarily. The Babylonian, Kidinnu of Sippar, calculated the duration of the year as 365 days, five hours, forty-one minutes and sixteen seconds.[1] Aristarchus of Samos discovered that the earth and the planets turn around the sun which, like the fixed stars, remains motionless. His system, it is true, was to be rejected by Hipparchus and Ptolemy, who were to adopt the geocentric formula, perpetuated up to the times of Copernicus. Dicearchus drew a map of the world. Eratosthenes of Cyrene calculated the circumference of the earth, which he reckoned, almost exactly, at 24,660·5 miles; he studied the tides, proved that Europe, Asia and Africa together form an island, and claimed that it would be possible to reach India by travelling westward from Spain. Euclid published his eight books of geometry; a little later, Apollonius of Perga, at the court of Pergamon, inaugurated trigonometry. And Alexandria, putting into practice the discoveries of science, built on the island of Pharos a lighthouse nearly four hundred feet high, provided with concave mirrors.

Medicine assumed a definite scientific character; the motor nerves were distinguished from the sense nerves, arterial circulation was studied, thanks to the dissection of corpses and even, it is said, by vivisection, which may have been occasionally permitted at Alexandria in the IIIrd century on those condemned to death. Zoology and the natural sciences also developed. Chemistry and physics alone, despite the atomist theory put forward by Democritus, made no progress after Archimedes, owing to the lack of research instruments.

Everywhere in Egypt, Asia and Greece a similar trend dominated the arts and influenced thought, that of triumphant individualism which, freeing the Hellenized peoples from prejudices of race, nationality, language and religion, prepared them, despite the wars waged by economic and political imperialism, to unite in a single civilization based on two essential ideas; respect for the individual conscience and the universal value of reason and moral conceptions. These ideas reached their highest

[1] The error was only seven minutes sixteen seconds.

expression in the IInd century BC in the work of the Greek, Polybius, the greatest historian of antiquity, who, free from all national preoccupations, envisaged the historic evolution of all the Hellenized peoples as leading them towards a universal empire of which, for him, Rome was the centre and the culmination.

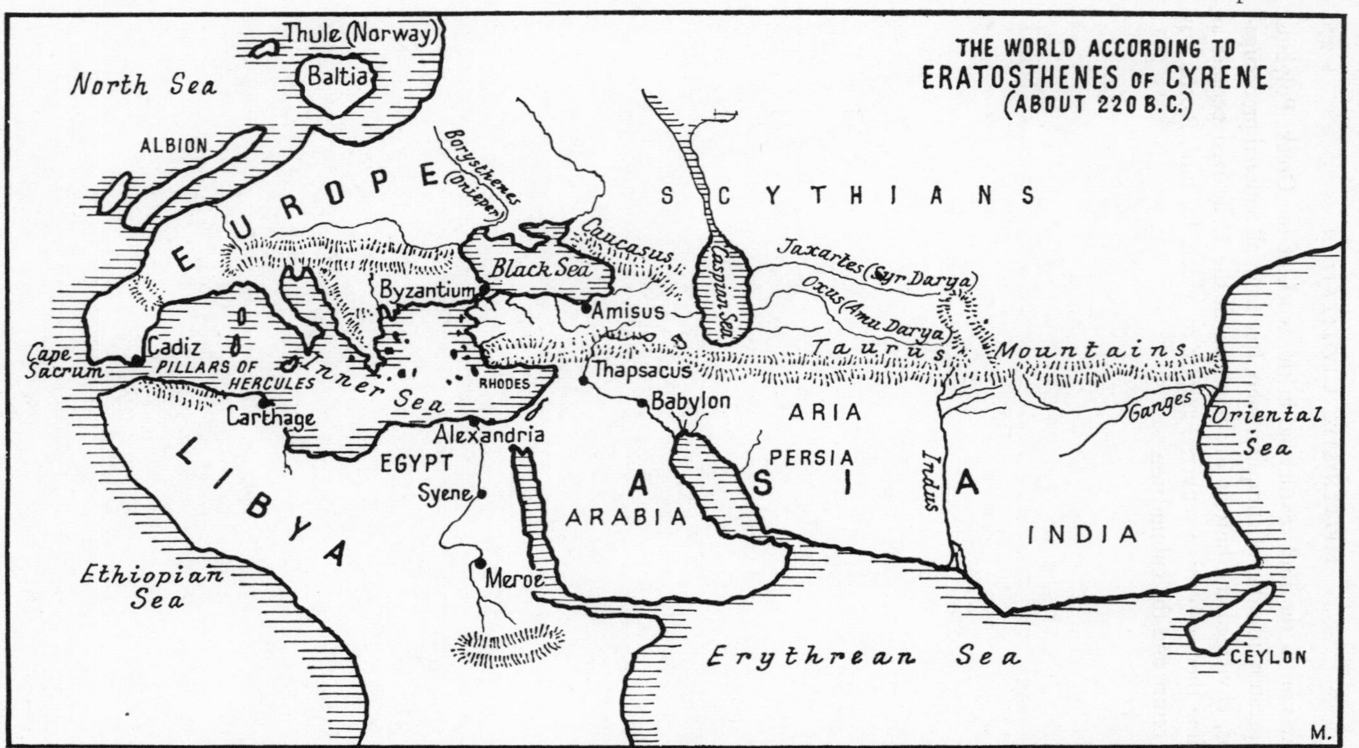

Eratosthenes made geography a science. He regarded the earth as a globe floating in the centre of the universe. He uses meridians and parallels for the first time and divides his map of the world into degrees of latitude.

BOOK VIII

The Triumph of Rome. IInd and Ist Centuries BC

CHAPTER XXXVII

ROME GAINS THE MASTERY OF THE SEAS

THE period which began after the first Punic War was marked by a double policy of hegemony. Antiochus III, King of Asia (223–187 BC)[1], profiting by the decline of the Maurya dynasty which was evident in India after the great reign of King Asoka (233 BC), was to make a supreme military effort to restore his empire; and Rome, which had acquired a dominant maritime position in the central Mediterranean by its victory over Carthage, was making ready to assume, once and for all, the mastery of the seas in the West.

ANTIOCHUS III AIMS AT HEGEMONY BY THE RESTORATION OF A CONTINENTAL EMPIRE

Profiting by the war about to break out again between Rome and Carthage (220 BC) and by the internal crisis in Egypt at the beginning of the reign of Ptolemy IV (221 BC) Antiochus III attempted an invasion of Egypt which, had it succeeded, would have assured him mastery both of Syria and of the Red Sea. But, after taking possession of the Egyptian lands in Syria, he was brought to a halt at Raphia in 217 BC.

Renouncing his plan, he turned once more toward the continent. From 212 to 204 BC, with a powerful army of a hundred thousand infantry and twenty thousand cavalry, he undertook a series of campaigns in Central Asia and recovered Armenia, Parthia and Bactria for his empire. In 206 BC he tried to re-conquer the Punjab. He failed, but concluded a treaty of alliance with the princes of the Indus which gave him trade advantages and war-elephants. His victories permitted Antiochus III to revert to his plans for economic and maritime hegemony. Master of the Oxus regions, he controlled the important caravan trade of Central Asia. But the key of sea-borne trade was still Egypt, although her position had lessened in importance after the loss of Syria. To seize from her the mastery of the seas, Antiochus III resolved first of all to expel her from the

[1] The Kingdom of the Seleucids never had a name. It is referred to by the title of its kings, whether as Kings of Syria or of Asia.

Aegean where her alliance with Pergamon had firmly established her.

It was here that the alliance concluded with Philip V of Macedon should have assumed its full importance. Threatened on the Adriatic by Rome and cut off from the Aegean by the alliance of Egypt and Pergamon, Philip V had tied his destinies to those of the Seleucid Kingdom in the East and had approached Carthage in the West. The coalition of Asia, Macedonia and Carthage countered the supremacy of Egypt in the eastern Mediterranean and of Rome in the central Mediterranean by a plan designed to assure the predominance of the Seleucid Kingdom in Nearer Asia and of Carthage in the central and western Mediterranean. To carry out this plan, Philip V employed all his resources in the construction of a great navy. The Phoenician and Macedonian fleets were to make common cause against the squadrons of Egypt and Pergamon, and, in view of the inevitable struggle, the diplomacy of both coalitions did its best to attract Rhodes and Byzantium, the two great Greek naval powers, one keeping watch and ward over the access of Syria to the Aegean and the other guarding the Straits.

ROME AIMS AT THE MASTERY OF THE SEAS
THE SECOND PUNIC WAR

While these great events were taking place in the East, Rome was making ready for her decisive struggle against Carthage. But first she had to eliminate the danger of invasion that threatened Italy from a coalition of Cisalpine Gauls and Belgian tribes from the farther side of the Alps. Rome took the initiative and conquered the valley of the Po (225 BC). Now able to rely upon her Alpine frontier which protected her on the European side she turned resolutely seaward. What Rome wanted was Spain and its rich silver mines. She assembled two invasion armies at Pisa and at Lilybaeum, and had fleets ready to transport them. Her pretext was the defence of the rights of Marseilles which had been threatened by Carthage in Spain.

In order to paralyse Carthage, Rome, declaring herself the champion of Greek interests in Sicily, appealed for the support of Syracuse in the central Mediterranean. In reply, Hannibal denounced the barbarism of Rome and proclaimed himself the representative of Hellenic civilization; he undertook a propaganda campaign, assisted by the Greek historian Sosyles and a whole court of Sicilians who had grouped themselves around him.

The war was preceded by an ideological campaign.

Carthage occupied Saguntum in Spain, which she was entitled to do by the treaty of the Ebro; but Rome declared war (219 BC). Carthaginian diplomacy, however, had won precious allies in the Gauls. Threatened from the north, Rome was forced to use the armies which she had made ready for the invasion of Spain to defend her northern frontiers, while Hannibal's army reached Italy by forced marches, crossed the Alps, joined up with the rebellious Gauls and crushed the Roman legions in the battles of Lake Trasimene and Cannae (216 BC). The Roman defeats led to the defection of Syracuse which, on the death of Hieron II (215 BC), joined the Carthaginian camp. Hannibal, holding out his hand across the Adriatic to Macedonia, concluded a military alliance with Philip V against Rome.

While Hannibal was invading Italy, Antiochus III marched against Egypt. The year 217 BC saw almost simultaneously the two great battles of Lake Trasimene in Italy and of Raphia on the Egyptian frontier. Antiochus III, less fortunate than Hannibal, did not succeed in breaking the resistance of Ptolemy IV whose armies had just been reorganized by the incorporation of Egyptians in their ranks in place of Greek mercenaries. Egypt remained inviolate. But the battle of Raphia, although won, had cost Ptolemy too dearly to allow him to dream of exploiting his victory.

The victorious resistance of Egypt could not, therefore, bring any improvement to the almost desperate plight of Rome. Militarily alone, before the coalition of Carthage supported by Syracuse, Macedonia and Antiochus III, then at the height of his power, Rome nerved herself for an immense effort. Renouncing the party struggles that rent her, she granted full powers to the dictator Fabius Maximus and demanded that all her citizens should hand over, as a loan, all the gold, silver and bronze that they possessed. The intervention of the little Greek power, the Aetolian League, came opportunely, since it prevented the disembarkation in Italy of the Macedonian army which Hannibal was expecting in order to take decisive action against Rome.

Fearing the victory of Philip V, which would have delivered all Greece into his hands, the Aetolian League formed a close alliance with Rome and Pergamon. The two conflicts, Rome against Carthage, and Asia and Macedonia against Egypt and Pergamon, thenceforward merged in a general war. Its fate was decided by the Aetolian League which paralyzed the armies of Philip V and kept them in Greece at the critical moment. Thanks to the respite thus granted, the Roman people, united in a common outburst of patriotism, triumphed. Hannibal was driven out of Italy and the offensive, carried over into Sicily, took Syracuse (211 BC), while the

Roman fleets and armies in Spain captured first Cartagena (209 BC) and then Gades (206 BC).

The balance of forces having changed, Philip V, engaged against the Aetolian League, sued for peace (205 BC) and, thinking to gain an advantage, committed the error of sharing with Rome[1] the coastwise state of Illyria. Thus Rome installed her forces at Pharos (in the northern part of present-day Albania) whence she was able to dominate the Adriatic.

Vanquished Carthage had to give up the struggle (202 BC), cede Spain and its mines to Rome, hand over her fleet and agree to pay the expenses of the war.

From then on, Rome reigned without a rival over the whole Mediterranean from the Pillars of Hercules to the Macedonian coast of the Adriatic. Her magnificent effort had made her the greatest naval and military power of the times.

ROME INTERVENES TO DEFEND THE GREEKS AND EGYPT AGAINST MACEDONIA

At the time of the fall of Carthage, a child, Ptolemy V, ascended the throne of Egypt (203 BC). Judging Rome to be exhausted by her long struggle with Carthage, Antiochus III immediately concluded an agreement with Philip V for the partition of the Egyptian Empire. Philip V, believing himself assured against Rome by the treaty which he had just signed, took possession of the northern shore of the Hellespont which had always been in the possession of Egypt (202 BC). Egypt did not react. But Byzantium and Pergamon, fearful of being crushed between Macedonia and Asia, and Rhodes, which feared the closing of the Straits, resisted Philip and appealed to Rome. The Roman fleet appeared in the Straits, preceded by an ultimatum demanding that Philip respect the freedom of the Greeks and the integrity of the Egyptian possessions. The Achaean League, which had been joined by the maritime cities of Corinth, Megara and Sicyon, allied itself with Rome to defend the freedom of the seas. The Roman legions disembarked in Greece and defeated the Macedonian army at Cynocephalae in Thessaly (197 BC). Philip V was defeated and obliged to hand over his entire fleet to Rome and pay her an indemnity of a thousand talents.

After this brilliant triumph, in which she had played the part of guardian of Greek independence and protector of Egypt, Rome evacuated Greece without demanding any territorial annexations. It was enough for her to have destroyed the fleet of Macedonia as well as that of Carthage.

[1] It may be recalled that it had become a vassal of Rome in 225 BC.

Henceforward, only Greek and Egyptian fleets, allies of Rome, cruised the seas.

Rome was to impose her naval supremacy over the whole East.

THE NAVAL SUPREMACY OF ROME TRIUMPHS OVER THE CONTINENTAL EMPIRE OF ANTIOCHUS III

There remained only one hostile power facing Rome, the power of Antiochus III who had just completed the restoration of a great continental empire stretching as far as India and Bactriana. He held, in addition, all the eastern shores of the Mediterranean, from Thrace to Palestine, with the exception of the possessions of Pergamon and Rhodes. But he had committed the irreparable error of not intervening against Rome at the time of the Macedonian war. He had now to support alone all the weight of the inevitable conflict. The last act of the great duel, commenced long before by the Persian wars, between the Asiatic continent, represented by the King of Antioch, and the sea, of which this time Rome appeared as the champion, was about to take place.

The possession of the Straits had been the cause of the war between Rome and Macedonia; it was also to lead to the struggle between Rome and Antiochus III. Master of the Persian Gulf, and of Syria whence he had an outlet on the Red Sea, Antiochus III had now to get possession of Pergamon and Byzantium to complete the conquest of the coastline of his empire and to dominate the Black Sea. In 197 BC he occupied Ephesus, the advance port of Pergamon, and in 196 BC installed himself on the Hellespont. Foreseeing war, Hannibal, ready to take up arms once more against Rome, sought refuge at the court of Antiochus.

Rome could not abandon the Straits and Pergamon to Antiochus III without compromising her naval supremacy. As previously she had called on Philip V, she now called upon Antiochus III to relinquish the territories he had just occupied and respect the integrity of the Egyptian possessions and the liberty of the Greeks. On his refusal, war broke out. Greece was its theatre.

Divided by social conflicts, the Greeks were also divided between the belligerents, whose diplomacy sought to exploit their dissensions. Rome declared herself defender not only of the freedom of the seas but of the interests of the property-owning and mercantile classes; Pergamon, Byzantium, Rhodes and the Achaean League, then dominated by Corinth, turned to her. Antiochus III, on the other hand, supported the popular party. The Aetolian League, in which the democrats had just triumphed, and the party of social reforms throughout the whole country allied themselves to the King of Asia, from whom they naïvely expected the realization of their revolutionary aspirations.

Thus the great struggle for hegemony, which ranged land and sea against one another, assumed in Greece the form of a civil war.

Rome won. The peace of Apamea (188 BC) gave her the fleet of Antiochus; Pergamon got all the coasts of Asia Minor, with the exception of Southern Caria and Lycia which went to Rhodes. All the Greek cities of Asia outside the kingdom of Pergamon had their freedom recognized. Antiochus III kept only the Syrian sea-coast. Rome saddled him with immense reparations but, this time also, renounced any territorial annexations. It was enough for her to have driven back the King of Asia from the sea, where henceforth Roman supremacy was uncontested. Egypt and the Greek cities now passed into the Roman sphere of influence. Rome became the protector and arbiter of all the Mediterranean states.

CHAPTER XXXVIII

ROMAN IMPERIALISM AND THE DECLINE OF THE EASTERN STATES

INTERNATIONAL POLITICAL EVOLUTION

RIVALRY between Rome and the great Oriental states was now no longer possible. All the cards were stacked in favour of Rome. International trade, by uniting all the coastal peoples of the Mediterranean into a single Mediterranean economy, centred all its active forces on Rome which, since the peace of Apamea, dominated the seaways without a rival. In her national army she had at her disposal a military power which no state could hope to resist. Roman democracy, now in full expansion, possessed, like the Greek cities of the Vth century BC, a power of growth which contrasted most strikingly with the signs of dissolution shown by the ancient Oriental states. Hellenism, concentrated on the sea, that is to say on Rome, was disintegrating Asia and even Egypt, despite her strong national tradition. The Kingdom of the Seleucids, in its maritime provinces, was dominated by Hellenism, whose influence extended as far as the Euphrates; in the ancient regions of Iran, on the other hand, the attraction of Iranian Zoroastrianism was directly opposed to Greek influences; as to the former oriental provinces of the Empire, cut off by Parthia from the coastal regions, they were irremediably lost, despite the Hellenistic influences which had penetrated there after Alexander's conquests; they were to be irresistibly drawn into the political and economic orbit of India.

The great design of the Achaemenid kings, continued by Alexander and the Seleucids, to create a continental empire looking both towards the Mediterranean and the Far East had finally failed. Driven towards the sea, the kings of Antioch could no longer hold their own save by creating a naval power; but the power of Rome and the centrifugal tendencies which permeated their lands as a result of Mediterranean trade condemned in advance the great effort they were to make.

Greece was exhausted, and was disintegrating into social factions. Only the great trade centres of Rhodes, Byzantium and Pergamon were still active and vigorous. But their naval and trading activities necessarily tied them to the Mediterranean; they had either to come to terms with the naval supremacy of Rome or submit to it.

Macedonia, intensely Hellenized, could only play a leading political role by unifying and assimilating Greece. But the check to her Greek policy had been complete; she could no longer withstand the supremacy of Rome, now mistress of the seas.

Alone among the Oriental states, Egypt had preserved her national unity. But the Hellenization of her ruling classes had created a deep division between the intellectual élite, the business community and the government officials on the one hand, and the mass of the people on the other. The extension of the Egyptian Empire which, during the first half of the IIIrd century BC, had included the Cyclades, the coasts of Asia Minor and of Syria, had led to the predominance of the Hellenized elements; but the prosperity which this had given to the great cities of the Delta, the Red Sea ports and Egyptian agriculture and industry, had created a balance between the Greek and Egyptian elements, on which Egypt had built up her supremacy. Alone of all the Oriental monarchies, she could have become a great Mediterranean land- and sea-power, because of the bond she had achieved between Hellenism and the civilization of the ancient East, and between her maritime economy and her solid agricultural and industrial structure.

Her position between the Mediterranean and India and her favourable trade balance had made her, in the reigns of Ptolemy I and Ptolemy II, the greatest power of her time. It would then have been possible to pose the question which of the two naval hegemonies, the Egyptian or the Roman, would have won the day. The alliance concluded with Rome would have been able to ensure a system of balance had the two states had equivalent military forces. But since the reign of Ptolemy III (246–221 BC) it had become clear that such a balance did not exist. The armed forces of Egypt were too exclusively naval. After the brilliant victories of Ptolemy II, the Egyptian army had begun to lose the supremacy which it had held in the East for sixty years.

The breakdown of the balance of power, precipitated by the weakness first of Egypt and then of the Seleucid Kingdom, unsettled not only international relations but also the internal evolution of the two states which had until then been the leaders: Rome and Egypt.

Rome, intoxicated by the possibilities opening before her, embarked on an imperialist policy. Egypt, eliminated from the international scene, tried to preserve the wealth she had acquired by withdrawing into autarchy. Lack of political balance was grafted on to lack of economic balance. The period of great international crises was beginning.

ROMAN IMPERIALISM

The wars against Carthage, Macedonia and the Seleucid Kingdom had an immense influence on the internal structure of the Roman state. For the first time in history a democratic republic had become the mistress of a territorial empire. The annexation of Sicily (241 BC), of Corsica and Sardinia (237 BC) and of Spain (202 BC) created for the Romans difficult problems of public law.

In the course of these wars the principle of power had been greatly modified according to the needs of the moment. After the defeat at Cannae democracy had relinquished the control of affairs to the Senate and, since then, Rome had been governed by an oligarchy.

Without modifying the republican constitution of the state the Senate had endowed it with imperial institutions. It had raised permanent armies in which, alongside the citizen legions, were contingents furnished by the allied and subject peoples. The army ceased to be exclusively a nation in arms. Its maintenance necessitated large resources. Imitating the Ptolemies, Rome had first sought them by establishing customs duties and a salt monopoly. But soon, far from being an expense, war—after the final victory over Carthage—had become a source of enormous profits. Rome derived a considerable revenue from the war indemnities imposed on the vanquished states. Carthage was forced to pay an annual tribute of two hundred talents for fifty years; vanquished Macedonia had been burdened with an indemnity of a thousand talents, and Antiochus III, by the peace of Apamea, had agreed to pay the exorbitant sum of fifteen thousand talents in twelve annual instalments. To administer this imperial treasure, which was outside the control of the elected magistrates, the Senate had created, on the Hellenistic model, a financial administration distinct from the republican institutions. The influence of the citizens on the destinies of the state had thereby been considerably reduced.

THE ADVENT OF CAPITALISM IN ROME

As a result, the influence of the financiers had rapidly become of overwhelming importance. Not only did Rome now have at her disposal enormous resources, but the vast booty brought back by her generals from the wars in the East had given the Roman oligarchy fluid wealth for which no use could be found in Rome itself. The pillage of the conquered countries made Rome the greatest financial centre of the times.

In order to make profitable use of these resources, Roman capitalism, in the IInd century BC, was to spread throughout the East. It was to find a wide field for exploitation in the farming of provincial taxes, in supplies to the army and fleet and in great public works.

In order to tender for these enterprises, the speculators (*publicani*) founded share companies which became so popular that in 180 BC the first Stock Exchange was opened in Rome. Speculation became a fever among the Romans; smallholders sold their lands to gamble on the stock market.

In 179 BC the port of Rome was rebuilt on the model of the port of Alexandria. In 178 BC the Spanish silver mines were put up for tender and there was a rush of emigrants from Rome to this Eldorado of the ancient world. In 172 BC the system of tenders was extended to the exploitation of the state lands. Rome adopted a completely free-trade policy which even broke away from the principle cf state monopoly of mining, which the Oriental monarchies had applied, and allowed the capitalists to take over the uncontrolled exploitation of all the wealth of the republic. Their ascendancy over public life was rapidly to become all-powerful. The ferocious avidity with which the speculators exploited the state lands provoked a terrible revolt in Sardinia and Corsica (170 BC), which was repressed with the most atrocious cruelty. The Sardinians, thrown by thousands on the slave markets, were bought for a song by the capitalists, who employed them to exploit the public lands that they had leased. The shameless enslavement of the Sardinian population paved the way for the great social crisis in Italy, since the exploitation of the soil by slaves was to reduce smallholding to a dangerous degree.

Capitalism thrived on war, slaves, booty and the supply-contracts that these involved. It was to make the whole civilized world a prey to the Romans. Immediately after the signature of the peace of Apamea, the party of the moneyed classes put before the Senate a plan for an imperialist policy based on wars of conquest and exploitation. War was to become a financial enterprise for the Romans, under the all-powerful guidance of a few hundred families.

THE ANNEXATION OF MACEDONIA

Trying to find some compensation for his defeat, Philip V turned once more to Greece, obsessed by the idea of extending Macedonian rule over the whole Aegean Sea, where, since the peace of Apamea, the influence of Egypt and the Seleucid kings had been replaced by that of Pergamon and Rhodes.

In Greece the social situation was very serious. At Sparta, in 195 BC, Nabis had successfully led a popular revolution which had been carried out in a most ferocious manner. Sparta, since then, had been the centre of the 'communist' party which, throughout Greece, had been the cause of revolutionary upheavals. The Achaean League, on the other hand, had declared for the property-owning classes. The Stoics, as democrats, had taken the side of the people. Greece, torn by conflicting ideologies, became involved in bitter class struggles.

From the foundation of their dynasty the Macedonian kings had professed Stoic ideals. Philip V, intervening in the social struggles in Greece, ranged himself on the side of the people. Rome, on the other hand, declared herself the protector of the property-owning classes.

At the time when Antiochus III had been forced to sign the peace of Apamea, Philip V, fearing the supremacy of Pergamon in the Aegean, had occupied a part of the Thracian Chersonese in order to wrest from her the control of the Straits. Pergamon at once appealed to Rome, who called on Philip to abandon the Chersonese (188 BC). Philip could only obey, but did not give up his policy of intervention in Greece. In the reign of his son, Perseus, this policy resulted in a fresh war against Rome (171 BC). Before attacking Macedonia, Rome appealed for the alliance of Rhodes. But the imperialism of the Roman financiers, which penetrated everywhere as if in a conquered country, alarmed Rhodes who refused to involve herself fully. The King of Antioch allied to Perseus preferred rather than come to his help against Rome, to invade Egypt, subject the country to a terrible devastation and annex it to his states (170–168 BC).

In 168 BC the Macedonian army was crushed at Pydna. This victory was followed by an atrocious campaign in Illyria, in which Rome reverted to the most barbarous methods of war which the oriental states had long renounced. Perseus died in internment in a city of Latium, and Macedonia, after horrible devastation, was completely annexed, thanks to the influence of the capitalists who coveted the country's mines.

THE DECLINE OF RHODES

Rhodes, who had not given proof of all the required submission, lost all her possessions in Asia Minor. Roman finance, in order to wrest from Rhodes her role as the great market of capital, set up Delos, where the

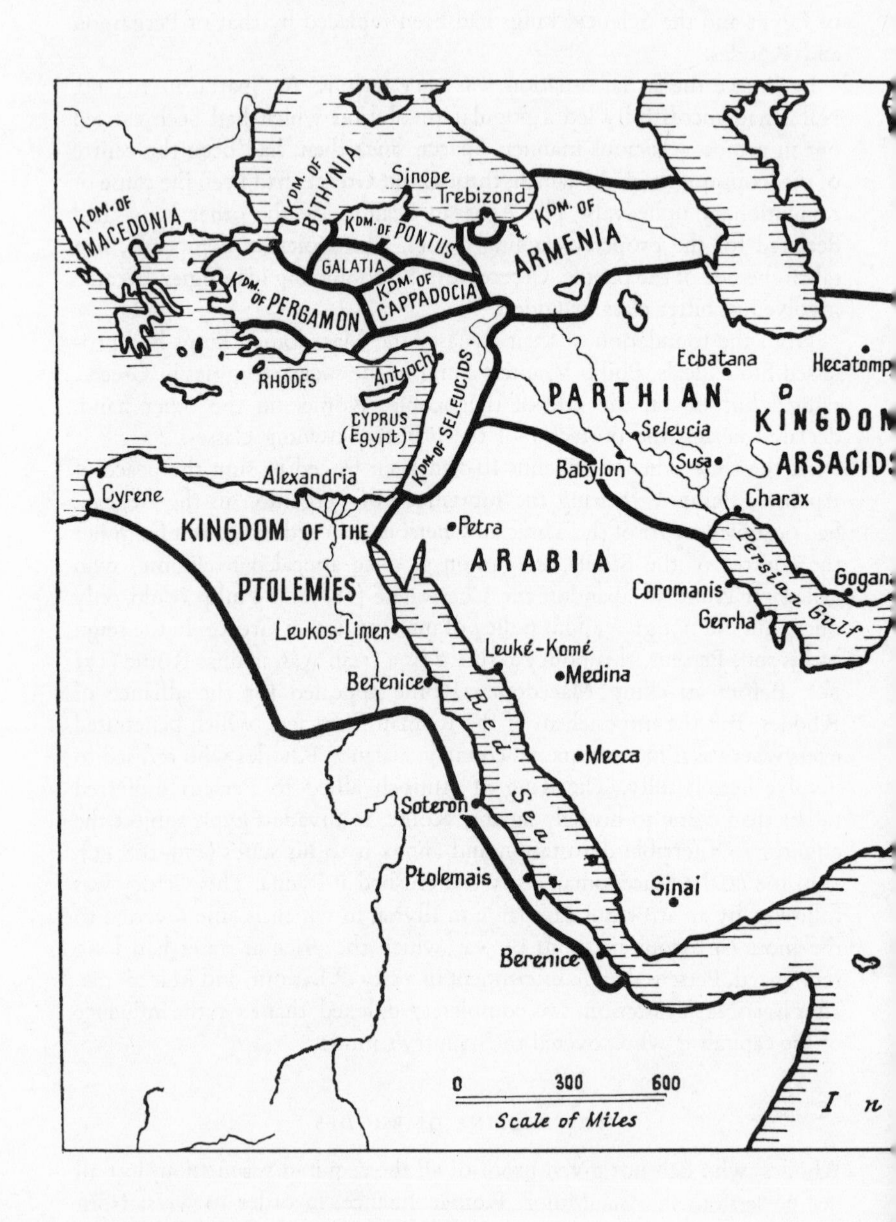
KDM. OF MACEDONIA
KDM. OF BITHYNIA
Sinope
Trebizond
KDM. OF PONTUS
KDM. OF ARMENIA
GALATIA
KDM. OF PERGAMON
KDM. OF CAPPADOCIA
RHODES
Antioch
KDM. OF SELEUCIDS
CYPRUS (Egypt)
Ecbatana
Hecatomp
PARTHIAN
KINGDOM
ARSACIDS
Seleucia
Susa
Babylon
Charax
Cyrene
Alexandria
KINGDOM OF THE PTOLEMIES
Petra
ARABIA
Persian Gulf
Coromanis
Gerrha
Gogana
Leukos-Limen
Leuké-Komé
Medina
Berenice
Red Sea
Mecca
Soteron
Ptolemais
Sinai
Berenice
0 300 600
Scale of Miles
In

Map No. 23

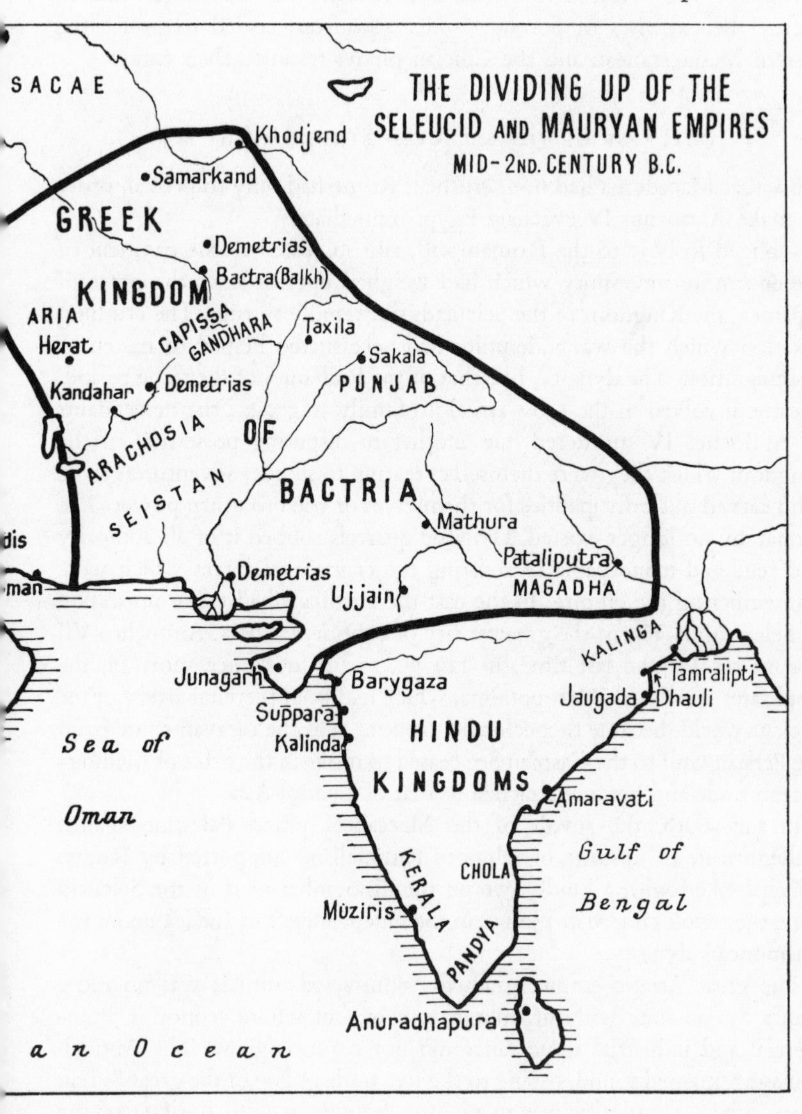
THE DIVIDING UP OF THE
SELEUCID AND MAURYAN EMPIRES
MID-2ND. CENTURY B.C.
SACAE
Khodjend
Samarkand
GREEK
KINGDOM
OF
BACTRIA
Demetrias
Bactra (Balkh)
ARIA
Herat
CAPISSA
GANDHARA
Taxila
Sakala
PUNJAB
Kandahar
Demetrias
ARACHOSIA
SEISTAN
Mathura
Pataliputra
MAGADHA
dis
man
Demetrias
Ujjain
KALINGA
Junagarh
Barygaza
Tamralipti
Jaugada
Dhauli
Suppara
Kalinda
HINDU
KINGDOMS
Sea of
Oman
Amaravati
Gulf of
Bengal
CHOLA
KERALA
Muziris
PANDYA
Anuradhapura
an Ocean

slave trade was concentrated, as a rival free port. Delos became the centre of Roman banking. From then on Rhodes rapidly declined. Roman commerce was diverted to Delos, and Rhodes was no longer able to defray the expenses of her navy. Her squadrons ceased to police the eastern Mediterranean and the Cilician pirates resumed their forays.

COLLAPSE OF THE SELEUCID KINGDOM (168 BC)

Now that Macedonia had been crushed, Rome had only to give an order to make Antiochus IV evacuate Egypt immediately.

Obliged to bow to the Roman will, and subjected to the payment of the enormous indemnity which had weighed upon it since the peace of Apamea, the Kingdom of the Seleucids slid rapidly to ruin. The crushing taxation which the war indemnity had necessitated helped to hasten its disintegration. The dynasty, like that of the Ptolemies of the same period, became involved in the most atrocious family tragedies; the descendants of Antiochus IV murdered one another in disputing possession of the kingdom which they were themselves tearing to shreds; adventurers arose who carved out principalities for themselves or tried to usurp power. The monarchy no longer existed. Dynastic quarrels robbed it of all authority and rendered it incapable of resisting the centrifugal forces which were dismembering the empire. In the east the Parthians had taken possession of Seleucia-on-Tigris, the greatest city of continental Asia. Antiochus VII was to try for the last time, in 129 BC, to set foot once more on the Euphrates. He failed. Mesopotamia, which had been the vital artery of the ancient world, became thenceforth a frontier, and the caravan route from the Persian Gulf to the Caspian Sea ceased to move in the orbit of Mediterranean trade and became attached to that of Central Asia.

In the south, the revolt of the Maccabees pitted Palestine against Hellenism in an upsurge of religious nationalism. Supported by Rome, which looked with a kindly eye on the dismemberment of the Seleucid state, the revolt ended, in 152 BC, in the independence of Judaea under the Hasmonean dynasty.

The great Asiatic empire gradually contracted until it was no more than a Syrian state without military power, but whose economic, commercial and industrial importance did not cease to grow. The Antioch coinage remained sound, owing to the free trade policy of the great Syrian cities, whose prosperity was in no way bound up with the fate of the monarchy. Closely integrated in the Mediterranean economy, they tried to break the bonds that linked them to the court. Thus, in the IInd century

BC, these cities easily accepted the rule of *condottieri* who set themselves up as tyrants, giving the cities, by this very fact, their own autonomy.

The Seleucid kings, driven back on all sides, none the less continued to tear themselves to pieces in terrible palace dramas; they ended by being no more than petty princes of Antioch, while the eastern half of the ancient Persian Empire, under the Parthian dynasty of the Arsacids, progressively freed itself from Greek influence. Of the Hellenistic kingdoms only Egypt, despite the loss of her empire and her political decline, still retained the semblance of a great power. The vicissitudes of her history involved her in a policy of autarchic state socialism which was one of the strangest economic and social experiments of ancient times.

CHAPTER XXXIX

THE EGYPTIAN CRISIS: FROM AUTARCHIC STATE SOCIALISM TO ROMAN PROTECTORATE

STATE SOCIALIST CENTRALIZATION

UP to the second half of the IIIrd century BC Egypt had ruled the seas, thanks to her naval supremacy. The wise organization of her central administration and her sound fiscal structure had assured her a considerable advantage over her adversaries during the Syrian wars. But little by little the centralizing policy of the Ptolemies had become—as earlier under the Ancient and New Empires—a hindrance to the normal operation of her administration because of the control which it exercised over all the activities of the state. The plethora of red tape stifled initiative, evaded responsibility and paralysed authority. The administrative machine affected even the king himself.

To found their absolutism on a legitimate basis, the Ptolemies had reverted to the ancient conception of the divine right of power that the Saite kings had abandoned. Ptolemy II (285–246 BC) had already reverted to the theory of theogamy, once again associating his dynasty with the great line of the Pharaoh-Gods who had given Egypt universal supremacy in the XVth century BC. But by this very fact the cult once again appeared as the source of power. To escape the tutelage of the priests, the king had been compelled to take firmly in his own hands the control of the cults and, as an innovation in tradition, had united them in a 'state church', annually convoking the High Priests of the country under his chairmanship in a national synod.

But this synod, created in order to subject the priests and even the dogmas to royal control, rapidly became a political force.

As for the administration, it became a state within the state; in order to assure the strict control of everyday affairs, a system of legal arbitration had been organized, but, instead of confiding it to independent judges, the

Ptolemies had committed the error of putting it in the hands of the officials themselves. The result was that the administration had become a privileged body which passed judgment on itself and was thus able to evade the royal authority.

Conflicts arose between the priests, whose properties, as in Persian times, were administered by the state, and the administration. The synod demanded the restoration of their sacred domains to the temples. A crisis was inevitable.

This was the more serious inasmuch as it coincided with a slow but unavoidable disintegration of the army. Composed for the most part of Greek or Gaulish[1] mercenaries, and therefore without contact with the people, it too became a privileged body endowed with 'benefices' in land and settlement rights which weighed heavily upon the people. As every privileged army, it soon lost its combat value. It suffered its first defeats in 245 BC when Egypt lost the Cyclades. The Ptolemies had then tried to rebuild a national army, but instead of reverting to conscription as in the times of Egyptian greatness they had formed it of career soldiers whose maintenance was a heavy charge upon the budget. This army saved Egypt at the battle of Raphia in 217 BC but it was not able to sustain the demands that were then made on it.

THE ECONOMIC CONSEQUENCES OF THE LOSS OF THE EMPIRE

During the reigns of Ptolemy III (246–221 BC) and Ptolemy IV (221–203 BC) Antiochus III had robbed Egypt of her richest Asiatic provinces. This was an irreparable loss to the treasury and to the prosperity of the country which thenceforward lost the control of continental trade. In 202 BC Egypt lost the Hellespont and, in consequence, her supremacy in the Black Sea; in 200 BC Phoenicia was taken from her and in 197 BC the island of Samos. Pergamon, her former ally, had for long supplanted her as mistress of the coasts of Asia Minor, and she thus found herself excluded from the Aegean. Certainly, the friendship that linked her to the Roman republic allowed her to maintain a very strong position. But the Treaty of Apamea (188 BC) gave Rome the naval supremacy which Egypt had lost and, at the same time, deprived Egypt of her role as leader of international trade. Rhodes replaced Alexandria as a financial centre and dominated the trade with Syria. The result was a very serious economic crisis which, together

[1] They were recruited in the kingdom of the Galatians (Celts) which was formed about 275 BC in Asia Minor.

with the fiscal difficulties provoked by the loss of the Empire, precipitated the conflict which was brewing between the civil authority, Greek in tradition, and the priests, who were still the representatives of Egyptian tradition.

THE PRIESTS BECOME A PRIVILEGED NOBILITY

In order to win back the support of the priesthood the state, weakened by its defeats, agreed, at the end of the IIIrd century BC, to restore to the temples the free administration of their estates. The priests at once reverted to their traditional policy and, in the name of their sacred mission, tried to evade the temporal authority of the state. The donations, which all the kings from the times of Ptolemy V had never ceased to grant them, no longer sufficed; they demanded fiscal immunity which, by relieving their lands and the temple personnel from taxes, deprived the king of very considerable resources. The taxes which the temples no longer paid had to be met by the people. But the economic crisis had already resulted in widespread pauperism, and poverty had reduced the birth-rate and led to the exposure of children, a custom which the Egyptians had learned from the Greeks. The increase in land taxes meant that the state could no longer find tenants. Large amounts of land remained uncultivated and the king was compelled to lease them to the temples at a very low rate since they alone, thanks to their exemption from taxes, could still find tenant-farmers. The temples, which because of their immunity had become almost autonomous states, were organized on a seigniorial basis and adopted the capitalist system of the times; they negotiated life-leases with their tenants, which later became hereditary, so that the former free farmers became tied to the soil. Meanwhile, the workshops on the sacerdotal estates were developed and the temples, with their enormous wealth, once more resumed their banking activities.

This economic policy of the Egyptian temples was taking place at the same time as the Roman capitalists were organizing, by means of slave-workers, the industrial exploitation of their estates.

The competition of the temples with the industries of the cities led to an anti-clerical movement among the urban middle classes.

FISCAL POLICY LEADS TO AUTARCHY

The state, however, reacted. Cost what it might, it had to have resources. The unsuccessful wars had exhausted the gold reserves; direct taxation had reached its ceiling and there could no longer be any question of increasing it. It only remained to have recourse to indirect contributions. The fiscal policy of monopoly inaugurated in the IIIrd century first for oil and then for salt was extended, and customs protection, first introduced for trade reasons, became a means of raising taxes. The system of entry duties and quotas became general. The consequence was a reduction of imports which led naturally to a decline in exports. So, while the customs duties forced up the cost of living, wages went down. The Egyptian trade balance, which had always been favourable, showed a deficit. The reserves of precious metals being exhausted, a monetary crisis was added to the problem of the fiscal deficit. From the end of the IIIrd century, on the eve of the great wars against Antiochus III, the minting of gold had been abandoned and the silver content, till then scrupulously maintained, was slightly reduced. Once this step had been taken, devaluation of the coinage was bound to follow. Under Ptolemy VI (180–145) BC, after the invasion of Egypt by Antiochus IV and during the dynastic quarrels which the Egyptian defeat caused among the pretenders to the throne, the coinage was devalued by 75%, while the taxes on the sale of land and property were raised from 5% to 10% *ad valorem.*

Bad money drives out good. Prices rose and the economic and social crisis increased. Then there was a radical reform. Save at Alexandria where, economically separated from the rest of the country, silver coinage continued to be used, the tetradrachms were withdrawn and replaced by copper coins worth no more than a tenth of their nominal value. The exchange rate was fixed, and the silver coins reserved for foreign trade alone. Egypt was to be cut off from the rest of the world by an insuperable customs barrier, and the whole economic life of the country concentrated at Alexandria, which formed an autonomous customs zone. The country became a vast field for exploitation and all its wealth was drained away to the metropolis. The Ptolemies resolutely set out on the path to controlled economy and autarchy, and, in consequence, towards a social policy of restraint and absolutism.

THE DYNASTY IS CUT OFF FROM THE PEOPLE

Now that Alexandria was cut off from Egypt, the monarchy entirely changed in character. Since Ptolemy I it had rapidly become assimilated and while keeping Greek, the international language, as the language of government it had inherited, together with the dynastic ideas of the Pharaohs, the ancient Egyptian ideas of public law which required the exercise of strict justice as the foundation of monarchical power.

But when in the times of Ptolemy IV (221-203 BC) the Pharaoh became to all intents and purposes king of Alexandria he cut himself off from the people, which led immediately to the typical vices of those dynasties that do not represent a nation but only a family: internecine quarrels and palace crimes. Ptolemy IV massacred his entire family (221 BC). Customs were introduced at court which Egypt had never known; Ptolemy V (203–180 BC) put to death all those who offended him, and his autocratic policy developed hand in hand with an oppressive state socialism.

State socialism transformed absolutism into autocracy. New legal theories attributed to the king ownership of all the lands of the kingdom and asserted the royal omnipotence over the people who were regarded as having no other rights than those the Pharaoh deigned to recognize. The monarchy became a tyranny. The theory of the divine right of kings was invoked to justify an unbridled absolutism. The idea of force replaced that of justice, which led to the disappearance of that conception of the legal nature of power which inspired respect for the monarchy while at the same time imposing limitations on it. It was because the legality of power had been abolished that dynastic quarrels ensued. The throne, since it rested upon force, belonged to whoever could take it. A similar crisis had arisen toward the end of the Ancient Empire, when state socialism had led to palace plots against Pepi I, and at the close of the New Empire, when state socialism had engulfed the empire in the plots against Rameses III. A similar dynastic decadence was repeated under the Ptolemies. The abandonment of the moral principles upon which power had hitherto been based explains the policy of social constraint and favouritism which was not desired by the king but which he was compelled to carry out by the omnipotent bureaucracy, in order to assure the yield of the autarchic economic system into which he had been driven by the fiscal crisis.

THE POLICY OF SOCIAL CONSTRAINT

The devaluation of the coinage could only furnish the profits expected for the revenue if the agricultural and industrial production of the country yielded a sufficient surplus to provide large exports which could be sold against hard currencies.

The burden of taxes drove the peasant from the land into the towns where he was to increase the numbers of the proletariat. The land tax, therefore, produced little. The state, unable to take direct action against the passive resistance of the people, armed the tax officials with great powers and made them personally responsible for the tax-yield. The people reacted with violence to the violence which necessarily ensued. The king reacted by imposing penalties of exceptional severity; debtor-slavery, abolished since the VIIIth century BC, was restored in the harshest form it had ever known for those who failed to pay their taxes: public sale as slaves. Meanwhile, the king placed the farmers under the jurisdiction of the officials upon whom they depended. Like the sacerdotal estates, the crown lands were now exempt from the common law; and the consequences were not slow in making themselves felt. The free peasants who had occupied them became semi-slaves. To prevent the tenants from abandoning their lands, the state replaced short-term leases by leases of ten and twenty years which soon became life-tenancies and then hereditary tenancies. Tenants were forbidden to leave their villages. The Egyptian people, tied to the soil, passed under the jurisdiction of the great landowners, the temples or the tax officials. Riots and strikes broke out.

It was at this time that Egypt was attacked by Antiochus IV. She was unable to repel the invasion and was entirely occupied by the foreign armies who organized a systematic pillage (170–168 BC).

On Roman orders Antiochus IV evacuated Egypt; but when Rome had thus restored her liberty, Egypt was no more than a Roman protectorate.

CONTROLLED ECONOMY DESTROYS INDIVIDUAL LIBERTY

After the evacuation by Antiochus IV the misery of Egypt was at its height. The internal coinage, in the form of copper tokens, had only a fictitious value. The exchange rate was fixed by royal decree and prices kept stable by rigorous autarchic measures. The frontier was closed to all transactions, and trade with the outside world could only be carried on through the intermediary of the state and by the port of Alexandria.

This meant the ruin of the merchant cities of the Delta. But Alexandria, cut off from the economic system of Egypt, preserved its splendour. Apart from its being the great market for the Indian trade, the king exported corn, cloth, leather and wool which the administration had received as tax payments or had bought with devalued money. No longer having liquid capital to compete with the encroachments of Roman capitalism, the Ptolemies exploited the soil of Egypt and the labour of her people as their capital. But in order for the state to obtain from national production—bought with token money at imposed prices and resold abroad for hard currency—sufficient resources for the maintenance of the court, the fleet, the army and the administration, it had to drain the country of its riches and reduce the people to the lowest possible standard of life. The state thus found itself compelled to direct the entire economy of the country towards those products which were of the greatest benefit to it. Trade between private persons was greatly reduced, private industry was curtailed and the social intervention of the state increased continually. The invasion had ruined the country. Large areas of land remained untilled and uninhabited, and the state was forced to restore them to cultivation at all costs, in order to make them productive and draw taxes from them. An edict prescribed that, in every village, the abandoned lands should be handed over to the richest landowners on condition that they paid the taxes on them. In return, it granted them the right to levy taxes on the other inhabitants. Thenceforward, the rich men became local tyrants who reduced the people to slavery; and to prevent taxpayers from escaping their obligations they were compelled by law to remain in their places of origin. Thus a class of privileged landowners was interposed between the people and the king. Liberty and legal equality were destroyed. The rural population was congealed into a hereditary status, while in the cities the worker-proletariat, which was employed more and more in workshops exploited by the state or under its direct control, saw its living standards continually reduced by the fall in wages caused by social retrogression. The active middle classes, which no longer found any field for their activities in the country, went to Alexandria. The priests and officials became an oligarchy of nobles with their own laws, fiscal privileges and a special status.

STATE SOCIALISM DESTROYS THE ROYAL POWER IN FAVOUR OF AN OLIGARCHY

With its transformation into a noble caste, the oligarchy assumed the powers of the king. The centralization of authority, made necessary by the more and more arbitrary state socialism, concentrated, during the IInd century BC, all the provincial powers in the hands of governors and all the powers of the central government in those of an *epistrategos*, who was at the same time Minister of the Interior, of the Crown Lands, of Public Works and of War; his authority only stopped short of the finances which were centralized under a *dioecete*. So, as at the close of the Ancient and the New Empires, the governors seemed like princes, while the *epistrategos* and *dioecete* became Mayors of the Palace. Autarchic state socialism, having destroyed the liberty and prosperity of the citizens, ended by ruining the royal power itself to the advantage of a privileged oligarchy.

BOOK IX

The Great Roman Crises. IInd and Ist Centuries BC

CHAPTER XL

FROM CAPITALISM TO DEMAGOGY

EXPLOITATION OF THE EAST BY ROMAN CAPITALISM

THE reduction of Macedonia to a Roman province meant the final triumph of Rome in international affairs and, in Rome itself, the seizure by capitalism of the control of the state. Rome was to impose her protectorate over the Greco-Oriental world, but this protectorate was, in reality, to be that of Roman finance.

In Rome, the Senate was aware of the danger to the Republic of power passing into the hands of the speculators. It tried to oppose it. In order to check the excessive power of the speculators, it ordered the temporary closure of the Macedonian mines, which had been the reason for the annexation of the country. To restore its credit with the *Comitia*, the Senate tried to conciliate the middle classes by suppressing the tax on incomes. Henceforward, Rome lived upon the immense wealth procured by her conquests.

This demagogic measure was the supreme error of the senatorial oligarchy. On the one hand, it involved Rome in a policy of world exploitation from which she was no longer able to withdraw; having no taxes, Rome could only live by putting pressure on other countries. The Senate thus guided the Republic along the very road which it had wished to avoid, for the policy of financial exploitation necessarily gave the leading place in the state to the capitalist class, without whose support such a policy was impossible. On the other hand, by suppressing the tax, the Senate also suppressed the control that the *Comitia* had exercised up till then on internal and external policy by voting the budget, especially the military credits. The Senate thus gave the deathblow to democracy and opened the way to demagogy, upon which, thanks to their immense resources, the capitalists were to rely.

There was no longer any limit to the shameless exploitation to which the governors and speculators were to subject the provinces and even the 'protected' countries. In order to profit from the immense revenues which they derived from the farming of the taxes, the companies of speculators soon monopolized all banking throughout the provinces. The Greek cities, ruined by requisitions, had no alternative but to borrow from the Roman bankers in order to meet their demands, and thus delivered themselves into their hands. Governors and speculators operated in complete freedom; their abuses could, in fact, only remain unpunished despite the law passed in 149 BC, since a commission of senators had been appointed to judge them, so that they thus found themselves both judges and accused.

The tutelage of Roman finance extended even to the Seleucids who, in order to pay their annual instalments to Rome, were forced to subscribe to loans granted by the Roman bankers themselves. Even the Ptolemies, degraded like the Seleucids by dynastic plots and crimes, were forced to look to Rome for a ruinous protection.

SOCIAL CRISIS IN GREECE

The financial exactions of the Roman capitalists resulted in a serious social crisis in Greece which united in a single ideology popular claims and Greek patriotism, now directed against Rome, an enemy both in the political and social field. The proletariat of the great industrial city of Corinth assumed power in the Achaean League, till then dominated by the property-owning party, and simultaneously involved it in revolt against Rome and in radical reforms; abolition of debts, emancipation of slaves, and heavy taxation of the wealthy classes. Rome intervened. Her armies crushed the Achaean forces, and the Senate, in order to terrorize the revolutionaries, ordered Corinth to be razed (146 BC). The Roman army took advantage of this order to sack the city with a brutality which provoked an outburst of anger in all the Hellenized lands.

Carthage, which had also revolted, suffered the same horrible fate. In the same year the two great cities were totally destroyed and their entire population, accounted among the most civilized in the world, was massacred or sold at public auction by avid and unscrupulous generals. Almost all the lands of Boeotia were confiscated to the profit of Rome, and the Greek cities were subjected to tribute; only Athens, Sparta and Delphi were spared and admitted as allies.

Horrified by such misdeeds and uneasy at the universal hatred which was accumulating against Rome, formerly considered as the protector of the Greeks, the Senate loyally undertook a reform of the government of the Empire, which aimed at limiting the discretionary powers of the governors. A law fixed the total sum of the taxes due from each province, and a great effort was made to give them a legal status which would protect them from the exactions of politicians and speculators.

SOCIAL CRISIS AT ROME

But the Senate at once found itself faced by the party of the 'knights' (*equites*), that is to say the wealthy classes, dominated by the speculators and the business men. Roman imperialism, in the hands of the capitalists, had been the source of fabulous profits for them, which they did not intend to renounce.

Rome was thus divided into three parties. The nobility, or the party of the senatorial families, represented the governing oligarchy which furnished governors for the provinces and had immense resources of land at its disposal. The party of the *equites*, that is to say of high finance and business, had very great financial resources and held banking and the companies of the speculators in its hands; and, finally, there was the popular party, made up of the urban and rural proletariat. As for the middle-classes, formerly made up of smallholders and well-to-do craftsmen, they had almost entirely disappeared, ruined by the great landed proprietors and the industrialists of the party of the *equites*.

Thus, save for the classes enriched by war and conquest, there existed only a numerous and ruined proletariat, which made its pressing claims heard on all sides. In Rome, the urban plebs, reduced to unemployment by the extension of slave-labour, demanded frumentary laws to reduce the cost of bread; the rural population, dispossessed by the great landowners, demanded land. The middle classes of the Italian regions most recently conquered who did not enjoy Roman citizenship wanted to be admitted into the Roman political body and take their part in the control of affairs.

Up till 146 BC—the year of the sack of Corinth and Carthage—Rome had been governed by the nobles, supported by the *equites*. Their coalition had been powerful enough to oppose the distribution of lands demanded by the rural plebs. Refusing to make the sacrifices indispensable to restore a middle class of smallholders, the nobles had preferred to make sure of the votes of the popular party in the *Comitia* by creating a clientèle bought by doles and by electoral corruption. But the provincial reforms which aimed at limiting the illicit profits of the speculators had ranged high finance against the Senate. The property-owning coalition was broken and the *equites* turned to the proletariat to obtain, with its aid, a majority in the *Comitia*. To preserve the liberty of exploiting the provinces, the financiers were ready to sacrifice to the people the great landed estates of the nobles and the resources of the state.

This alliance 'of the left' was soon to break up. A revolutionary ferment was brewing, nourished by the unrest in the Greek world. The terrible revolt of slaves which broke out in Sicily in 135 BC and which was only crushed after three years of conflict provoked great repercussions in the popular party; the constitution of a revolutionary front, formed by the proletariat and the slaves, was openly preached. Everyone felt the need for action. In Rome, under the influence of Stoic ideas, members of the nobility made themselves champions of the popular claims. Plans were drawn up which included vast distributions of land taken from the great senatorial estates.

But in 133 BC the king of Pergamon, Attalus III, died, bequeathing his kingdom to Rome. The patrician, Tiberius Gracchus, whose Stoic education had convinced him of the need for social reform, held at this time the office of tribune. He proposed to hand over to the people control of this legacy of immense value, and at the same time introduced the draft of an agrarian law providing for distribution of lands to the proletariat. He was at once assassinated by bands in the pay of the nobles.

While Rome thus found herself suddenly on the brink of civil war, Aristonicus, the natural son of Attalus III, refused to recognize his father's testament as valid, entered Pergamon, called the people and the slaves to arms and carried out the social reforms advocated throughout Greece by the revolutionary party. He cancelled debts, freed the slaves and granted citizenship to foreigners and freedmen. These reforms provoked considerable repercussions, which reached as far as Rome itself. The Senate, claiming its legacy, entered the struggle; but it needed several years before it could take possession of the kingdom of Pergamon. In 123 BC this kingdom was at last annexed and became the province of Asia. It was immediately subjected to shameless exploitation by the speculators. During these events the social unrest at Rome had been constantly growing. With increasing violence the people demanded a distribution of lands. The *peregrini*, especially the Italians, whose numbers continued to grow in Rome, demanded citizenship which would enable them to participate in the benefits of the agrarian laws which were felt to be inevitable. Their insistence was so great that in 126 BC the expulsion of all the *peregrini* from Rome was mooted. The tabling of a fresh project for the agrarian law in

123 BC by Gaius Gracchus led to serious unrest. The nobles responded by having Gaius Gracchus assassinated.

Rome about now was involved in fresh wars, this time in the West. As protector of Marseilles, she had been called on in 154 BC by the great Greek city for help against the Celts of the interior. In 125 BC, threatened by the great Gaulish state of the Arveni, Marseilles had again appealed for aid. Four years of campaigning (125–121 BC) were needed to drive back the Gauls. This war came at just the right moment to bring some satisfaction to the Roman plebs. Roman colonies were settled at Aix and at Narbonne and a new province was created, encircling Marseilles and its colonies, which extended over the whole of Provence and linked Italy to the Roman possessions in Spain. In 112 BC a fresh conflict arose, this time in Africa. Roman merchants had been massacred in the states of Jugurtha, King of the Numidians. The Senate wanted peace. But the financiers, in order to open a fresh field for their activities, supported the war. They hinted to the people the possibility of further distributions of land in Africa, and the war was undertaken. But the Senate conducted it half-heartedly. This was the chance for the *equites* to try their strength. In 108 BC, despite the opposition of the Senate, they persuaded the *Comitia* to grant the consulate and the command of the armies in Africa to Marius, an obscure 'knight' of Arpinum. The coalition of finance and the popular party thus deprived the Senate of its dominant position in the *Comitia*; it gave way before the threat of violent revolution. For the first time, Marius, in order to recruit his legions, appealed to the citizens who did not pay the electoral tax, so that his army was made up of poor men. The legions were no longer to be the nation in arms, but a career army, avid of booty and in the pay of its generals.

A soon as he had conquered the Numidians, Marius was ordered to march against the Germans.

The Cimbri and the Teutones, setting out from the Cimbrian peninsula (Denmark), had crossed Moravia and clashed with the Celts settled on the Danube. In 109 BC they had appeared on the Rhine, which they crossed, and then, moving southward, reached the Rhône valley and in 105 BC clashed with a Roman army which they completely defeated. Panic broke out in Italy and the people were already making ready to flee before the invaders when Marius crushed the Teutones at Aix in 102 BC.

He returned to Rome as a saviour. At this time fresh slave revolts had broken out in Sicily (103–101 BC) and the unrest among the Roman proletariat was at its height. The *Comitia* ordered distribution of lands in Africa, in Corsica and in the Po valley. As the Senate resisted, Marius,

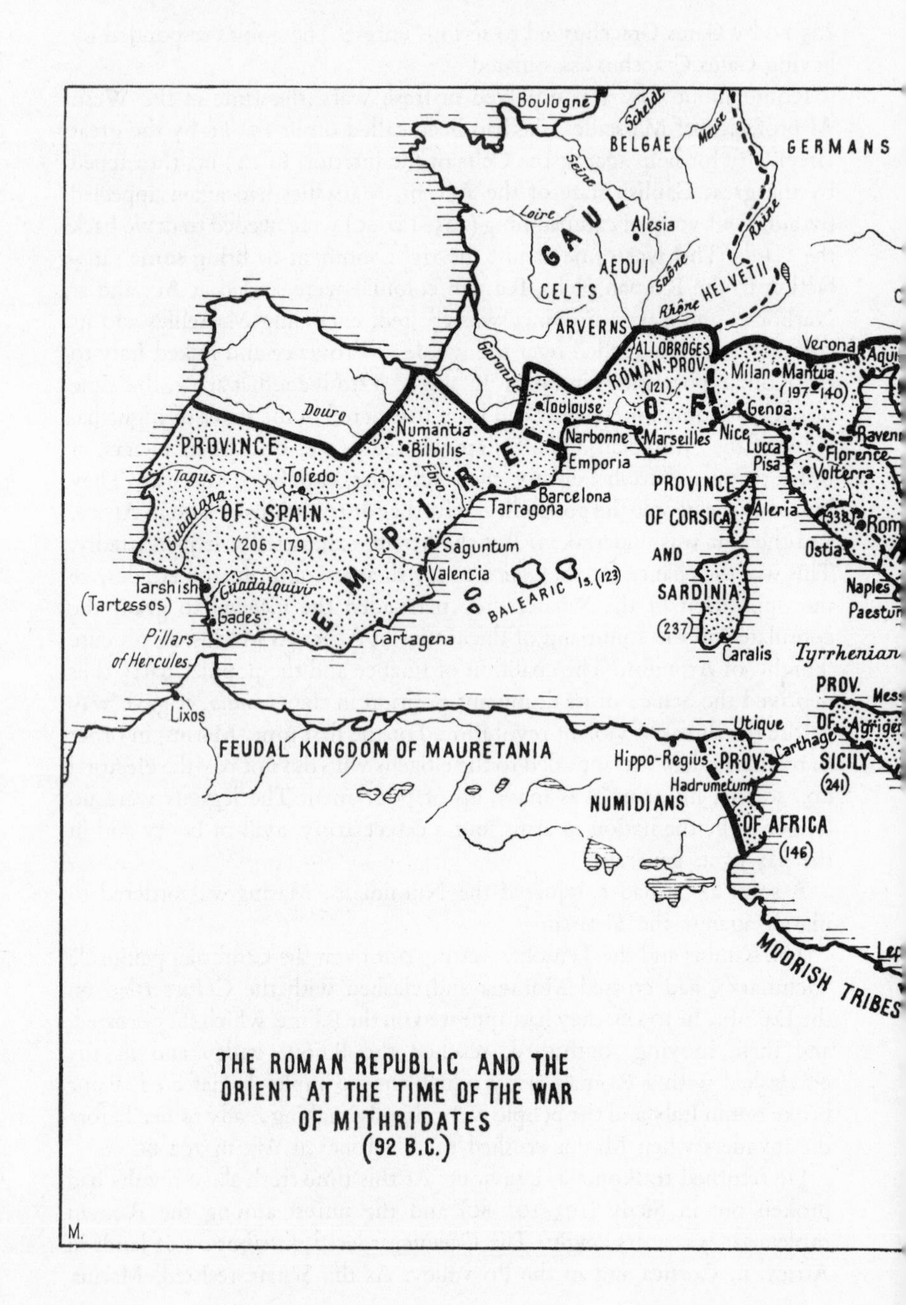

THE ROMAN REPUBLIC AND THE ORIENT AT THE TIME OF THE WAR OF MITHRIDATES (92 B.C.)

Map No. 24

SCYTHIANS
SARMATIANS
Tanais
Olbia
DACIANS
Panticapea
Phanagoria
Tiraspol
Theodosia
Cherson
Istros
(Danube) Ister
Dioscurias
Salona
ILLYRIA
Odessa
Pontus Euxinus
Phasis
Mesembria
THRACE
Apollonia
Sinope
Trebizond
Byzantium
Chalcedon
Amasea
Heraclea
KGDM. OF
K. OF
Brundisium
(148) PROVINCE OF
Abdera
Nicomedia
BITHYNIA
PONTUS
MACEDONIA
Salonica
Cyzicus
GALATIA
K. OF ARMENIA
Sestos
Lampsacus
PROV. OF
Pessinus
Abydos
ASIA
Thurii
Croton
Pergamus
(129)
KGDM. OF CAPPADOCIA
Cyme
Magnesia
Sardes
ACHAIA
Smyrna
K. OF THE PARTHIANS
Colophon
Ephesus
Iconium
Priene
PISIDIA (Pirates)
Tarsus
Alexandria
(146) Corinth
Athens
Seleucia
Ionian Sea
Miletus
LYCIA
Attalia
Seleucia
Antioch
DELOS
RHODES
Patara
Arvad
Halicarnassus
SELEUCID KGDM.
CRETE
Salamis
Beirut
Itanos
CYPRUS (Egypt)
Damascus
Tyre
PALESTINE
Jerusalem
Cyrene
Alexandria
Mendes
Gaza
KGDM. OF THE
Naucratis
Pelusium
Petra
K. OF THE PTOLEMIES
Memphis
Ailana
NABATAEANS
NOMAD TRIBES
Philoteras
Red Sea
Ptolemais
Thebes
Leuke-Kome

then consul for the sixth time, had a law voted by the *Comitia*, *De Majestate*, to compel it to give way. This permitted any citizen guilty of a crime against the majesty of the Roman people to be put to death. It was to deliver over to Marius and to the popular party of which he was the representative the lives and properties of all citizens. Horrible massacres ensued. Between the Senate and the democratic party civil war broke out, which degenerated into a proletarian revolution.

The terrified *equites* made common cause with the nobles. The revolt was crushed and a government of the right succeeded the coalition of the parties of the left.

It was soon to find itself faced with the most terrible social crisis known to the ancient world.

THE WAR OF MITHRIDATES AND THE CRISIS OF REPUBLICAN INSTITUTIONS

The disappearance of the kingdom of Pergamon left the field free in the Black Sea region to the king of Pontus, the energetic and ambitious Mithridates VI. He profited by it to incorporate into his possessions the Greek cities on the southern shores of the Euxine and made the great port of Sinope his capital. Menaced by the Scythians, Olbia, Panticapea and the other Greek cities of the Crimea had called on him for aid. He soon found himself the head of a great Greek state. All the northern and southern coasts of the Euxine belonged to him; from Trebizond he controlled the mines of the Caucasus and his alliance with Armenia opened to him the Mesopotamian route which placed him in direct contact, by way of Seleucia-on-Tigris and the kingdom of the Parthians, with Central Asia and India.

Mithridates did not want to come into conflict with Rome. The Senate, too, desired peace. But the speculators pressed for war. They obtained from the king of Bithynia—who since the Peace of Apamea had become a vassal of Rome—the closure of the Straits. This was to force Mithridates into war. He invaded Cappadocia, threatening the former territories of Pergamon, now the province of Asia. Rome ordered him to renounce his conquests (92 BC). In reply, he penetrated still further into Asia Minor, called to arms all the democrats of the Greek lands and ordered the massacre of all Italians resident in the coastal districts of the Aegean. The Greek and Asiatic population, exasperated by Roman exactions, enthusiastically replied to his appeal; eighty thousand Italians were massacred. A little later, Mithridates disembarked at Athens, where he set up his headquarters. Boeotia and the Peloponnesus rallied to him. To ensure the mastery of the Aegean, he made an alliance against Rome with the pirates of Crete and Cilicia.

The war took on the semblance of a democratic crusade. Everywhere Mithridates liberated slaves, abolished debts and granted citizenship to *metoikoi* and foreigners.

This great revolutionary ferment in the Greek world which had rallied around Mithridates had profound repercussions in Rome and throughout all Italy. In 92 BC, the year in which the king of Pontus challenged Rome, Drusus, reverting to the plan of the Gracchi, proposed to the *Comitia* that citizenship be granted to all Italians. He too perished, assassinated by the order of the nobles. All Italy thereupon grouped itself into a close federation and rose against Rome which, being then involved against Mithridates and the pirates, was to experience one of the most dramatic moments of her history.

The revolt of the countries of Greece and Asia Minor, where Roman finance had invested so much capital, led to a financial crisis at Rome, quickly followed by a fiscal crisis. Even more, the disturbance to shipping caused by the pirates and the Italian war led to a famine in the capital which immediately provoked popular riots. In order to find resources, the Senate, imitating the policy of the Ptolemies, secularized the goods of the temples and devalued the currency by fifty per cent. The result was a panic on the money exchanges which made the financial situation even more precarious.

Faced with the difficulties which had arisen because of the hatred she had aroused on all sides, Rome sent Marius against the rebellious Italians and Sulla against Mithridates. The Italians were vanquished. But their defeat marked their victory, for Rome was to give way and grant them citizenship *en bloc*. Italy, henceforward, formed a single and united democratic state.

CHAPTER XLI

FROM DEMAGOGY TO DICTATORSHIP

MARIUS AND SULLA

IN Rome the end of the Italian war also meant the triumph of the popular party which assumed power in 87 BC. Civil war immediately broke out. Marius, returning victorious from his campaigns, again took over the leadership of the democratic party, entered Rome with his troops and organized a terrible massacre of aristocrats.

The popular party, however, carried out some constructive work. It re-established a sound currency, set about the creation of a higher education on the Latin model and prepared for a great distribution of lands in Campania. While this was going on, Sulla triumphed over Mithridates and imposed the enormous tribute of twenty thousand talents on his lands as war reparations (85 BC), while he himself and his army carried out a systematic pillage of everything of value in Greece. With unlimited resources at his disposal, Sulla, at the head of troops gorged with booty, again marched on Italy. In 82 BC he forced his way into Rome and assumed power. The democratic party continued the struggle in Italy and then in Spain, while Sulla, the leader of the aristocrats, had himself nominated dictator by the *Comitia* and, in his turn, carried out horrible massacres.

Sulla's political plan was to establish finally the rule of the nobles by restricting the political rights of the people and setting up unified institutions for Italy. To achieve this double aim, he endowed all the municipalities with a local administration entrusted to four elected magistrates, increased the number of permanent courts, and associated the political with the religious power by trying to turn the body of pontiffs into an independent clergy recruited by co-option, which was to constitute the basis of a governing oligarchy. Furthermore, he wanted to revert to the ancient institutions and hand the government over to the Senate.

But the Senate hesitated. Sulla abdicated (79 BC).

The civil war immediately flared up again. A terrible slave revolt led by the Thracian Spartacus broke out. It was found necessary to mobilize ten legions, whose command was entrusted to Crassus, the wealthiest man in Rome and at that time head of the democratic party. He only triumphed after a terrible carnage (73–71 BC).

Mithridates, meanwhile, supported in Greece by the revolutionary parties and at sea by the pirates, resumed the struggle.

Lucullus, sent against him, first wanted to pacify the country by repressing the abuses of the speculators which had created an inextinguishable hatred for Rome. But the speculators reacted by stirring up revolutionary troubles in Lucullus' army.

In Rome, anarchy was in full sway. The financial party once again formed a coalition with the popular party. The Senate, which Sulla had for a time restored to power, was again defeated. The *Comitia* appointed to the consulate men who had managed to win the favour of the masses by the most shameless demagogic measures. Crassus, the most typical representative of speculative finance, and Pompey, who was for the first time entering the political field, were elected consuls in 70 BC.

The situation grew even more serious, since sensational financial scandals discredited the property-owning classes and demoralized public opinion. There was a passionate outcry at trials which revealed vast frauds against the marine insurance companies by shipowners who, after having laden their ships with earth, insured them as carrying cargoes of grain and then sank them at sea, crew and all. During this time Rome, blockaded by the pirates, was suffering from famine and the seriousness of the social situation led to a flight of capital.

POMPEY GIVEN FULL POWERS

In 67 BC the *equites* managed to induce the *Comitia* to confer on Pompey supreme command in the Mediterranean. Unity of command at once produced results. Pompey finally defeated Mithridates, put an end to the unlucky Seleucid kingdom, which had fallen to pieces in the hands of *condottieri*, making it the Province of Syria (64 BC), and destroying the pirates' fleets; while Cicero, consul in 63 BC, checked at Rome the conspiracy of Catiline who had tried to take over power by force, put an embargo on gold and halted the flight of capital which the fear of social revolution had provoked. By his victories and his conquests, Pompey raised the revenues of the Republic from eight thousand to fourteen thousand talents.

Rome appeared to be saved. But the tributes imposed on the subjected provinces were so heavy that they could only pay them by contracting loans at high interest with the Roman bankers themselves. Thanks to this subterfuge, the instalments continued to be paid for a certain number of years, but a tremendous financial crash was to result which threw the Republic into the crisis in which it was to perish.

Already it was on its death-bed. Demagogic over-bidding had ended by uniting all power in Pompey's hands. He would, it seemed, have been able to proclaim a monarchy with himself as king; but Caesar, a resolute demagogue, entered the lists. Civil war seemed on the eve of breaking out again, but the party chiefs, rather than fight it out, preferred to come to an agreement. In 60 BC Caesar, leader of the popular party, Crassus, who had become the leader of the *equites*, and Pompey, who relied upon his troops, secretly came to an understanding to share power under the mask of the sovereignty of the people.

THE FIRST TRIUMVIRATE
POMPEY, CAESAR AND CRASSUS

Despite the exploitation of the subject lands the Republic, after the terrible crises which it had gone through, was short of money. To find some, and to obtain the considerable resources that their policy required, the triumvirs turned their gaze on Egypt. Crassus and Caesar wanted to annex it without delay. But in the meantime Ptolemy XIII came to Rome to ask for aid in the dynastic conflicts between himself and other members of the royal family (59 BC). To buy over influential senators and especially Caesar —who cost him six thousand talents—he had to underwrite enormous loans from a syndicate of bankers under Draconian conditions, and assure himself the aid of the Roman governor of Syria—who demanded ten thousand talents. Ptolemy left to its fate Cyprus, the last Egyptian naval base outside Africa, which the *Comitia* simply voted to annex (58 BC) on the proposal of Cato, who made seven thousand talents out of the deal.

Thanks to these fabulous bribes, Caesar abandoned his project for the annexation of Egypt and extracted from the Senate a law which made Ptolemy 'the friend and ally of the Roman people'. Rome then maintained Ptolemy XIII on his throne despite the violent opposition of the people of Alexandria, but compelled him to accept the Roman banker Postumus, nominated by the syndicate of his creditors, as his Minister of Finance; in addition, a Roman garrison was sent to Alexandria to keep watch on the usurious interest on the debt.

Egypt thus passed from the protection of the Roman Republic to that of the Roman financiers—bankers and politicians—who, since the advent of the triumvirate, disposed of the world in more sovereign a manner than any autocrat had done.

But power required armies, as well as money. To obtain them, the triumvirs, under cover of a vote from the *Comitia*, shared out the Empire. Caesar obtained the government of Gaul, Crassus that of Syria and Pompey that of Spain (59 BC).

The whole world now felt that the Republic no longer existed. Even Cicero himself, the most illustrious representative of the republican idea, who was at this moment composing his great political work *De Republica* seemed to be waiting for and desiring the advent of a sort of parliamentary monarchy, with Pompey as monarch and the Senate as parliament.

CHAPTER XLII

FROM DICTATORSHIP TO EMPIRE

I. CAESAR TRIES TO ESTABLISH THE MONARCHY

THE division of the Empire among the three members of the triumvirate marked the end of republican institutions. Each of the triumvirs pursued his own individual policy. Personal power had come to stay.

Caesar, before he left for Gaul, declared himself the champion of democratic ideas by proposing a series of laws: one envisaged the distribution of lands in Campania, another provided for the publication of the minutes of Senate meetings in an official gazette, and a third fixed the legal salaries of provincial governors and set up a strict procedure for trials of offences concerning the misappropriation of public funds. His programme seemed settled: a social policy, control of the Senate by public opinion, imperial institutions. The Senate opposed the promulgation of these laws and replied to the fresh problems that had arisen with the narrow conservatism which had already involved Rome in the most sanguinary crises. The whole destiny of the Roman Empire is evident in these two trends of thought.

CAESAR CONQUERS GAUL

Having taken his stand in social and imperial affairs, Caesar left for Gaul, convinced that he would find there a base for the power which he sought. The Gauls were at this time passing through a crisis in their evolution. Although they all shared in the same Druidic cult which gave unity to their civilization, they were divided into peoples at different stages of development. In the south and centre, the Arveni and the Aedui, organized on an aristocratic basis, were subject to democratic influences; in the north, on the other hand, the less developed Belgae were still living under a regime of tribal royalty. But over and above the various states, a federation of all the Celtic peoples of Gaul had been formed, represented by a

Great Council in which all their delegates met and which took decisions for their common defence. The Celtic states comprised not only Gaul and a part of the island of Britain, but also the Danube valley, where the Gauls had come into contact with the Hellenistic world. During the wars of the *diadokoi* at the beginning of the IIIrd century BC Gallic tribes had even invaded Asia Minor where they had settled in Cappadocia and formed there the Kingdom of the Galatians. Incorporated into the Province of Asia after the defeat of Mithridates, these Gauls, after gracing the slave markets of Rome, provided her with excellent regular soldiers. On the Danube, from the IIIrd century BC, the Celts had also shown themselves to be able traders. On the confines of the Roman Empire, they had developed a trade-route which linked up in Gaul with the important Rhône route. From the Channel coasts, the Belgae were in communication by sea with the island of Britain, and Boulogne, farther south, was on the way to becoming a port. Thus there was already in Gaul sufficient trade to justify the minting of gold coins in imitation of Hellenistic types. Under the stimulus of the Gauls, a continental economy was being organized in Europe, in the basins of the Danube and the Rhône, entirely based on Greek commerce. The Rhine marked its limits.

The Germans, who occupied the whole of the plain country between the Rhine and the Elbe, were in a much more rudimentary stage of civilization. Semi-nomads, knowing nothing of the private ownership of land, they carried out no commercial transactions and were divided into tribes isolated from one another. Their religion, devoted to the forces of nature, was ignorant of any moral ideas. For centuries they were continually on the move. After having crossed Europe from Denmark to the Danube, they had been driven northward again by the Celts. The Cimbri and the Teutones, withdrawing westwards, had tried to penetrate into Gaul by the Rhône valley. Marius had driven them back, after crushing their forces at Aix. Since then they had kept up a constant pressure on the Rhine, where the Belgae lived in a state of perpetual war with them.

The Celtic world, lying between German barbarism and Mediterranean civilization, represented in the time of Caesar the continental civilization of a Europe in course of formation, centred around a religion of high moral tendencies and having great trade-routes which enveloped the Roman Empire from the Black Sea to the Atlantic Ocean. Since the IVth century BC the Celts had several times tried to advance towards the Mediterranean, invading Greece, Italy and finally the coast of Provence where, on the appeal of Marseilles, Rome had set up the Roman 'Province' to hold them back.

When Caesar appeared in Gaul in 58 BC the Arveni, who occupied the south of the country, and the Aedui, settled in the centre, were struggling for supremacy, both of them meanwhile bedevilled by the social conflict which was ranging the common people against the great landowners. A popular party had been formed, which foreshadowed the end of the seigniorial régime and the advent of tyrannies relying on the people. Caesar was to exploit these dissensions cleverly. In order to have the Arveni at his mercy, he conceded the title of 'brothers' to the Aedui. Meanwhile, the pressure of the Germans was making itself felt in the east. The Helvetians, in order to escape from it, sought permission to cross the 'Province'. Caesar refused, defeated them on the Morvan and drove them back toward Switzerland. It was then that the Great Council of the Gauls, on the proposal of the Aedui, called on Caesar to aid them against the Germans. The Roman legions immediately moved into action and drove back the invaders in the Belfort gap. The defence of Gaul against the Germanic menace took Caesar's armies into the north of the country. Once installed in the heart of Gaul, he extended his authority as far as the shores of the Atlantic and declared himself the protector of the property-owning classes, thereby provoking a reaction hostile to the Romans. For even if he had thus assured himself of the collaboration of the aristocrats, he had by this very fact associated the democratic movement with the cause of national independence. In Belgium, however, where the less advanced stage of social evolution had not yet ranged the people against the nobles and where the kings still held uncontested authority, the whole country rose against the Roman menace. In 54 BC all the Belgian tribes rose in revolt, soon followed by the popular masses throughout the country (52 BC). Save for the aristocracy, which seems to have remained above the battle, Gaul was solidly united under the leadership of the chief of the Arveni, Vercingetorix.

It was a merciless war. In 50 BC, after killing hundreds of thousands of Gauls and reducing at least as many to slavery, Caesar was master of the country.

The conquest of Gaul is one of the essential facts in the history of the ancient world. It made Rome, whose authority henceforth extended over all western Europe—Italy, Gaul and Spain—the greatest territorial state of the Mediterranean basin.

CRASSUS IS DEFEATED BY THE PARTHIANS

While Caesar was annexing Gaul to the Roman Empire, Crassus was undertaking the conquest of the Parthian kingdom. His aim was to install

Rome on the Tigris and thus give her control of the continental route to India and the caravan routes to the Far East. These were at that time of ever-growing importance because of the development of China which, after having attained her unity in the form of a strongly centralized monarchy, was also pursuing an imperialist policy and trying to extend her control over the great trade-routes of Central Asia.

Crassus was killed while fighting the Parthians in 53 BC. Their king, Orodes, then founded on the Tigris the new capital of Ctesiphon, and laid the foundations of a power which confirmed the orientation of Mesopotamia towards Asia. The defeat of Crassus has a historical importance as great as Caesar's conquests. For if the one extended Roman rule over the whole western European continent, the other finally closed the road from Rome to Asia. Thenceforward, the Roman Empire was destined to retain in the east a maritime and mercantile character and in the west a territorial character. Moreover, by uniting in a single state all the coastlands of the Mediterranean, Rome was to move the centre of Mediterranean trade to the banks of the Tiber.

The defeat of Crassus was therefore to have the most serious consequences for the Roman Empire. Syria and Asia Minor, by remaining cut off from Mesopotamia, with which they had been so closely associated from the economic point of view, prevented the control by the Empire of the great trade route between the Mediterranean and continental Asia; this led to a lack of economic balance and to the fiscal crises from which Rome suffered continually and which were to weigh so heavily upon her destinies.

THE STRUGGLE BETWEEN POMPEY AND CAESAR

The triumvirate had not put an end to the social unrest at Rome. The death of Crassus in 53 BC and the rebellion of Gaul in 52 BC had made the situation critical. The Senate nominated Pompey as sole consul, with full powers to restore order. But the Senators soon became suspicious of the popularity which Pompey enjoyed in Italy. They suspected him of wanting to make use of the armies of Spain to set up a monarchy to his own advantage. None the less, the Senate and Pompey, who did not have the intentions imputed to him, made common cause against Caesar who was the real danger to the nobles of the Republic. The Senate was considering recalling Caesar when he appeared in Italy with his army. The Senate wanted to revert to a legal régime but Caesar, on the other hand, intended to retain the government of Gaul as Pompey had kept that of Spain.

When the Senate refused to grant it to him, he crossed the Rubicon (49 BC) and entered Rome a few days later at the head of his troops. Civil war immediately broke out again. Pompey, defeated at Pharsalia (48 BC), fled to Egypt where he was assassinated. Caesar, who had followed him there, established himself at Alexandria. Following the example of Alexander, he had himself recognized as the son of Ammon. Having thus become legitimate sovereign of Egypt, he married in 48 BC the young queen Cleopatra, who was disputing the throne at this time with her brother Ptolemy. A son, Caesarion, was born of the union of the Roman conqueror and the Queen of Egypt. Under the personal authority of Caesar, a plan was drawn up envisaging the union of the only two great Mediterranean states still existent, the Egyptian Monarchy and the Imperial Republic of Rome.

CAESAR AIMS AT MONARCHY

It seems that Caesar had conceived the idea of founding a hereditary monarchy in favour of his son Caesarion. The fact that Caesar had only called upon western provincials such as Spaniards and Gauls to fill the Senate seats in Rome, and that he did not grant citizenship to the eastern provinces, the richest and most civilized in the Mediterranean, even though he had chosen his heir in Egypt and had had himself acknowledged as 'son of Ammon', seems to show that far from wanting to make the East a Roman possession he was dreaming of organizing the Empire in the form of a federation of states—on the model of the Empire of Alexander—which would have united under his sole rule and under Roman supremacy the Empire of Rome and Egypt and perhaps also the former Seleucid kingdom which Caesar hoped to restore by the conquest of Parthia.

To carry out this vast project Rome would have to become a monarchy. Caesar, while all the time fighting victoriously in Africa and Spain, prepared for it by a series of large-scale reforms. He attempted a complete refashioning of the social order; attacking the crucial problem of the 320,000 unemployed and state-assisted persons which weighed upon Rome like a perpetual threat, he expropriated the great estates of the nobility and endowed 20,000 families with land. He thus laid the foundation for a new middle class; 80,000 proletarians also received lands in Italy and the provinces, so that the number of persons on the dole was reduced to 150,000. To aid the petty bourgeoisie, burdened with debt as a result of the civil war and ruined by capitalism, he proclaimed a moratorium which suspended payment obligations for small arrears of rent and cancelled the interest on overdue payments. But the formidable power of the capitalists still remained. Caesar tamed it by subjecting the companies of speculators and the banks to a rigorous control, and to prevent future abuses in tax-farming methods he handed tax-collection over to a service directly created by the state.

Aware that he could not disarm the hostility of the nobles, he determined to make it powerless by transforming the Senate into a consultative Council of the Empire, to be composed thenceforward of nine hundred members by the introduction of new men, provincials from Gaul and Spain, centurions and sons of freedmen who were personally devoted to him. The *Comitia*, on whom Caesar hoped to base his power, in reality lost all authority and were only convened to vote the frumentary laws designed to create a spectacular propaganda for the new régime. The number of former republican magistratures was increased.

Rome ceased to be the mistress of the Empire to become the residence of the dictator, master of the state.

The new central government was formed around the person of the dictator. Chief of the army, he alone appointed its officers. Supreme Judge, he reserved the functions of that office for himself. He entrusted Egyptian officials with the task of giving a financial administration to the Empire. A state budget was created; provincial budgets were published in Rome and in the districts concerned; the taxes, payable in money, were standardized. For the empire, Rome was no longer to be a master who exploited but a sovereign who governed.

To make Rome a great capital Caesar replanned her as a modern city, well built, well administered, according to a grandiose plan which was not to be completed until the 1st century AD; and to make her equal with the great Hellenistic cities he tried to attract the Hellenized élite by founding public libraries.

It seemed that, according to Caesar's ideas, Italy was to become the nucleus to which the western provinces would gradually be attracted.

To make Italy itself a centralized and unified state, the status of all municipalities and colonies was made uniform; administratively autonomous, they were governed by two elected magistrates, who were at the same time heads of the administration and of justice. Commissioners, armed with full powers, were entrusted with the task of unifying local laws on the basis of Roman civil law.

Sicily and the Narbonnese were granted rights of citizenship and considered an integral part of the Roman national state. Inspired by Egyptian models, Caesar surrounded Italy with a customs barrier in order to allow her to develop economically. To give her financial supremacy, he reserved for Rome the monopoly of minting gold.

Even as Alexander had tried to make the Macedonian colonists the cement of his Empire, so Caesar wished to give his Empire a framework by means of the Roman proletariat, whom he sent to found colonies in all the principal centres. In the East they were to be rapidly absorbed, but in the West, where the colonies marked the beginnings of a huge urban policy, their language was spontaneously accepted by the local peoples because of its universality.

The immense task carried out by Caesar could only be crowned by the establishment of a monarchy.

One dynasty alone remained which, despite its decadence, still represented the conception of monarchy by divine right upon which all the oriental empires had been founded, the dynasty of the Ptolemies. By uniting himself to it through his marriage with Cleopatra, Caesar declared himself the legitimate heir of the Pharaohs and of Alexander, from whom the Ptolemies derived their power. The Egyptians considered sovereignty as a direct issue of the divinity; pantheist and Stoic ideas made the Greeks admit that the divine spirit is more especially manifested in great men, and therefore a number of Greek cities had granted Caesar the epithet of 'divine' in thanks for his restoration of peace. The whole East was ready, unanimously, to accept the formation of a Julian dynasty.[1]

But the Romans had still to be convinced. Caesar had already brought Cleopatra with her court to Rome; he wore the costume of the Hellenistic kings, and he erected, on the model of the Pharaohs, a shrine in the name of Jupiter Julius, putting up his own statues in the temples, and dedicated to Cleopatra, Queen and Goddess, a temple of Venus Genetrix.[2] Encouraging the diffusion of the legend of his divine origin, he set up a special priesthood to celebrate the cult of 'Caesar, the Living God'. The only thing that remained to be done, in order to transport the Pharaonic monarchy to Rome, was for him to take the title of King. The Senate seemed disposed to grant it to him, when he fell under the daggers of Brutus and the conspirators (44 BC). Brutus represented the Roman oligarchy and its privileges even more than he did the republican ideal, which he did not dissociate from the right of the senatorial party to exploit the world for its own profit. Had he not himself ruined the city of Salamis in Cyprus by his usurious loans?

By the assassination of Caesar, Rome avoided the monarchy which

[1] Caesar belonged to the *gens Julia*.
[2] Venus Genetrix is Venus regarded as Goddess-Mother.

would have subordinated her interests to those of the Empire. But by refusing the monarchical formula which Caesar had proposed, without suggesting any other possible régime, she plunged once more into civil war.

II. ANTONY AND OCTAVIAN: HELLENISTIC MONARCHY AGAINST ROMAN DICTATORSHIP

THE CAESARIAN TRIUMVIRATE

The assassination of Caesar once again plunged the world into the crisis which it seemed to have escaped. Was there to be a universal monarchy based on the ideas of natural law which had been developed in the Hellenistic world, or an empire kept in subjection by the Roman aristocracy? At Rome the republican party was revived; Cicero made the Senate proclaim a general amnesty and the abolition of the dictatorship. But the republican solution was no longer possible since, valid for Rome and just possible for Italy, it did not correspond to the necessities of the Empire. As formerly when Demosthenes was struggling against Philip, so now the republican party, by repudiating the monarchical idea, did not realize that it was defending an outworn formula. By demanding, with the support of the Senate, a return to republican institutions it aimed perhaps at restoring liberty to Rome, but it imposed slavery upon the Empire as a whole. Henceforth Rome was indissolubly a part of the Empire. The Roman people, moreover, being now cosmopolitan and formed of both citizens and resident aliens, no longer considered the Republic as synonymous with liberty; they saw in it only capitalist oppression and the triumph of the class privileges of the senatorial party. Caesar had given them land and democratic reforms; the popular party—as well as all the Hellenistic East which saw in the monarchy the end of Roman exactions—was for Caesar. Civil war broke out. Cleopatra, taking Caesarion with her, left Rome hurriedly for Alexandria. In Rome, the magistrates, to whichever party they belonged, once more battened upon the quarry of the Empire, disputing the government of the provinces. Octavian, Caesar's adopted son, took possession of Rome and in October 43 BC concluded an agreement with the two other representatives of the Caesarian party, Lepidus and Antony, by which they united in a constituent triumvirate. Masters of power, they divided the armies and the provinces and attacked the republican party with horrifying proscriptions, in the course of which Cicero perished. Senators and *equites* were put to death by the thousand.

The capital and income of the wealthy classes were subjected to taxes that amounted to expropriation. In 42 BC Caesar was proclaimed a god. The monarchical party had won the day.

Octavian installed himself at Rome, where the Senate bowed to his omnipotence. Lepidus departed for the province of Africa. Antony settled at Ephesus; determined, like each of his colleagues, to win the Empire for himself alone, he prepared for the struggle by increasing the tribute of the Asian provinces in order to provide himself with an immense war chest.

Antony, distant from Rome, was soon to be won over by the East, where only a single power remained—Egypt. Under the inspired guidance of Cleopatra, Egypt was to return to the lists and dispute with Rome the mastery of the Hellenistic world.

THE RETURN OF EGYPT TO THE SCENE

With astonishing clear-sightedness, Cleopatra realized that if Egypt were to have any chance of playing an international role, the autarchy which was threatening her position must be broken. The monopoly of the Royal Bank, as also the monopolies of oil and salt, were suppressed and freedom of trade, including freedom of the money market, was restored. On the state lands perpetual leases were abolished and the lands reverted to public tender. These radical reforms, which allowed Egypt to take her place once more in international trade, could only succeed by the restoration of a sound currency. The monarchy must therefore have sufficient resources at its disposal. Cleopatra achieved this at a single stroke; by abolishing the immunity of the temples, placing the sacerdotal estates under state administration and re-establishing the budget of the cults. As to the liquidation of the crushing loans that Ptolemy XIII Auletes had earlier underwritten at Rome, Caesar had already made their settlement possible by reducing the usurious terms that he himself, the governor of Syria and the syndicate of Roman bankers had been able to wrest from the harried king.

No such far-reaching economic, fiscal and social reform had ever before been carried out. But to make it possible Cleopatra needed to have at her disposal a military power that Egypt no longer possessed. She went to ask it of Antony. She left for Tarsus, where Antony was at that time in residence, and in 41 BC she brought him with her to Alexandria where he soon afterwards married her.

Antony then threw off the mask and aimed openly at the establishment of a monarchy directly associated with Hellenistic tradition.

But his policy rekindled the civil war in Rome. The Senate dominated by Octavian did not hesitate, in order to weaken Antony, to sacrifice the richest parts of the Empire by inciting Orodes, king of the Parthians, whose armies had defeated Crassus, to attack Antony. The opportunity of restoring the Persian Empire was unique; Orodes conquered Antioch, Jerusalem and Syria, and was preparing to penetrate into Asia Minor when Antony reacted. To drive back the menace from Asia, he appealed to the unity of the maritime peoples. Then, having driven the Parthian armies back from the coasts, he restored a chain of petty monarchies along the whole length of the eastern Mediterranean and the Black Sea in order to keep them in check. In 37 BC Herod was installed as king of Jerusalem. Pontus, Cilicia and Cappadocia were restored as kingdoms. Caesarion was recognized both as Caesar's heir and, conjointly with Cleopatra, ruler of Egypt, while the great market-town of Damascus in Syria was restored to Egyptian rule.

The policy of Cleopatra had triumphed. Egypt once more assumed her supremacy in the East. Reverting to her traditional policy, Egypt was already aiming at mastery over Syria which Herod, only just enthroned, wanted to dispute.

Over and above the oriental monarchies re-created by his will alone Antony appeared as the monarch of an Empire envisaged as a federation of states.

By this time the triumvirate was falling to pieces. Lepidus, who had quarrelled with Octavian, was deprived of the government of Africa. The world had now only two masters; Octavian who held the West and Antony who held the East.

Antony aimed at the mastery of the world by ensuring the supremacy of the East. That was why, reverting to the great political projects of Alexander and Caesar, he set out to conquer the kingdom of the Parthians, the crossroads where the great trade-routes from India, Armenia and the Caucasus met those which, through Central Asia, led to China.

But this new dream of empire ended in disaster. Once again the reunion of the continent and the sea in a single empire proved to be impossible.

Defeated on the continent, Antony turned once more seaward. Reverting to Ptolemaic policy, he decided with Cleopatra's aid to build his power on the naval and commercial supremacy of Egypt. In 34 BC he incorporated southern Syria, Phoenicia and Cyprus into Egypt while granting to the children he had had by Cleopatra dominion over Armenia, northern Syria, Cyrenaica and even Media, which he still dreamed of conquering.

A vast dynastic Empire was being built up in the East, with Egypt as its centre, while a great wave of moral and cultural renascence, which was to have lasting results, passed through all the Hellenized lands.

THE TRIUMPH OF OCTAVIAN

While Antony was unifying the East under the leadership of Egypt, Octavian had entrenched himself firmly in the West. Here there was no tradition favouring monarchy. Octavian had to appear as a dictator, speaking in the name of Roman power. He was, however, preparing a personal power by making Italy and the provinces that he held swear personal loyalty to him. The conflict between Octavian and Antony, between West and East, was inevitable. In 32 BC Rome declared war on Cleopatra.

Once again naval supremacy decided the issue. After the defeat of Antony's fleet at Actium in 31 BC the Empire of the East, which rested solely on the Roman forces of Antony, collapsed. Octavian entered Alexandria as a victor. Antony and Cleopatra committed suicide and the fabulous kingdom of the Pharaohs was incorporated into the Roman Empire, of which Octavian, with the title of Augustus, was to become sole master.

III. ROME AN INTELLECTUAL CAPITAL

During the great period of crisis in which Rome had built up her empire, and her democratic institutions had been submerged by demagogy, she was to know an intellectual development which reflected all the trends of her dramatic history.

The theatre held a leading place, but it was a theatre of great popular spectacles; the circus became a means of propaganda exploited by the party leaders who offered sumptuous pantomimes to the mob: magnificent and picturesque processions of camels, lions, tigers and other wild animals, troops in brilliant uniforms, and those terrible gladiatorial combats which the dictators made fashionable in order to sate the sadism of the Roman populace. The comedy of manners, introduced by Plautus in imitation of the Alexandrians, was replaced by coarse farces, the *atellanae*, which drew their inspiration from satire on public morals, and pantomimes which brought to the stage topical events, even going so far as to depict the amorous adventures of Caesar himself.

Satires attacked the political masters of the hour with verve and venom.

But while the mob thronged these spectacles and saturated itself with politics, the élite was becoming Hellenized and turning to Greek culture. Only Alexandrian literature was discussed in the fashionable salons. Political and legal eloquence modelled itself on the flowery and inflated 'Asian' schools or professed the sober atticism of Demosthenes. Legal studies were exposed to the pervasive influence of the ideas of natural law based on Hellenistic conceptions. Even the most conservative of the Romans, Varro, a landowner hostile to cosmopolitanism and international trade, was none the less an encyclopaedic spirit, fully imbued with Greek philosophy. Like the oriental sovereigns, statesmen wrote their memoirs. The *Commentaries* of Caesar are the political apologia of a democrat conquering the world. Contemporary history became a science. Sallust studied the causes of the democratic revolution which was taking place before his eyes.

Cicero, who had tried to form a third and moderate party, both conservative and liberal, midway between the aristocratic and senatorial party and the democrats, was the greatest spirit of his time. In his view, Rome should not dominate the Empire, but protect it. Like Socrates, Cicero was a citizen of the world. By the influence which he had over his contemporaries, he might be compared with Voltaire and the Encyclopaedists. His treatise on rhetoric is an essay on the philosophy of art. In *De Republica* and *De Legibus* he tries to establish a metaphysical basis for law and preaches a reform of the Roman constitution which should reconcile aristocracy and democracy. But the voice of reason is unheeded in times of crisis. Cicero was a voice crying in the wilderness; the empire, whatever may have been the influence of Cicero on the policy of Augustus, was founded on immediate interest, which led it into terrible dramas, and not on philosophical views which might have been able to give it a stable basis.

The more far-seeing among the élite began to understand this. But Roman society, freed from all restraint, was no longer capable of thought. It acted, driven on by blind and unreasoned forces. Thus, divorced from the mob, a world of dilettantes was created which gave itself up to disinterested studies. The elegant and sceptical Atticus, a literary dilettante as well as an usurer, lived in his magnificent library like a sophisticated man of the world who read everything but wrote nothing. The Cisalpine aristocrat, Cornelius Nepos, frequented the fashionable salons, while writing historical compilations.

In intellectual circles, however, thought attained remarkable heights. The provincial Catullus, the most perfect representative of dilettantism, practised 'art for art's sake and set up his complete individualism in opposition to the masses. While the city was echoing to the cries of the riotors, he excelled himself, like the Alexandrians, in lyrics of amorous passion, half erudite and half *galante*.

The thinking of this period is dominated by the great figure of Lucretius who, isolated in a proud withdrawal, wanted to ignore Rome for the universe. Instructed in all that the philosophy of the ancient world could give, he tried to understand the meaning of life and, as a disciple of Epicurus, ended in anti-religious positivism. He preached materialism and denial of the existence of God in opposition to popular mysticism: an atomist, he developed before Descartes the theory of universal mechanism, believed in the permanence of matter, in an infinity of worlds and in the natural evolution of beings: detached from the affairs of the moment, he preached a moral doctrine of resignation and the cult of knowledge. In contrast to the mystical and religious thought of the East, Lucretius was the noblest product of Roman materialism which, in his works, was able to rise to a proud scientific vision of the universe.

PART THREE
THE ERA OF THE EMPIRES

BOOK XI

The Roman Empire up to the Crisis of the 3rd Century AD

CHAPTER XLIII

INDIA, CENTRE OF WORLD TRADE

GREATNESS AND DECADENCE OF THE MAURYA EMPIRE

IN the VIth century BC a great idealist movement swept through Asia, represented by Buddha in India and by Lao-Tse in China. It followed Zoroastrianism, which had arisen in the VIIth century BC, and corresponded to the outburst of mysticism which, in the Saite period, had triumphed in Egypt and spread to Greece, where Plato was to sum up in beautiful prose the universal cycle of idealism. In the IVth century, when trade which was becoming more and more international in character bound India closely to the West, Aristotle was to replace Plato's idealism with a more realistic conception contemporary with the conquests of Alexander, and Mencius in China provided the monarchical system then in course of development with a pragmatist doctrine based upon a revised Confucianism.

This was the period when India and China took shape as great monarchical states, after an evolution similar to that of the Hellenistic lands. In 321 BC Chandragupta had founded the Maurya dynasty in the Ganges basin and rapidly extended his rule over all northern India, including the valleys of the Ganges and the Indus. He installed there a monarchy based on divine right, probably inspired by Hellenistic principles which Chandragupta had inherited from Alexander. Seleucus I had tried in vain to re-incorporate the Indian provinces in his Empire but, having failed to do so, he had concluded with the Maurya kingdom a treaty of alliance which maintained friendly trade relations between the two kingdoms and ceded the province of Gedrosia (Baluchistan) to Chandragupta.

Throughout the IIIrd century BC the Maurya Empire continued to grow in power. During the reign of King Asoka (274–237 BC), which marked its zenith, it extended over the Malabar coast, where the ports became of considerable importance, and covered all central India. The south of India alone escaped, and the Dravidian maritime states, Kerala, Pandya, Chola, enjoyed great prosperity because of their position half-way between Arabia and Egypt on the one hand and northern India and Indonesia on the other.

After the conquests of Asoka, India became the richest and most populous empire in the world, but it formed, from the political and from the racial and social viewpoints, an extremely incongruous unity. Asoka, while unifying power as far as was possible, respected the cultural and social divergencies of his lands by dividing them into vice-royalties: Punjab, Malva, Kalinga and Deccan. The principle of government, as formerly in the Persian empire, was respect for local autonomy, the town or village forming an administrative unit.

BUDDHISM CONQUERS ASIA

To offset this disparity, Asoka tried to give a moral unity to his lands. After the blood-stained campaigns necessitated by his conquests he was converted to Buddhism and his whole reign, thenceforward, was dominated by mystical and charitable ideals. A great current of mysticism and social unity was to engulf India at the same time as the cult of Isis was developing in Egypt and Stoicism spread through the Hellenistic world the theories of natural law which were to serve as the basis for the social legislation of the Greek cities. In India the two trends were combined. Asoka was a monk-king who translated mysticism into politics. In Greece, the reforms carried out under the pressure of proletarian claims assumed a revolutionary form; in India, similar reforms, introduced by the king as a charitable bequest, became an integral part of his design for moral virtues and universal love. Asoka wished the government to give an example of virtue by practising a policy of social assistance. He had wells dug to give drinking water to the people and planted fruit-trees along the roads which were being built; he founded hospitals for men and even for sick animals, and encouraged the cultivation of medicinal plants. He published decrees calling on the people to practise moral virtues, religious toleration and humanity to slaves.

A royal code of laws was drawn up and its execution confided to senior magistrates; this was based not on the need for maintaining order but, as in Egypt, on equity and moral virtues; instructions, almost similar to those given to their officials by the Ptolemies at the same period, reminded the king's representatives that their mission was to protect those whom they governed and that they must behave mildly and justly even with men who had been sentenced by the courts and with barbarian peoples.

These edicts of Asoka, which are amongst the noblest efforts of humanity to ensure the triumph of a moral code of universal charity, were based on both Buddhist and Brahmanic conceptions and could therefore be applied to all Hindus, whatever their religion.

It was however around the Buddhist faith that Asoka tried to rally his peoples. In 253 BC—at the time when the Ptolemies in Egypt were convoking the first councils of High Priests of all the cults in order to form them into a national church—he convened in his magnificent capital of Pataliputra a Buddhist council to organize the evangelization of the world. It was presided over by his brother, who had taken monastic orders. This policy of evangelization undertaken by Asoka, and designed to spread the Buddhist faith over the entire universe, corresponded to the attempt at religious universalism undertaken at exactly the same time in Alexandria by Egyptian and Greek theologians, who tried to give the whole Eastern world a single religion by uniting the solar and nature cults in the single worship of Serapis. Buddhist missionary monks were sent to Ceylon, to Kashmir, into Gandhara and into Central Asia; and a royal edict set up a plan for the conversion of the Hellenistic states ruled over at that time by Antiochus II in Syria, Ptolemy II in Egypt and Antigonus Gonatas in Macedonia.

All India, Burma and the island of Ceylon were converted to Buddhism. But in Egypt, Syria and Macedonia the Buddhist missionaries failed, because the mystery cults had already given pious souls the religion of salvation which they craved, and the solar syncretism fulfilled that need for universalism which was then felt throughout the whole civilized world.

Thus, although born of the Indo-European genius, Buddhism found no echo among the peoples, in great part Indo-European, of the Greco-Oriental world; it was on the other hand to conquer all Asia.

INDIAN TRADE TURNS TO THE SEA AND THE WEST

In the IIIrd century BC India was the great religious centre of the world. It was also its greatest commercial centre. Its influence on Western policy was, as we have seen, decisive. Possession of the trade-route to India, either by land or sea, was the aim of the wars which ended by draining the resources of the kingdoms of the Seleucids and the Ptolemies. Diplomatic missions converged on Pataliputra. The Seleucid king was the ally of Asoka, and the Ptolemies sent scientific and trade missions, ambassadors and savants to India. In the IInd century BC Egyptian navigators, no longer depending on Arabian middlemen, came in their own ships to the ports of India.

The current of trade, which linked India and Egypt and which made Alexandria the market for Indian produce, integrated India with the maritime economy and, in consequence, with Mediterranean economy of which it seemed at this time to be an inseparable part.

Despite its wealth, the Maurya dynasty enjoyed only an ephemeral existence. It was extinguished, leaving no descendants, in 185 BC. The Empire of Asoka, like that of Alexander, fell to pieces at the very moment when the Peace of Apamea (188 BC) marked the decline of the Seleucid Empire. Their simultaneous downfall meant a change of balance in Central Asia to the benefit of the two states which were being formed there during the wars that followed the death of Alexander: the Iranian kingdom of the Parthians and the Greek kingdom of Bactria.

CHAPTER XLIV

THE PARTHIAN KINGDOM AND THE GREEK KINGDOMS OF CENTRAL ASIA

THE PARTHIAN KINGDOM OF THE ARSACIDS

ALEXANDER the Great had conquered all the ancient Persian Empire. During the wars of the *diadokoi*, the greater part of Nearer Asia had fallen to the share of Seleucus. The Hellenistic policy of Alexander and his successors had met with lively opposition from the Iranians for religious reasons. Mazdaism, imbued with the mystical and moral ideas of Zoroastrianism, exercised a greater and greater ascendancy over ancient Media which had been its birthplace and which had already under the rule of the Achaemenids shown tendencies to a religious nationalism, similar to that of the Jewish people.

These tendencies had culminated in the formation of a Persian national state in northern Media, the kingdom of Atropatene based on the religion of Zoroaster, and, from Media, the movement had spread to the district of Persis. About 250 BC, taking advantage of the war in which Antiochus II was engaged against Egypt, Arsaces had founded, to the south-east of the Caspian Sea, the independent kingdom of Parthia, with a mixed population of Iranians and Scythians, these last being however a branch of the Iranian race.

At first, Arsaces had made Zadracarte on the Caspian his capital, and had assured himself control of the ports of that sea which put him in direct touch with the Caucasus.

About 200 BC the Arsacids took possession of Ecbatana. Thenceforward, they controlled both the land and the sea routes that linked the Caucasus to India, as well as the caravan route from Mesopotamia to China. These two great trade-routes met at Hecatompylos. The Arsacids soon moved their capital there, and the city developed greatly under Mithridates I (174–136 BC).

After the collapse of the Seleucid power under Antiochus IV, the

Arsacids took possession of the great metropolis of Mesopotamia, Seleucia-on-Tigris, which had replaced Babylon as the commercial centre of Nearer Asia. This conquest—which only became final in 129 BC—made them masters of all the continental communications of the West with India and the Far East. Parthia, thenceforward, formed part of the Hellenistic and Mediterranean economy because of her control of the Tigris, and also of the economy of Central Asia by Hecatompylos, while the Caspian Sea linked her to the Caucasus and the Russian plains. Parthia dominated continental trade even as Egypt dominated sea-borne trade.

CONTINENTAL CHARACTER OF PARTHIAN CIVILIZATION

This explains the composite character of the Parthian civilization. Iranian by religion, it was subject to the attraction of Hellenistic trade which then extended as far as India. The golden coins minted by the Arsacids were of Hellenistic type.

But because she did not control the coasts of the Mediterranean, Parthia did not continue the cosmopolitan civilization of the Persian Empire of the Achaemenids. Her culture was closely related to the Median culture, which was purely landowning. From the social viewpoint also she differed from the Hellenistic states. Essentially continental, she experienced the great urban evolution which was at that time changing so deeply all the maritime states of Nearer Asia. Despite the great cities that she possessed, she remained on the whole a feudal, landowning country. Her trade was concentrated on the international trade-routes in the large cities that had preserved a cosmopolitan character and where Greek was in current use as a business language. But it was the language of continental trade, Aramaic, then widespread from the Tigris to the Mediterranean, and not Greek, the language of sea-borne trade, which—alongside Iranian—was to be adopted as the official language of the Arsacids. Outside these strongly Hellenized ways of communication, the people remained grouped under a seigniorial régime, to the maintenance of which the influence of the Magi contributed. This phenomenon recalls Palestine in the times of Solomon when, outside Jerusalem which was an international trade centre, the people remained attached to the soil and to the national religion represented by prophets hostile to all foreign influences.

It was not, therefore, as in the Mediterranean countries, the cosmopolitanism of the cities which determined the civilization of the Parthian kingdom, but the religious and national sentiment of the countryside. For almost five centuries (250 BC–226 AD) the Parthian kingdom, under the rule of its priest-kings, reacted against Hellenism and turned more and more to Mazdaism, the traditions of which were to be finally elaborated by the Sassanids, in the 3rd century AD, in the religion and doctrine of the *Avesta*, an expression of a moral code as exalted as the Christian religion.

Thanks to its strong feudal army, the kingdom of the 'Magikings' resisted Roman ascendancy. By the defeats that it inflicted on Crassus and Antony, it prevented Rome from taking over control of the western land-route to the East. It was thus to exercise a decisive influence on the destinies of the Roman Empire.

THE GREEK KINGDOM OF BACTRIA (BACTRIANA)

The formation of the Parthian kingdom cut the Seleucid Empire off from its eastern provinces of Bactria and Sogdiana. The Greek governor of Bactria, Diodotus I, profited by this to assume the royal title (250 BC). The Seleucids did not, however, have to renounce control of the caravan route on which Bactra was one of the key-points. Seleucus II, and later Antiochus III, tried to keep the way to Central Asia open. For a time Parthia was reconquered by Antiochus III, who led his armies as far as the Punjab. But these successes were only ephemeral, and the Seleucids had to be content with a policy of alliance with the Indian dynasty of the Mauryas and a theoretical sovereignty over Bactria.

The decline of the Seleucid kingdom after the Peace of Apamea (188 BC) and the collapse of the Maurya Empire, which disintegrated after the dynasty became extinct in 185 BC, opened possibilities of extension both to the Parthian kingdom and to Bactria; the former profited by them to lay hands on Mesopotamia and the latter to impose its rule on the Indus valley. Politically divided, India none the less remained an economic force of essential importance. The ancient capital of Pataliputra in the Ganges valley and the city of Ujjain, which dominated the route from the Ganges to the ports of the western coast, were economic and intellectual centres of great influence. Their wealth quite naturally tempted the Greek kings of Bactria, masters of the route that linked India to China. Under Demetrius II, the kingdom of Bactria became a vast state which stretched from the Aral Sea to the Indian Ocean, including Afghanistan and all the Indus basin.

THE GRECO-BUDDHIST CIVILIZATION OF THE GREEK KINGDOMS OF ASIA

This Greek Empire, created in the midst of Central Asia, soon lost its unity. Torn between the attraction of the sea to the south and the continent to the north, it at once broke into fragments. From 175 BC Greek usurpers carved themselves kingdoms out of it, where Greek influence was only maintained by the sovereign dynasties surrounded by a few hundred Hellenized officials. These Greek kings were soon conquered by the advanced Hindu culture. One of the most important of them, Menander, who had installed himself at Pataliputra, was to become, if one is to believe the *Conversations of Milinda*,[1] a convinced Buddhist.

During his reign the port situated on the estuary of the Indus, and which at that time bore the Greek name of Demetriad, enjoyed an astonishing prosperity because of its links with Alexandria. The sea kept the Greek kingdom of India in touch with Hellenism.

There thus developed in the Greek states of India and Bactria a Greco-Buddhist civilization. The gold coins that they struck had inscriptions in both languages and the art of the period bears traces of this double inspiration.

In this economic complex formed during the whole IInd century BC by the Greek kingdoms of India and Central Asia it was the sea which played the leading role, because the distant influence of Alexandria drew the caravans from Central Asia to the Indus valley. These Greek kingdoms thus remained the outposts of Western influence as far as Central Asia, since Alexandria remained the determining factor of the prosperity of the caravan cities founded by Alexander in Bactria and Sogdiana.

Though checked on the continent by the Parthians, Greek influence came back by way of the sea and extended its ascendancy into Central Asia, moving up the Indus valley. There it soon clashed with the formidable competition of China which, at the zenith of the expansionist force given it by its monarchical unity and industrial activity, was then undertaking a policy of commercial imperialism. A fresh struggle was about to take place between the influence of the sea and that of the continent, and this time it was the continent that was to win.

[1] A classic work of Hindu literature written in the 2nd century AD.

CHAPTER XLV

THE ADVENT OF THE CHINESE EMPIRE

THE economic importance of the kingdoms of Parthia and Bactria was due to their position midway between the West, India and China. And since the development of the West and China were simultaneous, this explains the vitality of the great trade-routes by which contact between the Mediterranean and the Far East was maintained.

THE TSIN ORGANIZE THE MONARCHY (256–202 BC)

The Chinese monarchy was formed in the IVth century BC on the ruins of the great feudal Empire of the Chou, and to the advantage of the kingdom of Tsin, situated in the west of China at the point where the caravan routes ended.

After more than a century of great wars the Tsin finally rejected the sovereignty, which had in any case become nominal, of the Chou and emerged as masters of all northern China. They at once undertook the struggle against the southern kingdom of the Tsu and conquered it in the most atrocious manner. In 221 BC the king, Tsin-Che-Huang, succeeded in uniting China and took the title of Emperor.

He immediately enforced a policy of monarchical centralization. The former feudal lords disappeared and were replaced by royal agents. The Empire was divided into thirty-six governments, each administered by a civil governor, a military commandant and a superintendent of finances. A central government was organized under the authority of a Prime Minister, who presided over the administration entrusted to a corps of officials. Writing and standards of measure were unified. A pitiless repression of feudal wars brought internal security, and to prevent their recurrence all the strongholds of the local princes were destroyed.

On the other hand, the construction of the Great Wall was commenced in 215 BC to protect China against the nomad Huns in the north who had begun to move southward and westward.

The southern kingdom of the Tsu, inhabited by a people akin to the

Annamites, was divided into four governments. The country, still very backward, was exploited by the suppression of the seigniorial system, by the irrigation of the valley of the Tsing, an affluent of the Yang-Tse, which rendered 620,000 acres available for cultivation, and by a systematic agricultural colonization.

Hien-Yang, the capital of the Tsin Empire, the caravan-market which kept China in touch with India and the West, became a great city.

But China, though united under a single dynasty, had no racial, linguistic, economic or social unity. Civilization was much more advanced in the north than in the south. The consolidation of the divergent regions of the vast Chinese Empire into a political unit required a policy of pitiless absolutism. This soon provoked rebellions from which the dispossessed feudal lords hoped to profit.

On the death of the Emperor Tsin-Che-Huang (210 BC) a general revolt broke out. Civil war rent the country. The generals fought among themselves to obtain power. Their struggles ended, in 202 BC, in the supremacy of the Han family.

THE LIBERAL MONARCHY OF THE HAN (202 BC–AD 220)

The advent of the Han, who came from the south of the country, led to extensive reforms.

A penal code was published, based on the *lex talionis* and on equity. Imperial courts replaced the former local jurisdictions. Justice, rendered without class distinction, aimed above all at assuring the security of persons and goods. The nobles finally lost their ancient legal and social privileges.

Taxation was standardized in the form of a tithe and a poll-tax payable by all males from the ages of fifteen to fifty-six. A special contribution was levied for the upkeep of the army. In order to provide for the government of their Empire, the Han at first divided it into appanages entrusted to the royal princes and fiefs held by hereditary seigneurs who did not have sovereign rights but enjoyed the status of officials graded and paid by the king. The salary of these governor-princes, paid half in kind and half in money, varied from 3,000 to 120,000 measures of wheat and from 800 to 9,000 pieces of money annually. It was to some extent a compromise, covering the transition period from the feudal system to centralized monarchy. It evolved towards pure and simple bureaucracy which ended by eliminating the hereditary status of the governors and high officials and by introducing a régime very similar to that of Egypt under the centralized monarchies of the Ancient and New Empires and which was still existent under the dynasty of the Ptolemies. Aristocracy of birth was replaced by a non-hereditary administrative nobility.

The stability of power led quite naturally to the disappearance of the régime of force upon which the Tsin had relied. A conception of the state was created, based on law, which little by little eliminated all differences between victors and vanquished.

The consequence was that the civil administration took precedence over the military authority and the provinces of the Empire were handed over entirely to the civil powers.

The central government, under the authority of the Prime Minister, was divided into administrative departments; justice, education and cults, war (which controlled both army and police), arbitration (charged with keeping watch over the good conduct of officials towards the people and the state), agriculture, and public works. Peace and the facility of communications between all parts of the Empire led to increased internal trade and, with it, urban life. In the cities a needy proletariat made its appearance alongside the merchant classes. The action of trade exercised an influence parallel with the influence of the central administration; mobility of goods caused hereditary tenures to disappear, while at the same time the state suppressed the last traces of the seigniorial régime. The peasant, until then tied to the soil, was emancipated. This resulted in a great exodus to the cities, despite all the efforts made by the king to improve agriculture. The proletariat accumulated in the cities and soon created a social problem. It was solved, as in Rome at about the same time, by the establishment of agricultural colonies made up of the unemployed, and also, as in Greece, by social laws establishing state-aid for old and infirm persons, widows and orphans.

Humanitarian ideas penetrated law, and the archaic principle of the *lex talionis* was eliminated from the penal code.

The economic progress of the Empire led naturally to monetary reform. The Tsin had created a very heavy copper coinage. In 175 BC the Han introduced a new coinage ten times lighter. By a happy coincidence, copper mines were opened in 130 BC as a state monopoly.

By the normal course of evolution bureaucracy and social laws necessitated ever increasing resources, and taxation became more and more important. To obtain the necessary funds the state had recourse, as in the Egypt of the Ptolemies, to a fiscal monopoly of salt.

As the state became more centralized, the central power continued to strengthen its position in order to face up to its growing obligations. The monarchy thus evolved rapidly towards absolutism. And thenceforward, as in Egypt, it tried to justify its omnipotence by giving itself a religious basis. The Emperor declared himself the emissary of heaven and took the titles of 'master of heaven' and 'son of heaven'. In 165 BC a royal priesthood was created which soon took a leading place at court. As at Babylon, it tried through astrology to find in the stars laws which presided over human destinies and, in consequence, royal policy. By astrology the priests obtained a great influence over policy.

Wu-Ti (140–87 BC) raised absolutism to its highest point and, relying upon the doctrine which made the king the representative of the divine power on earth, he fixed as basic principles of government: reason, equity, reciprocity, leniency.[1]

The state, thenceforward, relied upon the class of *literati*. Officials were appointed after an examination. The state itself prepared them at its schools. Like the *Museum* at Alexandria, the Academy of Hien-Yang, founded in 124 BC, became a scientific centre with fifty savants versed in foreign languages, history, astrology and the natural sciences. The king, the provincial governors and the former lords, who still constituted a social aristocracy, surrounded themselves with savants. As the state became more centralized private law evolved, quite naturally, towards individualism. In 127 BC the right of primogeniture was suppressed; this reform put an end to the aristocracy as a social class.

THE POLICY OF ECONOMIC AND TERRITORIAL EXPANSION

The economic development of China drove her to a policy of expansion. The frontiers of the Empire were extended as far as the sea by the conquest of the kingdom of Canton (111 BC); a road, defended by military posts, linked it to the capital. A fleet was launched on the China Sea. The Empire assumed a maritime character.

It immediately set out to win the mastery of the seas. In 108 BC it established itself in Korea, whose western coasts were organized in four provinces. The administrative capital was set up at Ping-Yang on the Ta-Tong and a systematic colonization of the country was undertaken by the despatch of sixty thousand Chinese families, representing more than 400,000 individuals. Korea was thenceforth won for Chinese civilization.

The Empire also extended its frontiers to the south along the coasts of Annam which, from the IInd century BC, had been deeply influenced by the civilizing force of China, whence it had accepted Buddhism.

[1] In Egypt and at Babylon it was justice.

In 57 BC China entered into relations with Japan, where civilization was still in its beginnings. The islands of the Japanese Archipelago were at this time divided into about a hundred petty tribal kingdoms, in which a land-owning and aristocratic type of society had been created. China imposed a sort of sovereign protectorate over the island of Kyu-Shu, which put an end to the isolation of Japan.

At the same time as she was extending her dominion along all the coast, from Annam to Korea, China was also trying to extend her control over the caravan-routes which linked her to the West. She sent missions into Central Asia, which revealed to her the great market for cotton goods in the Indus valley. The Chinese missions reached Bactra, Ctesiphon-on-Tigris, the Ural region and the Indus, and a vigorous trade sprang up between China, the producer of silk, and the kingdom of Bactria, the great supplier of horses.

It was about this time that the itineraries of the two main caravan-routes were fixed, the southern route by Khotan and Bactra and the northern by Karachar to Samarkand, Merv and the Caspian Sea.

By these two routes China came into contact with the West, whence she imported the vine. Western craftsmen and artists flocked to Hien-Yang and Chinese civilization made a great step forward which was reflected in its art and literature.

Mastery of the caravan-routes henceforward determined the foreign policy of China. To control them she had to make herself safe from the forays of the Huns from the north and, on the west, to drive back the Greek kings of Bactria who also aimed at dominating trade.

The Huns, barbarian nomads who had settled in Northern Mongolia, had begun to move westward about 165 BC. The Chinese Emperors at first tried to get them to settle, by introducing them to new needs so as to civilize them, and at the same time to open vast markets for Chinese goods. But this pacific policy failed. It was therefore necessary to undertake military expeditions against the Huns, which drove them back to the north. The Great Wall was garrisoned with a guard of 600,000 men and fortified cities were founded along the frontiers of Mongolia.

Against the Greek kingdom of Bactria, Wu-Ti made an alliance with the Scytho-Sarmatian peoples of the Urals. China was at this time a prey to urban over-population and the emperor levied an army among the workless and organized an expedition which, with the support of the Scythians, advanced as far as the Indus. The caravan cities of present-day Turkestan were occupied. A fortress was built at Karachar, and China extended her protectorate over Central Asia as far as the Aral Sea.

THE END OF THE GREEK KINGDOMS OF ASIA

While China was taking possession of Turkestan, the Huns, in their migration westward, clashed with the Aryan people of the Tokharians who had settled to the north of the Aral Sea. Driven westward, they in turn drove the Scythians back to the Jaxartes, which they crossed, making forays into the kingdom of Bactria. The invasion of the Scythians in 135 BC and the Tokharian invasion which followed it under pressure from the Huns put an end to the Greek kingdom of Bactria. The Scythians settled in eastern Iran where they mingled with the Parthians. The Greeks were driven back to Kabul and the Punjab, which broke up into a number of petty states.

About 80 BC the Scytho-Parthians or Sacae began to penetrate into the valley of the Indus and spread gradually along the whole Persian Gulf and the Lower Indus valley. Between 80 and 30 BC they slowly conquered the whole Punjab, annexing one after the other the little Greek kingdoms which still held out there. Their disappearance marked the end of Greek influence in Central Asia. Henceforward Chinese culture was to be dominant.

THE EMPIRE EVOLVES TOWARDS STATE SOCIALISM

The Chinese expansion of the second half of the IInd century BC assured China both the mastery of the sea from Korea to Annam and that of the caravan-routes as far as the Aral region and the borders of India.

This resulted in an intensification of trade and industry. The manufacture of silk attained enormous proportions and its export became a considerable source of profit. The capital of the Empire, a commercial centre where the caravan-routes from the West ended, as well as the road from Canton and the Huang-Ho river, became the international market for silk which, about this time, made its triumphal entry into the West.

The development of sea and river shipping made the Yang-Tse river the great trade artery of the country. The ports of Kuang-Tung, Fu-Kien and Cho-Kiang flourished, and all along the two rivers, the Yang-Tse and the Huang-Ho, urban civilization developed rapidly.

This commercial activity necessitated, in addition to the former copper coins, the minting of coins in silver and tin.

Monetary economy and a liberal trade policy led to the acquisition of great fortunes. The wars carried on by China in Central Asia and along the coasts, the building of fleets and roads, resulted, as at Rome, in the creation of a class of industrialists enriched by state contracts. Financial speculation began to appear. The capitalists, in order to make profitable use of their money, leased land, thus reducing smallholding. In the cities, the craftsmen were unable to stand up to the capitalist enterprises. The ruin of the middle classes reduced the tax yield; and despite the immense wealth of the ruling classes, the state lacked resources. The tax authorities, reduced to despair, resorted to drastic methods. The lands of taxpayers who could not pay their dues were seized. The result was an aggravation of the crisis caused by the exodus of dispossessed peasants to the towns, where the growth of a proletariat of ruined country-people and workless artisans began to assume disquieting proportions.

The state which, up till then, had only imposed the land-tithe, tried to re-establish its finances by taxing liquid capital. A capital levy was decreed. Capitalists and merchants were required to make an annual declaration of their means and were taxed at five per cent. This tax, extremely heavy for the period, created such a flight of capital that the death penalty had to be introduced against defaulters; and if Chinese sources are to be believed, in 115 BC several tens of thousands of persons (clearly a much exaggerated figure) were executed for violation of the fiscal laws.

The Empire then set out resolutely on the road to economic state socialism. Following a similar evolution to that in which Egypt had involved herself fifty years earlier, China, forced by fiscal necessity, created one after the other a series of state monopolies: alcohol, fermented drinks and cast iron, in addition to the salt monopoly which had been in force since 130 BC.

Urged on by budget crises, the administration inaugurated a traffic in honorific titles, permitted the redemption of judicial sentences, at first for minor crimes and soon after even for those involving the death penalty. The wealthy classes were thus placed above the law, and money rapidly demoralized not only the state officials but the whole structure of society.

THE CRISIS OF STATE SOCIALISM

Quite naturally, as the monarchy developed the theory of state socialism it also evolved towards autocracy. While the venality introduced by the tax system, always short of money, destroyed the moral bases of the social order, state socialism, by freeing the executive power from the legitimate basis upon which it had been founded, delivered the throne over to struggles that degenerated into palace dramas as in Ptolemaic Egypt. Force, the only basis of autocratic absolutism, took the place of law; and Sinan-Ti (73–49 BC) announced the new order which marked its advent: 'We are no longer in the times,' he declared, 'of government by virtue and education. The learned men understand nothing of the needs of the times.'

At the very moment when Caesar, crossing the Rubicon, was marching on Rome, a political and social crisis was beginning in China, which was to open a period of foreign wars, civil conflicts and violent social unrest.

PART THREE
THE ERA OF THE EMPIRES

BOOK XI

The Roman Empire up to the Crisis of the 3rd Century AD

CHAPTER XLVI

THE NATIONALIST AND ARISTOCRATIC REACTION UNDER AUGUSTUS (27 BC–AD 14)

AUGUSTUS FOUNDS THE EMPIRE

CAESAR had wished to reign over a cosmopolitan empire and to associate Rome with the thousand-year-old tradition of the Hellenistic monarchies.

Augustus, in reaction to such ideas, wished to become the representative of an essentially Roman policy. He relied upon the western provinces and was forced to come to an understanding with the Senate. He had to transform the military dictatorship which he exercised into a legal power.

Remaining the only titular representative of the powers of the triumvirate, he seemed the legitimate head of the state which he at once undertook to reorganize. He reformed the Senate, which had been decimated by the proscriptions, and ordered a census of the citizens, who at that time numbered more than four million. He then proclaimed the abolition of debts to the state. This done, he stated that he would re-establish the Republic in its former institutions and would renounce his powers (27 BC). The Senate at once restored them to him for ten years, and was later to renew them until his death in AD 14. Thus the Roman Empire was born.

Legally, the Republic still existed. Augustus, endowed with all power by a legal decision of the *Comitia* and the Senate, was not, legally, any more than its representative.

But in reality the Republic no longer existed. The *Comitia*, which had at one time formed the basis of power, no longer held any authority. From time to time a law would formally renew the powers of the Emperors at their accession; but, voted by the Curiate *Comitia*, which for a long time past had done nothing save validate wills, the Republic could no longer be anything more than a legal fiction without political significance.

During the reign of Augustus the *Comitia* were still called upon, for form's sake, to confirm the appointment of magistrates proposed by the emperor. But in the reign of Tiberius this semblance of power which still remained to the people was transferred to the Senate. The sovereignty of the people had foundered in the great demagogic crisis of the dictatorships.

As to the Senate, at one time composed of former magistrates elected by the people, it had become a simple assembly of nobles, nominated or approved by the Emperor from amongst the citizens of the first class of the census.

Thus the Senate was no longer the ancient council which had evolved from the sovereignty of the people: it was an oligarchy of rich nobles nominated by the Emperor and which confirmed him in supreme power in the name of the people with whom it no longer had any bond.

In reality, the legal rights that the Emperor demanded from these fictitious *Comitia* and from a Senate made up of his own nominees were only a compromise between the military dictatorship which had been acquired by force and the senatorial oligarchy which also aimed at imposing its will upon the Empire.

In the times of the Republic sovereignty had belonged to the people. During the Empire it was held by the Emperor in his quality as representative of the people and confirmed by a rich oligarchy among whom he was the leading member (*princeps*). The Senate represented neither Rome nor the Empire; it was, in fact, only the guardian of the interests of the aristocratic class.

The former republican magistrates, nominated by the Senate on the proposal of the Emperor, were henceforward freed from any control by the people that had formerly elected them; they were the representatives of the Emperor and the oligarchy with which he shared his power.

THE POLICY OF ARISTOCRATIC AND NATIONALIST REACTION

The great demagogic crisis had therefore ended by destroying Roman democracy in favour of an aristocratic and authoritarian system, to which the new social régime of the Empire was adapted. Henceforward, society was divided into classes of varying legal status. First were the senators and their families, who possessed a million *sesterces*[1]; only they had the right to be appointed provincial governors and generals—with the exception of the Commander-in-Chief, the Pretorian Prefect, who was nominated

[1] That is to say about 275,000 gold francs.

directly by the Emperor from among the *equites*—and they had the privilege of being judged only by their peers. Then came the *equites*, the knights; these were all citizens whose property amounted to 400,000 *sesterces*; they could attain to the higher ranks of the army. The ordinary citizens were subdivided into two categories; the Italians who alone could become junior officers in the legions, and the others who could serve only in the ranks. But all were henceforward deprived of all political rights; they became once more a mass of plebeians. But even this plebeian mass, under the Empire, seemed an aristocracy in comparison with the resident aliens.

The latter were themselves divided into classes by Augustus. The westerners, including the Africans, upon whom he had relied during the civil war, held a privileged position. Citizenship was freely granted them and senators were frequently chosen from amongst them. The orientals however, excluded from the Senate, were looked on by Augustus with manifest disfavour. Greeks and Syrians could, however, obtain citizenship individually by imperial concession. But the Egyptians, who had disputed the mastery of the world with the Romans, were relegated to the class of *dedidicii* (dispossessed) and equated with freedmen who had been emancipated without the solemn ceremonies having been observed, and were never able to obtain citizenship. Egypt became an imperial appanage over which the Emperor ruled as legitimate Pharaoh and was to become in his view a field for exploitation.

Last of all were the slaves, who were reduced to the hardest conditions. Deprived of all rights, they were subjected to pitiless legal sanctions taken from the most archaic forms of Roman law; the murder of a master by one of them involved the death of all his slaves. The most severe restrictions were imposed on enfranchisement. The primitive and brutal Roman law reacted against the humane conceptions of Hellenistic law; the ancient Greek conception of a slave as 'a living tool' was henceforth imposed upon the whole Mediterranean world.

In many respects the Empire, as conceived by Augustus, marks an aristocratic and nationalist reaction against the democratic and cosmopolitan tendencies which had triumphed in the East.

Until 241 BC the Republic, as it enlarged its conquests, had also extended the right of citizenship. After the social wars it had been granted to all Italians. Caesar had granted it to Sicily and Provence. Under Augustus, on the contrary, reaction triumphed. He set up the superiority of the Romans, the master race, in opposition to the democratic theories which regarded all men as equal. To maintain this superiority he forbade certain forms of intermarriage and to assure the Romans the domination of the world he undertook a policy of increasing the birth-rate, refusing full civic rights to women who had not had three children, punishing bachelors by prohibition to inherit, restoring the power of the paterfamilias and expelling bastards from the civic body.

THE ZENITH OF ROMAN CULTURE

The reactionary policy of Augustus created no movement of hostility in the Empire. The restoration of peace, after the terrifying excesses of the civil war, seemed like the height of felicity. A great outburst of patriotic pride exalted all those who, as citizens, had participated in Rome's triumph. In the provinces Augustus was acclaimed as the restorer of order and prosperity. Ever since the IInd century BC all the Hellenistic monarchies had foundered in the worst kinds of disorder. The Greek intellectual world accepted the primacy of Rome, which had in any case taken lessons from it. Rome became the centre of all the spiritual forces of the Empire and 'Roman civilization' reached its zenith.

In the reign of Augustus it might well have been thought that Rome would replace Alexandria as an intellectual centre. To achieve this, Augustus declared himself the protector of writers. The court and high society followed his example. Maecenas played the part of a Minister of Fine Arts. Horace, son of a freedman, probably an oriental, and Virgil, son of a farmer from the outskirts of Mantua, were treated as equals by the Emperor.

The Romanized Italians brought a great contribution to Rome. Like Claudius Nepos and Catullus, Virgil and Titus Livius were Cisalpine Gauls enflamed by the Roman patriotism that characterizes the literature of the century of Augustus.

None the less, this flame of patriotism and national pride, which was mingled with attachment to the Emperor, did not mean any intellectual break with the Hellenistic tradition. Titus Livius was influenced by Polybius as Virgil was by Theocritus. Horace himself, so representative of the moral mediocrity of the Romans, was the most perfect of cosmopolitans. His studies at Athens had put him into contact with Hellenistic culture and the moderation which he preached in a Rome that had only just emerged from the horrors of the civil war recalled, though in a minor key, what the Egyptian moralists of the Saite and Hellenistic epochs had declared to be the great principle of social and moral conduct. The intellectual and social life of Rome recalled more and more that of Alexandria which it tried to rival in refinement. The elegant Tibullus, the polished and passionate Propertius, the gallant and gracious Ovid were real Alexandrian poets writing in Latin. Rome by her cosmopolitanism exercised an irresistible attraction for the Hellenized intellectual élite. Greek writers, even if they did not settle in Rome, made themselves known there, stayed there and gave readings there. Diodorus of Sicily published his universal history and Dionysius of Halicarnassus wrote in Greek a history of primitive Rome. Caecilius, born of Jewish slave parents, became one of the principal Greek literary critics of the time. Strabo, a native of Pontus, after studying in Caria, at Rome and at Alexandria, summarized all the historical and geographical knowledge of his time.

The nationalist reaction, therefore, even if it aimed at giving Rome an incontestable primacy, did not shut out all influences from without. From the intellectual point of view, Rome received far more from the Empire than she gave it. She thus asserted herself not as the conqueror, but as the capital, of the ancient Hellenistic world.

THE END OF FINANCIAL CAPITALISM AND THE ECONOMIC DUALITY OF THE EMPIRE

As soon as he had assured himself of power, Caesar had set out to reduce the ascendancy of large-scale capitalism. He organized a system of control of the banks and suppressed the system of tendering for the collection of taxes by the companies of speculators. The speculators retained only the farming of the customs duties which were low (2·5%). Like the fiscal taxes, they were levied at the frontiers and between certain areas of the Empire.

Augustus continued a similar policy, tending to free the state from the influence of large-scale capitalism which, in the previous century, had been preponderant in politics.

The measures taken by Caesar had already shown themselves to be of real efficacy. The restoration of peace and the establishment of provincial budgets had greatly helped to shield public life from financial speculation. But the capitalist oligarchy still remained a powerful force, thanks especially to its exploitation of the mines.

The mines in ancient times played the role that big business plays in our own times. The ancient oriental monarchies had always taken care not to lose control of their mineral wealth. In Egypt, in Lydia, in Macedonia, mining had always been a state monopoly. But the influence of Greek free-trade doctrines had led Rome to hand over first the Spanish, and then the Macedonian and Asian, mines to private exploitation. The metal market, which was the foundation of ancient economy, thus passed into the hands of the Roman financiers. Augustus, who was unwilling to allow this hidden power of the great capitalists who were capable of holding in check the power of the Emperor himself to continue to exist, reverted to the standpoint of the oriental monarchies and re-established the state monopoly of mining.

The suppression of tax-farming by Caesar and the institution of the mining monopoly by Augustus put an end to the economic disorders which had thrown the world into the terrible crises of the IInd and Ist centuries BC. After the time of Augustus the capitalist oligarchy ceased to be a state within the state; financial speculation, no longer kept alive by the activities of the companies of speculators, ceased to excite the populace, and the financial trials no longer revealed great scandals as in the time of the civil wars. The union of the Mediterranean states in a single empire also contributed very largely to create a sound financial situation by ending the abuses caused by the loans underwritten at the Roman banks by the kings of Antioch and Alexandria; there were no longer bank crashes such as Rome had known at the time of the Mithridatic war.

The nationalization of the mines—that is to say of heavy industry—did not, however, induce Augustus to introduce a policy of controlled economy. Once he had removed the mines from the control of the financial interests, he practised the widest possible liberalism and avoided any intervention in the economic organization of the Empire.

The end of large-scale financial capitalism, which had never been practised in the East, did not greatly change the economic life of the eastern provinces. But it had very great consequences on the economic evolution of Rome. Finance, in the strict sense of the word, lost the great role which it had played for more than a century in international affairs. For Rome was not an industrial centre nor a great trade mart, but a banking centre. The reforms of Augustus took from her the role of dispenser of capital which, no longer able to be employed in profitable state-tenders or tax-farming, returned to the economic centres of the East and especially to Egypt, the more so since the disappearance of the autarchic régime of the Ptolemies and the restoration of peace had restored to international trade and the India route an activity that recalled the best days of the IIIrd century BC.

Augustus tried, moreover, to encourage the economic expansion of the Empire towards India. The Suez canal, which had become silted up, was put back into operation. A Roman fleet was sent into the Red Sea to recover control of the sea-route to India and China, which had been taken over by the Arabs. But Aden controlled navigation, and Rome could not overcome the hostility of the Nabatean Arabs who, from Petra, controlled the traffic in the north of the Red Sea. Unable to conquer them by force, Rome tried a customs tariff war against Arab competition and later made an alliance with Abyssinia[1] which, settled on the Somali coasts, was rapidly expanding in naval power. The method which was to prove the most effective was to be that of free trade which, under the successors of Augustus, was to lead to an unprecedented prosperity of the Mediterranean trade with India and China.

While the disappearance of Roman high finance had restored normal economic life to the East, it had on the other hand released large capital sums which the senators and *equites* invested in land or in the colonization of the western provinces which were to know an extraordinary development in the 1st century AD because of their integration into international economic life.

On the whole, the economy of the West remained predominantly agricultural. The flourishing cities in Gaul and Spain certainly provided a great stimulus to trade but—except in the maritime cities—it was not, as in the East, international in character. The principal source of wealth remained landed property. Consequently a landowning aristocracy played a leading role. The senators, great landowners, always felt themselves far closer to the squires of Gaul and Spain than to the merchants of the East.

Thus the economic duality was evident from the very begining between the West, where land was all-important, and the East where trade was master. This economic divergence was superimposed on very marked political, social and linguistic differences. In the West, which had become Latinized under Roman influences, the ideas of natural law, widespread in the East, never took root. The West was therefore to become a stable foundation for conservative and aristocratic policy against the influences of the Hellenistic lands whence democratic and monarchical ideas had come to Rome.

The Empire thus appeared to be made up of two clearly distinct parts; a continental bloc formed of Italy, Gaul and Spain, with which Latin Africa was closely associated, and a vast maritime entity made up of the former Hellenistic states.

These two sections were, none the less, strongly knit into a single whole through the unifying influence of the Mediterranean, which Augustus made into a Roman lake by adding to the Empire Mauretania in Africa, Thrace in Europe and Cilicia and Cappadocia in Asia Minor.

[1] Abyssinia had remained in direct contact with Egyptian civilization through the kingdom of Meroe in southern Nubia, created by the last Pharaoh of the Ethiopian dynasty after the conquest of Egypt by Assyria (655 BC).

HELLENISTIC INFLUENCE

Despite the Senate which represented the landed oligarchy of the West, the Empire was to find itself subjected to the influence of the Hellenized provinces.

The status of the inhabitants of the Empire was not, as we have seen, homogeneous. The Roman citizens were organized in institutions of republican origin and subject to the Roman courts. The resident aliens, on the contrary, lived according to their national laws. The Empire, as formerly royal Rome, now possessed two communities of subjects; citizens, and non-citizens who became, legally, plebeians of a sort. But it was precisely these plebeians, made up for the most part of Greeks and orientals, who depended most closely on the Emperor. The imperial provinces, that is to say those most recently annexed, had very few citizens. It was therefore for the aliens (*peregrini*) that the Emperor was to create first and foremost the imperial institutions which were to end by extending over the entire Empire. It was to adjudicate in the disputes between resident aliens subject to different laws that Augustus extended the Greek system which referred such disputes to juries made up of assessors who did not belong to the nationality of the contestants; and it was for those courts that he was to establish a standard procedure.

The imperial law introduced everywhere the principles of Hellenistic public law; paid governors and officials, tax on land revenue and poll-tax, land-survey. In order to administer those finances which were outside the control of the Senate, the Emperor adopted the financial methods of Egypt, renounced tax-farming and drew up an annual budget of receipts and expenses.

These wise institutions, by being extended to the former provinces, took the place of the archaic system of the Republic.

Not even in Rome did the Emperor dream of retaining the summary administration of the Republic. To turn his capital and all Italy into a modern state, he created organs of government adapted from Hellenistic public law; a City Prefect, assisted by a Prefect of Police and a Prefect of Supply responsible for the provisioning of the city, was put at the head of the administration of Rome, and executive committees were set up to look after the streets, the aqueducts and the public buildings of Italy.

In every way, therefore, Greco-Oriental public law invaded the Empire. It was equally so in private law. The idea of property became changed; usufruct and mortgage were adopted from Greek law and the law of contract was simplified.

Nothing, not even the nature of the Imperial power itself, escaped the influence of the eastern provinces. Like Caesar, Augustus wished to provide a religious basis for the Empire. He would have liked it to be purely Roman. But Roman paganism, though it spread slowly in the West, could not become the cement of the Empire. Without mysticism and without a moral code it found itself unable to supplant the oriental cults so deeply rooted in the hearts and emotions of their adepts. Thus it was that the cult of the Emperor was formed spontaneously in the East.

For the eastern provinces the Emperor was not the first of the citizens (*princeps*); he was a sovereign. Exploited and humiliated by the Roman senatorial party and the *equites*, the peoples of the East felt nothing but hatred for the Roman aristocracy. But the Emperor had restored peace. Caesar and Antony had treated the East with understanding. It was they who, won over to the monarchical idea, represented the Imperial power for the eastern provinces. Augustus was unknown to them. He had passed through them as a military conqueror, but the reaction from the Caesarian system which he represented seemed to have escaped the Hellenistic lands. They saw in him a master, but also a protector. That is why, like Caesar, Augustus was declared 'divine' by the Hellenistic provinces. In each city a priest was appointed to celebrate the cult of the Emperor and in each province the delegates of the cities met annually to elect the provincial priest of the Emperor. These assemblies became centres of loyalism, not Roman but imperial. Distributed throughout the Empire, they soon took on a political role since their envoys brought their resolutions to Rome.

The East thus imposed upon the Empire the idea of power by divine right, which was to win over Rome and give her that state cult in which all the ancient monarchies had found the source of their legality. At the same time it created spontaneously by the interpretation of the religious assemblies of the provinces the first political organs which were to put the Emperor in touch with public opinion.

Ignoring Rome, which continued to live behind the hollow facade of republican institutions long inefficient and out-of-date, it was around the person of the Emperor himself that the Empire, eager for unity, rallied.

The Emperor may well have been an instrument of the senatorial oligarchy and may well have considered the provinces as fields for exploitation for the Roman master race, but the Empire refused to look on him in this way. The Emperor, obliged to grant institutions to the Empire, found himself bound to submit to the imperial cult, the provincial assemblies and Hellenistic public law.

Thus the provinces were rapidly to appear as the real foundation for an almost monarchical power of the Emperor, and it was upon the provinces that he was to rely in the now inevitable struggle with the senatorial oligarchy. This provincial—that is to say imperial—policy of the Emperor won him the implacable hostility of the Senate, which had no intention of renouncing its class privileges. Thus between the Imperial power, drawn onward by the unity of the Empire, and the Senate, prisoner of its own privileges and obstinate in its national and reactionary policy, the break was to become more and more complete.

Involved and drawn on by the provinces, which were grouped around him in a sentiment of monarchical loyalty, the Emperor made himself the champion of the emancipation of the resident aliens and appeared to the people, hostile to the privileges of the Roman aristocracy, as the protector of liberty. So, quite naturally, the monarchical policy of the Emperors was to become liberal.

CHAPTER XLVII

THE CONFLICT BETWEEN MONARCHY AND OLIGARCHY UNDER THE CAESARS AND THE FLAVIANS (AD 14–96)

SENATORIAL OPPOSITION UNDER TIBERIUS

THE break between the Emperor and the oligarchy began in the reign of Tiberius (AD 14–37). Like Augustus, Tiberius was a great Roman aristocrat whose family had given the democratic party its more fiery leaders since the times of Appius Claudius. Supported by the army, which he had commanded brilliantly during his campaigns in Germany, Tiberius, who had been a military man until he came to power, proved to be a great administrator. He introduced a strong centralizing policy. The council of friends created by Augustus was transformed into a permanent imperial council. The great public offices which he founded were entrusted to Hellenized freedmen and, under their stimulus, soon became ministries under the control of the Pretorian Prefect, who was himself transformed into a Prime Minister and Imperial Chief Justice. The policy of supporting the middle classes, which had ranged the senators against Caesar, was revived to meet the gravity of the social situation. The capitalists, in order to find outlets for their capital, had never stopped leasing lands, and the need for credit among the impoverished middle classes had made interest rates rise to a dangerous extent. Capitalist exploitation, which had just led to the outbreak of a rebellion in Gaul, threatened to destroy all that remained of the lower middle class in Italy. To save it, Tiberius created a fund of a hundred million *sesterces*[1] in order to provide it with cheap credits. The capitalists, hampered in their speculations, immediately united against the Emperor and fostered conspiracies against his person, as they had formerly done against the Gracchi. Tiberius retired to his villa on Capri and commenced a struggle to the death against the nobility, relying on the Pretorian

[1] That is to say 27,500,000 gold francs.

cohorts which he was unwise enough to billet at the very gates of Rome. Executions followed confiscations. Spanish and Gaulish senators replaced the Roman senators whom the Emperor had put to death.

However, under Tiberius, the conflict, more social than political, was not so much between the Emperor and the Senate as an institution as between the Emperor and a section of the oligarchy.

THE BREAK BETWEEN THE SENATE AND THE EMPEROR CALIGULA

The conflict was to spread in the reign of Caligula (37–41). This time, the principle of power itself was in question.

Caligula had been brought up in the household of Antony's daughter, surrounded by Egyptian counsellors. They had inculcated the idea that the Emperor was the 'shepherd of the peoples', a 'living God'. The ascendancy of Egypt, which had been so strong under Caesar and Antony, revived once more under Caligula. He had a temple erected in Rome to the great Egyptian goddess Isis who was adored throughout all the Hellenistic East, and, following the example of the Ptolemies, married his own sister. Openly reviving the policy of Caesar, he aimed at being accepted by the whole Empire in the character of a monarch by divine right, which he already possessed as Pharaoh of Egypt. The Senate reacted, which led to a tragic dilemma; the Senate wanted to retain for Rome, represented by its aristocracy, the mastery over a subject Empire; the Emperor, relying upon the Empire, aimed at monarchy. The two principles were irreconcilable. So, while in the provinces the liberal and beneficent imperial policy restored prosperity and security, at Rome a pitiless duel was waged between the Emperor and the Senate.

Just when he was making ready to leave for Egypt, which he doubtless wished to make the foundation of monarchical power, Caligula, who had meanwhile gone mad, was murdered. The Senate declared the office of *princeps* abolished and announced its intention once again to take the government of the Empire into its own hands. But the people of Rome, far from supporting it, rose, and it was to the cry of 'Liberty' that the Pretorians brought to the throne Caligula's uncle, Claudius (41–54). Inaugurating a pernicious custom, the new Emperor donated, as a gift on the occasion of his accession, fifteen thousand *sesterces* to every soldier of his Pretorian guard.

The Senate was powerless and had to give way. The Empire having no legal basis, a fresh element of disorder was revealed; the ten thousand Pretorians, who alone were able to impose their will by force, asserted their demands in face of the legal power of the Senate; demands which henceforth all the Emperors had to take into account.

THE LIBERAL AND MONARCHIC POLICY OF CLAUDIUS

The reign of Claudius was an important era in the history of Rome. The Empire began to be based more and more on monarchical institutions and the government was centralized. Relying on assistants who were not Romans, Claudius created, on the example of Egyptian administration, a centralized and specialized government. During his reign a Ministry of Finance was set up and, after it, a Ministry of the Imperial Treasury. A controller of vehicles was placed at the head of a Ministry of Communications, which was to develop the network of imperial roads on the model formerly carried out by the kings of Lydia and Persia. The Chancellery was organized, with departments for correspondence, petitions, legal questions and preparatory studies.

His ministers, Polybius, Pallas, Narcissus and Callixtus, were Hellenized freedmen, as were also their subordinates. They were completely loyal to the monarchy and without any trace of Roman republican tradition. They strove with all their influence for the creation of a hereditary and dynastic power. It was one of them, Pallas, the main inspirer of his policy, who caused Claudius to marry Agrippina, since she was a descendant of Augustus.

Under the influence of these provincial ministers, the imperial policy quite naturally ceased to appear as the exploitation of the provinces for the benefit of Rome and tended to make all subjects equal before the Emperor. 'He had decided,' writes Seneca, 'to see in togas (that is to say as citizens) all Greeks, Spaniards, Gauls and Britons.' From AD 48 Claudius, despite his weaknesses, showed himself one of the most far-seeing statesmen of antiquity. In a speech to the Senate he stated that 'the cause of the greatness of Rome is her generosity'. Some Aeduans were made senators and the first non-Italian consul was appointed.

As it freed itself from the oligarchy, so the imperial power became liberal and democratic. Like Caesar, Claudius adopted the ideas of natural law which had triumphed in the East for the past two centuries. A series of laws forbade the granting of loans to minors, freed women from the guardianship of their next-of-kin and prohibited them from standing as security for their husbands, protected sick slaves from the cruelty of their masters and widened testamentary freedom. And as if he had found a fresh legitimacy in his liberalism, Claudius renounced methods of terror, proclaimed a general amnesty and abolished the horrible law *de majestate* which had given a legal basis to proscriptions since the times of Marius.

NERO'S ABSOLUTISM

The plans for a hereditary monarchy drawn up by Pallas were nullified by the terrible palace plots hatched by Agrippina. After having had Claudius poisoned and Britannicus, who should legally have succeeded him, set aside, she arranged for the Pretorian guards to bring her son Nero (54–68) to the throne. The imperial power was on the point of foundering in murder and palace revolutions at the very moment when Seneca was preparing for the advent of a constitutional empire. Seneca, who belonged to a family of local magistrates of Cordova,[1] wished to replace the conception of personal royalty supported by the Hellenized officials by that of a monarchy in which the legislative power would be divided between the Emperor and a Senate made up of representatives of all the provinces.

THE ECONOMIC AND SOCIAL SITUATION

The Eastern provinces, then at the height of their prosperity, became of greater and greater importance in the state. The India trade-route, which ended at Alexandria, and which was the vital artery of the foreign trade of the Empire, was entirely in the hands of Egyptians and Syrians. Through Egypt, Rome strengthened her relations with India, whose first ambassadors, sent by the King of Pandya, reached Rome in AD 26; a little later, a second embassy, this time from Ceylon, was received by Claudius. Seaborne trade between Alexandria and India became regular. Every year, in July, profiting by the monsoons, a fleet of a hundred and twenty ships, with archers on board for their defence, left Berenice on the Red Sea for the ports of the Indus estuary and Malabar, loaded with wine, copper, lead, tin and slaves. It returned to Egypt in November, bringing back from the great markets of Barygaza and Muziris precious cargoes of pepper, pearls, diamonds and cotton goods.

From the Indus and Malabar, trade-routes led to the Bengal coast, where the trade currents of the Mediterranean met those from the Malay Archipelago and China.

The subjects of the Empire settled in great numbers in India where they formed an important element, especially at Muziris.

Silk reached Rome by the caravan routes of Turkestan, either by the

[1] Cordova was in the former state of Tartessos.

Indian route or by way of Mesopotamia. The reign of Nero marks the peak of Mediterranean trade with Asia, which was never again to become so prosperous until the 19th century of our own times.

But it was a curious fact that this important trade which, furthermore, usually accounted for a large deficit in the Roman trade-balance, had no effect on the economic development of the West. The great Roman capitalists who were interested in it did not try to find outlets in it for their capital like the orientals, but hastened to buy lands in Italy, in the western provinces and in Africa. So that in the West this great economic expansion was marked, in the first century AD, by a considerable growth not in fluid capital but in fortunes in land.

The consequence was twofold. On the one hand, by investing their wealth in landed property the Roman capitalists withdrew it from trade and restricted the financial opportunities of Rome and, on the other, greatly increased the gap between the economic structures of East and West where landed capitalism, since it could only expand to the detriment of smallholding, soon became a social danger.

The monopolizing of land was so great in the time of Nero that six Roman capitalists had been able to acquire half the province of Africa. They entrusted the administration of their domains to companies which settled there a number of small free farmers transformed by contract into hereditary serfs. This system, it is true, suppressed the scandalous abuses of slave exploitation; but the omnipotence of the owners of these *latifundia* reduced the tenants to terrible straits and their complaints were ceaselessly being expressed in petitions to the Emperor.

The capitalist magnates had succeeded in by-passing the authority of the local magistrates, and were entirely dependent on the Imperial procurator of the province, which was in practice equivalent to recognition of their seigniorial autonomy. This capitalist ascendancy was also evident in Italy, where the *latifundia* and the workshops, exploited by the capitalists by the use of slave labour, plunged the country into an ever more serious economic and social crisis. Peasants and free craftsmen, deprived of the means of gaining their livelihood, went to swell the Roman proletariat which soon became a menace to public order. Furthermore, the large-scale capitalist exploitation of agriculture raised problems of supply by reducing grain production in favour of more profitable harvests. Rome henceforward had to import grain. To prevent the provisioning of Rome from falling into the hands of speculators the Emperors had entrusted it to the Prefects of Supply, and Claudius had centralized grain imports at the port of Ostia. But state intervention falsified grain prices, disorganized the market and once more the small producers were the sufferers.

These first symptoms of state intervention were complicated by fiscal problems. Since the time of Caesar the currency had remained stable. A constant relation had been maintained between the Roman and Egyptian currencies. But the extravagances of Caligula and Nero had led to a fiscal crisis which the state had resolved by resorting to financial manipulation. The consequence had been a rise in prices which had brought numbers of small proprietors to bankruptcy. To aid them, the government of Nero rounded off the credit institutions intended to help the middle classes by an organization of mortgage banks. At the same time, Nero began the struggle against the great property owners, which added an economic and social conflict to the political differences between the Emperor and the Senate. On one pretext or another, Nero condemned to death the six greatest landowners of Africa and confiscated their enormous domains for the benefit of the treasury.

Thenceforward, the struggle became even more bitter. The Emperor had the provinces behind him and, in Italy, the non-privileged classes; ranged against him were about a hundred senatorial families.

The constitutional monarchy proposed by Seneca could not provide a solution for a conflict which, once again, had become a trial of strength. Seneca was condemned to death and Nero, who countered the Senate by an absolutist and demagogic policy, let himself be involved in horrible demagogic spectacles, which ended, it is not known how, in the burning of Rome (AD 64), for which the Christians were held responsible. Their religion made them appear as the enemies of the Emperor who claimed a divine character. The first Roman persecution of the Christians was the result; it only cost the lives of a relatively limited number of victims, amongst whom it seems we must include the apostles Peter and Paul.

THE MYSTICAL MOVEMENT. PERSECUTION OF THE CHRISTIANS AND ABOLITION OF FREEDOM OF THOUGHT

The reasons for this persecution are to be found as much in the moral as in the political crisis through which Rome was passing at this time.

In the course of the two preceding centuries, the eastern provinces had witnessed the gradual formation of a mystical movement which found expression in the mystery cults. Since the IInd century BC belief in the immortality of the soul and the Judgment of men in another world had become almost universal. Rome became little by little deeply influenced by the oriental cults. From as early as 204 BC temples had been built there to the great Egyptian divinities, Isis and Serapis, and the mysteries of Dionysus, which were confused with those of Osiris, enjoyed a great vogue; the masses of slaves sold in Rome after the wars against Mithridates had spread the mysteries of Attis. Under Claudius, the cult of Isis, after having been proscribed in the last years of the Republic, was favoured by the Emperor and became more and more confused with that of Ceres, the ancient mother-goddess, the cult of the Roman plebeians. The spring festival of Attis, with its great manifestations of mourning for the death of the god and of rejoicing for his resurrection, was officially introduced into Rome. Nero had had himself initiated by the king of Armenia into the cult of Mithras, which was henceforward to enjoy especial favour in the imperial palace.

Mithraism, a new form of Mazdaism, the official cult of the Achaemenids, was very similar to the Hellenistic and oriental mysteries. Like the adepts of Osiris, the initiated of Mithras believed in a future life, preached a code of human solidarity and justice, and announced the resurrection of the body on the Day of Judgment.

Mithraism had won over Cappadocia and upper Mesopotamia but had never had any influence in the Hellenized countries or in Egypt, faithful to their own mysteries which were, however, very similar to those of Mithras. But it spread in Rome and in the western provinces of the Empire where Hellenistic mysticism had not penetrated.

This wave of Mithraism, which the soldiers and the slaves captured in the wars against the Parthians had spread throughout the West in less than a century, marked the victory of oriental mysticism throughout the whole Mediterranean basin.

It was an aspect of the crisis that cannot be undervalued. Like all the Hellenistic cults, Mithraism preached that power was derived directly from God. The Mithraic adepts were monarchists and believed that the monarch was the elect of the great creator-god. The mysteries of Mithras, therefore, like all the other oriental cults, favoured the absolutist policy of the Emperors. But it was about the same time that the Christian teaching reached Rome. 'To believe in immortality,' wrote Seneca, 'what is needed? That a man rise from the dead!' And the first Christians appeared, in the reign of Caligula, announcing that a man-god was born who, after having been put to death, had risen from the dead and that he would return to preside at the Last Judgment.

The announcement of the coming of the Messiah, awaited throughout the East since the first century BC, was to exercise a strange fascination over all the faithful of the mysteries, all of whom believed in a God of redemption. But, alone of all the mystic cults, Christianity did not bring with it a monarchical metaphysic. Monothesists like the Jews, hostile to the pantheism upon which the idea of the divinity of the Emperor was founded, the Christians appeared as dangerous enemies of the monarchy by divine right towards which the Empire was tending. Their triumph would deprive the Emperor of the support of the mysticism upon which, in Rome as formerly in Egypt, dynastic policy wished to base the legitimacy of absolute power. They must therefore be extirpated as a ferment of anarchy and disorder. Persecution was carried on not only against their religious ideas but also against all those who threw a shadow of doubt on the absolutist policy of the Emperor. In the time of Tiberius a censorship had been set up at Rome. In his reign it had already persecuted republican historians; it had had Cremutius Cordus put to death and had ordered the destruction of the works of Labienus. Under Claudius the censorship had been abandoned. The Emperor, a partisan of liberal ideas, had shown a leaning towards the constitutional plans drawn up by Seneca, whom he had made Nero's tutor. But the condemnation of Seneca to death, followed by that of Lucan, the poet who had celebrated Pompey and the republican resistance to Julius Caesar, had marked a return to a régime of the most rigorous censorship. In this atmosphere political writers totally disappeared. Science, it is true, continued to flourish to a certain extent; the censorship did not stop the Cisalpine, Pliny the Elder, from continuing at Rome the traditions of the great Hellenistic scientific school, nor the Spaniard Quintilian from trying to carry out a reform of education in a professional and practical sense. But science itself could not live without independence. By suppressing freedom of thought Rome renounced the right to be the intellectual capital of the Empire. The Greek élite abandoned the capital after the first persecutions of Tiberius, and while in Rome intellectual life declined into a literature of salons and poetasters, it was in the provinces, where the administration of Claudius had installed a liberal régime, that the tradition of Hellenistic culture continued, which, though it took refuge in the great schools, was none the less to suffer an eclipse of half a century.

THE CRISIS OF POWER

The whole policy of the Emperor was dominated by a single idea, to transform the imperial power into a monarchy by divine right. Naturally enough he relied upon the eastern provinces to further this great design.

Caligula, when he attempted his *coup d'état*, had, like Alexander, looked to Egypt for the confirmation of his divine character. Nero, for his part, first wanted to conciliate the Greeks. In AD 67 he solemnly proclaimed the liberty of the Greeks at the Isthmian Games and ordered the cutting of the Corinth Canal in order to assist the economic recovery of Greece.

The break between the Emperor and the Senate showed the bankruptcy of the system of Alexander. But if the Emperor had degraded himself by his crimes, the Senate on its side had lost all credit in the Empire. Outside the aristocracy of which it was the symbol, it appeared to no one as the legitimate source of power.

The Roman aristocracy however was far from aware of this. It thought it possible to restore a republican government to power. In AD 68 the governors of Gaul, Spain, Germany and Africa, who had control of the legions, rose in the name of the Senate. Thus encouraged, the Senate proclaimed Nero a public enemy; and after the suicide of the Emperor, the senators brought to power one of their own adherents, Galba, the Governor of Spain, whom his legions had already proclaimed Emperor.

The Senate thus broke the tradition which had created a sort of dynastic status for the family of the Caesars. By nominating Galba, it asserted itself as the dispenser of the supreme power and reverted to the oligarchic principle pure and simple; but at the same time admitted its impotence because, by ratifying the *coup d'état* of the Spanish legions, it opened the way to military *pronunciamentos*.

Galba at once showed himself the loyal tool of the oligarchy. The principal act of his reign was to appoint a commission of enquiry to revise the expropriations and the donations made by Nero. The Senate only looked at the crisis from the viewpoint of its own immediate interests.

The Roman plebeians at once revolted. The Pretorians made common cause with the people. Galba was assassinated and Otto, an old friend of Nero, was brought to the throne in 69 AD.

A period of military *coups-d'état* began once more. In the provinces the legions, following the example of the Spanish legions, named their leaders as Emperors; the Army of the Rhine, Vitellius; the Army of the East, Vespasian. Civil war broke out throughout the Empire. Italy was invaded first by the legions of Vitellius and then by those of Vespasian. Vespasian took Rome by storm and the Senate, resigned to the fact, recognized him as Emperor, after the whole of the East had already recognized him.

THE FLAVIANS TRY TO INSTALL A MONARCHY OF DIVINE RIGHT (AD 69–96)

Once in control of authority, Vespasian attempted a constitutional reform which seems to have been based both on oriental and Stoic ideas.

The Senate was transformed into a sort of Imperial Council. First purged by the expulsion of the unworthy, it was reconstituted by the nomination of some hundreds of Senators from Italy, Gaul, Spain and Africa and an occasional oriental. Vespasian, a Roman, thought of the Empire as formed essentially of the Latinized West.

While he was thus trying to transform the Roman nobility into an imperial nobility, Vespasian enlarged the Roman national state by extending citizenship to the whole of Spain. But at the same time he once more accepted from Egypt the idea of the divine right of power. After his accession to the throne, he called his sons Caesars, regarded them as his heirs and considered himself the founder of a dynasty. In the collaboration which he established between himself and the Senate, the Emperor claimed the lion's share. He aimed at absolutism.

Vespasian found in Rome a most serious financial situation; the treasury deficit was forty milliards of *sesterces*. He at once set himself to restore the finances but did not call on the aid of the Senate, which would have hampered him; he thus provoked its opposition. Without halting in his plans, he deprived the Senate of its right to dispose of the public lands and had them annexed to the crown, undertaking a systematic exploitation of them according to Hellenistic methods. Egypt was subjected to a pitiless fiscal exploitation. The treasury deficit was finally made good.

Domitian, therefore, found at his accession a stable financial situation. An excellent administrator, he derived thereby a power which enabled him to assert officially his absolutist aims. He proclaimed himself *dominus et deus* (master and god), surrounded himself with oriental pomp and had an immense palace built.

In order to maintain his monarchical policy he had necessarily to obtain the support of the East; for the first time an Asiatic was appointed consul. The Emperor himself celebrated the cult of Isis and he had a stadium and an Odeum built in Rome on the model of the Hellenistic cities.

At the same time the middle classes began to enter the higher ranks of the administration.

But in the attempt to find a stable base for their omnipotence the Flavians soon found themselves faced with the same obstacles as had Nero: the Roman aristocracy, the monotheist cults and freedom of thought.

Proscription was therefore again employed against the Senators, and persecutions flared up against Christians and Jews. In AD 94 an imperial edict expelled all the philosphers from Rome. Amongst them was the former Phrygian slave, Epictetus. He took refuge in Epirus, where he lived in poverty, but he drew to him a number of disciples, one of whom, the Bythinian Arrian, was to record his teaching in his *Colloquies*. The Stoic moral code of the Greek slave gave an answer to the destructive rage of the Roman Emperor. It was to have an immense influence on the intellectual élite of the 2nd century AD.

In AD 96 Domitian was assassinated.

The attempt to establish the Empire on a basis of absolute monarchy had failed. The Senate once more found itself the sole legal source of power. But it had been profoundly changed during the reigns of the Flavians. The Roman oligarchy had been swamped by the provincial families, for whom Rome was above all the capital of the Empire and the residence of the Emperor. The republican tradition did not exist for these Gauls, Spaniards and Africans, who were to take a leading place in Rome and become some of her last writers and her greatest Emperors.

The former republican aristocracy had played its part. It had been replaced by an imperial aristocracy, almost exclusively Latin and western.

Rome and her western provinces became a unit, untouched by the monarchical and mystical influences of the East.

The dualism between the Latin provinces and the Greek provinces was thereby to become greatly accentuated.

CHAPTER XLVIII

THE ROMANIZATION OF THE WEST

THE ROMANIZATION OF GAUL

ROME clearly wanted to base her power on the Western provinces. The work of civilization that she accomplished there was so extensive that it left an indelible mark on the whole history of Europe.

Mediterranean civilization had penetrated into Gaul from the VIth century BC through the great Greek city of Marseilles. Marseilles, though incorporated into the 'Province' by Caesar and soon to be rivalled by the Roman colony of Narbonne, was to remain the great economic and intellectual centre of Gaul. Its celebrated Greek school attracted not only Celts but Italians. Nîmes, colonized by Greeks from Egypt who had been sent there by Augustus, rapidly acquired considerable importance as a river-port. Arles and Narbonne became important local centres. The mixture of Greeks, Celts and Romanized provincials led to a flowering of Provençal civilization. Orange, Aix, Vienne, became flourishing market towns; Béziers, a famous wine-growing centre. Toulouse, where schools were founded in imitation of those of Marseilles, exerted considerable intellectual influence. At the confluence of the Rhône and the Saône, Lyon, promoted to the rank of capital of the Gauls, became a great centre of business and international trade, frequented by Greeks, Syrians and other Orientals. On the upper Rhône, Geneva developed as the end of the Alpine trade-route.

The occupation of the island of Britain by Claudius conferred real importance on the port of Bordeaux. Roman trade thenceforth expanded along the Atlantic coasts.

In the interior of the country, along the routes that linked the North Sea, the Rhine and the Rhône, secondary towns were founded, to which Rome gave a kernel of international population: Bourges, Clermont, Autun, Sens, Rheims and Lutetia, the future Paris, with its famous corporation of Seine river-men. Boulogne, the ancient Celtic port, was promoted to the rank of military harbour.

In the north, Bavai, Arras and Tournai were staging-posts on the great roads, and Tongres an important crossroads to the legionary camps at Xanten and Nijmegen and to the headquarters of the Armies of Germany, Mayence and Cologne, which were regarded as among the most important cities of the West. The route from Lyon to the Rhine gave importance to the city of Arlon, a business centre whose merchants used to go as far as Rome to sell the cloth of Menapia, and to Trèves, which was to become the capital of the Gauls in the 4th century.

A middle class was formed in these cities, in which Roman, Hellenized and Celtic elements were mingled. Latin was the language of the army, the administration, business and education. Schools were opened at Autun, Rheims, Trèves and Bordeaux where the humanities and grammar, as well as law, were taught. Thus Roman and Hellenistic thought penetrated to the most distant limits of the Empire. The former local aristocracy became Latinized, adapted themselves to the local magistratures and became traders. Celtic students were prepared for careers in the highest posts of the administration. They were to give Rome the Emperor Antoninus.

Rome drew up great plans for the cities, endowed with theatres, temples, baths, aqueducts and water supply, on the model of the great Hellenistic cities.

Industry developed. Merchants, at first Romans and orientals and then Celts, travelled throughout the country; they exported livestock and woollen clothing to Rome and sent cheapjack goods to Germany. The trade balance of Gaul became favourable. The country grew rich. In the countryside luxurious villas were built by great Roman or Romanized Gallic landowners. In the cities Syrians and other orientals introduced currency markets and soon camels, used for goods transport, trod the roads of Gaul; and fruit-trees, imported from Asia, were acclimatized in the country.

Everywhere the former Gallic huts were replaced by farms built on the Roman model. The use of window-glass, copied from Syria and Egypt, the manufacture of which was established in Gaul itself, became common. Central heating was installed in dwelling-houses.

The importance of the cities grew rapidly. In the south of Gaul they soon became predominant. In the north there had always been few cities. Numerous villas grew into townships, but their character remained rural.

The former rivalries and distinctions between the petty Gallic states were effaced. Druidism, persecuted by Rome which saw in it an element of resistance to her penetration, disappeared little by little, save in Armorica.

Peace reigned, and with it comfort and prosperity. City government was organized throughout Gaul. None the less, there were few cities which possessed *Comitia*. In general, the aristocratic Gallic system was maintained and the cities were governed by self-opting *curiae*. Rome, in fact, pacified Gaul by relying upon the landowning classes. But the mercantile middle-class, united in free corporations, was of real importance in the development of the country.

Every year, in April, the three provinces of Gaul sent their delegates to Lyon, to the Assembly of the Gauls; each of them also held regularly its provincial assembly, as also did the 'Province' which had already been annexed half a century before the time of Caesar.

Little by little society evolved. The family, formerly patriarchal, became limited to the restricted group of parents and children under the authority of the father; private property encroached more and more on the former commons and the earlier political nobility was transformed into a class of landowners. Local chiefs ceased to form an oligarchy of nobles, and became magistrates elected by the property-owning middle classes or nominated by the higher authorities. The Gaulish cult, without disappearing, gradually allowed itself to be submerged by Roman paganism while waiting to give way altogether, from the 2nd century onward, to Christian teaching.

THE ROMANIZATION OF SPAIN

Spain had been influenced by oriental and Greek civilization earlier than Gaul. From the IXth century BC the Phoenicians had penetrated there, followed in the VIth century by the Greeks. The kingdom of Tartessos on the Guadalquivir, enriched by its silver-mines, had had an advanced type of civilization since the Xth century BC. Since then it had never ceased to carry on an active and prosperous trade with the East.

Spain had never had any ethnic unity. In the south the Iberians and in the north the Celts had settled there, mingling with the native Ligurians. The population was divided into a number of little states. Rome had conquered Spain during and a little after the second Punic War. The conquest had been carried on in pitiless fashion. It ended in the division of the country into two provinces, Tarragona and Baetica which corresponded to the former kingdom of Tartessos. The country had been crushed by taxation and the Roman capitalists had seized on the silver, iron, copper and lead mines.

By making mining a state monopoly, the Empire had undoubtedly expropriated the mines from the Spaniards but it had also delivered them from Roman high finance. Thanks to that, the political régime was regularized and the peace of the Empire brought great prosperity to Spain and favoured the integration which the exploitation of her mines and the activity of her ports had long been preparing. A large number of oriental merchants came to settle in the country. Roman colonies formed the basis for important cities or developed those which already existed. Besides Cordova, in the former state of Tartessos, and the port of Cartagena, founded by the Phoenicians, the ports of Valencia, Tarragona, Barcelona, Emporia and, in the interior of the country, the cities of Saragossa and Segovia became economic and intellectual centres where Greeks, Ligurians, Iberians and Romans mixed. The city régime helped to develop the ruling classes and Romanize the country. It was to give Rome two of her greatest Emperors, Trajan and Hadrian.[1] In the 1st century AD Greco-Roman penetration, finding the ground already well prepared, made Spain one of the principal centres of Latin culture. The famous Stoic Seneca, the pedagogue Quintilian, the epigrammatist Martial, the geographer Pomponius Mela, the agriculturalist Columella, were all Spaniards. It was therefore quite comprehensible that Vespasian should have granted citizenship to all Spaniards. The Latin language was as widespread as in Gaul; it had become the language of the educated classes, as well as of business and administration. But well before the time of the Roman Empire the sea had already brought to Spain a culture that still remained alive and it was doubtless to preserve that tradition that Vespasian specially authorized the official use of local languages in Spain.

THE ROMANIZATION OF BRITAIN

From Gaul, Roman rule had extended to the great island of Britain (AD 43) which was economically indispensable to Gaul and Spain because of its tin mines. The Celtic population lived there, as in Gaul, in tribes which were less developed in the north where the royal régime survived, whereas in the south the oligarchic régime already existed. The Highlands of Scotland were never conquered.

In England the Romans built a double road-network with its hub at London. Here, even before the conquest, a sort of city existed which,

[1] Marcus Aurelius, born in Rome, was also of Spanish origin.

thanks to the repression of Frisian piracy and the presence of a Roman fleet in the Channel, had been a famous business centre from the 1st century onward. Supply bases created for this fleet led to the formation of Dover, Lympne and Sandwich which kept in touch with one another by beacons. In the north a large number of military posts were founded along the coast to protect the island from the forays of the Frisians and, from the 3rd century onward, the Saxons. Roman colonies later became the cities of Gloucester, York and Lincoln; the origin of Chester was a legionary camp.

The tin mines, which had already been worked for centuries, became a state monopoly. Agriculture was developed and led to the construction of elegant villas by the great landowners along the shores of the Channel, and smallholding increased. Livestock from the island was exported to the port of Boulogne and imports from Gaul introduced more refined manners to the islanders. In Britain, Romanization was largely the work of the legionaries sent by Rome as garrisons, of merchants who kept up a constant trade with the mainland, and of the Roman Channel Fleet manned for the most part by Menapians from the Flanders coast.

Being essentially an agricultural country, Britain was not Romanized as completely as Spain and Gaul. The Celts of Hibernia (Ireland) and Caledonia (Scotland), who were not included in the conquest, remained untouched by Roman influence.

ROMANIZATION IN CENTRAL EUROPE

Romanization of the Danubian provinces was much less deep than in the West. In Rhaetia (present-day southern Bavaria, eastern Switzerland and the Tyrol) three Roman municipalities were founded, one of which, Augsburg, was the capital of the province; Coire (Chur) was to retain its Roman organization until the time of Charlemagne; but they remained market towns governed by the local nobles. Great roads linked Como with the Rhine in one direction and Salzburg in the other. The soldiers stationed on the Danube and the activity created along the roads kept the population in touch with the Empire. The Romansch dialect, which has survived on the Upper Rhine, recalls the Roman occupation.

In Noricum (upper Austria, Carinthia, and Styria) colonies had been settled since the time of Augustus in the midst of Illyrian populations mixed with Celts, who had already been subject to Greek influences by way of the Danube and Macedonia. Roman centres were formed around the camps; Salzburg and Celje in Slovenia were merchant cities which had sprung up at important crossroads.

In Pannonia (Cis-danubian Hungary, Croatia and Slovenia), where the amber route that linked the Adriatic and Baltic Seas crossed the Danube, military camps were set up, one of which was the origin of Vienna, but despite the arsenal at Sirmium (Mitrovica), where towards the end of the 3rd century an imperial palace was built, Romanization was weak. It was not much stronger in Moesia (Serbia) where a number of Roman military camps fringed the Danube. Many Moesians served in the army and one of them was to become the Emperor Aurelian. In Moesia Inferior, Rome found and supplanted the former Greek colonization along the Black Sea coasts. She even extended her rule temporarily as far as the Crimea, where the Greek cities retained their autonomy under her suzerainty.

Dalmatia was, quite naturally, drawn to Rome. Salona and Zara became important ports. Diocletian was later to build there an immense palace. Its ruins still exist at Split (Spalato).

Epirus, where since the VIth century BC the Greeks of Corinth and Corfu had founded the ports of Apollonia and Epidamnus (Durazzo), was Romanized naturally enough, because of the close links it had with Italy.

THE ROMANIZATION OF AFRICA

Romanization was extensive on the African coasts where, since the fall of Carthage, economic life was centred on Rome.

Cyrenaica remained subject to Greek and Egyptian influences, but Tripolitania and Tunisia on the other hand were profoundly affected by Roman rule. In the times of its splendour Carthage had introduced there the Phoenician municipal régime. Rome had restored Carthage after its destruction and, in the time of Caesar, it was once more a great centre of trade. Bizerta, Suse, Gabes and Leptis Magna became important cities.

In Numidia the legionary camps were the origin of cities which later became Roman municipalities; in the 1st century twelve such cities were created and by the end of the Empire there were forty-five of them, of which the ruins of Timgad attest the splendour.

Rome consolidated her power by relying on her colonists and on the property-owning classes which rapidly became Latinized. Roman engineers systematically exploited the soil and introduced, in present-day Algeria, irrigation techniques borrowed from Egypt. Africa became the great granary of the Empire. It is true that, alongside the Latinized élite, the common people continued to speak the Punic dialect. One of the most famous of the Emperors, Septimius Severus, came from this African people with whom he had kept so closely in touch that his sister caused a scandal in Rome by her ignorance of Latin.

Further westward, towards the Atlantic Ocean in Mauretania (western Algeria and Morocco), Rome only enforced a political occupation. Some towns were founded on the coast and even, like Volubilis, in the interior. But the local chiefs remained independent, vassals of the Empire, and in the 4th century AD were no longer considered as subjects but as confederates.

Thus Rome adapted herself with great flexibility to the level of civilization of the peoples incorporated into the Empire. She assimilated them by relying on the property-owning middle class and by creating great agricultural and commercial wealth through the system of free trade. Customs zones divided the Empire, it is true, but the moderate duties, which were simply fiscal in aim, did not exceed 2·5%. On the other hand, Rome put an end to the scandalous abuses of capitalism by restricting its sphere of operations. The nationalization of the great mining industry, coupled with the policy of free trade and economic liberty in all other fields, gave the Empire a balanced prosperity whose benefits were extended to all the provinces. This was shown by the astonishing architectural magnificence of the cities which were built on the principles of Hellenistic town-planning. At no period of history, save perhaps in the 19th century of our own times, was the world covered to such an extent by cities, all freely administered by their own population of property-owners and business men, amongst whom the veterans formed a class of notables. Everywhere where the Roman temples and porticoes arose, culture, spread by the schools, flourished. Raising the level of its people by a liberalism the more remarkable in that it followed a period of war and rapine, Rome extended over the whole Mediterranean world the two great achievements of oriental civilization; individual emancipation and the sense of the universal.

CHAPTER XLIX

THE LIBERAL AND UNIVERSAL EMPIRE OF THE ANTONINES (96–192)

ATTEMPT TO FORM A CONSTITUTIONAL EMPIRE UNDER NERVA

AFTER the terrible crisis which ended in the murder of Domitian it seemed that the monarchy would be rejected. The Senate, made up of western senators hostile to the monarchical notions of the East, adopted the constitutional ideas proposed by Seneca. Having made sure this time of the support of the Pretorians, it raised to the throne one of its own members, the Roman aristocrat Nerva (96–98).

However, once on the throne Nerva was no longer the representative of the Roman oligarchy. The transformation of the Senate into an imperial assembly allowed the Emperor, in full agreement with it, to abandon both the Roman national state and the aristocratic principle. In internal affairs, Nerva was able to revert to the democratic policy of Tiberius, Nero and the Flavians, and to distribute lands to poor citizens and organize a plan for aid to needy children without incurring the opposition of the senators.

Since the time of Vespasian, Italians had no longer been serving in any numbers in the legions. With the exception of the Pretorians, the army was made up of provincials. Thenceforward the provinces, by the threat of military *coups d'état*, were to seize authority from Rome. This threat was the more serious in that recruitment to the armies was rapidly becoming regional. Loyal to their generals or to the Emperor, the legions were a democratic and provincial factor who knew nothing of the Roman aristocracy. The Empire could therefore only continue to exist by halting their progress towards the seizure of power.

Whereas, from Augustus to Nero, every Emperor had chosen his successor from among his own relations, Nerva introduced the more worthy principle of adoption, which Antoninus was to take up again. His choice fell on Trajan (98–117), a Spanish general descended from a family of magistrates from Gades.

The adoption of Trajan by Nerva, a result of the need to calm the apprehension of the legions who feared to see the power once again seized by the Roman oligarchy, marked a decisive step in the history of the Empire.

By the accession of Trajan the imperial power was removed once and for all from Rome. The Empire ceased to be Roman and became universal.

All the Emperors, save for very rare and transient exceptions, were henceforward to be provincials.

Trajan followed the constitutional path marked out by his compatriot Seneca, and tried to share the power between the Emperor and an enlarged Senate representing the entire Empire. Under the Antonines almost half the senators were provincials, and—a considerable innovation—Greeks and a large number of Africans took their place in the Senate.

The share of the Senate in the exercise of power should not, however, be over-estimated. Its role in administrative affairs was reduced to that of a consultative council, the Emperor alone bearing all responsibility. However, by ratifying the adoption of an heir presumptive, it gave an indispensable legal sanction to the stability of the imperial power.

THE MONARCHICAL POLICY OF THE ANTONINES

This legal sanction was valid only for Rome. For the Empire, the Senate scarcely existed. It was for that reason that the Antonines, like the Flavians, were drawn by the monarchical idea as it still existed in Egypt and in the Parthian kingdom.

Egypt had not been incorporated into the Empire. It formed, under the sovereignty of the Emperor, a monarchy of divine right, based on the cult of the god Serapis.

It was evidently this centuries-old monarchical conception that impelled the Antonines to seek a legal sanction of their power in divine right.

Trajan had already had himself represented with the attributes of the god of Gades, Hercules, whom he considered his patron. His coins bore the sun as an emblem. Hadrian (117–138) took the title of 'Olympian', hitherto reserved to Jupiter, the solar god. Making an important step forward, he adopted Serapis as official god of the Empire. At the same time he practised a policy of enlightened absolutism. Like Caesar and Caligula, at the moment of transforming the Empire into a monarchy of divine right, Hadrian looked to Egypt as an example. But opposition revived in the Senate. Antoninus (138–161) and Marcus Aurelius (161–180) reverted to the constitutional principle in order to avoid conflict. Antoninus sought the support of the cultivated classes in the provinces and encouraged state-aided education in the large cities in order to improve the cultural level of the property-owning classes to whom he freely granted Roman citizenship.

Marcus Aurelius, imbued with Stoic ideals, wished to make the Empire an egalitarian monarchy wherein the Emperor would be the supreme interpreter of the general will. The Empire appeared to him as a unity of which the Emperor was the representative. But this incarnation of the Empire necessarily led him towards the hereditary monarchical conception. He nominated as his heir his son Commodus (180–192).

On his coming to the throne, Commodus affirmed the divine character of the monarchy in his proclamation to the troops: 'I am born Emperor', he told them. 'My father has risen to heaven'. As in Egypt, the sovereign became a god and the hereditary principle was affirmed.

This was not merely the affirmation of a simple rule of succession, but the inauguration of a new conception of power as a whole. The Emperor declared himself the mediator between gods and men. Even as all men are equal before the great creator-god, so they should be equal before the divine absolutism of the Emperor. The principle of a social hierarchy, upon which Augustus had founded the Empire, was repudiated, and, as if he wished to confirm this, Commodus gave the office of Pretorian Prefect, which had become that of Prime Minister, to Cleander, a former Phrygian slave.

It was evident that the Senate, threatened in both its political and its social prerogatives, would react with vehemence. An open struggle broke out once more against the Emperor, who replied by terrorism. The policy of appeasement, so long and so wisely pursued by the Antonines, foundered in civil war and ended with the assassination of Commodus.

LIBERAL AND DEMOCRATIC POLICY

The absolutism of the Antonines, in which power found its origin and justification in itself by divine right, was accompanied—as Egyptian absolutism had formerly been—by a policy of justice and equality. The central power perfected its institutions, the Emperor's offices became state services, and the bureaucracy, where the *equites* were from now on to make careers for themselves, was organized according to the regulations of Egyptian public law. The executive committees, till then made up of senators, were handed over to experts. The hierarchy of office replaced

HIBERNIA
BRITAIN
London
SAXONS
LOWER GERMANIA
VANDALS
GERMANIA
Cologne
Bonn
AGRI DECUMATES
BELGIUM
Paris (Luteta)
LYONNAIS
Orleans
UPPER GERMANIA
RHETIUM
Ratisbon
Carnuntum
Vienna
QUADI
AQUINCUM
NORICUM
PANNONIA
UPPER
LOWER
Cantabrian Sea
Geneva
Augsburg
Lyons
Aquileia
Sirmium
AQUITAINE
Vienne
Milan
ALPS
Genoa
Bordeaux
Arles
Ravenna
DALMATIA
UPPER MOESIA
León
SPAIN
Toulouse
NARBONNAIS
Nice
Rimini
Salona
Braga
Ebro
Marseilles
Narbonne
Barcelona
Tarragona
CITERIEURE
Bilbilis
Douro
Emporia
Aleria
CORSICA
ITALY
Rome
Ostia
Lissus
Salonica
Lisbon
LUSITANIA
Tagus
Tortosa
Naples
Brindisi
MACEDONIA
Toledo
Saguntum
Valencia
BALEARIC IS.
SARDINIA
Cagliari
Tarentum
EPIRUS
ACHAIA
BAETICA
SICILY
Rhegion
Corinth
Tarshish (Tartessos)
Cordova
Cartagena
Messina
Gades
Agrigentum
Syracuse
Ceuta
Caesarea
Hippo Regius
Carthage
Inner
TINGITANE MAURETANIA
CAESAREAN MAURETANIA
Cirta
NUMIDIA
PROCONSULAR
Volubilis
MOORS
Sabratha
Oea
Leptis
AFRICA
THE ROMAN EMPIRE UNDER THE ANTONINES
2ND. CENTURY A.D.
Frontiers of the provinces
Frontiers of the lands conquered by Augustus (Lower Germania) and by Trajan (Armenia and Mesopotamia for a limited period.

Map No. 25

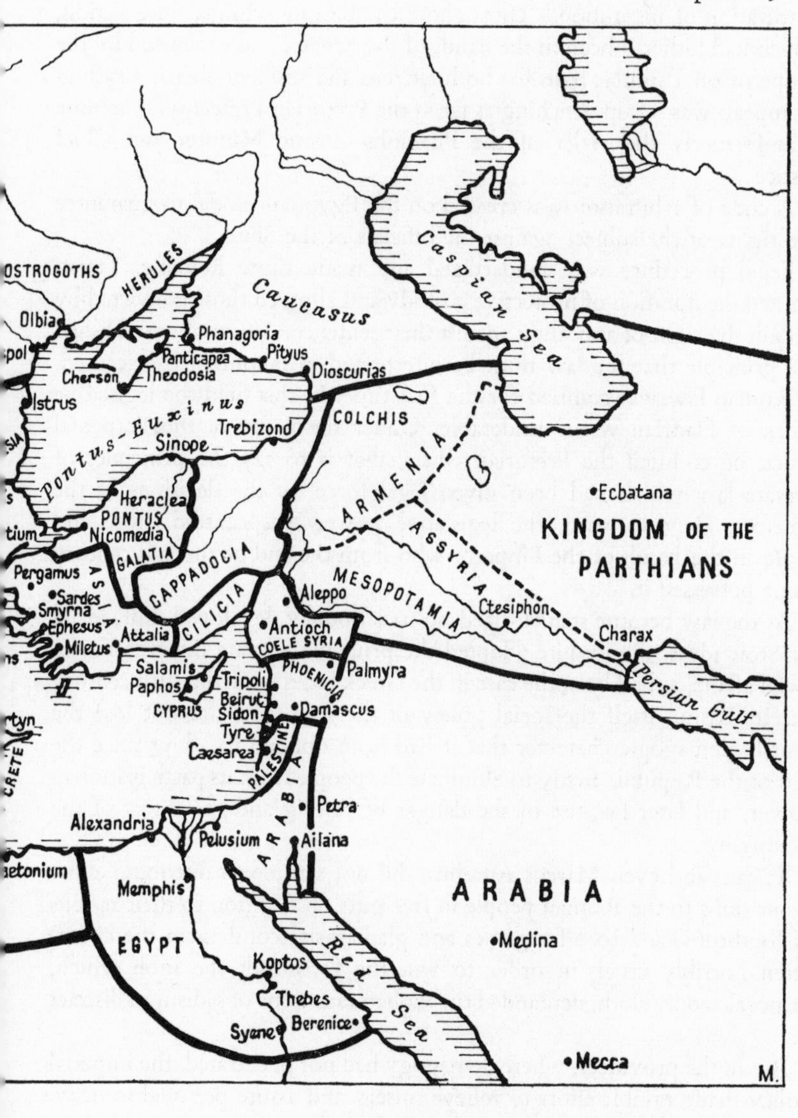
OSTROGOTHS
HERULES
Olbia
Caucasus
Caspian Sea
Phanagoria
Panticapea
Pityus
Cherson
Theodosia
Dioscurias
Istrus
Pontus-Euxinus
COLCHIS
Trebizond
Sinope
ARMENIA
Heraclea
PONTUS
Nicomedia
Ecbatana
KINGDOM OF THE
PARTHIANS
GALATIA
ASSYRIA
CAPPADOCIA
Pergamus
Sardes
Smyrna
Ephesus
Miletus
ASIA
CILICIA
Aleppo
MESOPOTAMIA
Ctesiphon
Attalia
Antioch
COELE SYRIA
Charax
Salamis
Paphos
CYPRUS
Tripoli
Beirut
Sidon
PHOENICIA
Palmyra
Persian Gulf
Damascus
Tyre
Caesarea
CRETE
PALESTINE
ARABIA
Petra
Alexandria
Pelusium
Ailana
Memphis
ARABIA
EGYPT
Medina
Koptos
Red Sea
Thebes
Syene
Berenice
Mecca
M.

that of class, and individual merit replaced rights acquired by birth.

The organization of the central power was accompanied by the standardization of institutions. Throughout the Empire criminal jurisdiction, which had hitherto been in the hands of the Senate, was organized by the Emperor on a similar basis for both citizens and resident aliens; a system of appeals was set up, reaching as far as the Pretorian Prefect who became —as formerly the vizier of the Pharaohs—Prime Minister and Chief Justice.

A code of arbitration was created on the Egyptian model to guarantee the rights of the subject against the officials of the State.

Legal procedure was standardized and made more humane. Trajan limited the duration of protective custody and allowed those convicted by default the right of appealing against their sentence. Antoninus established the principle that the law must be interpreted in favour of the accused.

Roman law was codified for the first time. In this field the legislative work of Hadrian was considerable. Under the name of the Perpetual Edict, he codified the Pretorian edicts, that is to say the principles of private law which had been given legal force by the decisions of the praetors. Henceforward, the legislative power was centred more and more in the hands of the Emperor who from the end of the 2nd century alone possessed it.

As the law became standardized, so social policy developed. Influenced by Stoic ideas, the Empire adopted the principle of state intervention in social affairs, as had been the case in the Greek cities since the IIIrd century BC. In Rome itself the social policy of the Emperors did not lose the grossly demagogic character that it had been obliged to adopt since the end of the Republic firstly to eliminate the people from its participation in power, and later because of the danger of rioting and the threat of the Pretorians.

Trajan, and even Marcus Aurelius, did not scruple to distribute enormous sums to the Roman people in free gifts, in addition to their rations of foodstuffs, and to offer games and gladiatorial combats in the circus, often horribly cruel, in order to win the favour of the mob which, demoralized by sloth, demanded the violent emotions of sadism to distract it.

But in the provinces, where demagogy had not penetrated, the imperial policy made a noble effort to relieve misery and assure personal security. The conception of natural law, which had flourished in Egypt in the XIVth century BC under the reign of Horemheb, reappeared. It corresponded, moreover, to the universal movement of public opinion in the

Hellenized provinces, as can be seen from the discourse of Dio of Prusa addressed to the Emperor Trajan on the duties of the prince and his responsibility to the human race.

Under Trajan, small inheritances were exempted from taxation; in Italy funds were created for the support of poor children and loans granted to young married couples to help them establish themselves, while in all municipalities the magistrates were ordered to look to the education of young girls who were without means. Marcus Aurelius created a Praetor of Guardianships to assure the protection of minors.

The state subsidized the city school-systems and intervened to alleviate the misery caused by large-scale catastrophes.

The lot of slaves was made easier; the law forbade masters to inflict the death penalty; badly treated slaves could demand to be put up for sale.

Laws applicable to all the inhabitants of the Empire gradually eliminated the differences that existed between the legal status of resident aliens and citizens.

Public law followed an evolution similar to that of private law. The principles of government in the cities were made more and more uniform. The system of nominating magistrates by the property-owning classes was introduced universally. The régime of the city was extended. In all the provinces, groups of villages were systematically united into cities which had complete control of their own affairs. On the Rhine, on the Danube and as far as Dacia—conquered by Trajan—the municipal régime caused the last vestiges of the seigniorial system to disappear and called to public life the middle classes which formed the real foundation of the Empire.

Superior to the cities, the provincial assemblies served as intermediaries between the people and the Emperor. They passed resolutions and controlled the activities of provincial governors. Never, as a whole, had the Mediterranean world lived under such liberal institutions.

From the times of Trajan to those of Marcus Aurelius (98–161) the Empire was a mosaic of autonomous cities administered by the middle class. The Emperor by his social legislation assured the people a greater and greater security of life.

Thus a balance was established between the Emperor and the varied classes of the population, which assured the unity of power, the freedom of the citizens and the protection of the unfortunate and the handicapped.

INTELLECTUAL RENAISSANCE

The advent of a liberal régime under the Antonines revived an intense intellectual life in Rome. The death of Domitian had provoked a reaction of public opinion against despotism. The satires of Juvenal, which scourged the parasites, the hypocrites, the men of letters in the pay of power or wealth, the egoistic nobility, the playboys and the easy ladies, give a biting picture of the times.

The liberal empire, that fruitful period when, as Tacitus wrote, 'man could think as he pleased and say what he thought', restored the dignity of life and revived the intellectual forces of the Roman élite. Care for the common weal and free discussion of the imperial policy inspired literature: 'You order us to be free,' wrote Pliny the Younger to Trajan, 'and thus you make us men and citizens'.

The society corrupted by despotism which appears in the satires of Juvenal and that depicted in the correspondence of Pliny the Younger under the Antonines are worlds apart; a few years of liberty had been enough to revive in men a sense of their responsibility and restore to morals a humanity and an honesty that had not existed since the times of Augustus.

The century of the Antonines was less favourable to literature than to history and science. Tacitus searched for an explanation of his own times in the study of the past; Pliny the Younger sought out the bases for the best form of government and found them in liberalism; Florus described the epoch of Augustus, and Suetonius wrote *The Lives of the Caesars*, based on documents from the imperial archives placed at his disposal by Hadrian.

The Greek élite, expelled from Rome by Domitian, flocked back and, after a century of decadence, Greek literature revived. Dio of Prusa returned to Rome under Trajan; he did not hesitate to remind the Emperor of the responsibilities of power and to make public the refusal of the Hellenized lands to accept ever again a government that would consider the Empire as a field for exploitation for the benefit of Rome alone. Plutarch, who in his *Parallel Lives* and his philosophical works had drawn up a balance sheet of ancient civilization, came to lecture in Rome. Greek rhetoricians and philosophers flocked to Rome from all parts.

The Alexandrian Appian, appointed Treasury Counsel, wrote a Roman history there; the Asiatic Pausanias, in his *Description of Greece*, a sort of tourist guide, laid the foundations of archaeology; Arrian published the *Discourses* of Epictetus, of whom the Emperor Marcus Aurelius was the most distinguished disciple, and wrote a history of Alexander the Great.

Lucian, the last of the rationalists, in his *Dialogues of the Dead*, attacked the vague mysticism which was overwhelming all classes of society.

But this intellectual renaissance bore in itself the seeds of decadence.

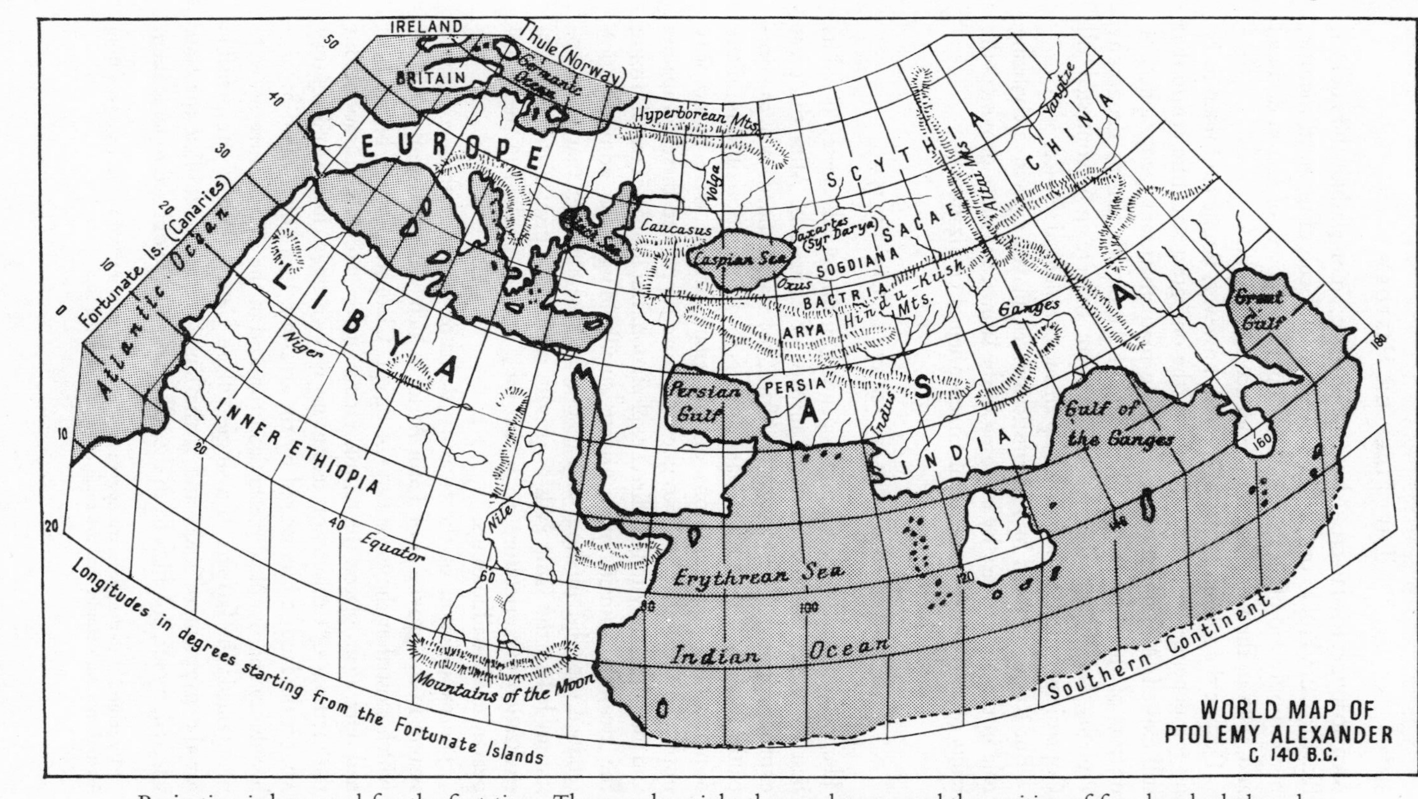

Projection is here used for the first time. The map has eight thousand names and the position of four hundred places has been determined by latitude and longitude. Ptolemy shows the Indian Ocean as a land-locked sea bounded by a southern continent joined to China, an idea based on vague tales of the existence of Japan and the Pacific islands.

Men no longer tried to create but to popularize; among fashionable authors, like the Latin Fronto or the Greek Aristides, the cult of form, of rhetoric, marked only too often their lack of depth; the power of reason declined and, with it, the value and independence of thought.

Despite the splendour of this period, however, Rome continued to be no less dependent on the influence of the one great scientific centre that still existed, Alexandria. All the leading mathematicians, geographers or doctors of the time taught or studied at Alexandria. In his geography Ptolemy formulated theories which were to remain uncontested till Copernicus[1]; and Galen summed up all ancient medical science.

But Rome, inspired by Hellenistic sources, played a decisive civilizing role in the 2nd century by bringing to the latinized western provinces the fruits of thirty-five centuries of Greco-oriental civilization.

FISCAL NEEDS LEAD TO STATE CAPITALISM

The social policy of the Empire depended on the middle classes. It did its best to protect them against the inroads of capitalism. After the great expropriations made by Nero in Africa, the state handed over to companies formed of groups of tenant-farmers the exploitation of its immense domains. But the conditions of the tenant-farmers were in no way improved thereby. The Antonines therefore suppressed these companies and introduced a system of direct exploitation. But instead of transforming the treasury domains into private smallholdings, the administration retained capitalist methods and it soon became apparent that state capitalism led to the same evils as private capitalism, insofar as the industrialization of agriculture, to which they tended, resulted in the disappearance of smallholdings.

The exploitation of the treasury domains by the state introduced a system in the provinces of Latin Africa which was very similar to that which existed at the same time in Egypt. Cleopatra, it may be recalled, had once again placed the temple estates under state administration. But the methods of exploitation had in no way changed. In the 2nd century AD, on the lands administered by the treasury, leases once again became hereditary and the fiscal methods introduced in the IInd century BC were maintained; the farmers of a single village were collectively responsible for the payment of taxes and if the lands remained untilled the state selected, by lot, colonists from the village who were obliged to lease them

[1] By returning to the geocentric system Ptolemy, however, marked a great regression from Eratosthenes who taught that the earth turned around the sun.

and pay rent and taxes on them. The Emperors continued to make use of this procedure which ended by reducing the peasants to slavery, but which gave a high yield to the state. Thus the manorial administration set up by the authorities, while increasing the revenue, led to an extension of the Egyptian system to the great treasury estates in Africa and elsewhere.

Fiscal necessity led to a tragic conflict between the liberal tendencies of the imperial policy which tried to protect the middle classes and the more and more tyrannical ascendancy of the treasury. The terrible cancer which was to eat away the Empire at the end of the third century was being prepared by the introduction of state capitalism.

Its results began to make themselves felt in Egypt in the 2nd century. Violent peasant revolts broke out which were soon transformed into a national uprising. To appease it Antoninus granted Egypt a less oppressive fiscal system, but it was in vain, since the evil lay in the methods themselves and not in the degree of severity with which they were applied. Shackled by state capitalism, the measures taken in favour of the rural classes were all inoperative. Hadrian allowed whoever wished to occupy the lands left untilled on the state domains in Africa, favoured the agricultural co-operatives to which the treasury lands were let out and encouraged long-term leases in order to assure the tenant of the benefits of soil improvement. But the long-term leases led to serfdom and the co-operatives facilitated the institution of communal responsibility of the peasants to the Treasury which, on the Egyptian model, was to be introduced throughout the Empire at the end of the 3rd century.

Since the state itself practised a system of capitalist exploitation, it was impossible to halt the progress of large private properties. Thus the impoverishment of the rural middle classes was a characteristic feature of the 2nd century. In the struggle between the measures taken by the Treasury, making use of state socialist methods, and the political ideas aimed at supporting the middle classes, it was the Treasury that won, since the fiscal needs of the Empire compelled it, despite the will of the Emperors and the force of public opinion, to tread the fatal road which, in the IInd century BC, had brought Egypt to ruin.

ROME LOSES CONTROL OF THE IMPERIAL ECONOMY

In the 2nd century AD an industrial crisis was added to the already imminent agricultural crisis. The constitution of the Empire in the 1st century, the organization of the western provinces and the stimulus given to commerce by peace and free-trade throughout the Mediterranean area had led to great industrial prosperity; over-production followed, and this became more and more evident in the 2nd century as the middle classes became more impoverished and their purchasing power diminished. The crisis was above all felt in Italy, because of the competition of the more progressive industries of Asia Minor and Syria.

Large-scale Roman capitalism had multiplied certain more profitable kinds of rural production, especially viniculture, in Italy. The result was a crisis in over-production of wines which was the more serious in that free trade made it possible for oriental wine to outprice Italian wine even on its home market. In AD 92 Domitian, in an attempt to remedy the crisis, had led the way towards state intervention, the first step towards controlled economy; he ordered half the vines in the provinces to be rooted up. Such measures were bound either to end in a régime of autarchy or to fail, which was the case. In the 2nd century Italy, swamped by slave-labour, slumbered in economic decadence, more and more dependent on the provinces which she had conquered and against whose economic superiority the policy of free-trade prevented her from struggling.

Rome, the imperial capital, had become the most populous city of the Empire. But her growth was not due, like that of Alexandria or Antioch, to her trade activity. Swollen by an immense proletariat, in part of servile origin, in part of farmers ruined by agrarian capitalism, she could not offer them work since she was not a centre of industrial production. A sterile consumer, inhabited by slothful *rentiers* and a proletariat maintained by state largesse, Rome ceased to govern and sank into slothful indolence.

TRAJAN INAUGURATES A POLICY OF ECONOMIC BALANCE

In reality, the whole economic life of the Empire was in the hands of the eastern provinces. The trade of Alexandria with India and China continued to develop. In the 2nd century Roman, that is to say Egyptian, vessels sailed directly to Ceylon and thence to the mouth of the Ganges. Egyptian and Syrian merchants went as far as China. About the year 100 Marinus of Tyre described the silk route which by way of Antioch, Ecbatana, Merv and Bactra reached the Stone Tower on the Chinese slopes of the Pamirs, where the Syrian merchants went to receive the bales of silk brought from the Far East.

But this great trade with Asia was mainly an import trade. In the time of Pliny, northern India alone took from the Empire more than a hundred million *sesterces* annually. Transactions with China were almost entirely carried on at a deficit, since Rome was unable to send back by the silk route the weighty produce of her iron, lead and copper mines which constituted her main wealth.

The deficit in the Roman trade balance was due partly to the industrial decline of Egypt during the first two centuries BC and which the exploitation of the country by the Roman treasury only accentuated—Egypt no longer produced return freights—and partly to the fact that Rome and the western provinces, though great consumers of precious metals, spices and silk, produced very little for export.

This deficit in the trade balance had to be paid for in gold and the Empire produced little gold. The Nubian mines had been lost and those of Asia Minor and Thrace were almost exhausted.

To all these causes which impaired the economic balance of the Empire must be added the serious harm resulting from Roman dependence on the great continental trade-routes. The profits of the traffic between China and Central Asia and Rome went to the caravan cities and the kingdom of the Parthians.

All these factors meant that Rome was short of gold.

Shortage of the precious metal had already been the cause of the fiscal crisis under Nero. Trajan seems to have been perfectly aware of it, and his foreign policy, as formerly that of the Hellenistic states, was determined by the need to give the Empire a stable economic balance.

But first of all the gold that the Empire needed must be found. Dacia (Rumania) possessed important gold-bearing deposits; Trajan set out to conquer it. By this he also gained possession of a vast province which made him master of the mouths of the Danube; and the traffic of Dacia increased the importance of the great trade-route that brought the Greek ports on the Black Sea into touch with the northern provinces.

A mass of Roman colonists, attracted by the exploitation of the mines, came to settle in Dacia, where Trajan, abandoning the monopolistic policy that the Empire had practised since Augustus, inaugurated a system of small-scale mining. Hadrian later introduced the same method into Portugal.

Thanks to the gold of Dacia, Rome enjoyed, up to the time of Commodus, a certain monetary stability. But it was not enough to assure reserves of precious metals for the state; it was also necessary to keep them as the result of a steady trade balance. Rome could only attain this by gaining control of the trade-routes, not only by sea but also by land, to India and China.

In order to do this, Trajan annexed Edessa which, together with Palmyra and Damascus, was one of the great continental markets on the caravan routes. To control the Red Sea he incorporated into the Empire the kingdom of the Nabatean Arabs.

Finally, to complete and round off his plan, he undertook a great military campaign which ended in the conquest of Mesopotamia and Armenia. The frontiers of the Empire were advanced to the Persian Gulf in the south and the Caspian Sea in the north. Thus all the trade-routes which led to the Mediterranean, the Black Sea and the Caucasus were under Roman control; all Nearer Asia was associated with the Mediterranean economy. A large-scale trade policy with Asia became possible. In order to launch it Trajan sent an embassy to India.

The conquests of Trajan, though beneficial to the economy of the Empire, in no way improved the economic situation of the capital. The occupation of Dacia gave, in fact, a new life to the continental trade-route formed by the Danube, the Rhine and the Rhône, and Italy ceased to be the meeting point of the traffic between East and West.

The direct communication established by the Black Sea and the great rivers with the continental provinces of Europe gave increased importance to Asia Minor and the Straits. Syrian merchants were scattered throughout all western Europe where they supplanted the Italian traders, and Syrian industry found immense new outlets. The provinces of Asia Minor with their flourishing ports of Sinope and Trebizond on the Black Sea, and Ephesus and Smyrna on the Aegean, open both to the west by the Mediterranean and the Danube and to the East by Mesopotamia and the routes of Central Asia, attained a prosperity that almost made them rivals of the Syrian cities.

The economic policy of Trajan in the East would have needed a great military effort. In the 3rd century the Parthian Empire had a magnificent revival under the dynasty of the Sassanids. It could only expand if it possessed Mesopotamia and thus the Persian Gulf route to the Caucasus. The struggle for the final mastery of the basin of the Euphrates and Tigris was therefore bound to be very hard. The eternal conflict between the continental and maritime economy for the possession of the trade routes of Nearer Asia seemed as if it would begin once more.

HADRIAN ADOPTS A PACIFIC POLICY

But the Empire was just then turning towards an essentially peaceful civilization. War far from being, as it had been in the last years of the Republic, a source of profit involved enormous expenses. The army was recruited with greater and greater difficulty from amongst prosperous peoples who had lost the habit of serving in its ranks. In order to complete the effectives of the Roman army, which were not actually very large since they did not exceed 350,000 men, barbarians were enrolled. Furthermore, the legions which were stationed in the regions where they were recruited became more and more sedentary in character and could no longer be sent far from their bases. That was why Hadrian, abandoning the great trade policy of Trajan, preferred to give up Mesopotamia and withdraw the Roman frontiers to the Upper Euphrates. Public opinion unanimously approved this peaceful policy, which it believed to be eternal.

The Empire surrounded itself with a frontier-wall, behind which it stationed its troops in too thin a cordon. It was thenceforward to limit its activities to assuring the maintenance of the *status quo*.

The great economic plan of Trajan, which aimed at the mastery of all the traffic on the continental routes of Nearer Asia, was abandoned. After Hadrian, Marcus Aurelius, who fully understood its importance, wanted to recover Mesopotamia. But he failed, and tried to compensate for this by establishing direct maritime relations between the Empire and China. In AD 166 he sent Roman traders on an embassy to the court of the Han to settle there. But the terrible crisis in which the Empire was to become involved prevented this from having any useful result.

RETREAT FROM LIBERALISM UNDER MARCUS AURELIUS

During the second half of the 2nd century the town-planning expenses of the cities, the social-welfare laws and public education all weighed heavily on the municipal budgets. Their deficit became endemic; the Emperor was forced to intervene. To watch over the financial administration of the cities, Marcus Aurelius added an Imperial Curator to the number of municipal magistrates.

This was the first step along the road to state socialism. The consequences were felt immediately. Jurisdiction in the cities was in the hands of local magistrates, the 'two men' (*duoviri*), elected by the property-owning middle-class. From the time of Marcus Aurelius, the system of co-option to the *curiae* freed these *duoviri* from the control of public opinion; instead of being judges representing the middle classes they became in reality representatives of a curial oligarchy. Their power at once became arbitrary. Despite the humanitarian laws in force, they began to introduce, especially for the common people, the penalty of mutilation. The 'notables', invested by Marcus Aurelius with the government of the cities, were at once transformed into a sort of nobility who acted as if they were above the law. They behaved towards the mass of the *humiliores* (common people) as *honestiores* (persons of distinction).

Thus fiscal difficulties led the Stoic Emperor, Marcus Aurelius, to renounce the liberalism of his predecessors, and the Stoic egalitarianism which he preached ended in the formation of an administrative class which immediately claimed privileges for itself and become a nobility.

THE FISCAL CRISIS UNDER COMMODUS

The state socialism introduced by Marcus Aurelius was transformed under Commodus (180–192) into absolutism. The opposition of the Senate was at once revived. The political crisis which ensued was complicated by the monetary crisis due to the continual flight of gold. The lack of metal reserves, at a moment of serious political unrest, led Commodus to devalue the currency by 30%. The result was a rapid rise in living costs which, in certain parts of the Empire, increased almost threefold. In order to appease the social unrest resulting from this, Commodus published a maximum price tariff; the only result was an even greater disorganization of trade, a halt in production, a diminution in tax yield and a lowering of wages. To avoid the discontent which was rumbling in the army, the pay of the troops had to be increased. The supplementary burden that this placed upon the exchequer could not be compensated for by the benefits of devaluation. It led to complete collapse.

After a century of peace and prosperity, the Empire found itself suddenly involved in a political, economic and fiscal crisis which seemed insoluble. In 192 Commodus, who had gone mad, was assassinated, and a new dynastic war broke out.

CHAPTER L

FROM LIBERALISM TO ANARCHY (193–235)

AUTHORITARIAN ABSOLUTISM UNDER THE SEVERI

THE assassination of Commodus once again brought to the fore the question of the central power. The Senate, in the absence of any legitimate principle of succession, reverted to the idea that it was itself the legitimate representative body of the Empire and elected Pertinax (193) to the throne. This time it was not a Roman aristocrat but the son of a freedman whom the Senate hoped to make its instrument. But Pertinax was assassinated in his palace by the Pretorians, who put the Empire up to auction. The armies of Britain, Syria and Illyria responded by nominating their generals as Emperors. After four years of civil war Septimius Severus, a general of Punic origin supported by the army of Illyria, marched on Rome (193) which, weary of disorders and hoping for security, welcomed him enthusiastically.

Septimius Severus (193–211) at once put into force a policy of authoritarian absolutism. The Senate, the only obstacle to absolute power, immediately opposed him. Conflict broke out once more. It soon degenerated into a terrible social struggle, in the course of which Septimius Severus, and after him Caracalla (211–217), worked unceasingly to destroy the aristocracy of birth and the aristocracy of money.

Hundreds of senators and thousands of *equites* were put to death and their goods confiscated. The proscriptions of the two Emperors ended in a wholesale destruction of the nobility and the upper classes and the confiscation of their possessions. It was one of the most bloody social revolutions that had ever taken place.

The destruction of the aristocracy, that is to say of all those families whose origin or wealth made them a social power, went hand in hand with the creation of a new order which established a total and implacable authority imposed on all alike.

The institutions of the Empire were rigidly unified to the sole benefit of the Emperor. An egalitarian legal formula was drawn up which divided society into classes in the interests of the state alone. The liberalism of the Antonines which had marked the zenith of the Empire—and which had been growing weaker since the times of Marcus Aurelius—was finally abandoned for a policy of state socialism. A new social era had begun.

ABOLITION OF DEMOCRACY

This radical unification of the institutions of the Empire was obtained by a far-reaching reform of municipal institutions. Similar forms of local government were introduced throughout the Empire. Even Alexandria and the Egyptian cities, which had till then preserved their Ptolemaic institutions, were endowed with a municipal senate. The new organization, it is true, was closer to the Ptolemaic than to the Greco-Roman system. The *Comitia* in which the citizens had formerly elected the magistrates had been suppressed by Marcus Aurelius. Since then the *curiae*, or senates, had been placed under the control of a *curator* (custodian) appointed by the Emperor, and had become councils of notables which co-opted their own members and chose the municipal magistrates from amongst themselves. On these municipal oligarchies Septimius Severus superimposed commissions of ten members responsible for the collection of taxes. The Empire abandoned the formula of democracy based on the census, which associated the taxpayers with the executive power, in order to adopt the oligarchic system formerly put into effect in Egypt at the time of the great state socialist reforms of the Ptolemies.

The duties of the *curiae*, thus transformed, were singularly limited. Their administrative and judicial competence was practically annulled and handed over to the *curator* of the city.

This vast reform, which made the status of the inhabitants of the Empire uniform from the shores of the North Sea and the Danube to the Euphrates and as far as Aswan, was completed by the Antonine Constitution of Caracalla (212) which extended to all the peoples of the Empire, with only a few exceptions, the status of Roman citizens. Henceforward, a single law was applicable in all the provinces; over and above the former local taxes which continued to exist, a uniform tax of 5% on inheritances was enforced throughout the Empire. The status of citizen, however, brought no new rights to the provincials, since the population was deprived of all participation in the political life of the state; it did no more than impose the same fiscal obligations on all the 'subjects' of the Emperors.

Carrying on the work of his father, Caracalla wanted to make all his subjects practise the same religion, that of the great solar god of Alexandria, Serapis. The shadow of Egypt spread more and more over the Empire. But Rome, which did not possess the moral unity of ancient Egypt, could not impose an imperial religion save by extirpating the Christian monotheism which was becoming more and more widespread in the eastern provinces. Religious persecutions, of an essentially political character, were begun. They were to cease, it is true, after 217, under the influence of the oriental prefects who soon imposed restraint on the bloodthirsty African Emperors.

EGALITARIAN STATE SOCIALISM

Septimius Severus, married to a Syrian, assured the domination of eastern ideas over the state by entrusting the Pretorian Prefecture to the great Syrian jurist, Papinian. The East again took on the preponderant role both in the economic and in the intellectual life of the Empire which it had played since the 2nd century.

From the time of Marcus Aurelius this had taken the form of a return to the policy of economic expansion over Mesopotamia. This, however, ended in total failure with serious consequences, since the offensive of the Empire in Asia involved it in a series of uninterrupted and exhausting wars against the Parthian monarchy.

Despite possession of the Dacian goldmines, the fiscal crisis remained latent under the Severi. In order to assure a certain monetary stability, Septimius Severus had been forced to revalue the gold reserves, which resulted in a devaluation of the coinage by more than 25%. This, however, could be no more than a palliative, for the irremediable vice of the Roman economy—its adverse trade balance—remained.

In social affairs, the absolutist policy of the Severi went hand in hand with a continual trend towards humanitarian ideas. It marked the triumph of natural law (*jus gentium*), which had been elaborated during the Hellenistic period and which, through the work of Papinian and his successor Ulpian, also a Semite, swamped the imperial law.

Papinian, in his famous *Responsa*, established the classic doctrine of Roman law on the foundation of Greco-Oriential individualism. Ulpian was to complete his work during the reign of Alexander Severus by a reform of the criminal law which was to suppress the penalty of confiscation of goods of those who had been sentenced, so that the punishment should not fall upon their heirs.

The individualism which triumphed in private law corresponded in public law to an egalitarian tendency which arose out of the policy of destroying the privileged classes and the radical reform of the bureaucracy, which opened the way to all public offices to men risen from the ranks. Thenceforward soldiers, all of them provincials, could be found occupying the highest civil and military posts and reaching even as far as the throne. After the dynasty of the Severi, the Emperors were frequently soldiers of low extraction, amongst them the greatest Emperors of the 3rd century, Aurelian and Diocletian.

The holding of high office by men without the prestige of birth led to the introduction of a whole hierarchy of honorific titles;[1] thus an administrative nobility was formed on the ruins of the former senatorial aristocracy, and this, little by little, became transformed into a governmental oligarchy.

STATE SOCIALISM STIFLES THE INDIVIDUAL

The enormous political and social transformation which took place under the Severi was egalitarian and humanitarian; it was inspired both by respect for human personality and by desire for social unity. But these two principles, both a result of Stoic ideas, soon came into conflict. The individual was sacrificed to society which was confounded with the state. In less than a century, the humanitarian doctrines ended in the enslavement of the citizens to the advantage of the omnipotent state. Those who suffered the most were the classes without property, whom nevertheless the state socialist policy aimed at protecting and emancipating.

The basis of this evolution, which recalled very closely what had taken place in Egypt in the IInd century BC, was to be found in the legal theory formulated by the Greek Callistrates. Studying the relations between the state and its citizens, he finally considered all activities which could have a bearing on public affairs and on property itself as social functions directly subject to the authority of the Emperor. This conception, which is at the root of all state socialist policy, is founded on the idea that the state is a living entity, formed by the union in a single group of all the citizens of whom the Emperor is the representative. The state thus assumes a personality which is superimposed on that of the citizens. In their individual activities the citizens are considered firstly as members of the state and only incidentally as separate individuals. Individual liberty, therefore, no longer appears legitimate save within limits set by the state. This theory of the primacy of the state was substituted for that of natural rights which had been consecrated by the *jus gentium*. Thus the imperial omnipotence,

[1] It was first introduced under Marcus Aurelius.

while it asserted in the name of equality the principle of individualism sanctioned by private law, formulated, at the same time and in the name of that same equality, the state socialist theory which was rapidly to stifle the individual and give the deathblow to the intellectual culture which the liberalism of the Antonines had revived.

It was in the name of this principle, which subjected all economic and social activity to the authority of the state, that Septimius Severus inaugurated his state socialist policy, by which democracy was suppressed and replaced by economic corporatism. Every citizen was of value to the state by reason of his office. It was therefore the trade or profession which constituted the essential activity of every man, and the corporation was to become the framework of society. The corporations, till then autonomous, were put under imperial control, which endowed them with uniform regulations throughout the Empire. A controlled economy was being established.

Since the possession of property was considered a public office, the Emperor systematized the obligation of property-owners to guarantee the state the resources necessary for the accomplishment of its social mission. It was thus led to adopt the Ptolemaic system, imposing on the *decurions* the payment of taxes due from their city, even were it from their personal fortunes. Formerly representatives of their fellow-citizens, the *decurions* were thus reduced to being no more than state agents forming a sort of fiscal aristocracy. To compensate them for this responsibility the Emperor granted them privileges which, as well as putting them in a position that enabled them to carry out their duties efficiently, made them a class superior to the ordinary taxpayer. The egalitarianism of the social policy combined with the absolutism of the state thus ended by creating a privileged oligarchy out of the richest citizens.[1]

ULPIAN TRIES TO ESTABLISH A CONSTITUTIONAL MONARCHY

The death of Caracalla, assassinated at the beginning of a campaign against the Parthians (217), led to a fresh dynastic crisis. Macrinus, the Pretorian Prefect, was elected Emperor by a part of the army, but he too was soon assassinated. The principle of heredity prevailed and a descendant of Caracalla, a solar priest at Edessa to whom the name of his god Elagabalus[2] had been given in derision, was raised to the throne at the age of fourteen (218–222). Surrounded by princesses, who reigned in his

[1] The *curiales* formed a hereditary aristocracy which could only co-opt members from the senators, the *equites*, the army or members of corporations; each must possess a hundred thousand *sesterces*. It was a prosperous middle class.

[2] Usually known as 'Heliogabalus,' though 'Elagabalus' is more correct. His real name was Varius Avitus.

name, he introduced the most arbitrary absolutism. The highest offices were given to his house-servants. At the age of eighteen he was assassinated by his soldiers, and his cousin Alexander Severus (222–235), still almost a child, succeeded him.

After the terror exercised by Septimius Severus and Caracalla and the follies of Elagabalus, absolutism seemed condemned. Under the direction of the Prefect Ulpian, who was devoted to Stoic ideas, a fresh attempt was made to install a constitutional Empire. In Ulpian's system the Emperor held the executive power, assisted by a Council of seventy members, of whom twenty were legal experts, and shared the legislative power with the Senate, which appointed its own members on the recommendation of the consuls. The Senate nominated the higher officials, Prefects and Governors of Provinces. The conception of the Emperor-God was abolished and the regal ceremonies suppressed. The Emperor became a sovereign ruling with the aid of a self-opting oligarchy.

There was complete tolerance in religious matters. Attracted by oriental mysticism, Alexander Severus placed statues of the great mystics, including one of Jesus, in the palace chapel.

But if Ulpian changed the form of the government, he could not change the state socialist evolution of the imperial policy. Under Alexander Severus corporatism was systematized and made universal. The corporative form was imposed on all trades and become an official and obligatory organism. The first state monopolies were formed, notably that of purple. The state, in order to organize the loans which it granted free to the people, became a banker. Technical education was stressed more and more and the public authorities encouraged the development of mechanics. Public warehouses were established to help trade. The state granted subsidies to cities to allow them to erect magnificent buildings, and in Rome, where the Emperors had already constructed sumptuous edifices, the state organized the lighting of the baths which remained open to the public in the evenings.

Social life attained a level of comfort that it had never before known and which the common people were able to enjoy more and more.

THE END OF INDIVIDUALIST SOCIETY

As wealth expanded, so also did culture. The state did its best to make it available to all social classes by creating bursaries for poor students, by paying teachers and granting pensions to doctors. But it could well have been said that this popularization of studies took from them all their depth.

The period of great discoveries was over. Culture became commonplace and mediocre and all local originalities disappeared. Everywhere the same taste triumphed, the same books were read, the same clothing worn, the same art practised. The world became uniform.

Doubtless this was the price that had to be paid for the magnificent internationalism of Roman civilization which made it possible for the subjects of the Emperor to travel freely from the coasts of Britain to the Asiatic frontiers and find themselves able to be understood everywhere in one or other of the two universal languages, Latin in the West, Greek in the East, both of which were known by all educated men. The free exchange of goods, the same currency, the same law, made the whole Mediterranean world into a single state where the Roman citizen was everywhere at home.

Was it this ease and comfort that withered the forces of the soul? Whatever the reason, philosophy gave no answer; the schools of Athens, Pergamon, Smyrna and Ephesus enjoyed, without doubt, a great international fame, Greek professors were summoned at great expense to the cities of Gaul, and a magnificent veneer of culture spread over all the Empire; but beneath this veneer the spirit was being extinguished.

One powerful intellectual force alone remained, the moral code that attracted all the most eminent men and aroused the enthusiasm of the élite; either the Stoic code of morals, detached from all mysticism, which, from the slave Epictetus to the Emperor Marcus Aurelius, professed that man must find within himself his own justification and the power to live a life based on humanity and idealism; or the mystic morality of the mysteries which led the masses to a belief in the immortality of the soul, personal piety and faith, which outlined a religion of abstinence, devotion and chastity; or above all the Christian moral code which, in the eastern provinces and as far as Rome itself, exercised on the élite as well as on the masses an ascendency which persecution only served to increase.

The most characteristic feature of the intellectual evolution of the early 3rd century was that it was moving farther and farther from the rational and towards the mystical; this movement was parallel to the social evolution which had caused the recoil of individualism before the ideals of equality and uniformity. Egalitarianism, an offshoot of humanitarianism, led to the emancipation of slaves. Society grew more and more democratic and, at the same time, became grouped into little social units. The idea of association was immensely extended, uniting men of the same trade or the same locality; associations of soldiers, N.C.O.'s and officials were created everywhere. Thus society itself prepared the framework that the state was to use to enchain it. The ease of existence, the general well-being, led to a decline in the birth-rate. The exodus from the countryside to the towns continued to increase; the land lacked workers and land ownership tended to become concentrated in a few hands. Vast estates were formed on which, from the time of Marcus Aurelius onwards, barbarians brought into the Empire were settled as tenants.

Industry also was concentrated, leading to a decline in the number of artisans, mainly in metallurgy and brick-making.

The general well-being made it difficult to obtain recruits for the army. On the other hand, the fiscal crisis caused the military expenses to weigh more and more heavily on the state budget. In order to attract volunteers, and at the same time to reduce expenses, Alexander Severus settled soldier-workers on the frontiers, giving them grants of land. But an army of this sort loses its mobility, and its will to fight becomes rapidly impaired, which necessitates a continual increase in its numbers.

The upkeep of a professional army, the constant increase in bureaucracy, swelled the state budget beyond all measure; fiscal difficulties became endemic.

It was at this time that war broke out once more against the Persian dynasty of the Sassanids who from 226 had replaced the former Parthian Empire. The legions had to be recalled from the Rhine and the Danube to meet the enemy offensive. But the frontiers were left unguarded and the barbarians began to force their way into the Empire. The Franks, who then made their first appearance in history, crossed the Rhine, and the Alamanni the Danube. The Empire was no longer powerful enough to enable it to fight on the northern and eastern frontiers at the same time.

Alexander Severus tried to save himself from the barbarians by treaties and subsidies, but the army rejected this policy of capitulation and the Emperor was killed by his legions on the Rhine in 235.

The attempt at constitutional monarchy had failed. In order to succeed, it should have been able to rely on a real community of interest between the Emperor and the people. But the representative governments of the cities had been destroyed. Everywhere the elective principle had been replaced by the principle of authority. Thenceforward, the constitution of Ulpian could be only a façade. The search for a constitutional legal basis founded on an oligarchic senate could only appear to the people as an attempt to restore the aristocracy. It ended by ruining the idea of the hereditary monarchy which it had attempted to assert.

The death of Alexander Severus left the Empire in absolute confusion. A terrible period of anarchy began. It was to last for fifty years (235–284).

CHAPTER LI

FROM ANARCHY TO AUTHORITARIANISM (235–305)

ANARCHY

FROM 235 to 268 the Empire passed through a terrible crisis which plunged it into complete anarchy. The sovereign power no longer existed. The Senate appeared only as the defender of an outworn aristocratic régime. Constitutional monarchy was no longer possible, since in the provinces all political life had been suppressed. Hereditary monarchy could not function because of the opposition of the Senate. Only force remained, and it was to seize power wherever it could, either to exploit or to restore the Empire. In thirty-three years the Senate and the armies elected no less than twenty-three Emperors.

Rent asunder, the Empire fell to pieces; and civil wars, by leaving the frontiers unguarded, left it open to the inroads of the barbarians.

The whole world was then in flux. At the beginning of the 3rd century strong pressure from the Huns was again felt on the frontiers of China. But the Chinese Empire held firm. The thrust turned westward. The Eastern Huns, settled north of China, drove back the Western Huns who were living a nomadic life near the Altai Mountains, and a great movement resulted from east to west, first in the whole Caspian region and later in the area of the Black Sea.

About the same time, the Germans in the north of Europe began to move southward in search of land. Harassed by the Scythians, who in their turn were under pressure from the Huns, the Goths crossed the Danube, invaded Thrace and Greece, took Corinth, launched their ships on the Black Sea, penetrated into Asia Minor and sacked Ephesus. The Vandals entered Thrace after the Goths, the Alamanni crossed the Rhine and advanced as far as Auvergne and Italy. The Franks overran Gaul and their raids reached as far as Spain. In Africa, the Berbers attacked the Roman colonists. In the East the Persians, who were trying to reconquer the Syrian coasts, took Antioch.

Wars between pretenders for the throne ruined the provinces. Alexandria was sacked; the treasuries and revenues of the cities were confiscated by the army leaders and the victorious soldiers gave themselves up to pillage.

In the midst of all this ruin and anarchy Rome, where the former Pretorian Prefect Philip the Arab, secretly a Christian, was then in power, celebrated its millenary with great pomp in 248.

Various attempts were made to restore the central authority.

The generals Decius (249–251) and Valerian (253–260) wished to re-establish the Empire on a Roman nationalist basis; this reaction against their Semitic predecessors incited them to unleash a ferocious persecution of the Christians. But Valerian was taken prisoner by the Persians and his son, Gallienus (260–268), in order to restore internal peace reverted to a policy of tolerance and granted the Christians liberty of worship.

In the midst of these attempts to restore the central power, Postumus in 260 created a separate Empire in Gaul, to which Spain and the island of Britain were soon united, and succeeded in driving back the barbarians; while in the East the Prince of Palmyra, Odaenathus, a vassal of Rome, drove back the Persians across the Euphrates and then set out to conquer the East for himself (262); he left to his queen, Zenobia, who succeeded him, the richest provinces of the Empire, Asia Minor, Syria and Egypt. All the great Asian trade thus passed under the control of Palmyra which, in a few years, amassed huge gold reserves.

This crisis not only destroyed the political structure of the Empire, but greatly altered it. The army of farmer-soldiers became a useless militia and the Emperors compelled the great landowners to provide them with men conscripted from among their tenants. The landowners thus found themselves invested with an authority that was to transform them into *seigneurs.*

The cities threatened in their security surrounded themselves with ramparts and, unable to maintain long-distance contacts, withdrew into purely local activities. The slaves, profiting by the troubles, freed themselves. Poverty led to brigandage, and in order to defend themselves the landowners organized their own police forces.

The troubles due to the economic and political unrest plunged the Empire into fiscal and monetary anarchy. From 256 onward the silver coins were so adulterated that they contained 95% alloy; they were no more than copper tokens covered by a thin film of precious metal. As the Emperors were unable to impose a fixed exchange rate, living costs, between 256 and 280, rose by a thousand per cent.

THE MILITARY ABSOLUTISM OF AURELIAN

In the midst of such terrible chaos the armies of Illyria, which were the strongest force remaining in the Empire, proclaimed their general, Aurelian, the son of a simple farmer of Pannonia, as Emperor (270–275).

Aurelian and his army saved the Empire. In three years his victorious troops again took their stations on the Rhine and the Danube, to which the frontiers of the Empire were finally withdrawn, abandoning Dacia and its goldmines. But Gaul was restored to the Empire, and Palmyra occupied and razed to the ground; its immense gold reserves enabled the Emperor to mint coins. Rebellious Egypt was subjugated, but at the cost of violence that seriously affected the prosperity of Alexandria. Order was re-established everywhere by court-martial methods. To obtain the resources that he needed, Aurelian extorted them from the rich, whom he detested. To assure the provisioning of Rome, the bakers' guild was declared a state service. Large areas of land had remained untilled as a result of the wars; the *decurions* were compelled to restore them to cultivation and to pay the taxes on them. But by imposing these burdens on the wealthy classes, Aurelian encouraged the concentration of vast estates in the hands of the great landowners and thus prepared the way for their domination over the rest of the population. The accumulation of property in a few hands was increased even more by the sale of large areas of crown lands carried out for the benefit of the Treasury.

In the midst of anarchy, power assumed an essentially personal character and the idea of hereditary succession took firmer and firmer root. Decius, Gordian and Valerian had associated their sons with them as co-emperors, and Gallienus had succeeded his father Valerian. The need for fighting on two fronts also introduced the custom of naming two Emperors, one taking control of the western provinces, the other of the eastern. Thirty years of military rule ended in the triumph of absolutism, to which the senators, excluded from army commands by Gallienus, were no longer able to make any opposition.

Aurelian rebuilt the Empire, re-established order and temporarily restored a sound currency. But the restoration was more apparent than real. The great current of trade to Asia, which had created the prosperity of the eastern provinces, was ruined. In the course of the terrible crisis, which for thirty years had destroyed all security within the Empire, trade with India and China had withered away; the sack of Alexandria and the ruin of Antioch, taken and destroyed by the Sassanid King, Shapur I, in 261, had prevented its recovery.

In internal affairs, it was not enough to have restored order to the Empire by authoritative methods; it was necessary to restore a normal balance and to replace the military dictatorship by a regular government. The absolutism which existed *de facto* had to become legitimate and find itself a moral and legal basis.

Aurelian wanted to provide this by proclaiming a monarchy of divine right based on the solar cult. A new college of priests was established and a temple consecrated to the glory of the Sun and the Emperor who had himself called a god. Withdrawn from the people, he surrounded himself with a pompous ceremonial in imitation of the Persian court. In order to realize his absolutism to the full, the Emperor claimed to control all activities, not only political, economic and social, but religious as well. It was in the name of this authority that Aurelian, although a pagan, intervened in the doctrinal conflicts which already divided the Christians, in order to impose orthodoxy upon them.

It seemed that the monarchical theory, by which Egypt had lived for three thousand years, must be imposed upon the Empire. But such a theory had to rely upon a universally accepted religion. Paganism was in its death throes. Aurelian, a native of Illyria where Christianity had only recently penetrated, did not understand that the religious revolution which was taking place in the Empire was making Christianity the dominant idea of his times.

STATE SOCIALIST REORGANIZATION OF THE EMPIRE BY DIOCLETIAN

Like most of his predecessors Aurelian was assassinated. The absence of a law of succession plunged Rome into a fresh crisis of anarchy during which Tacitus, an elderly Senator nominated by the Senate (275–276), Probus, an Illyrian soldier (276–282), Carus the Pretorian Prefect (282–3) and after him his two sons, successively held the throne until the general staff nominated as Emperor Diocletian (284–305), one of its members and the son of a Dalmatian freedman. Diocletian was appointed not so much for his military abilities as for his proved statesmanlike capacities. He undertook a radical reconstruction of the Empire.

In order to give a more direct authority to the sovereign power and to assure its continuity, Diocletian divided the Empire into two large governments, the West, including Africa, and the East, with Egypt; on the one hand all the Latin-speaking provinces (the Danubian lands excepted), and on the other the Hellenized world. The sovereignty was shared between two Emperors. Diocletian took the East for himself and handed over the West to Maximian. Of the two Emperors, equal in rank, the elder had the primacy of prestige and alone possessed legislative power. Each, during his lifetime, adopted his successor whom he associated effectively with his power. Thus the death of one of the Emperors would not leave the executive power vacant. It was noteworthy that the hereditary principle, which had begun to be accepted, was set aside in favour of the most worthy. Maximian passed over his own son in favour of Constantius Chlorus whom he adopted.

The Empire, thus presided over by a college of Emperors each possessing parallel authority, was ensured a more direct and firmer administration. It was, furthermore, to be reinforced by a new provincial structure.

Each of the two governments was divided into two Prefectures; the eastern government into the Prefecture of the East, comprising Thrace, Asia Minor, Syria and Egypt, and the Prefecture of Illyria (present-day Greece and Serbia[1]), while the western government was divided into the Prefecture of the Italys comprising Italy, the Danubian lands and Latin Africa, and that of the Gauls, comprising Gaul, Spain and Britain.

These Prefectures were themselves divided into six dioceses placed under the rule of vicars and the dioceses in their turn were sub-divided into provinces of reduced extent under civil governors. In the whole Empire there were ninety-six. The former national units were broken up; Egypt, henceforward, formed three provinces and Italy a dozen.

In order to invest the administration with a more direct authority and link it more closely to the Emperor, the Prefectures were given governments of their own and a definite separation was established between the civil and military powers.

At the head of each Prefecture was a Pretorian Prefect[2] to whom the vicars of the dioceses and the governors of the provinces were directly responsible.

In each Prefecture almost all the civil, judicial, administrative and financial powers were united in the hands of the Pretorian Prefect. As Chief of Police he controlled the courts and as Judge of Appeal he could revise their sentences; the civil administration was subject to his sole authority, as well as public education, the postal services, the control of the professional corporations and the fixing of market prices; though he did not command the army, he presided over its administration, was

[1] The Prefecture of Illyria only existed intermittently up to the end of the 4th century: more often it was attached to the Prefecture of the Italys.

[2] It will be recalled that previously there had been only one Pretorian Prefect for the whole Empire, though at times there had been two, and sometimes three, persons who bore the title.

responsible for recruiting, supply and payment of the troops and officers; finally, he administered the finances, collected the taxes, paid the officials and controlled all public expenses.

Every Prefecture thus enjoyed an administrative autonomy which assured the proper functioning of the more and more numerous state services.

The central government, held firmly in the hands of the Emperor in each of the two Empires, reserved to itself the administration of the capital, the military command, the chancellery, foreign affairs, the administration of the crown lands and state workshops, the currency, and the appointment of higher officials and army officers.

This administrative decentralization of the Empire, therefore, did not endanger its cohesion. The Emperor closely supervised the Prefects, vicars and governors by appointing alongside them a secretary-general who was directly responsible to the Imperial Chancellery to which he had to report.

The army was considerably strengthened. The best troops were withdrawn from the frontiers to serve as garrisons in the interior, both to maintain order and so that they could be sent rapidly wherever the need was felt.

Unity between the two Empires, completely separated from one another, had to be maintained by unity of legislation which was entrusted to the elder Emperor.

The executive power was thus closely centralized in the hands of the Emperors. No sort of contact any longer existed between them and the mass of the people. Power, henceforward, came exclusively from above. The last vestiges of political democracy, on which the Empire had in former times relied in the cities and provinces, disappeared. In the cities, the *decurions* existed only to supervise the municipal administration and to assure the normal tax yield. The provincial assemblies, it is true, still remained but, whereas formerly they had been composed of delegates from cities that freely administered their own affairs, they were now no more than meetings of officials or representatives of the bureaucratic oligarchy of the *curiales* (*decurions*).

The powers which the municipal *curiae* had lost in the administrative, legal and fiscal fields were now entirely concentrated in the hands of the state. A far-reaching reform of jurisdiction and taxation resulted.

Justice became exclusively the prerogative of the Emperor or of the officials to whom he delegated his powers. Administered by the governors, it was organized in stages; appeals went as far as the Pretorian Prefect and the Emperor. Procedure, thus made uniform, became more flexible and was simplified under the influence of the Eastern law-schools. But the fiscal administration, by standardizing the methods of procedure, involved so many expenses and delays that justice became bureaucratic, slow and burdensome.

The finances underwent a profound reorganization. Till then the budget had been drawn up by relating, in principle, expenses to revenues, but in fact its deficit had become endemic, leading to frequent and serious crises. The constant devaluation of the coinage had totally unbalanced the fiscal system. Over and above the taxes on the citizens—5% on inheritances, 5% on the enfranchisement of slaves, the poll-tax levied on all males from 18 to 65 years of age, and the land-tax—each provincial city paid, from the time of its incorporation into the Empire, a fixed tax in the nature of a tribute; but, since this tax was immutable, the devaluation of the coinage had ended by making it insignificant. In the 3rd century the state had substituted for it requisitions in kind. But this had proved no more than a palliative. Diocletian suppressed these local tributes and made the basis of assessment uniform throughout the Empire.

At the same time he modified the principle of budgeting in order to assure a balance.

Henceforward taxation was to be calculated in a manner to cover foreseen expenses. In order to be able to assess with certainty the total of receipts, the cities, after a general census of goods, were divided into small fiscal units, each representing the same revenue yield. It was thus enough to divide the total of expenses by the number of fiscal units to arrive at a constant budget balance, though it must rapidly have been realized that, where finances are concerned, the essential is not to fix the total of the taxes but to collect them, since the most authoritative state socialism cannot compensate for the inability of the taxpayers to pay.

The monetary system, till then based solely on gold, was reformed and, in order to ease the gold shortage, it was established on the basis of a fixed relation between gold and silver.

The Empire, standardized and simplified on these new foundations, made a further break with the past by abandoning Rome as its capital.

Rome, too distant from the northern frontiers, which were more and more threatened by the barbarians of central Europe, was abandoned for Milan. The Senate, although the Western Emperors in the 4th century maintained the tradition of having their constitutions ratified by it, was reduced to the status of a municipal council limited to administering the city and the university. Involved in the gradual decline of Italy as a whole,

Rome had in any case ceased to be the centre of the Empire. The Roman people, demoralized by the demagogic methods by which the Emperors had purchased its loyalty and which exhibited to the world the abject spectacle of its passion for the sadistic and bloody pageantry of the amphitheatre, was no more than a mass of parasites on the Imperial Treasury. The senatorial order, after having carried on for three centuries a baneful and sterile opposition, was no longer an active force, though it remained a danger to power established on absolutist monarchy. By leaving Rome, the Emperor freed himself both from the Roman proletariat and the Roman senators; at the same time he escaped from the tutelage of the Pretorian guards, who had for long claimed to exercise their influence upon the palace; they were finally to be abolished by Constantine in 312.

Transformed into a monarchy, the Empire broke the ancient bond that had united it with Rome, formerly the glorious capital of the Republic.

The creation of a new capital in the East, at Nicomedia, which was, some thirty years later, to be abandoned for Byzantium, the ancient Greek mistress of the Straits, was a fact no less important than the abandonment of Rome; it marked the incontestable primacy of the oriental world, now completely Hellenized, in the Empire. The greatest industrial centres—Alexandria, Antioch, Ephesus, Byzantium—were in the East. It was in the East, by far the richest part of the Empire, that the trade with India and China was concentrated. From the intellectual viewpoint, the East was still dominant. The law-schools of Beirut, Alexandria and Caesarea-of-Palestine exercised an influence over legal science the more decisive in that the school of Rome had lost its former importance. It was at Beirut that the Gregorian and Hermogenian codices were drawn up, summarizing the immense work carried out by Diocletian in both public and private law. Beirut also became the seat of the official archives, where all the acts of the Emperor of the East were registered.

Finally, an essential factor, it was also in the East—in Egypt, in Syria, in Asia Minor and in Greece—that Christianity, attracting all the adepts of the former pagan mysteries, had incontestably triumphed.

The work of Diocletian, despite the restoration that it effected, contained a mortal danger for the Empire. By dividing it into two parts, which differed in language as well as in economic and social structure, without a single central organ to unite them in a single whole, it threatened the whole imperial edifice with collapse. Only the elder Emperor, whose authority was preponderant, assured its cohesion. The unity of the Empire rested exclusively an the imperial prestige. That power must, therefore, be both authoritarian and mystical. It was bound to revert to the oriental conception of a monarchy by divine right and to be based on an imperial cult, as Aurelian had wished it to be.

The solar cult, now much influenced by Iranian Mithraism, which had extended its ascendancy over the Western provinces, was proclaimed the state religion. The two Emperors were described as "sons of gods and creators of gods"[1]—that is to say their power made them divine and adoption by them gave this divine character to the Caesars whom they adopted. Absolutism had therefore necessarily to be reinforced by religious unity within the Empire; in 303 Diocletian ordered all the Christian churches to be closed and the Holy Books confiscated. The most severe persecution known to the Empire then began.

Considering his work to have been completed, Diocletian abdicated in 305 and made Maximian abdicate also. They should have had as successors the two Caesars whom they had adopted, Galerius, a general of Dacian origin, for the East and Constantius Chlorus, a former Pretorian Prefect of Illyrian origin, for the West. But the son of Maximian at once claimed the throne. The system of adoption of the most worthy once more showed itself incapable of becoming the basis for succession in the Empire.

[1] Diocletian was presented as the descendant of Jupiter and Maximian as the descendant of Hercules, both solar gods.

BOOK XII

The Christian Empire and the Germanic Invasions (4th and 5th Centuries)

CHAPTER LII

JESUS AND THE ORIGINS OF CHRISTIANITY

JEWISH ORIGINS

OF all the peoples of the ancient world the Jews alone had accepted a stricter and stricter monotheism.

It seems that it was during their long sojourn in Egypt that monotheism assumed amongst them that purely spiritual character purged of all symbolism that it has possessed since the times of Moses. Perhaps the influence of the ideas of Amarna was not alien to it. But it is impossible to contest the direct and very deep influence of Egyptian thought on the Commandments of God which, after Sinai, became the basis of the Jewish moral code. Without renouncing the cult celebrated 'on the high places' the Jewish people, after settling in Palestine, little by little became united around the great national god, Jahvé (Jehovah.)

His character as a jealous God did not cease to be affirmed under the influence of the prophets. But the kings, from Solomon onward, while regarding Jahvé as the royal god and the Jewish God *par excellence*, tended for reasons of policy to admit, even in the temple, the religions of those peoples with whom they were trying to establish economic or political relations. The whole history of the Jews is dominated by the struggle between the kings, who tried to make Palestine a part of the great current of international life, and the prophets who, fearful of the contamination of foreign religious ideas, tried to keep it closed to all outside influences and from all commercial life, in order to keep the Jewish people isolated as a community of peasants around their exclusive God, Jahvé.

The monotheistic religion of the Jews did not, however, represent an advanced religious form. It conceived God as a master, and associated with his worship an exalted moral code based on the 'Tables of the Law' and restricted to the faithful of Jahvé alone; it did not believe in a life to come.

Solomon made Jerusalem a great international mart and introduced the first monarchical institutions, which were modelled on those of Egypt; Egyptian thinking thus brought into Judaea the first ideas of the Egyptian moral code of the time as taught by the moralists Ptah-hetep, Ani and Amenemope. The prophets reacted against the royal policy, but were not entirely deaf to the influence of the Egyptian moralists, though refusing to accept from them the idea of the after-life.

The afflictions which fell upon Palestine in the Assyrian and neo-Babylonian periods and which culminated in the capture of Samaria by Sargon in 722 BC and of Jerusalem by Nebuchadnezzar in 586 BC turned the thinking of the prophets into new channels. Politically annihilated, the Jewish people, the elect of God, could no longer conceive the triumph of Jahvé save on a purely spiritual plane. Isaiah for the first time broke the national structure of the religion of Israel and elevated it to the idea of a universal religion. Meanwhile, the prophets who looked for an explanation of the afflictions of their people found it, like Amos and Hosea, in the moral degradation of its upper classes, or like Jeremiah in its unfaithfulness to Jahvé and in its religious materialism. The Jewish religion, thenceforward, became receptive to the highest moral principles.

The exile was to bring the religious ideas of the Babylonians into still closer contact with the Jewish people and to put them in touch with Mazdaist influences, which were then spreading the moral and mystical ideas of Zoroaster, based on the antagonism between good and evil.

Jerusalem, restored by Cyrus, king of Persia, in 538 BC as a district of the satrapy of Damascus, was to be transformed according to the constitution imagined by Ezekiel into a small theocratic state ruled by a hereditary High Priest and a sacerdotal aristocracy. The cult of Jahvé which alone was official became obligatory under pain of death, and Judaea was governed by a clerical caste embalmed in a rigid national conformity.

For two centuries Jerusalem lived voluntarily isolated from the world under the rule of the Law, which was founded on the authority of Moses as shown in the Pentateuch, a composite miscellany of documents drawn up in the IXth and VIIIth centuries BC, and completed by Deuteronomy in 621 BC and by the sacerdotal code which dates from about 400 BC.

The conquest of Palestine by Alexander in 331 BC put an end to the isolation of Jerusalem. A pawn in the Hellenistic wars, Palestine was annexed to the Egypt of the Ptolemies (320 BC) and was subject to Egyptian influence. Then, in 200 BC, annexed to the Seleucid Empire by Antiochus III, Jerusalem became a Hebrew island in the midst of a country which was becoming more and more Hellenized. From then on, the influences of

Egypt and Hellenism met there and, incidentally, became increasingly interpenetrated. These influences were the more active in that, while Jerusalem was still the centre of the Jewish religion it no longer represented all the thinking of Israel. Since the capture of Jerusalem and Samaria the Jews had been scattered throughout the world. The exile had settled them in Mesopotamia and the greater number of them had remained there after the restoration of the Jewish state by Cyrus. Others had emigrated to Egypt with the prophet Jeremiah and under the Saite dynasty a Jewish community had been established at Elephantine. In the course of the Hellenistic wars a constant emigration, encouraged by a very high birth-rate, had driven the Jews throughout the whole eastern Mediterranean where, from the peasants that they had been in Palestine, they had become merchants and traders. The Ptolemies and the Seleucids encouraged them to settle in Alexandria and Antioch because of their intelligence.

The Jews of the *diaspora* became Hellenized and took part in the great international cultural movement. Soon it was no longer Jerusalem but Alexandria that was the centre of Jewish thought. In the beginning of the 3rd century BC the translation of the Bible into Greek (the Septuagint) was undertaken there. Jews travelled all over the known world. It was after a long voyage that Ben Sirah wrote, about 170 BC, the *Ecclesiasticus* permeated through and through by the moral ideas of Egypt. This was the period when Egyptian ideas were predominant throughout the whole Greco-Oriential maritime world in the mystery cults which spread the conceptions of the after-life and the judgment of souls by the gods, while, in the north of Nearer Asia, similar beliefs were introduced by Zoroastrianism.

Jerusalem too was affected by Hellenistic civilization and the Jewish people became divided into two parties; the nationalist party, conservative and fanatically Jahvist, and the Hellenistic party which, supported by the king of Antioch, was favourable to the currents of world thought. A terrible civil war resulted which became transformed, under the leadership of the Maccabees, into a war of independence (166 BC). It ended, in 142 BC, by the recognition of a kingdom of Jerusalem by the king of Antioch. As at the time of Solomon, the royal policy at once made Judaea emerge from her isolation and left her open to ideas from the outer world. But the eternal conflict began again between the party of the king, who however was then the High Priest, which was drawn onward by the current of cosmopolitanism, and the puritan party, supported by the scribes who wished to keep Palestine sheltered from the outside world. The war of independence led to an astonishingly creative period in Jewish thought. The book of Daniel, the first of the Apocalypses and all the literature associated with it—the Proverbs, the visions of Enoch &c.—which developed the theme of the Messianic destinies of Israel, all date from this time.

Though continuing to defend its monotheism fanatically, the Jewish people became receptive to the ideas of the times. Considerable borrowing has been noted in the Biblical writers, sometimes even word for word, from the thought, the moral code and the religious sentiment of Egypt. Belief in eternal life, in the judgment of souls represented by the Egyptian symbol of the weighing of the heart, belief in heaven and hell, and in angels, the conception of the dualism between good and evil, the idea of the Last Judgment and the resurrection of the dead taken from Mazdaism, and the announcement of the coming of the Messiah, were at that time accepted by Jewish thinkers and became essential features of Jewish teaching.

All the oriental, Egyptian and Greek mystical ideas met at the crossroads of Palestine; in the 1st century BC it was the greatest centre of religious syncretism in the eastern world.

The struggle was so intense between the royal party and the puritan party that the latter, in 64 BC, appealed to Pompey, who had returned victorious from the Mithridatic war, to put an end to the monarchy. Pompey intervened and Jerusalem, incorporated into the province of Syria, became once more, under its High Priests, a sacerdotal city. The puritan party sacrificed the prosperity and development of the country to its programme of conservatism.

The monarchy, suppressed by Pompey, was restored by Antony. In 37 BC Herod was granted the throne of Palestine, with the title of Ally of Rome. During his reign Jerusalem was again to become a great capital. Herod revived the splendours of Solomon. He built a sumptuous temple and surrounded himself with a cosmopolitan court. His kingdom extended to the Mediterranean and the Red Sea. The port of Caesarea which he founded soon became one of the main economic, intellectual and legal centres of the Roman Empire, and aimed at reviving the prosperity that Tyre had formerly enjoyed as a transit point to Central Asia and India. The economic renascence of Palestine afforded Herod considerable resources. In rivalry to Cleopatra he pursued an imperialist policy in Syria and declared himself the protector of Athens. His court, like that of Alexander, was one of the centres of international thought and its influence was the more widespread in that all the colonies of the *diaspora* had remained in touch with Jerusalem, paid tithes to it and accepted its authority.

Though faithful to the religion of Jahvé, Herod was not looked on favourably by the puritan party which obstinately supported the theocratic formula. Thus his death in 4 BC marked, as formerly that of Solomon, the dismemberment of his magnificent kingdom.

Judaea once more became a Roman province under a procurator who nominated the High Priest. But Rome granted to Jerusalem, as to all the colonies of the *diaspora*, complete religious autonomy and special privileges to the Jewish religion.

In Jerusalem the struggle between the political factions was at this time more intense than ever. The priestly and aristocratic class, which formed the Sadducean party, represented the conservative spirit in all its purity, refused to admit the imported beliefs in the immorality of the soul, the future life, the dualism between good and evil, but accepted the guardianship of Rome, relying on it for the strict maintenance of the social and doctrinal *status quo*. The Scribes, or Pharisees, formed the intellectual élite; they had adopted the ideas introduced in the IInd century on angels and demons, the resurrection of the dead and the advent of the Kingdom of God; but they were nationalists, and their extreme wing, consisting of the party of the Zealots, openly preached rebellion against Rome. From the moral point of view, they were divided; some professed the age-old ideas and weie, in particular, supporters of the right of a husband to repudiate his wife; others, drawn into the great individualist current of the times, adopted the Egyptian thesis of monogamy and the reciprocal fidelity of married couples.

The people, however, were carried away by mystical ideas mainly represented, since the beginning of the 1st century, by the sect of the Essenes. This sect was notable for its ascetic ideals. There had formerly been ascetics among the Jews from as early as the time of the Judges and the Essene sect was therefore founded on an ancient Jewish tradition. But it was permeated by Iranian ideas, which had perhaps come from Ephesus, and by the Pythagorean ideas which were then in vogue throughout the Greek lands, and the moral and mystical pietistic ideas which had triumphed in Egypt. While continuing to adhere to the Jewish law, the Essenes rejected the formalism of the cult and wished to attain eternal life by the practice of virtue and renunciation. They represented in Palestine the tendency which the Isiac and Dionysiac mysteries represented in the pagan cults. But their absolute monotheism freed them from all the claptrap that encumbered the pagan mysticism and bogged it down in a sort of magic; their spirituality, purged of all symbols, put them into direct contact with the idea of God; their purity and their asceticism permitted them to reach a moral height which surpassed that of any of the mysteries, even the Isiac. Cut off from this world's goods, they renounced private property for the benefit of the community to which they belonged, took their meals in common after prayer, and recommended sobriety, chastity, purity of morals, and meekness, and considered celibacy as a state superior to marriage; on the social plane, they considered all men to be equal and repudiated slavery.

Their religion admitted dualism between Good, represented by God, and Evil, which they assimilated to matter; they believed in angels and in the future life and made personal salvation the aim of their existence. Finally, they announced the imminent coming of the Messiah. The idea of the Messiah, which seems to have been expressed for the first time by Zoroaster, was then widespread throughout the East. In the Ist century the Assyro-Babylonians, then annexed to the Parthian Empire and won over to Mazdaist doctrines, announced the Messiah as a man-god born in a supernatural manner and who, having come into the world in order to save it, must rise again after his death. At Jerusalem, save among the priestly class which remained refractory, the Messianic idea had for long been accepted and had been preached by the prophets; a whole apocryphal literature was devoted to it. Daniel had prophesied his coming with the clouds of heaven. In the Ist century BC the Pharisees conceived the Messiah as a king; some taught that his reign would last a thousand years and would end with the Last Judgment, while others considered that his appearance would mark the end of the world and the advent of the Kingdom of God.

But the people awaited him in the semblance of one of those men of God preaching and practising good who, like John the Baptist, purified and initiated the faithful by the ceremony of baptism—similar to the rites of the Isiac and Hellenistic mysteries—and by calling on them to repent.

The Essenes, fervent adherents of the Messianic idea, did not conceive of the Messiah as did the Pharisees on the national, but on the universal, plane. With them, under the combined influence of all the mystical ideas of the times, Jewish thinking, made free and spiritual, was preparing to conquer the world.

JESUS

It was in a humble craftsman's household belonging, it seems, to Nazareth in the former kingdom of Israel—in that Galilee considered by Jerusalem as lost to orthodoxy—that towards the end of the reign of Herod there was born in the small and insignificant township of Bethlehem the Messiah so eagerly awaited.

After a sojourn in Egypt, caused according to tradition by a persecution by the anti-Messianic party—the Massacre of the Innocents—and about which we have no information, Jesus passed his boyhood obscurely, far from the strife of the parties and the schools, at Nazareth. Then, led like the prophets by the spirit of God, he had himself baptized in the waters of Jordan by John the Baptist, who preached repentance and the imminent coming of the Kingdom of Heaven. Jesus then retired to the wilderness where he experienced the temptation of the spirit of evil. After the imprisonment of St. John he returned to Galilee, to Capernaum on the shores of the Lake of Gennesareth, and, like John, he preached: 'Repent ye, for the Kingdom of Heaven is at hand'. Followed by a few fishermen, former disciples of John, he travelled throughout Galilee, teaching in the synagogues, announcing the Kingdom of Heaven and, like the ancient prophets, healing the sick.

After the Sermon on the Mount, his moral code was defined; blessed are the poor in spirit, the meek, the merciful, the peacemakers, those that weep and those that hunger and thirst after righteousness, for theirs is the Kingdom of Heaven.

Immortality of the soul, won not by sacrifices and the practices of the cult, but by renunciation, submission to the divine will, and charity; these became the foundation of Christian morals.

Certainly Jesus did not mean to be outside the law; he recommends its observance in all its precepts. But though admitting the temple offering, he pays no heed to sacrifice and all his teaching has a moral basis.

His moral code was not specifically Jewish, but universal. He made no distinction between men of differing nationality or even of differing religion, and preached that God would accept more favourably the good Samaritan than the hard-hearted Jew. As an individualist, he not only considered all men as equal before God, but also preached the equality of the sexes, demanded strict monogamy and conjugal fidelity, recommended the indissolubility of marriage and only allowed the repudiation of a wife for adultery.

The moral code of Jesus never tries to amend human institutions, which it accepts as an expression of man's justice; it goes beyond law, recommends the return of good for evil, and love of one's enemies. It is remarkable that the moral code of Jesus deals very little with the social problems so passionately discussed in the Hellenistic world of his times. Conduct towards others is summed up in two precepts which, however, embrace all the others: love one another, and do not do to another what you would not wish him to do to you. Virtue, for Jesus, was not a social matter, but one of conscience and, like prayer, was the nobler the more it was hidden.

Jesus, in fact, disdained material contingencies. Care for the morrow mattered little to him. In the midst of the mercantile civilization of his time he recalls men to the primacy of the spiritual by isolating it. In the midst of party struggles and civil wars he calls on man to listen not to the voice of authority but to that of God which he hears in the depths of his heart.

He replies to the world's violence with charity, to the loosing of passions by chastity. But he remains aloof from asceticism and thus avoids pessimism.

His thinking is like a balm; it possesses an infinite charm that comes from that deep inward feeling that leads, with angelic simplicity, to love. The moral code of Jesus, taken to its ultimate conclusions, is far from hate and far from formalism. It isolates the notion of the divine and purifies it from all that men have added to it of rules and formulae which conceal emptiness of spirit.

That is why he rejects all dogmatism. He does not observe the Sabbath, because the Sabbath is not observed by the priest in the temple and nature is the greatest of temples. The Temple at Jerusalem is nothing for him save a house of prayer. The authority of the priests, no matter how worthy of reverence, cannot override the authority of conscience; it is the practice of good and not dogma that makes religion.

The voice of Jesus, which only few men heard, was to find a tremendous response throughout the world.

It marked the culmination of that unwearying moral effort accomplished by men ever since it had first been made evident in Egypt, three thousand years before, in works of charity. This culmination was of irresistible power and of an infinite sweetness, since it was presented in a truly human guise and was addressed in a manner all could understand to individual consciences. It was not tied to any cult, did not refer to any earlier belief. Purged of all symbolism and even freed from all metaphysic, its vision of God was not obscured by any rites, by secret initiations or by learned dogmas, but made evident by love. It was offered to all men of good will whom it called to faith, hope and charity.

But the Jewish law demanded respect for dogma. The behaviour of Jesus seemed sacrilegious to the priests who ruled as sovereigns over the little theocracy of Jerusalem. So, according to the Law, the Sanhedrin sentenced him to death. Pilate, the Roman governor, had no authority in Jerusalem over religious matters; it was in vain that he advised the Elders to reprieve Jesus on the occasion of the Feast of the Passover; the law was applied in all its rigour and Jesus perished on the cross.

His martyrdom, crowning a life entirely devoted to peace and love, was to assure his triumph by revealing to men his Messianic and consequently divine character. The idea of God the Redeemer, which was the basis of all the pagan mysteries, was to bring to the Messiah and his doctrine of love the great mystical ecstasy which was astir in the world. A new era began with the poignant drama of Golgotha.

THE PROPAGATION OF CHRISTIANITY AND CHRISTIAN SYNCRETISM

While the preaching of Jesus set the crown on the far-reaching religious evolution that had been evident among the mass of the people in Palestine, the Jews of the *diaspora* devoted themselves to a great effort of proselytism. Philo of Alexandria, about AD 30, tried, by employing the methods of Egyptian symbolism, to correlate Jewish ideas with Greek philosophy. The Jewish preaching exercised an undoubted attraction; the Sabbath day of rest was adopted by almost all the cults, and some of the mysteries correlated Jahvé with Dionysus; but it aroused, on the other hand, a hostile reaction, above all among the Greeks who accused the Jews of atheism because they refused to admit the existence of the pagan gods. The monotheism of the Jews, which drove them to live in closed communities, laid them open to the charge of hating the human race, and their intransigence, which was the natural result of their belief in a single God, earned them the hatred of the pagans, amongst whom religious tolerance was then general.

In Rome, however, the influence of the Jews was considerable. In 37 Caligula created again for Agrippa, grandson of Herod the Great, the kingdom of Judaea, and Claudius in 44 restored its former frontiers. Since Egypt was now reduced to the status of a minor power under the suzerainty of the Emperors, Palestine should have been called upon to play, as a vassal kingdom and an ally of Rome, an important role. But on the death of Agrippa (44), Rome sent a Roman Procurator back to Caesarea, though leaving the government of Jerusalem to the High Priest.

The first act of the restored sacerdotal régime was to undertake a persecution of the Christians who formed a sect in Jerusalem without, however, separating from the Jewish church. The Christians, leaving Jerusalem, began to preach their doctrine throughout the world.

It was at this time that Paul appeared; he was a Pharisee of Palestinian origin, a tentmaker at Tarsus the former university city of the Seleucids, where the Peripatetic and Stoic schools had flourished for the last three centuries. Paul had had a rabbinical education at Jerusalem and a Hellenic one at Tarsus. While on his way to Damascus to arrest some Christians sentenced by the Sanhedrin he was converted to the teachings of Jesus. He was to become the great apostle of the new sect. By rejecting circumcision—which had always been repugnant to the Greeks—and the dietary taboos, he freed Christianity from its specifically Jewish features and made it possible for it to play a universal role. At Antioch, the ancient Seleucid capital, the first Christian community among the Gentiles was founded and there the name of 'Christians' was first used. Other communities followed, in Cyprus, in Asia Minor and at Salonica. Athens, which remained the centre of Greek philosophy, received Paul with respect but remained unconvinced. At Corinth, on the contrary, which was very much under the influence of the Egypto-Oriental mysteries, a Church was formed. An important community was created at Ephesus, in that centre of mysticism and cosmopolitanism where, since the settlement of the Iranian Magi by Darius, an ascetic movement had existed which had perhaps been the origin of the sect of the Essenes in Palestine.

It was therefore in the great cosmopolitan and trading cities of the Hellenized East, so deeply permeated by the Isiac mysticism, that Christianity found enthusiastic supporters among the pagans already deeply affected by the Jewish preaching of the *diaspora*. From Antioch and Ephesus, Christianity spread rapidly in Phrygia where the mysteries of Attis (or Men) had prepared the people for the idea of a Redeemer-God; it also reached Edessa, where the king was the first sovereign to be converted, and upper Mesopotamia, where Zoroastrianism had already created a favourable atmosphere. Tradition has it that the Apostle Thomas, following the trade-route, travelled as far as the Parthian kingdom and perhaps even India, where he is said to have converted, in the upper Ganges region, Prince Mathoura, satrap of the Sacian kings who were at this time founding a powerful empire in Central Asia and India.

Thanks to the Jewish *diaspora*, the Christian teaching spread in a few years over all the eastern and central Mediterranean. The Christians had not yet broken away from the synagogue, despite the persecutions to which they had been subjected in Palestine; and Jewish proselytism was at first confused with Christian preaching.

At Rome, where a Christian community had been founded, there appeared, as at Alexandria, a strong anti-Semitic movement which was hostile to both Jews and Christians, both of whom were regarded as atheists and enemies of the human race.

After the great fire which devastated Rome in AD 64 during the reign of Nero the first persecution broke out, in the course of which the apostles Peter and Paul perished. A similar hostility between Jews and Greeks was the cause of a riot at Caesarea in 66 which, owing to the activities of the extremist party of the Zealots, degenerated into a general rising against the Romans; throughout Palestine Romans and Greeks were pitilessly massacred, and a new war of independence began. The Jews of Mesopotamia came to the aid of Jerusalem, which was soon besieged by a Roman army while, within the walls, a terrible civil conflict was unleashed between the nationalists and the aristocrats who favoured Rome. In 70 the city was taken and burnt. The population was massacred, crucified, sent to forced labour in the mines of Egypt, or sold into slavery throughout the Empire. The Jewish colonies lost their privileges and the Jews were reduced to the status of *dediticii*, subjects of the lowest class, ranked with the lowest category of freedmen.

The terrible suppression of the revolt, the first great reaction of paganism against Judaeo-Christian monotheism, marked the end of Jewish proselytism. The communities of the *diaspora*, after everywhere ransoming the Jews sold into slavery in order to restore them to liberty, withdrew into themselves, piously conserving the rigorous monotheism for which their people had sacrificed all.

But even after the destruction of Jerusalem, the *diaspora* still remained a great centre of Jewish thought. Flavius Josephus, with magnificent courage, undertook to explain to the Greeks the standpoint of his people in his *History of the Jewish War*, written in Greek. His *Jewish Antiquities*, a polemic against the anti-Semites, introduced Jewish monotheism into universal literature and thus helped to pave the way to Christianity. In 95 some members of the Imperial family were executed by Domitian for having adhered to 'the Jewish superstition'.

While the ruin of Jerusalem checked the Jewish proselytism and restored to Judaism, despite the efforts of Flavius Josephus, its character as a national religion, Christianity had already laid the foundations of its first institutions, and Paul, in his letters to the Christian communities, had fixed the mystic doctrine of Christianity; by his voluntary death and by his resurrection, the Christ, who had come into the world to save mankind, had redeemed the human race from original sin, provoked by the sin of Adam. The infinity of human weakness was proclaimed in contrast to the omnipotence of God.

About the year 70 the Gospels of Matthew and Mark were written in Greek, and Luke, a Hellenized doctor of Antioch, composed the Third Gospel and the Acts of the Apostles which are its sequel. About 100 the Gospel according to St. John was published, also in Greek, perhaps based on an older version. The doctrine of the Trinity, the basis of Christianity, began to take form. Jesus appeared in it as the Son of God and his divinity was added to that of Jahvé and the Holy Spirit—the 'Breath of God' known to the Old Testament—thus outlining the idea of a God in three persons, the Father, the Son and the Holy Spirit. But this affirmation was still without any philosophical explanation.

While the doctrine was being outlined, the communities were becoming organized. In his *Epistle to the Corinthians* Paul begins to replace the itinerant preachers by a resident and organized clergy and orders the Christians to settle their disputes among themselves, like the Jews of the *diaspora*, and puts at their head elders, *episcopoi* or *presbuteroi*, assisted by deacons, deaconesses and widows.

Under Domitian, despite the persecutions (93–95), the Christians possessed, in addition to the local communities, a general organization. Clement, in the name of the Roman community, had already intervened in an internal dispute which was dividing the Church of Corinth.

At the same time as the extension of Christianity, paganism too had evolved and had grown closer to it. The Stoic moral code of Epictetus and Marcus Aurelius cannot be distinguished in fundamental principles, save that it did not share it humility, from the Christian moral code. Democratic ideas, the result of natural law, corresponded to the ideas of human equality professed by the Christians.

The conquest of the western provinces by Mithraism spread there the idea of the redemption of men by a Saviour-God.

In the East, the whole world believed in eternal life and in the Kingdom of God. The idea of a divinity, conceived as an abstract and omnipotent being, both creator and saviour, was the basis of the solar cult of Serapis which had become an official religion of the Empire. The conception of a divine being, of whom the Egyptians had made a trinity composed of the divine spirit diffused throughout the world, of the creative consciousness and of the saviour, had become implanted wherever the Isiac mysteries had penetrated. The cult of Isis, 'Lady of perpetual succour', mother of the infant-god Horus (called Harpocrates by the Greeks), victor over Seth the spirit of evil, had caught the imagination of the masses. The processions of 'the navigation of Isis' (March 5th) in her search for the body of Osiris, and of the 'invention of the Goddess' (in autumn), who found her husband killed and dismembered by Seth, the mysteries representing the death and resurrection of Osiris celebrated according to the Egyptian rites, and the *attidea* (22nd-24th March), when the people of Rome enthusiastically fêted the resurrection of the Syrian god Attis, united immense crowds in great manifestations of collective piety.

All the cults were becoming merged. 'We do not believe,' wrote Plutarch, 'that the Gods are different in each nation.'

Theological discussions began among the adherents of Serapis and Isis as to whether Horus, the son of Osiris, was inferior to his father or if he had existed, like him, from all eternity.

Judaism had not benefited from this deep evolution of paganism since its abstract monotheism could not merge with the emotional mysticism of the mysteries. Christianity, on the other hand, by announcing the glad news of the coming of the Messiah, dead and risen from the dead, appealed to the feelings of the masses who flocked to him simply because he was so attractively different from the symbolic divinities of the mysteries. He was a God who had been one of the people, dead on the cross like a slave out of love for men. The Gospels, filled with tenderness, offered to their piety the love of a child-God, of a Virgin Mother, of a resurrected Saviour. Christianity united in a single cult the great creator-god and the Divine Redeemer; it heralded the triumph of good over evil, the victory of God over Satan; and its moral code, which paid no heed to social differences and preached the pacifism for which the Empire was thirsting, corresponded to all the trends of the times. It satisfied the aspirations of the solar cult devoted to Serapis, creator-god and redeemer, and of Mazdaism, which awaited the advent of good triumphant over evil, as well as those of the countless mystery cults which looked towards the life to come. The angels gave satisfaction to the pantheist faith that looked for the presence of God in all things. The moral code of the Gospels crowned the moral ideas that had originated in Egypt and Iran. The Messiah, announced by Zoroaster, by the Sibyls, by the Jewish prophets, had at last been granted to men. And in the midst of the crises which were convulsing the world the proclamation of the Kingdom of God gave a supreme hope to men. The slaves and the humble found in Christian equality their moral liberation and their rehabilitation. By a few simple, human and tender ideas, stripped of archaic symbols, confused doctrines and obscure rites, and permeated with love, Christianity brought the answer to consciences afflicted by the moral and social crisis and gave them hope after the century of blood and iron that humanity had experienced at the time of the birth of Jesus.

The Greek language, in which Christianity was expressed, made it accessible to all.

But in order to conquer the world Christianity had to impose its monotheism. Irremediably ranged against pantheism, it had to reject the worship of the Emperor. The first Emperors had exempted the Jews from the observance of this cult. But the evolution of power towards absolutism by divine right under the Flavians made inevitable a clash between the Imperial thesis and the Christian doctrines. The recalcitrant Christians seemed to be rebels, enemies of the Empire. The Jewish war, ending with the capture of Jerusalem, increased the official reaction against Christianity. Imperial edicts declared the very name of Christian to be a crime.

The advent of the Antonines inaugurated a liberal policy; the edicts against the Christians were not annulled, but only the public profession of Christianity was forbidden.

The Christians, however, defended themselves, and applied to the Emperor in order to justify their faith. In 180 a Christian school was opened at Alexandria which was to become a rival to the *Museum*. Thenceforward, the attraction of Christianity was felt not only among the masses but also among the intellectual élite, and the two most powerful philosophical movements of the time, Stoicism and Platonism, converged on the new doctrine.

Meanwhile Christianity continued its task of internal organization. The *Doctrine of the Twelve Apostles*, written in Greek about AD 80, organized the cult, giving rules for baptism, communion, fasting and prayer. Theology was being formed. Justin, who had been born in Samaria, began to philosophize about the Trinity. The Assyrian Tatian, the Athenians Aristides and Athenagoras, Theophilus of Antioch and Irenaeus of Smyrna, who was to become Bishop of Lyon, built up a system of orthodox Christian thought in opposition to the ancient philosophy and to counter the heresies which tried to explain dogma by philosophy. It was in Egypt, in Asia Minor and at Rome that heresies first appeared among the syncretists. Gnosticism tried to find in the Gospels and the Old Testament a verification of the philosophical ideas of the time; pessimism, which showed itself in the *gnosis* by the dualism between spirit and matter, seemed inspired by Buddhist influences probably brought from India, with which Alexandria was then in constant trade relations. It was at Carthage that the first great Latin voice was raised in defence of the new faith. The Numidian Tertullian (150–230), who had been brought up in the Roman Stoic doctrine, preached passionately a moral code so inflexible that it led him into heresy. None the less, he exercised a decisive influence on the Church.

Stoic with Tertullian, Christianity remained Jewish in the apocalyptic literature provoked by the persecutions of Domitian. The Apocalypse of St John, conceived in Hebrew under the inspiration of the prophets Ezekiel and Zachariah, but written in Greek, inaugurated a genre which expressed both the hope and the terror caused by the persecutions, and announced the end of the world which was to see the triumph of Christ. In contrast to these mystical extravagances St Clement, who appeared at the end of the 2nd century as head of the Christian school at Alexandria, introduced into Christianity, with his Athenian love of reason, Platonic thinking. A pupil of the most famous schools of Greece, Syria, Italy, Palestine and Egypt, permeated through and through with Greek philosophy and oriental mysticism, he regarded Christianity as the culmination of ancient thought and claimed that Hellenistic reason and morals derived from the same divine revelation as the religion of Jesus.

Christianity thus became the centre of the syncretism of the thought of the ancient world.

It thus cut itself off sharply from Judaism and remained untouched by the excesses of Greek anti-Semitism which led to such terrible massacres at Alexandria and the dreadful repression of the last Jewish revolt in 132–136, caused, it is said, by the construction of a pagan temple in Jerusalem by order of Hadrian. Access to Jerusalem was forbidden to the Jews under pain of death. The Jews, martyrs of their purely spiritual monotheism—which was not understood by the mystics who were attracted by the humanized monotheism of the Christians—and treated as atheists by the pagans and as rebels by the Emperor, began their painful exile.

Christianity, on the other hand, despite persecution, went on to a rapid triumph in the 2nd century. But this triumph, because of the diversity of those whom it attracted, divided the new religion into sects which quarrelled amongst themselves under the influence of earlier religious ideas. Thus a real polemical literature developed which thundered against the heresies. But despite all these divisions the *Acts of the Martyrs*, which were handed on from one church to another, exercised an irresistible attraction for the faithful who became inflamed by their example. They were certainly one of the main factors which helped the Church, in its heroic period, to preserve its unity.

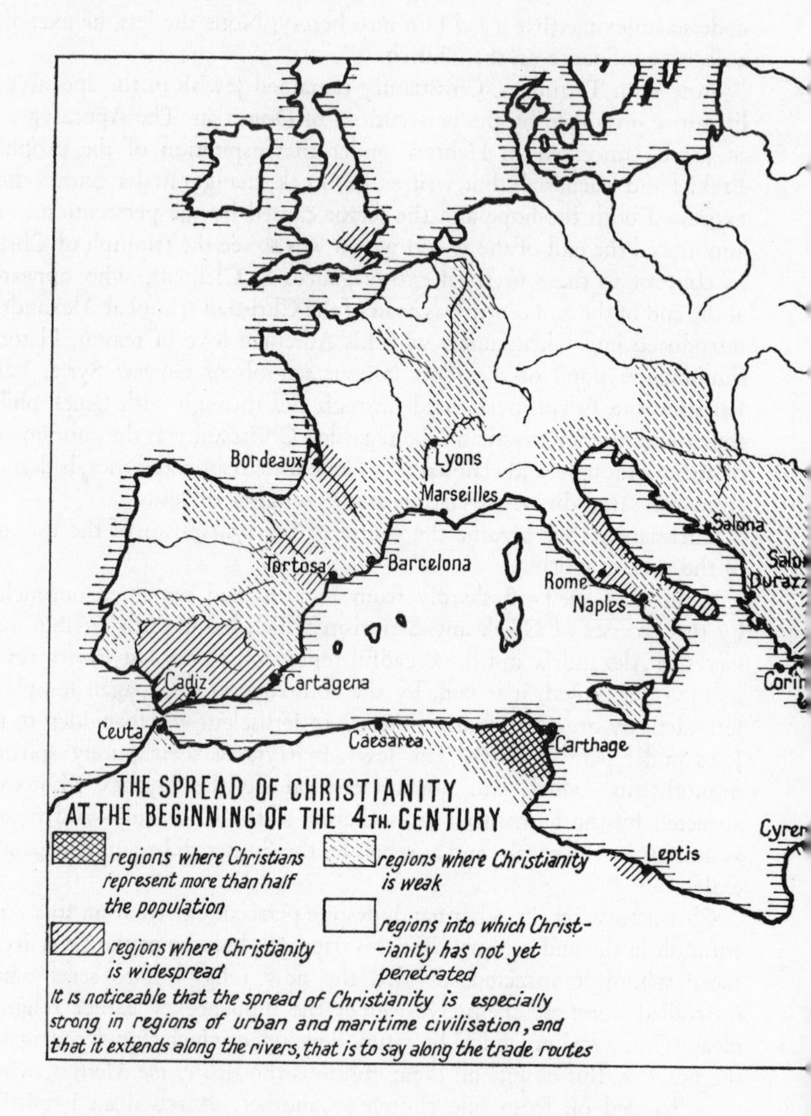

THE PERIOD OF REORGANIZATION IN THE CHURCH

The advent of the Severi meant strong centralization in religious as well as political affairs. Septimius Severus, reverting to the conception of monarchy by divine right, based his restoration of order on an anti-liberal and authoritarian policy; anything is preferable to disorder, and

Map No. 27

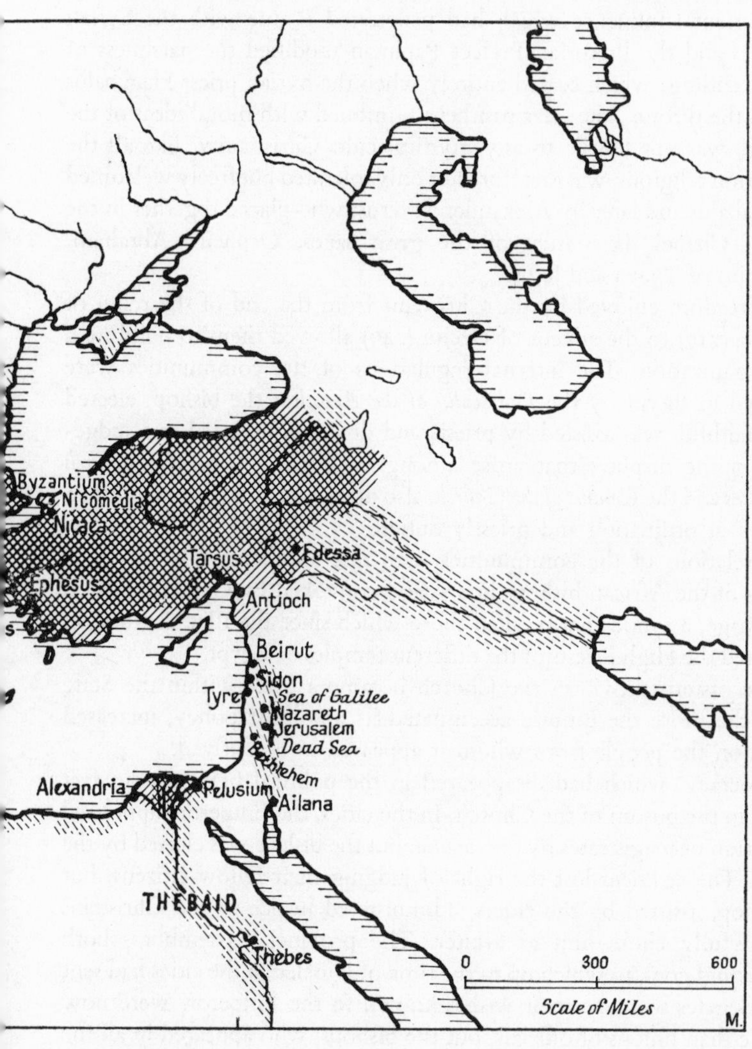

authority must be uncontested in all fields. All dissidents must be crushed. The logical consequence was a revival of the persecution of the Christians.

Caracalla, in his constitution which granted universal rights of citizenship (212), intimated his desire to see all men united in a single religion, that of the great god Serapis, in whom were syncretized Zeus, Jupiter, Apollo, Ammon, Osiris, Baal and Mithras. A paganism advancing towards a pantheist monotheism was opposed to Christian monotheism.

The oriental influence which had penetrated Rome with the Syrian princesses and the Pretorian Prefect Papinian modified the harshness of the persecutions, which ceased entirely when the Syrian priest Elagabalus came to the throne. The solar pantheism, imbued with moral ideas of the after-life, was not hostile to any mystical cult. Christianity, like all the redemption religions, was therefore not only tolerated but freely welcomed by Elagabalus and later by Alexander Severus, who placed together in the Imperial Chapel the statues of the great sages, Orpheus, Abraham, Apollonius of Tyana and Jesus.

The freedom enjoyed by the Christians from the end of the reign of Caracalla (217) to the advent of Decius (249) allowed them to build up a solid organization. The internal regulations of the communities were organized in Egypt by the *Didascalia of the Apostles*; the bishop, elected by the faithful, was assisted by priests and deacons; he acted as a judge-arbiter in the disputes that arose among his parishioners. The *Church Ordinances* and the *Canons of the Church*, also drawn up in Egypt, established the rules of ordination and priestly duties.

The relations of the communities with one another led in 216 to a meeting of the African bishops in a synod convoked by Cyprian, bishop of Carthage, a synod that recalled those which since the IIIrd century BC had united the High Priests of the different temples of Egypt.

In the eastern provinces the Church became a State within the State which, the more the Empire accentuated its absolutist policy, increased its hold on the people from whom it appeared to be derived.

Democracy, which had disappeared in the political field, was in fact revived in the bosom of the Church. In the cities, the Emperor suppressed the election of magistrates by the *comitia*, but the bishop was elected by the faithful. The *decurions* lost the right of judging their fellow-citizens, but the bishop, assisted by the elders, administered justice to the Christians who lawfully chose him as arbiter. The provincial assemblies, both religious and civil, to which up to the time of Diocletian the cities had sent their delegates to make their wishes known to the Emperor, were now no more than unions of officials, but the bishops, who appeared in all the cities as the elected representatives of the people, were united in synods which were to play a leading role in the life of the Empire.

Excluded from political life, the people had no longer any interest in the state, which more and more appeared to them as an oppressive and pitiless tax-collector, and turned to the Church. The election of a bishop became, in the cities, the mainspring of municipal life, so much so that it sometimes led to serious rioting. At Rome, the Christian community was so ardent in its beliefs that it became divided into parties according to differing doctrinal trends. Thus for example the dissidents, after violent riots, protested against the election of the bishop Calixtus (217–222) and elected an anti-bishop Hippolytus, the theologian who had brought the teachings of the Alexandrian catechists to the capital.

Basing its organization on that of the liberal Empire, the Church built up a structure which made it a considerable temporal power.

While the Empire was crushing the individual by its state-socialist theories the Church, relying entirely on individual conscience, made itself the champion of human personality, of individualism.

As it became transformed into a power which originated in the people itself, the Church continued to elaborate its doctrine and took its place as a great intellectual force which absorbed and revived ancient thought. The rapprochement which had already been outlined on the Jewish side by Philo and on the Christian side by Clement became even more evident among the savants of the 3rd century. At Alexandria a close parallelism appeared between the doctrines professed by the pagans and by the Christians. Origen, born of Christian parents in 185, the disciple and successor of Clement as head of the Alexandrian school, gave an encyclopaedic character to his teaching which combined Christian doctrine with Hellenistic philosophy. In his teaching, exegesis took on a scientific and philosophical character; he commented on Biblical texts, giving them, according to the traditions of Egyptian theology, both a material and an allegorical sense. In order to demonstrate the Christian verities, he appealed as much to reason as to faith. Continuing along this path he was to be condemned as a heretic (231), but his influence persisted in Alexandria with Bishop Dionysus the Great, and spread throughout the East by the teaching he was to give at Caesarea and at Tyre.

The symbolic method of Origen was broken down at Antioch where a school of literal exegesis was founded. But it too was not able to avoid heresy.

Certain propositions of the Bishop of Antioch, Paul of Samosata, were to pave the way to the heresy of Arius of Alexandria, the trinitarian heresy *par excellence*. The Christian belief in God the Father, God the Son and God the Holy Spirit found its theological explanation in the 2nd and 3rd centuries in the teaching of Theophilus of Antioch, Origen and Tertullian; God is one, because the Divine Nature is one; God the Father, by thought, is made evident in God the Son, that is to say that the Son is the consciousness, the *logos*, of the Father; the Holy Spirit, which proceeds from the Father, is 'the life-giving Spirit of which the Prophets have spoken'.[1]

From the 2nd century the heresies, under the influence of philosophy or of Jewish or pagan religious ideas, provided differing explanations; some, by presenting the Trinity as a single God of whom the three persons would be purely nominal aspects, reverted to the rigorous monotheism of the Jews; others, by separating the three persons or by subordinating one to another, reverted to polytheist conceptions. The upholders of Arianism were among the partisans of this thesis and were those who defended it with the greatest skill and tenacity; they were deeply to trouble the Church throughout the whole of the 4th century. The Councils of Nicaea in 325 and Constantinople in 381 condemned both these heresies. The fact that the Goths and the Vandals were converted at this time explains why they were supporters of Arianism, a historical fact that was to have the most serious consequences at the time of the barbarian invasions.

By contrast to this great spiritual movement that was being felt in the Church, paganism seemed incapable of producing anything except romances—that of *Daphnis and Chloe* had a great vogue—or works of historical erudition, like those of Dio Cassius, Herodian or Diogenes Laertes, the historian of the ancient philosophers.

It was left to an Egyptian of Lycopolis to give to expiring pagan thought a fresh force drawn from the inheritance of Egyptian mysticism. A student at Alexandria, Plotinus (204–270) had been a pupil of the Platonist Sakkas and the Christian Origen. His work, which borrowed its name, the *Enneads*, from the ancient heliopolitan theology, was immense. It studied the world, the moral code, the soul, reason and the nature of Being. Cut off from all material preoccupations, Plotinus saw reality only in spiritual life. Like Plato, he wished to free the soul from the body; like the Egyptian theologians, he tried to attain to God in order to live in Him. To do this, he immersed himself in the exclusive love of God and demanded revelation of the truth through ecstasy. By its contact with Egyptian mysticism, Platonism, with Plotinus and even more with his disciple Porphyry, became a religion.

Christianity had its Holy Book, the Bible. Porphyry found the basis of Neo-Platonic revelation in the ancient oracles. His deep religious feeling, his exalted spirituality, his moral code of charity and renunciation,

[1] St Augustine, defining the theology of the Trinity, was later to consider that the Son proceeds from the Father by intelligence and that the Holy Spirit proceeds from the will of the Father and the Son.

made of this reviver of paganism a Christian who refused to become one.

The ancient world, thenceforward, was carried along by a single mystical current. Christianity and paganism were now only the expression of the same moral ideal. The advent of a universal religion, so desired by the Emperors, was at hand. But it needed the terrible crisis of the 3rd century to make triumphant Christianity, laden with all the religious thought and the moral conceptions of earlier centuries, the sole religion of the Empire.

CHAPTER LIII

CONSTANTINE AND THE TRIUMPH OF THE CHURCH

HEREDITARY MONARCHY

DURING the struggle which rent the Empire after the abdication of Diocletian, Constantine, relying on the antipathy that the religious persecutions had aroused on all sides and understanding the dynamic force of the new religion, turned to Christianity. In 313, by an ordinance promulgated at Milan, he proclaimed freedom of worship for the Christians. At the same time he proclaimed himself the protector of the Church, presided at its Councils and intervened to calm the disputes which arose among the Christians. In 324, when Constantine triumphed, Christianity triumphed with him.

Once he was master of the Empire, Constantine continued the policy of Diocletian. But he substituted for the succession of the most worthy the principle of hereditary monarchy which was to be instituted by the accession of his sons, Constantius and Constans, as Emperors of the East and West.

In the reign of Constantine, Christianity became the religion of the Emperor. Paganism, however, was not proscribed. On the contrary, equality was rigorously maintained between the Christian and the pagan cults. The Emperor, Protector of the Church, continued, by retaining the title of Pontifex Maximus, to be head of the pagan priesthood. This title was only to be abandoned at the end of the 4th century when, in 380, Christianity was to become the sole religion of the state.

CHRISTIANITY THE STATE RELIGION

The adoption of Christianity did not bring any change in the conception of power. The Emperor ceased to be considered as a god, but his authority remained no less divine and the rites of adoration in his honour remained unchanged. The idea of power by divine right was introduced into Christianity. The Empire was to add it to Christian doctrine, which had till then developed aloof from all temporal authority. The fact that Christianity had been adopted by the Empire as its official religion at a time when the monarchical conception of the king-god was triumphant meant that this theory was included in the first forms of Christian public law, which were directly related to the theory of power formerly drawn up by Egyptian theology. It was to mean fresh power for Christianity. Having come from the people, it had hitherto been constituted outside the secular power and even in opposition to it. Now that it had become the official religion, it was to appear as the foundation and sanction of the monarchy.

Paganism, broken into divergent cults and mysteries, did not form a single and organized force. Christianity was, on the contrary, by definition, a single and undivided Church. Its unity was to facilitate its introduction into the structure of the state. As formerly in Egypt, there was henceforth to be in the Empire a religious administration alongside the civil administration. But—and this was a considerable innovation—the religious authority remained completely separate from the civil authority. The only link between them was the Emperor.

The Church thenceforth became a state administration; it was merged into the structure of the Empire as reorganized by Diocletian.

There was a bishop in every city and a metropolitan in each province. But while the governors of the provinces were officials nominated by the Emperor, the bishops and metropolitans preserved the character that the Church had given them of prelates elected by the faithful. The governors were chiefs imposed from above, the bishops pastors chosen by the people. Though citizens, the Christians were primarily the faithful of the Church, which immediately took precedence over the civil powers.

The Empire took over the provincial synods of the bishops as a regular institution precisely at the moment when the former provincial assemblies had lost all contact with the people. The bishops thus became the real representatives of the cities. To keep the Church under control the Emperor instituted, above the provincial synods, oecumenical councils where, in principle, all the bishops of the Empire met under his presidency. A new power appeared whose members, enjoying a sacred prestige, were not appointed by the Emperor but by the whole of the population, by the community of the faithful, without distinction of class or census. Intended as instruments of absolutism,[1] the oecumenical councils introduced into

[1] Like the synods created in Egypt by the Ptolemies in the IIIrd century BC.

the Empire the principle of representative power on which the Church had been formed in the cities. Its very name, *ecclesia*, which had meant in Athens the assembly of the citizens, was the affirmation that it was nothing other than the total of the faithful. By introducing the Church into the structure of the State, at the very moment when the latter was taking the form of a state-socialist and totalitarian monarchy, the Emperor himself caused the rise, against the imperial power, of a new force independent of himself and originating in the people, from which he was to ask for the legitimacy that the Roman institutions had not been able to give him.

The Church alone, by the unity—at least in theory—of its doctrine and by its monotheism, was to take its place as the true founder of a hereditary monarchy which, by claiming to hold its power from God, was able to justify its absolutism by a universally accepted doctrine.

But absolutism, by looking for support in the Church, at the same time imposed a restraint upon itself. The Emperor was able to behave as the master of the Church, but the Church in reply was able to impose its discipline upon him since, though the Church could live without the Empire, the Empire, henceforward, could not be conceived without the Church.

THE CHURCH CREATES A NEW PUBLIC LAW

Once it had been promoted to become a service of the state, the Church asserted itself as an autonomous force. The Oecumenical Council of Nicaea, held under the presidency of Constantine in 325, officially assumed supreme jurisdiction in doctrinal matters by condemning the heresy of Arius, and organizing an executive power by conferring primacy on the bishops of Rome, Alexandria and Antioch, the ancient and still revered capitals of the Roman, Egyptian and Seleucid Empires. In 381 the Council of Constantinople, while granting precedence to the Bishop of Constantinople over those of Alexandria and Antioch, recognized the primacy of the Roman Pope. Thus the Church created, within the structure of an absolutist Empire, an autonomous monarchical constitution.[1]

It is very curious to note that the Church achieved exactly the organization of power that had been preached by the Stoics since the time of

[1] The primacy of the Bishop of Rome, who like the Bishop of Alexandria had the title of Pope, was still only doctrinal. After the Council of Nicaea (325) the Pope of Rome had to approve the doctrinal decisions of the Councils. In the second half of the fifth century the Bishops of Constantinople, Alexandria and Antioch held the title of Patriach. The Patriarchs, like the Pope of Rome, ordained the metropolitans and bishops of their territories and held powers of jurisdiction over them.

Seneca. Democratic in the recruitment of the clergy and especially of the bishops, aristocratic in the manner in which it conferred on them rights of legislation and administration, monarchical in its hierarchy which gave precedence to the Bishop of Rome, it avoided, on the other hand, thanks to the celibacy of the bishops, the rule of heredity. It achieved the formation of an aristocracy, which could not become transformed into an oligarchy since, having originated in the people, it was constantly being renewed, and a monarchy which, since it was not subject to dynastic necessities, avoided autocratic absolutism. Furthermore, the leaders of the Church, even though they were elected by the people, did not exercise their power in the name of the people who had elected them, but in that of God himself; their power was both clothed in the majesty conferred on them by their sacred calling and subject to the highest of responsibilities, which they had assumed before God. The rules of power were, for them, merged with those of private morality. A fresh element had found its way into public law.

In its temporal organization, the Church thus seemed to have combined in a perfectly coherent whole the elective and representative principles, as they had been conceived in the Greek cities; government by an aristocracy of morals, as had been proposed by the Pythagoreans; a monarchy of the most worthy, as desired by the Stoics; and the power by divine right which, for more than thirty centuries, had given an uncontested legitimacy to the Egyptian Pharaohs.

Even as Christian morality represented the culmination of Greco-oriental thought, so the public law upon which the Church was built, and whence was to emerge in the course of centuries all the principles of government of the European peoples, was revealed as a syncretism of all the theories of power evolved in the ancient world.

THE BEGINNINGS OF CANON LAW

The abandonment of Rome by the Emperors of the West, who were to reside for most of the time at Milan and, in the 5th century, at Ravenna, handed over the ancient capital of the Empire, with all the prestige still associated with its name, to the 'Pope'.

A new capital thus appeared in the Empire, the capital of the Church, Rome, seat of the Premier Bishop of Christianity. Invested with powers which transcended strictly religious limits, the Church was rapidly endowed with institutions which separated it more and more from the authority of the Emperor. It was to elaborate them within the framework of the Empire, making use of the means that the Empire placed at its disposal, but without letting itself become absorbed.

Equating the bishops and the civil governors, Constantine recognized their right of disciplinary jurisdiction over the clergy, and by accepting the custom that had grown up in the Christian communities he conceded them powers of arbitration among the faithful. Thus endowed with powers of jurisdiction the clergy was transformed into a privileged class.

By conferring on the bishops the properties confiscated from the pagan temples the Emperor made the Church the great economic power of the time.

In order to possess all the attributes of an autonomous government, it only remained for the Church to have its independent legislative power recognized. This took place in the 4th century.

In 314 the Council of Ancyra confirmed the right of the Church to lesiglate in its own affairs, as it had already been doing even before it was officially recognized, by defining the effects of the most serious of religious penalties—excommunication. About 320 the Council of Neo-Caesarea established rules of entry to the deaconate and in 341 the Council of Antioch laid down the legal status of the episcopate and the properties of the Church. These rules, accepted by the Emperor, became an integral part of the public law of the Empire.

The clergy, henceforth, formed an entirely separate class, not only because it was devoted to religion alone, but also because it lived under its own laws.

The Church thus broke the legal unity of the Empire. Among the new units which were constituted it became the most powerful until in the end it asserted itself over all the others.

THE SUCCESSORS OF CONSTANTINE AND THE PAGAN REACTION OF JULIAN

The installation of a hereditary monarchy was not to take place without a crisis. The tradition was not yet sufficiently established to prevent a dynastic struggle breaking out on the death of Constantine in 337 between the Emperor's sons and the other members of the imperial family. After a massacre of almost all the latter, it ended in a division of the Empire between the sons of Constantine, Constantius who received the East and Constans the West.

The adoption of Christianity as the state religion was also to cause serious disorders by bringing the doctrinal quarrels which passionately divided the Christians into the political field.

The heresy of Arianism, already condemned in 325, revived and threatened to destroy Christian unity. Influenced by the rationalism and polytheism of the ancient Greek philosophies, Arianism became widely accepted in the East.[1] The Emperor Constantius declared himself in favour of it, whereas Constans with the whole of the Western Church supported the orthodox creed.

The religious war which seemed about to break out between the two brothers was only avoided by inciting a common hatred among all Christians. In 346 persecution, changing sides, was organized against the pagans. Now that it had triumphed, the Church refused to the pagans the boon of toleration which it had demanded for itself after 313. The temples were sacked; but the pagan religion, however, was not proscribed.[2]

United to the temporal power, the Church adopted its weaknesses. Transformed into an economic force, it became diverted from its exclusively divine mission and, by accepting the policy of persecution against which it had previously revolted with such magnanimity, denied its magnificent doctrine of love.

The privileges and the wealth which it had been granted made it subject to human passions; it gently slid into the groove of tradition, filled with blood and tears, and thus found itself involved in the political struggle.

The death of Constans rekindled the civil war. Constantius ended by extending his rule over the West and thus for a moment re-established the unity of the Empire (353).

In order to avert wars of succession he adopted as Caesar, that is to say as heir to the throne, his cousin Julian (355).

Julian was a mystic; with a tendency to piety, he had at first wanted to enter holy orders, but the persecutions undertaken against the pagans and the heretics, the intolerance displayed by the Church, alienated him from Christianity. He turned to philosophy and became a fervent neoplatonist, a disciple of Plotinus and Porphyry, whose doctrines, under the influence of Iamblichus, assumed more and more the nature of a mystical religion.

After victorious wars in Gaul, where he drove back fresh invasions of Franks and Alamanni, he threw off the mask, allowed himself to be pro-

[1] This trinitarian heresy, by considering the Son as inferior to the Father, gives a distinct personality to each of the three persons of the Trinity, thus threatening monotheism.

[2] This was not to take place until 392; and it was only under Justinian that, in 529, the fact of being a pagan became punishable by death.

claimed Emperor by his troops (360) and declared himself the restorer of paganism and tolerance.

Christianity was abandoned as the official religion and replaced by the solar cult; liberty of religion was proclaimed and the bishops were requested to cease persecuting the heretics, for the Christians were already persecuting each other.

The opposition which he inevitably aroused soon forced Julian to take, in his turn, measures against the Christians, who were excluded from education and state service. But even while fighting against the Church, Julian was deeply influenced by it. He was compelled to organize a pagan clergy on the Christian model, establish a budget for the cults and create charitable institutions modelled on those of the Christian communities.

Paganism could only react against Christianity by imitating it.

Even as Julian had revolted against the Church because he wished it more exclusively devoted to its moral code of charity and love, so too he revolted against state socialist oppression. Tolerant in religious matters, he tried also to return to political liberalism by reacting against authoritarian policy. He reduced taxes, restored to the municipalities the properties taken from them by previous Emperors and eased the fiscal obligations of the *decurions*.

But he was prematurely killed while fighting the Persians. His death in 363 put an end to his dreams of mystical idealism. It extinguished both the dynasty of Constantine and the last flame of paganism which now expired in beauty.

CHAPTER LIV

THE TOTALITARIAN EMPIRE

THE VALENTINIAN DYNASTY (363–392)

THE death of Julian, the last representative of the dynasty of Constantine, left the Empire without heirs. It was the army that brought to the throne the Pannonian general Valentinian (364–375) without anyone contesting its right to do so, since by a legal fiction the army was considered to represent the people.

Reverting to the division of the imperial power, Valentinian kept the West for himself and handed the East over to his brother Valens (364–378). His successors in the West were his sons Gratian (375–383) and Valentinian II (383–392). But after Valens had died without heirs, Gratian nominated the Spaniard Theodosius I (379–392) as ruler of the East. Valentinian II also died without heirs and the sons of Theodosius reigned, Arcadius in the West and Honorius in the East. The principle of hereditary monarchy was finally introduced.

THE ARMY BECOMES DENATIONALIZED

Although assured of a stable dynastic succession, the Empire was tottering under the blows of the barbarians who continued to cross the Rhine and the Danube. The Roman armies were now too weak to hold them back.

After the great crisis of the 3rd century the army had been reorganized by Diocletian. But the growing decline in the birth-rate, coupled with terrible epidemics and a half-century of civil wars, had led to a considerable fall in the population.[1] This, combined with pacifist sentiment, had checked voluntary recruitment. The only solution was to enrol barbarians and to introduce as a normal method of recruiting the obligation already imposed on the great landowners to levy recruits among their tenants. This system meant that the army very soon became little more than a social cesspool, since the landowners naturally sent their worst

[1]. From seventy millions in the 1st century it had fallen to fifty millions.

Germanic Ocean
Suevian Sea
WENDS
BRITAIN
SAXONS
LOMBARDS
FRANKS
Cologne
Tongres
Boulogne
BURGUNDY
VANDALS
Britannic Ocean
ALAMANNI
MARCOMANNI
QUADI
Treves
Rouen
Paris
Tours
GAUL
PANNONIA
HUNS
SARMATIA
Atlantic Ocean
Lyons
ITALY
Padua
Aquileia
PREFECTURE
SEPTIMANIA
Milan
Verona
Bordeaux
Vienne
Genoa
Ravenna
Salona
DACIA
OF
Marseilles
Narbonne
Nice
Ancona
Oporto
Florence
Adriatic Sea
SPAIN
Barcelona
THE
Tarragona
CORSICA
Rome
ITALY
Salonica
MACEDON
Valencia
BALEARIC Is.
Lisbon
Toledo
Naples
Tarentum
SARDINIA
Inner
Tuscan Sea
GAULS
Ionian Sea
Cordova
Messina
Rhegium
Malaga
Carthagena
PREFECTURE
Gades
Catania
Sicilian Sea
Palermo
Syracuse
Ceuta
Sea
Carthage
Caesarea
Lixos
Hadrumetum
OF ITALY
Lambaesa
AFRICA
Libyan Sea
THE ROMAN EMPIRE
ON THE EVE OF
THE INVASIONS c 390 A.D.
Leptis
Magna
MOORS
Frontiers of the Empire and of Sovereign States.
Frontiers of the three prefectures-(of the Eastern
Prefecture and the Prefectures of Italy and of the Gauls)
Frontiers of the dioceses, subdivisions of the prefectures.
Frontiers of the provinces, subdivisions of the dioceses.

Map No. 28

HUNS
HERULES
OSTROGOTHS
Caucasus
Panticapea (Kertch)
Dioscurias
Phasis
Cherson (Sebastopol)
Theodosia
Istrus
Black Sea
Sinope
Constantinople
Trebizond
PONTUS
KINGDOM OF ARMENIA
PERSIAN KINGDOM OF THE SASSANIDS
Caspian Sea
Pergamus
ASIA
Smyrna
Ephesus
Tarsus
Edessa
Antioch
Apamaea
CYPRUS
Palmyra
Beirut
Sidon
Tyre
Damascus
EASTERN PREFECTURE
ORIENT
Caesarea
Gaza
Bostra
Persian Gulf
Petra
Alexandria
Ailana
Paraetonium
Memphis
EGYPT
ARABIA
Red Sea
Koptos
M.

men to join it. Despite the privileges attached to it, the profession of arms became disreputable. After the crisis of the 3rd century the Empire reorganized its defences and decided to draw back the Rhine and Danube frontiers, abandoning the ancient *limes* that had protected the great trade-routes and military communications represented by the two rivers.

But even on this shortened front the Empire was unable to hold fast; not that the external pressure increased, but that the internal power of resistance continued to grow weaker. The civil wars that followed the abdication of Diocletian and the death of Constantine had given an opportunity for the Franks and Alamanni to cross the Rhine again, and the Goths to cross the Danube. Julian restored the situation in Gaul and, after him, Valentinian and Valens also made a great military effort to save the Empire.

But the army remained insufficient. In 376 the Empire once again experienced the after-effects of one of those great movements of peoples from the Asiatic confines. The Huns, resuming their march westward, crossed the Volga, driving before them the Ostrogoths and then the Visigoths who, for a century past, had been settled on the northern shores of the Black Sea. Valens, who was short of troops, could not defend the Danube. He allowed the Visigoths to cross the river and granted them lands in the northern Balkans. But the Goths, attracted by the rich sea-coast provinces, pushed on southward. Their number was not large; not more than a hundred thousand. But the Roman army, badly manned and made up of not very mobile infantry, was unable to stop them. They invaded Thrace and defeated at Adrianople the troops commanded by the Emperor Valens, who was killed on the field of battle. Then they advanced as far as the walls of Constantinople (378).

Theodosius authorized the Visigoths to settle in the Empire. Rather than fight them, he decided to make use of them as mercenaries. They were thus introduced into the Roman army as 'federates' under the command of their national leaders. In default of having at its disposal an adequate national army, the Empire became barbarized.

The individual enrolment of barbarians in the armed forces had already been a danger to the Empire, but, grouped as they were in special units, the barbarians continued to live according to their tribal laws and caused the reappearance of the system of personal law, which had entirely disappeared since the constitution of Caracalla (212). Marriage between the barbarians and Roman women, it is true, assimilated them fairly rapidly; but in 370 Valens forbade mixed marriages. Thenceforth the barbarians became unassimilable islands, a situation the more dangerous in that they had been charged with the defence of the Empire. After the incorporation of the Visigoths as 'federates' the position became even worse. This time the barbarians not only formed isolated legal groups but whole nations preserved their own nationality and their own leaders, and were only attached to the Empire by treaties concluded with their kings. These peoples were the Roman armies.

The Roman troops of farmer-soldiers were quartered in fortified camps spread out along the frontier which the Empire had given up trying to defend by a system of unbroken front. The conception of an elastic defence in depth necessitated the placing of troops in the provinces at a considerable distance from the frontier. The role of mobile forces was assigned to the federated barbarians. To assure their maintenance, the State compelled the large landowners to give up to them a third of their estates. Not only did the barbarians thus peaceably invade the European provinces, where units of Franks, Alamanni, Alans and Goths were stationed, but they even infiltrated into the high command. Since the democratic reforms of the Severi, soldiers could attain high command and barbarians, often scarcely Romanized, rapidly achieved high rank.

BUREAUCRATIC STATE SOCIALISM

In order to restore the central power after the great crises of the 3rd century Diocletian had organized the Empire on a state-socialist basis, even though decentralized. Bureaucracy, rigidly graded, was looked upon as the great instrument of absolutism.

The ascendancy of the Church as well as that of the great landowners over the population drove Valentinian I to enforce even more rigorously the graded status of civil and military offices. The administrative machine, rigid in its immutable code of rules, was superimposed on the country, which it was able to dispose of without hindrance. The consequence of this system, which recalls that of the state-socialist periods in Egypt, was twofold. On the one hand the state services lost all contact with the population which was regarded only from a fiscal and administrative point of view, and on the other the Emperor, unable to show his authority save through the agency of the bureaucratized services, was himself integrated into the administration as a piece of the machine that had been created to serve him. As during the period of state socialism five centuries earlier under the Ptolemies, bureaucracy killed initiative, the over-rigid grading suppressed individual responsibility and prevented the activities of the Emperor and his ministers, and even those of the Pretorian Prefects, from making themselves felt. The administration became a body without a soul, a ponderous and ruinous machine which functioned automatically, as if in a vacuum, and which was completely organized to ensure the strict execution of the regulations, even if they were outdated or contrary to the aim for which they had been intended.

Bureaucracy, complicated by countless departments of transmission and verification without direct yield, became swollen out of all measure. The salaries of the officials placed an increasingly heavy burden on the treasury. The whole administration ended by being dominated by fiscal preoccupations alone.

This congealed body, formed by the officials, became transformed little by little into a social caste.

The theory of absolutism had already brought under the authority of the state all activities, even commercial ones. This evolution, which had been broadly outlined since the times of the Severi, was greatly accelerated after the crises of the 3rd century.

Since the times of Aurelian the Emperors had introduced a regime of controlled economy, which was shown on the social plane by an intransigent corporatism and an economic organization established on bureaucratic principles. Each individual was regarded as an official and was assigned a definite position in society, and heredity of functions enforced in a manner intended to preserve the framework so laboriously erected.

But hereditary of function led quite naturally to the increased recruitment of officials from a single class. It therefore inevitably became transformed into a hereditary oligarchy.

Undoubtedly very many *curiales*, artisans and free peasants were still able to slip into the lower grades of the administration and thus, after a more or less long period, to escape from their hereditary grouping; but once they had become officials, these newcomers, at the end of their term of office, became members of the senatorial order which was henceforth open to all state functionaries. This high dignity, which was now extended to thousands of families, no longer gave them the right to sit in the Senate. But, however humble their origin, it threw wide open to their descendants an administrative career which allowed them to aspire to the highest offices. The officials were thus transformed into a distinct class that kept the representatives of the wealthiest and most famous families out of state service to its own advantage. It was famous lawyers or eminent officials who, in the East, held the reins of power.

In the West, however, where landed property was predominant, the bureaucrats were faced with the power of the aristocracy of birth which retained the privilege of holding the most important offices. Democratic in the East, aristocratic in the West, the administration became transformed into a ruling oligarchy. Throughout the Empire officials of whatever rank formed a privileged class.

The transformation of the officials into an oligarchy vitiated the very principle upon which the government of the Empire was based.

The administrative machine had been constructed to assure imperial absolutism and to suppress any power that could in any way oppose it. But in the West about thirty large landowning families managed to monopolize the higher offices, and throughout the Empire subordinate functions, though without becoming hereditary in law, passed into the hands of the families of officials. The principle of promotion by seniority existed, as well as the obligation to recruit senior state functionaries from the law-school pupils. But members of the senatorial order were admitted to them in preference to all other citizens. In a number of services the offices became family inheritances which allowed their holders to transmit them to relatives or even to sell them.

The officials, once they had become an oligarchy, transformed the laws on disputes, created to ensure respect for the rights of the Emperor and of those administered, into a class justice; based on the principle of judgment of subordinates by their official superiors, it ended by escaping entirely from the imperial authority. The officials formed, henceforth, a sort of nobility, designated by various titles and honorifics attached to their rank. The Pretorian Prefects bore the title of 'Eminence', the ministers and army generals were 'Illustrious' and 'Your Power'; then came the 'Magnificents' (*spectabiles*), vicars, professors of universities and generals of the second class; finally governors, senior officials and, in general, functionaries who had retired after forty years of service were 'Most distinguished' (*clarissimi*).

Even as the state officials now formed the senatorial order, so the municipal magistrates (*decurions*) and the presidents of corporations formed the equestrian order, which formerly had been composed of the rich or well-to-do bourgeoisie.

The whole of society was reorganized on state-socialist principles; men took their rank in it according to the position they held in the administrative machine.

Created under the influence of egalitarian and democratic principles, the administration produced a new aristocracy which, after the reign of Theodosius I, was to paralyze and dominate the power of the Emperor.

Since the times of Diocletian the higher civil administration was no longer recruited save from the classes that it had itself created. The army, on the other hand, passed more and more under the rule of the barbarians who even attained the rank of Commander-in-Chief. Theodosius made a Vandal, Stilicho, the Chief of all the Roman military forces and the most important personage of the Empire, and a Moor, Gildo, became the commander of the army of Africa.

In the 4th and 5th centuries the upper ranks of the bureaucracy represented the elegant and cultured society of the Empire, as can be seen from the reports and correspondence of Symmachus, Prefect of Rome in 384. Symmachus was a man of the world, gracious and refined, a cultivated and able orator, but incapable of understanding the significance of the tragic events that were about to happen. Rendered insensitive by the possession of wealth and honours, as were all the men of his class, he did not even seem to suspect that the Empire was threatened from all sides, from without as well as from within, and that an immense effort would be needed to stand fast in the war against the barbarians. The profound moral and social changes of the times passed him by. He thought only of keeping what he possessed. His conservatism was not, however, pure and simple egotism, but rather the expression of an outworn ideal. Symmachus, with eyes fixed on the past, had remained a pagan as had many men of his class. And as the Emperor Gratian had suppressed in 382 the subsidies hitherto granted to the pagan religion, these men had themselves assumed the expense of maintaining the services of that religion. They were priests of Mithras or of Isis, as pious people had formerly been. They were unable to accept Christianity, since for them it represented the expression of social tendencies of which they disapproved. They remained loyally and sincerely attached to liberal principles and to the rights of man, which state-socialism, of which they were the high dignitaries, was trampling underfoot. The great historian Ammianus Marcellinus belonged to this circle. They were interested in the things of the spirit and had fine editions published of the classics; but they no longer belonged to the times, to which they were in many ways superior. Their archaism made them live on the fringe of the society of their contemporaries, upon whom they no longer had any influence. They were the symbol of a class expiring in a conservatism that isolated them before condemning them to oblivion.

THE CHURCH IN THE STATE

While bureaucracy was sapping the power of the Emperor, the authority of the Church was growing greater. After the great religious crisis caused by the pagan revival of Julian, the Emperors Valentinian and Valens in order to restore peace proclaimed freedom of religion. But the triumphant Church was to impose on the Empire a policy of religious intolerance.

Despite the momentary revival during the reign of Julian, pagan thought had lost all dynamism. The only active intellectual force was Christianity, which was felt in all fields. All values were revised from a Christian viewpoint.

During the reign of Constantine, Eusebius wrote at Caesarea a History of the Church in Greek, and Lactantius at Nicomedia an essay on the philosophy of history in Latin, in which he presented historical events as ordained by the Divine Providence. Political events assumed a moral and religious significance, involved a lesson and a divine admonishment. Christian literature was thus directly inspired by the Jewish prophets.

Parallel with this movement was the mystical reaction within the fold of Christianity itself against the wealth of the Church, the privileges of the clergy and the luxury in which the prelates lived. The ascetic movement, born in Egypt in the 3rd century, which drew the hermits to the desert in search of simplicity and renunciation, exerted a more and more powerful influence, and this led, at the beginning of the 4th century, to monasticism.

While the Church, which had now become one of the principal powers of the state, was being granted the properties confiscated from the pagan temples and was obtaining fiscal privileges for the clergy, the Dalmatian St Jerome and the Asiatics St Basil and St John Chrysostom arose as moralists and judges and saw in the invasions a chastisement sent by God to punish Roman society for its corruption and moral laxity. With a violence that recalls the prophet Hosea, John Chrysostom launched out on an almost revolutionary denunciation of the corruption of luxury, to which he contrasted the ascetic ideal of the monks of the Thebaid. St Basil founded monastic communities in Pontus, and St Jerome, dismayed by the struggle against temptation and the crisis of mysticism, included in a single hatred the laxity of morals and the ancient thinking which he held responsible for it. Asceticism, according to him, is opposed to aristocracy of thought—still very close to Hellenistic philosophy—and to social aristocracy. 'The Church', he proclaims, 'is not born of the Academy or the Lyceum, but of the humblest of the people.'

However, St Jerome, himself a writer, published the Vulgate[1], and laid the foundations of that school of exegesis to which the mediaeval monks were to remain faithful. He wanted thought to free itself from all that

[1] An edition of the Bible.

is not God and therefore tried to replace Homer and Virgil by the Bible, and Pindar by David.

With St Jerome, monasticism penetrated the West where, on the initiative of the hermits Paul and Hilarion, monks began to travel through the country preaching renunciation. A large number of religious thinkers, horror-stricken by the misfortunes into which the invasions had plunged the world and disillusioned at seeing Christian society continue in the same errors as the pagans, took refuge in contemplation and prayer.

In the midst of this fever of mysticism, ancient philosophy expired and with it knowledge. Lactantius, still permeated with ancient culture, was able to look on Christ as the corner-stone of the edifice adumbrated by such great thinkers as Socrates, Plato, Lucretius, Cicero and Seneca in their efforts to find truth. He would have liked to adapt knowledge to the new faith but was obliged to reject the theories of evolution and atomism in order to remain faithful to the doctrines of the Bible. The new dogmas which were then formed crystallized all thought. They were to stifle for ten centuries all free research, which had in any case been in full decline since the middle of the 2nd century. But the ancient philosophies had penetrated society so deeply that, even when they had been abandoned, they continued to exercise a considerable influence in the bosom of the Church itself. Its doctrine, made up of an amalgam of biblical ideas and Platonist conceptions, gave rise to impassioned disputes which originated in the philosophical and religious ideas of the past and which resulted in the growth of new heresies: Manicheism (296), inspired by Zoroastrian ideas; Donatism (311) which sapped the unity of the Church in Africa; Arianism, of rationalist origin and opposed to the supernatural, and Pelagianism (411) which denied the necessity of grace.

The Church defended itself against these centrifugal tendencies and, having become a state religion, it adopted totalitarian methods. Athanasius, Bishop of Alexandria, thundered against Arianism and appealed to the principle of religious authority, going so far as to oppose the authority of the Emperor and to refuse to admit that liberty of religious belief which Tertullian in the previous century had demanded so clamourously for the Christians.

The Church was divided on this important question of religious toleration. St Hilary, Bishop of Poitiers, in his struggle against Arianism would not resort to passion or to force, but relied on scholasticism. He adapted Aristotelian logic to points of faith and to the sacred texts and thus initiated the methods of the *Summae* and the treatises of the Middle Ages. Like the Stoics, he remained the apostle of human feeling; in its name he rejected the use of force and refused to admit any intermingling of religion with politics. 'God, master of all,' he wrote, 'has no need of forced obedience or of constrained worship.' But the magnificent tolerance, a legacy of ancient times, that Hilary professed was too much in contradiction with state-socialist and authoritarian theories to be accepted by his own times. Victorious Christianity would not agree to allow to pagans and heretics—since it alone possessed the truth—the liberty which it had earlier demanded for itself. Moreover, the barbarians converted to Christianity brought with them their lack of culture and the brutality of primitive men incapable of understanding what freedom of belief could be. Commodian raised against the Jews and pagans the most terrible cry of hatred that had ever sounded in ancient times; it would have made Jesus, who came into the world to teach men to love one another, tremble.

The African St Augustine, the greatest spirit of his times, but none the less a product of them, was to adapt the doctrine of the Church to totalitarian and authoritarian ideas, declaring himself in favour of a state religion and against liberty of belief and appealing to the secular arm to repress heresy. By claiming an absolute and uncontested authority for the Church, he asserts its pre-eminence over the State. In *The City of God* he dissociates the Church from the Empire and places it outside and above the temporal power. St Augustine was thus able to save it from the ruin in which the Empire was about to be involved and to put it in a position where it would be able to continue, on the spiritual plane, the work of universalism that was to remain the great achievement of the Roman Empire. The Emperor could only adapt his policy to the intolerance demanded by the greater part of Christian opinion; Valens, after first proclaiming liberty of belief, had suspect books burnt and persecuted philosophers for magic or sorcery. Soon the heretics were being hunted down by the Church as formerly the Christians had been by the pagan Emperors.

Theodosius, however, made one more attempt to save the principle of toleration. He appointed pagans to high office and put an end to the persecutions of the heretics. But Ambrose, Bishop of Milan, using as pretext a massacre which had taken place at Salonica after a riot, excommunicated the Emperor. The spiritual power asserted itself over the temporal. So great was its ascendancy that the Emperor was forced to submit. Fearing for his salvation, he made himself the instrument of the intolerance that Ambrose demanded. Measures against the pagans and heretics were strengthened, and the temple of Serapis at Alexandria, the greatest shrine of pilgrimage of the ancient world, was destroyed in 391.

CHAPTER LV

THE EMPIRE SPLITS INTO THE CONTINENTAL WEST AND THE MARITIME EAST

STATE SOCIALIST ECONOMY

THE safety of the Empire did not depend solely on the defence of its frontiers. It depended above all on internal conditions; the stability of the central power and the economic balance.

Diocletian and Constantine had been perfectly aware of this. So the far-reaching reform of the imperial power had been accompanied by a policy aimed at restoring to the Empire that economic balance so often compromised by its trading deficit and the monetary crises resulting from it.

Trajan and Aurelian had both temporarily solved the serious monetary crises with which they had been faced by an influx of fresh gold, in the one case from the Dacian mines and in the other from the treasury of the Queen of Palmyra.

A similar solution was no longer possible in the times of Diocletian. Either the Empire must adopt a trade policy able to give it an economic balance capable of competing with the free trade of the outside world, or it must put an end to the drain on its gold by organizing an imperial economy based on its own resources, that is to say a policy of autarchy. Regarding the problem only from the fiscal viewpoint, Diocletian quite naturally chose the second of these alternatives, which had already been foreshadowed in the state socialist policy followed by all the Emperors since the Severi. In order to keep the currency stable, Diocletian had built up considerable gold reserves. In order to maintain them he put into general practice the system introduced by Aurelian—and earlier made use of by the Egyptian Pharaohs—of paying officials and soldiers not in money but mainly in kind. He had thus made use of the grain, oil and food products obtained from the treasury lands and avoided too heavy expenses in cash. This method created a twofold economy; an economy in kind practised by the state and a monetary economy, almost wholly reserved for trade. The economy in kind drove the state, in order to produce what it needed without depleting its gold reserves, to build arsenals and weaving workshops, to organize huge bakeries for the victualling of the main cities and to construct granaries, amongst which the general warehouses of Ostia were the most important. By using the produce of its own lands more and more the state considerably restricted the market for agricultural produce. The military suppliers and officials, provisioned by the state, ceased to buy on the local markets. The purchasing power of the rural population was affected, and private agriculture, producing less and less for sale, tended towards a closed economy, above all in those districts where the cities did not provide an outlet for agricultural produce. Large-scale landowning which, from the close of the 2nd century, had continually gained ground, since it was better adapted to the system of closed economy than smallholding, extended more and more and led to the formation of great concentrations of land, while trade was driven into the cities.

CONTROLLED ECONOMY LEADS TO SOCIAL RESTRAINT

To assure the yield of the taxes and to control production in such a manner as to ensure an autarchic economic balance, the state was driven to develop the corporatism which the Severi had introduced. More and more, personal activities were considered from the viewpoint of their social yield and were grouped into corporations. The state assumed control of the associations of common interests—especially numerous in the Hellenized provinces—which united landowners, artisans, workers and soldiers. They were all transformed into official bodies entrusted with various public services and were made obligatory and hereditary, while their members were declared collectively responsible for the tasks assigned them.

Society was crystallized into closed groups. Individual liberty was seriously curtailed. The members of the various corporations were so closely bound together that the law forbade them to alienate their property and their slaves to any save their colleagues, in order that the guarantee of collective responsibility imposed on them by the state should not be weakened. The corporation itself, endowed with a civic personality, acquired, in relation to its members, rights of succession and inherited their goods in the event of a lack of heirs.

In the countryside a similar evolution was taking place. Here the cell was not the corporation; it was the domain or the village.

The domain was a unit, represented by its owner, responsible to the state for the taxes from all its tenants; and to guarantee the owner the workers he needed all the occupants of his lands were tied hereditarily to their duties. The farmer, whether a tenant engaged by contract, a barbarian settled on the domain, or even a slave, was tied to the soil which he cultivated. In a similar way, the farmhands and craftsmen on the domain were tied in perpetuity to their jobs.

In the villages the landowners[1] were declared collectively responsible for the yield of the taxes, and to ensure the standard yield both from taxes and cultivation, landowners, tenants, craftsmen, journeymen and slaves were compelled to remain in their employment and their villages, by a system similar to that in force in Egypt at the end of the Ptolemaic period.

This régime, which has been given the name of 'colonization', was not created by any law, but appeared in 332 as an almost universally established fact. Although it hardened society into a mould which could not be broken, it did not in theory change either the political status or the private law under which the Roman citizen lived. In fact, the 'colonist' (*colonus*), unable to leave his land or to marry outside the domain or the village or to alienate his property without the authorization of the landowners upon whom he was dependent, passed completely into the civil authority of the landowner. A seigniorial régime was formed, which restored to law a patriarchal and collective character and which substituted for the legal equality affirmed by the civil law a graded social régime crystallized in the heredity of duties, that is to say in separate legal classes. The perpetual bond thus created between men and the soil greatly modified the idea of the law of property and the law of contract. The fluidity of property which had marked the individualist system was replaced by immobilization and inalienability; testamentary rights were curtailed and the land, instead of being a benefit of which its owner could freely dispose, henceforth imposed upon its occupier, whether he was a landowner or not, a separate juridical status.

THE WESTERN EMPIRE DEVELOPS A SEIGNIORIAL RÉGIME

The consequences of this great change were no less serious in the political than in the social field. The class of great landowners, responsible and privileged, stood midway between the state and the people; and since the treasury, whose methods became more brutal as the taxes became more

[1] Villages of free peasants continued to exist, especially in Egypt, throughout the 4th century.

difficult to collect, appeared to the taxpayers as their main enemy, the small landowners, incapable of resistance to the arbitrary and omnipotent officials, sought the protection of the great landowning seigneurs and sold their lands, in order to take them back once more as *coloni*. Freedom disappeared before the need for security.

In the West, where agriculture was all-important, the great landowners became so powerful that they refused to pay their taxes to the *decurions* of the cities. In 338 Constans, at their request, began to allow certain of the great landowners to become directly dependent on the authority of the provincial governors. This system was to spread little by little and to become general in the 5th century. Not only the cities but also the great domains became separate administrative units. The seigneurs, by the very fact that they were not subject to the common law, were transformed into a privileged class. Soon, abusing their power, they imposed their patronage, despite the formal prohibition to do so, over the small landowners and even over whole villages which they incorporated into their domains.

The autarchic reforms, especially since the time of Diocletian, therefore contributed to destroy the middle classes upon which the Empire had been built and perverted the administrative system created by state socialism by creating a landholding aristocracy which was to undermine the imperial authority that the state-socialist policy had intended to make absolute.

THE EAST RESISTS STATE SOCIALISM

In the East the reforms of Diocletian and his successors were far from having so great an influence. This was because the economy of the East was essentially commercial whereas in the West landowning was predominant. The Empire of the West was a continental block; the Empire of the East, on the contrary, was conditioned by its maritime character and by the numerous and wealthy class of merchants and business men. Throughout the Empire it was Greeks, Syrians, Egyptians, Illyrians and Jews who held the monopoly of trade and navigation. In the West the cities, of recent formation save on the shores of the Mediterranean, had not been able to revive after the terrible economic and political crisis of the 3rd century. A large number of them, which had only just begun to develop, were reduced to the state of military and administrative townships. A few centres of trade alone managed to survive on the sea-coasts and along the rivers. The Italian cities were decadent. Rome itself was now no more than a great city, sterile and parasitic. In the East, on the other hand, almost all the cities were markets of greater or lesser importance. In Asia Minor and in Syria an active middle class had become wealthy through industry. A few great commercial centres, such as Alexandria, though greatly in decline since the 3rd century, Antioch, Constantinople and Ephesus, created throughout the eastern provinces an important movement of internal and external trade, favoured by the trade-routes to India and China.

A monetary and commercial economy extended widely around these cities. Buying in their own environs the produce that they needed, they prevented the development of the manorial and closed economy and assured markets for the smallholders. This helped them to escape the patronage of the great landowners who were not powerful enough to free themselves from the control of the prosperous cities on which they were dependent. The ascendancy of the seigniorial régime, which was only evident in the rural areas, and the influence of the economy in kind practised by the state therefore effected the East far less than the West.

Thus the Empire was split economically as well as politically. In the eastern provinces, of Greek speech, the urban régime, the business middle-classes and smallholding, despite its decline, managed to survive; the current of trade checked the expansion of state socialism and safeguarded individual liberty, despite the obstacles imposed by the state.

In the western provinces, of Latin speech, where landowning was predominant, the seigniorial régime rapidly took root, smallholding disappeared, and economy in kind increased more and more to the detriment of monetary economy which, however, continued to hold its own, thanks to the activities of the merchant classes, on the coasts and in the cities of Gaul, Spain and Africa.

Navigation, by linking Constantinople, Antioch and Alexandria with Marseilles, Cartagena and Carthage, maintained commercial activity around the Mediterranean and prevented the unity of the Empire from being broken. From the ports the eastern merchants made their way into all the provinces, ascending the rivers and settling in the cities where they formed corporations which, however, remained free since trade always escaped imperial tutelage; they hastened the diffusion of Christianity which, from the 2nd century onward, had won over the cities and was slowly penetrating into the countryside where the peasants, being isolated, were less ready to accept it.[1]

[1] The word *paganus*, a peasant, came to mean a pagan.

THE REVIVAL OF TRADE RESTORES MONETARY ECONOMY

Economy in kind had only been introduced by Diocletian because of the shortage of ready money at the disposal of the Empire.

But during the 4th century peace and security little by little revived trade and, with it, monetary economy, thanks to the stimulus of the great markets of the eastern provinces. Trade restored to fluid property, and especially to money, great possibilities of profit. The gold that had been hidden or hoarded during the time of troubles began to reappear.

Economic wealth consists above all in the circulation of goods. In anarchic and troubled periods gold becomes the one secure form of wealth and disappears from circulation. But the return of a normal trade régime brings gold back into circulation, since it is indispensable to commercial operations.

Thus the Empire which had no money left in the times of Diocletian once more had an abundant circulation of gold and silver by the middle of the 4th century. Business prosperity allowed the state to increase customs dues to $12\frac{1}{2}\%$. Enormous quantities of ready money flowed into its coffers and economy in kind was gradually abandoned. In 360 the state began to resume payment of officials and officers in money. By the middle of the 5th century all salaries were paid in cash.

The wealth of the state was thus closely linked with the economic life of the Empire, fertilized by the great merchant cities of the Hellenized provinces.

DECLINE OF INDIVIDUALISM

The new tendency, in which law concerned itself mainly with social preoccupations, necessarily meant a check to the advance of individualism. It was in the times of Constantine that this crisis in legal evolution became apparent. Roman law was subject to a twofold influence. On the one hand, the individual was at last freed from all that remained of collective family responsibility; the power of the *paterfamilias* disappeared, marriage required only the consent of those about to be married and no longer that of their parents, sons could dispose freely of their inheritances and women rejected all forms of guardianship. But on the other hand, the collective sense of family which had been destroyed was replaced by a social collectivity in the form of the corporation, which absorbed the individual, and the collective unity of the state which, in the name of public interest, imposed its will over that of the citizens.

The idea of property was transformed. Far from appearing an unlimited and exclusive right, it was no longer considered legitimate except insofar as it served the community, that is to say the state.

The state, the corporation, the domain, the village, all arrogated to themselves or were given rights over private property. Members of a unit could no longer dispose of their property outside their own group. In the villages, vacant lands were officially handed over to neighbouring landowners on condition that they paid the taxes on them. The law made a strange step backward by tying men to the soil by perpetual bonds, and created, alongside individual property, communal properties superimposed on it, setting out limitations and bond-services and many rules of succession.

Thus the individual became more and more merged into the group, which stifled his personality and reduced him to the role of a unit forming part of a state-socialized society.

But, after the adoption of Christianity as a state religion, the people of the Empire were composed not only of citizens but also of believers. These two notions tended to become confused, and the intolerance of the Church compelled the state to consider only Christian citizens as full citizens. Pagans, heretics, apostates and Jews were rejected from the civic community; the law burdened them with restrictions which, in the 6th century, were to go so far as to forbid them to receive inheritances. As in the times of primitive collectivity, religion once again became the condition and the sanction of law.

Together with its individualist character, the civilization of the Empire was also rapidly losing its universalism.

CHAPTER LVI

THE GERMANIC INVASIONS

THE SPLIT BETWEEN EAST AND WEST

ON the death of Theodosius I (395) the Empire passed to his two sons, Honorius (395–423) who was nominated to reign in the West, and Arcadius (395–408) in the East. Theodosius had placed Honorius, who was then a minor, under the guardianship of Stilicho, Generalissimo of the armies of the West, who had availed himself of office to become, like all the high officials of his time, one of the greatest landowners of the Empire.

After the reign of Theodosius the split between the West and the East was to become even more evident.

The division of the imperial budget into two distinct budgets, one for the West and the other for the East, revealed to how great an extent the East provided almost all the fiscal resources of the Empire.

When, after the death of Theodosius (395), the greater part of Illyria, with the silver mines of Macedonia, was attached to the East the budget of the Empire of the West fell to about two million gold *solidi*[1], that is to say a third of the budget at the disposal of the Emperor of the East.

In the preceding chapter we have already followed the formation of the seigniorial domains since the reign of Constantine. The large landowners who were charged with collecting the taxes for the Emperor, amongst whom were all the high officials, tried to evade this duty by declaring that their *coloni* were unable to pay. In order to compensate for the yield which it had lost, the treasury put even greater pressure on the small landowners who, in order to escape, 'recommended' to the seigneurs that they too should become *coloni*. The seigniorial regime, therefore, continued to expand; and the land tax, which Diocletian and his successors had wanted to stabilize by handing over its collection to the landowners, became more and more exiguous in their hands and the receipts to the treasury diminished to a dangerous extent.

[1] The gold *solidus* weighed 4·48 grams and was therefore worth 15·43 gold francs.

To supply the treasury with fresh resources Valentinian I, continuing the policy of state-socialist centralization, confiscated two-thirds of the municipal revenues. The financial situation of the cities was seriously affected and their poverty encouraged the ascendancy of the landed aristocracy. The state, for its part, scarcely profited at all by this enormous access of wealth, since the high-ranking officials continued to pillage the treasury lands and carve out for themselves vast domains, as Stilicho himself had done, which became more and more like autonomous lordships. The resistance put up by the administration had no other effect than to drive the landowners into making common cause with the barbarians against the Empire. In the western provinces it was impossible to prevent them from appropriating the most valuable resources of the state, which was now stricken to death.

The policy of state-socialist absolutism, practised since Diocletian, ended, after a century, in dismembering the Empire to the profit of the high administration which it had relied on to restore the central power, and in transforming the officials into a landed aristocracy. In the western provinces, which had crumbled into a patchwork of lordships which had no ties with the cities, only two powers now existed: the armies of the federated barbarians, and the Church.

The federated armies were the military structure of the Empire. Valentinian III, being short of resources, could only keep 30,000 troops under arms[1] and found himself compelled to apply to the barbarian chiefs to take service under him with their troops. They very soon took on the guise of *condottieri*.

The power of the Church increased as that of the Empire diminished.

Since the 2nd century the Bishop of Rome had held first place in the hierarchy of the Church; Rome was to some extent the capital of the Christian world and its prestige overshadowed that of the Imperial residence, which had been transferred to the great provincial cities.

In 378 the Emperor, by confirming the decision of a synod (348) which conferred on the Pope the jurisdiction over appeals from trials by canon law judged by the Metropolitans, ceased to be regarded in the West as Head of the Church.

The Church thus freed itself from the temporal power and organized itself independently.

The situation in the East was quite different. The wealth of the commercial and industrial cities and the fiscal resources that they provided

[1] Their maintenance cost a million gold *solidi* out of a total budget of two millions. In 470 there were no more than 12,000 soldiers in Italy.

furnished the Emperor with a solid foundation, upon which Arcadius did not hesitate to rely in order to resist the forces that were trying to seize power; the great landed proprietors, the administrative oligarchy and the Church.

Thanks to the yield of the taxes, due in large to the commercial activities of the great cities of the East, Arcadius could both keep the internal administration firmly in his hands and restore to his army, less barbarized than in the West,[1] the mobility it had lacked since the crisis of the 3rd century by reorganizing the fleet which was entrusted with its supply and communications.

Thus, while the continental and landholding West was falling to pieces, the East, maritime and commercial, retained a firm imperial structure.

The pressure of the Germans, driven onward by the Huns, was making itself felt more and more heavily on the frontiers of the Empire, from the Danube to the North Sea. It was bound to breach them at the point at least resistance, that is to say in the West.

THE BARBARIANS IN THE EMPIRE

After the death of Theodosius the guardianship exercised by Stilicho, Generalissimo of the West, over the two Emperors did not prevent the two parts of the Empire from each having its own policy. In the East where it was in the hands of the Pretorian Prefect, the Gaul Rufinus, a struggle for supremacy broke out between Stilicho and Rufinus. Stilicho wished to keep for the Empire of the West the eastern part of the Province of Illyria, with its silver mines, which Rufinus claimed for the East. This was no doubt only a pretext because, after Rufinus had been murdered (395) by order of Arcadius, Stilicho gave way. None the less, fearing lest Stilicho should become all-powerful in the Empire, the ministers of Arcadius sent against him the leader of the Illyrian militia, Alaric, who was both Chief of the Visigoths and a Roman general.

Alaric entered Italy. After a bloody battle, Stilicho, with the aid of four thousand pounds of gold, took Alaric into his service. But the murder of Stilicho by his own soldiers soon restored Alaric to freedom. Thenceforward, he no longer acted as a Roman general but as a Gothic chief and demanded from the Emperor Honorius the right to settle his Visigoths in Pannonia. Honorius refused and the conflict broke out again. Alaric

[1] In 401, in the East, the barbarians were expelled from the army; but in the course of the 5th century they had again to be admitted because of the lack of men.

declared Honorius dethroned from his imperial dignity and set up against him as Emperor a senior official, Attalus (409), who appointed Alaric Generalissimo. Alaric, however, was not deceived by his own fraud; in order to come to terms with the real Emperor, he soon betrayed Attalus without, however, making Honorius weaken; then, in fury, he sacked Rome (410) and pressed forward into southern Italy in order to cross over into the rich province of Africa. He died on the way, and was succeeded by his brother-in-law, Athaulf. But not having enough ships to make the crossing into Africa, Athaulf retraced his steps northward with his army and people, passed into Gaul and settled at Narbonne, where he married Galla Placidia, the sister of Honorius, declaring that he wished to restore the greatness of Rome by Gothic arms. But Honorius refused to treat with a Gothic King settled on the coasts of Provence who could assure himself of the mastery of the seas. Athaulf then again made Attalus Emperor in order to obtain from him a confirmation of his command, but having no fleet he was unable to provision his army. Athaulf was driven out of Provence by famine and crossed into Spain where he died, after recommending Wallia, who was to succeed him after a short period of anti-Roman reaction, to remain a faithful servant of Rome.

At this time the West was in complete anarchy. Under pressure of the Huns who had reached the Danube, the Vandals, the Alans, the Suevi and the Burgundians broke into Gaul, destroying Trèves, Strasbourg, Rheims and Amiens.

Usurpers appeared in Gaul, in Spain and in Africa.

It only remained for Honorius, whose forces in Gaul were weak, to look to Wallia for aid. He authorized Wallia to settle in Aquitaine, between the Loire and the Garonne, where he could not threaten the Mediterranean coasts, and charged him to drive back the barbarian invasions, thus matching against the German tribes the army of a Gothic king, a 'federate' of the Roman Empire.

The Empire was disintegrating, and the imperial power was only sustained by the immense prestige that it enjoyed.

The prestige of the Pope, however, continued to grow greater. Above the powers of the Emperor, of the usurpers and of the barbarian chiefs the power of the Pope remained uncontested and immutable in the midst of the storm. The Church was adapting itself to the new world which was being formed in the West. In 417, at the height of the crisis, the priest Paul Orosius published a *Universal History*, in which he described the sack of Rome by Alaric as a punishment for its vices, and predicted, with marvellous foresight, the advent of a new form of Empire, under the authority of the Pope, conceived as a confederation of semi-independent states made up of barbarians and Romans.

The Church was making ready to maintain in the West the unity of the Empire that the Imperial power was no longer able to preserve.

STRENGTHENING OF THE CENTRAL POWER IN THE EAST

While the Empire of the West was foundering, the Empire of the East, on the other hand, more and more detached from the western provinces, recovered and in the reign of Theodosius II (408–450) experienced a period of renascence.

The decline of the West made Constantinople the uncontested centre of the Mediterranean world. In 425 Theodosius reorganized the University that Constantine had founded. Thenceforward, the teaching was not only in Latin, but also in Greek which brought Alexandrian Hellenism to the capital of the Empire. Greek found its way into the administration and completely supplanted Latin as the cultural language of the Eastern provinces. Ammianus Marcellinus (about 390), a native of Antioch and the continuator of Tacitus, still wrote in Latin, but after him Olympiodorus, Zosimus, the Thracian Priscus and the Palestinian Malchus were to write the history of their times in Greek. The most important Pretorian Prefect of the reign was the Greek poet Cyrus, a native of Panopolis in Egypt.

Constantinople, however, was not the capital of a Greek Empire; she claimed to be the centre of the universal Empire and took up once more the role that Rome had played in the centuries of her greatness. Thus Latin remained, alongside Greek, as an official language. It was in Latin, in 438, at the time when the Empire of the West was being overrun by the Vandals, that Theodosius II published at Constantinople the first official codex of Roman law, a monument which, despite its imperfections, proved to what extent the Empire remained faithful to its destinies.

In the East, which was the cradle of Hellenistic law and the country of the greatest of the Roman jurists, law had preserved its doctrinal and scientific character. The Syrian city of Beirut, where the great tradition of the Pretorian Prefects Papinian and Ulpian was preserved, became the premier school of Roman law.

The juridical work accomplished by Theodosius, now that the West was becoming barbarized, was the most shining proof of the superiority of the civilization preserved in the East, thanks to its social structure and its economic balance.

Theodosius II, pursuing a policy in accord with his resources, tried to avoid interminable struggles with the barbarians even at the price of a tribute, such as that which he offered about 430 to Attila who had then appeared at the head of his Hunnic hordes on the frontiers of the Empire.

In the East, Theodosius met with the aggression of the Sassanid Kings who, profiting by the blows which the barbarians were dealing the Empire, tried to conquer Syria and install themselves on the Mediterranean. He abandoned to the Sassanids the kingdom of Armenia,[1] which gave them access to the Black Sea. By the peace of 442 Theodosius reverted to the treaties signed after the death of Julian in 363. This peace conceded freedom of worship to the Christians throughout the Persian kingdom and re-opened to Byzantine trade the routes to India and China by way of Mesopotamia and the Caspian area.

THE EMPIRE LOSES MASTERY OF THE SEAS

In the first twenty years of his reign Theodosius had taken care not to become involved in the wars that were devastating the West. As long as they did not threaten the safety of the seas, they did not impinge upon the vital interests of the East. But in 427 the Vandals, after passing from Gaul into Spain under their king Genseric, occupied the port of Cartagena whence, thanks to the large number of ships that they found there, they were able to cross into Africa and in 439 captured the great naval base of Carthage. From then on the Vandals were masters of the Central Mediterranean. Sardinia, Corsica and the Balearic Islands fell, one after the other, into their hands (455).

The Empire was now threatened in its sea communications, that is to say in the vital principle of its economic life.

Theodosius II was no longer able to stand aside. The Constantinople fleet was sent against the Vandals, but did not dare to join battle with the squadrons of Carthage at the disposal of Genseric (441). At the same time Attila, breaking the treaty that he had signed, crossed the Danube. All the forces of the Empire were called on to resist the terrible invasion of the Huns. The Byzantines suffered some resounding defeats. But, thanks to his financial resources, the Emperor was able to buy their retreat in 447.

Once settled in Pannonia, Attila, sole King of the Huns from 445 onward, surrounded himself with a court of 'illustrious' Romans (*claris-*

[1] Armenia had been partitioned in 387 between Persia and the Roman Empire. The Empire from then on abandoned its political pretensions to Armenia, but under Theodosius II took an interest in its intellectual development; it was then that the Armenian alphabet was invented at Constantinople and a translation of the Bible was published which marked the beginning of Armenian literature.

simi) who had passed over to his service. A little later he claimed an imperial princess for his wife and, after the failure of his attempt against the East, demanded that Gaul should be given to him as her dowry. When he obtained no satisfaction, he invaded Gaul. Aetius, who was then in command of the remains of the Roman armies, appealed to the 'federates', who were as much menaced as the Empire itself, for their aid against the Hunnic hordes and their many allies. The Visigoths, the Burgundians and the Franks rallied to him. Attila was defeated at the Catalaunian Fields near Troyes in 451. He then withdrew towards Italy which he knew to be incapable of defence. Pope Leo the Great advanced to meet him; an epidemic had broken out among the Huns, and the Emperor of the East had just entered the war against them. Attila left Italy. In 453 his death delivered the Empire from the greatest danger it had hitherto known. All that remained of the Hunnic deluge was a few survivors settled in southern Russia who, reinforced by other elements of the same race, were later to reappear in history under the name of Bulgars.

East and West then joined forces for the final struggle against Genseric to reconquer the mastery of the seas.

But the West was a prey to ever increasing anarchy. Valentinian III (425–455), who had been struggling, not without courage, against the great lords who had formed a coalition with Aetius, wanted to get rid of the generalissimo before engaging in a war against Genseric; he killed Aetius with his own hand, but was himself assassinated a short time after (455), having fallen victim to a conspiracy of the nobles against whom he had tried to protect the state. Genseric profited by this to take the offensive. He conquered Rome, which he sacked methodically but without massacres. The game was up. It was in vain that Majorian (457–461) tried to deliver the Empire of the West from the calamitous rule of the great landowners and their ally, the Suevian barbarian Ricimer, then generalissimo of the Roman armies. Assassinated by the order of Ricimer, Majorian was succeeded by one of the great landowners, Severus (451), during whose reign the Empire was overrun by the barbarians. The Visigoths left Aquitaine to settle in the coastlands of Spain, occupying the ports they had long coveted; the Burgundians, whom Aetius had settled in Savoy, took possession of Lyon; the Franks and the Alamanni advanced into Northern and Eastern Gaul; Armorica (Brittany) became a virtually independent kingdom, while the island of Britain, which the Roman legions had evacuated in 442, passed finally into the power of the Anglo-Saxons.

Disorder was at its height. Almost all the coasts of Africa and Spain had been conquered and the great seaport cities of Carthage and Cartagena were in the hands of the barbarians. The West lost its richest provinces and the commercial prosperity of Constantinople was directly affected.

The death of Theodosius II (450), who left no heir, led to a troubled period in Constantinople. The Master of the Militia, Aspar, an Alan barbarian chief, wielded power there, as the Masters of the Militia, Aetius and Boniface, had at the same time wielded power in Gaul and in Italy. Being able to dispose of the crown as he wished, Aspar, without even referring to the Emperor of the West, who was then Valentinian III, granted it to a Thracian soldier, Marcian (450–457).

But the idea of the legitimacy of power was by then so implanted in Constantinople that Marcian, in order to have the *coup d'état* that had brought him to the throne recognized, found it opportune to have himself crowned Emperor by the Patriarch of Constantinople, after marrying Pulcheria the sister of Theodosius.

This was a date of primary importance in the history of European institutions. The legitimacy of monarchy by divine right was established on a double principle; on the one hand hereditary and on the other through confirmation by the Church. As formerly in Egypt the High Priest of Ammon consecrated a king in the absence of heirs, so now the right of confirming the imperial power, first exercised at Rome by the Senate and later by the army, was recognized as belonging to the Church.

The Emperor Leo (457–474), another Thracian soldier who succeeded Marcian, had his ascent to the throne made legitimate in a similar manner; the tradition of consecration became implanted, thus avoiding the intestine quarrels which had so often been caused by dynastic heirs.

The naval defeat by Genseric and then the war against the Huns had prevented Constantinople from intervening in the West after 441. Since then, the situation had become stable. Leo made a great effort to re-establish the imperial authority in the West. But since it was necessary first of all to restore the imperial power that had fallen into the hands of the Masters of the Militia, Leo sent the son-in-law of the Emperor Marcian, Anthemius (467–472), to Rome to be invested with the imperial purple. Meanwhile he devoted the entire resources of the Empire to rebuilding the fleet. In 468 eleven hundred ships left Constantinople to wrest from the Vandals the mastery of the seas and restore it to the Empire. But the fleet was badly commanded and was disastrously defeated.

COLLAPSE OF THE EMPIRE OF THE WEST

The Empire of the West was now lost. Without control of the central Mediterranean, Constantinople could do nothing for Rome. Power fell into the hands of the great landlords, and civil war broke out. Ricimer had the Emperor Anthemius murdered, and called on the colourless aristocrat Olybrius to occupy the throne (472). But Ricimer was murdered in his turn, Olybrius died soon afterwards, and the Burgundian Gondebaud, soon to become king of his own people and who had been nominated generalissimo by Olybrius, placed on the throne an obscure personage, Glycerius (473), who was to become a tool in his hands.

Constantinople at once reacted and set up in opposition a Roman, the Master of the Dalmatian Militia, Julius Nepos. But the personality of the Emperor was no longer of any importance; the imperial power no longer existed. Julius Nepos could do nothing. The generalissimo Orestes, a Pannonian who had once been Attila's secretary, had his son, Romulus Augustulus, proclaimed Emperor in 475.

The naval victory of the Vandals now began to make its effects seriously felt. The barbarian army billeted in Italy was badly provisioned, since Rome no longer held control of communications by sea. It revolted, and brought to the throne its leader, a scarcely Romanized barbarian,[1] Odoacer (476).

A barbarian and a supporter of the Arian heresy, Odoacer could not dream of wearing the imperial purple. In agreement with the Roman Senate, he declared that one Emperor was sufficient for the Empire. He sent the imperial insignia to Constantinople and contented himself with the title of king, which his soldiers had conferred on him. The Emperor Zeno, who was then reigning at Constantinople, recognized Odoacer's right to administer Italy and conferred on him the aulic dignity of Patrician. The unity of the Empire was legally re-established to the advantage of the Emperor of the East alone. In the West, the Empire was to take the form of a federation of kingdoms under barbarian kings, vassals of Constantinople.[2]

POLITICAL AND RELIGIOUS SCHISMS

While the split was taking place between the eastern and western provinces of the Empire, the Church, reacting to the political, social and intellectual divergencies that increasingly separated the two parts of the Empire, was in its turn involved in internal struggles.

At Rome, in contrast to the imperial power which was disintegrating,

[1] Odoacer was a German of the tribe of the Scyrri, settled on the Hungarian plain.

[2] In 476 only Odoacer and the Burgundian king, Gondebaud, recognized the suzerainty of the Emperor.

the Pope firmly maintained the unity of the Church. Only the short-lived heresy of Pelagianism, which denied original sin and the necessity for grace, came to trouble its orthodoxy.

At Constantinople, on the other hand, where the Emperor had kept his rich and prosperous provinces firmly in his hands, the Church was divided by furious controversies. Recalling the disputes which had been raised in Egypt about the nature of Horus, violent polemics broke out between the schools of Alexandria and Antioch on the subject of the incarnation and the two natures of Christ. The Alexandrians, still influenced by Egyptian mysticism, tended to minimize his human nature and to stress his divine nature alone. This doctrine, monophysism, met with lively opposition at Antioch. The Patriarch Nestorius of Constantinople, who belonged to the Antioch school, declared that the Virgin Mary was not the Mother of God, but only mother of Jesus in his human form; and his supporters, influenced by the Greek rationalism of the school of Antioch, finally saw in Christ only a man singularly inspired by God. The Church was divided between these two theories. In 431 the Council of Ephesus condemned Nestorianism; at the end of the reign of Theodosius II monophysism, supported by the Emperor and widespread in Egypt and Syria, seemed to have triumphed.

But at Rome, then in the throes of anarchy, the voice of Pope Leo (449) was raised to re-establish the spiritual unity of the Church by defining the doctrine of the incarnation; the two natures, he asserted, were united without merging in the person of Christ, who was both 'perfect God and perfect man'. In 451 the same year that Leo the Great made Attila retreat from Rome the Council of Chalcedon confirmed the doctrine of the Pope and condemned monophysism, without however succeeding in putting an end to the religious strife.

Nestorianism remained triumphant among the Christians who, in Asia, carried the word of the gospel beyond the confines of the Empire; it was in its Nestorian form that Christianity was to expand in Central Asia and as far as China, an event of great importance for its future destinies.

In the Roman East, on the other hand, monophysism retained a dominant influence. At a time when the barbarians were destroying the political unity of the Empire, the Church too seemed very close to dissolution.

Its unity had been formed within the framework of the Empire. Would it be able to survive the dismemberment of that framework?

Without doubt, the Church was not the daughter of the Empire. It had overflowed its frontiers, conquered Armenia and Chaldaea, won over the Goths, who were evangelized in the 4th century by the monk Ulfilas, and, through the Goths, Christianity had been handed on to the Alamanni, the Burgundians and the Vandals, even before the invasions. But in the independent countries of the Empire the Church was very soon divided into distinct factions. From 384 onward the Christians of Armenia formed an autonomous community and in 424 those of Chaldaea in their turn became separate. As for the barbarians, converted at a time when Arianism was triumphant in the East, they remained faithful to it and could not be wooed back to orthodoxy nor, even more definitely, to obedience to the Pope.

As had already occurred in the evolution of the history of Egypt, political centralization, in the Roman Empire, was accompanied by religious unity. The dismemberment of the Empire seemed as if it must entail, following a similar precedent, the dismemberment of the Church.

BOOK XIII

The Empire after the Invasions

CHAPTER LVII

THE GERMANS IN THE EMPIRE: FROM THE 5TH TO THE 7TH CENTURY AD

THE GERMANS ACCEPT ROMAN INSTITUTIONS

By sending the imperial insignia back to Zeno, Odoacer had in law restored the unity of the Empire; but while the eastern provinces and Italy retained the organization given them earlier by Diocletian and Constantine, the West, occupied by the barbarians, had broken up into a number of states under hereditary dynasties.

Pannonia was occupied by the Ostrogoths; Italy, with Dalmatia and parts of Noricum and Rhaetia, formed the kingdom of Odoacer; the Burgundians held the valley of the Rhône as far as the Durance, Savoy and Franche-Comté; a Visigoth Kingdom extended over Spain, Provence and western Gaul as far as the Loire; Galicia and northern Portugal were in the hands of the Suevi; Latin Africa, with Sardinia, Corsica and the Balearic Islands, formed a Vandal kingdom; northern Gaul between the Loire and the Somme was held by a former Roman general, Syagrius, who had proclaimed himself a king; further north, the Salian Franks and the Ripuarian Franks, and to the east the Alamanni, held the rest of Gaul. Finally, in the island of Britain the invasion of the Angles and Saxons had driven the Celts westward or made them emigrate to the peninsula of Brittany.

The years that followed brought a series of wars between the barbarian kings, which were to lead to important changes in the political geography of Europe.

In 486–487 the kingdom of Syagrius was conquered by Clovis, king of the Salian Franks.

The Emperor Zeno feared Odoacer, even though he had granted him the title of Patrician. He appointed the king of the Ostrogoths, Theodoric, as Imperial Commissary for Italy and sent him against Odoacer, by the same token removing Theodoric to a safe distance from Constantinople.

In 493 Odoacer was killed and Theodoric installed himself in the ancient imperial capital of Ravenna.

The West was to retain this political organization until the reign of Justinian.

It must not, however, be thought that the installation of barbarian dynasties in the former provinces of the Empire had put an end to its existence in the West.

Undoubtedly certain parts had been lost. In the island of Britain the Angles and Saxons, in Africa the Vandals and in Spain the Visigoths did not acknowledge the authority of the Emperor. But the other kings, even if they were considered as such by their own peoples, gloried in being generals or commissaries of the Emperor and solicited from him the titles of Patrician or Consul.

The barbarian vassals of the Empire were considered to be the Emperor's subjects and levied armies for his service.

It must be remembered that the number of these barbarians was relatively small. The Ostrogoths, who had settled in Italy in the midst of a population of four or five millions, numbered scarcely a hundred thousand, of whom twenty thousand were warriors; the Visigoths in Spain were no more numerous. In rich Africa, inhabited by five or six million people, there were not more than eighty thousand Vandals; the Burgundians in the Rhône valley were not more than twenty-five thousand, of whom five thousand were warriors. Of the whole population of the Empire, which amounted to above fifty millions, the Germans were not more than a million and in the provinces where they had settled, with the exception of those on the outermost fringes, they probably represented less than five per cent of the population.

This explains why their settlement in the Empire did not change Roman institutions. The system of personal law, which had reappeared since the barbarians had been admitted into the armies as federates, meant that Roman citizens and barbarians lived side by side, each according to their own customs. This had been a regular Roman practice since the times of Valentinian I and Valens.

The barbarians' customary law was, however, more or less influenced by Roman law. The Ostrogoths, 'federates' of the Empire since 454, were Christianized and Romanized to the point that when Theodoric settled at Ravenna their customs had for the most part disappeared under the influence of Roman law.

Among the Visigoths and the Burgundians, the Germanic customs were transformed into written law after contact with the Empire. At Toulouse,

Euris (466–484) had had the Visigothic Code drawn up in Latin. Gondebaud at the end of the 5th century promulgated, also in Latin, the Law of the Burgundians. Both these peoples were thoroughly Romanized. Settled on the soil of the Empire as allied soldiers, the Germans, dispersed among the Romans, acquired the idea of landed property and adopted Latin as their official language.

The Ostrogoths, the Burgundians, and even the Visigoths and the Vandals, formed the military element in the population. The Roman system of the *tertia* obliged every landowner to hand over a third of his estates to the troops, and the Germans, once settled in the Empire, were granted lands proportionately to the social rank which they held among their own people. Where the Vandals and the Visigoths formed independent kingdoms, they benefited from tax exemption. But the Burgundians and the Ostrogoths, whose kingdoms formed part of the Empire, did not enjoy any privileges because of their race. In the 6th century the Visigoths and the Burgundians began, moreover, to be assimilated with the Roman citizens, while the Vandals and the Ostrogoths were to disappear together with their state.

The German kings carried on their government surrounded by Roman officials. The law-schools at Toulouse, Lyon and Autun continued their activities and it was Roman jurists whom the barbarian kings called upon to codify the Germanic customs. The German chiefs had replaced the Roman authorities or had superimposed themselves on them, but they governed in a similar manner and made use of existing institutions. The Goths, the only Germans who had made use of writing before abandoning their national tongue,[1] possessed a translation of the Bible into Gothic, written in the 4th century, but they had no further literature.

In Italy Theodoric was so thoroughly imbued with Roman civilization that his court, of which all the principal writers of the time, Boethius, Cassiodorus and Ennodus, were members, conferred on Latin literature a last period of glory.

On the other hand, the barbarians brought about a rapid decay in Roman institutions and social usages, because of the ruin caused by the disorganization of economic life after the invasions, and the crudity of their manners which spread even among the aristocracy into which they had penetrated as landlords.

The Germans brought nothing specifically new with them, but they barbarized the Empire. In 417 Orosius, who had lived amongst them,

[1] Only the Saxons published their laws in the 7th century in the Saxon language and in Runic characters.

described them thus: 'The Goths are perfidious but chaste; the Alans more debauched but less perfidious; the Franks are liars but hospitable; the Saxons are horribly cruel but have an admirable purity of customs'. They were, in every sense of the word, primitive peoples. But the social decadence was not due to them alone. It was also due to the evolution towards a seigniorial régime which had affected the West since the times of Constantine. The lack of security during the period of the invasions had accelerated this process. The great landowners imposed their patronage on whole villages, transforming into *coloni* the neighbouring smallholders who sought their protection and arrogating to themselves the right of jurisdiction over the tenants of their domains.

The individualism of Roman law had not stood up to this social transformation; the *coloni*, tied to the lands of their lord, could not marry outside the domain without his consent and without paying him an indemnity. The Theodosian code could evidently not be applied to a population rapidly slipping towards such a régime of hereditary gradations.

The subdivision of the Empire among autonomous kings had decapitated the administration; only the provincial institutions continued to function, and even these were more or less disorganized, while the great central services had ceased to exist.

Therefore it was necessary, once the period of anarchy was over, to proceed to a general refurbishing of Roman law. Some Gallo-Roman jurists had drawn up a number of compilations for the use of judges, which adapted the law to the needs of the moment. These were the 'Roman Law of the Visigoths' of 506, known as the *Breviary of Alaric*, and, about the same period, the 'Roman Law of the Burgundians' or Papian. Roman law, as it was known to the Middle Ages up to the end of the 11th century, was thus established; the *Breviary of Alaric* was the basis of 'written law' in the French Midi. At the same time the barbarian customs were becoming Romanized so quickly that in the course of the 7th century the Visigothic king Recceswinth (649–672) published as 'Visigothic Law' a real Roman code, suppressing the law of persons between Germans and Romans. All that remained of the Germanic customs was the archaic *wehrgeld*[1], which came at just the right moment to take its place in the seigniorial régime which was being formed.

The situation was undoubtedly altogether different in the frontier areas of the Empire where the barbarians, by constant infiltration or by the

[1] Every crime or misdemeanour could be cleared by a certain sum paid to the victim or his family; this is what was called *composition*, or *wehrgeld*.

immigration of whole peoples, had settled in large numbers, submerging or destroying the Romanized population whose place they took. In the island of Britain, in Flanders, in the countries of the Rhine and Danube, the influence of the barbarians prevailed to such an extent that their languages took the place of the Latin dialects, and the Roman institutions were almost totally wiped out by the primitive customs which they brought with them.

THE SOCIAL STATUS OF THE NON-ROMANIZED GERMANS

The Germans, before their contact with the Empire, had had no knowledge of writing, of money or even of trade. They had no clergy. Their rudimentary religion, devoted, like that of all primitive peoples, to the forces of nature was devoid of any moral preoccupations.

Some of the Germans had however already been subjected to civilizing influences. Centuries of contact with the Greeks and Iranians had given the Scythians an art and a primitive culture which was especially evident among the Goths. But the northern Germans had known no form of civilization, even as a reflection of that of other peoples. They lived in tribes, bound by strict collective responsibility of religion and blood. The group alone was of importance. Law and morals did not extend beyond its compass. The individual did not exist as a legal concept. If a dispute arose between groups, it could only be settled by war. Each group was composed of families or *sippes* which included all the descendants of a common ancestor. In the monogamic families, created by wife-purchase, the authority of the father or the ancestor was omnipotent.

From this point of view, the evolution of the Germans was more advanced than that of the Slavs who, at this time, were settled on the plains of northern Russia. Paternal authority envisaged as a legal concept was not yet known. Only force ruled. Thus they abandoned old people at the end of winter on the floes floating down the rivers in order to get rid of them. As late as the 8th century the Wends sacrificed women on the death of their husbands. Certain German tribes, it is true, especially the Scandinavians, had not yet attained the régime of the patriachal family. Old people were excluded from the community, but instead of being put to death, as among the Wends, they were collected together into huts and given food.

It thus seemed that the further north the greater the degree of barbarism.

In the time of Caesar, the Germans who lived on the Rhine were still ignorant of the private ownership of land. The land occupied by the tribe

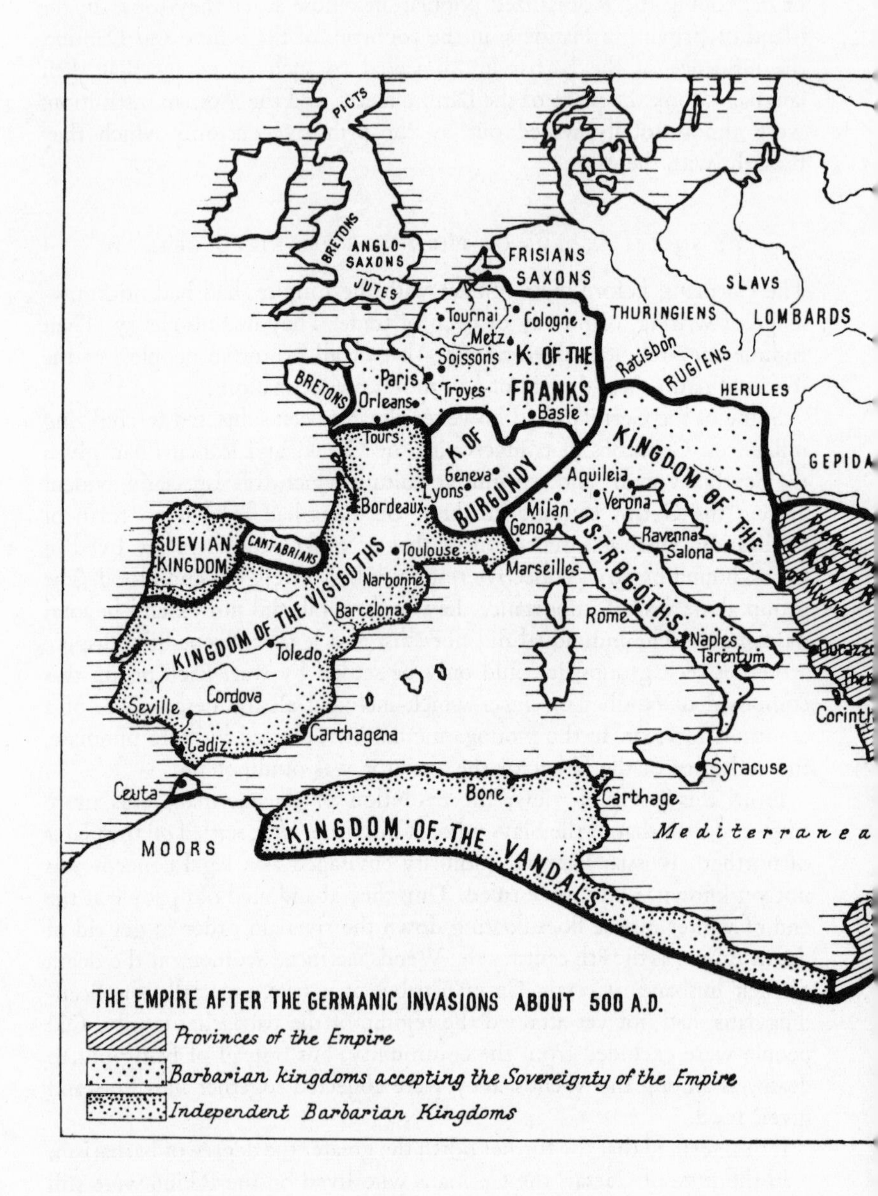

THE EMPIRE AFTER THE GERMANIC INVASIONS ABOUT 500 A.D.

Map No. 29

HUNS
ALANS
GOTHS
HEPHTALITES
(WHITE HUNS)
Caspian Sea
Olbia
Phanagoria
Panticapea (Kertch)
Theodosia
Cherson
(Sebastopol)
Phasis
Black Sea
Trebizond
Sinope
Tope
Hecatompylos
Ecbatana
Nicomedia
Nicaea
Cyzicus
ROMAN EMPIRE
PERSIAN
EMPIRE
Alexandretta
Aleppo
Antioch
Smyrna
Ephesus
Miletus
Ctesiphon
Charax
Hira
Persian Gulf
Palmyra
Tripoli
Beirut
Sidon
Tyre
Damascus
Caesarea
Petra
Alexandria
Pelusium
Ailana
ARABIA
Memphis
Medina
Koptos
Thebes
Red Sea
Syene
Mecca
M.

was divided between the families and redistributed periodically. In the time of Tacitus, the same tribes, having been obliged to settle down when faced by the Roman frontiers, were slowly becoming civilized. Rudimentary houses took the place of huts and formed the first private property. Stock too began to be apportioned to the families, amongst whom the use of the tribal lands was divided according to the number of draft animals that each family possessed. This system was introduced into England by the Angles and Saxons and was to prevail there in certain districts up to the 13th century.

The social nucleus of Germanic society was the *sippe*, composed of a minority of free men who formed the aristocracy, numerous retainers—men without family or the remnants of conquered peoples—and also slaves captured in war. The nobles and their retainers formed the army.

The tribe was represented by its warriors in arms, who met in assemblies to choose their chiefs, or settle disputes which the families submitted to the people's judgment.

By the time that the Franks began to settle in the Empire, a certain military organization had already begun to be superimposed on the purely family system; 'hundreds', or groups of a hundred families, formed the framework of the army and, consequently, of the people. It was amongst these hundreds that the first judicial organization, though only for arbitration in disputes, appeared; it was not intended to assure respect for equity but rather the security of the group.

Justice was rudimentary and formalist, as among all primitive peoples; it was limited to a 'conjuration' of members of the disputant groups who took oath together to affirm their rights; the largest group won the case, since the will of the gods was made manifest by this ceremony.

After forcing their way into the Empire, the Salian Franks settled between the Scheldt and the Lys, the Ripuarian Franks along the lower Rhine, and the Alamanni in Alsace and the former Rhaetia. The Roman population was driven back before them and they occupied the lands which had been abandoned and founded villages there. The chiefs took up residence in the great villas. That was why Clovis was born at Tournai in a villa once belonging to the Imperial Treasury. But since the country, from the 3rd century onwards, had been many times devastated by the Franks before they finally settled there, a large number of small towns and Roman villas were no more than ruins.

The founding of villages had given rise to a new form of unity based on proximity alongside the former unity of the *sippe* based on blood relationship.

The land was first divided amongst the hundreds which, thenceforward, formed territorial divisions; within the hundreds it was shared out among the *sippes* and then among the individual families, who took possession of it. The former nobility was thus transformed into a landed aristocracy.

The land, since it was a common patrimony, was inalienable and could only be allotted to men, since women, on marriage, would have caused it to pass out of the family.

In default of blood heirs, the village community made the neighbour the natural heir. This rule of succession, based on proximity, was suppressed about 575 by an edict of Chilperic; but the collectivity of family property still existed among the Franks and the Alamanni in the 7th century.[1]

THE FRANKISH MONARCHY

Once settled on the land, the Frankish tribes naturally organized themselves in a military manner and the choice of a permanent army leader from the most powerful of the *sippes* led, in the 5th century, to the emergence of royalty. It was an elective, aristocratic and military monarchy. A king of the Salian Franks, a member of the Merovingian family, took part in the battle of the Catalaunian Fields as a federate. The Salian kings thenceforward tried to move southward. Another Merovingian, Childeric, appeared on the Loire, but Syagrius drove him back to Tournai. But from 486 onwards Clovis took possession, city by city, of the territory of the Roman state of Syagrius. Twenty years later, the petty king of Tournai had conquered almost all of France from the Alamanni, the Burgundians and the Visigoths.

He was able to do this because he had the support of the bishops. Clovis was a pagan, but the Burgundians and the Visigoths were heretics. That was the reason why the Church made Clovis, married to a Burgundian princess who was a Catholic, its champion against the heretics. Converted in 506, he was to become the instrument of the orthodoxy which had ensured his triumph.

The great conflict that divided the West at this time was not, in fact, between Romans and barbarians, but between orthodoxy and Arianism. The Church preferred a frankly pagan barbarian, whom it could make a Catholic, to the Burgundian and Visigoth kings, who were Christians but Arians. Furthermore, no feeling of racial community existed among the Germans. Himself a German, Clovis halted the thrust of the Alamanni

[1] This evolution towards private property in land corresponds exactly to the evolution which took place among the Kassites after the XXth century BC, when they settled in the Babylonian Empire.

which threatened Gaul with far-reaching Germanization; a recently converted pagan, he restored Christian unity and established the Frankish monarchy in Paris, based on a close alliance between king and church.

In 507 the battle of Vouille, when the Visigothic king Alaric II was driven back, delivered almost the whole of Gaul to Clovis, with the exception of Brittany, and the Mediterranean coast which was shared between the Ostrogoths and the Visigoths.

Twenty-five years later Provence and Septimania were incorporated into the Frankish kingdom. Clovis thus assured himself possession of the great port of Marseilles and the cities of Provence, which were to play a preponderant role in the economic and political development of his kingdom up to the time of the Islamic invasion.

The dominions of Clovis were of a hybrid character. In the north, the Franks occupied those provinces of present-day Belgium which have remained Flemish; they lived there in accordance with their national customs. From Tournai to the Loire, Clovis had installed, in the villas of the Roman Treasury, Frankish chiefs and soldiers who had rapidly been assimilated into the Roman population. South of the Loire, Gaul had remained entirely Gallo-Roman.

It was in the north of the Frankish kingdom that the Germanic customs were preserved most faithfully. They had perhaps already been collected in the German language before the times of Clovis, but they were drawn up in Latin apparently during his reign to form the Salic Law. It was no more than a code of criminal law, a tariff of 'compositions' (*wehrgeld*), intended to replace private war; Roman influence was entirely absent.

The conquests of Clovis did not give the Franks a dominant position in the kingdom. The Merovingian kings lost interest in their own people, the greater number of whom remained settled in Flanders, even to the point of not trying to convert them. It was only in the 7th century that Aquitanian missionaries, St Remacle and St Armand, converted the Franks. The Salic Law had very little influence in Gaul. Applied fully in the north, and jointly with Roman law in Central France, it was unknown south of the Loire.

On the other hand, Roman institutions were imposed on the Germans. There are marked traces of them in the law of the Ripuarian Franks, which was drawn up in the 6th and 7th centuries, as also in the law of the Alamanni, which was codified by Clotair II (584–628).

It is very important, if one is to understand the social and political history of Gaul under the Merovingians and Carolingians, to take account of this duality, Germanic in the north, Gallo-Roman in the south. In these two regions, so profoundly divergent and living under diametrically opposed laws, a double juridical evolution took place. In the north, the Germanic régime of collective property moved towards family property, following a process which more and more broke up the primitive groups; in the south, the Roman régime of individual property was being dissolved into a seigniorial system, within which the collectivity of the family was re-established. These contrasting evolutions, progressive among the Germans who were passing from tribal collectivity to private property and decadent among the Gallo-Romans whose individualist society was disappearing as it was submerged by the manorial organization, merged in Carolingian times into a single system which was to be that of seigniorial feudalism.

As long as the Germans and the Gallo-Romans had differing social organizations, the system of personal law continued to exist; that is to say, each of them lived according to his own national law. When the evolutions to which each of them was subject merged and united them in a single social organization this system of 'personality' disappeared in favour of 'territoriality', that is to say that the territory and not the nationality of its occupants decided their legal status.

The Frankish kings soon lost their Germanic character. They became very wealthy because of the confiscation of the lands of the Roman Treasury, and being surrounded by Roman officials they ceased to be elected kings and became, in accordance with the imperial conception of power, absolute sovereigns.

The wealth of Provence, its cities, its trade, the yield of the taxes and the trade-dues, ended by concentrating the interests of the Merovingian monarchy in the south. The Frankish population, forgotten in the north, continued its evolution towards seigniorial landed property without playing the slightest role in the destinies of *Francia*.

Henceforward the king lived at Paris, Soissons, Metz, Rheims or Orleans. His policy was dictated by Roman Gaul and by the Church, over which he ruled like the Emperor at Constantinople. He adapted himself to the Roman system of government, whose officials continued to administer the finances and collect the taxes. As under the Empire, the administration remained secular.

On the whole the Roman institutions, though greatly watered down, survived the invasion.[1] The cities kept their governors, under the title of

[1] The central organs of the administration disappeared. Thus, the Pretorian Prefecture of the Gauls, which had numbered a thousand officials at its administrative centre, no longer existed. In the middle of the 6th century the Merovingian courts no longer possessed ministers of the imperial type.

'counts';[1] their jurisdictions and their corporations remained, and the state still retained the fiscal basis on which the payment of its officials depended. Monetary economy remained as before, as well as trade which was mostly in the hands of Syrians and Jews.

Despite the decadence into which they had fallen since the 3rd century and which, in the north and centre of Gaul, had reduced them to a few thousand inhabitants each, the cities still formed, in the south, the framework of the economy of the country. Along the coasts, along the rivers and the great trade routes, international and seaborne trade were concentrated on Marseilles, Fréjus, Arles, Orange, Lyon and Toulouse.

Through Marseilles, Gaul remained in contact with Cartagena, Carthage, Alexandria, Constantinople, Antioch and Ephesus, the principal cities which maintained the unity of Mediterranean trade which was entirely centred in the East. The coinage of all the barbarian kingdoms made use of the Byzantine gold piece as a standard; only the Anglo-Saxons, separated from the economy of the Empire, lived on a silver standard.

Silk, spices, papyrus, glass and luxury products were imported from the East, and as return freight Marseilles shipped wood, textiles, cloth, garments and also slaves captured from the Saxons, the Thuringians and the far distant Wends. Verdun and Marseilles were the main slave markets. But the Gaulish glassworks, so celebrated in the 4th century, had disappeared, a characteristic sign of the economic decadence after the invasions.

Besides religious unity, seaborne trade promoted among all the Mediterranean countries as well as among the barbarian kingdoms an economic unity which helped to maintain the idea of the unity of the Empire and encouraged the absorption of the invaders by Roman civilization.

VANDAL AFRICA

Even in Africa, where Genseric had founded an independent kingdom which had from the start refused to accept the authority of the Emperor, the Vandals were absorbed. They came as conquerors, confiscated the lands of the Roman landowners and handed them over to the barbarian aristocrats, who settled in the country as a privileged military minority. None the less, Roman civilization rapidly assimilated them. In 442 Genseric, whom the Emperor had just recognized as an independent king, crushed an insurrection of the Vandal nobility who had determined to maintain their aristocratic organization according to Germanic custom. Even as he

[1] The Roman title of 'count' (*comes*) meant Companion of the Emperor.

aimed at taking the place of the Emperor, so he intended to become an absolute sovereign in the Roman manner. He made Latin the official language of the kingdom and surrounded himself at Carthage with a court modelled on that of Constantinople.

Like the Emperors, the Vandal kings wished to base their power on the Church whose unity they aimed at upholding within their kingdom. And, being Arians, they indulged in ferocious persecutions of the Catholics. These were to contribute greatly to their rapid downfall.

The course of events in the Roman Empire of the West was similar to what had taken place in the Seleucid Kingdom in the IInd and Ist centuries BC. The provinces, by becoming semi-independent states, wrested from the monarchy its exclusive sovereign right and feudalized it. A centrifugal movement broke up the Empire before destroying it. Some of the provinces even detached themselves entirely. But even as Hellenism survived the dismemberment of Seleucid Asia, so too did *Romania* continue to exist even in those regions which, like Africa, had broken with the imperial authority, because the economic unity created by the sea combined in a single whole those states which had built themselves up on the ruin of the Empire of the West, and the Byzantine Empire which had maintained the imperial tradition.

CHAPTER LVIII

JUSTINIAN RECONQUERS THE MEDITERRANEAN

THE SITUATION IN THE EAST DURING THE 5TH CENTURY
THE DECLINE OF EGYPT

WHILE the Empire of the West was breaking up into Romanized barbarian kingdoms, the Empire of the East passed through a very severe internal crisis during the 5th century. The extension of the manorial régime and of 'colonization' had ended, especially in Egypt, by subjecting the mass of the people to a small minority of large landowners. The social evolution commenced by the state-socialist policy of the Ptolemies had reached its culmination. In the course of the IInd century BC autarchic state-socialism had imposed on Egypt a policy of controlled economy which ended by cutting the country off from the rest of the world. Only Alexandria remained directly in contact with international trade. The result had been the quick decline of all the Egyptian cities of the Delta, formerly so wealthy and populous, and the exodus of all the active middle class to Alexandria. In the countryside there remained only peasants, priests, officials and landowners. The Hellenized élite was thus totally separated from the mass of the people, which was attached to the great domains by hereditary tenures.

Cleopatra had broken the autarchic structure of Egypt, but from the time of Augustus onward the Emperors had again taken up the fiscal methods of the Ptolemies for their own advantage, and the Egyptian population had become more and more exploited by the Treasury and the great Hellenized landowners who gradually took over all the higher posts in the administration.

Cleopatra's reforms had come too late to restore the Egyptian cities to their former activity. Urban civilization was already too deeply in decline for it to be revived. Yet for thirty centuries past Egypt had been essentially a land of cities, in the sense that her economic, artistic, moral and political activities had been dominated by their influence. The extinction of the urban era in Egypt, which took place under the Roman Empire, led to an enormous decrease in the population. From eight to ten millions at the time of the Ptolemies, it was no more, at the time of the emergence of Islam, than six millions, amongst whom about two hundred thousand were Hellenized. The greatness and wealth of Alexandria concealed the utter ruin of Egypt, which was never to recover from the autarchic state-socialist policy of the Ptolemies, continued, in the form of fiscal exploitation, by the Roman Emperors.

The consequence was twofold, social and economic. From the social viewpoint, the people, reduced to serfdom but still preserving their earlier individualist aspirations, were ranged in opposition to the landed proprietors. A strong class antagonism arose between the *coloni* and their lords. The *coloni* spoke Egyptian (Coptic) and their piety, which was now manifested in their Christian sentiments as formerly it had been shown in their Osirian mysticism, centred around the clergy. The landowners, on the contrary, spoke Greek and held all the high administrative posts. So this social opposition took the form of an Egyptian national reaction against the Greek aristocracy. On the other hand the clergy, relying upon the people, tried to take over power in a struggle with the landed and administrative aristocracy supported by the government in Constantinople. The seigniorial régime thus provoked two opposite currents in Egypt, one of the priests and the other of the nobles, both of which tended towards the feudalization of the country; but by neutralizing one another, they allowed the Emperor to retain his power unbroken. Quite naturally, this social and national opposition went hand in hand with a religious opposition. The people, not only the people of the countryside but also the proletariat of Alexandria, were enthusiastic supporters of monophysism which had become imbued in the 5th century with that Neoplatonic mysticism so closely allied to the religious sentiments of ancient Egypt; the Greek aristocrats, on the contrary, remained faithful to Catholic orthodoxy. This fact made the monophysite controversy exceptionally serious during the 5th century; its social character explains the riots and massacres to which the religious conflict continually gave rise.

Monophysism thus became in Egypt the centre of the popular and national movement. The people rejected Greek influence. But it had lost its élite, and the revival of Egyptian literature in the Coptic language was lamentably weak. Its most famous representative was Chenudi, who was to become the great Egyptian saint; he was both a mystic and a revolutionary. He aimed at slaughtering the Greek landlords, lawyers and writers in Egypt, whom he accused of being pagans or heretics; social hatred mingled with nationalist sentiment and religious fanaticism.

The Patriarch of Alexandria, who aspired to the domination of Egypt, made himself the champion of monophysism, supported by the clergy and the people.

Social decline went hand in hand with economic decline. The ruin of the cities deprived Egypt of the great industrial activity she had formerly enjoyed. Alexandria suffered the effects; but it none the less remained the main centre of international trade between the Empire and the markets of India. Koptos, in Upper Egypt, was in direct communication with the Red Sea by the Wadi Hammamat, and the port of Leukos-Limen (the former Qoseïr) also retained its importance as a stage on the Eastern trade-route. The Indian trade remained in the hands of Egyptian merchants. But whereas in the 2nd century Egyptian ships sailed directly to the Indian port of Muziris and the island of Ceylon, and Roman merchants settled at Barygaza and even at Canton, the Egyptian ships in the 5th century, whose home-port was Ailana on the Red Sea, did not sail beyond the port of Adulis in Abyssinia; navigation had declined to what it had been under the Ancient Empire, when it did not adventure farther than the Land of Punt. Abyssinia, on the other hand, had taken a leading place in international trade. Its ships sailed to Ceylon and frequented the ports of Arabia and the Persian Gulf. It was through Adulis that the silk from China, from which the Syrian cities derived their wealth, was imported into the Empire. An important colony of Egyptian merchants had settled at Adulis, through whom Christianity penetrated into Abyssinia in the 4th century.

NATIONAL REACTION IN SYRIA

In Syria the situation was quite different. The Seleucid Empire had been dismembered, but without involving in its ruin the prosperity of the wealthy cities of the Syrian coast. Urban civilization had preserved Greek influence among them to a much greater extent than in Egypt. The great business activities of the Phoenician cities and the new cities created by the Seleucids had kept abreast of the cosmopolitan current, which was the vehicle of Hellenism. Beirut, seat of the famous law-school, was one of the principal centres of Hellenistic thought. In the countryside, however, the seigniorial régime had expanded and led to similar consequences as in Egypt; the rural population had little by little been reduced to serfdom by the great landed proprietors against whom it looked for help from the clergy. A similar antagonism therefore appeared there between the Hellenized landlords and the clergy who supported the people in its struggle against social oppression and in reaction against Hellenism. Syriac literature revived and, as in Egypt, the nationalist movement was associated in Syria also with the monophysite heresy.

PALESTINE

In Palestine, on the other hand, monophysism failed. The Patriarch of Jerusalem remained faithful to Catholic orthodoxy. It was only in Palestine that the native population had remained hostile to Christianity. Only the Hellenized middle classes had had any influence on the Church and there, as elsewhere, the Hellenized classes in the 5th century remained for the most part attached to orthodoxy. Palestine became one of the centres of Hellenism; Gaza, in particular, took on the aspect of a Greek city.

RE-ESTABLISHMENT OF THE CENTRAL POWER IN THE EASTERN EMPIRE BY REACTION AGAINST STATE-SOCIALISM

The social and religious situation of the eastern provinces, the richest in the Empire, exercised a decisive role in the destinies of the Empire of the East in the 5th and 6th centuries. Two forces met and clashed there; the landed aristocracy, against whom the ardent hostility of the enslaved peoples became more and more aroused, and the population of the cities. The latter, represented in its dealings with the state by the petty local aristocracy of the *curiales*, landowners to whom entry into the mercantile professions was denied, were economically dominated by the businessmen who, because of their control of international trade, formed the essential element of the economic life of the Empire.

The Empire of the West had become involved in irremediable decline by the triumph of the class of landed proprietors who had turned themselves into *seigneurs*. In the East the influence of the cities won the day. Constantinople was a great international mart, a centre of banking with a prosperous industry. Salonica, Corinth, the many cities of Asia Minor and the Syrian cities, amongst which Antioch held pride of place, Gaza in Palestine, and in Egypt Alexandria, the busiest port of the Mediterranean, constituted the real backbone of the Empire. They were to determine the policy of the 5th century Emperors in their task of reconstituting the central power.

At the time when Odoacer in Rome overturned the puppet Emperor

Romulus Augustulus (476), Zeno the Isaurian seized the throne of Constantinople. He had, it seems, formerly been a pirate whom the Emperor Leo (died 474) had made use of to fight against the over-powerful minister Aspar, who was supported by the Ostrogothic federated troops. The advent of Zeno did not lead to any dynastic crisis. Such was still the imperial prestige that Odoacer, master of Rome, sent him the imperial insignia and recognized him as overlord.

The unity of the Empire was thus legally re-established to the benefit of the Emperor of Constantinople. The critical phase of the invasions was past. The East had emerged from it intact. The crisis that was just over seemed to contemporaries comparable with that which had dismembered the Empire in the 3rd century. The reconstruction of the Empire was to be courageously undertaken by the Emperors.

While the Ostrogoths devasted the Balkan provinces, Zeno sent the most powerful of their chiefs, Theodoric, to Italy. He installed himself at Ravenna where, being very much Romanized, he gave his court and government an imperial character. He soon gathered under his sovereignty all the barbarian kings, and the Empire of the West seemed to have been restored in the form of a federation of kingdoms.

The cruel and bloodthirsty Zeno had as successor a palace official, the Epirote Anastasius (491–518) whom the widowed Empress brought to the throne by marrying him. He set himself methodically to the task of reconstructing the Empire. Understanding that the greatest danger that threatened it was the dismemberment of the country under the seigniorial régime, he undertook to defend smallholding against the ascendancy of the great landed proprietors and to favour the activity of the cities, thanks to which the Empire of the East still had considerable financial resources. The existence of these great commercial centres was, moreover, an essential condition for the maintenance of rural smallholding, because of the outlets they assured to agricultural produce.

To restore the life of the cities, Anastasius I broke away from the state-socialist policies which had been adopted by Constantine and his successors and helped, by reducing the crushing privileges of the treasury, to save individual initiative from the authoritarian rule that had stifled it. A first reform suppressed the collective responsibility of the *curiales* in fiscal matters and handed over the collection of the taxes to special officials. It is enough to recall the legal and social consequences that this collective responsibility of the *curiales* had caused to understand how important was its suppression, because it restored to them the free disposition of their goods and properties.

He then tried to improve the administration of the cities by restoring to them a certain measure of political life. The municipal officials entrusted with buying grain for the supply of the cities were elected by the bishops and the landowners from among the officials of the provincial government. The 'defender' of the city, who had hitherto been appointed by the Emperor, was thenceforward also elected by the bishops, the great landowners and the *curiales*. The bishops were also charged with the supervision of military supplies in order to avoid the abuses which had crept in. The bishop, himself elected by the community of Christians, found himself entrusted with a sort of guardianship over the administration which the Emperor was trying to free from the extortions and peculations which had crept in to it.

Valentinian I had handed over to the treasury two-thirds of the municipal revenues. Anastasius made use of these resources to benefit the cities themselves.

As to the manorial economy, organized on the basis of 'colonization', there could be no question of suppressing it; it was far too closely linked with the fiscal organization of the Empire. But in order to prevent an increase in the enslavement of the rural population, a law established that peasants were to be attached to the soil as *coloni* only if they had held the same tenure for the past thirty years. Furthermore, instead of becoming enslaved *coloni*, they preserved their liberty and remained capable of possessing and, in consequence, of disposing of their properties without any intervention by their lord. This was a further application of the principle which had caused Anastasius to suppress the collective responsibility of the *curiales* to the treasury; in the cities and in the countryside the Emperor tried to restore to the middle classes the free disposition of their goods and properties, of which they had been deprived by the state-socialist policy.

The fiscal policy of Anastasius was on a par with his social policy. On coming to the throne he remitted unpaid taxes to debtors, lightened the burdens that weighed upon the poorer classes and tried to revive by subsidies the regions devastated by war or in difficulties because of bad harvests.

Anastasius was able to check the drift towards state-socialism and the seigniorial régime only because the East had retained its international commercial activity, to which the restoration of order after the great invasions gave an upsurge of prosperity.

The Sassanid kings had control of the land- and sea-routes which led to India and China by way of Central Asia and the Persian Gulf; they kept a strict mopopoly of them and imposed heavy duties on the trade in silk, spices and precious stones imported from the East and greatly hampered Roman exports to Asia.

Roman commerce could, however, still escape this control by making use of the Red Sea route.

The Empire remained in contact with India through Abyssinia, despite the decline of its merchant marine. Peace and good administration of the finances under Anastasius encouraged trade with the East.

The weakness of Rome had always been the deficit in its trading balance. The Empire of the East faced up to this danger by encouraging the development of luxury industries at Antioch, Beirut and Tyre and, in general, in all the cities of Asia Minor and Syria, whose exports and whose role as international markets for wine, purple, worked leather and gold- and silversmiths' work caused the precious metals that assured its monetary stability to flow into the Imperial treasury. Their prosperity kept busy the port of Alexandria, the market for spices and papyrus, while the bank of Constantinople made great profits by organizing the necessary business credits.

On his accession Anastasius had found the treasury greatly depleted by the ruinous war of 458 against the Vandals. But after twenty-seven years of his reign the treasury possessed a reserve of twenty-three million gold *solidi*, which was undoubtedly due to his excellent financial administration. However, when it is taken into account that the annual revenue did not exceed seven million gold *solidi*, it is clear that the prosperity of the treasury could only have come from the economic prosperity that the Empire was then experiencing. The Imperial Treasury doubtless made considerable profits from its credit operations, advancing state funds to business men at 6% interest. The customs houses did not benefit only from the dues on imports and exports, since Anastasius, by attaching *commerciarii* to the customs administration, men who were commissioned to supervise state trade operations, was probably trying to put the sums received from the customs to profitable use.

The abundance of liquid capital shows that in his reign the trade balance must have been for the most part favourable. The result was soon felt throughout the whole Mediterranean area; the revival of monetary economy which took place in the West at the end of the 5th century could only have been due to the revival of trade between the eastern cities and the West.

Restoration of the finances permitted Anastasius to re-organize the army. In the 4th century barbarians had been excluded from it. But voluntary recruitment did not provide enough men. In the 5th century the Empire had to have recourse once again to the barbarians, not to engage them under their own chiefs as armed bands in the service of the Empire but to enrol them in the cavalry regiments under the command of Roman officers.

RELIGIOUS CONFLICTS

The restoration of the imperial power met, however, with a very serious obstacle; the unity of the Empire was breaking up. In Egypt and Syria, social conflicts and national movements destroyed the homogeneity of the culture which had been formed in the eastern Mediterranean since Hellenistic times. Greek was gradually replaced by Coptic and Syriac. The feeling of imperial unity diminished. Since the 4th century the arbitrary nature of the administrative oligarchy which had been created by authoritarian state-socialism had led to a great decline in manners and customs. In the provinces of Asia torture became more and more common, if not in law then at least in criminal practice. Brutality became the general rule, despite the triumph of Christianity. It is true that contradictory currents divided society; Anastasius, for instance, forbade gladiatorial combats in the circuses; but on the whole the moral decadence was evident. Education was in decline; so too was thought.

The breaking up of the Empire was accompanied by more and more serious religious conflicts. Monophysism, which had become a national religion in Egypt, conquered Antioch during the reign of Anastasius, while the Patriarchs of Constantinople and Jerusalem, even though in conflict with the Pope, remained Catholic. The school of Edessa declared for the Nestorian heresy, which had a firm footing in Persia. In the West the Arian heresy triumphed with Theodoric, suzerain of all the Germanic courts.

Among the barbarian kings, Clovis alone was converted to Catholicism. It may be well imagined how important this conversion was for Rome at a time when the Church was torn by internal dissensions so serious that they led everywhere to riots, assassinations and even terrible massacres.

The Emperor Anastasius was himself a monophysite by conviction and also, doubtless, by policy, since Egypt and Syria, the provinces upon which the whole economic life of the Empire depended, were monophysite. In order not to break with the Patriarchs of Alexandria and Antioch he came into conflict with the Pope, Symmachus (died 514), who declared him a heretic. The break between the Pope and the Emperor led to the defection of Theodoric, the sole link between the imperial authority and the barbarian kingdoms of the West. At Constantinople itself, the people sided violently with the Catholic Patriarch against the monophysite Emperor, who only with difficulty suppressed a revolt in the army and the fleet.

JUSTINIAN RECONQUERS THE EMPIRE (527–565)

On the death of Anastasius in 518 there was a reaction against monophysism and the influence of the eastern provinces. Two thirds of the Empire of the East, especially all those regions which were Hellenized, were Catholic. A rough Illyrian soldier, Justin I, of Latin speech, urged on by his nephew Justinian who was intriguing for power, was elected Emperor.

Justinian succeeded him in 527. He was to undertake the restoration of the Empire by force of arms, conceiving it as a Mediterranean state dependent on the sea and its economic interests.

The excellent government of Anastasius had restored enormous financial and military power to the Empire. The currency was stable and the economic prosperity considerable.

Justinian looked on the restoration of the Empire from a twofold viewpoint; maritime and economic on the one hand, religious on the other; the Empire must recover its supremacy over all the Mediterranean lands and the touchstone of its unity must be religious orthodoxy.

This probably explains why Justinian turned to Gaul, the only one of all the barbarian states which was Catholic, for support. Without doubt, Gaul was less important for Constantinople than Spain or Africa, and the Merovingian court was less civilized than those of the Vandal, Visigoth or Ostrogoth kings. But the Merovingian kings were supported by Rome and accepted by the Roman populations because they were Catholics.

On the contrary the other German kings who had remained faithful to Arianism were detested by their Roman subjects, not because they were barbarians but because they professed the heresy of Arius. To restore the Empire, Justinian had to be accepted by the Roman populations and any conflict with the Pope would have made this impossible.

The war he was about to undertake was therefore to assume both a political and a religious character. It was to aim at restoring the unity both of the Empire and of the Church.

Before involving himself in this war, however, Justinian re-established peace on his eastern frontiers (532) by putting an end to the war with the Persians which the Empire had been carrying on for six years without decisive results.

His first move was to attack Carthage, the key to the Central Mediterranean. An invasion army was disembarked in Africa by a fleet of five hundred ships, and the Vandal kingdom, which had lost its pristine military vigour, collapsed. The possession of Carthage restored mastery in the Mediterranean to Constantinople, and the squadrons of Justinian occupied Corsica, Sardinia and the Balearic Islands.

Assailed from both Sicily and Dalmatia, Italy was then re-conquered from the Ostrogoths (525–540). Taking advantage of a civil war then raging in the Visigoth kingdom, the Byzantines occupied the coasts of Spain, with the ports of Malaga and Cartagena and the great city of Cordova. The rest of the country was left to the Visigothic kings.

However Totila, king of the Ostrogoths, took the field again in 541. Since his people had suffered enormous losses during the war, he hit upon the idea of getting fresh recruits for his army by appealing to the Italian population. To obtain the troops he needed, he liberated the slaves on the great estates *en masse* and to gain the support of the *coloni* he freed them from the forced labour and the dues that they owed to the great landlords. He thus created common interests between the Goths and the rural classes in Italy; this explains the considerable military effort that Byzantium had to make in order to reconquer the country a second time (552).

At first Justinian had appealed to the Franks against the Goths. In order to conciliate them he had recognized their possession of Provence in 538, which they had had ceded to them by the Ostrogoths who, like Justinian, had been seeking their alliance. But, profiting by the war, the king of the Franks, Theodobert, pursued an independent policy and, to the detriment of both belligerents, had taken possession of a considerable portion of Piedmont and Venetia and made himself master of Noricum. He was even dreaming of conquering Constantinople at the head of a Germanic confederation (545) and of restoring the Empire to his own advantage, when Justinian halted him by inciting the Lombards against Theodobert's allies the Gepidi on the middle Danube.

Twenty years of war restored to Justinian almost all the maritime provinces of the former Empire. Only Provence remained in the hands of the Franks; but they were already reverting to a policy of friendship with the Emperor. The Mediterranean had once again become a Roman sea.

JUSTINIAN TRIES TO RESTORE THE RELIGIOUS UNITY OF THE EMPIRE

Now that the Empire had been restored in its most essential features, it remained to assure its cohesion by restoring its religious unity; but here a fresh conflict arose which endangered the whole work of Justinian. Arianism, it is true, was destroyed. But in the bosom of the orthodox Church, the terrible question of monophysism, which had caused a schism between the East and the West (from 484–518), remained a serious threat to the unity of the Empire. Even in the capital itself, it divided the 'parties' into which the Constantinople mob was divided, the party of 'the blues' standing for orthodoxy and 'the greens' for monophysism.

Monophysism held absolute mastery in Egypt and in Syria. The Empress Theodora, who was a monophysite, managed to get one of her protégés, Vigilius, installed on the pontifical throne of Rome. Justinian took advantage of this to try to reconcile Catholics and monophysites by proposing a christological formula which should satisfy both sides. He obtained the support of the Catholics, but the monophysites remained intransigent; for them, the conflict went beyond religion; they were not only separated from Rome by dogmatic differences, but were also opposed to Constantinople in an indomitable social and national resistance.

Since he was unable to reconcile them by persuasion, Justinian launched very severe persecutions against them, especially in Egypt. These only succeeded in aggravating the conflict still more.

For his part Vigilius, obliged to take into account the religious susceptibilities of the West and the interests of the great landed proprietors of Italy who demanded the radical abolition of the social reforms of Totila, began to adopt a policy of opposition to the efforts at conciliation made by Justinian and to contest the Emperor's right to interfere in matters of dogma. Justinian did not hesitate; Vigilius was arrested and taken to Constantinople where he bowed to the wishes of the Emperor (553). But if monophysism had made common cause with the interests of the proletariat, orthodox Catholicism was closely bound up with the great landowners. Therefore it was not enough to make the Pope give way on dogmatic formulae, but it was also necessary to regain the confidence of the landed aristocracy. That was why, in 554, Justinian sent Vigilius back to Rome, as the bearer of a pragmatic sanction that restored the forced labour dues of the *coloni* which had been suppressed by Totila and gave back to the great landowners the slaves whom the Gothic king had freed.

The efforts of Anastasius to prevent the enslavement of the rural population and the troubles of the time of Justinian had a profound influence on the social evolution of Italy. The peasants ceased to be tied to the soil and, in the course of the following centuries, the *coloni* system was gradually replaced by a system of leasehold tenures, in which contracts concluded for less than thirty years did not allow the proprietor to reduce to the status of *coloni*, that is to say serfs, the occupants of his domain, as happened in all the former western provinces of the Empire.

The reaction of the Emperors to the ascendancy of the *seigneurs* thus became one of the essential causes why serfdom was only to spread to a small extent in Italy.

The concession that he had made to the great magnates allowed Justinian to have consecrated as successor to Vigilius a Pope of his own choice, Pelagius, who was a docile tool of imperial policy and collaborated fruitfully with the Byzantine administration in the restoration of Italy, which had been devastated by twenty years of war.

There still remained the indomitable opposition of the monophysites to prevent religious unity from being restored in the Empire. All the achievements of Justinian were henceforth compromised; the Empire was a union of provinces under the imperial authority, but it was not the bloc, cemented by a common ideology, of which Justinian had dreamed.

THE CIVIL CODE

While he was once again conquering the Empire, Justinian, like the great statesman he was, was modifying his institutions to new needs. His legislative work was immense. It was crowned in 529 by the promulgation of the Justinian Code,[1] drawn up by a commission of jurists under the chairmanship of the learned Tribonian. A second commission collected all the legal texts, of doctrine and of jurisprudence, in the compilation known as the *Digest* (or *Pandects*) in 533; a manual, intended for students, was also published under the title of *The Institutes*. The legislative work of Justinian himself after 534 was collected under the title of the *Novellae*. Thenceforward, Roman law, freed from the archaisms which encumbered it, became a rational corpus of doctrines, deeply influenced by the evolution of the social ideas of the time. The individualism of classical law was breached by humanitarian conceptions, in the name of which the will of the parties was in many cases modified by the law; measures taken to limit the total of rents, to reduce interest rates despite the agreement of the parties concerned, are symptomatic of a profound change in the idea of law; without its being expressed, the theory known in our own days as 'abuse of law' may be discovered in the Code of Justinian.

The Code and the Digest are the greatest works of legislation that have ever been carried out. The enormous mass of work that they entailed,

[1] We have only the second edition, which appeared in 534.

the technical perfection of the Latin language,[1] the knowledge to which they bear witness, are the most striking illustration of the intellectual vitality of Constantinople at that time.

ABANDONMENT OF AUTHORITARIANISM

Justinian did not want merely to codify the law; he wished to make it a living force and to restore to the population the civic life from which it had been excluded by state-socialist policy.

The inspirer of his reforms was the great Pretorian Prefect, John of Cappadocia. They aimed at breaking the growing influence of the great landowners, whose feudal tendencies were becoming a real danger to the Empire.

These reforms, which covered the whole organization of public life, were not carried out without causing tumultuous reaction among the people of Constantinople. Greens and blues, though enemies in religion, at once united in opposition. A formidable riot broke out against the Emperor which, stirred up by the dynastic intrigues of the nephews of the Emperor Anastasius, soon took the form of a popular uprising. It was quenched in blood by Belisarius, but it helped to overthrow John of Cappadocia (541) who was already the object of the indomitable hatred of the landed aristocracy.

All that remained of the social policy of John of Cappadocia after his fall was condensed by Justinian in his Pragmatic Sanction of 554. Forced to make concessions, he restored to the great Italian landowners all their social power. But he tried to keep two forces in being which were opposed to them; the cities, to which he restored the autonomous political life which they had lost since the times of Septimius Severus, and the bishops. The *curiae* once again took over the administration of the cities; but the body of active citizens was not re-established, as formerly, on the basis of the persons electorally qualified. For two centuries past public life in the cities had centred on the election of the bishop. In order to restore to the citizens the sense of the Empire that their elimination from public life had caused them to lose, there was only one thing to do; to give the bishop, the elected of the faithful, a predominant place in the civic body. In all cities the *curator*, till then appointed by the Emperor, was from now on to be elected by the bishop and the city notables. Also, in order to limit the development of the administrative oligarchy, Justinian confided the

[1] Under the influence of John of Cappadocia, Greek became the official language of the Empire; the greater part of the *Novellae* are written in Greek.

control of the imperial officials to the bishops. This measure was of immense significance, for it helped to make the Roman Pope a sort of arbiter and judge over the whole administration of Italy. Going farther along the road which led to the participation of the citizens in the government than even the Antonines had done, Justinian renounced the appointment of provincial governors and handed that over also to the election of the bishops and notables, and entrusted the provincial assemblies with supervising their activities. Since the cities now once more possessed an electoral body of notables, the provincial assemblies became, as at the beginning of the Empire, their representative organs. Finally, to revive in Rome, now decadent and depopulated, the ancient imperial tradition a political role was reassigned to the Senate which, however, was no longer anything more than the organ of the landed aristocracy.

State socialism, inaugurated by the Severi and developed by Diocletian and Constantine, experienced a set-back; a public opinion reappeared in the political life of the Empire, limited, it is true, to the notables and the bishops; though it must not be forgotten that the bishops were themselves elected by the community of the faithful. Thus, imperial policy from Anastasius to Justinian broke away from authoritarian theories and restored to the Empire that contact with the people which alone could revive the sentiment, formerly so powerful, of belonging to the Roman community.

ECONOMIC MERCANTILISM

The political work of Justinian was carried on despite threats on all the frontiers of the Empire. In the north the Gepidi, the Lombards and the Slavs were ceaselessly making forays into the Balkans, and in the east Chosroes, who had not renounced the idea of conquering Syria, violated the peace signed in 532 and resumed hostilities in 540.

The struggle on the Persian frontier was the more serious in that it disorganized the economic life of the Empire. The silk woven in the Syrian cities arrived by the caravan routes of Central Asia, over which Persia had control. The resumption of the war against Persia caused a serious crisis in the silk-weaving industry. To prevent its ruin, Justinian transformed it into a state monopoly. Economic liberalism once again had to give way to controlled economy. It was, however, only a temporary policy. In 552, after silk-worms had been introduced into the Empire and acclimatized there, the government abandoned its monopoly and once more encouraged private industry.

By producing silk within the Empire, instead of being obliged to buy it from China, the Empire considerably improved its trade balance and successfully consolidated its commercial equilibrium.

INTELLECTUAL AND ARTISTIC RENAISSANCE

Under Justinian, Constantinople reached the zenith of her greatness. Politically mistress of the Mediterranean and a great economic power, she also experienced a fresh intellectual renaissance which was shown not only by the publication of the Code but also by the creation of new art forms exemplified in S. Sophia, perhaps the boldest work of ancient and mediaeval architecture and one of the most beautiful buildings of all time. The abandonment of authoritarianism led to a revival of literary activity which recalled the great periods of the Roman Empire without, however, continuing them, for the Justinian renaissance developed exclusively under the aegis of Christianity. In 529 the closing of the schools in Athens, where the teaching of Neo-Platonist philosophy had till then continued to survive, meant a final break with pagan thought. Intellectual life could no longer be conceived save in the framework of Christian dogma.

With Procopius and Caesarius the study of history began a new era in which social and financial problems were examined; John the Lydian published a treatise on the administration of the Empire; John of Ephesus wrote a history of the Church. A whole swarm of epigrammatists continued—as Christians—the Hellenistic tradition; the Egyptian Dioscoros restored to Greek poetry a last ray of glory in the land of the Pharaohs and Malalas for the first time made use of demotic Greek in his works.

It seemed that the Empire was on the threshold of a new period of greatness.

THE CRISIS AFTER JUSTINIAN

On the death of Justinian in 565, however, war broke out on all the frontiers of the Empire. In the east the Persians again took the offensive, still aiming at possession of the Syrian coast. Justin II made an alliance against them with the Turks, who had just settled in Sogdiana (569), and at the same time provoked an insurrection in Armenia. In the north the Slavs and the Avars,[1] heralding a fresh wave of invasions, overran Pan-

[1] The Avars were a Hunnic people who, defeated by the Turks in Mongolia, had penetrated into eastern Europe about the end of the reign of Justinian, where, after destroying the Gepidi, they reduced the Slavs in Rumania to slavery.

nonia, whence the Lombards, the most barbarous of all the Germans who had invaded the Empire, were driven to attack Italy.

In Gaul and in Spain, the Franks and Visigoths at once freed themselves from the imperial authority.

Paralyzed by the bitter war he was obliged to wage in the East against the military power of the Sassanids, the Emperor abandoned to the Pope the task of guarding Italy, while Byzantine diplomacy tried to gain the Franks as allies against the Lombards.

In 577 Tiberius Constantine, being unable to send troops to the aid of Rome, advised the Senate to appeal for aid to the Merovingian kings, and in 583 the Emperor Maurice, the first Greek to occupy the throne, sent fifty thousand gold *solidi* to Queen Brunhilda to gain her support against the Lombard invaders. At the same time, he installed exarchs endowed with viceregal powers in Italy and in Africa to meet the danger.

The combined efforts of the Byzantines and the Franks could not free Italy from the Lombards. They remained masters of the greater part of the peninsula, but in the 7th century they renounced Arianism for Catholicism and began to be Romanized.

During the wars which followed the reign of Justinian the Empire showed serious signs of disintegration. The great landed proprietors again raised their heads and the cities in the threatened provinces tried to defend themselves by raising local militias. In the Crimea, the Turks took possession of Panticapaea (Kertch) in 576, while Cherson (Sebastopol) and the other Greek cities, which had always kept, even under the suzerainty of the Empire, their former municipal governments, took on the semblance of little autonomous republics, which they retained up to the 9th century.

Internal disorders aggravated the external crises. In 602 a military revolt placed on the throne Phocas who had Maurice executed and established a reign of terror. The people revolted. Heraclius, son of the exarch of Africa, appeared before Constantinople with an imperial fleet. Phocas was put to death and Heraclius invested with the imperial purple (610–641).

The Persians, taking advantage of the internal troubles of the Empire, resumed the war and, after defeating the imperial armies, captured Antioch, Damascus and Jerusalem (614), where they burnt the Holy Sepulchre. They soon appeared at Chrysopolis (Scutari), opposite the capital. Another Persian army, profiting from the hostility of the monophysite population to the Emperor and the Greeks, occupied Egypt.

The Empire seemed to be lost.

RESTORATION OF THE EMPIRE BY HERACLIUS

Heraclius bought off the barbarians in the Balkans with funds requisitioned from the churches and, proclaiming a Holy War against Persia, saved the Empire by setting out for the conquest of the Holy Places. In 629 Syria and Egypt were re-conquered. Persia was crushed and Heraclius returned to Constantinople in triumph. India sent ambassadors to him with presents; the king of the Franks, Dagobert, hastened to do him homage. The restored Empire—Visigothic Spain having alone recovered independence—was at the height of its glory.

But it remained undermined by the deep-rooted evil of religious schism. This more than ever concealed a social and national struggle between Greeks and orientals. The religious, social and national hatred between the two camps became irreconcilable, more violent than the hatred which had formerly divided Christians from pagans.

To restore peace Heraclius had recourse to a twofold policy, social and religious.

The Persian invasion of Asia Minor had been accompanied by confiscations and massacres. The class of large landed proprietors, which had been a threat to the Empire and had aroused the violent hostility of the peasant populations, was almost totally destroyed; Heraclius did not allow it to be recreated. He took possession of its lands and settled there, as free peasants, the best men of his armies. Asia Minor thus became covered by smallholdings, each perpetually under the obligation to furnish a soldier to the Empire. In 679 Constantine IV was to extend the same system to Thrace, after confiscating the great seigniorial estates there.

This great social regeneration was accompanied by administrative reform. The various regions of settlement for these soldier-peasants became *themes*,[1] which were to serve as a framework for the provincial administration. The central government was reorganized and divided into ministries; the department of the finances undertook the control of the currency and the treasury, taxes, customs dues and military expenses under the supervision of a controller-general of finances; the chancellery, foreign affairs, the posts, the court, became rigidly centralized ministries; the Emperor, who was the direct head of the army, constituted the liaison between the various state departments.

The Empire was thus socially and administratively regenerated. The Emperors had won their struggle against the landed aristocracy. The richest provinces once again had a solid social structure founded on smallholding;

[1] The word *theme* means 'region of settlement'.

the bureaucratic state-socialism which had stifled the imperial power while at the same time breaking it up among the prefectures was overthrown and replaced by a central government in which the Emperor held the control firmly in his own hands.

The social question and at the same time the religious conflict were finally put an end to in Asia Minor.

But monophysism remained powerful in Syria and in Egypt where the privileged class of Greek proprietors still remained face to face with the hostile population of Syrian and Coptic *coloni*.

In order to overcome the danger of cleavage that was threatened by this religious division in the eastern provinces of the Empire, Heraclius tried to find a conciliatory formula. He thought that he had found it in monotheism, which taught that the two natures of Christ were merged in one and a single will. But the Patriarch of Jerusalem rejected it as heretical and, after the death of Heraclius, the Papacy declared itself of the same opinion. The conflict appeared insoluble; the truth was that it went far beyond questions of doctrine.

Despairing of a solution, Heraclius tried to reconcile the Christians among themselves by inciting them to a common hatred. At the time of the capture of Jerusalem by the Persians, the Jews had welcomed these newcomers. Heraclius ordered the Jews to be baptized and demanded the dismissal of Jewish officials. A wind of antisemitism swept through Christendom. At the other end of the Mediterranean, the Visigothic King Siselbut (612–620) also adopted measures of persecution against the Jews, forbidding their religion and expelling them from almost all public and private professions. But the persecutions did no more than create fresh causes for unrest within the Empire. A large number of Jews, who had held a role of primary importance in the economic life of the Empire, sought refuge in Arabia where at this time Mohammed was preaching a new religion.

Thus, although the Empire had retained a strong cohesion in Asia Minor, it was weakened by a feeling of religious hatred when it was unexpectedly learnt, in 634, that the Arabs had captured the citadel of Bostra which defended the Jordan valley and therefore the way into Syria.

The fate of the Empire and of the world was at stake.

CHAPTER LIX

IN THE WEST, THE CHURCH BECOMES THE SUCCESSOR TO THE EMPIRE

THE CHURCH EXTENDS ITS TEMPORAL AUTHORITY

DURING the invasions the Church of Rome had never ceased struggling with tireless energy to safeguard its unity and to impose orthodox Christianity on the waves of barbarians that overran the Empire. By supporting the pagan Clovis against the Burgundian and Visigothic kings, Christian but heretic, the bishops ensured the triumph of Roman orthodoxy in Gaul and sealed the alliance of the Church with the Merovingian monarchy.

In Italy the authority of the Pope even invaded the temporal domain; in 554 a *novella* of Justinian made the imperial officials subject to the control of the bishops. During the crisis which followed the reign of Justinian the Emperors themselves, by obtaining from the Church—which possessed immense wealth in Sicily—an undertaking that it would be responsible for the expenses of the imperial administration in Italy, to some extent handed over to it the government of that country. As to the clergy, the legislation of Justinian had rigidly subjected them to the jurisdiction of the bishops (546).

Gregory the Great, who was enthroned in 590, appeared the real arbiter of peace by assuming, at the request of the Emperor, the defence of Rome against the Lombards; at the same time, by asserting himself as the immediate chief of all the bishops of the West, he introduced into the Church an authority which gave it all the features of a monarchy.

Thus, while the East was torn between the supporters and adversaries of monophysism, the Pope assured the strict doctrinal unity of the Church in the West and watched over its independence.

The Church also continued to extend its juridical prerogatives in Gaul. In 506 the Council of Agde forbade clerics to cite other clerics before the civil tribunals and organized mixed courts presided over by a count and a churchman to settle disputes between clergy and laymen. In 614 the Council of Paris, intervening in the domain of public law, forbade civil judges from hearing causes in which priests were involved. The same year Clotair II, submitting docilely, confirmed this decision and went so far as to abandon to the bishops' courts the administration of low justice in all affairs between clerics and laymen.

Thus the Church gradually extended its sway over all classes.

Even though becoming a part of national institutions, especially in Gaul, the Church still preserved its universal character. The bishops and the founders of monasteries were rarely nationals; with a few rare exceptions they were, generally speaking, Romans or even Hellenized persons permeated with oriental culture. The Monastery of St Victor, founded at Marseilles at the beginning of the 5th century by Jean Cassien who had been a monk at Bethlehem, in Egypt and at Constantinople, and the Monastery of Lerins, founded by Honorat, introduced Egyptian asceticism into Gaul, where it was to have a great influence.

MONASTICISM

It was in these monasteries, as in that of Monte Cassino founded by St Benedict about 525, that the monks who were to evangelize the pagans and bring monasticism to the northern countries were trained.

Monasticism, which originated in the East, was to develop to an extraordinary degree in the 6th century. It was not so much the bishops as the kings and aristocrats who competed in the foundation of monasteries. They were to play an essential role in the history of Christianity.

If the bishops were the high officials of the Church, it was the monks who made up the army which was to set out to conquer the pagan world. In the beginning of the 5th century the Angles, the Saxons and the Jutes, who came from the districts around the Elbe, had invaded England. An implacable struggle took place between them and the British Celts who defended themselves tenaciously for five hundred years. When they were finally defeated, the Celts were forced to withdraw into Ireland, Cornwall and Wales or to emigrate to Armorica, which from that time took the name of Brittany, while the Anglo-Saxons founded seven little kingdoms in England, amongst which Wessex soon gained the supremacy.

While these ferocious struggles were going on Pope Gregory the Great sent the monk Augustine to England. He converted the Saxon king Ethelbert to Catholicism and induced him to accept the religious authority of Rome. Thus the Saxon kingdoms were organized in the Christian faith and, from the middle of the 6th century, Rome possessed two archbishoprics in England—Canterbury and York.

The evangelization of England was of especial importance in the history of the Papacy. As Imperial Rome had formerly won its Empire by force of arms, so Christian Rome also laid the foundations of an Empire, but by the peaceful propagation of the faith.

With Christianity, Latin came to England, and also Greek; Roman law formed the basis of Canon Law and in the bishops' schools the writings of the Fathers of the Church, saturated with classical culture, became the basis of education. Christianity continued the work of the Empire and spread Roman civilization which was itself only the western form of Greco-Oriental civilization.

By their conversion to Christianity the barbarians became participants in the classical tradition.

The evangelization of England had also another aspect. While on the cultural plane it meant the conquest of new peoples by classical and Roman culture, on the political plane it meant a break between Rome and the old order.

Till then Christianity had been identified with the Empire; the churches which had been formed outside its frontiers, in Armenia, in Persian Mesopotamia, had become detached from Rome. On the contrary, by founding bishropics and monasteries in England, the Pope extended outside the former confines of the Empire an authority which, by separating itself completely from that of the Emperor, seemed a sort of theocratic sovereignty. The spiritual power, divorced from political considerations, put into practice the thesis of St Augustine on the primacy of spiritual power. England constituted a real fief of Rome and Rome was to make this fief a favoured land.

In 668 the Italian Pope sent as Archbishop of Canterbury Theodore of Tarsus, a Greek monk famous for his erudition; his collaborator, Adrian, was an African versed in Latin and Greek letters. The abbeys and monasteries founded in England were thenceforth to become the only centres of Greco-Latin culture preserved in the western Church after the 6th century.

THE CULTURAL ROLE OF THE CHURCH

The cultural role abandoned by the Empire was now taken over by the Church; and, what was even more remarkable, while the Empire split up into national states the culture spread by the Church was entirely international.

THE MAP KNOWN AS ST ALBANS
(8th century A.D.)

Map No. 30

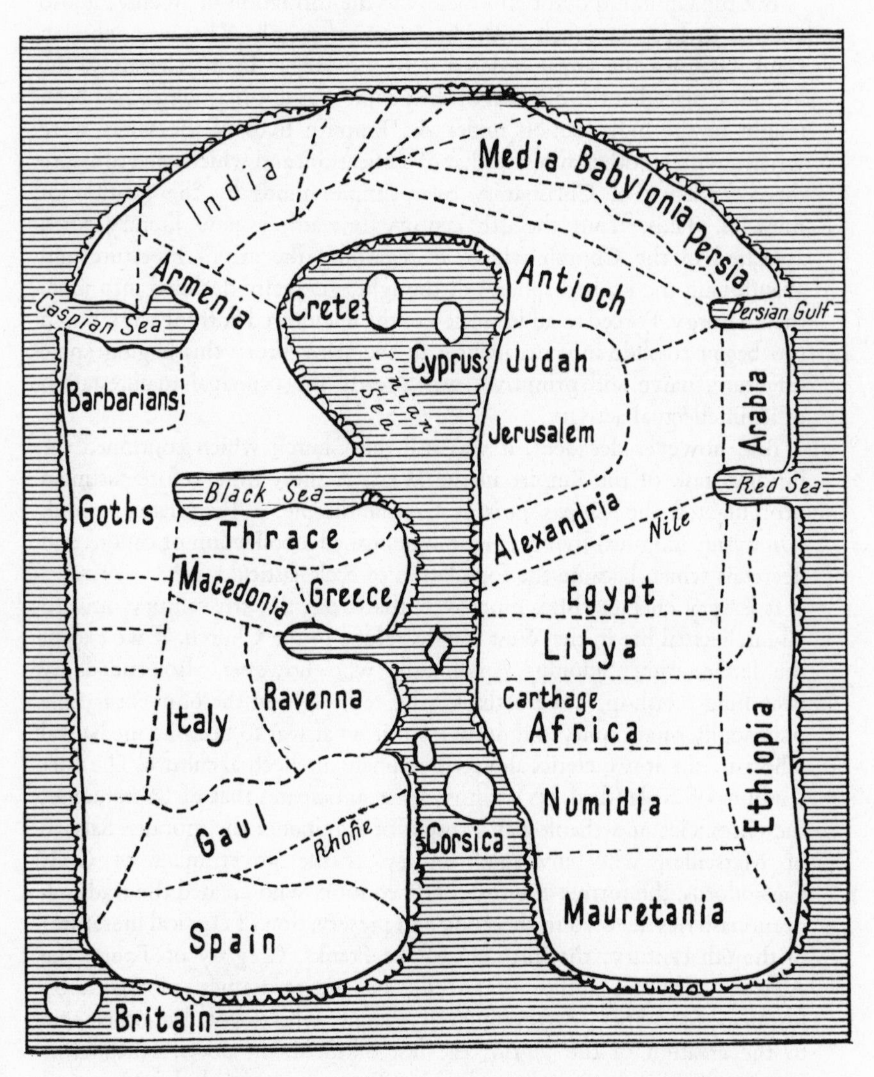

This map displays the intellectual decline of Gaul after the Germanic invasions. The scientific knowledge of ancient times has long been forgotten.

The élite which it created was formed by the study of the ancient classics, following the methods of instruction recommended by St Augustine.

But the Church did not aim merely at the formation of an élite; it also wanted to keep in touch with the common people. That was why, in Gaul, Gregory the Great ordered it to use vulgar Latin. Certainly, the literature placed at the disposal of the people was not that which had been taught in the high schools under the Empire; lives of the saints were written with no other aim save that of edification, and which tried to assure the ascendancy of Christianity over simple minds by the relation of miracles. Thus, from the 4th century onward, a new literary form appeared in the Church which, disregarding the art of literature and abandoning the exalted spheres of thought, gradually declined into mere thaumaturgy. Forced to address itself to the uncultured faithful, the Church too began to slide into decadence. In the 7th century this hagiographic literature, naïve and primitive, was already the principal manifestation of its intellectual activity.

But, however decadent, it was still the Church which continued the juridical task of the Empire in the West. A short time before Justinian promulgated the *Corpus Juris* at Constantinople, a Roumanian monk (Dionysius Exiguus) living at Rome published a collection of canons and decretals which became the foundation of ecclesiastical law.[1]

It is very characteristic, moreover, that from the 5th century onward all intellectual life in the West sought refuge in the Church. If we except the letter-writer Sidonius Apollinaris, who however also ended by becoming a bishop, and Boethius, who rethought in the 6th century the philosophy of antiquity and drew from it what was to become mediaeval scholasticism, it was clerics alone who upheld intellectual culture. The poet Paulinus of Nola (died 431), whose verse anticipates that of La Fontaine; the chronicler and theologian Prosper of Aquitaine; the moralist Salvian of Marseilles, who envisaged history as the government of God; Cassiodorus, the former minister of Theodoric, who created the tradition of monasteries devoted to the study and preservation of classical literature; in the 6th century: the historian of the Franks, Gregory of Tours; the African Corippus, author of an epic on the reconquest of Africa by Justinian; St Avitus, Metropolitan of Vienne, who devoted another epic to the creation of the world; the last of the Latin poets, Fortunatus; Isidore of Seville, an encyclopaedist like Pliny, who wrote the last Universal

[1] Dionysius Exiguus used, as the basis for his chronology, the Alexandrian Easter computations, thus introducing the Christian era with an error of several years. Christ was born from four to seven years before the Christian era as thus calculated.

History of antiquity for the use of the people; all these were clerics and most of them bishops.

While the Pope, thanks to the prestige which he enjoyed and the influence he exercised throughout the West, was making ready to assume the role formerly played by the Emperor, the Church arrogated to itself the spiritual and cultural direction of the national states which had been born within the framework of the Empire. The break between West and East became more and more final. In the West, authority, now transferred from the temporal to the spiritual plane, became theocratic.

BOOK XIV

The Asiatic Empires from the 1st to the 7th Century AD

CHAPTER LX

ASIA UP TO THE CRISIS OF THE 3RD CENTURY. THE HAN EMPIRE AND THE SACIAN EMPIRE

REPERCUSSIONS OF WORLD TRADE

THe parallelism that existed between the histories of the Mediterranean countries and the great civilized countries of Asia—India and China—in the course of the first three centuries after Christ was not the work of chance. The same factors determined their history; on the one hand the movements of the nomad peoples which dominated the vast expanses from the China Sea to the Atlantic Ocean and which caused the great waves of invasion, and on the other the international trade-routes whose importance grew from the VIth century BC onward and which ensured a traffic between the peoples upon which their social structure was dependent.

The evolution of China was closely related to that of the West. The Persian policy of eastward economic expansion under Darius coincided with the reforms which led to the disappearance of the last vestiges of closed economy in the Tsin kingdom, where the caravan routes of Central Asia ended. The period of development of international trade in the Hellenistic era corresponds to the advent of the liberal Empire of the Han in China.

At the end of the IInd and in the Ist century BC the Hellenistic states were in decline and the Near East was torn between the Mediterranean dominated by Rome in the West and the Asiatic continent over which China was extending her supremacy in the East.

After the conquest of the kingdom of Canton (111 BC) China obtained an outlet to the sea. Navigation developed along the coasts and a century later Egyptian merchants from Alexandria appeared in Chinese ports. On the continent China controlled the caravan routes of Central Asia, set up a resident at Kashgar with the title of 'Protector-General of the Western

Regions' (60 BC) and entered into direct relations with India and the regions around the Caspian Sea and the Urals.

Similar problems arose in Rome and in China owing to the universal character of trade in the Ist century BC. In both, capitalism led to a lack of economic balance which created serious social unrest. The Han dynasty tried to guard against it by a policy of autocratic absolutism, as Rome did by dictatorship. The proclamation of a new political order by Siuan-Ti (73–49 BC), which replaced the government 'of education and virtue' by a régime of force, coincided with the proscriptions of the expiring Roman Republic; and when Augustus gave a new structure to the Roman Empire after seizing power as the result of civil war, the usurper Wang-Mang (AD 9-23) attempted a far-reaching social reform in China.

In China as in Rome the unrest caused by capitalism and demagogy led to a severe political crisis and the moral decadence of the ruling classes.

Rome, a maritime Empire, tried to restore the balance by a free-trade policy and tempered democracy; China, a continental Empire, while affirming the principles of natural law which had triumphed at Rome, tried to stabilize order and ensure social content by a new distribution of land.

THE SOCIAL REFORMS OF WANG-MANG IN CHINA (AD 9–23)

The reforms attempted by Wang-Mang amounted to a social and ideological revolution.

They were based on moral principles. 'The nature of heaven and earth', said Wang-Mang, 'ensures that man is precious'. Because of the natural equality of men, the Emperor in the year AD 9 decreed the abolition of slavery and the emancipation of all serfs. Noting that landed property had become concentrated in the hands of the rich families, he initiated a vast expropriation of large estates; all families which owned more than 1482 acres were deprived of the excess by confiscation if they did not include at least eight males. The lands thus obtained were divided amongst the people and declared inalienable so that they could not be taken away again.

A policy to reduce living costs was inaugurated. Decrees fixed maximum prices. In order to standardize the price of wheat, the state bought in those provinces where it was abundant and sold in those where it was scarce.

Taxation was reorganized on a new basis. Henceforward, taxation would not fall upon land values alone but also on business and professions, to the extent of 10%. Taxpayers had to make an annual declaration of their possessions, any fraud involving confiscation of goods and a sentence of a year's forced labour.

The coinage was recast.

The status of officials was revised and their actions subjected to a control commission which had power to confiscate their personal fortunes for abuses committed in the exercise of their duties.

The army was reorganized on the basis of the conscription of one man in thirty.

Towards capitalism Wang-Mang took up an attitude similar to that of Augustus. The Roman Emperor had decreed mining to be a state monopoly. Wang-Mang also, to check the ascendancy of capitalism, made trade in metals a state monopoly; but otherwise industry and commerce were encouraged and even as Tiberius had organized credits for the middle classes, so Wang-Mang, several years before him, laid down the basis for popular credit facilities at the rate of 3% per month (36% per annum), a very high rate by comparison with the practice of the Mediterranean countries. Caesar had controlled banking; Wang-Mang tempered free-trade by a control of the markets for raw materials and silver.

Finally, the officials were reorganized on Confucian principles.

But the administration, which had to be greatly developed because of these reforms, became plethoric; fiscal needs multiplied and the state was compelled to increase taxation.

The destruction of the large estates aroused vigorous opposition to Wang-Mang. The inalienability of the soil, moreover, was shown to be incompatible with an economic régime based on private trade. From the year 12 the sale of land had again to be permitted; and it soon appeared that the transformation of all the political, social and economic foundations of the Empire was leading to a crisis which was the more severe in that the power of Wang-Mang, won by usurpation, was considered by his enemies to be devoid of legitimacy.

CRISIS IN THE EMPIRE AND RESTORATION OF THE HAN DYNASTY (AD 23–220)

The resultant weakening of the Empire made it incapable of resisting the pressure of the Huns which was continually being exerted on its northern frontiers. The northern provinces of China were overrun by the invaders. The population withdrew towards the centre of the country. The caravan routes were cut. Thus economic crisis aggravated the social consequences of the exodus of refugees. The people rose and the usurpation of power by the generals in the invaded and threatened provinces plunged the

Empire into anarchy. Misery led to a real *jacquerie*; the peasants marched on the capital and took it, and the Emperor, who had wanted by his reforms to ensure the well-being of his subjects, was put to death by thepeople.

In the midst of these troubles the Han dynasty, which had been deposed by Wang-Mang, recovered power. Kwang-Wu-Ti did his best to overcome the crisis by reducing taxes and greatly diminishing state expenses. Nine-tenths of the officials, among whom were five hundred sub-prefects, were dismissed and the tax on incomes abolished. The land tax, which was the sole tax to be retained, was reduced to a thirtieth of the value of the property. The local armies were disbanded.

Finally, after thirty years of effort, order was restored. But the crisis had been so severe that the population, which according to the census of the year AD 2 had been fifty millions, had declined to twenty-one millions. Furthermore, internal disorders had cost China her Empire; all her possessions in Central Asia and along the coasts were lost.

The restoration of the central power was to restore to China not only peace and order, but prosperity and power. In AD 42 Tonkin was conquered, and China regained mastery of the seas along all her coasts. In 70, after the Mongol invasions had been checked by the settlement of the Huns as 'federates' along the northern confines of the Empire, control was re-established over the caravan routes of Central Asia and the Chinese resident reappeared at Kashgar, despite the opposition of the Sacian Empire which at this time had a firm hold on Bactria and all northern India.

The Chinese Empire once again extended from the China Sea to the Jaxartes and from Korea to Tonkin. A generation later the Chinese Empire could match its sixty million subjects with the seventy million inhabitants of the Roman Empire and in Asia the 'Chinese peace' corresponded to the 'Pax Romana' which reigned in the times of Trajan from the Atlantic Ocean to the Persian Gulf.

Between these two great pacific and liberal empires a constant current of trade existed, which assured their mutual prosperity. But no spiritual contact was ever established between the Mediterranean basin and China.

The famous 'silk road'—which started from Antioch and ended, by way of Ecbatana, Merv, Bactra and the Pamir Plateau, at the Stone Tower—kept the Syrian merchants in touch with the Chinese sellers of silk, who came there from Lo-Yang, the new capital of the Han. But there was no exchange of ideas as there was of goods, since the influence of India which from the intellectual and religious point of view was dominant in Chinese thought intervened between Rome and China.

THE FIRST HUNNIC INVASIONS

While the two great Empires of Rome and China were being built up during the 1st century BC vast movements were taking place among the nomadic hordes of northern Asia and Europe.

Drawn by the rich and civilized lands the Germans in Europe and the Huns in Asia tried to force their way southward, the former into the Mediterranean regions and the latter into the valley of the Huang-Ho.

In Europe the Cimbri and the Teutones, who descended from the Cimbrian peninsula (Denmark) by way of Bohemia and Moravia into the Danube valley, clashed with the Celts, who forced them to move westward in search of a line of least resistance, and crossed the Rhine in 109 BC; the Teutones continued down the Rhône valley looking for lands and were crushed by Marius in Provence; while the Cimbri, who had penetrated into Italy by the Brenner Pass, were halted at Vercelli in 101.

At the same time, more than six thousand miles away, the Huns were moving on the northern frontier of China. The Han dynasty had succeeded in stabilizing the Eastern Huns, by permitting them to settle north of the Great Wall; but the Western Huns, driven westward, had taken with them the Alans and had caused two great migrations, one to the north of the Caspian and the other towards Bactria.

The wave of the Alans and Huns flowing towards the Urals and the Volga clashed with the Scythians. Driven back towards the Black Sea, they menaced the Greek cities there and helped to push westward the Cimbri and the Teutones who, about the same time, clashed with the Celts in the Danube valley. In 109 BC, at the time when the Germanic tribes crossed the Rhine, the Scythian princes appealed to Rome as suppliants asking, but in vain, to be admitted into the Empire.

In the region of the Aral Sea the Huns, in their southward emigration, met with the U-Sun people with whom the Chinese hastened to conclude an alliance.[1] The combined efforts of the Chinese and the U-Sun armies crushed the Huns in a pincer movement and about 60 BC inflicted so terrible a defeat on them that the Hunnic thrust southward was completely checked and their drive westward gradually weakened.

At the time when the Hunnic invasion of Central Asia was checked, the counter-effects which it had caused led to consequences of considerable importance. During the IInd century BC, when the great movement of the Western Huns began to be felt, the Sacae, who had settled to the east of the Aral Sea, were gradually driven back to the Jaxartes.

[1] The U-Sun seem to have been Indo-Europeans.

The Sacae were an Aryan people who formed, it seems, the link between the Scythians settled in the Caspian region and the Tokharians in Turkestan. Some of them had already formed part of the 15th satrapy of the Persian Empire. The city of Alexandria Eschata (Khodjend), founded by Alexander on the great bend of the Oxus, and the close proximity of the Greek kingdom of Bactria put them into direct touch with the Hellenic and Parthian civilizations; the movement of the caravans which left Khodjend for China, by way of Kandahar and Turfan, brought them under Chinese influence and, through the passes of the Hindu-Kush, they were in communication with the Upper Indus basin.

THE SACIAN INVASION OF BACTRIA AND INDIA

Pressed by the Huns, the Sacae, about 130 BC, invaded the rich kingdom of Bactria, driving the Greeks back towards Kabul and the Punjab. In 80 BC they captured Kabul, crossed the Peshawar pass and took Taxila, the capital of the Upper Indus region, quite close to the city of Nicaea, which had been founded by Alexander.

In 30 BC the last Greek kingdom in the eastern Punjab succumbed. After the conquest of Bactria, the Sacae continued their movement towards the sea, west of the Hindu-Kush, entered the Parthian Empire and settled in the province of Seistan (Baluchistan) where, since they were kin to the Parthians, they were rapidly assimilated. From Seistan they continued towards Sind where, going upstream, they joined forces with other Sacae who were coming down from the Punjab. India was unable to resist the invasion. The Empire of the Mauryas which, up to 189 BC, had united the whole northern part of the Indian sub-continent, was broken up into little states, exceedingly prosperous and civilized, but politically subject to the influence of the Parthian Empire and the Greek kingdom of Bactria. The Sacae settled in the Parthian province of Seistan took the place of the Greek monarchs and became masters of the Indus basin; they were quite naturally to extend their influence over the valley of the Ganges. From the beginning of the Ist century there was a Sacian satrap on the Upper Ganges; and tradition has it that it was a Parthian prince, Mathoura, who was converted to Christianity by St Thomas.

THE SACIAN EMPIRE

As they extended their rule over the highly civilized countries of Bactria, Parthia and India, the Sacae, already deeply permeated by influences from all sides, were soon assimilated by the civilization of the conquered countries.

The Kushan dynasty, of Sacian race, was installed at Kabul. It was to preside over two centuries of greatness of the Sacian Empire. It had been converted to Buddhism.

At the beginning of the 1st century AD the Kushan dynasty reigned over an immense state which extended over the Indus and Ganges basins, Seistan, and the former Greek kingdom of Bactria up to the Aral Sea, and included the caravan cities of Bactra, Samarkand, Khodjend and Kashgar. A great civilization flourished in this composite Empire, of which the Hindu coast of Malabar at one time formed part; a civilization made up of Indian, Greek and Parthian elements under the dominant influence of Buddhism.

In the 1st and 2nd centuries AD the Sacian Empire was an essential factor in international trade. The port of Barygaza in Malabar played a leading role in the sea-borne communications of India with Rome, as did the port of Muziris, farther south, in the Dravidian state of Kerala. Western influence was predominant there. About AD 60 the coins of the Sacian Empire bore bilingual inscriptions, in Greek and Parthian, and were struck with the effigies of the Emperors Augustus and Claudius. Export to the Roman Empire of pearls, spices, medicaments, indigo and cotton goods became so important that whole fleets of ships left Alexandria for India, profiting by the monsoons. The Hindu trade-balance was very favourable; Pliny valued its excess over Roman exports at a hundred million *sesterces* annually.

India was the necessary staging-post for trade between Rome and China, not only by sea, but also by the caravan routes to which the Sacians controlled the access. This period of almost universal peace in the first two centuries after Christ, Roman in the West, Chinese in the East, gave India a prodigious economic impulse. The Indus valley became one of the main industrial centres of the world and the great international market for cotton goods, even as China was for silk. It was because the Roman Empire developed its industry far less than China and India that its trade-balance came to show such a dangerous deficit and its gold reserves, formerly amassed by the Hellenistic states, ended by draining away to Asia. In the 2nd century sea-borne trade was obviously more important than continental trade. The little Dravidian states of southern India, Kerala with the great port of Muziris oriented westward; Pandya with the port of Korkai; Chola and Ceylon became great economic powers. Alexandria sent ships to Malabar and the Indus, with the assurance of good freights, but Roman shipping, though it sometimes reached the mouth of the Ganges seldom went further than the port of Muziris. It was the Dravidians who made themselves the great sea-carriers from India to China, as formerly the Phoenicians and then the Greeks had done between West and East, and who controlled the great sea-routes to the Far East. Embassies set out from Pandya and Ceylon for Rome; Egyptian merchants reached the ports of the Ganges and from there China.

The movement of trade from the West to the East also favoured, though to a lesser degree, the caravan routes. So, in the middle of the 1st century at the height of her power, China established a protectorate over the little Tokharian kingdoms which fringed the Chinese frontier along the great caravan routes as far as the Sacian Empire. When the Chinese Resident, who had disappeared at the time of the great crisis in the Empire following the reign of Wang-Mang, reappeared at Kashgar in AD 70 there was a clash between the two great Asiatic states. China, in the flood-tide of expansion, tried to extend westward and install herself on the frontiers of the Parthian Empire in order to prevent control of her exports by the Sacae. A Chinese army of seventy thousand men advanced as far as the Indus, but could not hold out there; China was compelled to share the mastery of the trade-routes of Central Asia with the Sacae.

The control exercised by the Parthians and the Sacae over the continental trade-routes led, in the 2nd century, to diplomatic negotiations between the Emperor Marcus Aurelius and the Emperor Jenn-Si (166) for the establishment of direct sea communications between Rome and China. These led to the establishment of a trade-route from Alexandria to Kattigara, a port thought to have been situated in the estuary of the Red River, whence a route, following the coast, led by way of Canton to northern China.

Rome exercised a decisive influence on India because she was India's main customer; but none the less she was unable to introduce either Christianity or her intellectual and artistic ideas into India. In this, as in trade, India gave much more, during the first two centuries of our era, than she received. She was, at that time, perhaps the greatest intellectual centre of the world. Greek and Iranian played an important role in the 1st century, but it was Sanskrit that was the language of thought, literature and science. In the first two centuries the intellectual development of India equalled that of the Hellenistic world in the IIIrd and IInd centuries BC. Without having borrowed them from the Greeks, Hindu science discovered the theorem of Pythagoras, formulated a theory of numbers, developed arithmetical science (the cube and the square root) and higher algebra. Its progress was as brilliant in philosophy as in literature and the arts; erotic poetry, music and the dance flourished alongside the epic literature which, in the Mahabharata and the Ramayana whose tradition went back to ten centuries before Christ, gave India in the IVth century BC its great national epics comparable with the Iliad and the Odyssey.

India was also intellectually unified in a religious syncretism composed of Brahmanism, Jainism and Buddhism. Biographies of the Buddha finally determined its character; and a council summoned by King Kanishka (78–110) established the orthodoxy of Buddhism under the influence of the Mazdaist ideas which had triumphed during the Sacian rule.

In the 2nd century AD the Sacian Empire, which had been more and more won over by Indian culture, withdrew farther and farther from western influences even in the economic field. After 190 the currency bore only Indian inscriptions and emblems recalling the cult of the god Shiva. The Sacian satraps of Malabar, which was the terminal point of the Alexandrian trade, made use only of Sanskrit. Moreover, the crisis which afflicted Rome at the end of the 2nd century by weakening the ties of India with the West weakened also the Sacian Empire. But what finally determined the end of its power was the advent of the Sassanid dynasty in the Iranian kingdom (226) which undertook an expansionist policy and seized Bactria, and therefore the control of the continental transit trade which till then had been in Sacian hands.

CHAPTER LXI

THE CRISIS OF THE CHINESE EMPIRE IN THE 3RD CENTURY AND THE INVASION OF THE HUNS

THE INTERNAL CRISIS

THE Chinese Empire, restored by the Han dynasty after the great social crisis of the reign of Wang-Mang (AD 23), was to know a period of great prosperity in the first two centuries AD. The liberal régime then in force allowed the maximum development of its economic life. The invention of paper dates from this time. Its manufacture was widespread; it was to pass from China to Samarkand, where the Arabs were to find it in the 8th century.

But, as in the Roman Empire, and as earlier in the Egyptian Ancient and New Empires, centralization evolved into bureaucracy, the administration became divorced from the people and an oligarchy of high officials was created. It was mainly recruited from the personnel of the court whose size and ceremonial were constantly increasing; the palace eunuchs, who formed the closest entourage of the Emperor, acquired great influence in the state and were awarded the most honourable and lucrative posts.

The decadence of the administration, due to the plethoric development of state services, resulted in a great increase in expenditure. The treasury became the foundation of the state; taxes had continually to be made heavier and the oligarchy transformed its functions into hereditary fiefs, involving an open venality of offices.

As in all centralized Empires, the power monopolized by an oligarchy rapidly forced the country into a governmental crisis. An opposition party was formed, a party at once political, social and mystical, which advocated the idealism of Lao-Tse in opposition to the lust for pleasure of the ruling classes. Even as Christianity was then being organized into a Church which was independent of Roman institutions, so also in China Taoism created a priestly hierarchy which was independent of the official structure of the state.

In 184 a revolution broke out which aimed at seizing the power from the civil authorities and handing it over to the Taoist clergy. The supporters of Taoism refused to obey the governors and organized themselves in a Church under the spiritual authority of a religious leader. It was the signal for a terrible civil war. The government replied to the Taoist rising by proscriptions and mass decapitations. But in 189 the President of the Supreme Court of Justice took the part of the insurgents and had two thousand palace eunuchs massacred.

The Emperor at this time was a child. The generals seized power and China was plunged into chaos.

About the same time the death of Commodus (192) led to the great crisis of military anarchy at Rome. The general Septimius Severus had just installed his military government (193) when in 196 the general Tsao-Tsao proclaimed himself protector of China and made the Emperor a mere tool.

At Rome, the Severi restored forty years of peace and order; but on the death of Alexander Severus in 235 the great crisis began, in the course of which the Empire was broken up into several states; the Asiatic provinces under the kings of Palmyra, and Gaul and Britain under separate Emperors set themselves up as independent states. The Germanic invasions began, the Goths crossed the Danube, and the Alamanni and the Franks the Rhine. The situation could only be stabilized in 270 by the authoritarian rule of Aurelian and later (283) of Diocletian.

The history of China followed, step by step, a similar evolution to that of Rome.

Military anarchy, after a few years, led to the break-up of the Empire into three kingdoms (221): in the north-west the kingdom of Wei with the caravan capitals of Chang-Ngan and Lo-Yang, which exercised a protectorate over Central Asia; in the south-east the kingdom of Wu, which held all the coasts of Nankin as far as the confines of Annam; and lastly, in the south-west, the kingdom of Choü, the most isolated.

For sixty years China was in the throes of civil war which caused such devastation that the population fell to twenty-nine million inhabitants.

Finally, in 280, the Mayors of the Palace of the kingdom of Wei restored the unity of China and founded the Tsin dynasty (280–419).

The restoration affected by the Tsin, as purely military as that of Aurelian at Rome, did not interrupt the state-socialist and oligarchic development of the Empire which had been evident before the crisis.

Absolutism produced autocracy. Following the normal development, autocracy, by substituting force for law, took from the monarchy its legitimate basis. The dynasty thenceforward foundered, as had earlier the Ptolemies and the Seleucids, in family crimes and palace intrigues. The high administration having become an affair of the oligarchy, offices were sold to the highest bidder; the subjects of the Emperor, considered as merely a flock to be fleeced, became the prey of the most brutal fiscal oppression.

Destroyed from above, the Empire fell to pieces.

The ruin of the central power had similar consequences in China as it had had in the Roman Empire; incapable of resisting the pressure of the barbarians, China was given over to the invasions of the Huns and Mongols, even as Rome was left exposed to the invasions of the Germans.

CHINA INVADED BY THE HUNS

As in the West, it was not so much the invasions that destroyed the Empire as that the Empire, being weakened, was no longer able to hold back the pressure of the barbarians. Even as at Rome the destruction of the Empire was to commence by the settlement of the federate Goths in the Danubian provinces, so also in China it was the Huns settled as federates north of the Great Wall who delivered the first blow.

The collapse of Chinese power destroyed the protectorate that it exercised over Central Asia and left the way open to the Western Huns. Resuming their movement southward and westward, they clashed with the U-Sun in the region of the Caspian, and crossed southern Russia, reducing the Alans to servitude and driving before them the Goths who, crossing the Danube, were to settle within the Roman Empire and lead to its ruin.

Thus the Roman Empire was profoundly shaken by the collapse of the Chinese power, the direct cause of the Gothic invasion.

The two Empires, though without being aware of it, were complementary. The proclamation of a Hun as Emperor in northern China in 308 was the first step in the great invasions which started the movement of the Germanic and Slavic tribes of eastern and central Europe and culminated in the terrible raid by the Huns of Attila.

The Hunnic usurper, allied by marriage to the Han dynasty, after arrogating to himself the imperial title, announced his intention of restoring the Chinese Empire. In 311 his troops captured the capital of Lo-Yang after terrible massacres. The Tsin dynasty, abandoning all northern China to the Mongols, took refuge at Nankin which, from 318 to 589, was to become the capital of all that remained of the Empire.

All the continental provinces were abandoned to the Huns; the southern provinces, which lived from the sea and whose urban way of life and trading activities were carried by the great Yang-Tse river as far as the frontiers of China, escaped the rule of the barbarians. The centre of Chinese civilization shifted and was henceforth to remain in the maritime provinces of the Empire.

All the continental part of the country, the north and the west, was on the contrary to go through a period of complete decadence under the rule of the nomads who settled there. Depopulated, its cities sacked and destroyed, its people massacred, it none the less went on living according to its former Chinese institutions; but these only served to enable the invader to impose on the people the double scourge of conscription and arbitrary taxation which, added to the famines caused by the invasions and the breakdown of trade, plunged the country into poverty and constant anarchy.

DISMEMBERMENT OF THE EMPIRE

While the imperial family of the Tsin drew from the wealth of the maritime provinces the means they needed to rebuild a power able to defend itself against invasion, the continental provinces, from Shantung down to beyond Canton, were divided into six hostile kingdoms in the hands of Turco-Mongol dynasties organized on the ruins of the Chinese Empire, like the Germanic kingdoms in the Roman Empire of the West. Involved in continual wars against one another, the Hunnic kingdoms were assimilated by the Chinese as rapidly as the kingdoms created by the Germans in Gaul and Spain became Latinized. Even as Christianity was imposed on the Germans, Buddhism in China, from 390 onward, entirely conquered the Huns.

In the midst of the political and economic decadence of the Turco-Mongol kingdoms, the mystical movement born in the 2nd century with the organization of the Taoist church spread widely. In the invaded parts of China it became merged with a philosophical movement directly inspired by Lao-Tse which preached passivity. Despair at the destruction of all values was elevated to a doctrine and left the way open to Buddhist ideals. Everywhere Taoist and Buddhist monasteries were founded, in which the finest minds of the time took refuge. At the moment when the Christian Church was triumphing in the Roman Empire, a great wave of religious proselytism appeared in China. Apostles went as far as Korea to preach the new religion which was to bring to the people the consolation of the after-life.

Thanks to mysticism and monasticism, intellectual civilization did not succumb in the midst of political decline. On the contrary, the 4th century was, under the stimulus of religious feeling, a period of flourishing Chinese sculpture and painting.

One cannot but be struck by the similarity between the break-up of the Chinese Empire and that of the Roman Empire. In both cases it was the agricultural, continental provinces which were conquered in the invasions. In both cases it was the maritime part of the Empire, where city life and trade were paramount, which escaped decadence and dismemberment. As Lo-Yang, the ancient capital, was abandoned for Nankin, the greatest port of the Empire, so Rome itself was supplanted by the great port and market of Constantinople.

The wave of mysticism and Buddhist monasticism which flooded China in the 4th century found its counterpart in the great wave of mysticism and Christian monasticism which spread through the Roman Empire in the 5th century.

While still surviving along the coasts, Chinese civilization lost much of its power of expansion. In Korea the ascendancy of China was obliterated. In the place of the Chinese provinces there appeared in northern Korea an autonomous kingdom, Kokuli, of which a former Chinese administrative centre, the important city of Ping-Yang, became the capital. The incorporation of all northern and central Korea into the Empire of the Han, which had lasted for more than a century, had however definitely won over the country for Chinese civilization. The kingdom of Kokuli was to remain a cultural centre for the little south Korean states, Silla which occupied all the south-east, and Paik-Che which held the south-western coast.

THE YAMATO KINGDOM IN JAPAN

The overlordship imposed by China over Japan in the Ist century BC also disappeared. In the 1st century AD a tribal royalty, of a type somewhat similar to that which China itself had known in the Chou epoch about 1200 BC, began to take form. The seigniorial royalty set up in the island of Kyu-Shu spread northward and, probably about the end of the 1st century, reached Yamato which became the capital of the first great Japanese state.[1]

[1] The traditional history of Japan traces the present Japanese dynasty back to this Yamato dynasty whose origin is officially fixed at 660 BC, but it seems that historically it dates in reality from the first century AD.

The Yamato kingdom was formed by the union of aristocratic clans, each ruled by a hereditary family under which seigniorial families disposed of the land; in their domains the semi-serf population was tied to the soil or formed hereditary and specialized corporations of certain trades: weavers, armourers, soldiers, priests. There seem to have been few slaves.

The seigniorial clans were graded in order of importance and grouped under ducal dynasties, themselves vassals of the imperial dynasty. This type of society, manorial and feudal, whose Shinto religion was dedicated to the forces of nature, especially the sun goddess, became progressively more civilized by contact with China and Korea. In the 1st century it turned seaward and, as the Normans were later to do in Europe, the Japanese carried out forays against Korea, where a Japanese enclave, the little state of Meniana, was set up on the southern coast as soon as decadent China could no longer assure safety of navigation. Pirate fleets setting out from Meniana continually attacked the rich and civilized coastlands of Korea. But through these very expeditions Japan came into contact with Chinese civilization and became ready to receive it.

CHAPTER LXII

THE SASSANID EMPIRE AND THE DOWNFALL OF THE SACIAN EMPIRE

THE PARTHIAN KINGDOM

THE Parthian Kingdom, which had been formed in the times of the Seleucids, had known a period of great prosperity, thanks to its position midway between Rome and India. After the check to the policy of Caesar and Antony in the East, Augustus had given up the idea of incorporating Mesopotamia into the Roman Empire and a policy of friendship between Rome and Ctesiphon existed for a century. The protectorate over Armenia, which controlled the communications of the Black Sea with Central Asia through the Caspian region, was the only thing that disturbed, about 50 BC, the good understanding between Rome and the Parthians; in the end Armenia remained a vassal of the Parthians and the Arsacid dynasty retained the mastery of all Nearer Asia from the Black Sea to the Indus.

In order to restore Roman trade, Trajan had formed the great plan of advancing the frontiers of the Empire beyond the Tigris and eventually to the Persian Gulf. But his death in 117 had meant the abandonment of his policy. Hadrian renounced the conquests of Trajan and concluded peace with the Parthian king Osroes in 123.

War with Rome was, however, rekindled over Armenia in the reign of Marcus Aurelius; the Roman army advanced as far as Ctesiphon and burnt it. In order to keep back the Arsacids, Septimius Severus built a great Roman arsenal at Nisibis. In 199 the Romans again burnt the capital, Ctesiphon.

The Roman Empire and the Arsacid dynasty thus wasted their military power in a fruitless duel which left them rivals in the field.

THE ADVENT OF THE SASSANIDS

While the Arsacids were exhausting themselves in the struggle against

Rome, a princely dynasty descended from a priest of Persepolis, which dreamed of restoring to Persia the greatness she had known under the Achaemenids, was set up in Persis. In 226 Ardashir I revolted against his suzerain, Artaban V, captured Ctesiphon and founded the Sassanid dynasty.

In contrast to the Roman Empire which in the 3rd century was foundering in the great crisis of anarchy, the Sassanids tried to give their states a mystic unity founded on the ancient national religion of Persia, Mazdaism, in its Zoroastrian form. Modelling themselves on ancient Persia, they restored to vigour the Achaemenid traditions which had never entirely disappeared under the Arsacids.

Sassanid Persia was organized on the twofold basis of theocratic absolutism and aristocracy.

The monarchy, in accordance with the ancient tradition, declared that it held its power from the great god Ahura-Mazda. The king, surrounded by immense ceremony, relied upon an organized Church, of which he appointed the High Priest, who in turn appointed all the 'Magi' of the priestly hierarchy. The sanctuaries, where fire was worshipped as the symbol of Ahura-Mazda, became huge landed estates. The clergy formed a privileged class, exempted from the land-tax and from military service; they constituted the first order of the state. Their influence on the people was immense; they intervened in all the activities of life with rites celebrated at births, weddings and funerals, they heard confession and gave absolution; they held a monopoly of education which was organized for the nobles and the middle classes of the cities; they provided the royal judges. Mazdaism, the state religion served by a fanatical clergy, was obligatory, in theory at least for it did not penetrate either into Armenia or Iraq where the Nestorian heresy continued to be the only religion.

Like Christianity at the same period, Mazdaism was troubled with heresies based on the ancient philosphies. The Magi, supported by the state, organized the severest persecutions against the sectaries, as also against the faithful of other religions.

The most important of the Mazdaist heresies was Manicheism (from 242) which regarded good and evil as forces independent of one another. It was to spread, to the detriment of Christianity, as far as the West and to have an immense influence in Central Asia, where it was the vehicle of Persian influence. Mani, its initiator, was executed as a heretic.

The Sassanid Empire was ruled by a landed aristocracy; though absolute, it was feudal. Vassal kings and governors of the frontier marches formed a sovereign nobility. As formerly in Persia, seven privileged families held the high military and civil offices by hereditary tenure. It was a survival of the ancient Persian feudalism.

Four nobles, known as kings, formed the highest caste in the hierarchy of nobles, which was crowned by the 'King of Kings'. After them came the highest of the officials, the Vizier and his ministers: the High Priest, the Guardian of the Sacred Fire, the Commander-in-Chief, the Chancellor, the Minister of Finances, Agriculture and Trade, the Minister of the Royal Domains; after them came the viceroys of the four governments of the Empire.

Below the ruling nobility ranked the great *seigneurs* who lived on their lands and under whose authority the local landlords formed a chivalrous caste that provided recruits for the Persian cavalry; they were the representatives of government in the villages and, as such, collected the taxes for the king. The district chiefs were recruited from amongst them. Under the authority of the great landlords the peasants, tied to the soil, were almost in a state of serfdom; they served in the infantry which was of little military value.

This semi-serfdom of the rural population was the result of a twofold evolution; one facet, which was evident in the under-developed districts to the east of Mesopotamia, had transformed the serfs into semi-free peasants; the other, in those regions where the peasants had been emancipated during the Hellenistic period, had reduced the free peasants, under the influence of absolutist state-socialism, to the status of *coloni* tied to the soil under the rule of the landlords who had become a privileged class.

Alongside the nobility and the serfs who formed the agricultural population, the people of the cities possessed a special status. Not noble, but free, they were made up of artisans and merchants who paid a personal tax, were exempt from forced labour and military service, and possessed their own laws. The social constitution of Sassanid Persia was, in fact, very similar to that which existed in the West in the 12th century AD.

The cities were important industrial centres. Tabriz, Shapur, Rei, Merv and Herat manufactured fabrics for export. Trade also played an important role. Silk came to them from China by the caravan routes of Central Asia, and also from India by sea. Sassanid commerce, in return, exported to China and India Babylonian carpets, Syrian jewellery, coral and pearls from the Red Sea, fabrics from its own cities and woven stuffs from Egypt.

This economic activity of the Persian cities formed the essential element of the prosperity of the Sassanids.

The finances were supplied by the land-tax, based on a land survey, and the poll-tax.

Justice derived from the king. The privileged classes, however, clergy and nobility, were judged by their peers. In the countryside justice was administered by the priests. It was somewhat rudimentary in character, both cruel and summary, and made extensive use of ordeals and the death penalty.

THE IMPERIAL POLICY OF THE SASSANIDS

The importance of the Sassanid Empire from the 3rd to the 7th century was due to the ruin of the two empires of Rome and China which, up to the time of the simultaneous crises in the 3rd century, had exercised, the one in the West and the other in the East, undisputed leadership. It was their weakness that enabled the Sassanid dynasty to carry out an extensive programme that aimed at nothing less than the restoration of the Empire of Darius, by giving it, as Darius himself had done, an economic basis.

The Sassanids continually sought to gain control of the trade-routes from the Mediterranean to India and the Far East.

They tried, in vain it is true, to recover a foothold on the Syrian coast. But though they renounced Syria easily enough, they never ceased to struggle against Rome to assure themselves the protectorate over Armenia, in order to control the traffic from the Black Sea to Central Asia.

Theodosius I ended by ceding to the Persians practically all Armenia, thus inaugurating a policy of friendship between the courts of Constantinople and Ctesiphon. At the end of the 4th century the position of the Sassanids was so strong in the West that the Emperor Arcadius, on his death-bed, put his heirs under the protection of Yezdigird I.

Halted in their drive towards the Mediterranean, the Sassanids, on the other hand, succeeded in penetrating deeply into Central Asia. As soon as he came to power, Ardashir I turned against the Sacian Empire which extended over northern India and the former Greek kingdom of Bactria as far as the Aral Sea. All Bactria was conquered. Deprived of the control of the caravan routes, the Sacian Empire collapsed.

The monopoly of the caravan routes by Persia, which China, paralysed by the terrible crisis of anarchy through which she was then passing, was unable to contest, changed the economic balance of the great powers.

The Parthian Empire had played only a secondary role in international trade; the Sassanid Empire, on the other hand, wielded a real economic supremacy in Asia. Without doubt, the very serious decadence of China considerably diminished the importance of the caravan routes to the Far East. The Sassanid prosperity was not, therefore, equal to that either of the Sacian Empire or that which the Empire of Bagdad was to know later, thanks to the revival of Chinese trade. But Central Asia remained, none the less, of capital importance for the communications between the West and India and, furthermore, the silk trade with China was never completely interrupted.

From the time of Ardashir I the Sassanid dynasty tried also to develop Persia's internal economic power. Like the Seleucids, Ardashir was a great city-builder; and his successor Sapor I, by constructing an immense dam on the Karun, systematically exploited and irrigated the lands of Susiana.

But however great the importance of economic questions, they were bound, as everywhere at this time, to become involved with religious questions.

The hostility between Persia and Rome was considerably augmented after the adoption by Constantine of Christianity as the state religion. The political conflict was henceforth identified with the religious conflict.

Throughout the Sassanid Empire the Christians were regarded as friends of Rome, and bloodthirsty persecutions were often carried out against them. Sapor II, to spite Constantinople, welcomed the Nestorian heretics who were fleeing from the Empire. This was of primary importance in the history of Christianity; for it was in its Nestorian form that Christianity penetrated Asia along the caravan routes and reached Mongolia and China. Asiatic Christianity was thus to develop in Asia outside the framework of the Catholic Church.

DESTRUCTION OF THE SACIAN EMPIRE

The expansion of Sassanid power, favoured by the eclipse of China, led to the downfall of the Sacian Empire. Created by Scythian invaders, the Sacian Empire had been based on the economic control of the trade-routes and caravan cities of Central Asia, and the basins of the Indus and the Ganges. Its downfall marked the end of the economic supremacy of India in Central Asia, but not the destruction of her prosperity or her civilization. The basins of the Indus and Ganges, liberated from Sacian rule, broke up into little independent states which looked to the great city of Pataliputra, at one time the capital of the Hindu dynasty of the Mauryas.

Around this Ganges basin state, which retained a great prestige in all northern India, a Hindu national unity was once more constituted. Little by little the princes of the Ganges passed under the suzerainty of the sovereigns of Pataliputra. In 308 Prince Chandragupta, sovereign of Magadha, who was perhaps akin to the ancient and illustrious dynasty of the Mauryas, restored, by a marriage with the heiress of the kingdom of Pataliputra, the political unity of the Ganges basin and took the title of 'King of Kings' (320). His son, Sandragupta (339), undertook to establish a Hindu Empire by force of arms. In a few years he conquered the Punjab and Central India as far as the Deccan. The economic power at his disposal was thus certain to attract to him the kings of Kabul and the Tokharian princes of Central Asia who lived from the proceeds of the Indian trade to Europe and the Far East, as also the kings of Ceylon whose ships linked Malabar with the Chinese coast.

HINDU RENAISSANCE UNDER THE GUPTA DYNASTY

India was to regain for about a century the immense economic and intellectual expansion that she had known in the times of the Maurya Empire.

The Gupta dynasty marked the peak of Hindu civilization. The intellectual centres of the 4th century were indisputably on the one hand Antioch and Alexandria, and on the other Pataliputra on the Ganges and the city of Ujjain near the Malabar coast.

Malabar, with its great port of Barygaza, was, it will be recalled, one of the essential trade centres of India with the West.

The decline of China turned Hindu trade definitely towards the Mediterranean, which explains why, under the Gupta dynasty, the influence of Alexandria was so deeply evident at Ujjain, where Hellenistic mathematics and astronomy flourished. The Hindu renaissance in the time of the Guptas was complementary to the renaissance felt throughout the Roman Empire from the reign of Constantine to that of Theodosius I and, to a great extent, was associated with it.

The economic vigour of India in the 4th century was quite naturally accompanied by a great development of individualism, both social and intellectual. The ideas of natural law and the social preoccupations which were then triumphant in the Roman Empire found equally wide credit in India and were shown especially in the foundation of free hospitals.

Art flourished as a result of the wealth and refinement of life. Painting was to know one of its greatest periods. Literature with its court poetry, erotic, learned and elegant, lyricism, didactic tales, theatrical presentations with choruses, music and dancing, fables, stories and romances had as great a vogue in India as the *fin-de-siècle* literature of Alexandria two centuries before.

But in Alexandria, from the 3rd century onward, the profane arts had been replaced by religious thought. Christian mysticism succeeded Neo-Platonic mysticism. So also in India; though profane literature shone with a lively brilliance, it was religion that became the basis of intellectual life. China was still searching for her way after the terrible Mongol invasions, and Buddhist monks from China came to India to be initiated into the holy mysteries in the famous Hindu monasteries, even as the *literati* flocked to the schools of Ujjain to learn the scientific knowledge that had come there from Alexandria and which, through their agency, penetrated as far as the coasts of the China Sea.

CHAPTER LXIII

RESTORATION OF THE CHINESE EMPIRE

THE TIME OF TROUBLES IN CHINA

THE history of China after the crises of the 3rd century is dominated by two great historical facts. One, of universal importance, was the eclipse of the two Empires whose supremacy had given the world two centuries of prosperity and peace. The other was the invasions of the Huns, and later the Turks, in Central Asia.

The Roman Empire, which ended by dissolving into an anarchy caused by the internal decadence of the West and the Germanic invasions suffered an eclipse until its restoration by Justinian in 527.

The same was true of China, which renounced until the 6th century the leadership which she had held in Asia before the great crisis of the 3rd century. Thereafter, China lived in isolation. Sheltered from the Hunnic invasions, which devasted Central Asia and northern India from the close of the 4th century, she found a new way of life. Broken up politically under the rule of Mongol dynasties, she absorbed her conquerors. This slow work of assimilation, the essential factor of her renascence, was accomplished in so complete a manner that in the 6th century the kings of Oe, of Manchu origin, who ruled over the former capitals of Chang-Ngan and Lo-Yang, decreed the exclusive use of the Chinese language and Chinese dress throughout their vast kingdom.

None the less, the assimilation of the barbarians was not accomplished without producing a catalytic influence on Chinese civilization. The Mongol courts, where the ruling class mostly lived, remained centres of unrestrained barbarity. There were constant murders and intrigues. They could only be compared with the courts of the Germanic kings set up in the Roman Empire. The decadence caused by barbarism among the upper classes led to a profound social degeneration. Anarchy and the annihilation of the population which was almost complete in some regions—in the valley of Oe after the invasions only two out of every hundred inhabitants remained alive—halted all economic life and destroyed all security. The same phenomenon of grouping about local lords, which was the origin of the seigniorial régime in Western Europe, took place also in continental China, where smallholding disappeared, absorbed by the great estates.

Intellectual and moral activities, still so remarkable in the 4th century, gradually subsided. The monasteries, which had been founded under the influence of mystical idealism, changed little by little into great landed estates, more concerned with their temporal power than with religious speculation. The clergy, having become an aristocracy, allowed themselves to be tainted, as in Merovingian Gaul, by the corruption which was rife at court and among the ruling classes. The mystical current of Buddhism was replaced by a clerical policy of domination by the monasteries over the people of the countryside. None the less, it was in these monasteries that all that remained of civilization still survived, and a great school of painters and sculptors flourished in them during the 5th century. The barbarized kingdoms of the north and west slid slowly into a purely landholding régime, dominated by the nobility and the monasteries.

In the south, on the contrary, where the Tsin had maintained a national dynasty, the economic activity of the great coastal cities dominated social and political evolution. But trade remained confined to the sea-coasts and the valleys, where the Chinese farmers, thanks to the outlets which remained open to their produce, preserved their smallholdings. In the interior of the provinces, where the greatly weakened power of the Nankin Emperors could not make itself felt, the nomad invaders disorganized the country. The central power, sapped by its weakness, was a prey to internal disorders which, in 420, led to the overthrow of the Tsin dynasty by a general who founded the Sung dynasty (420–479).

THE INVASION OF CENTRAL ASIA BY THE HUNS

The internal crisis which China went through from the 4th to the end of the 6th century was both the cause and the consequence of the invasion of Central Asia by the Huns; the cause, since the internal collapse of the Empire made it possible for the Huns to cut the silk route by settling in Chinese Turkestan; the consequence, because once this route had been cut, continental China, isolated from the outside world, since it could find no outlet for its exports, could only turn to a purely manorial and closed economy, that is to say to the seigniorial régime.

About 425 the Hephtalite Huns, settled to the east of the Caspian Sea, invaded Bactria which they soon wrested from the Sassanids; about 490 they crossed the passes of the Hindu-Kush and invaded India, which was then experiencing one of the most brilliant periods of her history under the Gupta kings.

THE FALL OF THE GUPTA DYNASTY AND THE CRISIS IN PERSIA

The invasion of India by the Huns was carried out with the greatest atrocity; cities were sacked and the Buddhist monasteries destroyed. The Gupta Empire collapsed and on its ruins a Hun khan extended his rule, as the Sacian princes had done before him, from the Malabar coast to the Aral Sea.

The establishment of the Huns in Bactria had only been made possible by the social crisis that Persia was then undergoing.

The Sassanid Empire, founded on the antinomic principles of absolute monarchy and aristocratic feudalism, was to end in a crisis. The royal policy, aimed entirely at ensuring the economic prosperity of the country and in consequence the development of the cities, therefore led to the emancipation of the rural classes. The great improvement of farming, especially in Susiana, by encouraging the market for agricultural produce destroyed the manorial régime of closed economy upon which the seigniorial system depended.

Thus the economic policy of the monarchy aroused the opposition of the landed aristocracy and of the priestly sanctuaries which were the largest landowners in the country. The king countered by strengthening his absolutist methods.

The crisis broke out in the reign of Yezdigird I (399–420). The economic policy of the Sassanids led them quite naturally to show favour to foreign merchants. Yezdigird I on his accession to the throne gave up the religious persecutions and adopted a tolerant policy which ensured him great popularity among the Semitic and Christian people of Iraq, and also abroad, especially at Constantinople, but which earned him the hatred of the clergy. He perished as the victim of a plot, and his son Bahram V (420–438) revived the religious persecutions. Christians sought refuge in the Roman Empire and aroused there a hatred for Persia which gave the Emperor Theodosius II a pretext to attack. In 422 Persia had to sign a peace recognizing religious liberty for the Christians. But such a peace, imposed by the enemy, was to seem even more odious to the Persian nationalists, who now reacted. Under their influence Yezdigird II (438–457) reverted to the policy of intolerance and tried to impose Mazdaism on the Armenian Christians by force. The Huns, however, at this time had triumphed in Bactria, and the Persian bishops thought the time ripe to oppose Zoroastrianism openly. The Germanic invasions prevented the Emperor of Constantinople from intervening. Yezdigird II took advantage of this to proclaim the obligatory practice of Zoroastrianism. An insurrection broke out among the Christians which set off a revolt of the peasants reduced to serfdom by the monasteries and landed seigneurs, and Persia was plunged into social revolution.

The country was then faced with serious economic difficulties as a result of the occupation of Bactria by the Huns to whom the kings of Persia were forced to pay tribute (484). The opposition of the nobility further weakened the dynasty.

In the midst of such internal and external crises the popular movement of the peasants who wished to free themselves from serfdom and to obtain land assumed a mystical and religious character and continued to grow. The Nestorian Christians, persecuted within the Roman Empire, looked for asylum in Persia and increased the confusion already existing; and just at this time Mazdak, a social Utopian who claimed to be Mani, formed a religious sect which aimed at establishing complete community of goods and women, the abolition of all privileges and absolute prohibition of slaughter, even of animals for food.

POLITICAL REFORM IN PERSIA

King Kavadh (488–531), paralyzed by the opposition of the nobles, favoured the teaching of Mazdak and declared himself an adherent of his doctrines. The nobles overthrew him and he fled temporarily to the Huns (497) but was soon able to restore his authority.

The social revolution had thrown Persia into inextricable anarchy. After a terrible massacre of the communists, the king first restored internal order by reconstituting the family and property. The landed nobility had been greatly weakened by the communist revolution. Kavadh took advantage of this to break its power, which was hostile to his own. The functions of Prime Minister had been appropriated by the most powerful of the land-owners in the kingdom; Kavadh reduced his powers and in order to free the country from the ascendancy of the *seigneurs* he divided it into four large civil governments directly responsible to the sovereign. The nobles were compelled to pay the land-tax, to assure which a land-survey was established.

Chosroes (531–579) carried on the work of his father by completing the destruction of the privileges of the high nobility. The office of generalissimo, which was still in the hands of the former feudal nobles, was abolished; the army was divided into four commands corresponding to the administrative districts created by Kavadh; to the governors of these districts the four hereditary 'kings', who had continued to exist as a feudal legacy, were made subordinate. A new administrative nobility replaced the former military and landowning nobility; the monarchy triumphed over the seigniorial-feudal régime. The army itself, which hitherto had retained its aristocratic structure, passed under the direct authority of the king; barbarian prisoners of war, whose loyalty was assured by a small grant of land and who were forced to do hereditary military service, henceforward formed its backbone.

Heraclius, in the great social reform that he carried out in Asia Minor after the Persian invasion, was inspired by the model of Kavadh and Chosroes I, but his reform was greatly superior to that which they had carried through in Persia, since Heraclius built up his army of nationals, whereas Chosroes entrusted the destiny of his lands, as Rome had done in its decadence, to foreign barbarians.

Thanks to the social and political stability which he had restored to Persia, the influence of Chosroes in foreign affairs became very great. In 540, turning against Justinian who was then engaged in the conquest of the Mediterranean provinces, he seized Antioch and deported into Persia thousands of Syrian artisans who contributed greatly to give that country, still suffering from the effects of the recent social convulsions, a revival of economic and intellectual vigour.

A great wave of Hellenic influence affected Persia at this time. It was encouraged by Chosroes who aimed, while breaking down the political privileges of the nobility, at creating an absolute monarchical power and who welcomed international culture. Opposite Ctesiphon he constructed a new city on the Greek model, 'the Roman city', where Greek and Syrian savants, fleeing from the religious persecutions of Heraclius, translated into Persian the geography of Ptolemy and the great encyclopaedias.

The growing power of Justinian made it impossible for Chosroes to extend westward. He concluded a 'fifty-year peace' with Constantinople (561)[1] and concentrated all his forces against the Huns of Central Asia in order to reconquer the rich province of Bactria which they had seized from Persia.

[1] It was broken in 572.

PERSIA AND THE TURKS CRUSH THE HEPHTALITE HUNS

The Turks, of Mongol race, came originally from the Altai region where they exploited the iron mines. They lived there under the rule of the Avars—or Juan-Juan—who had created a vast Empire on the northern frontiers of China stretching from the Aral Sea to Manchuria. About 545 the Manchu Kings of Oe, one of the barbarian kingdoms established in the former Chinese Empire, had made an alliance with their Turkish vassals against the Avars, who were the most primitive of nomads. The Avars, attacked on the east by the Manchus and on the West by the Turks, were crushed. The remnant of their tribes then flowed back across Asia westward, where shortly afterwards they crossed the Volga and appeared on the Danube.

The kings of Oe thus made themselves masters of all Mongolia, and the Turks extended their rule from the Caspian Sea as far as the Gulf of Petchili.

Chosroes, in his turn, made an alliance with the Turks against the Hephtalite Huns who, attacked in Bactria both from the west and from the north, were annihilated in 560. This was the end of the great conquests of the Huns, and the destruction of the Hun khanate of Bactria dealt the death-blow to the Hunnic race.

Chosroes again incorporated Bactria into his Empire, while Sogdiana passed into the power of the Turks.

WAR BETWEEN PERSIA AND CONSTANTINOPLE FOR THE TRADE ROUTES

Chosroes had recovered control of the caravan routes. He now wanted to complete his conquest by gaining possession of the Indian sea-route, which was held by the Roman Empire. He succeeded in doing this by making a conquest of the Yemen. Thenceforward the Red Sea was at his mercy. All the trade of the Roman Empire with India and the Far East came under his control. Justin II, who succeeded Justinian in 565, could not accept such a tutelage. He turned to the Turks who, as neighbours of Persia, had not failed to come into conflict with their former allies on the subject of the caravan routes, of which they held the eastern parts. Justin II now offered them his alliance (572).

A war to the death broke out between Constantinople and Persia for the possession of the great international trade-routes.

It spelt disaster for Constantinople. Chosroes II captured, one after the other, Edessa, Antioch and Damascus, penetrated into Asia Minor and, after taking Caesarea of Cappadocia, occupied Chalcedon directly opposite Constantinople. If Chosroes II had had a fleet, the capital of the Roman Empire would have fallen. The sea saved it. Continuing his conquests southward, Chosroes entered Jerusalem in 614 and carried away the Holy Cross, and in 619 conquered Egypt. Byzantium lost the richest provinces of her Empire.

But while they were triumphing over Constantinople, the Sassanids were giving way under the blows of the Turks who, about 597, took possession of Bactria and its rich merchant-cities. This meant the collapse of the Sassanid economic policy. The crisis which followed deprived Persia of her continental communications with Asia and allowed the Emperor, Heraclius, to recover his lost provinces. Defeated Persia was forced, in 629, to restore to Byzantium all her conquests and the 'True Cross'.

Driven back from the coasts of the Mediterranean and deprived of the control of the routes of Central Asia, which were occupied by her enemies, Persia lost the mainspring of her power. The result was soon felt. The economic decline of the cities allowed the landed aristocracy to raise its head; the political anarchy that resulted ruined all that was left of the kingdom.

In 632 Yezdigird III ascended the throne. Four years later the Arab invasion burst on the Byzantine and the Persian Empires, both of which were exhausted by the fruitless wars they had been waging and by the internal dissensions which were rending them.

INDIA BECOMES FEUDAL

The destruction of the Hephtalite khanate of Bactria by the Persians and Turks (560) freed India from Hunnic domination. She was left divided into a number of little states, formerly vassals of the Hephtalite Huns, which now recovered their independence. During the one hundred and fifty years of Hunnic rule the seigniorial dismemberment of northern India had continually progressed. The cities, cut off from the outer world, were ruined and depopulated. Pataliputra, the famous capital on the Ganges, had no more than a thousand inhabitants. The country was given over to a régime of closed economy, seigniorial feudalism had spread and the landed aristocracy had become dominant. Thus, freed from the Huns, India was no longer centred on the ancient metropolis of Pataliputra, but around the warrior princes of Thanesvar, a little state situated in the mountains between the Ganges and the Indus basins.

A feudal state was formed. In 606 Prince Harcha founded the Hindu dynasty of Vardhana by uniting under his rule all northern and central India as far as the Deccan. Northern India, however, was never to recover its former prosperity.

India under Harcha was no more like the India of the Gupta kings than Carolingian Gaul was like the Roman Empire. The central administration had disappeared. Commerce was dead. The Indus, formerly a great industrial centre, became, like the Ganges valley, a country of landed *seigneurs* and peasants. Harcha was no more than a feudal king elected by his peers. There was no longer a fixed capital and the king went from domain to domain, living from the revenue of his estates wherever he happened to be.

All intellectual life was concentrated in the monasteries and was limited to mystical thought. King Harcha himself wrote Buddhist hymns. India no longer sent her cotton goods and spices far abroad, but she was still a great religious centre. By contact with her the Turks, masters of Bactria and Sogdiana, were converted to Buddhism, and Chinese monks still came to India as to the Holy Land.

There still existed, however, several cities which maintained a considerable prosperity through their trade with the Sassanid and Byzantine Empires. In Malabar, the port of Barygaza remained a great international market and an intellectual centre. The little kingdom of Vallabhi in the Malabar peninsula lived by trade with the West. But these were rare exceptions. In the interior of the country, save for Kanaudj, the seat of an important trade fair in the Upper Ganges region, the cities fell into decadence; the most famous amongst them were no more than religious centres where Buddhist monasteries multiplied and where the ascetics of the Brahmanic, Jain or Shivaist cults, living among the ruins, vied with one another in austerity and fanaticism.

In reality, king Harcha only presided over a feudal federation temporarily grouped under his personal sovereignty, and his death in 647 put an end to his kingdom.

Thus India was to find herself feudalized, dismembered and powerless to resist when the threat of Islam confronted her in 711.

RESTORATION OF THE CHINESE EMPIRE

While northern China was broken up into feudal kingdoms, the southern kingdom looked definitely seaward, to India. Navigation between China and India was dependent on the important staging-post of Kattigara on the Red River; the Song (420–479) captured it and subjected the Champa to their protectorate, thus controlling the sea-route from China to Ceylon. Agriculture revived in the valleys; the nomads who were disorganizing the country were driven back across the Yang-Tse. The sea-coast and river ports again enjoyed great prosperity. But the dynasty of the Song usurpers, who governed as autocrats, was wiped out in a series of palace dramas. They were dethroned in 479 by a military *coup d'état*, to the advantage of the Tsi (479–502) who foundered in similar abuses and were themselves replaced by the Liang (502–549). The restoration of normal conditions and the return to honest government did not, however, prevent their succumbing to a palace revolution which brought the Ch'en dynasty (549–589) to the throne.

The Nankin Empire was no more than a façade. The dynasty, super-imposed on the country, no longer had any ties with it. The wealthy classes no longer gave any thought save to their own interests. The Empire no longer possessed the political cohesion or the military force necessary to resist the assaults which were to come from the north.

In the north the assimilation of the barbarian kingdoms revived Chinese national unity. Security was restored and, with it, the silk industry. Despite the occupation of Bactria by the Huns, a certain trade activity was resumed and caravans of silk merchants again took the road to Central Asia. The kingdom of Oe, where the caravan routes ended, was the first to emerge from seigniorial torpor. The decadence of civilization and the barbarity of Mongol customs had brought with them a brutality and materialism in which the mystical movement, which had resulted in the foundation of the great Buddhist monasteries at the end of the 3rd century, changed its character. Encumbered by riches, Buddhism had become temporal and clerical, and a gross thirst for worldly and sensual pleasures reigned everywhere. The kings of Oe, in the course of the 5th century, reacted against this corruption of morals. In 498 they went so far as to decree a completely dry régime, the sale or consumption of alcohol entailing the death penalty.

The crushing of the Huns in Bactria by the alliance of the Persians and Turks about 560 restored security to the caravan routes. The economic life of China thereby received an enormous stimulus. Close relations were established between the maritime economy of the southern kingdom and the continental economy of the northern. China once again formed an economic unity, based both on the coastal ports and the Central

Asian trade routes, which presaged the restoration of her political unity.

The renewal of trade caused the closed economy, and consequently the seigniorial régime, to disappear gradually in the kingdoms of the north. A political and social movement in opposition to feudal ascendancy resulted. The monasteries, which had reduced the tenants on their immense domains to serfdom, were attacked by the peasants. The kings of Oe confiscated the monastery lands and forbade any Chinese who had not passed the age of military conscription to enter holy orders. As the feudal and seigniorial structure was broken up, the kings of Oe again formed a royal army on a conscript basis.

They were soon powerful enough to undertake the conquest of the other Mongol kingdoms of the north, which they united under their rule in the course of the 6th century.

Masters of northern China, the kings of Oe, drawn to the ports of the Nankin kingdom, undertook their conquest and in 589, after several political upheavals in the course of which the House of Oe was overthrown by its prime minister who founded the dynasty of the Sui, China was again united.

REFORMS OF THE SUI DYNASTY (581–619)

Having restored the political unity of China, the Sui tried to restore peace, order and intellectual and economic prosperity by far-reaching reforms. The Emperor announced the return to a pacific régime: 'Let those who are illustrious by their warlike energy,' he ordered, 'return to a study of the classics.' China was to know a renaissance of antiquity. The ancient classics were collected in libraries set up in the former capitals of Chang-Ngan and Lo-Yang. An encyclopaedia, in seventeen thousand volumes, was published by the state. Under the influence of this intellectual revival, public opinion reacted against the formal clericalism of the Buddhist monks and there was a renewed outburst of Taoist idealism, while the *literati* restored Confucius to honour. Buddhism reformed itself and, influenced by the mysticism of India, made ready to take up once more its role as a great spiritual force.

The criminal code was redrafted and penalties made less harsh. A general amnesty was proclaimed.

Taxes were reduced by a third and forced-labour dues by a half.

Since centralization of power went hand in hand with individualism, lands were distributed in the proportion of a little under three-and-three quarter acres[1] per adult in order to revive smallholding. They were taken from the confiscated estates of the great landowners.

Thus the restoration of the monarchy coincided with a broadly democratic policy and with a considerable expansion of trade, both by sea and by the routes of Central Asia.

The imperialist policy of the Sui Emperors led them to undertake great military expeditions against Korea in 611 and 614. These ended in disaster. The great losses in men and the enormous expenses which they entailed led to revolts, in the course of which the Sui dynasty foundered in anarchy. The former local dynasties profited from this by trying to recover their sovereignty, and the governors of the provinces, imitating them, proclaimed themselves independent.

However this purely political anarchy, the last convulsion of the dispossessed ruling families, did not last. General Li-Yuan (620–629) seized power and founded the Tang dynasty, under which China was to know a fresh period of greatness.

GREATNESS OF THE CHINESE EMPIRE UNDER THE TANG (620–907)

After the restoration of the Empire, the peoples of the caravan regions of Turfan, as well as the states of Tonkin, which were both economically dependent on China, hastened to do homage. China, restored internally, recovered her position of supremacy. The Tang, inaugurating an imperialist policy, conquered all eastern Mongolia. Turkestan, Annam, Champa and the Khmer kingdom acknowledged their suzerainty.

Chinese merchants settled in all these countries. In 631 Japan, which was still not very civilized but where Buddhism had been introduced from the middle of the 6th century onward, opened her frontiers in 631 to Chinese artisans, artists and *literati*, who brought with them Confucian moral ideas. Korea, converted to Buddhism about 528, once again passed into the sphere of Chinese influence. Tibet, whose kings were allied by marriage with the Tang dynasty, accepted Chinese suzerainty.

About 630 the Empire extended from the China Sea to the Tarim basin, whence its protectorate reached as far as the Caspian, and from the Gobi desert to Kashmir.

Chinese economic supremacy was based on her political supremacy. Both were the less disputed since the collapse of Sassanid Persia, vanquished

[1] 'un hectare et demi' = 3·7066 (English) acres (Translator).

in the west by Heraclius and in the east by the Turks; and the economic decline of India, now feudal and dormant, gave China the mastery over all Asia.

It seemed as if the world was to be shared, as during the first two centuries AD, between two powers, Constantinople in the West and the Chinese Empire in the East. But whereas at that time the Roman Empire had been the great centre of influence, this time it was China which became the great centre of attraction.

THE GREAT OWNERSHIP REFORMS

The enormous influence exercised by the Chinese Empire over Asia was accompanied by a far-reaching internal reform of a broadly democratic character.

Developing the Sui policy, which had aimed at restoring smallholding by expropriating the great estates, the Tang attempted a wholesale redistribution of land, reviving the great reform earlier carried out by Wang-Mang (between AD 9 and 23) by systematizing and expanding it still more.

All land was declared to be the property of the state and was expropriated. It was the largest and most radical reform ever made before the Russian Communist revolution of 1917.

The State had no intention of exploiting the land itself on state-socialist lines. On the contrary, it wanted to divide it among all Chinese. It was therefore laid down that the Emperor would give just under fifteen acres of arable land to every farmer of the age of twenty or over; for this the farmer would pay not a tax but an annual rent, but would not be able to sell his land, since that would remain the property of the state, to which it would revert on the death of the holder.

In return for the use of a part of the soil of the Empire, every state farmer was liable to military service.

Thus, through the reforms of Wang-Mang, the Sui and the Tang, a conception of property was created in China based on the idea that the land is a common benefit to which all men have a right, entirely different from the conception of the Roman law, which considered property as individual, absolute and exclusive.

In the maritime Empire of Rome, democratic evolution resulted in a capitalist and individual conception of landed property; property, whether fixed or movable, was regarded as one and the same legal conception and susceptible to private negotiation.

In the immense continental Empire of China, the essential factor, on the contrary, was the land. Democracy consisted essentially in assuring the right of every man to have the use of it. So, while trade remained liberal and capitalist, land became a source of common benefit and ceased to have a negotiable value.

Democracy was much more egalitarian in China than in Rome; the equality preached by natural law was attained there, since the vast majority of men were dependent on the land, by a common ownership of the soil and the right of every adult to have an equal share in its usufruct.

This egalitarian social reform, the culmination of a trend evident in China for six centuries past, was accompanied by the complete standardization of institutions throughout the Empire. The population was grouped into villages, the villages into cantons, the cantons into provinces; and military and police chiefs were attached to the local governors.

The central government kept the whole administration of the provinces firmly in its hands. It was put under the control of a directorate of three Ministers; the Commander-in-Chief, a Minister responsible for Internal Affairs, Agriculture and Justice, and another Minister who presided over Industry, Public Works and Transport. They controlled the nine 'palaces' which looked after the great departments of the administration: cults and education, the ancestors and family of the sovereign, the army and police, justice, finances, festivals and the treasury, arsenals, agriculture, and administrative personnel.

The state itself organized education and provided a structure for teaching by creating empire schools, an academy of specialists in all branches of knowledge, and an observatory charged with looking after the calendar and astronomical studies.

The cult was also subjected to extensive reform. A vast enquiry led to the suppression of monasteries and nunneries, of which there were thousands, with the exception of three Buddhist and two Taoist monasteries in the capital and one monastery of each cult in each province. Magic was strictly prohibited. Beyond that, absolute tolerance in religious matters was proclaimed; all religions could be practised and preached, Buddhism, Taoism and Zoroastrianism. A Zoroastrian temple was built in the capital in 631, and Christianity, in the form of the Nestorian heresy, penetrated China at this time (635).

None the less, a state cult was established which, up till then, had been celebrated only by the sovereign and the governors and in which the people were now called upon to participate; the harvest cult. It was evidently a survival of some very ancient nature worship.

As an official code of morals the state adopted the code of Confucius; equity, courtesy, 'reciprocity', were reintroduced as basic principles of the art of government. 'On high,' declared the Emperor, 'I fear the ever present surveillance of august Heaven; on earth, I take account of the views of the people and the officials who must heed this example.'

Finally, the law also was revised. A century after the promulgation of the Code of Justinian, the Tang published a new code based, like that of Justinian, on the principles of humanity and social unity (637). The law confirmed, legally, the equality that the Tang had introduced in the division of lands. All nobility by birth disappeared, to be replaced by a sort of non-hereditary administrative nobility very similar to that of the *illustres*, the *spectabiles* and the *clarissimi* of the later Roman Empire. The *literati* played a leading role in the state. In order to train them China, as formerly Egypt, founded an Imperial School for officials which soon had twelve thousand pupils from all classes, amongst them the children of vassal sovereigns. Administrative posts were granted after examinations which were open to all pupils. The way to wealth and honour was open to all Chinese.

CHINESE CIVILIZATION SPREADS TO JAPAN

Under the Tang dynasty China exerted an enormous influence upon all her neighbours, especially on Japan.

The development of navigation in the 4th century had assured Japan a very strong position in Korea. Intervening in the disputes between the Korean states, the Emperor of Japan, allied to the state of Paik-Che, tried to make Silla his vassal in the 5th century.

This close alliance between Paik-Che and Japan had a considerable influence on Japanese development. In the 3rd century Japan exchanged slaves for the fabrics, arms and bronze mirrors of Korea. By the end of the 4th century a wholesale emigration to Japan of scribes, craftsmen, painters and doctors from Paik-Che was organized. They introduced Chinese script and language to the court, formed a class of *literati* and entered the aristocracy in such great numbers that, in the 7th century, a third of the Japanese noble families claimed descent from Korean or Chinese immigrants. Whole villages of Koreans were settled in Japan.

Buddhism, which penetrated Korea in the 4th century, spread in the 6th to Japan with the Koreans, who were influenced in all fields by the ascendancy of Chinese civilization. But in the 6th century the kingdom of Silla conquered and annexed Paik-Che, the ally of Japan, and took possession of the Japanese enclave of Meniana. Japan was thus finally driven out of Korea.

MONARCHIC REFORMS OF THE YAMATO

Japan then turned to China and from 650 her relations with China were unbroken. The Emperor of Japan sent more and more pupils to attend the Chinese high schools; Chinese *literati* were invited in great numbers to Japan and a systematically Chinese-influenced élite was formed by the Emperors. The Yamato court was organized on the model of the Sui court, whose centralizing policy it imitated. In 607 the Emperor declared himself master of all Japan and organized around him, on the Chinese model, a court hierarchy in which the *literati* held a leading place.

The considered policy of the Emperor aimed at 'modernizing' Japan by imposing Chinese institutions.

In 646 Taikwa published an edict of four articles, which constituted a radical reform of Japan. It dispossessed the *seigneurs* of their domains, freed all the serfs, suppressed the corporations of artisans and proclaimed the freedom of professions; it replaced the hereditary feudal lords by royal governors, and introduced a system of citizenship and registration; forced labour and dues to the *seigneurs* were abolished and replaced by a land-tax payable in rice, by forced labour quotas due to the state and by a production-tax which could be paid in silk or any other article. The land taken from the nobles was to be divided amongst the former serfs. The feudal army was replaced by a royal army based on the conscription of one man in four, who was compelled to do military service for a year.

This revolution, theoretical and radical, was evidently not fully put into force, but it helped to accelerate the evolution of the monarchy. The feudal lords were not replaced by royal governors but, losing their sovereign powers, themselves became hereditary governors dependent on the Emperor. Their domains were not taken from them, but the supreme right of the Emperor was imposed on all the lands and the nobles only retained these lands, through all the grades of the feudal hierarchy, as direct fiefs of the crown.

The reform of property resulted in the emancipation of the tenant-serfs, making them free tenants directly dependent on the Emperor. The great communist reform attempted in China led, in Japan, to the diffusion of private property in the sense that all the cultivable lands of the seigniorial domains were surveyed and divided between the former serfs according to the number of the members of their families. In actual fact, the situation of the former tenants was not greatly altered.

The former feudal royalty thus made itself a monarchy over the whole country. The Emperor, adored as a god, proclaimed himself the descendant of the sun-goddess, whose cult became the state religion. A permanent capital was set up at Nara (710), with a palace, ministeries, state shops, residences for senior officials, temples and a university organized on the Chinese model and put in charge of professors trained in Chinese schools. The central government was composed of three Chancellors and a Council of three Ministers who presided over the great state services: Internal Affairs, Ceremonies, Civil Affairs, Labour, War, Justice, the Treasury and the Imperial Household. An imperial postal system was created. An administrative code, published in 668, fixed the status of the officials.

This extraordinary attempt to adapt Japanese feudal society to the needs of a centralized monarchy in complete imitation of China was one of the strangest political experiments ever to be attempted.

The new régime of the Tang was in full operation in China, and the Empire had reached the zenith of its political, economic and intellectual power when, in 638, ambassadors sent by the Sassanid king, Yezdigird III, presented themselves at the court of the Emperor Tai-Tsong (629–651) imploring him for aid against the Arabs who had just invaded Persia.

Islam was making its entry into world affairs. It was radically to affect their balance. A new era began in the history of all the peoples.

CHAPTER LXIV

THE END OF THE ERA OF THE EMPIRES

THE ERA OF THE EMPIRES

LOOKING at a map of the world in the 2nd century AD, the first thing that strikes one is that it is made up of a few very large states, and that all these states are connected by land- and sea-routes, punctuated by great ports and caravan cities whose influence extended far afield.

Two Empires dominated the world, the maritime Empire of Rome in the West and the continental Empire of China in the East. Between the two, on the sea-route from Alexandria to China, lay India the great economic and intellectual centre where influences from all parts of the world met and mingled. On the silk route, which stretched from the Chinese capital of Chang-Ngan to the Syrian cities, a chain of rich and prosperous cities stretched through Central Asia, Persia and Mesopotamia.

The Roman Empire and the Chinese Empire had both reached the peak of their evolution and had therefore become pacific in policy. The *pax Romana* corresponded to the Chinese peace. The era of great wars, which had stained the world with blood in the full crisis of growth from the IIIrd to the Ist century BC, had ended. An international balance had been attained throughout the world, which allowed each people to develop freely and to increase its wealth in full security of the morrow. Population reached a density it had never before known. Under the dynasty of the Antonines, the Roman Empire numbered seventy million inhabitants, all belonging to the same civilization, heirs to the experience of forty centuries of Oriental, Greek and Roman civilization. The former local patriotisms had merged into the great universal community of the Empire which inspired these magnificent verses to the glory of Rome by the Alexandrian Claudian: 'She alone has received the vanquished into her bosom and she alone keeps ward under a single name over the whole race of men. Mother but not queen, she calls her subjects citizens; she binds in sacred bonds the most distant lands. Thanks to her mildness, the foreigner may believe he is in his own country; we are all one people.'[1] This liberal universalism was achieved by the assertion of the rights of the individual; all the citizens of the Empire were equal before the law,[2] and respect for human rights had led to the triumph of that solidarity preached by the Stoics which dictated the social legislation of the Empire.

To express this common civilization, all the peoples united within the Empire had abandoned their national tongues and adopted two universal languages, Greek and Latin, which were known by all educated men.

The prevailing peace promoted an expansion of industry and commerce and this in turn increased the volume of wealth which was soon manifest in the magnificence of the cities, sumptuously built according to elaborate town planning. Comfort and civilization led to a universal refinement of manners and customs which had hitherto been restricted to the few. Universities and libraries popularized the discoveries made by science in the previous centuries, and schools, which were numerous in all the provinces of the Empire, brought a knowledge of Greco-Roman literature and philosophy even into the most recently Romanized regions.

In China the situation was analogous. The Han dynasty practised a liberal policy that recalled that of the Antonines; urban civilization, based on commercial activity, spread throughout the whole Empire, which numbered fifty million inhabitants, a wealth that encouraged its artistic and intellectual development, widely popularized by the schools and guided by a national academy. The individualist law had suppressed all the former privileges of birth and, as in Rome, had led to a sentiment of the equality of all men which was shown in the social field by the first humanitarian laws. Without doubt the continental character of the Chinese Empire gave its social conceptions a viewpoint different from the maritime Empire of Rome. Roman democracy was liberal, as was, at all periods, the democracy of the maritime states; in the Chinese Empire it was social, a characteristic to be found throughout history in continental democratic movements; the reform of ownership, which tended towards a sort of communism in land, was the basis of Chinese democracy. But, liberal in Rome, egalitarian in China, imperial policy in both cases aimed, under the influence of moral ideas, at individual emancipation.

In India civilization followed exactly the same evolution. Dominated by the great ports of Malabar and Bengal, it was both cosmopolitan and

[1] Claudian was a poet of the late 4th century. The Gaul Rutilius Namatianus wrote in 416: 'You have given a common fatherland to diverse peoples. The evil have gained by being conquered by you; and by offering to the vanquished a share of your laws, you have made the whole world a single city.'

[2] The Constitution of 212, which extended citizenship to the whole Empire, only confirmed what had already existed in fact, save for certain fiscal differences.

individualist, perhaps even more brilliant than in Rome and China. The capital, Pataliputra, rivalled the greatest cities of the world in splendour. Its high schools experienced an extraordinary upsurge of scientific thought, while art and literature passed through a period of great creative energy. Here too universalism and individualism, at that time the two great principles of civilization, were accompanied by humanitarian ideas which, in India, took the form of charity.

The Sacian Empire included both northern India and Bactria where the caravan cities prospered and in which the Greek, Persian, Hindu and Chinese civilizations mingled. Greco-Roman influence came from the sea through the Indian ports; that of China and Persia came from the land through the Syrian, Persian and Chinese merchants.

Between the Roman Empire and the Sacian Empire, Persia alone gave the impression of an essentially continental civilization. It displayed, in contrast to the cosmopolitanism of the great Empires on its frontiers, a pure and simple nationalism based on its traditional religion, Zoroastrianism. Certainly, the Persian cities were influenced by Hellenism, and the navigation of the Persian Gulf and of Syria put them in contact with the sea. But, despite the wealth that the Persians drew from their industry and from the transit trade along the trade routes on which their cities were situated, these cities had only a secondary influence on the country. Persia was above all an agricultural state. Thus it was, of all the great states of the time, the only one in which the people had not attained that individual emancipation that had triumphed in the rest of the world. The landed nobility continued to exist there, as in certain of the more isolated provinces of the Sacian Empire; but while outside Persia the cities were dominant, in Persia it was the nobility, under whose rule the enslaved peasants lived, that impressed its character on society. The sea had spread liberty everywhere save in Persia, where the land continued to impose its mastery; nationalism and a class-society made up the structure of the state.

Outside the four Empires that stretched from the Atlantic Ocean to the China Sea, the world was divided into two very well-defined zones. On all the coasts of Asia along the great sea-route from Alexandria to India and China, civilization penetrated through the cities which owed their existence to the sea. Flourishing ports had been founded on the coasts of Arabia, and on the borders of her deserts great markets were formed under the influence of the traffic which, from time immemorial, had linked Egypt by sea and land to Mesopotamia. The state of Meroë, founded in the middle of the Sudan in the VIth century BC by princes from Egypt, and Abyssinia, which had been for centuries in contact with the Egyptians coming from the Red Sea to the coasts of Punt, looked seaward; the Abyssinians took their place among the sea-going peoples and thus were influenced by Roman civilization. Between India and China, especially after the Chinese Empire had gained a foothold at Canton (111 BC), navigation, in the hands of the Dravidians of southern India, brought Hindu civilization to Burma, Indo-China and the Malay islands, while Chinese influence reached the coasts of Annam. That composite civilization which was to know so magnificent a flowering in Cambodia and the Khmer Empire also came from the sea.

But outside the maritime countries, in the immense continental spaces that stretched through central and eastern Europe, in all northern Asia, on the Tibetan plateaux and in vast Africa, civilization had not penetrated.

Central Africa, inhabited by black races and pygmies whose existence had been revealed by the caravans trading in ivory, remained mysterious. The peoples of East Africa were, however, to receive some fitful gleams of Egyptian civilization through contact with the Abyssinians.

Nomadic peoples wandered in Asia and in northern Europe, held in check in Asia by the Chinese and in Europe by the Roman Empire; Huns, Mongols, Turks and Tibetans in Asia, Germans and Scythians in Europe. These were pastoral and warrior peoples who made and unmade chaotic empires formed of tribes federated or subjected by some conquering clan; they did not write, did not trade, save when, as in the case of the Altai Turks, mines gave them the chance of selling the iron indispensable for the making of arms. They possessed a rudimentary civilization, forged metals and wove cloth; on contact with the Greeks, the Scythians of southern Russia became farmers and created an art which, by its perfection, is in sharp contrast to the crude work of other barbarians. The Ostrogoths, settled on the Danube, were also subject to the influence of Roman civilization which spread beyond the confines of the Empire. All these barbarians formed a vast human sea in movement, into which from time to time Chinese, Tokharian or Roman merchants ventured. But the only contact that the civilized states had with them was to drive them back when they attempted to cross their frontiers. It seemed that there was no possibility of contact with the barbarians. They had no cities; when nomadic, they formed great camps where they assembled their wagons and horses; when semi-sedentary, they lived in huts and formed villages similar to those which the central African negroes still construct today. Whatever their race, they were all grouped into tribes and families rigidly united; they totally ignored the individual, who existed only for the group. Human life had no value for them; every man who did not belong to their horde, if he came into conflict with them, must be either killed or reduced to slavery. The group, united by blood and divided rigidly within itself into classes, declared itself the enemy of all those not of its race. They lived from the labour of those who came to demand their protection, or of enemies conquered and enslaved. But their real activity was war, a pitiless war, for racialism knows no pity, and war was the basis of the only moral code they knew: total devotion to the racial community.

This strange and savage world lived on the fringes of the civilization which, separated from it by the Great Wall of China or the Roman *limes*, believed itself sheltered and secure.

THE CRISIS OF THE EMPIRES

This balance of the great empires, which seemed so stable, only lasted for the first two centuries AD. A series of crises undermined it. A political crisis, because of the evolution of centralized institutions leading towards a more and more pervasive state-socialism necessitating fiscal demands which ended, both in China and in the Roman Empire, by becoming so insistent that they crushed the individual for the benefit of the state. An economic crisis, because capitalism, the result of liberalism, led to the accumulation of great fortunes in a few hands and, by this very fact, created huge estates that reduced the rural population to serfdom. A social crisis, because of the development of humanitarian trends which necessitated a more and more tyrannical intervention of the state in economic organization. Combined with state-socialism, the theories of social solidarity ruined democracy to the advantage of egalitarianism and, at the same time, because of the more and more absolute powers assumed by the Emperor, but actually exercised by the officials, an oligarchy was created which was superimposed upon the mass of the people and ended by exploiting them for its own profit. Finally, a moral crisis, born of the conflict between mystical aspirations, Christian in the Roman Empire, Buddhist or Taoist in China, and the materialism which was promoted by wealth and the comforts of life.

The results of these crises led, in the two Empires which safeguarded the peace of the world, to an internal weakness which first became manifest in the break-down of equilibrium in the 3rd century and then, after the efforts at restoration made by authoritarian absolutism, in the impossibility of containing the pressure of the barbarians who swept, like a flood, over the civilized lands. The Germans invaded the Roman Empire, the Huns swept over the Chinese Empire and Central Asia and penetrated into India where their wave of destruction was to drown in its passage the great cities of the Indus and the Ganges.

The Hunnic wave, starting in Asia, was to die away in Gaul with Attila. But the first migrations prepared the way for others along the routes that the Huns had opened. In Europe the Slavs began to move and soon reached the Adriatic, while in Asia the Turkish tide began to flow; it was to cover Bactria and was only to stop on the shores of the Gulf of Oman and it drove into Europe the first Bulgar hordes who advanced as far as the walls of Constantinople.

The barbarian inundation stretched over almost all the civilized world. In Europe, however, Constantinople and the eastern maritime provinces, strongly buttressed by the great cities which still preserved a free population, resisted; the same was the case in China where, driven back on Nankin, the Imperial dynasty saved the maritime provinces of the south and the cities of the Yang-Tse from the barbarian invasions. In India only the little maritime kingdoms of the south, sheltered behind the high plateau of the Deccan, remained free from the scourge. Sassanid Persia, protected on the Mediterranean side by the rampart of the Roman Empire of the East, was able to save its Iranian and Mesopotamian provinces.

In the 6th century the barbarian kingdoms founded on the ruins of the Empires were absorbed, in the West by Roman and in the East by Chinese civilization, and a great effort at revival was undertaken, in the Mediterranean by Justinian who tried by recovering the mastery of the seas to restore the Roman Empire, and in China by the Sui who were able to restore its former territories and its unity to the Chinese Empire.

THE WORLD BREAKS UP: THE SEIGNIORIAL RÉGIME

The era of the Empires had ended. The world, broken and ruined materially and morally, was no longer what it had been in the 2nd century; it was no more than a heap of rubble, even if some pieces of the façade or even an entire wing had remained intact, like a ruined palace whence the brilliant and mannered life of its occupants has departed to make way for the misery of refugees camping in its debris.

The Roman Empire of the West, broken into a series of barbarian kingdoms, had fallen into utter decadence. Save on the coasts, where the great ports continued to exist, the depopulated cities now had only local importance; international relations were confined to a few important centres; the ascendancy of the land became more and more powerful and the countryside was covered with huge estates peopled by serfs; the landed aristocracy, into which large numbers of gross and primitive Germans had infiltrated, lost all traces of civilization; the regal dynasties themselves, despite the Roman officials who surrounded them, only with difficulty cast off their barbarian origins; save for the Church, only the cities retained what could be preserved of the former Roman civilization; individual liberty, education and trade could now be found only within their walls, which had become too wide for the population which they sheltered. The sea, however, still gave life. The ports remained in touch with Constantinople and the industrial cities of Asia Minor and Syria, whence, together with their goods, they received a breath of civilization; but though the coasts continued to preserve the ancient tradition, the continental provinces became dormant and were parcelled into the estates of the seigniorial régime, which broke the world into still smaller pieces even more rigidly withdrawn into themselves.

The unity of the Empire was no more. It was the Church that replaced it; under the authority of the Pope, religious unity was substituted for the former feeling of community within the Empire. Intellectual culture made way for mysticism; and while the great schools stagnated and had fewer and fewer pupils, more and more monasteries were founded as the centres or the reliquaries of the dying civilizations.

Byzantium, it is true, retained all its splendour, as St Sophia and the Code of Justinian bear witness. But it was a crumbling façade. The provinces of the eastern Empire, sheltered from invasion, were rent by religious schism; the seigniorial ascendancy of the Hellenized landlords provoked, in Egypt and Syria, a burning hatred among the enslaved population which took the form of a national reaction against the now detested Greeks.

In the East the cities preserved the Imperial unity; but their prosperity depended on their international contacts, that is to say on the sea. Roman navigation, of which Constantinople, the Syrian cities and Alexandria were the vital centres, was however much diminished. It no longer ventured beyond the Red Sea, where the Abyssinians, taking over the role of the earlier Egyptian mariners, established contact with India by sea. Direct contact between Alexandria and Asia was broken. The Mediterranean, whose attraction had formerly made itself felt so powerfully in India, lost its influence, both because of the decadence of the West and the decadence of Asia.

For Asia was just as deeply changed as Europe. All Central Asia was now no more than a vast Turkish Empire, which stretched from Lake Baikal to the Persian Gulf, where a warrior feudalism ruled and surrounded the Tokharian cities and the cities of Bactria, as decadent as those of Gaul.

The general insecurity, by breaking the contacts between China and the Persian Empire of the Sassanids, precipitated Persia into an economic crisis which, by ruining the urban centres, gave complete power to the landed aristocracy. Persia, parcelled out under a seigniorial régime, became feudal.

India had not recovered from the devastation caused by the Huns. Its greatest cities were now no more than miserable hamlets. The ports along the coastline alone survived. In the interior, the country, delivered from the Huns after the Turkish victories, was restored in the form of a feudal régime of warrior princes. As in the West, poverty and the collapse of civilized manners and customs gave rise to a great popular enthusiasm for mysticism, centred on the countless Buddhist and Brahmanic monasteries within whose walls all that remained of the brilliant Hindu civilization had taken refuge.

The sea, however, as in Europe, maintained activity wherever its influence extended and, with this activity, individual liberty and civilization. The ports of Malabar and Bengal welcomed vessels from Alexandria and Arabia. In southern India the Dravidian states which had been spared became the true representatives of Hinduism in the whole Bay of Bengal; but here too, as in the Mediterranean, trade lost its universal character and was restricted to a limited area.

Thus a similar evolution was taking place from Spain to China, which drove men towards a landowning and seigniorial régime, tied the people of the countryside to the soil in a servile or semi-servile condition, diminished the importance of the cities and broke the civilized world into small and isolated units. City life and international trade and, with them, intellectual culture were only preserved along the sea-coasts. The last states which were not yet barbarized were the maritime states, the Empire of Byzantium and the Dravidian kingdoms of southern India. Navigation, however, had considerably slackened. It no longer dominated the economic life of the world, and the landholding régime had destroyed its cosmopolitan character; the sea lost its pride of place to the land and shipping played only a secondary role, though still an important one since it alone still maintained international contacts; but its effects were none the less insufficient to impose on the world a civilization both universal and individualist in character, as it had during the first centuries after Christ. Universalism had lost ground to political and economic dismemberment; individualism had been destroyed, first by state-socialism and later by the triumph of the seigniorial régime.

There remained of the great civilization that was expiring only the religious factor, Christianity in Europe, Buddhism and Taoism in Asia; by regarding moral values as universal and individual conscience as the first condition of morality, it was to preserve, through the coming period of complete decadence, the fundamental principles of ancient civilization.

CHINA REMAINS THE ONLY EMPIRE

Of the whole world, China alone fully recovered after the crisis of the invasions. Driven back from the caravan routes, the activities of the Nankin Empire became more and more centred on the sea and, since the decadence of India extended also to her shipping, China at the beginning of the 6th century enjoyed an era of great maritime expansion, which for a short time extended as far as Ceylon (515).

In the north her immense territory absorbed the invaders, and the contact which her rivers kept open between the sea and the most remote parts of the Empire permitted her, while restoring her economic unity, to restore also her political unity (589).

None the less, the constant shrinking of international sea-borne communications accentuated her continental character, and the decline of the caravan trade, following the ruin of India and the insecurity caused by Turkish rule in Central Asia, isolated her in an imperial civilization in the midst of a disintegrating world. She extended her rule from Annam to Korea and forced the Tokharian cities of the Tarim valley to accept her protectorate. The immense Empire which she thus created formed an economic unity sufficient unto itself. So while the whole world was turning towards feudalism and becoming organized on the basis of the seigniorial régime, China, continuing her democratic evolution, sought a new balance in a collectivist reform of landed property.

The era of the empires was now no more than a memory. There remained in the world only one real Empire, China, which alone escaped the universal decadence to enter a period of political and intellectual greatness isolated from the rest of the world.

INDEX

Alexander's Empire

Corinthian League

Areas dominated by Greek cities

Kingdom of Epirus

Zone of Egyptian influence

Armenia

Carthaginian maritime empire

Tartessos

Etruria

Roman Republic

Arab kingdoms and tribes

Hindu kingdoms

Chinese kingdoms constituted in the old Chou Empire